50 Best Jobs for Your Personality

Second Edition

Part of JIST's Best Jobs® Series

Michael Farr and Laurence Shatkin, Ph.D.

Foreword by Kristine Dobson, President, Career 1 Consulting

Also in JIST's *Best Jobs* Series

- ❋ *Best Jobs for the 21st Century*
- ❋ *200 Best Jobs for College Graduates*
- ❋ *300 Best Jobs Without a Four-Year Degree*
- ❋ *200 Best Jobs Through Apprenticeships*
- ❋ *40 Best Fields for Your Career*
- ❋ *225 Best Jobs for Baby Boomers*
- ❋ *250 Best-Paying Jobs*
- ❋ *150 Best Jobs for Your Skills*

- ❋ *150 Best Jobs Through Military Training*
- ❋ *175 Best Jobs Not Behind a Desk*
- ❋ *150 Best Jobs for a Better World*
- ❋ *10 Best College Majors for Your Personality*
- ❋ *200 Best Jobs for Introverts*
- ❋ *150 Best Low-Stress Jobs*
- ❋ *150 Best Recession-Proof Jobs*

JIST Works
America's Career Publisher®

50 Best Jobs for Your Personality, Second Edition

© 2009 by JIST Publishing

Published by JIST Works, an imprint of JIST Publishing
7321 Shadeland Station, Suite 200
Indianapolis, Indiana 46256-3923

Phone: 800-648-JIST   Fax: 877-454-7839
E-mail: info@jist.com   Web site: www.jist.com

Some Other Books by the Authors

Michael Farr

The Quick Resume & Cover Letter Book

Same-Day Resume

Overnight Career Choice

100 Fastest-Growing Careers

Top 100 Careers Without a Four-Year Degree

Laurence Shatkin

Great Jobs in the President's Stimulus Plan

90-Minute College Major Matcher

Your $100,000 Career Plan

New Guide for Occupational Exploration

150 Best Recession-Proof Jobs

Quantity discounts are available for JIST products. Please call 800-648-JIST or visit www.jist.com for a free catalog and more information.

Visit www.jist.com for information on JIST, free job search information, tables of contents and sample pages, and ordering information on our many products.

Acquisitions Editor: Susan Pines
Development Editor: Stephanie Koutek
Cover and Interior Designer: Aleata Halbig
Cover Illustration: Comstock, Fotosearch Stock Photography

Interior Layout: Aleata Halbig
Proofreaders: Linda Seifert, Jeanne Clark
Indexer: Cheryl Lenser

Printed in the United States of America

14 13 12 11   9 8 7 6 5 4 3

Library of Congress Cataloging-in-Publication Data
Farr, J. Michael.
  50 best jobs for your personality / Michael Farr and Laurence Shatkin; foreword by Kristine Dobson.
    p. cm. -- (Jist's best jobs series)
  Includes index.
  ISBN 978-1-59357-657-8 (alk. paper)
  1. Vocational guidance--Psychological aspects. 2. Career development--Psychological aspects. 3. Personality and occupation. 4. Vocational interests. 5. Occupations--Psychological aspects. I. Shatkin, Laurence. II. Title. III. Title: Fifty best jobs for your personality.
  HF5381.15.F3618 2009
  331.702--dc22
                    2009006041

We have been careful to provide accurate information throughout this book, but it is possible that errors and omissions have been introduced. Please consider this in making any career plans or other important decisions. Trust your own judgment above all else and in all things.

Trademarks: All brand names and product names used in this book are trade names, service marks, trademarks, or registered trademarks of their respective owners.

ISBN 978-1-59357-657-8

This Is a Big Book, But It Is Very Easy to Use

Psychologists have long understood a principle that many of us consider just common sense: that people have an aspect called personality that makes them feel more comfortable in some situations than in others. People who have a certain personality feel more capable of doing certain things and dealing with certain problems; they also feel more accepted when they are among people with personalities similar to their own. This is especially true for one place where people spend a major portion of their time: at work. People want to feel that they fit in with the people and with the activities where they work.

If personality is the key to this feeling of fitting in, then you need to consider this question: *What kind of personality do you have?* Maybe you can come up with a few ways to describe yourself, such as "sunny," "energetic," "conscientious," "loyal," "outgoing," "funny," or "competitive." But what do those terms suggest for the kind of work you might enjoy and do well? What terms might be more useful?

Some Things You Can Do with This Book

This book can help you think about your personality in terms that have proven relevance to the world of work. You'll learn about the personality types that many psychologists and career development practitioners use to describe people and jobs. You'll take a quick assessment to help you clarify your dominant personality type. Then you'll dig into a gold mine of facts about the jobs that are the best fit for your personality type—and that are the best for other reasons, too, such as their wages and job openings. The lists of "best jobs" will help you zero in on promising careers, and the descriptive profiles of the jobs will open your eyes to career choices that previously you may not have known much about.

We all want to fit in somewhere. And there are probably several different careers where each of us could fit in. But why not do it in a *really good job?* That's what this book can help you choose.

Credits and Acknowledgments: While the authors created this book, it is based on the work of many others. The occupational information is based on data obtained from the U.S. Department of Labor and the U.S. Census Bureau. These sources provide the most authoritative occupational information available. The job titles and their related descriptions are from the O*NET database, which was developed by researchers and developers under the direction of the U.S. Department of Labor. They, in turn, were assisted by thousands of employers who provided details on the nature of work in the many thousands of job samplings used in the database's development. We used the most recent version of the O*NET database, release 13.0. We appreciate and thank the staff of the U.S. Department of Labor for their efforts and expertise in providing such a rich source of data.

Table of Contents

Summary of Major Sections

Introduction. A short overview to help you better understand and use the book. *Starts on page 1.*

Part I: Overview of Personality and Career. Part I is an overview of personality and of personality types. This section also explores the relationship between personality and career. *Starts on page 17.*

Part II: What's Your Personality Type? Take an Assessment. This part helps you discover your personality type with a short, easy-to-complete assessment. *Starts on page 23.*

Part III: The Best Jobs Lists: Jobs for Each of the Six Personality Types. The 141 lists in Part III show you the best jobs in terms of high salaries, fast growth, and plentiful job openings for each of the six personality types. Further lists classify the jobs according to education and training required and several other features, such as jobs with the highest percentage of women and of men and jobs with high rates of self-employment and many part-time workers. Although there are a lot of lists, they are easy to understand because they have clear titles and are organized into groupings of related lists. *Starts on page 33.*

Part IV: Descriptions of the 50 Best Jobs for Each Personality Type. This part provides a brief but information-packed description of the 50 jobs from each personality type that met our criteria for this book. Each description contains information on earnings, projected growth, education and training required, job duties, skills, related job titles, related knowledge and courses, and many other details. The descriptions are presented in alphabetical order within each personality type. This structure makes it easy to look up a job that you've identified in a list from Part III and that you want to learn more about. *Starts on page 129.*

Part V: Appendixes. Appendix A contains a list of occupations in this book and their two-letter personality codes. Appendix B lists the Guide for Occupational Exploration (GOE) interest areas and work groups. Appendix C defines the skills and the types of knowledge listed in the job descriptions in Part IV. Appendix D identifies resources for further career exploration. *Starts on page 451.*

Detailed Table of Contents

Foreword

When I wrote the foreword for the first edition of this book, I started by saying, *Whether you're a counselor or a career explorer, this book is a must-have resource!*

I'd like to take credit for the tens of thousands of copies that have been sold, but I am fairly certain that readers discovered the value of this fabulous resource for themselves. I have no doubt that *50 Best Jobs for Your Personality* will continue to be a popular reference for career guidance professionals and also for individuals who are in the process of choosing or changing their careers.

The O*NET content model as a whole and the in-depth descriptions of occupations that have grown out of that model are of huge significance. O*NET has provided career professionals and others the common terminology that was needed to communicate across disciplines about the world of work. This book, *50 Best Jobs for Your Personality,* takes great advantage of the O*NET occupational database. For counselors, the book is a ready reference that includes key descriptors of over 300 occupations, organized by the six career personality types ("RIASEC" or "Holland Codes") first described by John Holland. For the lay reader, there is a "How to Use This Book" section that will promote effective use in advancing individual career exploration. Though the focus is on personality type, the book is uniquely organized to encourage readers to consider a range of characteristics as they investigate potential careers.

As a career counseling professional, I have experienced firsthand the gratification that comes with helping individuals understand how their personal characteristics relate to occupational choice. I have witnessed the effects, both in terms of job satisfaction and of productivity, when there is a good match between an individual's personality and an environment that supports his/her personality traits. It's an exciting process, one that will be furthered through the use of this book.

Kristine Dobson
President, Career 1 Consulting

Introduction

Before we get started finding the best jobs for your personality type, here are a few things to know about the information in this book and how it is organized.

Where the Information Comes From

The information we used in creating this book comes from three major government sources:

❋ **The U.S. Department of Labor:** We used several data sources to construct the information we put into this book. We started with the jobs included in the U.S. Department of Labor's O*NET database. The O*NET includes information on about 950 occupations and is now the primary source of detailed information on occupations. One of the information topics the O*NET covers is the personality types that are discussed in this book. The Labor Department updates the O*NET on a regular basis, and we used the most recent one available, release 13. As it happens, in release 13 the data about personality types has been completely revised and updated. Because we also wanted to include earnings, growth, and number of openings—information not included in the O*NET—we used sources at the U.S. Department of Labor's Bureau of Labor Statistics (BLS). The Occupational Employment Statistics survey provided the most reliable figures on earnings we could obtain, and the Employment Projections program provided the nation's best figures on job growth and openings. These two BLS programs use a slightly different system of job titles than the O*NET does, but we were able to link the BLS data to most of the O*NET job titles we used to develop this book.

❋ **The U.S. Census Bureau:** Data on the demographic characteristics of workers came from the Current Population Survey (CPS), conducted by the U.S. Census Bureau. This includes our information about the proportion of workers in each job who are men and women, are self-employed, or work part time. As with the BLS data, we had to match slightly different sets of job titles, but we were able to identify CPS data for almost all the O*NET jobs.

❋ **The U.S. Department of Education:** We used the Classification of Instructional Programs, a system developed by the U.S. Department of Education, to cross-reference the educational or training programs related to each job.

Of course, information in a database format can be boring and even confusing, so we did many things to help make the data useful and present it to you in a form that is easy to understand.

How the Jobs in This Book Were Selected

Here is the procedure we followed to select the jobs we included in this book:

1. We began by creating our own database from the O*NET, the Census Bureau, and other sources to include the information that we wanted. This database covered 949 job titles, of which 812 were rated in terms of the six RIASEC personality types.

2. Although the O*NET was our source of data on the RIASEC personality types of occupations, we decided to base our best jobs lists on the system of job classification that the Department of Labor uses to report data for our other sources: the Standard Occupational Classification (SOC). The SOC system collapses several O*NET job titles; for example, the SOC job Accountants and Auditors combines two O*NET jobs, as the title indicates. In this example, the two O*NET jobs both have the same dominant RIASEC personality type, Conventional, so the personality type for Accountants and Auditors obviously is Conventional. Some other SOC jobs, however, combine O*NET jobs with differing RIASEC types, so we calculated the average of the ratings for the six RIASEC types to determine which type was dominant for these diverse SOC occupations. Thus we were able to determine the dominant RIASEC types for 733 SOC occupations.

3. We eliminated five jobs for which we lacked important information. (For example, we had no job-growth data for Farm Labor Contractors.) We eliminated an additional 14 jobs that are expected to employ fewer than 500 workers per year and to shrink rather than grow in workforce size. We also removed 51 jobs because they have annual earnings of less than $20,920, which means that 75 percent of workers earn more than the workers in these jobs.

4. For the remaining 663 occupations, we were able to create six lists of occupations, each representing one dominant RIASEC personality type. The six lists ranged in size from 285 jobs for the Realistic type to 29 for the Artistic type.

5. Because we wanted to identify 50 best jobs for each personality type, we needed a pool of more than 29 jobs for the Artistic type. Therefore, we added to this pool another 41 jobs for which Artistic was the highest-rated *secondary* personality type. As a result, you'll find some jobs on the Artistic job lists that also appear on lists for another RIASEC type, such as Political Scientists (which has Investigative as its dominant RIASEC type), Training and Development Specialists (Social), or Public Relations Specialists (Enterprising).

6. Next, for each of the six RIASEC-based lists, we ranked the jobs three times, based on these major criteria: median annual earnings, projected growth through 2016, and number of job openings projected per year.

7. We then added the three numerical rankings for each job to calculate its overall score.

8. To emphasize jobs that tend to pay more, are likely to grow more rapidly, and have more job openings, we selected the 50 job titles with the best total scores for each of the six RIASEC types. Because 17 Artistic jobs also appear on other lists, a total of 283 jobs (rather than 300) appear on the Part III lists, and they are the focus of this book.

For example, Accountants and Auditors is the Conventional job with the highest combined score for earnings, growth, and number of job openings, so Accountants and Auditors is listed first in our "50 Best Conventional Jobs" list even though it is not the best-paying Conventional job (which is Actuaries), the fastest-growing Conventional job (which is Financial Analysts), or the Conventional job with the most openings (which is Office Clerks, General).

Why This Book Has More Than 300 Job Descriptions

We didn't think you would mind that this book actually provides information on more than 300 jobs. As this introduction explains, the jobs on the Part III lists are based on the SOC job classification system, but in Part IV we describe the related O*NET jobs separately. This means that although we used 283 SOC job titles to construct the lists, Part IV actually has a total of 326 O*NET job descriptions.

Understand the Limits of the Data in This Book

In this book, we use the most reliable and up-to-date information available on earnings, projected growth, number of openings, and other topics. The earnings data came from the U.S. Department of Labor's Bureau of Labor Statistics. As you look at the figures, keep in mind that they are estimates. They give you a general idea about the number of workers employed, annual earnings, rate of job growth, and annual job openings.

Understand that a problem with such data is that it describes an average. Just as there is no precisely average person, there is no such thing as a statistically average example of a particular job. We say this because data, while helpful, can also be misleading.

Take, for example, the way we assign the jobs to the six personality types. We follow the ratings assigned by the O*NET database, which are based on analysis of the occupation's definition, core work tasks, types of knowledge used, and other information about the job. But workers with the same occupation title often work in different settings and have varying work duties, use varying kinds of knowledge, and vary in other ways that should influence the RIASEC type one would assign to their job. For example, Librarians who do research for a corporation have considerably different work tasks from the Librarians who work in a public library. Therefore, when we assign Librarians to the Conventional personality type, you should keep in mind that Librarians can also find niches within their profession that are compatible with other personality types. One way to identify the most likely alternative personality types is to look at the full RIASEC personality code (usually two or three letters) listed for the job in the Part IV description. The code for Librarians is CSE, meaning that Social and Enterprising are secondary personality types for this occupation.

Salary figures, which seem so precise, likewise summarize a great amount of variation. The yearly earnings information in this book is based on highly reliable data obtained from a very large U.S. working population sample by the Bureau of Labor Statistics. It tells us the average annual pay received as of May 2007 by people in various job titles (actually, it is the median annual pay, which means that half earned more and half less).

This sounds great, except that half of all people in that occupation earned less than that amount. For example, people who are new to the occupation or with only a few years of work experience often earn much less than the median amount. People who live in rural areas or who work for smaller employers typically earn less than those who do similar work in cities (where the cost of living is higher) or for bigger employers. People in certain areas of the country earn less than those in others. Other factors also influence how much you are likely to earn in a given job in your area. For example, Aircraft Mechanics and Service Technicians in the Detroit–Livonia–Dearborn, Michigan, metropolitan division have median earnings of $56,740, probably because Northwest Airlines has a hub in Detroit and its mechanics are unionized. By comparison, the Allentown–Bethlehem–Easton, Pennsylvania, metropolitan area has no major airline hub and only a small aircraft service facility with nonunionized workers. Aircraft Mechanics and Service Technicians there earn a median of only $31,540.

Beginning wages vary greatly, too, depending not only on location and size of employer, but also on what skills and educational credentials a new hire brings to the job.

Also keep in mind that the figures for job growth and number of openings are projections by labor economists—their best guesses about what we can expect between now and 2016. Those projections are not guarantees. A catastrophic economic downturn, war, or technological breakthrough could change the actual outcome.

Finally, don't forget that the job market consists of both job openings and job *seekers*. The figures on job growth and openings don't tell you how many people will be competing with you to be hired. The Department of Labor does not publish figures on the supply of job candidates, so we are unable to tell you about the level of competition you can expect. Competition is an important issue that you should research for any tentative career goal. The *Occupational Outlook Handbook* provides informative statements for many occupations. You should speak to people who educate or train tomorrow's workers; they probably have a good idea of how many graduates find rewarding employment and how quickly. People in the workforce can provide insights into this issue as well. Use your critical thinking skills to evaluate what people tell you. For example, educators or trainers may be trying to recruit you, whereas people in the workforce may be trying to discourage you from competing. Get a variety of opinions to balance out possible biases.

So, in reviewing the information in this book, please understand the limitations of the data. You need to use common sense in career decision making as in most other things in life. We hope that, by using that approach, you find the information helpful and interesting.

Data Complexities

For those of you who like details, we present some of the complexities inherent in our sources of information and what we did to make sense of them here. You don't need to know these things to use the book, so jump to the next section of the introduction if details bore you.

We selected the jobs partly on the basis of economic data, and we include information on earnings, projected growth, and number of job openings for each job throughout this book. We think this information is important to most people, but getting it for each job is not a simple task.

Earnings

The employment security agency of each state gathers information on earnings for various jobs and forwards it to the U.S. Bureau of Labor Statistics. This information is organized in standardized ways by a BLS program called Occupational Employment Statistics, or OES. To keep the earnings for the various jobs and regions comparable, the OES screens out certain types of earnings and includes others, so the OES earnings we use in this book represent straight-time gross pay exclusive of premium pay. More specifically, the OES earnings include each job's base rate; cost-of-living allowances; guaranteed pay; hazardous-duty pay; incentive pay, including commissions and production bonuses; on-call pay; and tips. The OES earnings do not include back pay, jury duty pay, overtime pay, severance pay, shift differentials, nonproduction bonuses, or tuition reimbursements. Also, self-employed workers are not included in the estimates, and they can be a significant segment in certain occupations. When data on annual earnings for an occupation is highly unreliable, OES does not report a figure, which meant that we reluctantly had to exclude from this book a few occupations such as Hunters and Trappers.

For each job, we report three figures related to earnings:

❋ The Annual Earnings figure shows the median earnings (half earn more, half earn less).

❋ The Beginning Wage figure shows the 10th percentile earnings (the figure that exceeds the earnings of the lowest 10 percent of the workers). This is a rough approximation of what a beginning worker may be offered.

❋ The Earnings Growth Potential figure represents the ratio between the 10th percentile and the median. In a job for which this figure is high, you have great potential for increasing your earnings as you gain experience and skills. When the figure is low, it means you will probably need to move on to another occupation to improve your earnings substantially. For the 283 SOC jobs in this book, the earnings growth potential ranges from a high of 59.9% for Music Directors and Composers to a low of 10.5% for Postal Service Clerks. Because the percentage figures would be hard to interpret, we use verbal tags to indicate the level of Earnings Growth Potential: "very low" when the percentage is less than 25%, "low" for 25–35%, "medium" for 35%–40%, "high" for 40%–50%, and "very high" for any figure higher than 50%. For the highest-paying jobs, those for which BLS reports the median earnings as "more than $145,600," we are unable to calculate a figure for Earnings Growth Potential.

The median earnings for all workers in all occupations were $31,410 in May 2007. The 283 SOC jobs in this book were chosen partly on the basis of good earnings, so their average is a respectable $45,793. (This is a weighted average, which means that jobs with larger workforces are given greater weight in the computation. It also is based on the assumption that a job with income reported as "more than $145,600" pays exactly $145,600, so the actual average is somewhat higher.)

The beginning (that is, 10th percentile) wage for all occupations in May 2007 was $16,060. For the 283 SOC jobs in this book, the weighted average is an impressive $28,118.

The earnings data from the OES survey is reported under the SOC system of job titles. As noted earlier in this introduction, the SOC system collapses some O*NET job titles, such as Accountants and Auditors. In Part IV of this book, where the O*NET job titles are described separately, you may notice that the salary we report for Accountants ($57,060) in Part IV is identical to the salary we report for Auditors. In reality, there probably is a difference, but this is the best information available.

Projected Growth and Number of Job Openings

This information comes from the Office of Occupational Statistics and Employment Projections, a program within the Bureau of Labor Statistics that develops information about projected trends in the nation's labor market for the next ten years. The most recent projections available cover the years from 2006 to 2016. The projections are based on information about people moving into and out of occupations. The BLS uses data from various sources in projecting the growth and number of openings for each job title: Some data comes from the Census Bureau's Current Population Survey and some comes from an OES survey. The BLS economists assumed a steady economy unaffected by a major war, depression, or other upheaval. They also assumed that recessions may occur during the decade covered by these projections, as would be consistent with the pattern of business cycles we have experienced for several decades. However, because their projections cover 10 years, the figures for job growth and openings are intended to provide an average of both the good times and the bad times.

Like the earnings figures, the figures on projected growth and job openings are reported according to the SOC classification. So, again, we had to exclude a few jobs from this book because this information is not available for them. As with earnings, some of the SOC jobs crosswalk to more than one O*NET job. To continue the example we used earlier, the Department of Labor projects growth (17.7%) and openings (134,463) for one SOC occupation called Accountants and Auditors, but in the Part IV job descriptions, we report these figures separately for the O*NET occupation Accountants and for the O*NET occupation Auditors. When you see that Accountants has a 17.7% projected growth rate and 134,463 projected job openings and Auditors has the same two numbers, you should realize that the 17.7% rate of projected growth represents the *average* of these two occupations—one may actually experience higher growth than the other—and that these two occupations will *share* the 134,463 projected openings.

The Department of Labor provides a single figure (22.9%) for the projected growth of 38 postsecondary teaching jobs and also provides a single figure (237,478) for the projected annual job openings for these 38 jobs. Because these college-teaching jobs are related to two different RIASEC types—Investigative and Social—and because separate *earnings* figures are available for each of the 38 jobs, we thought you'd appreciate having these jobs appear separately in the Part III lists in this book. If the trends of the last several years continue, none of these jobs can be expected to grow or take on workers at a faster rate than the other 37. Therefore, in preparing the lists and in the Part IV descriptions, we assumed that all of these college-teaching jobs share the same rate of projected job growth, 22.9%, and we computed a figure for their projected job openings by dividing the total (237,478) into 38 parts, each of which is proportional in size to the current workforce of the job.

While salary figures are fairly straightforward, you may not know what to make of job-growth figures. For example, is projected growth of 15% good or bad? Keep in mind that the average (mean) growth projected for all occupations by the Bureau of Labor Statistics is 10.4%. One-quarter of the SOC occupations have a growth projection of 3.2% or lower. Growth of 11.6% is the median, meaning that half of the occupations have more, half less. Only one-quarter of the occupations have growth projected at more than 17.4%.

Because the jobs in this book were selected as "best" partly on the basis of job growth, their mean growth is 13.9%, which compares favorably to the mean for all jobs. Among these 283 SOC jobs, the job ranked 71st by projected growth has a figure of 22.9%, the job ranked 141st (the median) has a projected growth of 15.4%, and the job ranked 212th has a projected growth of 10.6%.

The number of job openings for the 283 best jobs is slightly lower than the national average for all occupations. The Bureau of Labor statistics projects an average of about 35,000 job openings per year for the 750 occupations that it studies, but for the 283 SOC occupations included in this book, the average is about 35,700 openings. The job ranked 71st for job openings has a figure of about 37,800 annual openings, the job ranked 141st (the median) has about 14,300 openings projected, and the job ranked 212th has about 5,600 openings projected.

However, keep in mind that average figures for job openings depend on how BLS defines an occupation. For example, consider the college teaching jobs. The Office of Occupational Statistics and Employment Projections recognizes *one* occupation called Teachers, Postsecondary, and projects 237,478 annual job openings for this occupation. As explained earlier in this introduction, we divided this huge occupation into 38 separate occupations, following the practice of O*NET and of the Occupational Employment Statistics program. The average number of openings for all occupations changes substantially depending on whether you deal with college teachers as one or 38 occupations. So it follows that, because the way BLS defines occupations is somewhat arbitrary, any average figure for job openings is also somewhat arbitrary.

Perhaps you're wondering why we present figures on both job growth *and* number of openings. Aren't these two ways of saying the same thing? Actually, you need to know both. Consider the occupation Makeup Artists, Theatrical and Performance, which is projected to grow at the astounding rate of 39.8%. There should be lots of opportunities in such a fast-growing job, right? Not exactly. This is a tiny occupation, with only about 2,100 people currently employed. So, even though it is growing rapidly, it will not create many new jobs (about 400 per year). Now consider Secretaries, Except Legal, Medical, and Executive. This occupation is growing at the glacial rate of 1.2% now that many secretarial tasks are being handled by word processors, answering machines, and other kinds of office automation. Nevertheless, this is a huge occupation that employs almost two million workers. So, even though its growth rate is unimpressive, it is expected to take on about 240,000 new workers each year as existing workers retire, die, or move on to other jobs. That's why we base our selection of the best jobs on both of these economic indicators and why you should pay attention to both when you scan our lists of best jobs.

Education or Training Required

One set of lists in Part III organizes jobs on the basis of the amount of education or training that they typically require for entry. In Part IV, each job description includes a statement of the education or training requirements. We base these educational and training requirements on ratings supplied by the Bureau of Labor Statistics.

You should keep in mind that some people working in these jobs may have credentials that differ considerably from the level listed here. For example, although a bachelor's degree is considered the appropriate preparation for Cost Estimators, over one-quarter of these workers have no college background at all. Conversely, although Registered Nurses can begin working after earning an associate degree, over half have a bachelor's, and in fact career opportunities without the bachelor's are considerably more limited.

Some workers who have more than the minimum required education for their job have earned a higher degree *after* being hired, but others entered the job with this educational credential, and the more advanced degree may have given them an advantage over other job-seekers with less education. Some workers with *less* than the normal minimum requirement may have been hired on the basis of their work experience in a similar job. So don't assume that the one-line "Education Required" statement in the Part IV job descriptions gives a complete picture of how best to prepare for the job. If you're considering the job seriously, you need to investigate this topic in greater detail. Consider using some of the resources listed in Appendix D for further career exploration.

Other Job Characteristics

Like the figures for earnings, some of the other figures used to create the lists of jobs in this book are shared by more than one job title. Usually this is the case for occupations that are so small that BLS does not release separate statistics for them. For example, the occupation Sound Engineering Technicians has a total workforce of only about 16,000 workers, so BLS does not report a specific figure for the percentage of women workers. In this case, we had to use the figure that BLS reports for a group of occupations it calls Broadcast and Sound Engineering Technicians and Radio Operators. We relied on this same figure for four other jobs: Camera Operators, Television, Video, and Motion Picture; Film and Video Editors; Audio and Video Equipment Technicians; and Broadcast Technicians. You may notice similar figure-sharing among related jobs where we list the percentages of workers in specific age brackets.

Information in the Job Descriptions

We used a variety of government and other sources to compile the job descriptions we provide in Part IV. Details on these various sources are mentioned later in this introduction in the section "Part IV: Descriptions of the 50 Best Jobs for Each Personality Type."

How This Book Is Organized

The information in this book moves from the general to the highly specific. It starts by explaining how personality relates to career choice and presents a widely used model for making that connection. An assessment helps you focus on your dominant personality type (or types), and then you can consult a wealth of lists that itemize the best jobs for your personality type. These lists let you look at the jobs from several different perspectives—for example, which jobs pay the best, which jobs employ the most young people, and which jobs require an associate's degree for entry. Finally, you can get highly detailed information about any of these career choices in the fact-packed job descriptions that make up the last part of the book.

Part I. Overview of Personality and Career

Part I is an overview of how personality relates to careers—the basic theory, plus the six personality types that were originally described by John Holland and have since become the basis of many guidance resources. This section may clear up some misunderstandings you have about what personality means in the context of career choice, and it will help you understand a useful way of looking at yourself and the world of work.

Part II. What's Your Personality Type? Take an Assessment

You probably are not reading this book simply to educate yourself about career development theory. Rather, the odds are that you have a more practical goal: making a career choice. To help you, we've included a paper-and-pencil assessment that can help you clarify your dominant personality type or types. The Personality Type Inventory usually takes about 20 or 30 minutes to complete, but there is no time limit, nor are there any right or wrong answers.

After taking the Personality Type Inventory, you can use what you've learned about your personality type to identify a job that suits you well. This book makes that task easy because all of the information about jobs is grouped by the dominant personality type of the jobs. That means you don't have to waste time exploring jobs that are unlikely to be a good match for your personality. Also, because this book focuses on the 50 most rewarding jobs for each personality type, you don't have to complicate your search by considering jobs with low earnings or highly limited odds of being employed.

Part III. The Best Jobs Lists: Jobs for Each of the Six Personality Types

For many people, the 141 lists in Part III are the most interesting section of the book. Here you can see which jobs for each personality type are best in terms of high salaries, fast growth, and plentiful job openings and best when these three factors are combined. Other lists break out the best of each type according to the level of education or training required and several other features of the jobs and of the people who hold them. Look in the Table of Contents for a complete list of the lists. Although there are a lot of lists, they are not difficult to understand because they have clear titles and are organized into groupings of related lists.

People who prefer to think about careers in terms of economic rewards will want to browse the lists that show the best jobs in terms of earnings, growth, and openings. On the other hand, some people think first in terms of opportunities for young people or representation of women, and these readers will find other useful lists that reflect these interests.

We suggest that you use the lists that make the most sense for you. Following are the names of each group of lists along with short comments on each group. You will find additional information in a brief introduction provided at the beginning of each group of lists in Part III.

Best Jobs Overall for Each Personality Type: Jobs with the Highest Pay, Fastest Growth, and Most Openings

This group has four sets of six lists, and they are the ones that most people want to see first. The first set of lists presents, for each personality type, all 50 jobs that are included in this book in order of their total scores for earnings, growth, and number of job openings. These jobs are used in the more-specialized lists that follow and in the descriptions in Part IV. Three more sets of lists in this group present, for each personality type, specialized lists of jobs extracted from the best 50 overall: the 20 best-paying, the 20 fastest-growing, and the 20 with the most openings.

The Best Jobs for Each Personality Type with a High Percentage of Workers Age 16–24

This section provides lists of the jobs for each personality type that have the highest percentage of workers age 16–24. Each list is then re-sorted to present these youthful jobs in order of their total combined scores for earnings, growth, and number of openings. Thus there is a total of 12 lists in this section.

The Best Jobs for Each Personality Type with a High Percentage of Workers Age 55 and Over

The 12 lists in this section were assembled in the same manner as the lists in the previous section, except that these jobs have a high percentage of workers age 55 and over.

The Best Jobs for Each Personality Type with a High Percentage of Part-Time Workers

There are 12 lists in this group, and they extract the jobs from our 50 best jobs for each personality type that have a high percentage of part-time workers. Again, they are ordered first in terms of percentage of part-time workers, so you can easily find the jobs with the most opportunities for part-timers, and then they are re-sorted in order of their total combined score for earnings, growth, and number of openings.

The Best Jobs for Each Personality Type with a High Percentage of Self-Employed Workers

The 12 lists in this section show you the jobs that have the highest percentage of self-employed workers. Once again, the lists for the six personality types are re-sorted in order of the jobs' total combined scores for earnings, growth, and number of openings.

Best Jobs for Each Personality Type with a High Percentage of Women and of Men

For each personality type, you can see the jobs that have the highest percentage of workers who are women and workers who are men. In addition, each of the lists is re-sorted to show these predominantly-male or predominantly-female jobs ordered by their overall ranking on earnings, growth, and openings. That would make up 24 lists, but one personality type (Social) has no jobs with a high percentage of men, so this section includes 22 lists.

The Best Jobs for Each Personality Type Sorted by Education or Training Required

When considering a career choice, many people put a lot of emphasis on how long it takes to prepare for the job and what kind of preparation is appropriate—education, training, work experience. Just as it's important to choose a job that suits your personality, it can be helpful to choose learning goals that suit your preferences and abilities. Your financial circumstances also may shape your plans for career preparation because higher education can be expensive (even with financial aid) and the years you spend in college will postpone the years in which you will earn a salary. This set of lists sorts the jobs linked to each personality type into groups according to what preparation method is the fastest route to career entry. Within each group, the jobs are sorted by their overall ranking on earnings, growth, and openings.

Part IV. Descriptions of the 50 Best Jobs for Each Personality Type

This part of the book provides a brief but information-packed description of each of the 283 best jobs that met our criteria for this book. As noted earlier in this introduction, the jobs here are the O*NET equivalents of the SOC jobs named in the lists, so there are actually 326 job descriptions. The descriptions are divided into six groups, one for each personality type, and are presented in alphabetical order within each group. This structure makes it easy to look up a job that you've identified in a list from Part II or Part III and that you want to learn more about.

Note that 17 of the jobs on the Artistic lists in Part III actually have a different RIASEC type as their dominant personality type, as explained earlier in this introduction. Public Relations Managers is one such job; its dominant RIASEC type is actually Enterprising, but it also appears on Artistic lists in Part III. If you should look it up in the Artistic section of Part IV, you will find a note there telling you to look for Public Relations Managers in the Enterprising section of Part IV instead. Several jobs on the lists are related to multiple O*NET jobs, so we also provide notes to refer you to these jobs. For example, if you should turn to the Conventional section of Part IV to look up Surveying and Mapping Technicians (which appears on the Conventional lists), you will find a note there directing you to the descriptions of the related O*NET jobs: Mapping Technicians (Conventional) and Surveying Technicians (Realistic).

We used the most current information from a variety of government sources to create the descriptions. Although we've tried to make the descriptions easy to understand, the sample job description that follows—and the explanation of each of its parts—may help you better understand and use the descriptions.

Job Title →

Forest Fire Fighters

Data Elements →

- Personality Code: RS
- Education/Training Required: Long-term on-the-job training
- Annual Earnings: $43,170
- Beginning Wage: $21,530
- Earnings Growth Potential: Very high
- Growth: 12.1%
- Annual Job Openings: 18,887
- Self-Employed: 0.0%
- Part-Time: 1.3%

The job openings listed here are shared with Municipal Fire Fighters.

Summary Description and Tasks →

Control and suppress fires in forests or vacant public land. Maintain contact with fire dispatchers at all times to notify them of the need for additional firefighters and supplies or to detail any difficulties encountered. Rescue fire victims and administer emergency medical aid. Collaborate with other firefighters as a member of a firefighting crew. Patrol burned areas after fires to locate and eliminate hot spots that may restart fires. Extinguish flames and embers to suppress fires, using shovels or engine- or hand-driven water or chemical pumps. Fell trees, cut and clear brush, and dig trenches to create firelines, using axes, chain saws, or shovels. Maintain knowledge of current firefighting practices by participating in drills and by attending seminars, conventions, and conferences. Operate pumps connected to high-pressure hoses. Participate in physical training to maintain high levels of physical fitness. Establish water supplies, connect hoses, and direct water onto fires. Maintain fire equipment and firehouse living quarters. Inform and educate the public about fire

prevention. Take action to contain any hazardous chemicals that could catch fire, leak, or spill. Organize fire caches, positioning equipment for the most effective response. Transport personnel and cargo to and from fire areas. Participate in fire prevention and inspection programs. Perform forest maintenance and improvement tasks such as cutting brush, planting trees, building trails, and marking timber. Test and maintain tools, equipment, jump gear, and parachutes to ensure readiness for fire-suppression activities. Observe forest areas from fire lookout towers to spot potential problems. Orient self in relation to fire, using compass and map, and collect supplies and equipment dropped by parachute. Serve as fully trained lead helicopter crewmember and as helispot manager. Drop weighted paper streamers from aircraft to determine the speed and direction of the wind at fire sites.

← GOE Information

GOE—Interest Area/Cluster: 12. Law and Public Safety. **Work Group:** 12.06. Emergency Responding. **Other Jobs in This Work Group:** Emergency Medical Technicians and Paramedics; Fire Fighters; Municipal Fire Fighters.

← Skills

Skills: Repairing; Equipment Maintenance; Management of Personnel Resources; Operation Monitoring; Equipment Selection; Operation and Control; Systems Analysis; Operations Analysis.

← Education/Training Program(s)
← Related Knowledge/Courses

Education and Training Programs: Fire Science/Firefighting; Fire Protection, Other. **Related Knowledge/Courses:** Geography; Customer and Personal Service; Mechanical Devices; Public Safety and Security; Education and Training; Psychology.

Work Environment: Outdoors; very hot or cold; contaminants; hazardous conditions; minor burns, cuts, bites, or stings; using hands on objects, tools, or controls.

Work Environment

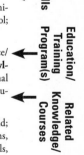

Here are some details on each of the major parts of the job descriptions you will find in Part IV:

❁ **Job Title:** This is the job title for the job as defined by the U.S. Department of Labor and used in its O*NET database.

❁ **Data Elements:** This information comes from various U.S. Department of Labor and Census databases for this occupation, as explained elsewhere in this introduction.

❁ **Summary Description and Tasks:** The bold sentences provide a summary description of the occupation. This is followed by a listing of tasks that are generally performed by people who work in this job. We followed the listing of tasks in the O*NET database, except that where necessary we edited the tasks to keep them from exceeding 2,200 characters.

❁ **GOE:** This information cross-references the Guide for Occupational Exploration (or the GOE), a system that organizes jobs based on interests and is used in a variety of career information systems. We use the *New Guide for Occupational Exploration,* as published by JIST. That book uses a set of interest areas based on the 16 career clusters developed by the U.S. Department of Education and used in a variety of career information systems. Here we include the major interest area the job fits into, its more specific work group, and a list of related job titles that are in this same GOE work group. This information will help you identify other jobs that relate to similar interests or require similar skills. You can find more information on the GOE and its interest areas in Appendix B.

❁ **Skills:** The government provides data on many skills; we decided to list only those that were most important for each job rather than list pages of unhelpful details. For each job, we identified any skill with a rating for level of mastery that was higher than the average rating for that skill for all jobs and a rating for importance that was higher than very low. If there were more than eight, we included only those eight with the highest ratings, and we present them from highest to lowest score (that is, in terms of by how much its score exceeds the average score). You can find definitions of the skills in Appendix C.

❁ **Education/Training Program(s):** This part provides the names of one or more programs for preparing for the job. The titles are based on the U.S. Department of Education *Classification of Instructional Programs.* A particular college major or training program may not have the identical title—for example, there probably is no college that offers a major called "Political Science and Government, General," but you are likely to find a major called "Political Science" or "Government." We derived this information from a crosswalk created by the National Crosswalk Service Center to connect information in the Classification of Instructional Programs (CIP) to O*NET job titles. We made various changes to connect the O*NET job titles to the education or training programs related to them and also modified the names of some education and training programs so they would be more easily understood. In 25 cases, we abbreviated the listing of related programs for the sake of space; such entries end with "others."

❋ **Related Knowledge/Courses:** This entry can help you understand the most important knowledge areas that are required for a job and the types of courses or programs you will likely need to take to prepare for it. For each job, we identified the highest-rated knowledge area in the O*NET database, so every job has at least one listed. We identified any additional knowledge area with a rating that was higher than the average rating for that knowledge area for all jobs. We listed as many as six knowledge areas in descending order.

❋ **Work Environment:** We included any work condition with a rating that exceeds the midpoint of the rating scale. The order does not indicate any condition's frequency on the job. Consider whether you like these conditions and whether any of these conditions would make you uncomfortable. Keep in mind that when hazards are present (for example, contaminants), protective equipment and procedures are provided to keep you safe.

How to Use This Book

This is a book that you can dive right into:

❋ **If you don't know much about what personality types are,** you'll want to read Part I, which is an overview of the theory behind using personality types as a way of making career choices. You'll also see definitions of the six personality types that are used in this book.

❋ **If you want to understand your own personality type,** you'll want to do the assessment in Part II. It takes only 20 or 30 minutes to complete and can guide you to jobs that suit you.

❋ **If you like lists and want an easy way to compare jobs,** you should turn to Part III. Here you can browse lists showing the 50 jobs for each personality type with the best pay, the fastest growth, and the most job openings. You can see these "best jobs" lists broken down in various ways, such as by amount of education or training required.

❋ **For detailed information about jobs,** turn to Part IV and read the profiles of the jobs. We include 326 jobs and itemize their major tasks, their top skills, their educational or training programs, and other facts you won't learn from the lists in Part III.

On the other hand, **if you like to do things in a methodical way,** you may want to read the sections in order:

1. Part I will give you useful background on how personality type can be a guide in choosing a career.

2. The assessment in Part II will help you identify your dominant personality type.

3. With a clearer understanding of your personality type, you can browse the appropriate lists of "best jobs" in Part III and take notes on the jobs that have the greatest appeal for you.

4. Then you can look up the descriptions of these jobs in Part IV and narrow down your list. Ask yourself, Do the work tasks interest me? Does the required education or training discourage me?

PART I

Overview of Personality and Career

Why Use Personality to Choose a Career?

Many psychological theorists and practicing career counselors believe that you will be most satisfied and productive in a career if it suits your personality. There are two main aspects of a job that determine whether it is a good fit:

❋ The nature of the work tasks and the skills and knowledge you use on the job must be a good match for the things you like to do and the subjects that interest you. For example, if you like to help other people and promote learning and personal development and if you like communication more than working with things or ideas, then a career in social work might be one that you would enjoy and do well in.

❋ The people you work with must share your personality traits so that you feel comfortable and can accomplish good work in their company. For an example of the opposite, think of how a person who enjoys following set procedures and working with data and detail might feel if forced to work with a group of conceptual artists who constantly seek self-expression and the inspiration for unconventional new artistic ideas.

Personality theorists believe that people with similar personality types naturally tend to associate with one another in the workplace (among other places). As they do so, they create a working environment that is hospitable to their personality type. For example, a workplace with a lot of Artistic types tends to reward creative thinking and behavior. Therefore, your personality type not only predicts how well your skills will match the demands of the work tasks in a particular job; it also predicts how well you will fit in with the culture of the work site as shaped by the people who will surround you and interact with you. Your personality type thus affects your satisfaction with the job, your productivity in it, and the likelihood that you will persist in this type of work.

One of the advantages of using personality as a key to career choice is that it is *economical*—it provides a tidy summary of many aspects of people and of careers. Consider how knotty a career decision could get if you were to break down the components of the work environment into highly specific aspects and reflect on how well you fit them. For example, you could focus on the skills required and your ability to meet them. Next you could analyze the kinds of knowledge that are used on the job and decide how much you enjoy working with those topics. Then you could consider a broad array of satisfactions, such as variety, creativity, and independence; for each one, you would evaluate its importance to you and then determine the potential of various career options to satisfy this need. You can see that, when looked at under a microscope like this, career choice gets extremely complex.

But the personality-based approach allows you to view the career alternatives from 40,000 feet. When you compare yourself or a job to certain basic personality types, you encounter much less complexity. With fewer ideas and facts to sort through and consider, the task of deciding becomes much easier.

Describing Personality Types

You probably have heard many labels that describe people's personalities: "He's a perfectionist." "She's a control freak." "He's a go-getter." "She's very self-confident." "He's pushy." "She's wishy-washy." "He has a short fuse." "She's a drama queen." The list could go on and on.

These everyday terms for personality types have some bearing on work, but they are not very useful for several reasons: They don't differentiate well between jobs (for example, self-confidence is useful in just about every job); some of them are too specific (for example, "control freak" focuses on one small aspect of how a person functions at work); and, worst of all, most of them are too negative for people to want to apply to themselves.

Now that it's clear what kinds of personality labels we *don't* want to use, let's consider what would characterize a useful set of personality types:

※ They should differentiate well between kinds of work.

※ They should differentiate well between people.

※ They should be broad enough that a small number of these categories can cover the whole universe of jobs and people.

※ They should have neutral connotations, neither negative nor positive.

The RIASEC Personality Types

During the 1950s, the career guidance researcher John L. Holland tried to find a meaningful new way to arrange the output of an interest inventory and relate it to occupations. He devised a set of six personality types that would meet the criteria listed in the previous section, and he called them Realistic, Investigative, Artistic, Social, Enterprising, and Conventional. (The acronym *RIASEC* is a convenient way to remember them.)

The following table shows how these labels apply to both people and work:

Personality Type	How It Applies to People	How It Applies to Work
Realistic	Realistic personalities like work activities that include practical, hands-on problems and solutions. They enjoy dealing with plants, animals, and real-world materials like wood, tools, and machinery. They enjoy outside work. Often they do not like occupations that mainly involve doing paperwork or working closely with others.	Realistic occupations frequently involve work activities that include practical, hands-on problems and solutions. They often deal with plants; animals; and real-world materials like wood, tools, and machinery. Many of the occupations require working outside and do not involve a lot of paperwork or working closely with others.
Investigative	Investigative personalities like work activities that have to do with ideas and thinking more than with physical activity. They like to search for facts and figure out problems mentally rather than to persuade or lead people.	Investigative occupations frequently involve working with ideas and require an extensive amount of thinking. These occupations can involve searching for facts and figuring out problems mentally.
Artistic	Artistic personalities like work activities that deal with the artistic side of things, such as forms, designs, and patterns. They like self-expression in their work. They prefer settings where work can be done without following a clear set of rules.	Artistic occupations frequently involve working with forms, designs, and patterns. They often require self-expression, and the work can be done without following a clear set of rules.
Social	Social personalities like work activities that assist others and promote learning and personal development. They prefer to communicate more than to work with objects, machines, or data. They like to teach, to give advice, to help, or otherwise to be of service to people.	Social occupations frequently involve working with, communicating with, and teaching people. These occupations often involve helping or providing service to others.
Enterprising	Enterprising personalities like work activities having to do with starting up and carrying out projects, especially business ventures. They like persuading and leading people and making decisions. They like taking risks for profit. These personalities prefer action rather than thought.	Enterprising occupations frequently involve starting up and carrying out projects. These occupations can involve leading people and making many decisions. They sometimes require risk taking and often deal with business.
Conventional	Conventional personalities like work activities that follow set procedures and routines. They prefer working with data and details rather than with ideas. They prefer work in which there are precise standards rather than work in which you have to judge things by yourself. These personalities like working where the lines of authority are clear.	Conventional occupations frequently involve following set procedures and routines. These occupations can include working with data and details more than with ideas. Usually there is a clear line of authority to follow.

Holland went further by arranging these six personality types on a hexagon:

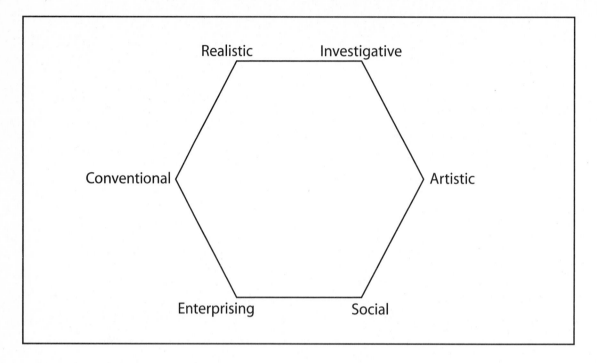

Figure 1: Holland's hexagon of personality types. (After Holland, A Theory of Vocational Choice, 1959.)

He used this diagram to explain that people tend to resemble one type primarily, but they may also have aspects of one or more adjacent types. Each personality type tends to have aspects of the types on the adjacent sides of the hexagon, but little in common with the type on the opposite side. Therefore, for example, a person might be primarily Realistic, with an additional but smaller resemblance to the Conventional type. Such a person would be described by the two-letter code RC and might be well suited to work as a Boilermaker or a Roofer (both coded RC). This person would have little in common with a Social personality type and likely would not be very happy or productive as a Special Education Teacher (coded SA). But this person could get along well with both Realistic and Conventional personalities and, to a lesser extent, with Investigative personalities.

Although Holland originally applied this model to academic advising, he soon extended it to the larger question of career choice. Since then, hundreds of researchers and practitioners have investigated the RIASEC framework and have applied it to real-life decisions and situations. Researchers have even found it useful for predicting who will have the most traffic accidents or what kinds of drug abuse people are likely to engage in. More relevant to the theme of this book, however, is the fact that a number of career decision-making assessments have been developed to help people determine what personality type best describes them (and perhaps an additional adjacent type or types that are also important). You can find one such assessment in Part II of this book.

Although the RIASEC scheme does a good job of covering the whole world of work, the symmetrical hexagon shape used to illustrate it may be a little misleading because when you count the different jobs in our economy and the number of people working in those jobs, you'll find that some sectors of the hexagon are much more heavily populated than others. Here is a breakdown of the 732 occupations in the Department of Labor's SOC classification for which we have both RIASEC codes and figures for workforce size:

Personality Type	Number of Occupations	Number of Workers 2006
Realistic	329	47,947,078
Investigative	79	6,503,428
Artistic	32	2,600,124
Social	107	22,554,382
Enterprising	91	28,477,616
Conventional	94	34,370,117

As the United States shifts from a manufacturing economy to an information economy, employment in the Realistic sector is declining and employment in the Investigative sector is growing, but a large imbalance is likely to continue for the foreseeable future.

The six sectors are asymmetrical in other ways, too. As you'll see when you look at the lists in Part III, Social jobs employ a lot more women than Realistic jobs do. Enterprising jobs employ a lot more men than do Conventional jobs. Likewise, there are differences when you consider where large numbers of young people and older people work.

The differences get really significant when you look at the amounts of education or training required by jobs linked to the various personality types. For example, for Realistic and Conventional jobs the most common entry route is on-the-job training, whereas for Investigative jobs a college degree is usually needed. John Holland and other researchers have explained that these differences reflect the different levels of cognitive complexity to be found in the jobs. Realistic jobs deal mainly with manipulating things physically—moving them, cleaning them, repairing them, and so forth. Conventional jobs deal mainly with data at the level of organizing it according to pre-determined patterns—filing it, keying it in, and so forth. Investigative jobs, on the other hand, deal mainly with ideas and solving problems mentally, so the level of cognitive complexity is high and a college education becomes a necessity.

You should not be troubled by this lack of symmetry in the RIASEC model (even if you are an Artistic type). It does not indicate a weakness in the theory. But it does create some problems for a book like this. Although we have attempted to give equal coverage to each of the six personality types, you will notice that some of the sets of lists in Part III are not of equal size. Also, since we identified the "50 Best Artistic Jobs" out of a pool of only 70 jobs (some of which have Artistic as a secondary personality type), when you scan that list you may want to concentrate on the higher-ranked choices. On the other hand, to create the list of the "50 Best Realistic Jobs," we sorted a pool of 285 jobs, so the best 50 truly represent the upper crust of that large group. These differences simply reflect the nature of the United States workforce.

No theory can perfectly describe the infinite variety of personalities to be found in our culture and the messy distribution of jobs that a free economy produces. You should note that the RIASEC scheme for describing personality types is not the only one that is used in career decision-making. However, it is the most popular and most thoroughly researched one, so it is the most appropriate one to use in this book.

Other Assessments with RIASEC Output

Apart from the assessment in Part II of this book, you may want to use any of these free assessments to explore your personality type in RIASEC terms:

❋ The O*NET Computerized Interest Profiler (for Windows), which you can download at www.onetcenter.org/CIP.html (the assessment in Part II is based on it)

❋ The University of Missouri's Career Center Career Interests Game at http://career.missouri.edu/students/explore/thecareerinterestsgame.php

❋ The Work Interest Quiz at www.myfuture.com/toolbox/workinterest.html

❋ The University of New Orleans's "What Is Your RIASEC?" checklist at www.career.uno.edu/pdfs/Career%20Interest%20Game.pdf

You also have a number of options if you are willing to pay a fee. For example, you can access John Holland's own Self-Directed Search at www.self-directed-search.com/.

Keep in mind that although all of these assessments produce outputs with RIASEC codes and some of them also link these codes to occupations, they will not necessarily produce the exact same output. Assessment of personality is not as exact a science as, say, chemistry. Neither is the task of linking personalities to occupations.

You should not regard the output of *any* personality assessment as the final word on what career will suit you best. Use a variety of approaches to decide what kind of person you are and narrow down the kinds of work you enjoy. Actual work experience is probably the best way to test a tentative choice.

PART II

What's Your Personality Type? Take an Assessment

In this section, you can take a Personality Type Inventory that will help you determine your primary RIASEC personality type and perhaps one or two secondary RIASEC personality types. It asks if you like or dislike various activities and then lets you score your responses. You can use your scores in the following sections of the book to identify specific highly rewarding jobs to explore.

It's easy to use the Personality Type Inventory—just turn the page and follow the directions beginning with Step 1. This is not a test, so there are no right or wrong answers. There is also no time limit for completing this inventory.

If someone else will be using this book, you should photocopy the inventory pages and mark your responses on the photocopy.

Note: This inventory is based on the O*NET Interest Profiler, Version 3.0, developed by the U.S. Department of Labor (DOL). The DOL's edition consists of several components, including the Interest Profiler Instrument, Interest Profiler Score Report, and Interest Profiler O*NET Occupations Master List. The DOL provides a separate Interest Profiler User's Guide with information on the Profiler's development and validity as well as tips for professionals using it in career counseling. Additional information on these items is available at www.onetcenter.org, which is maintained by the DOL. This Personality Type Inventory is a version of the DOL's O*NET Interest Profiler that uses its work activity items and scoring system but has shorter directions, format changes, and additional content.

Restrictions for use: This and any other form of the O*NET Interest Profiler should be used for career exploration, career planning, and vocational counseling purposes only, and no other use has been authorized or is valid. Results should not be used for employment or hiring decisions or for applicant screening for jobs or training programs. Please see the DOL's separate "O*NET User Agreement" at www.onetcenter.org/agree/tools for additional details on restrictions and use. The word "O*NET" is a trademark of the U.S. Department of Labor, Employment and Training Administration.

JIST Publishing offers a color foldout version of this assessment. It is called the *O*NET Career Interests Inventory* and is sold in packages of 25.

Step 1: Respond to the Statements

Carefully read each work activity (items 1 through 180). For each item, fill in just one of the three circles as follows:

If you think you would LIKE the activity, fill in the circle containing the L, like this:

(L)   (?)   (D)

If you think you would DISLIKE the activity, fill in the circle containing the D, like this:

(L)   (?)   (D)

If you are UNSURE whether you would like the activity, fill in the circle with the ?, like this:

(L)   (?)   (D)

As you respond to each activity, don't consider whether you have the education or training needed for it or how much money you might earn if it were part of your job. Simply fill in the circle based on whether you would like, would dislike, or aren't sure about the activity.

After you respond to all 180 activities, you'll score your responses in Step 2.

Would you LIKE the activity or DISLIKE the activity, or are you UNSURE?

		L	?	D
1.	Build kitchen cabinets	(L)	(?)	(D)
2.	Guard money in an armored car	(L)	(?)	(D)
3.	Operate a dairy farm	(L)	(?)	(D)
4.	Lay brick or tile	(L)	(?)	(D)
5.	Monitor a machine on an assembly line	(L)	(?)	(D)
6.	Repair household appliances	(L)	(?)	(D)
7.	Drive a taxicab	(L)	(?)	(D)
8.	Install flooring in houses	(L)	(?)	(D)
9.	Raise fish in a fish hatchery	(L)	(?)	(D)
10.	Build a brick walkway	(L)	(?)	(D)
11.	Assemble electronic parts	(L)	(?)	(D)
12.	Drive a truck to deliver packages to offices and homes	(L)	(?)	(D)
13.	Paint houses	(L)	(?)	(D)
14.	Enforce fish and game laws	(L)	(?)	(D)
15.	Operate a grinding machine in a factory	(L)	(?)	(D)
16.	Work on an offshore oil-drilling rig	(L)	(?)	(D)
17.	Perform lawn care services	(L)	(?)	(D)
18.	Assemble products in a factory	(L)	(?)	(D)
19.	Catch fish as a member of a fishing crew	(L)	(?)	(D)
20.	Refinish furniture	(L)	(?)	(D)
21.	Fix a broken faucet	(L)	(?)	(D)
22.	Do cleaning or maintenance work	(L)	(?)	(D)
23.	Maintain the grounds of a park	(L)	(?)	(D)
24.	Operate a machine on a production line	(L)	(?)	(D)
25.	Spray trees to prevent the spread of harmful insects	(L)	(?)	(D)
26.	Test the quality of parts before shipment	(L)	(?)	(D)
27.	Operate a motorboat to carry passengers	(L)	(?)	(D)
28.	Repair and install locks	(L)	(?)	(D)
29.	Set up and operate machines to make products	(L)	(?)	(D)
30.	Put out forest fires	(L)	(?)	(D)

____ **Page Score for R**

Would you LIKE the activity or DISLIKE the activity, or are you UNSURE?

		L	?	D
31.	Study space travel	Ⓛ	⑦	Ⓓ
32.	Make a map of the bottom of an ocean	Ⓛ	⑦	Ⓓ
33.	Study the history of past civilizations	Ⓛ	⑦	Ⓓ
34.	Study animal behavior	Ⓛ	⑦	Ⓓ
35.	Develop a new medicine	Ⓛ	⑦	Ⓓ
36.	Plan a research study	Ⓛ	⑦	Ⓓ
37.	Study ways to reduce water pollution	Ⓛ	⑦	Ⓓ
38.	Develop a new medical treatment or procedure	Ⓛ	⑦	Ⓓ
39.	Determine the infection rate of a new disease	Ⓛ	⑦	Ⓓ
40.	Study rocks and minerals	Ⓛ	⑦	Ⓓ
41.	Diagnose and treat sick animals	Ⓛ	⑦	Ⓓ
42.	Study the personalities of world leaders	Ⓛ	⑦	Ⓓ
43.	Conduct chemical experiments	Ⓛ	⑦	Ⓓ
44.	Conduct biological research	Ⓛ	⑦	Ⓓ
45.	Study the population growth of a city	Ⓛ	⑦	Ⓓ
46.	Study whales and other types of marine life	Ⓛ	⑦	Ⓓ
47.	Investigate crimes	Ⓛ	⑦	Ⓓ
48.	Study the movement of planets	Ⓛ	⑦	Ⓓ
49.	Examine blood samples using a microscope	Ⓛ	⑦	Ⓓ
50.	Investigate the cause of a fire	Ⓛ	⑦	Ⓓ
51.	Study the structure of the human body	Ⓛ	⑦	Ⓓ
52.	Develop psychological profiles of criminals	Ⓛ	⑦	Ⓓ
53.	Develop a new way to better predict the weather	Ⓛ	⑦	Ⓓ
54.	Work in a biology lab	Ⓛ	⑦	Ⓓ
55.	Invent a replacement for sugar	Ⓛ	⑦	Ⓓ
56.	Study genetics	Ⓛ	⑦	Ⓓ
57.	Study the governments of different countries	Ⓛ	⑦	Ⓓ
58.	Do research on plants or animals	Ⓛ	⑦	Ⓓ
59.	Do laboratory tests to identify diseases	Ⓛ	⑦	Ⓓ
60.	Study weather conditions	Ⓛ	⑦	Ⓓ

_____ **Page Score for I**

Would you LIKE the activity or DISLIKE the activity, or are you UNSURE?

		L	?	D
61.	Conduct a symphony orchestra	L	?	D
62.	Write stories or articles for magazines	L	?	D
63.	Direct a play	L	?	D
64.	Create dance routines for a show	L	?	D
65.	Write books or plays	L	?	D
66.	Play a musical instrument	L	?	D
67.	Perform comedy routines in front of an audience	L	?	D
68.	Perform as an extra in movies, plays, or television shows	L	?	D
69.	Write reviews of books or plays	L	?	D
70.	Compose or arrange music	L	?	D
71.	Act in a movie	L	?	D
72.	Dance in a Broadway show	L	?	D
73.	Draw pictures	L	?	D
74.	Sing professionally	L	?	D
75.	Perform stunts for a movie or television show	L	?	D
76.	Create special effects for movies	L	?	D
77.	Conduct a musical choir	L	?	D
78.	Act in a play	L	?	D
79.	Paint sets for plays	L	?	D
80.	Audition singers and musicians for a musical show	L	?	D
81.	Design sets for plays	L	?	D
82.	Announce a radio show	L	?	D
83.	Write scripts for movies or television shows	L	?	D
84.	Write a song	L	?	D
85.	Perform jazz or tap dance	L	?	D
86.	Direct a movie	L	?	D
87.	Sing in a band	L	?	D
88.	Design artwork for magazines	L	?	D
89.	Edit movies	L	?	D
90.	Pose for a photographer	L	?	D

____ **Page Score for A**

Would you LIKE the activity or DISLIKE the activity, or are you UNSURE?

		L	?	D
91.	Teach an individual an exercise routine	L	?	D
92.	Perform nursing duties in a hospital	L	?	D
93.	Give CPR to someone who has stopped breathing	L	?	D
94.	Help people with personal or emotional problems	L	?	D
95.	Teach children how to read	L	?	D
96.	Work with mentally disabled children	L	?	D
97.	Teach an elementary school class	L	?	D
98.	Give career guidance to people	L	?	D
99.	Supervise the activities of children at a camp	L	?	D
100.	Help people with family-related problems	L	?	D
101.	Perform rehabilitation therapy	L	?	D
102.	Do volunteer work at a nonprofit organization	L	?	D
103.	Help elderly people with their daily activities	L	?	D
104.	Teach children how to play sports	L	?	D
105.	Help disabled people improve their daily living skills	L	?	D
106.	Teach sign language to people with hearing disabilities	L	?	D
107.	Help people who have problems with drugs or alcohol	L	?	D
108.	Help conduct a group therapy session	L	?	D
109.	Help families care for ill relatives	L	?	D
110.	Provide massage therapy to people	L	?	D
111.	Plan exercises for disabled students	L	?	D
112.	Counsel people who have a life-threatening illness	L	?	D
113.	Teach disabled people work and living skills	L	?	D
114.	Organize activities at a recreational facility	L	?	D
115.	Take care of children at a day-care center	L	?	D
116.	Organize field trips for disabled people	L	?	D
117.	Assist doctors in treating patients	L	?	D
118.	Work with juveniles on probation	L	?	D
119.	Provide physical therapy to people recovering from an injury	L	?	D
120.	Teach a high school class	L	?	D

_____ **Page Score for S**

Would you LIKE the activity or DISLIKE the activity, or are you UNSURE?

		L	?	D
121.	Buy and sell stocks and bonds	Ⓛ	⍰	Ⓓ
122.	Manage a retail store	Ⓛ	⍰	Ⓓ
123.	Sell telephone and other communication equipment	Ⓛ	⍰	Ⓓ
124.	Operate a beauty salon or barbershop	Ⓛ	⍰	Ⓓ
125.	Sell merchandise over the telephone	Ⓛ	⍰	Ⓓ
126.	Run a stand that sells newspapers and magazines	Ⓛ	⍰	Ⓓ
127.	Give a presentation about a product you are selling	Ⓛ	⍰	Ⓓ
128.	Buy and sell land	Ⓛ	⍰	Ⓓ
129.	Sell compact discs at a music store	Ⓛ	⍰	Ⓓ
130.	Run a toy store	Ⓛ	⍰	Ⓓ
131.	Manage the operations of a hotel	Ⓛ	⍰	Ⓓ
132.	Sell houses	Ⓛ	⍰	Ⓓ
133.	Sell candy and popcorn at sports events	Ⓛ	⍰	Ⓓ
134.	Manage a supermarket	Ⓛ	⍰	Ⓓ
135.	Manage a department within a large company	Ⓛ	⍰	Ⓓ
136.	Sell a soft drink product line to stores and restaurants	Ⓛ	⍰	Ⓓ
137.	Sell refreshments at a movie theater	Ⓛ	⍰	Ⓓ
138.	Sell hair-care products to stores and salons	Ⓛ	⍰	Ⓓ
139.	Start your own business	Ⓛ	⍰	Ⓓ
140.	Negotiate business contracts	Ⓛ	⍰	Ⓓ
141.	Represent a client in a lawsuit	Ⓛ	⍰	Ⓓ
142.	Negotiate contracts for professional athletes	Ⓛ	⍰	Ⓓ
143.	Be responsible for the operation of a company	Ⓛ	⍰	Ⓓ
144.	Market a new line of clothing	Ⓛ	⍰	Ⓓ
145.	Sell newspaper advertisements	Ⓛ	⍰	Ⓓ
146.	Sell merchandise at a department store	Ⓛ	⍰	Ⓓ
147.	Sell automobiles	Ⓛ	⍰	Ⓓ
148.	Manage a clothing store	Ⓛ	⍰	Ⓓ
149.	Sell restaurant franchises to individuals	Ⓛ	⍰	Ⓓ
150.	Sell computer equipment in a store	Ⓛ	⍰	Ⓓ

____ **Page Score for E**

Would you LIKE the activity or DISLIKE the activity, or are you UNSURE?

		L	?	D
151.	Develop a spreadsheet using computer software	L	?	D
152.	Proofread records or forms	L	?	D
153.	Use a computer program to generate customer bills	L	?	D
154.	Schedule conferences for an organization	L	?	D
155.	Keep accounts payable/receivable for an office	L	?	D
156.	Load computer software into a large computer network	L	?	D
157.	Transfer funds between banks using a computer	L	?	D
158.	Organize and schedule office meetings	L	?	D
159.	Use a word processor to edit and format documents	L	?	D
160.	Operate a calculator	L	?	D
161.	Direct or transfer phone calls for a large organization	L	?	D
162.	Perform office filing tasks	L	?	D
163.	Compute and record statistical and other numerical data	L	?	D
164.	Generate the monthly payroll checks for an office	L	?	D
165.	Take notes during a meeting	L	?	D
166.	Keep shipping and receiving records	L	?	D
167.	Calculate the wages of employees	L	?	D
168.	Assist senior-level accountants in performing bookkeeping tasks	L	?	D
169.	Type labels for envelopes and packages	L	?	D
170.	Inventory supplies using a hand-held computer	L	?	D
171.	Develop an office filing system	L	?	D
172.	Keep records of financial transactions for an organization	L	?	D
173.	Record information from customers applying for charge accounts	L	?	D
174.	Photocopy letters and reports	L	?	D
175.	Record rent payments	L	?	D
176.	Enter information into a database	L	?	D
177.	Keep inventory records	L	?	D
178.	Maintain employee records	L	?	D
179.	Stamp, sort, and distribute mail for an organization	L	?	D
180.	Handle customers' bank transactions	L	?	D

____ **Page Score for C**

Step 2: Score Your Responses

Do the following to score your responses:

1. **Score the responses on each page.** On each page of responses, go from top to bottom and add the number of "L"s you filled in. Then write that number in the "Page Score" box at the bottom of the page. Go on to the next page and do the same there.

2. **Determine your primary interest area.** Which Page Score has your highest score: **R, I, A, S, E,** or **C**? Enter the letter for that personality type on the following line.

My Primary Personality Type: ___

You will use your Primary Personality Type *first* to explore careers. (If two Page Scores are tied for the highest scores or are within 5 points of each other, use both of them for your Primary Personality Type. You are equally divided between two types.)

- ❋ R = Realistic
- ❋ I = Investigative
- ❋ A = Artistic
- ❋ S = Social
- ❋ E = Enterprising
- ❋ C = Conventional

3. **Determine your secondary interest areas.** Which Page Score has your next highest score? Which has your third highest score? Enter the letters for those areas on the following lines.

My Secondary Personality Types: ___ ___

(If you do not find many occupations that you like using your Primary Personality Type, you can use your Secondary Personality Types to look at more career options.)

Step 3: Find Jobs That Suit Your Personality Type

Start with your Primary Personality Type. Turn to Part III and look at the Best Jobs lists for your type. Find lists that suit your particular priorities and see what job titles appear there. Don't rule out a job just because the title is not familiar to you.

When you find job titles that interest you or that you want to learn more about, turn to Part IV. The job descriptions there are grouped by Primary Personality Type and are listed alphabetically within each type. Of course, you can also look at jobs that are linked to one of your Secondary Personality Types.

If you want to find jobs that *combine* your Primary Personality Type and a Secondary Personality Type, turn to Appendix A. All 326 jobs described in Part IV of this book are listed there by their one- or two-letter personality codes. For example, if your Primary Personality Type is Social and your Secondary Personality Type is Enterprising, you would look in Appendix A for the letter S and then for jobs coded SE, such as Personal Financial Advisors and Training and Development Specialists.

You may discover that you can't find an appealing job in your Primary Personality Type that *also* is coded for one of your Secondary Personality Types. That is not necessarily a problem. John Holland himself has remarked, "You cannot expect a single job to satisfy all aspects of your personality." This is why we have hobbies. Use recreational time for activities related to your Secondary Personality Types. Volunteer work can be another outlet for these interests and abilities.

PART III

The Best Jobs Lists: Jobs for Each of the Six Personality Types

This part contains a lot of interesting lists, and it's a good place for you to start using the book. Here are some suggestions for using the lists to explore career options:

❋ The Table of Contents at the beginning of this book presents a complete listing of the list titles in this section. You can browse the lists or use the Table of Contents to find those that interest you most.

❋ We gave the lists clear titles, so most require little explanation. We provide comments for each group of lists.

❋ As you review the lists, one or more of the jobs may appeal to you enough that you want to seek additional information. As this happens, mark that job (or, if someone else will be using this book, write it on a separate sheet of paper) so that you can look up the description of the job in Part IV.

❋ Keep in mind that all jobs in these lists meet our basic criteria for being included in this book. All lists, therefore, are organized by personality type and emphasize occupations with high pay, high growth, or large numbers of openings. These economic measures are easily quantified and are often presented in lists of best jobs in the newspapers and other media. While earnings, growth, and openings are important, there are other factors to consider in your career planning. For example, location, having an opportunity to serve others, and enjoying your work are a few of many factors that may define the ideal job for you. These measures are difficult or impossible to quantify and thus are not used in this book, so you will need to consider the importance of these issues yourself. The resources listed in Appendix D may help you research these issues.

❋ All data used to create these lists comes from the U.S. Department of Labor. The earnings figures are based on the average annual pay received by full-time workers. Because the earnings represent the national averages, actual pay rates can vary greatly by location, amount of previous work experience, and other factors.

Best Jobs Overall for Each Personality Type: Jobs with the Highest Pay, Fastest Growth, and Most Openings

The four sets of lists that follow are the most important lists in this book. The first set of lists presents, for each personality type, the jobs with the highest combined scores for pay, growth, and number of openings. These are very appealing lists because they represent jobs with the very highest quantifiable measures from our labor market. The 283 jobs in these six lists are the ones that are described in detail in Part IV.

The three additional sets of lists present, for each personality type, jobs with the highest scores in each of three measures: annual earnings, projected percentage growth, and largest number of openings.

The 50 Best Jobs for Each Personality Type

These are the lists that most people want to see first. For each personality type, you can see the jobs that have the highest overall combined ratings for earnings, projected growth, and number of openings. (The "How the Jobs in This Book Were Selected" section in the Introduction explains in detail how we rated jobs to assemble this list.)

Although each list covers one personality type, you'll notice a wide variety of jobs on the list. For example, among the top 20 Investigative jobs are some in the fields of high technology, medicine, education, and business. Among the top 20 Conventional jobs are some in the financial, legal, technology, and health-care industries. We included each job's personality code, which indicates its primary and secondary (if any) personality types.

A look at one list will clarify how we ordered the jobs—take the Realistic list as an example. Civil Engineers is on the top of the list because it was the occupation with the best total score. The second-place job, Surveyors, has somewhat better projected job growth, but it has fewer projected job openings and considerably lower earnings, so its total score was lower than that for Civil Engineers. The other occupations follow in descending order based on their total scores. Many jobs had tied scores and were simply listed one after another, so there are often only very small or even no differences between the scores of jobs that are near each other on the list. All other job lists in this book use these lists as their source. You can find descriptions for each of these jobs in Part IV, beginning on page 129.

The 50 Best Realistic Jobs

Job	Personality Code	Annual Earnings	Percent Growth	Annual Openings
1. Civil Engineers	RIC	$71,710	18.0%	15,979
2. Surveyors	RCI	$51,630	23.7%	14,305
3. Computer Support Specialists	RIC	$42,400	12.9%	97,334
4. Construction and Building Inspectors	RCI	$48,330	18.2%	12,606
5. Radiologic Technologists and Technicians	RS	$50,260	15.1%	12,836
6. Correctional Officers and Jailers	REC	$36,970	16.9%	56,579
7. Plumbers, Pipefitters, and Steamfitters	RC	$44,090	10.6%	68,643
8. Surgical Technologists	RSC	$37,540	24.5%	15,365
9. Fire Fighters	RS	$43,170	12.1%	18,887
10. Automotive Service Technicians and Mechanics	RI	$34,170	14.3%	97,350
11. Biological Technicians	RIC	$37,810	16.0%	15,374
12. Electricians	RIC	$44,780	7.4%	79,083
13. Carpenters	RCI	$37,660	10.3%	223,225
14. Bus and Truck Mechanics and Diesel Engine Specialists	RC	$38,640	11.5%	25,428
15. Truck Drivers, Heavy and Tractor-Trailer	RC	$36,220	10.4%	279,032
16. Aircraft Mechanics and Service Technicians	RCI	$49,010	10.6%	9,708
17. Airline Pilots, Copilots, and Flight Engineers	RCI	$145,600+	12.9%	4,073
18. Mobile Heavy Equipment Mechanics, Except Engines	RC	$41,450	12.3%	11,037
19. Roofers	RC	$33,240	14.3%	38,398
20. Tile and Marble Setters	RCA	$38,720	15.4%	9,066
21. Brickmasons and Blockmasons	RCI	$44,070	9.7%	17,569
22. Aircraft Structure, Surfaces, Rigging, and Systems Assemblers	RC	$45,420	12.8%	6,550
23. Automotive Body and Related Repairers	R	$35,690	11.6%	37,469
24. Industrial Machinery Mechanics	RIC	$42,350	9.0%	23,361
25. Cardiovascular Technologists and Technicians	RIS	$44,940	25.5%	3,550
26. Captains, Mates, and Pilots of Water Vessels	REC	$57,210	17.9%	2,665
27. Operating Engineers and Other Construction Equipment Operators	RCI	$38,130	8.4%	55,468
28. Cartographers and Photogrammetrists	RIC	$49,970	20.3%	2,823
29. Water and Liquid Waste Treatment Plant and System Operators	RC	$37,090	13.8%	9,575
30. Painters, Construction and Maintenance	RC	$32,080	11.8%	101,140
31. Heating, Air Conditioning, and Refrigeration Mechanics and Installers	RC	$38,360	8.7%	29,719

(continued)

(continued)

The 50 Best Realistic Jobs

Job	Personality Code	Annual Earnings	Percent Growth	Annual Openings
32. Bus Drivers, Transit and Intercity	RS	$33,160	12.5%	27,100
33. Cement Masons and Concrete Finishers	RE	$33,840	11.4%	34,625
34. Sheet Metal Workers	R	$39,210	6.7%	31,677
35. Medical and Clinical Laboratory Technicians	RIC	$34,270	15.0%	10,866
36. Maintenance and Repair Workers, General	RCI	$32,570	10.1%	165,502
37. Electrical and Electronic Engineering Technicians	RIC	$52,140	3.6%	12,583
38. Telecommunications Line Installers and Repairers	RE	$47,220	4.6%	14,719
39. Athletes and Sports Competitors	RE	$38,440	19.2%	4,293
40. Architectural and Civil Drafters	RCA	$43,310	6.1%	16,238
41. Civil Engineering Technicians	RCI	$42,580	10.2%	7,499
42. Audio and Video Equipment Technicians	RIC	$36,050	24.2%	4,681
43. Electrical Power-Line Installers and Repairers	RIC	$52,570	7.2%	6,401
44. Security and Fire Alarm Systems Installers	RC	$35,390	20.2%	5,729
45. Telecommunications Equipment Installers and Repairers, Except Line Installers	RIC	$54,070	2.5%	13,541
46. Drywall and Ceiling Tile Installers	RC	$36,520	7.3%	30,945
47. Transportation Inspectors	RCI	$51,440	16.4%	2,122
48. Sailors and Marine Oilers	RC	$32,570	15.7%	8,600
49. Boilermakers	RC	$50,700	14.0%	2,333
50. Mechanical Drafters	RCI	$44,740	5.2%	10,902

The 50 Best Investigative Jobs

Job	Personality Code	Annual Earnings	Percent Growth	Annual Openings
1. Computer Software Engineers, Applications	IRC	$83,130	44.6%	58,690
2. Anesthesiologists	IRS	$145,600+	14.2%	38,027
3. Family and General Practitioners	IS	$145,600+	14.2%	38,027
4. Internists, General	ISR	$145,600+	14.2%	38,027
5. Obstetricians and Gynecologists	ISR	$145,600+	14.2%	38,027
6. Psychiatrists	ISA	$145,600+	14.2%	38,027
7. Surgeons	IRS	$145,600+	14.2%	38,027
8. Computer Software Engineers, Systems Software	ICR	$89,070	28.2%	33,139
9. Pediatricians, General	IS	$140,690	14.2%	38,027
10. Pharmacists	ICS	$100,480	21.7%	16,358
11. Computer Systems Analysts	ICR	$73,090	29.0%	63,166

The 50 Best Investigative Jobs

Job	Personality Code	Annual Earnings	Percent Growth	Annual Openings
12. Management Analysts	IEC	$71,150	21.9%	125,669
13. Network Systems and Data Communications Analysts	IC	$68,220	53.4%	35,086
14. Computer and Information Scientists, Research	IRC	$97,970	21.5%	2,901
15. Engineering Teachers, Postsecondary	IRS	$79,510	22.9%	5,565
16. Network and Computer Systems Administrators	ICR	$64,690	27.0%	37,010
17. Veterinarians	IR	$75,230	35.0%	5,301
18. Industrial Engineers	ICE	$71,430	20.3%	11,272
19. Environmental Engineers	IRC	$72,350	25.4%	5,003
20. Market Research Analysts	IEC	$60,300	20.1%	45,015
21. Dentists, General	IRS	$137,630	9.2%	7,106
22. Geoscientists, Except Hydrologists and Geographers	IR	$75,800	21.9%	2,471
23. Aerospace Engineers	IR	$90,930	10.2%	6,498
24. Medical Scientists, Except Epidemiologists	IRA	$64,200	20.2%	10,596
25. Environmental Scientists and Specialists, Including Health	IRC	$58,380	25.1%	6,961
26. Biochemists and Biophysicists	IAR	$79,270	15.9%	1,637
27. Biomedical Engineers	IR	$75,440	21.1%	1,804
28. Optometrists	ISR	$93,800	11.3%	1,789
29. Clinical, Counseling, and School Psychologists	ISA	$62,210	15.8%	8,309
30. Environmental Science and Protection Technicians, Including Health	IRC	$39,370	28.0%	8,404
31. Forensic Science Technicians	IRC	$47,680	30.7%	3,074
32. Hydrologists	IR	$68,140	24.3%	687
33. Industrial-Organizational Psychologists	IEA	$80,820	21.3%	118
34. Operations Research Analysts	ICE	$66,950	10.6%	5,727
35. Orthodontists	IRS	$145,600+	9.2%	479
36. Prosthodontists	IR	$145,600+	10.7%	54
37. Diagnostic Medical Sonographers	ISR	$59,860	19.1%	3,211
38. Medical and Clinical Laboratory Technologists	IRC	$51,720	12.4%	11,457
39. Electrical Engineers	IR	$79,240	6.3%	6,806
40. Podiatrists	ISR	$110,510	9.5%	648
41. Computer Hardware Engineers	IRC	$91,860	4.6%	3,572
42. Chemical Engineers	IR	$81,500	7.9%	2,111
43. Chemists	IRC	$63,490	9.1%	9,024
44. Electronics Engineers, Except Computer	IR	$83,340	3.7%	5,699

(continued)

(continued)

The 50 Best Investigative Jobs

Job	Personality Code	Annual Earnings	Percent Growth	Annual Openings
45. Nuclear Medicine Technologists	IRS	$64,670	14.8%	1,290
46. Atmospheric and Space Scientists	IR	$78,390	10.6%	735
47. Mathematicians	ICA	$90,870	10.2%	473
48. Mechanical Engineers	IRC	$72,300	4.2%	12,394
49. Physicists	IR	$96,850	6.8%	1,302
50. Survey Researchers	ICE	$36,820	15.9%	4,959

Jobs 2, 3, 4, 5, 6, 7, and 9 share 38,027 openings.

The 50 Best Artistic Jobs

Job	Personality Code	Annual Earnings	Percent Growth	Annual Openings
1. Multi-Media Artists and Animators	AI	$54,550	25.8%	13,182
2. Art, Drama, and Music Teachers, Postsecondary	SA	$55,190	22.9%	12,707
3. Architects, Except Landscape and Naval	AI	$67,620	17.7%	11,324
4. English Language and Literature Teachers, Postsecondary	SAI	$54,000	22.9%	10,475
5. Education Teachers, Postsecondary	SAI	$54,220	22.9%	9,359
6. Training and Development Specialists	SAC	$49,630	18.3%	35,862
7. Public Relations Specialists	EAS	$49,800	17.6%	51,216
8. Special Education Teachers, Preschool, Kindergarten, and Elementary School	SA	$48,350	19.6%	20,049
9. Technical Writers	AIC	$60,390	19.5%	7,498
10. Substance Abuse and Behavioral Disorder Counselors	SAI	$35,580	34.3%	20,821
11. Elementary School Teachers, Except Special Education	SAC	$47,330	13.6%	181,612
12. Public Relations Managers	EA	$86,470	16.9%	5,781
13. Writers and Authors	AEI	$50,660	12.8%	24,023
14. Communications Teachers, Postsecondary	SA	$54,720	22.9%	4,074
15. Self-Enrichment Education Teachers	SAE	$34,580	23.1%	64,449
16. Kindergarten Teachers, Except Special Education	SA	$45,120	16.3%	27,603
17. Foreign Language and Literature Teachers, Postsecondary	SAI	$53,610	22.9%	4,317
18. Philosophy and Religion Teachers, Postsecondary	SAI	$56,380	22.9%	3,120

The 50 Best Artistic Jobs

Job	Personality Code	Annual Earnings	Percent Growth	Annual Openings
19. Middle School Teachers, Except Special and Vocational Education	SA	$47,900	11.2%	75,270
20. Preschool Teachers, Except Special Education	SA	$23,130	26.3%	78,172
21. Art Directors	AE	$72,320	9.0%	9,719
22. Producers and Directors	EAC	$61,090	11.1%	8,992
23. Architecture Teachers, Postsecondary	SA	$68,540	22.9%	1,044
24. Marriage and Family Therapists	SAI	$43,600	29.8%	5,953
25. Secondary School Teachers, Except Special and Vocational Education	SAE	$49,420	5.6%	93,166
26. Adult Literacy, Remedial Education, and GED Teachers and Instructors	SAE	$44,710	14.2%	17,340
27. Biochemists and Biophysicists	IAR	$79,270	15.9%	1,637
28. Special Education Teachers, Middle School	SA	$48,940	15.8%	8,846
29. Interior Designers	AE	$43,970	19.5%	8,434
30. Interpreters and Translators	AS	$37,490	23.6%	6,630
31. Landscape Architects	AIR	$57,580	16.4%	2,342
32. Graphic Designers	ARE	$41,280	9.8%	26,968
33. Commercial and Industrial Designers	AER	$56,550	7.2%	4,777
34. Editors	AEC	$48,320	2.3%	20,193
35. Advertising and Promotions Managers	EAC	$78,250	6.2%	2,955
36. Music Directors and Composers	AE	$40,150	12.9%	8,597
37. Hairdressers, Hairstylists, and Cosmetologists	AES	$22,210	12.4%	73,030
38. Photographers	AR	$27,720	10.3%	16,100
39. Film and Video Editors	AEI	$47,870	12.7%	2,707
40. Anthropologists and Archeologists	IA	$53,080	15.0%	446
41. Fashion Designers	AER	$62,810	5.0%	1,968
42. Set and Exhibit Designers	AR	$43,220	17.8%	1,402
43. Sociologists	IAS	$61,140	10.0%	403
44. Makeup Artists, Theatrical and Performance	AR	$35,250	39.8%	392
45. Camera Operators, Television, Video, and Motion Picture	RA	$41,850	11.5%	3,496
46. Astronomers	IAR	$99,020	5.6%	128
47. Political Scientists	IAS	$91,580	5.3%	318
48. Fine Artists, Including Painters, Sculptors, and Illustrators	AR	$42,070	9.9%	3,830
49. Merchandise Displayers and Window Trimmers	AER	$24,830	10.7%	9,103
50. Broadcast News Analysts	ASE	$49,060	6.0%	1,444

The 50 Best Social Jobs

Job	Personality Code	Annual Earnings	Percent Growth	Annual Openings
1. Registered Nurses	SIC	$60,010	23.5%	233,499
2. Health Specialties Teachers, Postsecondary	SI	$80,700	22.9%	19,617
3. Physical Therapists	SIR	$69,760	27.1%	12,072
4. Dental Hygienists	SRC	$64,740	30.1%	10,433
5. Physician Assistants	SIR	$78,450	27.0%	7,147
6. Business Teachers, Postsecondary	SEI	$64,900	22.9%	11,643
7. Biological Science Teachers, Postsecondary	SI	$71,780	22.9%	9,039
8. Occupational Therapists	SI	$63,790	23.1%	8,338
9. Medical Assistants	SCR	$27,430	35.4%	92,977
10. Art, Drama, and Music Teachers, Postsecondary	SA	$55,190	22.9%	12,707
11. Law Teachers, Postsecondary	SIE	$87,730	22.9%	2,169
12. Mental Health Counselors	SIA	$36,000	30.0%	24,103
13. Substance Abuse and Behavioral Disorder Counselors	SAI	$35,580	34.3%	20,821
14. Computer Science Teachers, Postsecondary	SIC	$62,020	22.9%	5,820
15. Mathematical Science Teachers, Postsecondary	SIA	$58,560	22.9%	7,663
16. Economics Teachers, Postsecondary	SI	$75,300	22.9%	2,208
17. English Language and Literature Teachers, Postsecondary	SAI	$54,000	22.9%	10,475
18. Education Teachers, Postsecondary	SAI	$54,220	22.9%	9,359
19. Agricultural Sciences Teachers, Postsecondary	SIR	$78,460	22.9%	1,840
20. Psychology Teachers, Postsecondary	SIA	$60,610	22.9%	5,261
21. Vocational Education Teachers, Postsecondary	SR	$45,850	22.9%	19,313
22. Chemistry Teachers, Postsecondary	SIR	$63,870	22.9%	3,405
23. Fitness Trainers and Aerobics Instructors	SRE	$27,680	26.8%	51,235
24. Nursing Instructors and Teachers, Postsecondary	SI	$57,500	22.9%	7,337
25. Medical and Public Health Social Workers	SI	$44,670	24.2%	16,429
26. Physics Teachers, Postsecondary	SI	$70,090	22.9%	2,155
27. Self-Enrichment Education Teachers	SAE	$34,580	23.1%	64,449
28. Health Educators	SE	$42,920	26.2%	13,707
29. Radiation Therapists	SRC	$70,010	24.8%	1,461
30. Mental Health and Substance Abuse Social Workers	SIA	$36,640	29.9%	17,289
31. Preschool Teachers, Except Special Education	SA	$23,130	26.3%	78,172
32. Atmospheric, Earth, Marine, and Space Sciences Teachers, Postsecondary	SI	$73,280	22.9%	1,553
33. Instructional Coordinators	SIE	$55,270	22.5%	21,294

The 50 Best Social Jobs

Job	Personality Code	Annual Earnings	Percent Growth	Annual Openings
34. History Teachers, Postsecondary	SIA	$59,160	22.9%	3,570
35. Political Science Teachers, Postsecondary	SEA	$63,100	22.9%	2,435
36. Rehabilitation Counselors	SI	$29,630	23.0%	32,081
37. Physical Therapist Assistants	SRI	$44,130	32.4%	5,957
38. Architecture Teachers, Postsecondary	SA	$68,540	22.9%	1,044
39. Communications Teachers, Postsecondary	SA	$54,720	22.9%	4,074
40. Foreign Language and Literature Teachers, Postsecondary	SAI	$53,610	22.9%	4,317
41. Sociology Teachers, Postsecondary	SIA	$58,160	22.9%	2,774
42. Philosophy and Religion Teachers, Postsecondary	SAI	$56,380	22.9%	3,120
43. Marriage and Family Therapists	SAI	$43,600	29.8%	5,953
44. Graduate Teaching Assistants	SC	$28,060	22.9%	20,601
45. Training and Development Specialists	SAC	$49,630	18.3%	35,862
46. Anthropology and Archeology Teachers, Postsecondary	SI	$64,530	22.9%	910
47. Environmental Science Teachers, Postsecondary	SIA	$64,850	22.9%	769
48. Recreation and Fitness Studies Teachers, Postsecondary	S	$52,170	22.9%	3,010
49. Education Administrators, Preschool and Child Care Center/Program	SEC	$38,580	23.5%	8,113
50. Elementary School Teachers, Except Special Education	SAC	$47,330	13.6%	181,612

The 50 Best Enterprising Jobs

Job	Personality Code	Annual Earnings	Percent Growth	Annual Openings
1. Securities, Commodities, and Financial Services Sales Agents	EC	$68,430	24.8%	47,750
2. Financial Managers	EC	$95,310	12.6%	57,589
3. Computer and Information Systems Managers	ECI	$108,070	16.4%	30,887
4. Construction Managers	ERC	$76,230	15.7%	44,158
5. Lawyers	EI	$106,120	11.0%	49,445
6. Medical and Health Services Managers	ECS	$76,990	16.4%	31,877
7. Marketing Managers	EC	$104,400	14.4%	20,189
8. Personal Financial Advisors	ECS	$67,660	41.0%	17,114

(continued)

(continued)

The 50 Best Enterprising Jobs

Job	Personality Code	Annual Earnings	Percent Growth	Annual Openings
9. Public Relations Specialists	EAS	$49,800	17.6%	51,216
10. Social and Community Service Managers	ES	$54,530	24.7%	23,788
11. Sales Representatives, Wholesale and Manufacturing, Technical and Scientific Products	EC	$68,270	12.4%	43,469
12. Customer Service Representatives	ESC	$29,040	24.8%	600,937
13. Sales Managers	EC	$94,910	10.2%	36,392
14. Education Administrators, Postsecondary	ECS	$75,780	14.2%	17,121
15. General and Operations Managers	ECS	$88,700	1.5%	112,072
16. Employment, Recruitment, and Placement Specialists	ESC	$44,380	18.4%	33,588
17. Public Relations Managers	EA	$86,470	16.9%	5,781
18. Insurance Sales Agents	ECS	$44,110	12.9%	64,162
19. Detectives and Criminal Investigators	ECR	$59,930	17.3%	14,746
20. Property, Real Estate, and Community Association Managers	EC	$43,670	15.1%	49,916
21. Administrative Services Managers	EC	$70,990	11.7%	19,513
22. Advertising Sales Agents	ECA	$42,820	20.3%	29,233
23. Logisticians	EC	$64,250	17.3%	9,671
24. First-Line Supervisors/Managers of Construction Trades and Extraction Workers	ERC	$55,950	9.1%	82,923
25. Chief Executives	EC	$145,600+	2.0%	21,209
26. Education Administrators, Elementary and Secondary School	ESC	$80,580	7.6%	27,143
27. Training and Development Managers	ES	$84,340	15.6%	3,759
28. Compensation and Benefits Managers	ECS	$81,410	12.0%	6,121
29. First-Line Supervisors/Managers of Non-Retail Sales Workers	ECS	$67,020	3.7%	48,883
30. Police and Sheriff's Patrol Officers	ERS	$49,630	10.8%	37,842
31. First-Line Supervisors/Managers of Landscaping, Lawn Service, and Groundskeeping Workers	ERC	$38,720	17.6%	18,956
32. Natural Sciences Managers	EI	$104,040	11.4%	3,661
33. Real Estate Brokers	EC	$58,860	11.1%	18,689
34. Engineering Managers	ERI	$111,020	7.3%	7,404
35. First-Line Supervisors/Managers of Personal Service Workers	ECS	$33,900	15.5%	37,555
36. Real Estate Sales Agents	EC	$40,600	10.6%	61,232
37. Gaming Managers	EC	$64,410	24.4%	549

The 50 Best Enterprising Jobs

Job	Personality Code	Annual Earnings	Percent Growth	Annual Openings
38. Demonstrators and Product Promoters	ECR	$22,570	18.0%	32,779
39. First-Line Supervisors/Managers of Office and Administrative Support Workers	ECS	$44,650	5.8%	138,420
40. Meeting and Convention Planners	ECS	$43,530	19.9%	8,318
41. First-Line Supervisors/Managers of Food Preparation and Serving Workers	ECR	$28,040	11.3%	154,175
42. First-Line Supervisors/Managers of Police and Detectives	ESC	$72,620	9.2%	9,373
43. Directors, Religious Activities and Education	ESC	$35,370	19.7%	11,463
44. Flight Attendants	ESC	$61,120	10.6%	10,773
45. Gaming Supervisors	EC	$42,980	23.4%	4,602
46. Producers and Directors	EAC	$61,090	11.1%	8,992
47. Sales Engineers	ERI	$80,270	8.5%	7,371
48. Air Traffic Controllers	EC	$112,930	10.2%	1,213
49. First-Line Supervisors/Managers of Housekeeping and Janitorial Workers	ECR	$32,850	12.7%	30,613
50. Food Service Managers	ECR	$44,570	5.0%	59,302

The 50 Best Conventional Jobs

Job	Personality Code	Annual Earnings	Percent Growth	Annual Openings
1. Accountants and Auditors	CEI	$57,060	17.7%	134,463
2. Financial Analysts	CIE	$70,400	33.8%	29,317
3. Cost Estimators	CE	$54,920	18.5%	38,379
4. Executive Secretaries and Administrative Assistants	CE	$38,640	14.8%	235,314
5. Loan Officers	CES	$53,000	11.5%	54,237
6. Sales Representatives, Wholesale and Manufacturing, Except Technical and Scientific Products	CE	$50,750	8.4%	156,215
7. Database Administrators	CI	$67,250	28.6%	8,258
8. Compensation, Benefits, and Job Analysis Specialists	CE	$52,180	18.4%	18,761
9. Paralegals and Legal Assistants	CIE	$44,990	22.2%	22,756
10. Computer Specialists, All Other	CIR	$71,510	15.1%	14,374
11. Bill and Account Collectors	CE	$29,990	22.9%	118,709

(continued)

(continued)

The 50 Best Conventional Jobs

Job	Personality Code	Annual Earnings	Percent Growth	Annual Openings
12. Actuaries	CIE	$85,690	23.7%	3,245
13. Bookkeeping, Accounting, and Auditing Clerks	CE	$31,560	12.5%	286,854
14. Social and Human Service Assistants	CSE	$26,630	33.6%	80,142
15. Claims Adjusters, Examiners, and Investigators	CE	$53,560	8.9%	22,024
16. Dental Assistants	CRS	$31,550	29.2%	29,482
17. Legal Secretaries	CE	$38,810	11.7%	38,682
18. Pharmacy Technicians	CR	$26,720	32.0%	54,453
19. Brokerage Clerks	CE	$37,360	20.0%	10,826
20. Medical Secretaries	CS	$28,950	16.7%	60,659
21. Receptionists and Information Clerks	CES	$23,710	17.2%	334,124
22. Appraisers and Assessors of Real Estate	CE	$46,130	16.9%	6,493
23. Production, Planning, and Expediting Clerks	CE	$39,690	4.2%	52,735
24. Medical Records and Health Information Technicians	CE	$29,290	17.8%	39,048
25. Court Reporters	CE	$45,330	24.5%	2,620
26. Office Clerks, General	CER	$24,460	12.6%	765,803
27. Cargo and Freight Agents	CER	$37,060	16.5%	9,967
28. Librarians	CSE	$50,970	3.6%	18,945
29. Surveying and Mapping Technicians	CR	$33,640	19.4%	8,299
30. Purchasing Agents, Except Wholesale, Retail, and Farm Products	CE	$52,460	0.1%	22,349
31. Human Resources Assistants, Except Payroll and Timekeeping	CES	$34,970	11.3%	18,647
32. Police, Fire, and Ambulance Dispatchers	CRE	$32,660	13.6%	17,628
33. Budget Analysts	CEI	$63,440	7.1%	6,423
34. Compliance Officers, Except Agriculture, Construction, Health and Safety, and Transportation	CEI	$48,400	4.9%	15,841
35. Tellers	CE	$22,920	13.5%	146,077
36. Insurance Underwriters	CEI	$54,530	6.3%	6,880
37. Billing and Posting Clerks and Machine Operators	CE	$29,970	4.4%	81,885
38. Statisticians	CI	$69,900	8.5%	3,433
39. Medical Transcriptionists	CR	$31,250	13.5%	18,080
40. Interviewers, Except Eligibility and Loan	CES	$27,320	9.5%	54,060
41. Insurance Appraisers, Auto Damage	CRE	$51,500	12.5%	1,030
42. Secretaries, Except Legal, Medical, and Executive	CE	$28,220	1.2%	239,630
43. Dispatchers, Except Police, Fire, and Ambulance	CRE	$33,140	1.5%	29,793
44. Occupational Health and Safety Technicians	CR	$44,020	14.6%	886

The 50 Best Conventional Jobs

Job	Personality Code	Annual Earnings	Percent Growth	Annual Openings
45. Shipping, Receiving, and Traffic Clerks	CRE	$26,990	3.7%	138,967
46. Postal Service Mail Carriers	CR	$44,500	1.0%	16,710
47. Archivists	CI	$43,110	14.4%	795
48. Court, Municipal, and License Clerks	CE	$32,330	8.8%	16,163
49. Insurance Claims and Policy Processing Clerks	CE	$32,040	−1.3%	42,246
50. Loan Interviewers and Clerks	CE	$31,680	−0.9%	40,217

The 20 Best-Paying Jobs for Each Personality Type

In the following six lists you'll find the 20 best-paying jobs for each personality type that met our criteria for this book. These are popular lists, for obvious reasons.

If you compare these six lists, you may notice that some personality types have better income possibilities than others. For example, the best-paying Investigative and Enterprising jobs command much higher incomes than the best-paying Artistic and Conventional jobs. Keep in mind that these figures are only averages; there are a few artists (for example, think of movie stars) who are earning more than obstetricians. Also remember what we said earlier about how earnings can vary by region of the country and amount of experience and because of many other factors.

The 20 Best-Paying Realistic Jobs

Job	Annual Earnings
1. Airline Pilots, Copilots, and Flight Engineers	$145,600+
2. Civil Engineers	$71,710
3. Captains, Mates, and Pilots of Water Vessels	$57,210
4. Telecommunications Equipment Installers and Repairers, Except Line Installers	$54,070
5. Electrical Power-Line Installers and Repairers	$52,570
6. Electrical and Electronic Engineering Technicians	$52,140
7. Surveyors	$51,630
8. Transportation Inspectors	$51,440
9. Boilermakers	$50,700
10. Radiologic Technologists and Technicians	$50,260
11. Cartographers and Photogrammetrists	$49,970

(continued)

(continued)

The 20 Best-Paying Realistic Jobs

Job	Annual Earnings
12. Aircraft Mechanics and Service Technicians	$49,010
13. Construction and Building Inspectors	$48,330
14. Telecommunications Line Installers and Repairers	$47,220
15. Aircraft Structure, Surfaces, Rigging, and Systems Assemblers	$45,420
16. Cardiovascular Technologists and Technicians	$44,940
17. Electricians	$44,780
18. Mechanical Drafters	$44,740
19. Plumbers, Pipefitters, and Steamfitters	$44,090
20. Brickmasons and Blockmasons	$44,070

The 20 Best-Paying Investigative Jobs

Job	Annual Earnings
1. Anesthesiologists	$145,600+
2. Family and General Practitioners	$145,600+
3. Internists, General	$145,600+
4. Obstetricians and Gynecologists	$145,600+
5. Orthodontists	$145,600+
6. Prosthodontists	$145,600+
7. Psychiatrists	$145,600+
8. Surgeons	$145,600+
9. Pediatricians, General	$140,690
10. Dentists, General	$137,630
11. Podiatrists	$110,510
12. Pharmacists	$100,480
13. Computer and Information Scientists, Research	$97,970
14. Physicists	$96,850
15. Optometrists	$93,800
16. Computer Hardware Engineers	$91,860
17. Aerospace Engineers	$90,930
18. Mathematicians	$90,870
19. Computer Software Engineers, Systems Software	$89,070
20. Electronics Engineers, Except Computer	$83,340

The 20 Best-Paying Artistic Jobs

Job	Annual Earnings
1. Astronomers	$99,020
2. Political Scientists	$91,580
3. Public Relations Managers	$86,470
4. Biochemists and Biophysicists	$79,270
5. Advertising and Promotions Managers	$78,250
6. Art Directors	$72,320
7. Architecture Teachers, Postsecondary	$68,540
8. Architects, Except Landscape and Naval	$67,620
9. Fashion Designers	$62,810
10. Sociologists	$61,140
11. Producers and Directors	$61,090
12. Technical Writers	$60,390
13. Landscape Architects	$57,580
14. Commercial and Industrial Designers	$56,550
15. Philosophy and Religion Teachers, Postsecondary	$56,380
16. Art, Drama, and Music Teachers, Postsecondary	$55,190
17. Communications Teachers, Postsecondary	$54,720
18. Multi-Media Artists and Animators	$54,550
19. Education Teachers, Postsecondary	$54,220
20. English Language and Literature Teachers, Postsecondary	$54,000

The 20 Best-Paying Social Jobs

Job	Annual Earnings
1. Law Teachers, Postsecondary	$87,730
2. Health Specialties Teachers, Postsecondary	$80,700
3. Agricultural Sciences Teachers, Postsecondary	$78,460
4. Physician Assistants	$78,450
5. Economics Teachers, Postsecondary	$75,300
6. Atmospheric, Earth, Marine, and Space Sciences Teachers, Postsecondary	$73,280
7. Biological Science Teachers, Postsecondary	$71,780
8. Physics Teachers, Postsecondary	$70,090
9. Radiation Therapists	$70,010
10. Physical Therapists	$69,760

(continued)

(continued)

The 20 Best-Paying Social Jobs

Job	Annual Earnings
11. Architecture Teachers, Postsecondary	$68,540
12. Business Teachers, Postsecondary	$64,900
13. Environmental Science Teachers, Postsecondary	$64,850
14. Dental Hygienists	$64,740
15. Anthropology and Archeology Teachers, Postsecondary	$64,530
16. Chemistry Teachers, Postsecondary	$63,870
17. Occupational Therapists	$63,790
18. Political Science Teachers, Postsecondary	$63,100
19. Computer Science Teachers, Postsecondary	$62,020
20. Psychology Teachers, Postsecondary	$60,610

The 20 Best-Paying Enterprising Jobs

Job	Annual Earnings
1. Chief Executives	$145,600+
2. Air Traffic Controllers	$112,930
3. Engineering Managers	$111,020
4. Computer and Information Systems Managers	$108,070
5. Lawyers	$106,120
6. Marketing Managers	$104,400
7. Natural Sciences Managers	$104,040
8. Financial Managers	$95,310
9. Sales Managers	$94,910
10. General and Operations Managers	$88,700
11. Public Relations Managers	$86,470
12. Training and Development Managers	$84,340
13. Compensation and Benefits Managers	$81,410
14. Education Administrators, Elementary and Secondary School	$80,580
15. Sales Engineers	$80,270
16. Medical and Health Services Managers	$76,990
17. Construction Managers	$76,230
18. Education Administrators, Postsecondary	$75,780
19. First-Line Supervisors/Managers of Police and Detectives	$72,620
20. Administrative Services Managers	$70,990

The 20 Best-Paying Conventional Jobs

Job	Annual Earnings
1. Actuaries	$85,690
2. Computer Specialists, All Other	$71,510
3. Financial Analysts	$70,400
4. Statisticians	$69,900
5. Database Administrators	$67,250
6. Budget Analysts	$63,440
7. Accountants and Auditors	$57,060
8. Cost Estimators	$54,920
9. Insurance Underwriters	$54,530
10. Claims Adjusters, Examiners, and Investigators	$53,560
11. Loan Officers	$53,000
12. Purchasing Agents, Except Wholesale, Retail, and Farm Products	$52,460
13. Compensation, Benefits, and Job Analysis Specialists	$52,180
14. Insurance Appraisers, Auto Damage	$51,500
15. Librarians	$50,970
16. Sales Representatives, Wholesale and Manufacturing, Except Technical and Scientific Products	$50,750
17. Compliance Officers, Except Agriculture, Construction, Health and Safety, and Transportation	$48,400
18. Appraisers and Assessors of Real Estate	$46,130
19. Court Reporters	$45,330
20. Paralegals and Legal Assistants	$44,990

The 20 Fastest-Growing Jobs for Each Personality Type

From the six lists of 50 jobs that met our criteria for this book, these six lists show the 20 for each personality type that are projected to have the highest percentage increase in the numbers of people employed through 2016.

You will notice that just as income opportunities vary among the lists of the best-paying jobs, job opportunities vary among the personality types. The top Investigative and Social jobs have better opportunities (an average of about 40 percent growth) than do the top jobs in the other groups (an average of about 24 percent growth). This is partly because the kind of work done by Investigative and Social workers typically cannot be done by computers or by overseas workers. An aging population with greater need for medical and personal care also will demand more Investigative and Social workers.

The 20 Fastest-Growing Realistic Jobs

Job	Percent Growth
1. Cardiovascular Technologists and Technicians	25.5%
2. Surgical Technologists	24.5%
3. Audio and Video Equipment Technicians	24.2%
4. Surveyors	23.7%
5. Cartographers and Photogrammetrists	20.3%
6. Security and Fire Alarm Systems Installers	20.2%
7. Athletes and Sports Competitors	19.2%
8. Construction and Building Inspectors	18.2%
9. Civil Engineers	18.0%
10. Captains, Mates, and Pilots of Water Vessels	17.9%
11. Correctional Officers and Jailers	16.9%
12. Transportation Inspectors	16.4%
13. Biological Technicians	16.0%
14. Sailors and Marine Oilers	15.7%
15. Tile and Marble Setters	15.4%
16. Radiologic Technologists and Technicians	15.1%
17. Medical and Clinical Laboratory Technicians	15.0%
18. Automotive Service Technicians and Mechanics	14.3%
19. Roofers	14.3%
20. Boilermakers	14.0%

The 20 Fastest-Growing Investigative Jobs

Job	Percent Growth
1. Network Systems and Data Communications Analysts	53.4%
2. Computer Software Engineers, Applications	44.6%
3. Veterinarians	35.0%
4. Forensic Science Technicians	30.7%
5. Computer Systems Analysts	29.0%
6. Computer Software Engineers, Systems Software	28.2%
7. Environmental Science and Protection Technicians, Including Health	28.0%
8. Network and Computer Systems Administrators	27.0%
9. Environmental Engineers	25.4%
10. Environmental Scientists and Specialists, Including Health	25.1%

The 20 Fastest-Growing Investigative Jobs

Job	Percent Growth
11. Hydrologists	24.3%
12. Engineering Teachers, Postsecondary	22.9%
13. Geoscientists, Except Hydrologists and Geographers	21.9%
14. Management Analysts	21.9%
15. Pharmacists	21.7%
16. Computer and Information Scientists, Research	21.5%
17. Industrial-Organizational Psychologists	21.3%
18. Biomedical Engineers	21.1%
19. Industrial Engineers	20.3%
20. Medical Scientists, Except Epidemiologists	20.2%

The 20 Fastest-Growing Artistic Jobs

Job	Percent Growth
1. Makeup Artists, Theatrical and Performance	39.8%
2. Substance Abuse and Behavioral Disorder Counselors	34.3%
3. Marriage and Family Therapists	29.8%
4. Preschool Teachers, Except Special Education	26.3%
5. Multi-Media Artists and Animators	25.8%
6. Interpreters and Translators	23.6%
7. Self-Enrichment Education Teachers	23.1%
8. Architecture Teachers, Postsecondary	22.9%
9. Art, Drama, and Music Teachers, Postsecondary	22.9%
10. Communications Teachers, Postsecondary	22.9%
11. Education Teachers, Postsecondary	22.9%
12. English Language and Literature Teachers, Postsecondary	22.9%
13. Foreign Language and Literature Teachers, Postsecondary	22.9%
14. Philosophy and Religion Teachers, Postsecondary	22.9%
15. Special Education Teachers, Preschool, Kindergarten, and Elementary School	19.6%
16. Interior Designers	19.5%
17. Technical Writers	19.5%
18. Training and Development Specialists	18.3%
19. Set and Exhibit Designers	17.8%
20. Architects, Except Landscape and Naval	17.7%

The 20 Fastest-Growing Social Jobs

Job	Percent Growth
1. Medical Assistants	35.4%
2. Substance Abuse and Behavioral Disorder Counselors	34.3%
3. Physical Therapist Assistants	32.4%
4. Dental Hygienists	30.1%
5. Mental Health Counselors	30.0%
6. Mental Health and Substance Abuse Social Workers	29.9%
7. Marriage and Family Therapists	29.8%
8. Physical Therapists	27.1%
9. Physician Assistants	27.0%
10. Fitness Trainers and Aerobics Instructors	26.8%
11. Preschool Teachers, Except Special Education	26.3%
12. Health Educators	26.2%
13. Radiation Therapists	24.8%
14. Medical and Public Health Social Workers	24.2%
15. Education Administrators, Preschool and Child Care Center/Program	23.5%
16. Registered Nurses	23.5%
17. Occupational Therapists	23.1%
18. Self-Enrichment Education Teachers	23.1%
19. Rehabilitation Counselors	23.0%
20. Agricultural Sciences Teachers, Postsecondary	22.9%

The 20 Fastest-Growing Enterprising Jobs

Job	Percent Growth
1. Personal Financial Advisors	41.0%
2. Customer Service Representatives	24.8%
3. Securities, Commodities, and Financial Services Sales Agents	24.8%
4. Social and Community Service Managers	24.7%
5. Gaming Managers	24.4%
6. Gaming Supervisors	23.4%
7. Advertising Sales Agents	20.3%
8. Meeting and Convention Planners	19.9%
9. Directors, Religious Activities and Education	19.7%
10. Employment, Recruitment, and Placement Specialists	18.4%

The 20 Fastest-Growing Enterprising Jobs

Job	Percent Growth
11. Demonstrators and Product Promoters	18.0%
12. First-Line Supervisors/Managers of Landscaping, Lawn Service, and Groundskeeping Workers	17.6%
13. Public Relations Specialists	17.6%
14. Detectives and Criminal Investigators	17.3%
15. Logisticians	17.3%
16. Public Relations Managers	16.9%
17. Computer and Information Systems Managers	16.4%
18. Medical and Health Services Managers	16.4%
19. Construction Managers	15.7%
20. Training and Development Managers	15.6%

The 20 Fastest-Growing Conventional Jobs

Job	Percent Growth
1. Financial Analysts	33.8%
2. Social and Human Service Assistants	33.6%
3. Pharmacy Technicians	32.0%
4. Dental Assistants	29.2%
5. Database Administrators	28.6%
6. Court Reporters	24.5%
7. Actuaries	23.7%
8. Bill and Account Collectors	22.9%
9. Paralegals and Legal Assistants	22.2%
10. Brokerage Clerks	20.0%
11. Surveying and Mapping Technicians	19.4%
12. Cost Estimators	18.5%
13. Compensation, Benefits, and Job Analysis Specialists	18.4%
14. Medical Records and Health Information Technicians	17.8%
15. Accountants and Auditors	17.7%
16. Receptionists and Information Clerks	17.2%
17. Appraisers and Assessors of Real Estate	16.9%
18. Medical Secretaries	16.7%
19. Cargo and Freight Agents	16.5%
20. Computer Specialists, All Other	15.1%

The 20 Jobs with the Most Openings for Each Personality Type

From the six lists of 50 jobs that met our criteria for this book, this list shows the 20 jobs for each personality type that are projected to have the largest number of job openings per year through 2016.

Jobs with many openings present several advantages that may be attractive to you. Because there are many openings, these jobs can be easier to obtain, particularly for those just entering the job market. These jobs may also offer more opportunities to move from one employer to another with relative ease. Though some of these jobs have average or below-average pay, some also pay quite well and can provide good long-term career opportunities or the ability to move up to more responsible roles.

It is interesting but not surprising that job openings are dramatically more scarce in the Artistic list than in the other five lists; this is a category where keen competition for nonteaching jobs is the rule. If sales jobs were set aside, comparatively few openings also would be found among the Enterprising jobs; this also tends to be a competitive arena. The two personality types with outstanding figures for job openings are Conventional and Social.

On all the lists, the jobs that are expected to have the greatest number of openings tend to be those that require hands-on or in-person work—for example, truck drivers, teachers, salespeople, or cashiers. These workers are less likely to be replaced by technology or by overseas workers.

The 20 Realistic Jobs with the Most Openings

Job	Annual Openings
1. Truck Drivers, Heavy and Tractor-Trailer	279,032
2. Carpenters	223,225
3. Maintenance and Repair Workers, General	165,502
4. Painters, Construction and Maintenance	101,140
5. Automotive Service Technicians and Mechanics	97,350
6. Computer Support Specialists	97,334
7. Electricians	79,083
8. Plumbers, Pipefitters, and Steamfitters	68,643
9. Correctional Officers and Jailers	56,579
10. Operating Engineers and Other Construction Equipment Operators	55,468
11. Roofers	38,398
12. Automotive Body and Related Repairers	37,469
13. Cement Masons and Concrete Finishers	34,625

The 20 Realistic Jobs with the Most Openings

Job	Annual Openings
14. Sheet Metal Workers	31,677
15. Drywall and Ceiling Tile Installers	30,945
16. Heating, Air Conditioning, and Refrigeration Mechanics and Installers	29,719
17. Bus Drivers, Transit and Intercity	27,100
18. Bus and Truck Mechanics and Diesel Engine Specialists	25,428
19. Industrial Machinery Mechanics	23,361
20. Fire Fighters	18,887

The 20 Investigative Jobs with the Most Openings

Job	Annual Openings
1. Management Analysts	125,669
2. Computer Systems Analysts	63,166
3. Computer Software Engineers, Applications	58,690
4. Market Research Analysts	45,015
5. Anesthesiologists	38,027
6. Family and General Practitioners	38,027
7. Internists, General	38,027
8. Obstetricians and Gynecologists	38,027
9. Pediatricians, General	38,027
10. Psychiatrists	38,027
11. Surgeons	38,027
12. Network and Computer Systems Administrators	37,010
13. Network Systems and Data Communications Analysts	35,086
14. Computer Software Engineers, Systems Software	33,139
15. Pharmacists	16,358
16. Mechanical Engineers	12,394
17. Medical and Clinical Laboratory Technologists	11,457
18. Industrial Engineers	11,272
19. Medical Scientists, Except Epidemiologists	10,596
20. Chemists	9,024

Jobs 5, 6, 7, 8, 9, 10, and 11 share 38,027 openings.

The 20 Artistic Jobs with the Most Openings

Job	Annual Openings
1. Elementary School Teachers, Except Special Education	181,612
2. Secondary School Teachers, Except Special and Vocational Education	93,166
3. Preschool Teachers, Except Special Education	78,172
4. Middle School Teachers, Except Special and Vocational Education	75,270
5. Hairdressers, Hairstylists, and Cosmetologists	73,030
6. Self-Enrichment Education Teachers	64,449
7. Public Relations Specialists	51,216
8. Training and Development Specialists	35,862
9. Kindergarten Teachers, Except Special Education	27,603
10. Graphic Designers	26,968
11. Writers and Authors	24,023
12. Substance Abuse and Behavioral Disorder Counselors	20,821
13. Editors	20,193
14. Special Education Teachers, Preschool, Kindergarten, and Elementary School	20,049
15. Adult Literacy, Remedial Education, and GED Teachers and Instructors	17,340
16. Photographers	16,100
17. Multi-Media Artists and Animators	13,182
18. Art, Drama, and Music Teachers, Postsecondary	12,707
19. Architects, Except Landscape and Naval	11,324
20. English Language and Literature Teachers, Postsecondary	10,475

The 20 Social Jobs with the Most Openings

Job	Annual Openings
1. Registered Nurses	233,499
2. Elementary School Teachers, Except Special Education	181,612
3. Medical Assistants	92,977
4. Preschool Teachers, Except Special Education	78,172
5. Self-Enrichment Education Teachers	64,449
6. Fitness Trainers and Aerobics Instructors	51,235
7. Training and Development Specialists	35,862
8. Rehabilitation Counselors	32,081
9. Mental Health Counselors	24,103
10. Instructional Coordinators	21,294
11. Substance Abuse and Behavioral Disorder Counselors	20,821

The 20 Social Jobs with the Most Openings

Job	Annual Openings
12. Graduate Teaching Assistants	20,601
13. Health Specialties Teachers, Postsecondary	19,617
14. Vocational Education Teachers, Postsecondary	19,313
15. Mental Health and Substance Abuse Social Workers	17,289
16. Medical and Public Health Social Workers	16,429
17. Health Educators	13,707
18. Art, Drama, and Music Teachers, Postsecondary	12,707
19. Physical Therapists	12,072
20. Business Teachers, Postsecondary	11,643

The 20 Enterprising Jobs with the Most Openings

Job	Annual Openings
1. Customer Service Representatives	600,937
2. First-Line Supervisors/Managers of Food Preparation and Serving Workers	154,175
3. First-Line Supervisors/Managers of Office and Administrative Support Workers	138,420
4. General and Operations Managers	112,072
5. First-Line Supervisors/Managers of Construction Trades and Extraction Workers	82,923
6. Insurance Sales Agents	64,162
7. Real Estate Sales Agents	61,232
8. Food Service Managers	59,302
9. Financial Managers	57,589
10. Public Relations Specialists	51,216
11. Property, Real Estate, and Community Association Managers	49,916
12. Lawyers	49,445
13. First-Line Supervisors/Managers of Non-Retail Sales Workers	48,883
14. Securities, Commodities, and Financial Services Sales Agents	47,750
15. Construction Managers	44,158
16. Sales Representatives, Wholesale and Manufacturing, Technical and Scientific Products	43,469
17. Police and Sheriff's Patrol Officers	37,842
18. First-Line Supervisors/Managers of Personal Service Workers	37,555
19. Sales Managers	36,392
20. Employment, Recruitment, and Placement Specialists	33,588

The 20 Conventional Jobs with the Most Openings

Job	Annual Openings
1. Office Clerks, General	765,803
2. Receptionists and Information Clerks	334,124
3. Bookkeeping, Accounting, and Auditing Clerks	286,854
4. Secretaries, Except Legal, Medical, and Executive	239,630
5. Executive Secretaries and Administrative Assistants	235,314
6. Sales Representatives, Wholesale and Manufacturing, Except Technical and Scientific Products	156,215
7. Tellers	146,077
8. Shipping, Receiving, and Traffic Clerks	138,967
9. Accountants and Auditors	134,463
10. Bill and Account Collectors	118,709
11. Billing and Posting Clerks and Machine Operators	81,885
12. Social and Human Service Assistants	80,142
13. Medical Secretaries	60,659
14. Pharmacy Technicians	54,453
15. Loan Officers	54,237
16. Interviewers, Except Eligibility and Loan	54,060
17. Production, Planning, and Expediting Clerks	52,735
18. Insurance Claims and Policy Processing Clerks	42,246
19. Loan Interviewers and Clerks	40,217
20. Medical Records and Health Information Technicians	39,048

The Best Jobs for Each Personality Type with a High Percentage of Workers Age 16–24

In the following lists, we sorted the best 50 jobs for each personality type and included only those that employ the highest percentage of workers age 16–24. Workers in this age bracket make up 14.1 percent of the workforce, and jobs in the lists that follow include at least 10 percent of these workers.

Though young workers are employed in virtually all major occupations, and therefore in settings associated with all six personality types, you may notice that the jobs for the Realistic, Conventional, and Artistic personality types are considerably "younger" than those for the Investigative and Enterprising personality types. This largely reflects the fact that careers in the Investigative and Enterprising categories often require a lot of prior education or time spent rising through the ranks to a supervisory role, whereas on-the-job training requiring less commitment of time may be sufficient preparation for many jobs for the other personality types.

Keep in mind that the young people who hold the jobs listed in this section may not stay in those jobs, or even in jobs related to the same personality type, for a whole career. Some people are "late bloomers" who do not recognize at an early age what their personality type is and how to find a job appropriate to that type. Others may take a job related to an inappropriate personality type because it offers the opportunity to enter the labor market, earn some money, gain basic job skills, and acquire the experience necessary for moving up to a job that is a better fit.

Realistic Jobs with the Highest Percentage of Workers Age 16–24

Job	Percent Workers Age 16–24
1. Athletes and Sports Competitors	34.5%
2. Surgical Technologists	24.7%
3. Roofers	22.4%
4. Sailors and Marine Oilers	20.8%
5. Automotive Body and Related Repairers	19.0%
6. Cement Masons and Concrete Finishers	16.3%
7. Drywall and Ceiling Tile Installers	16.3%
8. Automotive Service Technicians and Mechanics	16.2%
9. Tile and Marble Setters	16.1%
10. Security and Fire Alarm Systems Installers	15.5%
11. Sheet Metal Workers	14.7%
12. Carpenters	12.8%
13. Plumbers, Pipefitters, and Steamfitters	12.8%
14. Computer Support Specialists	12.6%
15. Bus and Truck Mechanics and Diesel Engine Specialists	12.5%
16. Electricians	12.2%
17. Audio and Video Equipment Technicians	12.1%
18. Brickmasons and Blockmasons	11.7%
19. Boilermakers	10.7%
20. Biological Technicians	10.5%
21. Heating, Air Conditioning, and Refrigeration Mechanics and Installers	10.4%

Best Realistic Jobs Overall Employing 10 Percent or More Workers Age 16–24

Job	Percent Workers Age 16–24	Annual Earnings	Percent Growth	Annual Openings
1. Computer Support Specialists	12.6%	$42,400	12.9%	97,334
2. Plumbers, Pipefitters, and Steamfitters	12.8%	$44,090	10.6%	68,643
3. Electricians	12.2%	$44,780	7.4%	79,083
4. Automotive Service Technicians and Mechanics	16.2%	$34,170	14.3%	97,350
5. Carpenters	12.8%	$37,660	10.3%	223,225
6. Surgical Technologists	24.7%	$37,540	24.5%	15,365
7. Biological Technicians	10.5%	$37,810	16.0%	15,374
8. Tile and Marble Setters	16.1%	$38,720	15.4%	9,066
9. Boilermakers	10.7%	$50,700	14.0%	2,333
10. Athletes and Sports Competitors	34.5%	$38,440	19.2%	4,293
11. Bus and Truck Mechanics and Diesel Engine Specialists	12.5%	$38,640	11.5%	25,428
12. Brickmasons and Blockmasons	11.7%	$44,070	9.7%	17,569
13. Roofers	22.4%	$33,240	14.3%	38,398
14. Automotive Body and Related Repairers	19.0%	$35,690	11.6%	37,469
15. Audio and Video Equipment Technicians	12.1%	$36,050	24.2%	4,681
16. Sheet Metal Workers	14.7%	$39,210	6.7%	31,677
17. Security and Fire Alarm Systems Installers	15.5%	$35,390	20.2%	5,729
18. Heating, Air Conditioning, and Refrigeration Mechanics and Installers	10.4%	$38,360	8.7%	29,719
19. Cement Masons and Concrete Finishers	16.3%	$33,840	11.4%	34,625
20. Drywall and Ceiling Tile Installers	16.3%	$36,520	7.3%	30,945
21. Sailors and Marine Oilers	20.8%	$32,570	15.7%	8,600

Investigative Jobs with the Highest Percentage of Workers Age 16–24

Job	Percent Workers Age 16–24
1. Environmental Science and Protection Technicians, Including Health	28.0%
2. Forensic Science Technicians	28.0%

Best Investigative Jobs Overall Employing 10 Percent or More Workers Age 16–24

Job	Percent Workers Age 16–24	Annual Earnings	Percent Growth	Annual Openings
1. Forensic Science Technicians	28.0%	$47,680	30.7%	3,074
2. Environmental Science and Protection Technicians, Including Health	28.0%	$39,370	28.0%	8,404

Artistic Jobs with the Highest Percentage of Workers Age 16–24

Job	Percent Workers Age 16–24
1. Adult Literacy, Remedial Education, and GED Teachers and Instructors	17.4%
2. Self-Enrichment Education Teachers	17.4%
3. Photographers	16.4%
4. Hairdressers, Hairstylists, and Cosmetologists	14.5%
5. Camera Operators, Television, Video, and Motion Picture	14.1%
6. Film and Video Editors	14.1%
7. Sociologists	13.5%
8. Kindergarten Teachers, Except Special Education	13.2%
9. Preschool Teachers, Except Special Education	13.2%
10. Broadcast News Analysts	11.8%
11. Commercial and Industrial Designers	10.3%
12. Fashion Designers	10.3%
13. Graphic Designers	10.3%
14. Interior Designers	10.3%
15. Merchandise Displayers and Window Trimmers	10.3%
16. Set and Exhibit Designers	10.3%
17. Public Relations Specialists	10.1%

Best Artistic Jobs Overall Employing 10 Percent or More Workers Age 16–24

Job	Percent Workers Age 16–24	Annual Earnings	Percent Growth	Annual Openings
1. Public Relations Specialists	10.1%	$49,800	17.6%	51,216
2. Kindergarten Teachers, Except Special Education	13.2%	$45,120	16.3%	27,603

(continued)

(continued)

Best Artistic Jobs Overall Employing 10 Percent or More Workers Age 16–24

Job	Percent Workers Age 16–24	Annual Earnings	Percent Growth	Annual Openings
3. Preschool Teachers, Except Special Education	13.2%	$23,130	26.3%	78,172
4. Self-Enrichment Education Teachers	17.4%	$34,580	23.1%	64,449
5. Adult Literacy, Remedial Education, and GED Teachers and Instructors	17.4%	$44,710	14.2%	17,340
6. Interior Designers	10.3%	$43,970	19.5%	8,434
7. Film and Video Editors	14.1%	$47,870	12.7%	2,707
8. Hairdressers, Hairstylists, and Cosmetologists	14.5%	$22,210	12.4%	73,030
9. Commercial and Industrial Designers	10.3%	$56,550	7.2%	4,777
10. Set and Exhibit Designers	10.3%	$43,220	17.8%	1,402
11. Fashion Designers	10.3%	$62,810	5.0%	1,968
12. Graphic Designers	10.3%	$41,280	9.8%	26,968
13. Sociologists	13.5%	$61,140	10.0%	403
14. Camera Operators, Television, Video, and Motion Picture	14.1%	$41,850	11.5%	3,496
15. Photographers	16.4%	$27,720	10.3%	16,100
16. Merchandise Displayers and Window Trimmers	10.3%	$24,830	10.7%	9,103
17. Broadcast News Analysts	11.8%	$49,060	6.0%	1,444

Social Jobs with the Highest Percentage of Workers Age 16–24

Job	Percent Workers Age 16–24
1. Fitness Trainers and Aerobics Instructors	30.2%
2. Medical Assistants	19.5%
3. Self-Enrichment Education Teachers	17.4%
4. Physical Therapist Assistants	14.8%
5. Preschool Teachers, Except Special Education	13.2%
6. Health Educators	10.5%

Best Social Jobs Overall Employing 10 Percent or More Workers Age 16–24

Job	Percent Workers Age 16–24	Annual Earnings	Percent Growth	Annual Openings
1. Medical Assistants	19.5%	$27,430	35.4%	92,977
2. Physical Therapist Assistants	14.8%	$44,130	32.4%	5,957
3. Fitness Trainers and Aerobics Instructors	30.2%	$27,680	26.8%	51,235
4. Health Educators	10.5%	$42,920	26.2%	13,707
5. Preschool Teachers, Except Special Education	13.2%	$23,130	26.3%	78,172
6. Self-Enrichment Education Teachers	17.4%	$34,580	23.1%	64,449

Enterprising Jobs with the Highest Percentage of Workers Age 16–24

Job	Percent Workers Age 16–24
1. Customer Service Representatives	22.8%
2. First-Line Supervisors/Managers of Food Preparation and Serving Workers	21.4%
3. Demonstrators and Product Promoters	16.3%
4. Food Service Managers	14.2%
5. Gaming Managers	13.4%
6. Advertising Sales Agents	10.3%
7. Public Relations Specialists	10.1%

Best Enterprising Jobs Overall Employing 10 Percent or More Workers Age 16–24

Job	Percent Workers Age 16–24	Annual Earnings	Percent Growth	Annual Openings
1. Customer Service Representatives	22.8%	$29,040	24.8%	600,937
2. Gaming Managers	13.4%	$64,410	24.4%	549
3. Public Relations Specialists	10.1%	$49,800	17.6%	51,216
4. Advertising Sales Agents	10.3%	$42,820	20.3%	29,233
5. Food Service Managers	14.2%	$44,570	5.0%	59,302
6. First-Line Supervisors/Managers of Food Preparation and Serving Workers	21.4%	$28,040	11.3%	154,175
7. Demonstrators and Product Promoters	16.3%	$22,570	18.0%	32,779

Conventional Jobs with the Highest Percentage of Workers Age 16–24

Job	Percent Workers Age 16–24
1. Tellers	33.8%
2. Pharmacy Technicians	24.7%
3. Receptionists and Information Clerks	24.5%
4. Interviewers, Except Eligibility and Loan	20.9%
5. Bill and Account Collectors	19.8%
6. Medical Transcriptionists	19.5%
7. Office Clerks, General	19.1%
8. Surveying and Mapping Technicians	18.6%
9. Dental Assistants	18.5%
10. Shipping, Receiving, and Traffic Clerks	14.3%
11. Human Resources Assistants, Except Payroll and Timekeeping	12.3%
12. Cargo and Freight Agents	11.6%
13. Court Reporters	11.3%
14. Dispatchers, Except Police, Fire, and Ambulance	11.3%
15. Loan Interviewers and Clerks	11.3%
16. Police, Fire, and Ambulance Dispatchers	11.3%
17. Insurance Claims and Policy Processing Clerks	10.9%
18. Actuaries	10.5%
19. Social and Human Service Assistants	10.5%

Best Conventional Jobs Overall Employing 10 Percent or More Workers Age 16–24

Job	Percent Workers Age 16–24	Annual Earnings	Percent Growth	Annual Openings
1. Bill and Account Collectors	19.8%	$29,990	22.9%	118,709
2. Social and Human Service Assistants	10.5%	$26,630	33.6%	80,142
3. Actuaries	10.5%	$85,690	23.7%	3,245
4. Pharmacy Technicians	24.7%	$26,720	32.0%	54,453
5. Court Reporters	11.3%	$45,330	24.5%	2,620
6. Dental Assistants	18.5%	$31,550	29.2%	29,482
7. Cargo and Freight Agents	11.6%	$37,060	16.5%	9,967
8. Receptionists and Information Clerks	24.5%	$23,710	17.2%	334,124
9. Surveying and Mapping Technicians	18.6%	$33,640	19.4%	8,299

Best Conventional Jobs Overall Employing 10 Percent or More Workers Age 16–24

Job	Percent Workers Age 16–24	Annual Earnings	Percent Growth	Annual Openings
10. Human Resources Assistants, Except Payroll and Timekeeping	12.3%	$34,970	11.3%	18,647
11. Office Clerks, General	19.1%	$24,460	12.6%	765,803
12. Police, Fire, and Ambulance Dispatchers	11.3%	$32,660	13.6%	17,628
13. Tellers	33.8%	$22,920	13.5%	146,077
14. Dispatchers, Except Police, Fire, and Ambulance	11.3%	$33,140	1.5%	29,793
15. Shipping, Receiving, and Traffic Clerks	14.3%	$26,990	3.7%	138,967
16. Insurance Claims and Policy Processing Clerks	10.9%	$32,040	–1.3%	42,246
17. Interviewers, Except Eligibility and Loan	20.9%	$27,320	9.5%	54,060
18. Medical Transcriptionists	19.5%	$31,250	13.5%	18,080
19. Loan Interviewers and Clerks	11.3%	$31,680	–0.9%	40,217

The Best Jobs for Each Personality Type with a High Percentage of Workers Age 55 and Over

In the following lists, we sorted the best 50 jobs for each personality type and included only those that employ the highest percentage of workers age 55 and over. Workers in this age bracket make up roughly 15 percent of the workforce. We included occupations in the lists if the percentage of workers 55 and over was 15 percent or higher.

One use for these lists is to help you identify jobs that might be interesting to you as you decide to change careers or approach retirement. Some jobs are on the lists because they are attractive to older workers wanting part-time work to supplement their retirement income—for example, Tellers. Other occupations on the lists, such as several jobs in music (Artistic), medicine and science (Investigative), psychology (Social), and college teaching (several personality types), take many years of training and experience. People who are established in such careers often have many incentives to continue working at ages when workers in other fields are ready to retire. These jobs also may not be as physically demanding as some other jobs, especially compared to those linked to the Realistic personality type, and therefore may be easier for older workers to perform.

Realistic Jobs with the Highest Percentage of Workers Age 55 and Over

Job	Percent Workers Age 55 and Over
1. Bus Drivers, Transit and Intercity	38.2%
2. Transportation Inspectors	28.1%
3. Construction and Building Inspectors	26.8%
4. Maintenance and Repair Workers, General	25.3%
5. Surveyors	24.2%
6. Cartographers and Photogrammetrists	24.2%
7. Truck Drivers, Heavy and Tractor-Trailer	22.5%
8. Airline Pilots, Copilots, and Flight Engineers	22.4%
9. Industrial Machinery Mechanics	21.6%
10. Civil Engineers	20.6%
11. Water and Liquid Waste Treatment Plant and System Operators	19.9%
12. Medical and Clinical Laboratory Technicians	19.8%
13. Operating Engineers and Other Construction Equipment Operators	19.8%
14. Electrical and Electronic Engineering Technicians	19.6%
15. Civil Engineering Technicians	19.6%
16. Telecommunications Equipment Installers and Repairers, Except Line Installers	19.5%
17. Automotive Body and Related Repairers	18.4%
18. Captains, Mates, and Pilots of Water Vessels	18.3%
19. Bus and Truck Mechanics and Diesel Engine Specialists	17.4%
20. Mobile Heavy Equipment Mechanics, Except Engines	17.4%
21. Architectural and Civil Drafters	16.8%
22. Mechanical Drafters	16.8%
23. Electricians	15.9%

Best Realistic Jobs Overall Employing 15 Percent or More Workers Age 55 and Over

Job	Percent Workers Age 55 and Over	Annual Earnings	Percent Growth	Annual Openings
1. Civil Engineers	20.6%	$71,710	18.0%	15,979
2. Surveyors	24.2%	$51,630	23.7%	14,305
3. Construction and Building Inspectors	26.8%	$48,330	18.2%	12,606
4. Airline Pilots, Copilots, and Flight Engineers	22.4%	$145,600+	12.9%	4,073
5. Captains, Mates, and Pilots of Water Vessels	18.3%	$57,210	17.9%	2,665

Best Realistic Jobs Overall Employing 15 Percent or More Workers Age 55 and Over

Job	Percent Workers Age 55 and Over	Annual Earnings	Percent Growth	Annual Openings
6. Cartographers and Photogrammetrists	24.2%	$49,970	20.3%	2,823
7. Electricians	15.9%	$44,780	7.4%	79,083
8. Truck Drivers, Heavy and Tractor-Trailer	22.5%	$36,220	10.4%	279,032
9. Bus and Truck Mechanics and Diesel Engine Specialists	17.4%	$38,640	11.5%	25,428
10. Transportation Inspectors	28.1%	$51,440	16.4%	2,122
11. Automotive Body and Related Repairers	18.4%	$35,690	11.6%	37,469
12. Bus Drivers, Transit and Intercity	38.2%	$33,160	12.5%	27,100
13. Industrial Machinery Mechanics	21.6%	$42,350	9.0%	23,361
14. Operating Engineers and Other Construction Equipment Operators	19.8%	$38,130	8.4%	55,468
15. Telecommunications Equipment Installers and Repairers, Except Line Installers	19.5%	$54,070	2.5%	13,541
16. Architectural and Civil Drafters	16.8%	$43,310	6.1%	16,238
17. Electrical and Electronic Engineering Technicians	19.6%	$52,140	3.6%	12,583
18. Maintenance and Repair Workers, General	25.3%	$32,570	10.1%	165,502
19. Mobile Heavy Equipment Mechanics, Except Engines	17.4%	$41,450	12.3%	11,037
20. Water and Liquid Waste Treatment Plant and System Operators	19.9%	$37,090	13.8%	9,575
21. Medical and Clinical Laboratory Technicians	19.8%	$34,270	15.0%	10,866
22. Civil Engineering Technicians	19.6%	$42,580	10.2%	7,499
23. Mechanical Drafters	16.8%	$44,740	5.2%	10,902

Investigative Jobs with the Highest Percentage of Workers Age 55 and Over

Job	Percent Workers Age 55 and Over
1. Clinical, Counseling, and School Psychologists	35.0%
2. Industrial-Organizational Psychologists	35.0%
3. Physicists	33.3%
4. Management Analysts	30.1%
5. Veterinarians	28.4%

(continued)

(continued)

Investigative Jobs with the Highest Percentage of Workers Age 55 and Over

Job	Percent Workers Age 55 and Over
6. Dentists, General	27.4%
7. Orthodontists	27.4%
8. Prosthodontists	27.4%
9. Anesthesiologists	27.2%
10. Family and General Practitioners	27.2%
11. Internists, General	27.2%
12. Obstetricians and Gynecologists	27.2%
13. Pediatricians, General	27.2%
14. Psychiatrists	27.2%
15. Surgeons	27.2%
16. Optometrists	24.6%
17. Chemical Engineers	24.3%
18. Environmental Scientists and Specialists, Including Health	22.6%
19. Geoscientists, Except Hydrologists and Geographers	22.6%
20. Hydrologists	22.6%
21. Pharmacists	22.5%
22. Electrical Engineers	21.3%
23. Electronics Engineers, Except Computer	21.3%
24. Industrial Engineers	20.8%
25. Mathematicians	20.0%
26. Medical and Clinical Laboratory Technologists	19.8%
27. Operations Research Analysts	18.6%
28. Aerospace Engineers	18.5%
29. Computer Hardware Engineers	17.9%
30. Environmental Engineers	16.2%

Best Investigative Jobs Overall Employing 15 Percent or More Workers Age 55 and Over

Job	Percent Workers Age 55 and Over	Annual Earnings	Percent Growth	Annual Openings
1. Anesthesiologists	27.2%	$145,600+	14.2%	38,027
2. Family and General Practitioners	27.2%	$145,600+	14.2%	38,027
3. Internists, General	27.2%	$145,600+	14.2%	38,027
4. Obstetricians and Gynecologists	27.2%	$145,600+	14.2%	38,027
5. Psychiatrists	27.2%	$145,600+	14.2%	38,027
6. Surgeons	27.2%	$145,600+	14.2%	38,027
7. Pediatricians, General	27.2%	$140,690	14.2%	38,027
8. Pharmacists	22.5%	$100,480	21.7%	16,358
9. Management Analysts	30.1%	$71,150	21.9%	125,669
10. Veterinarians	28.4%	$75,230	35.0%	5,301
11. Industrial Engineers	20.8%	$71,430	20.3%	11,272
12. Environmental Engineers	16.2%	$72,350	25.4%	5,003
13. Environmental Scientists and Specialists, Including Health	22.6%	$58,380	25.1%	6,961
14. Dentists, General	27.4%	$137,630	9.2%	7,106
15. Geoscientists, Except Hydrologists and Geographers	22.6%	$75,800	21.9%	2,471
16. Clinical, Counseling, and School Psychologists	35.0%	$62,210	15.8%	8,309
17. Prosthodontists	27.4%	$145,600+	10.7%	54
18. Orthodontists	27.4%	$145,600+	9.2%	479
19. Aerospace Engineers	18.5%	$90,930	10.2%	6,498
20. Hydrologists	22.6%	$68,140	24.3%	687
21. Industrial-Organizational Psychologists	35.0%	$80,820	21.3%	118
22. Optometrists	24.6%	$93,800	11.3%	1,789
23. Medical and Clinical Laboratory Technologists	19.8%	$51,720	12.4%	11,457
24. Electrical Engineers	21.3%	$79,240	6.3%	6,806
25. Computer Hardware Engineers	17.9%	$91,860	4.6%	3,572
26. Physicists	33.3%	$96,850	6.8%	1,302
27. Electronics Engineers, Except Computer	21.3%	$83,340	3.7%	5,699
28. Operations Research Analysts	18.6%	$66,950	10.6%	5,727
29. Mathematicians	20.0%	$90,870	10.2%	473
30. Chemical Engineers	24.3%	$81,500	7.9%	2,111

Jobs 1, 2, 3, 4, 5, 6, and 7 share 38,027 openings.

Artistic Jobs with the Highest Percentage of Workers Age 55 and Over

Job	Percent Workers Age 55 and Over
1. Sociologists	37.8%
2. Art Directors	33.9%
3. Fine Artists, Including Painters, Sculptors, and Illustrators	33.9%
4. Multi-Media Artists and Animators	33.9%
5. Astronomers	33.3%
6. Writers and Authors	33.3%
7. Music Directors and Composers	27.3%
8. Marriage and Family Therapists	25.3%
9. Substance Abuse and Behavioral Disorder Counselors	25.3%
10. Architects, Except Landscape and Naval	23.4%
11. Landscape Architects	23.4%
12. Technical Writers	22.4%
13. Secondary School Teachers, Except Special and Vocational Education	22.2%
14. Adult Literacy, Remedial Education, and GED Teachers and Instructors	22.1%
15. Self-Enrichment Education Teachers	22.1%
16. Elementary School Teachers, Except Special Education	22.0%
17. Middle School Teachers, Except Special and Vocational Education	22.0%
18. Anthropologists and Archeologists	21.2%
19. Political Scientists	21.2%
20. Photographers	20.8%
21. Special Education Teachers, Middle School	19.5%
22. Special Education Teachers, Preschool, Kindergarten, and Elementary School	19.5%
23. Commercial and Industrial Designers	19.0%
24. Fashion Designers	19.0%
25. Graphic Designers	19.0%
26. Interior Designers	19.0%
27. Merchandise Displayers and Window Trimmers	19.0%
28. Set and Exhibit Designers	19.0%
29. Interpreters and Translators	18.7%
30. Public Relations Managers	18.1%
31. Editors	18.0%
32. Public Relations Specialists	17.6%
33. Training and Development Specialists	17.6%
34. Broadcast News Analysts	17.1%
35. Hairdressers, Hairstylists, and Cosmetologists	16.8%
36. Producers and Directors	15.4%

Best Artistic Jobs Overall Employing 15 Percent or More Workers Age 55 and Over

Job	Percent Workers Age 55 and Over	Annual Earnings	Percent Growth	Annual Openings
1. Multi-Media Artists and Animators	33.9%	$54,550	25.8%	13,182
2. Architects, Except Landscape and Naval	23.4%	$67,620	17.7%	11,324
3. Training and Development Specialists	17.6%	$49,630	18.3%	35,862
4. Public Relations Specialists	17.6%	$49,800	17.6%	51,216
5. Special Education Teachers, Preschool, Kindergarten, and Elementary School	19.5%	$48,350	19.6%	20,049
6. Technical Writers	22.4%	$60,390	19.5%	7,498
7. Elementary School Teachers, Except Special Education	22.0%	$47,330	13.6%	181,612
8. Public Relations Managers	18.1%	$86,470	16.9%	5,781
9. Self-Enrichment Education Teachers	22.1%	$34,580	23.1%	64,449
10. Substance Abuse and Behavioral Disorder Counselors	25.3%	$35,580	34.3%	20,821
11. Writers and Authors	33.3%	$50,660	12.8%	24,023
12. Middle School Teachers, Except Special and Vocational Education	22.0%	$47,900	11.2%	75,270
13. Art Directors	33.9%	$72,320	9.0%	9,719
14. Producers and Directors	15.4%	$61,090	11.1%	8,992
15. Secondary School Teachers, Except Special and Vocational Education	22.2%	$49,420	5.6%	93,166
16. Landscape Architects	23.4%	$57,580	16.4%	2,342
17. Marriage and Family Therapists	25.3%	$43,600	29.8%	5,953
18. Adult Literacy, Remedial Education, and GED Teachers and Instructors	22.1%	$44,710	14.2%	17,340
19. Interior Designers	19.0%	$43,970	19.5%	8,434
20. Special Education Teachers, Middle School	19.5%	$48,940	15.8%	8,846
21. Interpreters and Translators	18.7%	$37,490	23.6%	6,630
22. Hairdressers, Hairstylists, and Cosmetologists	16.8%	$22,210	12.4%	73,030
23. Anthropologists and Archeologists	21.2%	$53,080	15.0%	446
24. Graphic Designers	19.0%	$41,280	9.8%	26,968
25. Sociologists	37.8%	$61,140	10.0%	403
26. Commercial and Industrial Designers	19.0%	$56,550	7.2%	4,777
27. Editors	18.0%	$48,320	2.3%	20,193
28. Astronomers	33.3%	$99,020	5.6%	128
29. Set and Exhibit Designers	19.0%	$43,220	17.8%	1,402
30. Music Directors and Composers	27.3%	$40,150	12.9%	8,597

(continued)

(continued)

Best Artistic Jobs Overall Employing 15 Percent or More Workers Age 55 and Over

Job	Percent Workers Age 55 and Over	Annual Earnings	Percent Growth	Annual Openings
31. Fashion Designers	19.0%	$62,810	5.0%	1,968
32. Political Scientists	21.2%	$91,580	5.3%	318
33. Photographers	20.8%	$27,720	10.3%	16,100
34. Merchandise Displayers and Window Trimmers	19.0%	$24,830	10.7%	9,103
35. Broadcast News Analysts	17.1%	$49,060	6.0%	1,444
36. Fine Artists, Including Painters, Sculptors, and Illustrators	33.9%	$42,070	9.9%	3,830

Social Jobs with the Highest Percentage of Workers Age 55 and Over

Job	Percent Workers Age 55 and Over
1. Instructional Coordinators	30.4%
2. Education Administrators, Preschool and Child Care Center/Program	28.7%
3. Marriage and Family Therapists	25.3%
4. Mental Health Counselors	25.3%
5. Rehabilitation Counselors	25.3%
6. Substance Abuse and Behavioral Disorder Counselors	25.3%
7. Self-Enrichment Education Teachers	22.1%
8. Elementary School Teachers, Except Special Education	22.0%
9. Registered Nurses	21.0%
10. Medical and Public Health Social Workers	19.9%
11. Mental Health and Substance Abuse Social Workers	19.9%
12. Health Educators	18.3%
13. Training and Development Specialists	17.6%
14. Fitness Trainers and Aerobics Instructors	16.4%

Best Social Jobs Overall Employing 15 Percent or More Workers Age 55 and Over

Job	Percent Workers Age 55 and Over	Annual Earnings	Percent Growth	Annual Openings
1. Registered Nurses	21.0%	$60,010	23.5%	233,499
2. Mental Health Counselors	25.3%	$36,000	30.0%	24,103
3. Elementary School Teachers, Except Special Education	22.0%	$47,330	13.6%	181,612
4. Substance Abuse and Behavioral Disorder Counselors	25.3%	$35,580	34.3%	20,821
5. Training and Development Specialists	17.6%	$49,630	18.3%	35,862
6. Instructional Coordinators	30.4%	$55,270	22.5%	21,294
7. Mental Health and Substance Abuse Social Workers	19.9%	$36,640	29.9%	17,289
8. Fitness Trainers and Aerobics Instructors	16.4%	$27,680	26.8%	51,235
9. Medical and Public Health Social Workers	19.9%	$44,670	24.2%	16,429
10. Marriage and Family Therapists	25.3%	$43,600	29.8%	5,953
11. Health Educators	18.3%	$42,920	26.2%	13,707
12. Self-Enrichment Education Teachers	22.1%	$34,580	23.1%	64,449
13. Education Administrators, Preschool and Child Care Center/Program	28.7%	$38,580	23.5%	8,113
14. Rehabilitation Counselors	25.3%	$29,630	23.0%	32,081

Enterprising Jobs with the Highest Percentage of Workers Age 55 and Over

Job	Percent Workers Age 55 and Over
1. Demonstrators and Product Promoters	38.2%
2. Property, Real Estate, and Community Association Managers	35.2%
3. Real Estate Brokers	34.5%
4. Real Estate Sales Agents	34.5%
5. Chief Executives	31.5%
6. Natural Sciences Managers	30.9%
7. Education Administrators, Elementary and Secondary School	28.7%
8. Education Administrators, Postsecondary	28.7%
9. Lawyers	27.8%

(continued)

(continued)

Enterprising Jobs with the Highest Percentage of Workers Age 55 and Over

Job	Percent Workers Age 55 and Over
10. Directors, Religious Activities and Education	27.7%
11. Administrative Services Managers	27.1%
12. Insurance Sales Agents	27.1%
13. Gaming Supervisors	26.9%
14. First-Line Supervisors/Managers of Housekeeping and Janitorial Workers	25.7%
15. Engineering Managers	25.5%
16. Social and Community Service Managers	25.3%
17. Medical and Health Services Managers	24.7%
18. Flight Attendants	23.2%
19. Personal Financial Advisors	22.3%
20. Gaming Managers	22.0%
21. First-Line Supervisors/Managers of Personal Service Workers	21.4%
22. Construction Managers	21.1%
23. First-Line Supervisors/Managers of Non-Retail Sales Workers	21.0%
24. Sales Representatives, Wholesale and Manufacturing, Technical and Scientific Products	21.0%
25. First-Line Supervisors/Managers of Office and Administrative Support Workers	20.5%
26. General and Operations Managers	19.8%
27. Sales Engineers	19.7%
28. Advertising Sales Agents	18.5%
29. Logisticians	18.5%
30. Compensation and Benefits Managers	18.2%
31. Training and Development Managers	18.2%
32. Public Relations Managers	18.1%
33. Employment, Recruitment, and Placement Specialists	17.6%
34. Public Relations Specialists	17.6%
35. First-Line Supervisors/Managers of Construction Trades and Extraction Workers	17.4%
36. Meeting and Convention Planners	16.6%
37. Producers and Directors	15.4%
38. Financial Managers	15.1%

Best Enterprising Jobs Overall Employing 15 Percent or More Workers Age 55 and Over

Job	Percent Workers Age 55 and Over	Annual Earnings	Percent Growth	Annual Openings
1. Financial Managers	15.1%	$95,310	12.6%	57,589
2. Construction Managers	21.1%	$76,230	15.7%	44,158
3. Lawyers	27.8%	$106,120	11.0%	49,445
4. Medical and Health Services Managers	24.7%	$76,990	16.4%	31,877
5. Personal Financial Advisors	22.3%	$67,660	41.0%	17,114
6. Public Relations Specialists	17.6%	$49,800	17.6%	51,216
7. General and Operations Managers	19.8%	$88,700	1.5%	112,072
8. Social and Community Service Managers	25.3%	$54,530	24.7%	23,788
9. Employment, Recruitment, and Placement Specialists	17.6%	$44,380	18.4%	33,588
10. Sales Representatives, Wholesale and Manufacturing, Technical and Scientific Products	21.0%	$68,270	12.4%	43,469
11. Insurance Sales Agents	27.1%	$44,110	12.9%	64,162
12. Public Relations Managers	18.1%	$86,470	16.9%	5,781
13. Property, Real Estate, and Community Association Managers	35.2%	$43,670	15.1%	49,916
14. Advertising Sales Agents	18.5%	$42,820	20.3%	29,233
15. Education Administrators, Postsecondary	28.7%	$75,780	14.2%	17,121
16. First-Line Supervisors/Managers of Construction Trades and Extraction Workers	17.4%	$55,950	9.1%	82,923
17. Chief Executives	31.5%	$145,600+	2.0%	21,209
18. Logisticians	18.5%	$64,250	17.3%	9,671
19. Training and Development Managers	18.2%	$84,340	15.6%	3,759
20. Gaming Managers	22.0%	$64,410	24.4%	549
21. Administrative Services Managers	27.1%	$70,990	11.7%	19,513
22. Demonstrators and Product Promoters	38.2%	$22,570	18.0%	32,779
23. Education Administrators, Elementary and Secondary School	28.7%	$80,580	7.6%	27,143
24. First-Line Supervisors/Managers of Office and Administrative Support Workers	20.5%	$44,650	5.8%	138,420
25. First-Line Supervisors/Managers of Non-Retail Sales Workers	21.0%	$67,020	3.7%	48,883
26. Compensation and Benefits Managers	18.2%	$81,410	12.0%	6,121
27. First-Line Supervisors/Managers of Personal Service Workers	21.4%	$33,900	15.5%	37,555

(continued)

(continued)

Best Enterprising Jobs Overall Employing 15 Percent or More Workers Age 55 and Over

Job	Percent Workers Age 55 and Over	Annual Earnings	Percent Growth	Annual Openings
28. Natural Sciences Managers	30.9%	$104,040	11.4%	3,661
29. Engineering Managers	25.5%	$111,020	7.3%	7,404
30. Meeting and Convention Planners	16.6%	$43,530	19.9%	8,318
31. Directors, Religious Activities and Education	27.7%	$35,370	19.7%	11,463
32. Real Estate Sales Agents	34.5%	$40,600	10.6%	61,232
33. Gaming Supervisors	26.9%	$42,980	23.4%	4,602
34. Real Estate Brokers	34.5%	$58,860	11.1%	18,689
35. First-Line Supervisors/Managers of Housekeeping and Janitorial Workers	25.7%	$32,850	12.7%	30,613
36. Sales Engineers	19.7%	$80,270	8.5%	7,371
37. Flight Attendants	23.2%	$61,120	10.6%	10,773
38. Producers and Directors	15.4%	$61,090	11.1%	8,992

Conventional Jobs with the Highest Percentage of Workers Age 55 and Over

Job	Percent Workers Age 55 and Over
1. Librarians	39.0%
2. Archivists	32.5%
3. Court, Municipal, and License Clerks	30.4%
4. Cost Estimators	29.9%
5. Appraisers and Assessors of Real Estate	28.6%
6. Bookkeeping, Accounting, and Auditing Clerks	28.2%
7. Compliance Officers, Except Agriculture, Construction, Health and Safety, and Transportation	27.0%
8. Medical Records and Health Information Technicians	26.1%
9. Executive Secretaries and Administrative Assistants	25.5%
10. Legal Secretaries	25.5%
11. Medical Secretaries	25.5%
12. Secretaries, Except Legal, Medical, and Executive	25.5%
13. Postal Service Mail Carriers	24.2%
14. Purchasing Agents, Except Wholesale, Retail, and Farm Products	23.8%
15. Budget Analysts	23.0%

Conventional Jobs with the Highest Percentage of Workers Age 55 and Over

Job	Percent Workers Age 55 and Over
16. Interviewers, Except Eligibility and Loan	22.0%
17. Human Resources Assistants, Except Payroll and Timekeeping	21.9%
18. Sales Representatives, Wholesale and Manufacturing, Except Technical and Scientific Products	21.0%
19. Billing and Posting Clerks and Machine Operators	20.3%
20. Database Administrators	20.0%
21. Office Clerks, General	20.0%
22. Statisticians	19.7%
23. Production, Planning, and Expediting Clerks	19.2%
24. Receptionists and Information Clerks	19.2%
25. Accountants and Auditors	19.1%
26. Claims Adjusters, Examiners, and Investigators	18.9%
27. Insurance Appraisers, Auto Damage	18.9%
28. Occupational Health and Safety Technicians	18.4%
29. Social and Human Service Assistants	18.3%
30. Cargo and Freight Agents	18.2%
31. Court Reporters	18.2%
32. Surveying and Mapping Technicians	17.7%
33. Compensation, Benefits, and Job Analysis Specialists	17.6%
34. Insurance Claims and Policy Processing Clerks	16.7%
35. Shipping, Receiving, and Traffic Clerks	16.0%
36. Brokerage Clerks	15.9%
37. Tellers	15.9%
38. Financial Analysts	15.8%

Best Conventional Jobs Overall Employing 15 Percent or More Workers Age 55 and Over

Job	Percent Workers Age 55 and Over	Annual Earnings	Percent Growth	Annual Openings
1. Financial Analysts	15.8%	$70,400	33.8%	29,317
2. Accountants and Auditors	19.1%	$57,060	17.7%	134,463
3. Cost Estimators	29.9%	$54,920	18.5%	38,379
4. Database Administrators	20.0%	$67,250	28.6%	8,258

(continued)

(continued)

Best Conventional Jobs Overall Employing 15 Percent or More Workers Age 55 and Over

Job	Percent Workers Age 55 and Over	Annual Earnings	Percent Growth	Annual Openings
5. Compensation, Benefits, and Job Analysis Specialists	17.6%	$52,180	18.4%	18,761
6. Executive Secretaries and Administrative Assistants	25.5%	$38,640	14.8%	235,314
7. Sales Representatives, Wholesale and Manufacturing, Except Technical and Scientific Products	21.0%	$50,750	8.4%	156,215
8. Social and Human Service Assistants	18.3%	$26,630	33.6%	80,142
9. Receptionists and Information Clerks	19.2%	$23,710	17.2%	334,124
10. Bookkeeping, Accounting, and Auditing Clerks	28.2%	$31,560	12.5%	286,854
11. Claims Adjusters, Examiners, and Investigators	18.9%	$53,560	8.9%	22,024
12. Court Reporters	18.2%	$45,330	24.5%	2,620
13. Brokerage Clerks	15.9%	$37,360	20.0%	10,826
14. Medical Records and Health Information Technicians	26.1%	$29,290	17.8%	39,048
15. Medical Secretaries	25.5%	$28,950	16.7%	60,659
16. Office Clerks, General	20.0%	$24,460	12.6%	765,803
17. Appraisers and Assessors of Real Estate	28.6%	$46,130	16.9%	6,493
18. Legal Secretaries	25.5%	$38,810	11.7%	38,682
19. Surveying and Mapping Technicians	17.7%	$33,640	19.4%	8,299
20. Statisticians	19.7%	$69,900	8.5%	3,433
21. Tellers	15.9%	$22,920	13.5%	146,077
22. Production, Planning, and Expediting Clerks	19.2%	$39,690	4.2%	52,735
23. Purchasing Agents, Except Wholesale, Retail, and Farm Products	23.8%	$52,460	0.1%	22,349
24. Budget Analysts	23.0%	$63,440	7.1%	6,423
25. Cargo and Freight Agents	18.2%	$37,060	16.5%	9,967
26. Insurance Appraisers, Auto Damage	18.9%	$51,500	12.5%	1,030
27. Librarians	39.0%	$50,970	3.6%	18,945
28. Billing and Posting Clerks and Machine Operators	20.3%	$29,970	4.4%	81,885
29. Compliance Officers, Except Agriculture, Construction, Health and Safety, and Transportation	27.0%	$48,400	4.9%	15,841
30. Interviewers, Except Eligibility and Loan	22.0%	$27,320	9.5%	54,060
31. Occupational Health and Safety Technicians	18.4%	$44,020	14.6%	886

Best Conventional Jobs Overall Employing 15 Percent or More Workers Age 55 and Over

Job	Percent Workers Age 55 and Over	Annual Earnings	Percent Growth	Annual Openings
32. Human Resources Assistants, Except Payroll and Timekeeping	21.9%	$34,970	11.3%	18,647
33. Secretaries, Except Legal, Medical, and Executive	25.5%	$28,220	1.2%	239,630
34. Archivists	32.5%	$43,110	14.4%	795
35. Shipping, Receiving, and Traffic Clerks	16.0%	$26,990	3.7%	138,967
36. Postal Service Mail Carriers	24.2%	$44,500	1.0%	16,710
37. Court, Municipal, and License Clerks	30.4%	$32,330	8.8%	16,163
38. Insurance Claims and Policy Processing Clerks	16.7%	$32,040	−1.3%	42,246

The Best Jobs for Each Personality Type with a High Percentage of Part-Time Workers

Starting with the 50 jobs that met our criteria for each personality type in this book, we created lists that include those jobs with 15 percent or more part-time workers.

If you want to work part time, these lists will be helpful in identifying where most others are finding opportunities for this kind of work in the personality type most compatible with you. Many people prefer to work less than full time. For example, people who are attending school or who have young children may prefer the flexibility of part-time work. People also work part time for money-related reasons, such as supplementing income from a full-time job or working two or more part-time jobs because one desirable full-time job is not available.

If you are the Enterprising type of personality, you will note that few occupations suited to you have a lot of part-timers. Keep in mind that even in occupations where few people work part-time it may be possible for you to carve out a position for yourself that does not require a 40-hour work week.

Many of these jobs can be learned quickly, offer flexible work schedules, are easy to obtain, and offer other desirable advantages. Although many people think of part-time jobs as requiring few skills and providing low pay, this is not always the case. Some of these jobs pay quite well, require substantial training or experience, or are growing rapidly.

Realistic Jobs with the Highest Percentage of Part-Time Workers

Job	Percent Part-Time Workers
1. Athletes and Sports Competitors	39.1%
2. Bus Drivers, Transit and Intercity	34.1%
3. Surgical Technologists	20.8%
4. Cardiovascular Technologists and Technicians	17.3%
5. Radiologic Technologists and Technicians	17.3%

Best Realistic Jobs Overall Employing 15 Percent or More Part-Time Workers

Job	Percent Part-Time Workers	Annual Earnings	Percent Growth	Annual Openings
1. Cardiovascular Technologists and Technicians	17.3%	$44,940	25.5%	3,550
2. Radiologic Technologists and Technicians	17.3%	$50,260	15.1%	12,836
3. Surgical Technologists	20.8%	$37,540	24.5%	15,365
4. Athletes and Sports Competitors	39.1%	$38,440	19.2%	4,293
5. Bus Drivers, Transit and Intercity	34.1%	$33,160	12.5%	27,100

Investigative Jobs with the Highest Percentage of Part-Time Workers

Job	Percent Part-Time Workers
1. Engineering Teachers, Postsecondary	27.8%
2. Dentists, General	25.9%
3. Orthodontists	25.9%
4. Prosthodontists	25.9%
5. Clinical, Counseling, and School Psychologists	24.0%
6. Industrial-Organizational Psychologists	24.0%
7. Podiatrists	23.6%
8. Optometrists	20.8%
9. Environmental Science and Protection Technicians, Including Health	19.4%
10. Forensic Science Technicians	19.4%
11. Pharmacists	18.1%
12. Diagnostic Medical Sonographers	17.3%
13. Nuclear Medicine Technologists	17.3%

Best Investigative Jobs Overall Employing 15 Percent or More Part-Time Workers

Job	Percent Part-Time Workers	Annual Earnings	Percent Growth	Annual Openings
1. Pharmacists	18.1%	$100,480	21.7%	16,358
2. Engineering Teachers, Postsecondary	27.8%	$79,510	22.9%	5,565
3. Environmental Science and Protection Technicians, Including Health	19.4%	$39,370	28.0%	8,404
4. Dentists, General	25.9%	$137,630	9.2%	7,106
5. Clinical, Counseling, and School Psychologists	24.0%	$62,210	15.8%	8,309
6. Forensic Science Technicians	19.4%	$47,680	30.7%	3,074
7. Diagnostic Medical Sonographers	17.3%	$59,860	19.1%	3,211
8. Optometrists	20.8%	$93,800	11.3%	1,789
9. Industrial-Organizational Psychologists	24.0%	$80,820	21.3%	118
10. Orthodontists	25.9%	$145,600+	9.2%	479
11. Prosthodontists	25.9%	$145,600+	10.7%	54
12. Podiatrists	23.6%	$110,510	9.5%	648
13. Nuclear Medicine Technologists	17.3%	$64,670	14.8%	1,290

Artistic Jobs with the Highest Percentage of Part-Time Workers

Job	Percent Part-Time Workers
1. Adult Literacy, Remedial Education, and GED Teachers and Instructors	41.3%
2. Self-Enrichment Education Teachers	41.3%
3. Music Directors and Composers	37.0%
4. Hairdressers, Hairstylists, and Cosmetologists	31.1%
5. Interpreters and Translators	28.5%
6. Architecture Teachers, Postsecondary	27.8%
7. Art, Drama, and Music Teachers, Postsecondary	27.8%
8. Communications Teachers, Postsecondary	27.8%
9. Education Teachers, Postsecondary	27.8%
10. English Language and Literature Teachers, Postsecondary	27.8%
11. Foreign Language and Literature Teachers, Postsecondary	27.8%
12. Philosophy and Religion Teachers, Postsecondary	27.8%
13. Makeup Artists, Theatrical and Performance	26.3%
14. Kindergarten Teachers, Except Special Education	25.1%
15. Preschool Teachers, Except Special Education	25.1%

(continued)

(continued)

Artistic Jobs with the Highest Percentage of Part-Time Workers

Job	Percent Part-Time Workers
16. Sociologists	24.0%
17. Art Directors	22.5%
18. Fine Artists, Including Painters, Sculptors, and Illustrators	22.5%
19. Multi-Media Artists and Animators	22.5%
20. Photographers	22.1%
21. Writers and Authors	21.8%
22. Anthropologists and Archeologists	20.1%
23. Political Scientists	20.1%
24. Camera Operators, Television, Video, and Motion Picture	18.9%
25. Film and Video Editors	18.9%
26. Broadcast News Analysts	17.3%
27. Commercial and Industrial Designers	16.7%
28. Fashion Designers	16.7%
29. Graphic Designers	16.7%
30. Interior Designers	16.7%
31. Merchandise Displayers and Window Trimmers	16.7%
32. Set and Exhibit Designers	16.7%
33. Marriage and Family Therapists	15.4%
34. Substance Abuse and Behavioral Disorder Counselors	15.4%

Best Artistic Jobs Overall Employing 15 Percent or More Part-Time Workers

Job	Percent Part-Time Workers	Annual Earnings	Percent Growth	Annual Openings
1. Multi-Media Artists and Animators	22.5%	$54,550	25.8%	13,182
2. Art, Drama, and Music Teachers, Postsecondary	27.8%	$55,190	22.9%	12,707
3. English Language and Literature Teachers, Postsecondary	27.8%	$54,000	22.9%	10,475
4. Education Teachers, Postsecondary	27.8%	$54,220	22.9%	9,359
5. Substance Abuse and Behavioral Disorder Counselors	15.4%	$35,580	34.3%	20,821
6. Preschool Teachers, Except Special Education	25.1%	$23,130	26.3%	78,172
7. Communications Teachers, Postsecondary	27.8%	$54,720	22.9%	4,074
8. Kindergarten Teachers, Except Special Education	25.1%	$45,120	16.3%	27,603

Best Artistic Jobs Overall Employing 15 Percent or More Part-Time Workers

Job	Percent Part-Time Workers	Annual Earnings	Percent Growth	Annual Openings
9. Philosophy and Religion Teachers, Postsecondary...	27.8%	$56,380	22.9%	3,120
10. Self-Enrichment Education Teachers	41.3%	$34,580	23.1%	64,449
11. Architecture Teachers, Postsecondary	27.8%	$68,540	22.9%	1,044
12. Foreign Language and Literature Teachers, Postsecondary	27.8%	$53,610	22.9%	4,317
13. Writers and Authors	21.8%	$50,660	12.8%	24,023
14. Marriage and Family Therapists	15.4%	$43,600	29.8%	5,953
15. Art Directors	22.5%	$72,320	9.0%	9,719
16. Adult Literacy, Remedial Education, and GED Teachers and Instructors	41.3%	$44,710	14.2%	17,340
17. Interpreters and Translators	28.5%	$37,490	23.6%	6,630
18. Interior Designers	16.7%	$43,970	19.5%	8,434
19. Commercial and Industrial Designers	16.7%	$56,550	7.2%	4,777
20. Graphic Designers	16.7%	$41,280	9.8%	26,968
21. Hairdressers, Hairstylists, and Cosmetologists	31.1%	$22,210	12.4%	73,030
22. Music Directors and Composers	37.0%	$40,150	12.9%	8,597
23. Anthropologists and Archeologists	20.1%	$53,080	15.0%	446
24. Makeup Artists, Theatrical and Performance	26.3%	$35,250	39.8%	392
25. Sociologists	24.0%	$61,140	10.0%	403
26. Fashion Designers	16.7%	$62,810	5.0%	1,968
27. Film and Video Editors	18.9%	$47,870	12.7%	2,707
28. Photographers	22.1%	$27,720	10.3%	16,100
29. Set and Exhibit Designers	16.7%	$43,220	17.8%	1,402
30. Political Scientists	20.1%	$91,580	5.3%	318
31. Camera Operators, Television, Video, and Motion Picture	18.9%	$41,850	11.5%	3,496
32. Merchandise Displayers and Window Trimmers	16.7%	$24,830	10.7%	9,103
33. Fine Artists, Including Painters, Sculptors, and Illustrators	22.5%	$42,070	9.9%	3,830
34. Broadcast News Analysts	17.3%	$49,060	6.0%	1,444

Social Jobs with the Highest Percentage of Part-Time Workers

Job	Percent Part-Time Workers
1. Dental Hygienists	58.7%
2. Self-Enrichment Education Teachers	41.3%
3. Fitness Trainers and Aerobics Instructors	38.2%
4. Occupational Therapists	29.8%
5. Agricultural Sciences Teachers, Postsecondary	27.8%
6. Anthropology and Archeology Teachers, Postsecondary	27.8%
7. Architecture Teachers, Postsecondary	27.8%
8. Art, Drama, and Music Teachers, Postsecondary	27.8%
9. Atmospheric, Earth, Marine, and Space Sciences Teachers, Postsecondary	27.8%
10. Biological Science Teachers, Postsecondary	27.8%
11. Business Teachers, Postsecondary	27.8%
12. Chemistry Teachers, Postsecondary	27.8%
13. Communications Teachers, Postsecondary	27.8%
14. Computer Science Teachers, Postsecondary	27.8%
15. Economics Teachers, Postsecondary	27.8%
16. Education Teachers, Postsecondary	27.8%
17. English Language and Literature Teachers, Postsecondary	27.8%
18. Environmental Science Teachers, Postsecondary	27.8%
19. Foreign Language and Literature Teachers, Postsecondary	27.8%
20. Graduate Teaching Assistants	27.8%
21. Health Specialties Teachers, Postsecondary	27.8%
22. History Teachers, Postsecondary	27.8%
23. Law Teachers, Postsecondary	27.8%
24. Mathematical Science Teachers, Postsecondary	27.8%
25. Nursing Instructors and Teachers, Postsecondary	27.8%
26. Philosophy and Religion Teachers, Postsecondary	27.8%
27. Physics Teachers, Postsecondary	27.8%
28. Political Science Teachers, Postsecondary	27.8%
29. Psychology Teachers, Postsecondary	27.8%
30. Recreation and Fitness Studies Teachers, Postsecondary	27.8%
31. Sociology Teachers, Postsecondary	27.8%
32. Vocational Education Teachers, Postsecondary	27.8%
33. Physical Therapist Assistants	27.1%
34. Preschool Teachers, Except Special Education	25.1%
35. Medical Assistants	23.2%
36. Physical Therapists	22.7%
37. Registered Nurses	21.8%

Social Jobs with the Highest Percentage of Part-Time Workers

Job	Percent Part-Time Workers
38. Instructional Coordinators	19.7%
39. Physician Assistants	15.6%
40. Marriage and Family Therapists	15.4%
41. Mental Health Counselors	15.4%
42. Rehabilitation Counselors	15.4%
43. Substance Abuse and Behavioral Disorder Counselors	15.4%

Best Social Jobs Overall Employing 15 Percent or More Part-Time Workers

Job	Percent Part-Time Workers	Annual Earnings	Percent Growth	Annual Openings
1. Health Specialties Teachers, Postsecondary	27.8%	$80,700	22.9%	19,617
2. Physical Therapists	22.7%	$69,760	27.1%	12,072
3. Registered Nurses	21.8%	$60,010	23.5%	233,499
4. Dental Hygienists	58.7%	$64,740	30.1%	10,433
5. Physician Assistants	15.6%	$78,450	27.0%	7,147
6. Biological Science Teachers, Postsecondary	27.8%	$71,780	22.9%	9,039
7. Business Teachers, Postsecondary	27.8%	$64,900	22.9%	11,643
8. Medical Assistants	23.2%	$27,430	35.4%	92,977
9. Mental Health Counselors	15.4%	$36,000	30.0%	24,103
10. Occupational Therapists	29.8%	$63,790	23.1%	8,338
11. Substance Abuse and Behavioral Disorder Counselors	15.4%	$35,580	34.3%	20,821
12. Law Teachers, Postsecondary	27.8%	$87,730	22.9%	2,169
13. Self-Enrichment Education Teachers	41.3%	$34,580	23.1%	64,449
14. Art, Drama, and Music Teachers, Postsecondary	27.8%	$55,190	22.9%	12,707
15. Fitness Trainers and Aerobics Instructors	38.2%	$27,680	26.8%	51,235
16. Economics Teachers, Postsecondary	27.8%	$75,300	22.9%	2,208
17. Preschool Teachers, Except Special Education	25.1%	$23,130	26.3%	78,172
18. Agricultural Sciences Teachers, Postsecondary	27.8%	$78,460	22.9%	1,840
19. Mathematical Science Teachers, Postsecondary	27.8%	$58,560	22.9%	7,663
20. Computer Science Teachers, Postsecondary	27.8%	$62,020	22.9%	5,820
21. Rehabilitation Counselors	15.4%	$29,630	23.0%	32,081
22. Vocational Education Teachers, Postsecondary	27.8%	$45,850	22.9%	19,313

(continued)

(continued)

Best Social Jobs Overall Employing 15 Percent or More Part-Time Workers

Job	Percent Part-Time Workers	Annual Earnings	Percent Growth	Annual Openings
23. Atmospheric, Earth, Marine, and Space Sciences Teachers, Postsecondary	27.8%	$73,280	22.9%	1,553
24. Chemistry Teachers, Postsecondary	27.8%	$63,870	22.9%	3,405
25. English Language and Literature Teachers, Postsecondary	27.8%	$54,000	22.9%	10,475
26. Nursing Instructors and Teachers, Postsecondary	27.8%	$57,500	22.9%	7,337
27. Physical Therapist Assistants	27.1%	$44,130	32.4%	5,957
28. Physics Teachers, Postsecondary	27.8%	$70,090	22.9%	2,155
29. Psychology Teachers, Postsecondary	27.8%	$60,610	22.9%	5,261
30. Education Teachers, Postsecondary	27.8%	$54,220	22.9%	9,359
31. Graduate Teaching Assistants	27.8%	$28,060	22.9%	20,601
32. Architecture Teachers, Postsecondary	27.8%	$68,540	22.9%	1,044
33. History Teachers, Postsecondary	27.8%	$59,160	22.9%	3,570
34. Marriage and Family Therapists	15.4%	$43,600	29.8%	5,953
35. Political Science Teachers, Postsecondary	27.8%	$63,100	22.9%	2,435
36. Environmental Science Teachers, Postsecondary	27.8%	$64,850	22.9%	769
37. Anthropology and Archeology Teachers, Postsecondary	27.8%	$64,530	22.9%	910
38. Communications Teachers, Postsecondary	27.8%	$54,720	22.9%	4,074
39. Philosophy and Religion Teachers, Postsecondary	27.8%	$56,380	22.9%	3,120
40. Sociology Teachers, Postsecondary	27.8%	$58,160	22.9%	2,774
41. Foreign Language and Literature Teachers, Postsecondary	27.8%	$53,610	22.9%	4,317
42. Instructional Coordinators	19.7%	$55,270	22.5%	21,294
43. Recreation and Fitness Studies Teachers, Postsecondary	27.8%	$52,170	22.9%	3,010

Enterprising Jobs with the Highest Percentage of Part-Time Workers

Job	Percent Part-Time Workers
1. Demonstrators and Product Promoters	56.1%
2. Directors, Religious Activities and Education	25.2%
3. Flight Attendants	24.9%

Enterprising Jobs with the Highest Percentage of Part-Time Workers

Job	Percent Part-Time Workers
4. Customer Service Representatives	16.5%
5. Property, Real Estate, and Community Association Managers	16.1%
6. First-Line Supervisors/Managers of Personal Service Workers	15.8%
7. Real Estate Brokers	15.5%
8. Real Estate Sales Agents	15.5%

Best Enterprising Jobs Overall Employing 15 Percent or More Part-Time Workers

Job	Percent Part-Time Workers	Annual Earnings	Percent Growth	Annual Openings
1. Customer Service Representatives	16.5%	$29,040	24.8%	600,937
2. Property, Real Estate, and Community Association Managers	16.1%	$43,670	15.1%	49,916
3. Real Estate Sales Agents	15.5%	$40,600	10.6%	61,232
4. Directors, Religious Activities and Education	25.2%	$35,370	19.7%	11,463
5. First-Line Supervisors/Managers of Personal Service Workers	15.8%	$33,900	15.5%	37,555
6. Real Estate Brokers	15.5%	$58,860	11.1%	18,689
7. Demonstrators and Product Promoters	56.1%	$22,570	18.0%	32,779
8. Flight Attendants	24.9%	$61,120	10.6%	10,773

Conventional Jobs with the Highest Percentage of Part-Time Workers

Job	Percent Part-Time Workers
1. Dental Assistants	35.7%
2. Receptionists and Information Clerks	31.7%
3. Tellers	27.1%
4. Office Clerks, General	26.0%
5. Bookkeeping, Accounting, and Auditing Clerks	24.8%
6. Interviewers, Except Eligibility and Loan	23.4%
7. Medical Transcriptionists	23.2%
8. Librarians	21.2%
9. Pharmacy Technicians	20.8%

(continued)

(continued)

Conventional Jobs with the Highest Percentage of Part-Time Workers

Job	Percent Part-Time Workers
10. Brokerage Clerks	19.4%
11. Executive Secretaries and Administrative Assistants	18.9%
12. Legal Secretaries	18.9%
13. Medical Secretaries	18.9%
14. Secretaries, Except Legal, Medical, and Executive	18.9%
15. Archivists	18.4%

Best Conventional Jobs Overall Employing 15 Percent or More Part-Time Workers

Job	Percent Part-Time Workers	Annual Earnings	Percent Growth	Annual Openings
1. Executive Secretaries and Administrative Assistants	18.9%	$38,640	14.8%	235,314
2. Bookkeeping, Accounting, and Auditing Clerks	24.8%	$31,560	12.5%	286,854
3. Dental Assistants	35.7%	$31,550	29.2%	29,482
4. Receptionists and Information Clerks	31.7%	$23,710	17.2%	334,124
5. Medical Secretaries	18.9%	$28,950	16.7%	60,659
6. Pharmacy Technicians	20.8%	$26,720	32.0%	54,453
7. Brokerage Clerks	19.4%	$37,360	20.0%	10,826
8. Archivists	18.4%	$43,110	14.4%	795
9. Office Clerks, General	26.0%	$24,460	12.6%	765,803
10. Legal Secretaries	18.9%	$38,810	11.7%	38,682
11. Librarians	21.2%	$50,970	3.6%	18,945
12. Medical Transcriptionists	23.2%	$31,250	13.5%	18,080
13. Secretaries, Except Legal, Medical, and Executive	18.9%	$28,220	1.2%	239,630
14. Tellers	27.1%	$22,920	13.5%	146,077
15. Interviewers, Except Eligibility and Loan	23.4%	$27,320	9.5%	54,060

The Best Jobs for Each Personality Type with a High Percentage of Self-Employed Workers

About 8 percent of all working people are self-employed or own their own business. This substantial part of our workforce gets little mention in most career books.

The jobs in the lists in this section are selected from the 50 best jobs for each personality type, and all have 8 percent or more self-employed workers. Many jobs in these lists, such as the various types of artists, are held by people who operate one- or two-person businesses and who may also do this work part time. Those in other occupations, such as Carpenters, often work on a per-job basis under the supervision of others.

As you will see from these lists, self-employed people hold a wide range of jobs at all levels of pay and skill. Many are in the arts (Artistic), construction (Realistic), or health-care (Investigative) professions, but many other fields are also represented. Also, while the lists do not include data on age and gender, older workers and women make up a rapidly growing part of the self-employed population. For example, some highly experienced older workers set up consulting and other small businesses following a layoff or as an alternative to full retirement. Large numbers of women are forming small businesses or creating self-employment opportunities as an alternative to traditional employment.

Realistic Jobs with the Highest Percentage of Self-Employed Workers

Job	Percent Self-Employed Workers
1. Painters, Construction and Maintenance	42.2%
2. Tile and Marble Setters	33.8%
3. Carpenters	31.8%
4. Athletes and Sports Competitors	27.0%
5. Brickmasons and Blockmasons	24.5%
6. Drywall and Ceiling Tile Installers	23.0%
7. Roofers	20.1%
8. Automotive Service Technicians and Mechanics	16.8%
9. Automotive Body and Related Repairers	14.1%
10. Audio and Video Equipment Technicians	12.8%
11. Heating, Air Conditioning, and Refrigeration Mechanics and Installers	12.7%
12. Plumbers, Pipefitters, and Steamfitters	12.3%
13. Electricians	10.7%
14. Construction and Building Inspectors	9.4%
15. Truck Drivers, Heavy and Tractor-Trailer	8.8%

Best Realistic Jobs Overall with 8 Percent or More Self-Employed Workers

Job	Percent Self-Employed Workers	Annual Earnings	Percent Growth	Annual Openings
1. Construction and Building Inspectors	9.4%	$48,330	18.2%	12,606
2. Plumbers, Pipefitters, and Steamfitters	12.3%	$44,090	10.6%	68,643
3. Carpenters	31.8%	$37,660	10.3%	223,225
4. Electricians	10.7%	$44,780	7.4%	79,083
5. Truck Drivers, Heavy and Tractor-Trailer	8.8%	$36,220	10.4%	279,032
6. Automotive Service Technicians and Mechanics	16.8%	$34,170	14.3%	97,350
7. Tile and Marble Setters	33.8%	$38,720	15.4%	9,066
8. Athletes and Sports Competitors	27.0%	$38,440	19.2%	4,293
9. Painters, Construction and Maintenance	42.2%	$32,080	11.8%	101,140
10. Audio and Video Equipment Technicians	12.8%	$36,050	24.2%	4,681
11. Brickmasons and Blockmasons	24.5%	$44,070	9.7%	17,569
12. Roofers	20.1%	$33,240	14.3%	38,398
13. Automotive Body and Related Repairers	14.1%	$35,690	11.6%	37,469
14. Heating, Air Conditioning, and Refrigeration Mechanics and Installers	12.7%	$38,360	8.7%	29,719
15. Drywall and Ceiling Tile Installers	23.0%	$36,520	7.3%	30,945

Investigative Jobs with the Highest Percentage of Self-Employed Workers

Job	Percent Self-Employed Workers
1. Prosthodontists	51.3%
2. Orthodontists	43.3%
3. Industrial-Organizational Psychologists	39.3%
4. Dentists, General	36.6%
5. Clinical, Counseling, and School Psychologists	34.2%
6. Management Analysts	27.0%
7. Optometrists	25.5%
8. Podiatrists	23.9%
9. Network Systems and Data Communications Analysts	17.5%
10. Veterinarians	17.1%
11. Anesthesiologists	14.7%
12. Family and General Practitioners	14.7%

Investigative Jobs with the Highest Percentage of Self-Employed Workers

Job	Percent Self-Employed Workers
13. Internists, General	14.7%
14. Obstetricians and Gynecologists	14.7%
15. Pediatricians, General	14.7%
16. Psychiatrists	14.7%
17. Surgeons	14.7%

Best Investigative Jobs Overall with 8 Percent or More Self-Employed Workers

Job	Percent Self-Employed Workers	Annual Earnings	Percent Growth	Annual Openings
1. Anesthesiologists	14.7%	$145,600+	14.2%	38,027
2. Family and General Practitioners	14.7%	$145,600+	14.2%	38,027
3. Internists, General	14.7%	$145,600+	14.2%	38,027
4. Obstetricians and Gynecologists	14.7%	$145,600+	14.2%	38,027
5. Psychiatrists	14.7%	$145,600+	14.2%	38,027
6. Surgeons	14.7%	$145,600+	14.2%	38,027
7. Pediatricians, General	14.7%	$140,690	14.2%	38,027
8. Management Analysts	27.0%	$71,150	21.9%	125,669
9. Network Systems and Data Communications Analysts	17.5%	$68,220	53.4%	35,086
10. Veterinarians	17.1%	$75,230	35.0%	5,301
11. Clinical, Counseling, and School Psychologists	34.2%	$62,210	15.8%	8,309
12. Orthodontists	43.3%	$145,600+	9.2%	479
13. Prosthodontists	51.3%	$145,600+	10.7%	54
14. Industrial-Organizational Psychologists	39.3%	$80,820	21.3%	118
15. Dentists, General	36.6%	$137,630	9.2%	7,106
16. Optometrists	25.5%	$93,800	11.3%	1,789
17. Podiatrists	23.9%	$110,510	9.5%	648

Jobs 1, 2, 3, 4, 5, 6, and 7 share 38,027 openings.

Artistic Jobs with the Highest Percentage of Self-Employed Workers

Job	Percent Self-Employed Workers
1. Multi-Media Artists and Animators	69.7%
2. Writers and Authors	65.9%
3. Fine Artists, Including Painters, Sculptors, and Illustrators	62.6%
4. Art Directors	59.0%
5. Photographers	54.3%
6. Music Directors and Composers	44.7%
7. Hairdressers, Hairstylists, and Cosmetologists	44.5%
8. Makeup Artists, Theatrical and Performance	39.7%
9. Commercial and Industrial Designers	29.8%
10. Set and Exhibit Designers	29.8%
11. Producers and Directors	29.5%
12. Merchandise Displayers and Window Trimmers	28.6%
13. Interior Designers	26.3%
14. Graphic Designers	25.3%
15. Fashion Designers	23.6%
16. Interpreters and Translators	21.6%
17. Self-Enrichment Education Teachers	21.5%
18. Architects, Except Landscape and Naval	20.3%
19. Landscape Architects	18.5%
20. Camera Operators, Television, Video, and Motion Picture	16.9%
21. Film and Video Editors	15.9%
22. Advertising and Promotions Managers	13.4%
23. Editors	13.4%
24. Broadcast News Analysts	11.1%

Best Artistic Jobs Overall with 8 Percent or More Self-Employed Workers

Job	Percent Self-Employed Workers	Annual Earnings	Percent Growth	Annual Openings
1. Multi-Media Artists and Animators	69.7%	$54,550	25.8%	13,182
2. Architects, Except Landscape and Naval	20.3%	$67,620	17.7%	11,324
3. Writers and Authors	65.9%	$50,660	12.8%	24,023
4. Self-Enrichment Education Teachers	21.5%	$34,580	23.1%	64,449
5. Art Directors	59.0%	$72,320	9.0%	9,719
6. Producers and Directors	29.5%	$61,090	11.1%	8,992

Best Artistic Jobs Overall with 8 Percent or More Self-Employed Workers

Job	Percent Self-Employed Workers	Annual Earnings	Percent Growth	Annual Openings
7. Interior Designers	26.3%	$43,970	19.5%	8,434
8. Landscape Architects	18.5%	$57,580	16.4%	2,342
9. Interpreters and Translators	21.6%	$37,490	23.6%	6,630
10. Hairdressers, Hairstylists, and Cosmetologists	44.5%	$22,210	12.4%	73,030
11. Graphic Designers	25.3%	$41,280	9.8%	26,968
12. Music Directors and Composers	44.7%	$40,150	12.9%	8,597
13. Advertising and Promotions Managers	13.4%	$78,250	6.2%	2,955
14. Editors	13.4%	$48,320	2.3%	20,193
15. Commercial and Industrial Designers	29.8%	$56,550	7.2%	4,777
16. Film and Video Editors	15.9%	$47,870	12.7%	2,707
17. Set and Exhibit Designers	29.8%	$43,220	17.8%	1,402
18. Photographers	54.3%	$27,720	10.3%	16,100
19. Makeup Artists, Theatrical and Performance	39.7%	$35,250	39.8%	392
20. Camera Operators, Television, Video, and Motion Picture	16.9%	$41,850	11.5%	3,496
21. Fashion Designers	23.6%	$62,810	5.0%	1,968
22. Fine Artists, Including Painters, Sculptors, and Illustrators	62.6%	$42,070	9.9%	3,830
23. Merchandise Displayers and Window Trimmers	28.6%	$24,830	10.7%	9,103
24. Broadcast News Analysts	11.1%	$49,060	6.0%	1,444

Social Jobs with the Highest Percentage of Self-Employed Workers

Job	Percent Self-Employed Workers
1. Self-Enrichment Education Teachers	21.5%
2. Occupational Therapists	8.6%
3. Physical Therapists	8.4%

Best Social Jobs Overall with 8 Percent or More Self-Employed Workers

Job	Percent Self-Employed Workers	Annual Earnings	Percent Growth	Annual Openings
1. Physical Therapists	8.4%	$69,760	27.1%	12,072
2. Occupational Therapists	8.6%	$63,790	23.1%	8,338
3. Self-Enrichment Education Teachers	21.5%	$34,580	23.1%	64,449

Enterprising Jobs with the Highest Percentage of Self-Employed Workers

Job	Percent Self-Employed Workers
1. Real Estate Brokers	63.5%
2. Real Estate Sales Agents	60.2%
3. Construction Managers	56.3%
4. Property, Real Estate, and Community Association Managers	50.9%
5. First-Line Supervisors/Managers of Non-Retail Sales Workers	45.4%
6. Food Service Managers	44.8%
7. First-Line Supervisors/Managers of Landscaping, Lawn Service, and Groundskeeping Workers	44.1%
8. First-Line Supervisors/Managers of Personal Service Workers	38.6%
9. Personal Financial Advisors	30.9%
10. First-Line Supervisors/Managers of Housekeeping and Janitorial Workers	30.7%
11. Producers and Directors	29.5%
12. Gaming Supervisors	29.2%
13. Lawyers	26.7%
14. Insurance Sales Agents	25.5%
15. First-Line Supervisors/Managers of Construction Trades and Extraction Workers	24.4%
16. Chief Executives	22.0%
17. Demonstrators and Product Promoters	20.8%
18. Securities, Commodities, and Financial Services Sales Agents	17.7%
19. Gaming Managers	16.3%
20. Medical and Health Services Managers	8.2%

Best Enterprising Jobs Overall with 8 Percent or More Self-Employed Workers

Job	Percent Self-Employed Workers	Annual Earnings	Percent Growth	Annual Openings
1. Securities, Commodities, and Financial Services Sales Agents	17.7%	$68,430	24.8%	47,750
2. Construction Managers	56.3%	$76,230	15.7%	44,158
3. Medical and Health Services Managers	8.2%	$76,990	16.4%	31,877
4. Lawyers	26.7%	$106,120	11.0%	49,445
5. Personal Financial Advisors	30.9%	$67,660	41.0%	17,114
6. Insurance Sales Agents	25.5%	$44,110	12.9%	64,162
7. First-Line Supervisors/Managers of Construction Trades and Extraction Workers	24.4%	$55,950	9.1%	82,923
8. Property, Real Estate, and Community Association Managers	50.9%	$43,670	15.1%	49,916
9. Gaming Managers	16.3%	$64,410	24.4%	549
10. First-Line Supervisors/Managers of Non-Retail Sales Workers	45.4%	$67,020	3.7%	48,883
11. Food Service Managers	44.8%	$44,570	5.0%	59,302
12. Chief Executives	22.0%	$145,600+	2.0%	21,209
13. Real Estate Sales Agents	60.2%	$40,600	10.6%	61,232
14. Demonstrators and Product Promoters	20.8%	$22,570	18.0%	32,779
15. First-Line Supervisors/Managers of Personal Service Workers	38.6%	$33,900	15.5%	37,555
16. First-Line Supervisors/Managers of Landscaping, Lawn Service, and Groundskeeping Workers	44.1%	$38,720	17.6%	18,956
17. Gaming Supervisors	29.2%	$42,980	23.4%	4,602
18. Producers and Directors	29.5%	$61,090	11.1%	8,992
19. Real Estate Brokers	63.5%	$58,860	11.1%	18,689
20. First-Line Supervisors/Managers of Housekeeping and Janitorial Workers	30.7%	$32,850	12.7%	30,613

Conventional Jobs with the Highest Percentage of Self-Employed Workers

Job	Percent Self-Employed Workers
1. Appraisers and Assessors of Real Estate	32.7%
2. Medical Transcriptionists	9.7%
3. Accountants and Auditors	9.5%
4. Financial Analysts	8.3%

Best Conventional Jobs Overall with 8 Percent or More Self-Employed Workers

Job	Percent Self-Employed Workers	Annual Earnings	Percent Growth	Annual Openings
1. Financial Analysts	8.3%	$70,400	33.8%	29,317
2. Accountants and Auditors	9.5%	$57,060	17.7%	134,463
3. Appraisers and Assessors of Real Estate	32.7%	$46,130	16.9%	6,493
4. Medical Transcriptionists	9.7%	$31,250	13.5%	18,080

Best Jobs for Each Personality Type with a High Percentage of Women and of Men

We knew we would create some controversy when we first included the best jobs lists with high percentages of men and women in an earlier *Best Jobs* book. But these lists are not meant to restrict women or men from considering job options—one reason for including these lists is exactly the opposite. We hope the lists will help people see possibilities that they might not otherwise have considered. For example, we suggest that women browse the lists of jobs that employ high percentages of men. Many of these occupations pay quite well, and women who want to do them and are willing to undertake the education or training should consider them.

To create the lists, we sorted the jobs of each personality type that met the criteria for this book and included only those employing 70 percent or more of women or men. For the Realistic, Investigative, and Enterprising personality types, the list of predominantly male jobs is much longer than the list of predominantly female jobs. For the Social and Conventional personality types, you'll find the opposite to be true. In fact, there is no list for

Social jobs with a high percentage of men because no Social jobs employ 70 percent or more men. For the Artistic personality type, the lists are roughly equal.

We also produced "best overall" lists in which these predominantly male jobs and predominantly female jobs are sorted by their combined ranking in terms of annual earnings, percent growth, and annual job openings. In these lists, we list these facts for each job so you can compare their potential rewards.

In the following lists, if you compare the occupations employing a high percentage of women with those employing a high percentage of men, you may notice some distinct differences beyond the obvious. For example, you may notice that the jobs with a high percentage of women are growing somewhat faster than those with a high percentage of men. We've done the math and discovered that the difference is an average growth rate of 15.4 percent for the jobs that employ mostly women versus an average rate of 11.9 percent for the jobs that employ mostly men. The number of annual job openings shows a similar pattern. Occupations with a high percentage of men average 32,131 openings per year, while more than double that number of openings, 76,361, are projected on average for occupations with a high percentage of women.

This discrepancy reflects the trend that men have had more problems than women in adapting to an economy dominated by service and information-based jobs. Many women may simply be better prepared for these jobs, possessing more appropriate skills for the jobs that are now growing rapidly and have more job openings.

On the other hand, you may notice that on average the jobs with a high percentage of men have higher wages (an average of $56,065) than do the jobs with a high percentage of women ($36,553). This indicates that women interested in improving their earnings may want to consider jobs traditionally dominated by men. Remember that a time-honored gender imbalance is not always a barrier to women. Some employers are seeking female recruits to counterbalance a traditional male dominance.

Realistic Jobs with the Highest Percentage of Women

Job	Percent Women
1. Surgical Technologists	80.1%
2. Medical and Clinical Laboratory Technicians	78.1%
3. Cardiovascular Technologists and Technicians	72.9%
4. Radiologic Technologists and Technicians	72.9%

Best Realistic Jobs Overall Employing 70 Percent or More Women

Job	Percent Women	Annual Earnings	Percent Growth	Annual Openings
1. Radiologic Technologists and Technicians	72.9%	$50,260	15.1%	12,836
2. Surgical Technologists	80.1%	$37,540	24.5%	15,365
3. Cardiovascular Technologists and Technicians	72.9%	$44,940	25.5%	3,550
4. Medical and Clinical Laboratory Technicians	78.1%	$34,270	15.0%	10,866

Realistic Jobs with the Highest Percentage of Men

Job	Percent Men
1. Automotive Body and Related Repairers	99.4%
2. Cement Masons and Concrete Finishers	99.3%
3. Bus and Truck Mechanics and Diesel Engine Specialists	99.1%
4. Electrical Power-Line Installers and Repairers	99.1%
5. Roofers	98.9%
6. Mobile Heavy Equipment Mechanics, Except Engines	98.6%
7. Automotive Service Technicians and Mechanics	98.4%
8. Brickmasons and Blockmasons	98.4%
9. Operating Engineers and Other Construction Equipment Operators	98.3%
10. Plumbers, Pipefitters, and Steamfitters	98.2%
11. Electricians	98.1%
12. Carpenters	97.6%
13. Security and Fire Alarm Systems Installers	97.6%
14. Tile and Marble Setters	97.6%
15. Heating, Air Conditioning, and Refrigeration Mechanics and Installers	97.3%
16. Drywall and Ceiling Tile Installers	97.1%
17. Sheet Metal Workers	96.9%
18. Boilermakers	96.9%
19. Fire Fighters	96.5%
20. Industrial Machinery Mechanics	96.2%
21. Maintenance and Repair Workers, General	96.0%
22. Water and Liquid Waste Treatment Plant and System Operators	96.0%
23. Truck Drivers, Heavy and Tractor-Trailer	94.8%
24. Aircraft Mechanics and Service Technicians	94.7%
25. Painters, Construction and Maintenance	92.3%
26. Telecommunications Line Installers and Repairers	91.4%
27. Construction and Building Inspectors	91.2%
28. Cartographers and Photogrammetrists	90.1%

Realistic Jobs with the Highest Percentage of Men

Job	Percent Men
29. Surveyors	90.1%
30. Civil Engineers	88.1%
31. Captains, Mates, and Pilots of Water Vessels	85.2%
32. Sailors and Marine Oilers	85.2%
33. Transportation Inspectors	85.2%
34. Telecommunications Equipment Installers and Repairers, Except Line Installers	84.8%
35. Audio and Video Equipment Technicians	84.4%
36. Civil Engineering Technicians	79.4%
37. Electrical and Electronic Engineering Technicians	79.4%
38. Architectural and Civil Drafters	78.2%
39. Mechanical Drafters	78.2%
40. Airline Pilots, Copilots, and Flight Engineers	78.0%
41. Correctional Officers and Jailers	71.8%
42. Computer Support Specialists	71.1%

Best Realistic Jobs Overall Employing 70 Percent or More Men

Job	Percent Men	Annual Earnings	Percent Growth	Annual Openings
1. Civil Engineers	88.1%	$71,710	18.0%	15,979
2. Surveyors	90.1%	$51,630	23.7%	14,305
3. Computer Support Specialists	71.1%	$42,400	12.9%	97,334
4. Construction and Building Inspectors	91.2%	$48,330	18.2%	12,606
5. Correctional Officers and Jailers	71.8%	$36,970	16.9%	56,579
6. Plumbers, Pipefitters, and Steamfitters	98.2%	$44,090	10.6%	68,643
7. Captains, Mates, and Pilots of Water Vessels	85.2%	$57,210	17.9%	2,665
8. Cartographers and Photogrammetrists	90.1%	$49,970	20.3%	2,823
9. Automotive Service Technicians and Mechanics	98.4%	$34,170	14.3%	97,350
10. Airline Pilots, Copilots, and Flight Engineers	78.0%	$145,600+	12.9%	4,073
11. Electricians	98.1%	$44,780	7.4%	79,083
12. Fire Fighters	96.5%	$43,170	12.1%	18,887
13. Carpenters	97.6%	$37,660	10.3%	223,225
14. Transportation Inspectors	85.2%	$51,440	16.4%	2,122
15. Truck Drivers, Heavy and Tractor-Trailer	94.8%	$36,220	10.4%	279,032
16. Roofers	98.9%	$33,240	14.3%	38,398
17. Boilermakers	96.9%	$50,700	14.0%	2,333

(continued)

(continued)

Best Realistic Jobs Overall Employing 70 Percent or More Men

Job	Percent Men	Annual Earnings	Percent Growth	Annual Openings
18. Aircraft Mechanics and Service Technicians	94.7%	$49,010	10.6%	9,708
19. Bus and Truck Mechanics and Diesel Engine Specialists	99.1%	$38,640	11.5%	25,428
20. Painters, Construction and Maintenance	92.3%	$32,080	11.8%	101,140
21. Brickmasons and Blockmasons	98.4%	$44,070	9.7%	17,569
22. Automotive Body and Related Repairers	99.4%	$35,690	11.6%	37,469
23. Tile and Marble Setters	97.6%	$38,720	15.4%	9,066
24. Mobile Heavy Equipment Mechanics, Except Engines	98.6%	$41,450	12.3%	11,037
25. Industrial Machinery Mechanics	96.2%	$42,350	9.0%	23,361
26. Operating Engineers and Other Construction Equipment Operators	98.3%	$38,130	8.4%	55,468
27. Telecommunications Equipment Installers and Repairers, Except Line Installers	84.8%	$54,070	2.5%	13,541
28. Audio and Video Equipment Technicians	84.4%	$36,050	24.2%	4,681
29. Maintenance and Repair Workers, General	96.0%	$32,570	10.1%	165,502
30. Cement Masons and Concrete Finishers	99.3%	$33,840	11.4%	34,625
31. Electrical and Electronic Engineering Technicians	79.4%	$52,140	3.6%	12,583
32. Heating, Air Conditioning, and Refrigeration Mechanics and Installers	97.3%	$38,360	8.7%	29,719
33. Sheet Metal Workers	96.9%	$39,210	6.7%	31,677
34. Electrical Power-Line Installers and Repairers	99.1%	$52,570	7.2%	6,401
35. Security and Fire Alarm Systems Installers	97.6%	$35,390	20.2%	5,729
36. Telecommunications Line Installers and Repairers	91.4%	$47,220	4.6%	14,719
37. Water and Liquid Waste Treatment Plant and System Operators	96.0%	$37,090	13.8%	9,575
38. Architectural and Civil Drafters	78.2%	$43,310	6.1%	16,238
39. Civil Engineering Technicians	79.4%	$42,580	10.2%	7,499
40. Drywall and Ceiling Tile Installers	97.1%	$36,520	7.3%	30,945
41. Mechanical Drafters	78.2%	$44,740	5.2%	10,902
42. Sailors and Marine Oilers	85.2%	$32,570	15.7%	8,600

Investigative Jobs with the Highest Percentage of Women

Job	Percent Women
1. Medical and Clinical Laboratory Technologists	78.1%
2. Diagnostic Medical Sonographers	72.9%
3. Nuclear Medicine Technologists	72.9%

Best Investigative Jobs Overall Employing 70 Percent or More Women

Job	Percent Women	Annual Earnings	Percent Growth	Annual Openings
1. Diagnostic Medical Sonographers	72.9%	$59,860	19.1%	3,211
2. Nuclear Medicine Technologists	72.9%	$64,670	14.8%	1,290
3. Medical and Clinical Laboratory Technologists	78.1%	$51,720	12.4%	11,457

Investigative Jobs with the Highest Percentage of Men

Job	Percent Men
1. Mechanical Engineers	94.2%
2. Electrical Engineers	92.3%
3. Electronics Engineers, Except Computer	92.3%
4. Aerospace Engineers	86.9%
5. Biomedical Engineers	85.5%
6. Environmental Engineers	85.5%
7. Computer Hardware Engineers	83.8%
8. Computer Software Engineers, Applications	83.8%
9. Computer Software Engineers, Systems Software	83.8%
10. Network and Computer Systems Administrators	83.4%
11. Chemical Engineers	82.9%
12. Environmental Scientists and Specialists, Including Health	78.0%
13. Dentists, General	77.4%
14. Industrial Engineers	77.4%
15. Orthodontists	77.4%
16. Prosthodontists	77.4%
17. Network Systems and Data Communications Analysts	74.5%
18. Mathematicians	73.3%

Best Investigative Jobs Overall Employing 70 Percent or More Men

Job	Percent Men	Annual Earnings	Percent Growth	Annual Openings
1. Computer Software Engineers, Applications	83.8%	$83,130	44.6%	58,690
2. Computer Software Engineers, Systems Software	83.8%	$89,070	28.2%	33,139
3. Network Systems and Data Communications Analysts	74.5%	$68,220	53.4%	35,086
4. Network and Computer Systems Administrators	83.4%	$64,690	27.0%	37,010
5. Dentists, General	77.4%	$137,630	9.2%	7,106
6. Aerospace Engineers	86.9%	$90,930	10.2%	6,498
7. Environmental Engineers	85.5%	$72,350	25.4%	5,003
8. Prosthodontists	77.4%	$145,600+	10.7%	54
9. Industrial Engineers	77.4%	$71,430	20.3%	11,272
10. Orthodontists	77.4%	$145,600+	9.2%	479
11. Biomedical Engineers	85.5%	$75,440	21.1%	1,804
12. Computer Hardware Engineers	83.8%	$91,860	4.6%	3,572
13. Environmental Scientists and Specialists, Including Health	78.0%	$58,380	25.1%	6,961
14. Mathematicians	73.3%	$90,870	10.2%	473
15. Electrical Engineers	92.3%	$79,240	6.3%	6,806
16. Mechanical Engineers	94.2%	$72,300	4.2%	12,394
17. Electronics Engineers, Except Computer	92.3%	$83,340	3.7%	5,699
18. Chemical Engineers	82.9%	$81,500	7.9%	2,111

Artistic Jobs with the Highest Percentage of Women

Job	Percent Women
1. Kindergarten Teachers, Except Special Education	97.7%
2. Preschool Teachers, Except Special Education	97.7%
3. Hairdressers, Hairstylists, and Cosmetologists	93.4%
4. Makeup Artists, Theatrical and Performance	93.4%
5. Special Education Teachers, Middle School	83.5%
6. Special Education Teachers, Preschool, Kindergarten, and Elementary School	83.5%
7. Elementary School Teachers, Except Special Education	82.2%
8. Middle School Teachers, Except Special and Vocational Education	82.2%
9. Training and Development Specialists	71.5%

Best Artistic Jobs Overall Employing 70 Percent or More Women

Job	Percent Women	Annual Earnings	Percent Growth	Annual Openings
1. Training and Development Specialists	71.5%	$49,630	18.3%	35,862
2. Preschool Teachers, Except Special Education	97.7%	$23,130	26.3%	78,172
3. Elementary School Teachers, Except Special Education	82.2%	$47,330	13.6%	181,612
4. Special Education Teachers, Preschool, Kindergarten, and Elementary School	83.5%	$48,350	19.6%	20,049
5. Middle School Teachers, Except Special and Vocational Education	82.2%	$47,900	11.2%	75,270
6. Special Education Teachers, Middle School	83.5%	$48,940	15.8%	8,846
7. Kindergarten Teachers, Except Special Education	97.7%	$45,120	16.3%	27,603
8. Makeup Artists, Theatrical and Performance	93.4%	$35,250	39.8%	392
9. Hairdressers, Hairstylists, and Cosmetologists	93.4%	$22,210	12.4%	73,030

Artistic Jobs with the Highest Percentage of Men

Job	Percent Men
1. Camera Operators, Television, Video, and Motion Picture	84.4%
2. Film and Video Editors	84.4%
3. Architects, Except Landscape and Naval	77.8%
4. Landscape Architects	77.8%

Best Artistic Jobs Overall Employing 70 Percent or More Men

Job	Percent Men	Annual Earnings	Percent Growth	Annual Openings
1. Architects, Except Landscape and Naval	77.8%	$67,620	17.7%	11,324
2. Landscape Architects	77.8%	$57,580	16.4%	2,342
3. Film and Video Editors	84.4%	$47,870	12.7%	2,707
4. Camera Operators, Television, Video, and Motion Picture	84.4%	$41,850	11.5%	3,496

Social Jobs with the Highest Percentage of Women

Job	Percent Women
1. Dental Hygienists	98.6%
2. Preschool Teachers, Except Special Education	97.7%
3. Registered Nurses	91.3%
4. Medical Assistants	90.4%
5. Occupational Therapists	90.3%
6. Medical and Public Health Social Workers	82.6%
7. Mental Health and Substance Abuse Social Workers	82.6%
8. Elementary School Teachers, Except Special Education	82.2%
9. Physical Therapist Assistants	78.4%
10. Radiation Therapists	74.1%
11. Physician Assistants	71.7%
12. Training and Development Specialists	71.5%
13. Health Educators	70.5%

Best Social Jobs Overall Employing 70 Percent or More Women

Job	Percent Women	Annual Earnings	Percent Growth	Annual Openings
1. Dental Hygienists	98.6%	$64,740	30.1%	10,433
2. Medical Assistants	90.4%	$27,430	35.4%	92,977
3. Registered Nurses	91.3%	$60,010	23.5%	233,499
4. Physician Assistants	71.7%	$78,450	27.0%	7,147
5. Mental Health and Substance Abuse Social Workers	82.6%	$36,640	29.9%	17,289
6. Elementary School Teachers, Except Special Education	82.2%	$47,330	13.6%	181,612
7. Physical Therapist Assistants	78.4%	$44,130	32.4%	5,957
8. Preschool Teachers, Except Special Education	97.7%	$23,130	26.3%	78,172
9. Radiation Therapists	74.1%	$70,010	24.8%	1,461
10. Training and Development Specialists	71.5%	$49,630	18.3%	35,862
11. Medical and Public Health Social Workers	82.6%	$44,670	24.2%	16,429
12. Health Educators	70.5%	$42,920	26.2%	13,707
13. Occupational Therapists	90.3%	$63,790	23.1%	8,338

Enterprising Jobs with the Highest Percentage of Women

Job	Percent Women
1. Flight Attendants	74.2%
2. First-Line Supervisors/Managers of Office and Administrative Support Workers	72.2%
3. Employment, Recruitment, and Placement Specialists	71.5%
4. Directors, Religious Activities and Education	70.5%
5. Customer Service Representatives	70.4%

Best Enterprising Jobs Overall Employing 70 Percent or More Women

Job	Percent Women	Annual Earnings	Percent Growth	Annual Openings
1. Customer Service Representatives	70.4%	$29,040	24.8%	600,937
2. Employment, Recruitment, and Placement Specialists	71.5%	$44,380	18.4%	33,588
3. First-Line Supervisors/Managers of Office and Administrative Support Workers	72.2%	$44,650	5.8%	138,420
4. Directors, Religious Activities and Education	70.5%	$35,370	19.7%	11,463
5. Flight Attendants	74.2%	$61,120	10.6%	10,773

Enterprising Jobs with the Highest Percentage of Men

Job	Percent Men
1. First-Line Supervisors/Managers of Construction Trades and Extraction Workers	97.4%
2. Engineering Managers	92.7%
3. Construction Managers	92.2%
4. First-Line Supervisors/Managers of Landscaping, Lawn Service, and Groundskeeping Workers	92.0%
5. Police and Sheriff's Patrol Officers	87.2%
6. Air Traffic Controllers	87.0%
7. First-Line Supervisors/Managers of Police and Detectives	84.5%
8. Chief Executives	76.6%
9. Administrative Services Managers	75.6%
10. Detectives and Criminal Investigators	74.0%
11. Computer and Information Systems Managers	72.8%
12. First-Line Supervisors/Managers of Non-Retail Sales Workers	72.8%
13. Sales Engineers	72.8%

(continued)

(continued)

Enterprising Jobs with the Highest Percentage of Men

Job	Percent Men
14. Sales Representatives, Wholesale and Manufacturing, Technical and Scientific Products	72.8%
15. General and Operations Managers	70.9%
16. Securities, Commodities, and Financial Services Sales Agents	70.7%

Best Enterprising Jobs Overall Employing 70 Percent or More Men

Job	Percent Men	Annual Earnings	Percent Growth	Annual Openings
1. Securities, Commodities, and Financial Services Sales Agents	70.7%	$68,430	24.8%	47,750
2. Computer and Information Systems Managers	72.8%	$108,070	16.4%	30,887
3. Construction Managers	92.2%	$76,230	15.7%	44,158
4. General and Operations Managers	70.9%	$88,700	1.5%	112,072
5. Sales Representatives, Wholesale and Manufacturing, Technical and Scientific Products	72.8%	$68,270	12.4%	43,469
6. Chief Executives	76.6%	$145,600+	2.0%	21,209
7. Administrative Services Managers	75.6%	$70,990	11.7%	19,513
8. Air Traffic Controllers	87.0%	$112,930	10.2%	1,213
9. First-Line Supervisors/Managers of Construction Trades and Extraction Workers	97.4%	$55,950	9.1%	82,923
10. Detectives and Criminal Investigators	74.0%	$59,930	17.3%	14,746
11. First-Line Supervisors/Managers of Landscaping, Lawn Service, and Groundskeeping Workers	92.0%	$38,720	17.6%	18,956
12. First-Line Supervisors/Managers of Non-Retail Sales Workers	72.8%	$67,020	3.7%	48,883
13. Engineering Managers	92.7%	$111,020	7.3%	7,404
14. Police and Sheriff's Patrol Officers	87.2%	$49,630	10.8%	37,842
15. First-Line Supervisors/Managers of Police and Detectives	84.5%	$72,620	9.2%	9,373
16. Sales Engineers	72.8%	$80,270	8.5%	7,371

Conventional Jobs with the Highest Percentage of Women

Job	Percent Women
1. Executive Secretaries and Administrative Assistants	96.9%
2. Legal Secretaries	96.9%
3. Medical Secretaries	96.9%
4. Secretaries, Except Legal, Medical, and Executive	96.9%
5. Dental Assistants	95.4%
6. Receptionists and Information Clerks	92.7%
7. Medical Records and Health Information Technicians	92.0%
8. Human Resources Assistants, Except Payroll and Timekeeping	91.9%
9. Medical Transcriptionists	90.4%
10. Bookkeeping, Accounting, and Auditing Clerks	90.3%
11. Paralegals and Legal Assistants	89.1%
12. Billing and Posting Clerks and Machine Operators	88.1%
13. Insurance Claims and Policy Processing Clerks	87.6%
14. Tellers	84.8%
15. Librarians	84.2%
16. Interviewers, Except Eligibility and Loan	82.1%
17. Office Clerks, General	81.9%
18. Court, Municipal, and License Clerks	80.7%
19. Pharmacy Technicians	80.1%
20. Court Reporters	76.8%
21. Loan Interviewers and Clerks	76.7%
22. Brokerage Clerks	75.4%
23. Cargo and Freight Agents	75.4%
24. Occupational Health and Safety Technicians	73.4%
25. Archivists	72.4%
26. Compensation, Benefits, and Job Analysis Specialists	71.5%
27. Social and Human Service Assistants	70.5%

Best Conventional Jobs Overall Employing 70 Percent or More Women

Job	Percent Women	Annual Earnings	Percent Growth	Annual Openings
1. Executive Secretaries and Administrative Assistants	96.9%	$38,640	14.8%	235,314
2. Paralegals and Legal Assistants	89.1%	$44,990	22.2%	22,756

(continued)

(continued)

Best Conventional Jobs Overall Employing 70 Percent or More Women

Job	Percent Women	Annual Earnings	Percent Growth	Annual Openings
3. Compensation, Benefits, and Job Analysis Specialists	71.5%	$52,180	18.4%	18,761
4. Court Reporters	76.8%	$45,330	24.5%	2,620
5. Social and Human Service Assistants	70.5%	$26,630	33.6%	80,142
6. Dental Assistants	95.4%	$31,550	29.2%	29,482
7. Pharmacy Technicians	80.1%	$26,720	32.0%	54,453
8. Bookkeeping, Accounting, and Auditing Clerks	90.3%	$31,560	12.5%	286,854
9. Receptionists and Information Clerks	92.7%	$23,710	17.2%	334,124
10. Brokerage Clerks	75.4%	$37,360	20.0%	10,826
11. Medical Secretaries	96.9%	$28,950	16.7%	60,659
12. Legal Secretaries	96.9%	$38,810	11.7%	38,682
13. Medical Records and Health Information Technicians	92.0%	$29,290	17.8%	39,048
14. Office Clerks, General	81.9%	$24,460	12.6%	765,803
15. Librarians	84.2%	$50,970	3.6%	18,945
16. Occupational Health and Safety Technicians	73.4%	$44,020	14.6%	886
17. Cargo and Freight Agents	75.4%	$37,060	16.5%	9,967
18. Archivists	72.4%	$43,110	14.4%	795
19. Billing and Posting Clerks and Machine Operators	88.1%	$29,970	4.4%	81,885
20. Tellers	84.8%	$22,920	13.5%	146,077
21. Secretaries, Except Legal, Medical, and Executive	96.9%	$28,220	1.2%	239,630
22. Human Resources Assistants, Except Payroll and Timekeeping	91.9%	$34,970	11.3%	18,647
23. Insurance Claims and Policy Processing Clerks	87.6%	$32,040	–1.3%	42,246
24. Loan Interviewers and Clerks	76.7%	$31,680	–0.9%	40,217
25. Medical Transcriptionists	90.4%	$31,250	13.5%	18,080
26. Interviewers, Except Eligibility and Loan	82.1%	$27,320	9.5%	54,060
27. Court, Municipal, and License Clerks	80.7%	$32,330	8.8%	16,163

Conventional Jobs with the Highest Percentage of Men

Job	Percent Men
1. Surveying and Mapping Technicians	90.1%
2. Cost Estimators	87.3%
3. Computer Specialists, All Other	73.3%
4. Statisticians	73.3%
5. Sales Representatives, Wholesale and Manufacturing, Except Technical and Scientific Products	72.8%

Best Conventional Jobs Overall Employing 70 Percent or More Men

Job	Percent Men	Annual Earnings	Percent Growth	Annual Openings
1. Computer Specialists, All Other	73.3%	$71,510	15.1%	14,374
2. Cost Estimators	87.3%	$54,920	18.5%	38,379
3. Sales Representatives, Wholesale and Manufacturing, Except Technical and Scientific Products	72.8%	$50,750	8.4%	156,215
4. Surveying and Mapping Technicians	90.1%	$33,640	19.4%	8,299
5. Statisticians	73.3%	$69,900	8.5%	3,433

The Best Jobs for Each Personality Type Sorted by Education or Training Required

The lists that follow cover each personality type and separate the top 50 jobs that met the criteria for this book into lists based on the education or training typically required for entry. Next to each job title you'll find the job's annual earnings, percent growth, and annual job openings, and these measures are used to order the jobs within each grouping. Thus you can easily find the best overall jobs for a given level of education or training within a given personality type.

You can use these lists in a variety of ways. For example, they can help you identify a job that has higher potential than a job you now hold that requires a similar level of education.

You can also use these lists to figure out additional job possibilities that would open up if you were to get additional training, education, or work experience. For example, maybe you are a high school graduate working in a job associated with the Social personality type. There are many jobs in this field at all levels of education, but especially at higher levels. You can identify the job you're interested in and the related training you need (you'll find more details in Part IV) so you can move ahead while still working in jobs that are well suited to the Social personality type.

The lists of jobs by education should also help you when you're planning your education. For example, you might be thinking about a job within the Realistic personality type, but you aren't sure what kind of work you want to do. The lists show that Sheet Metal Workers need to get long-term on-the-job training and earn an average of $39,210, whereas Aircraft Structure, Surfaces, Rigging, and Systems Assemblers need only moderate-term on-the-job training but earn an average of $45,420. If you want higher earnings without lengthy training, this information might make a difference in your choice.

If you compare the different personality types, you'll note something that was discussed in Part I: some personality types (especially Investigative) offer most of their opportunities to people who are willing to get college degrees, whereas for other types (especially Realistic and Conventional) the most common entry route is on-the-job training.

The Education Levels

⁕ **Short-term on-the-job training.** It is possible to work in these occupations and achieve an average level of performance within a few days or weeks through on-the-job training.

⁕ **Moderate-term on-the-job training.** Occupations that require this type of training can be performed adequately after a 1- to 12-month period of combined on-the-job and informal training. Typically, untrained workers observe experienced workers performing tasks and are gradually moved into progressively more difficult assignments.

⁕ **Long-term on-the-job training.** This training requires more than 12 months of on-the-job training or combined work experience and formal classroom instruction. This includes occupations that use formal apprenticeships for training workers that may take up to four years. It also includes intensive occupation-specific, employer-sponsored training such as police academies. Furthermore, it includes occupations that require natural talent that must be developed over many years.

⁕ **Work experience in a related occupation.** This type of job requires experience in a related occupation. For example, First-Line Supervisors/Managers of Police and Detectives are selected based on their experience as Police and Sheriff's Patrol Officers.

⁕ **Postsecondary vocational training.** This requirement involves an amount of training that can vary from a few months to about one year. In a few instances, there may be as many as four years of training.

⁕ **Associate degree.** This degree usually requires two years of full-time academic work beyond high school.

* **Bachelor's degree.** This degree requires approximately four to five years of full-time academic work beyond high school.
* **Work experience plus degree.** Jobs in this category are often management-related and require some experience in a related nonmanagerial position.
* **Master's degree.** Completion of a master's degree usually requires one to two years of full-time study beyond the bachelor's degree.
* **Doctoral degree.** This degree normally requires two or more years of full-time academic work beyond the bachelor's degree.
* **First professional degree.** This type of degree normally requires a minimum of two years of education beyond the bachelor's degree and frequently requires three years.

Another Warning About the Data

We warned you in the Introduction to use caution in interpreting the data we use, and we want to do it again here. The occupational data we use is the most accurate available anywhere, but it has its limitations. For example, the education or training requirements for entry into a job are those typically required as a minimum—but some people working in those jobs may have considerably more or different credentials. For example, most Registered Nurses now have a four-year bachelor's degree, although the two-year associate degree is the minimum level of training the job requires.

In a similar way, people with jobs that require long-term on-the-job training typically earn more than people with jobs that require short-term on-the-job training. However, some people with short-term on-the-job training do earn more than the average for the highest-paying occupations listed in this book. On the other hand, some people with long-term on-the-job training earn much less than the average shown in this book—this is particularly true early in a person's career.

So as you browse the lists that follow, please use them as a way to be encouraged rather than discouraged. Education and training are very important for success in the labor market of the future, but so are ability, drive, initiative, and, yes, luck.

Having said this, we encourage you to get as much education and training as you can. It used to be that you got your schooling and never went back, but this is not a good attitude to have now. You will probably need to continue learning new things throughout your working life. You can do so by going to school, and this is a good thing for many people to do. But there are also many other ways to learn, such as workshops, certification programs, employer training, professional conferences, Internet training, reading related books and magazines, and many others. Upgrading your computer and other technical skills is particularly important in our rapidly changing workplace, and you avoid doing so at your peril.

An old saying goes, "The harder you work, the luckier you get." It is just as true now as it ever was.

Best Realistic Jobs Requiring Short-Term On-the-Job Training

Job	Annual Earnings	Percent Growth	Annual Openings
1. Sailors and Marine Oilers	$32,570	15.7%	8,600

Best Realistic Jobs Requiring Moderate-Term On-the-Job Training

Job	Annual Earnings	Percent Growth	Annual Openings
1. Correctional Officers and Jailers	$36,970	16.9%	56,579
2. Truck Drivers, Heavy and Tractor-Trailer	$36,220	10.4%	279,032
3. Aircraft Structure, Surfaces, Rigging, and Systems Assemblers	$45,420	12.8%	6,550
4. Roofers	$33,240	14.3%	38,398
5. Operating Engineers and Other Construction Equipment Operators	$38,130	8.4%	55,468
6. Painters, Construction and Maintenance	$32,080	11.8%	101,140
7. Cement Masons and Concrete Finishers	$33,840	11.4%	34,625
8. Maintenance and Repair Workers, General	$32,570	10.1%	165,502
9. Bus Drivers, Transit and Intercity	$33,160	12.5%	27,100
10. Drywall and Ceiling Tile Installers	$36,520	7.3%	30,945

Best Realistic Jobs Requiring Long-Term On-the-Job Training

Job	Annual Earnings	Percent Growth	Annual Openings
1. Plumbers, Pipefitters, and Steamfitters	$44,090	10.6%	68,643
2. Electricians	$44,780	7.4%	79,083
3. Fire Fighters	$43,170	12.1%	18,887
4. Boilermakers	$50,700	14.0%	2,333
5. Carpenters	$37,660	10.3%	223,225
6. Brickmasons and Blockmasons	$44,070	9.7%	17,569
7. Mobile Heavy Equipment Mechanics, Except Engines	$41,450	12.3%	11,037
8. Industrial Machinery Mechanics	$42,350	9.0%	23,361
9. Tile and Marble Setters	$38,720	15.4%	9,066
10. Automotive Body and Related Repairers	$35,690	11.6%	37,469
11. Athletes and Sports Competitors	$38,440	19.2%	4,293
12. Electrical Power-Line Installers and Repairers	$52,570	7.2%	6,401
13. Telecommunications Line Installers and Repairers	$47,220	4.6%	14,719

Best Realistic Jobs Requiring Long-Term On-the-Job Training

Job	Annual Earnings	Percent Growth	Annual Openings
14. Sheet Metal Workers	$39,210	6.7%	31,677
15. Audio and Video Equipment Technicians	$36,050	24.2%	4,681
16. Heating, Air Conditioning, and Refrigeration Mechanics and Installers	$38,360	8.7%	29,719
17. Water and Liquid Waste Treatment Plant and System Operators	$37,090	13.8%	9,575

Best Realistic Jobs Requiring Work Experience in a Related Occupation

Job	Annual Earnings	Percent Growth	Annual Openings
1. Captains, Mates, and Pilots of Water Vessels	$57,210	17.9%	2,665
2. Construction and Building Inspectors	$48,330	18.2%	12,606
3. Transportation Inspectors	$51,440	16.4%	2,122

Best Realistic Jobs Requiring Postsecondary Vocational Training

Job	Annual Earnings	Percent Growth	Annual Openings
1. Bus and Truck Mechanics and Diesel Engine Specialists	$38,640	11.5%	25,428
2. Surgical Technologists	$37,540	24.5%	15,365
3. Automotive Service Technicians and Mechanics	$34,170	14.3%	97,350
4. Architectural and Civil Drafters	$43,310	6.1%	16,238
5. Aircraft Mechanics and Service Technicians	$49,010	10.6%	9,708
6. Telecommunications Equipment Installers and Repairers, Except Line Installers	$54,070	2.5%	13,541
7. Mechanical Drafters	$44,740	5.2%	10,902
8. Security and Fire Alarm Systems Installers	$35,390	20.2%	5,729

Best Realistic Jobs Requiring an Associate Degree

Job	Annual Earnings	Percent Growth	Annual Openings
1. Radiologic Technologists and Technicians	$50,260	15.1%	12,836
2. Cardiovascular Technologists and Technicians	$44,940	25.5%	3,550

(continued)

(continued)

Best Realistic Jobs Requiring an Associate Degree

Job	Annual Earnings	Percent Growth	Annual Openings
3. Computer Support Specialists	$42,400	12.9%	97,334
4. Electrical and Electronic Engineering Technicians	$52,140	3.6%	12,583
5. Medical and Clinical Laboratory Technicians	$34,270	15.0%	10,866
6. Civil Engineering Technicians	$42,580	10.2%	7,499

Best Realistic Jobs Requiring a Bachelor's Degree

Job	Annual Earnings	Percent Growth	Annual Openings
1. Civil Engineers	$71,710	18.0%	15,979
2. Surveyors	$51,630	23.7%	14,305
3. Airline Pilots, Copilots, and Flight Engineers	$145,600+	12.9%	4,073
4. Biological Technicians	$37,810	16.0%	15,374
5. Cartographers and Photogrammetrists	$49,970	20.3%	2,823

Best Investigative Jobs Requiring an Associate Degree

Job	Annual Earnings	Percent Growth	Annual Openings
1. Environmental Science and Protection Technicians, Including Health	$39,370	28.0%	8,404
2. Diagnostic Medical Sonographers	$59,860	19.1%	3,211
3. Nuclear Medicine Technologists	$64,670	14.8%	1,290

Best Investigative Jobs Requiring a Bachelor's Degree

Job	Annual Earnings	Percent Growth	Annual Openings
1. Computer Software Engineers, Applications	$83,130	44.6%	58,690
2. Computer Software Engineers, Systems Software	$89,070	28.2%	33,139
3. Computer Systems Analysts	$73,090	29.0%	63,166
4. Network Systems and Data Communications Analysts	$68,220	53.4%	35,086
5. Network and Computer Systems Administrators	$64,690	27.0%	37,010

Best Investigative Jobs Requiring a Bachelor's Degree

Job	Annual Earnings	Percent Growth	Annual Openings
6. Aerospace Engineers	$90,930	10.2%	6,498
7. Market Research Analysts	$60,300	20.1%	45,015
8. Industrial Engineers	$71,430	20.3%	11,272
9. Environmental Engineers	$72,350	25.4%	5,003
10. Computer Hardware Engineers	$91,860	4.6%	3,572
11. Electrical Engineers	$79,240	6.3%	6,806
12. Biomedical Engineers	$75,440	21.1%	1,804
13. Electronics Engineers, Except Computer	$83,340	3.7%	5,699
14. Mechanical Engineers	$72,300	4.2%	12,394
15. Medical and Clinical Laboratory Technologists	$51,720	12.4%	11,457
16. Forensic Science Technicians	$47,680	30.7%	3,074
17. Chemical Engineers	$81,500	7.9%	2,111
18. Atmospheric and Space Scientists	$78,390	10.6%	735
19. Chemists	$63,490	9.1%	9,024
20. Survey Researchers	$36,820	15.9%	4,959

Best Investigative Jobs Requiring Work Experience Plus Degree

Job	Annual Earnings	Percent Growth	Annual Openings
1. Management Analysts	$71,150	21.9%	125,669

Best Investigative Jobs Requiring a Master's Degree

Job	Annual Earnings	Percent Growth	Annual Openings
1. Environmental Scientists and Specialists, Including Health	$58,380	25.1%	6,961
2. Geoscientists, Except Hydrologists and Geographers	$75,800	21.9%	2,471
3. Hydrologists	$68,140	24.3%	687
4. Industrial-Organizational Psychologists	$80,820	21.3%	118
5. Operations Research Analysts	$66,950	10.6%	5,727

Best Investigative Jobs Requiring a Doctoral Degree

Job	Annual Earnings	Percent Growth	Annual Openings
1. Computer and Information Scientists, Research	$97,970	21.5%	2,901
2. Engineering Teachers, Postsecondary	$79,510	22.9%	5,565
3. Medical Scientists, Except Epidemiologists	$64,200	20.2%	10,596
4. Biochemists and Biophysicists	$79,270	15.9%	1,637
5. Clinical, Counseling, and School Psychologists	$62,210	15.8%	8,309
6. Physicists	$96,850	6.8%	1,302
7. Mathematicians	$90,870	10.2%	473

Best Investigative Jobs Requiring a First Professional Degree

Job	Annual Earnings	Percent Growth	Annual Openings
1. Anesthesiologists	$145,600+	14.2%	38,027
2. Family and General Practitioners	$145,600+	14.2%	38,027
3. Internists, General	$145,600+	14.2%	38,027
4. Obstetricians and Gynecologists	$145,600+	14.2%	38,027
5. Psychiatrists	$145,600+	14.2%	38,027
6. Surgeons	$145,600+	14.2%	38,027
7. Pediatricians, General	$140,690	14.2%	38,027
8. Pharmacists	$100,480	21.7%	16,358
9. Veterinarians	$75,230	35.0%	5,301
10. Prosthodontists	$145,600+	10.7%	54
11. Orthodontists	$145,600+	9.2%	479
12. Dentists, General	$137,630	9.2%	7,106
13. Optometrists	$93,800	11.3%	1,789
14. Podiatrists	$110,510	9.5%	648

Jobs 1, 2, 3, 4, 5, 6, and 7 share 38,027 openings.

Best Artistic Jobs Requiring Moderate-Term On-the-Job Training

Job	Annual Earnings	Percent Growth	Annual Openings
1. Merchandise Displayers and Window Trimmers	$24,830	10.7%	9,103

Best Artistic Jobs Requiring Long-Term On-the-Job Training

Job	Annual Earnings	Percent Growth	Annual Openings
1. Interpreters and Translators	$37,490	23.6%	6,630
2. Photographers	$27,720	10.3%	16,100
3. Fine Artists, Including Painters, Sculptors, and Illustrators	$42,070	9.9%	3,830

Best Artistic Jobs Requiring Work Experience in a Related Occupation

Job	Annual Earnings	Percent Growth	Annual Openings
1. Self-Enrichment Education Teachers	$34,580	23.1%	64,449

Best Artistic Jobs Requiring Postsecondary Vocational Training

Job	Annual Earnings	Percent Growth	Annual Openings
1. Preschool Teachers, Except Special Education	$23,130	26.3%	78,172
2. Makeup Artists, Theatrical and Performance	$35,250	39.8%	392
3. Camera Operators, Television, Video, and Motion Picture	$41,850	11.5%	3,496
4. Hairdressers, Hairstylists, and Cosmetologists	$22,210	12.4%	73,030

Best Artistic Jobs Requiring an Associate Degree

Job	Annual Earnings	Percent Growth	Annual Openings
1. Interior Designers	$43,970	19.5%	8,434
2. Fashion Designers	$62,810	5.0%	1,968

Best Artistic Jobs Requiring a Bachelor's Degree

Job	Annual Earnings	Percent Growth	Annual Openings
1. Public Relations Specialists	$49,800	17.6%	51,216
2. Multi-Media Artists and Animators	$54,550	25.8%	13,182
3. Architects, Except Landscape and Naval	$67,620	17.7%	11,324
4. Technical Writers	$60,390	19.5%	7,498

(continued)

(continued)

Best Artistic Jobs Requiring a Bachelor's Degree

Job	Annual Earnings	Percent Growth	Annual Openings
5. Special Education Teachers, Preschool, Kindergarten, and Elementary School	$48,350	19.6%	20,049
6. Writers and Authors	$50,660	12.8%	24,023
7. Elementary School Teachers, Except Special Education	$47,330	13.6%	181,612
8. Secondary School Teachers, Except Special and Vocational Education	$49,420	5.6%	93,166
9. Substance Abuse and Behavioral Disorder Counselors	$35,580	34.3%	20,821
10. Kindergarten Teachers, Except Special Education	$45,120	16.3%	27,603
11. Landscape Architects	$57,580	16.4%	2,342
12. Middle School Teachers, Except Special and Vocational Education	$47,900	11.2%	75,270
13. Special Education Teachers, Middle School	$48,940	15.8%	8,846
14. Commercial and Industrial Designers	$56,550	7.2%	4,777
15. Adult Literacy, Remedial Education, and GED Teachers and Instructors	$44,710	14.2%	17,340
16. Editors	$48,320	2.3%	20,193
17. Graphic Designers	$41,280	9.8%	26,968
18. Set and Exhibit Designers	$43,220	17.8%	1,402
19. Film and Video Editors	$47,870	12.7%	2,707

Best Artistic Jobs Requiring Work Experience Plus Degree

Job	Annual Earnings	Percent Growth	Annual Openings
1. Training and Development Specialists	$49,630	18.3%	35,862
2. Public Relations Managers	$86,470	16.9%	5,781
3. Art Directors	$72,320	9.0%	9,719
4. Producers and Directors	$61,090	11.1%	8,992
5. Advertising and Promotions Managers	$78,250	6.2%	2,955
6. Music Directors and Composers	$40,150	12.9%	8,597
7. Broadcast News Analysts	$49,060	6.0%	1,444

Best Artistic Jobs Requiring a Master's Degree

Job	Annual Earnings	Percent Growth	Annual Openings
1. Marriage and Family Therapists	$43,600	29.8%	5,953
2. Anthropologists and Archeologists	$53,080	15.0%	446
3. Sociologists	$61,140	10.0%	403
4. Political Scientists	$91,580	5.3%	318

Best Artistic Jobs Requiring a Doctoral Degree

Job	Annual Earnings	Percent Growth	Annual Openings
1. Art, Drama, and Music Teachers, Postsecondary	$55,190	22.9%	12,707
2. Education Teachers, Postsecondary	$54,220	22.9%	9,359
3. English Language and Literature Teachers, Postsecondary	$54,000	22.9%	10,475
4. Philosophy and Religion Teachers, Postsecondary	$56,380	22.9%	3,120
5. Architecture Teachers, Postsecondary	$68,540	22.9%	1,044
6. Communications Teachers, Postsecondary	$54,720	22.9%	4,074
7. Foreign Language and Literature Teachers, Postsecondary	$53,610	22.9%	4,317
8. Biochemists and Biophysicists	$79,270	15.9%	1,637
9. Astronomers	$99,020	5.6%	128

Best Social Jobs Requiring Moderate-Term On-the-Job Training

Job	Annual Earnings	Percent Growth	Annual Openings
1. Medical Assistants	$27,430	35.4%	92,977

Best Social Jobs Requiring Work Experience in a Related Occupation

Job	Annual Earnings	Percent Growth	Annual Openings
1. Self-Enrichment Education Teachers	$34,580	23.1%	64,449
2. Vocational Education Teachers, Postsecondary	$45,850	22.9%	19,313

Best Social Jobs Requiring Postsecondary Vocational Training

Job	Annual Earnings	Percent Growth	Annual Openings
1. Fitness Trainers and Aerobics Instructors	$27,680	26.8%	51,235
2. Preschool Teachers, Except Special Education	$23,130	26.3%	78,172

Best Social Jobs Requiring an Associate Degree

Job	Annual Earnings	Percent Growth	Annual Openings
1. Dental Hygienists	$64,740	30.1%	10,433
2. Physical Therapist Assistants	$44,130	32.4%	5,957
3. Radiation Therapists	$70,010	24.8%	1,461
4. Registered Nurses	$60,010	23.5%	233,499

Best Social Jobs Requiring a Bachelor's Degree

Job	Annual Earnings	Percent Growth	Annual Openings
1. Elementary School Teachers, Except Special Education	$47,330	13.6%	181,612
2. Substance Abuse and Behavioral Disorder Counselors	$35,580	34.3%	20,821
3. Medical and Public Health Social Workers	$44,670	24.2%	16,429
4. Health Educators	$42,920	26.2%	13,707
5. Graduate Teaching Assistants	$28,060	22.9%	20,601

Best Social Jobs Requiring Work Experience Plus Degree

Job	Annual Earnings	Percent Growth	Annual Openings
1. Training and Development Specialists	$49,630	18.3%	35,862
2. Education Administrators, Preschool and Child Care Center/Program	$38,580	23.5%	8,113

Best Social Jobs Requiring a Master's Degree

Job	Annual Earnings	Percent Growth	Annual Openings
1. Mental Health Counselors	$36,000	30.0%	24,103
2. Physical Therapists	$69,760	27.1%	12,072
3. Mental Health and Substance Abuse Social Workers	$36,640	29.9%	17,289
4. Physician Assistants	$78,450	27.0%	7,147
5. Instructional Coordinators	$55,270	22.5%	21,294
6. Occupational Therapists	$63,790	23.1%	8,338
7. Marriage and Family Therapists	$43,600	29.8%	5,953
8. Rehabilitation Counselors	$29,630	23.0%	32,081

Best Social Jobs Requiring a Doctoral Degree

Job	Annual Earnings	Percent Growth	Annual Openings
1. Health Specialties Teachers, Postsecondary	$80,700	22.9%	19,617
2. Biological Science Teachers, Postsecondary	$71,780	22.9%	9,039
3. Business Teachers, Postsecondary	$64,900	22.9%	11,643
4. Art, Drama, and Music Teachers, Postsecondary	$55,190	22.9%	12,707
5. Computer Science Teachers, Postsecondary	$62,020	22.9%	5,820
6. Economics Teachers, Postsecondary	$75,300	22.9%	2,208
7. Agricultural Sciences Teachers, Postsecondary	$78,460	22.9%	1,840
8. Mathematical Science Teachers, Postsecondary	$58,560	22.9%	7,663
9. Psychology Teachers, Postsecondary	$60,610	22.9%	5,261
10. Chemistry Teachers, Postsecondary	$63,870	22.9%	3,405
11. Atmospheric, Earth, Marine, and Space Sciences Teachers, Postsecondary	$73,280	22.9%	1,553
12. Nursing Instructors and Teachers, Postsecondary	$57,500	22.9%	7,337
13. Physics Teachers, Postsecondary	$70,090	22.9%	2,155
14. Education Teachers, Postsecondary	$54,220	22.9%	9,359
15. English Language and Literature Teachers, Postsecondary	$54,000	22.9%	10,475
16. History Teachers, Postsecondary	$59,160	22.9%	3,570
17. Architecture Teachers, Postsecondary	$68,540	22.9%	1,044
18. Political Science Teachers, Postsecondary	$63,100	22.9%	2,435
19. Communications Teachers, Postsecondary	$54,720	22.9%	4,074
20. Anthropology and Archeology Teachers, Postsecondary	$64,530	22.9%	910
21. Environmental Science Teachers, Postsecondary	$64,850	22.9%	769

(continued)

(continued)

Best Social Jobs Requiring a Doctoral Degree

Job	Annual Earnings	Percent Growth	Annual Openings
22. Philosophy and Religion Teachers, Postsecondary	$56,380	22.9%	3,120
23. Sociology Teachers, Postsecondary	$58,160	22.9%	2,774
24. Foreign Language and Literature Teachers, Postsecondary	$53,610	22.9%	4,317
25. Recreation and Fitness Studies Teachers, Postsecondary	$52,170	22.9%	3,010

Best Social Jobs Requiring a First Professional Degree

Job	Annual Earnings	Percent Growth	Annual Openings
1. Law Teachers, Postsecondary	$87,730	22.9%	2,169

Best Enterprising Jobs Requiring Moderate-Term On-the-Job Training

Job	Annual Earnings	Percent Growth	Annual Openings
1. Customer Service Representatives	$29,040	24.8%	600,937
2. Advertising Sales Agents	$42,820	20.3%	29,233
3. Demonstrators and Product Promoters	$22,570	18.0%	32,779

Best Enterprising Jobs Requiring Long-Term On-the-Job Training

Job	Annual Earnings	Percent Growth	Annual Openings
1. Police and Sheriff's Patrol Officers	$49,630	10.8%	37,842
2. Flight Attendants	$61,120	10.6%	10,773
3. Air Traffic Controllers	$112,930	10.2%	1,213

Best Enterprising Jobs Requiring Work Experience in a Related Occupation

Job	Annual Earnings	Percent Growth	Annual Openings
1. Sales Representatives, Wholesale and Manufacturing, Technical and Scientific Products	$68,270	12.4%	43,469
2. Gaming Managers	$64,410	24.4%	549
3. Detectives and Criminal Investigators	$59,930	17.3%	14,746
4. First-Line Supervisors/Managers of Construction Trades and Extraction Workers	$55,950	9.1%	82,923
5. First-Line Supervisors/Managers of Non-Retail Sales Workers	$67,020	3.7%	48,883
6. First-Line Supervisors/Managers of Office and Administrative Support Workers	$44,650	5.8%	138,420
7. First-Line Supervisors/Managers of Food Preparation and Serving Workers	$28,040	11.3%	154,175
8. First-Line Supervisors/Managers of Landscaping, Lawn Service, and Groundskeeping Workers	$38,720	17.6%	18,956
9. First-Line Supervisors/Managers of Police and Detectives	$72,620	9.2%	9,373
10. First-Line Supervisors/Managers of Personal Service Workers	$33,900	15.5%	37,555
11. Gaming Supervisors	$42,980	23.4%	4,602
12. Real Estate Brokers	$58,860	11.1%	18,689
13. Food Service Managers	$44,570	5.0%	59,302
14. First-Line Supervisors/Managers of Housekeeping and Janitorial Workers	$32,850	12.7%	30,613

Best Enterprising Jobs Requiring Postsecondary Vocational Training

Job	Annual Earnings	Percent Growth	Annual Openings
1. Real Estate Sales Agents	$40,600	10.6%	61,232

Best Enterprising Jobs Requiring a Bachelor's Degree

Job	Annual Earnings	Percent Growth	Annual Openings
1. Securities, Commodities, and Financial Services Sales Agents	$68,430	24.8%	47,750
2. Personal Financial Advisors	$67,660	41.0%	17,114
3. Construction Managers	$76,230	15.7%	44,158

(continued)

(continued)

Best Enterprising Jobs Requiring a Bachelor's Degree

Job	Annual Earnings	Percent Growth	Annual Openings
4. Public Relations Specialists	$49,800	17.6%	51,216
5. Social and Community Service Managers	$54,530	24.7%	23,788
6. Employment, Recruitment, and Placement Specialists	$44,380	18.4%	33,588
7. Insurance Sales Agents	$44,110	12.9%	64,162
8. Logisticians	$64,250	17.3%	9,671
9. Property, Real Estate, and Community Association Managers	$43,670	15.1%	49,916
10. Sales Engineers	$80,270	8.5%	7,371
11. Directors, Religious Activities and Education	$35,370	19.7%	11,463
12. Meeting and Convention Planners	$43,530	19.9%	8,318

Best Enterprising Jobs Requiring Work Experience Plus Degree

Job	Annual Earnings	Percent Growth	Annual Openings
1. Computer and Information Systems Managers	$108,070	16.4%	30,887
2. Financial Managers	$95,310	12.6%	57,589
3. Marketing Managers	$104,400	14.4%	20,189
4. Medical and Health Services Managers	$76,990	16.4%	31,877
5. Sales Managers	$94,910	10.2%	36,392
6. Chief Executives	$145,600+	2.0%	21,209
7. Public Relations Managers	$86,470	16.9%	5,781
8. General and Operations Managers	$88,700	1.5%	112,072
9. Engineering Managers	$111,020	7.3%	7,404
10. Training and Development Managers	$84,340	15.6%	3,759
11. Education Administrators, Postsecondary	$75,780	14.2%	17,121
12. Education Administrators, Elementary and Secondary School	$80,580	7.6%	27,143
13. Natural Sciences Managers	$104,040	11.4%	3,661
14. Compensation and Benefits Managers	$81,410	12.0%	6,121
15. Administrative Services Managers	$70,990	11.7%	19,513
16. Producers and Directors	$61,090	11.1%	8,992

Best Enterprising Jobs Requiring a First Professional Degree

Job	Annual Earnings	Percent Growth	Annual Openings
1. Lawyers	$106,120	11.0%	49,445

Best Conventional Jobs Requiring Short-Term On-the-Job Training

Job	Annual Earnings	Percent Growth	Annual Openings
1. Bill and Account Collectors	$29,990	22.9%	118,709
2. Office Clerks, General	$24,460	12.6%	765,803
3. Receptionists and Information Clerks	$23,710	17.2%	334,124
4. Human Resources Assistants, Except Payroll and Timekeeping	$34,970	11.3%	18,647
5. Tellers	$22,920	13.5%	146,077
6. Interviewers, Except Eligibility and Loan	$27,320	9.5%	54,060
7. Postal Service Mail Carriers	$44,500	1.0%	16,710
8. Shipping, Receiving, and Traffic Clerks	$26,990	3.7%	138,967
9. Court, Municipal, and License Clerks	$32,330	8.8%	16,163
10. Loan Interviewers and Clerks	$31,680	−0.9%	40,217

Best Conventional Jobs Requiring Moderate-Term On-the-Job Training

Job	Annual Earnings	Percent Growth	Annual Openings
1. Bookkeeping, Accounting, and Auditing Clerks	$31,560	12.5%	286,854
2. Brokerage Clerks	$37,360	20.0%	10,826
3. Production, Planning, and Expediting Clerks	$39,690	4.2%	52,735
4. Social and Human Service Assistants	$26,630	33.6%	80,142
5. Pharmacy Technicians	$26,720	32.0%	54,453
6. Dental Assistants	$31,550	29.2%	29,482
7. Medical Secretaries	$28,950	16.7%	60,659
8. Billing and Posting Clerks and Machine Operators	$29,970	4.4%	81,885
9. Cargo and Freight Agents	$37,060	16.5%	9,967
10. Surveying and Mapping Technicians	$33,640	19.4%	8,299
11. Police, Fire, and Ambulance Dispatchers	$32,660	13.6%	17,628
12. Dispatchers, Except Police, Fire, and Ambulance	$33,140	1.5%	29,793
13. Secretaries, Except Legal, Medical, and Executive	$28,220	1.2%	239,630
14. Insurance Claims and Policy Processing Clerks	$32,040	−1.3%	42,246

Best Conventional Jobs Requiring Long-Term On-the-Job Training

Job	Annual Earnings	Percent Growth	Annual Openings
1. Claims Adjusters, Examiners, and Investigators	$53,560	8.9%	22,024
2. Purchasing Agents, Except Wholesale, Retail, and Farm Products	$52,460	0.1%	22,349
3. Compliance Officers, Except Agriculture, Construction, Health and Safety, and Transportation	$48,400	4.9%	15,841

Best Conventional Jobs Requiring Work Experience in a Related Occupation

Job	Annual Earnings	Percent Growth	Annual Openings
1. Executive Secretaries and Administrative Assistants	$38,640	14.8%	235,314
2. Sales Representatives, Wholesale and Manufacturing, Except Technical and Scientific Products	$50,750	8.4%	156,215

Best Conventional Jobs Requiring Postsecondary Vocational Training

Job	Annual Earnings	Percent Growth	Annual Openings
1. Court Reporters	$45,330	24.5%	2,620
2. Medical Transcriptionists	$31,250	13.5%	18,080
3. Insurance Appraisers, Auto Damage	$51,500	12.5%	1,030

Best Conventional Jobs Requiring an Associate Degree

Job	Annual Earnings	Percent Growth	Annual Openings
1. Paralegals and Legal Assistants	$44,990	22.2%	22,756
2. Medical Records and Health Information Technicians	$29,290	17.8%	39,048
3. Computer Specialists, All Other	$71,510	15.1%	14,374
4. Legal Secretaries	$38,810	11.7%	38,682

Best Conventional Jobs Requiring a Bachelor's Degree

Job	Annual Earnings	Percent Growth	Annual Openings
1. Financial Analysts	$70,400	33.8%	29,317
2. Accountants and Auditors	$57,060	17.7%	134,463
3. Database Administrators	$67,250	28.6%	8,258
4. Cost Estimators	$54,920	18.5%	38,379
5. Compensation, Benefits, and Job Analysis Specialists	$52,180	18.4%	18,761
6. Loan Officers	$53,000	11.5%	54,237
7. Budget Analysts	$63,440	7.1%	6,423
8. Appraisers and Assessors of Real Estate	$46,130	16.9%	6,493
9. Insurance Underwriters	$54,530	6.3%	6,880
10. Occupational Health and Safety Technicians	$44,020	14.6%	886

Best Conventional Jobs Requiring Work Experience Plus Degree

Job	Annual Earnings	Percent Growth	Annual Openings
1. Actuaries	$85,690	23.7%	3,245

Best Conventional Jobs Requiring a Master's Degree

Job	Annual Earnings	Percent Growth	Annual Openings
1. Statisticians	$69,900	8.5%	3,433
2. Librarians	$50,970	3.6%	18,945
3. Archivists	$43,110	14.4%	795

PART IV

Descriptions of the 50 Best Jobs for Each Personality Type

This part provides descriptions for all the jobs included in one or more of the lists in Part III. The book's introduction gives more details on how to use and interpret the job descriptions, but here are the highlights, along with some additional information.

- ✺ The job descriptions that follow met our criteria for inclusion in this book, as we describe in the Introduction. The jobs in this book scored among the 50 highest in each personality type for earnings, projected growth, and number of job openings. Many good jobs do not meet one or more of these criteria, but we think the jobs that do are the best ones to consider in your career planning.

- ✺ The job descriptions are arranged by personality type and in alphabetical order by job title within each personality type. This approach allows you to find a description quickly if you know its title from one of the lists in Part III. If you have not browsed the lists in Part III, consider spending some time there. The lists are interesting and will help you identify job titles that you can look up in the descriptions that follow.

- ✺ In some cases a job title that appears in Part III is linked to two or more different job titles in Part IV. For example, if you look for the job title Automotive Service Technicians and Mechanics, you will find it listed here alphabetically, but a note will tell you to see the descriptions for Automotive Master Mechanics and Automotive Specialty Technicians. Since these job titles are also listed alphabetically, you can find the descriptions easily.

- ✺ Refer to the Introduction, beginning on page 1, for details on interpreting the job descriptions' content.

- ✺ The section with GOE information includes a subsection titled Other Jobs in This Work Group to help you identify similar jobs. Not all of the jobs listed here are among the top 50 for each personality type.

- ✺ When reviewing the descriptions, keep in mind that the jobs meet our criteria for being among the top 50 jobs for each personality type based on their total scores for earnings, growth, and number of openings—but one or more of these measures may not be among the highest. For example, an occupation that has high pay may be included, even though growth rate and number of job openings are below average.

"Well," you might ask, "doesn't this mean that at least some 'bad' jobs are described in this part?" Our answer is yes and no. Some jobs with high scores for all measures, such as Securities, Commodities, and Financial Services Sales Agents—the Enterprising job with the highest total for pay, growth, and number of openings—would be a very bad job for people who dislike or are not good at that sort of work. On the other hand, many people would love working as Gaming Supervisors even though that job has lower earnings, a lower projected growth rate, and fewer openings. Descriptions for both jobs are included in this book.

Possibly somewhere a former securities sales agent works as a gaming supervisor and loves it. This person may even have figured out how to make more money (say, by getting hired in a very large casino), have a more flexible schedule, have more fun, or have other advantages not available to a securities sales agent.

The point is that each job is right for somebody, perhaps at a certain time in their lives. We are all likely to change careers and jobs several times, and it's not always money that motivates us. So browse the job descriptions that follow and know that somewhere there is a good place for you. We hope you find it.

Use the job descriptions in this section as one step in a continuing process of career exploration. When you find a job that interests you, turn to Appendix D for suggestions about resources for further exploration.

Realistic Occupations

Aircraft Mechanics and Service Technicians

- ❀ Personality Code: RCI
- ❀ Education/Training Required: Postsecondary vocational training
- ❀ Annual Earnings: $49,010
- ❀ Beginning Wage: $32,160
- ❀ Earnings Growth Potential: Low
- ❀ Growth: 10.6%
- ❀ Annual Job Openings: 9,708
- ❀ Self-Employed: 0.4%
- ❀ Part-Time: 2.1%

Diagnose, adjust, repair, or overhaul aircraft engines and assemblies, such as hydraulic and pneumatic systems. Read and interpret maintenance manuals, service bulletins, and other specifications to determine the feasibility and method of repairing or replacing malfunctioning or damaged components. Inspect completed work to certify that maintenance meets standards and that aircraft are ready for operation. Maintain repair logs, documenting all preventive and corrective aircraft maintenance. Conduct routine and special inspections as required by regulations. Examine and inspect aircraft components, including landing gear, hydraulic systems, and de-icers, to locate cracks, breaks, leaks, or other problem. Inspect airframes for wear or other defects. Maintain, repair, and rebuild aircraft structures; functional components; and parts such as wings and fuselage, rigging, hydraulic units, oxygen systems, fuel systems, electrical systems, gaskets, and seals. Measure the tension of control cables. Replace or repair worn, defective, or damaged components, using hand tools, gauges, and testing equipment. Measure parts for wear, using precision instruments. Assemble and install electrical, plumbing, mechanical, hydraulic, and structural components and accessories, using hand tools and

power tools. Test operation of engines and other systems, using test equipment such as ignition analyzers, compression checkers, distributor timers, and ammeters. Obtain fuel and oil samples and check them for contamination. Reassemble engines following repair or inspection and re-install engines in aircraft. Read and interpret pilots' descriptions of problems to diagnose causes. Modify aircraft structures, space vehicles, systems, or components, following drawings, schematics, charts, engineering orders, and technical publications. Install and align repaired or replacement parts for subsequent riveting or welding, using clamps and wrenches. Locate and mark dimensions and reference lines on defective or replacement parts, using templates, scribes, compasses, and steel rules. Clean, strip, prime, and sand structural surfaces and materials to prepare them for bonding. Service and maintain aircraft and related apparatus by performing activities such as flushing crankcases, cleaning screens, and lubricating moving parts.

GOE—Interest Area/Cluster: 13. Manufacturing. **Work Group:** 13.14. Vehicle and Facility Mechanical Work. **Other Jobs in This Work Group:** Aircraft Structure, Surfaces, Rigging, and Systems Assemblers; Automotive Body and Related Repairers; Automotive Glass Installers and Repairers; Automotive Master Mechanics; Automotive Service Technicians and Mechanics; Automotive Specialty Technicians; Bus and Truck Mechanics and Diesel Engine Specialists; Farm Equipment Mechanics; Fiberglass Laminators and Fabricators; Mobile Heavy Equipment Mechanics, Except Engines; Motorboat Mechanics; Motorcycle Mechanics; Outdoor Power Equipment and Other Small Engine Mechanics; Rail Car Repairers; Recreational Vehicle Service Technicians; Tire Repairers and Changers.

Skills: Repairing; Equipment Maintenance; Installation; Operation Monitoring; Troubleshooting; Operation and Control; Quality Control Analysis; Complex Problem Solving.

Education and Training Programs: Agricultural Mechanics and Equipment/Machine Technology; Aircraft Powerplant Technology/Technician; Airframe Mechanics and Aircraft Maintenance Technology/

Technician. **Related Knowledge/Courses:** Mechanical Devices; Design; Physics; Chemistry; Engineering and Technology; Transportation.

Work Environment: Noisy; contaminants; cramped work space, awkward positions; standing; using hands on objects, tools, or controls; bending or twisting the body.

Aircraft Structure, Surfaces, Rigging, and Systems Assemblers

- ❊ Personality Code: RC
- ❊ Education/Training Required: Moderate-term on-the-job training
- ❊ Annual Earnings: $45,420
- ❊ Beginning Wage: $25,050
- ❊ Earnings Growth Potential: High
- ❊ Growth: 12.8%
- ❊ Annual Job Openings: 6,550
- ❊ Self-Employed: 0.0%
- ❊ Part-Time: 1.9%

Assemble, fit, fasten, and install parts of airplanes, space vehicles, or missiles, such as tails, wings, fuselage, bulkheads, stabilizers, landing gear, rigging and control equipment, or heating and ventilating systems. Form loops or splices in cables, using clamps and fittings, or reweave cable strands. Align and fit structural assemblies manually or signal crane operators to position assemblies for joining. Align, fit, assemble, connect, and install system components, using jigs, fixtures, measuring instruments, hand tools, and power tools. Assemble and fit prefabricated parts to form subassemblies. Assemble, install, and connect parts, fittings, and assemblies on aircraft, using layout tools; hand tools; power tools; and fasteners such as bolts, screws, rivets, and clamps. Attach brackets, hinges, or clips to secure or support components and subassemblies, using bolts, screws, rivets, chemical bonding, or welding. Select and install accessories in swaging machines, using hand tools. Fit and fasten sheet metal coverings to surface areas and other sections of aircraft prior to welding or riveting. Lay out and mark reference points and locations for installation of parts and components, using jigs, templates, and measuring and marking instruments. Inspect and test installed units, parts, systems, and assemblies for fit, alignment, performance, defects, and compliance with standards, using measuring instruments and test equipment. Install mechanical linkages and actuators and verify tension of cables, using tensiometers. Join structural assemblies such as wings, tails, and fuselage. Measure and cut cables and tubing, using master templates, measuring instruments, and cable cutters or saws. Read and interpret blueprints, illustrations, and specifications to determine layouts, sequences of operations, or identities and relationships of parts. Prepare and load live ammunition, missiles, and bombs onto aircraft according to established procedures. Adjust, repair, rework, or replace parts and assemblies to eliminate malfunctions and to ensure proper operation. Cut, trim, file, bend, and smooth parts and verify sizes and fitting tolerances in order to ensure proper fit and clearance of parts. Install and connect control cables to electronically controlled units, using hand tools, ring locks, cotter keys, threaded connectors, turnbuckles, and related devices.

GOE—Interest Area/Cluster: 13. Manufacturing. **Work Group:** 13.14. Vehicle and Facility Mechanical Work. **Other Jobs in This Work Group:** Aircraft Mechanics and Service Technicians; Automotive Body and Related Repairers; Automotive Glass Installers and Repairers; Automotive Master Mechanics; Automotive Service Technicians and Mechanics; Automotive Specialty Technicians; Bus and Truck Mechanics and Diesel Engine Specialists; Farm Equipment Mechanics; Fiberglass Laminators and Fabricators; Mobile Heavy Equipment Mechanics, Except Engines; Motorboat Mechanics; Motorcycle Mechanics; Outdoor Power Equipment and Other Small Engine Mechanics; Rail Car Repairers; Recreational Vehicle Service Technicians; Tire Repairers and Changers.

Skills: Installation; Equipment Maintenance; Repairing; Quality Control Analysis; Equipment Selection; Operation Monitoring; Mathematics; Troubleshooting.

Education and Training Programs: Airframe Mechanics and Aircraft Maintenance Technology/ Technician; Aircraft Powerplant Technology/Technician; Avionics Maintenance Technology/Technician. **Related Knowledge/Courses:** Mechanical Devices; Design; Chemistry; Public Safety and Security; Production and Processing.

Work Environment: More often indoors than outdoors; hazardous equipment; standing; using hands on objects, tools, or controls; repetitive motions.

Airline Pilots, Copilots, and Flight Engineers

* Personality Code: RCI
* Education/Training Required: Bachelor's degree
* Annual Earnings: More than $145,600
* Beginning Wage: $56,540
* Earnings Growth Potential: Cannot be calculated
* Growth: 12.9%
* Annual Job Openings: 4,073
* Self-Employed: 2.5%
* Part-Time: 14.2%

Pilot and navigate the flight of multi-engine aircraft in regularly scheduled service for the transport of passengers and cargo. Requires Federal Air Transport rating and certification in specific aircraft type used. Use instrumentation to guide flights when visibility is poor. Respond to and report in-flight emergencies and malfunctions. Work as part of a flight team with other crew members, especially during takeoffs and landings. Contact control towers for takeoff clearances, arrival instructions, and other information, using radio equipment. Steer aircraft along planned routes with the assistance of autopilot and flight management computers. Monitor gauges, warning devices, and control panels to verify aircraft performance and to regulate engine speed. Start engines, operate controls, and pilot airplanes to transport passengers, mail, or freight while adhering to flight plans, regulations, and procedures. Inspect aircraft for defects and malfunctions according to pre-flight checklists. Check passenger and cargo distributions and fuel amounts to ensure that weight and balance specifications are met. Monitor engine operation, fuel consumption, and functioning of aircraft systems during flights. Confer with flight dispatchers and weather forecasters to keep abreast of flight conditions. Coordinate flight activities with ground crews and air-traffic control and inform crew members of flight and test procedures. Order changes in fuel supplies, loads, routes, or schedules to ensure safety of flights. Choose routes, altitudes, and speeds that will provide the fastest, safest, and smoothest flights. Direct activities of aircraft crews during flights. Brief crews about flight details such as destinations, duties, and responsibilities. Record in logbooks information such as flight times, distances flown, and fuel consumption. Make announcements regarding flights, using public address systems. File instrument flight plans with air traffic control to ensure that flights are coordinated with other air traffic. Perform minor maintenance work or arrange for major maintenance. Instruct other pilots and student pilots in aircraft operations and the principles of flight. Conduct in-flight tests and evaluations at specified altitudes and in all types of weather to determine the receptivity and other characteristics of equipment and systems.

GOE—Interest Area/Cluster: 16. Transportation, Distribution, and Logistics. **Work Group:** 16.02. Air Vehicle Operation. **Other Jobs in This Work Group:** Commercial Pilots.

Skills: Operation Monitoring; Operation and Control; Systems Analysis; Judgment and Decision Making; Troubleshooting; Science; Systems Evaluation; Monitoring.

Education and Training Programs: Airline/Commercial/Professional Pilot and Flight Crew Training; Flight Instruction. **Related Knowledge/Courses:** Transportation; Geography; Physics; Public Safety and Security; Psychology; Law and Government.

Work Environment: Indoors; noisy; contaminants; radiation; sitting; using hands on objects, tools, or controls.

Architectural and Civil Drafters

See Architectural Drafters (an Artistic job) and Civil Drafters (a Realistic job), described separately.

Athletes and Sports Competitors

- ❋ Personality Code: RE
- ❋ Education/Training Required: Long-term on-the-job training
- ❋ Annual Earnings: $38,440
- ❋ Beginning Wage: $15,210
- ❋ Earnings Growth Potential: Very high
- ❋ Growth: 19.2%
- ❋ Annual Job Openings: 4,293
- ❋ Self-Employed: 27.0%
- ❋ Part-Time: 39.1%

Compete in athletic events. Assess performance following athletic competition, identifying strengths and weaknesses and making adjustments to improve future performance. Receive instructions from coaches and other sports staff prior to events and discuss performance afterwards. Lead teams by serving as captains. Maintain equipment used in a particular sport. Represent teams or professional sports clubs, performing such activities as meeting with members of the media, making speeches, or participating in charity events. Participate in athletic events and competitive sports according to established rules and regulations. Attend scheduled practice and training sessions. Exercise and practice under the direction of athletic trainers or professional coaches in order to develop skills, improve physical condition, and prepare for competitions. Maintain optimum physical fitness levels by training regularly, following nutrition plans, and consulting with health professionals.

GOE—Interest Area/Cluster: 09. Hospitality, Tourism, and Recreation. **Work Group:** 09.06.

Sports. **Other Jobs in This Work Group:** Coaches and Scouts; Umpires, Referees, and Other Sports Officials.

Skills: Equipment Maintenance; Equipment Selection; Troubleshooting; Time Management; Learning Strategies; Active Learning; Judgment and Decision Making; Repairing.

Education and Training Program: Health and Physical Education, General. **Related Knowledge/Courses:** Therapy and Counseling; Communications and Media; Psychology; Sales and Marketing; Personnel and Human Resources.

Work Environment: More often outdoors than indoors; minor burns, cuts, bites, or stings; standing; walking and running; bending or twisting the body.

Audio and Video Equipment Technicians

- ❋ Personality Code: RIC
- ❋ Education/Training Required: Long-term on-the-job training
- ❋ Annual Earnings: $36,050
- ❋ Beginning Wage: $20,450
- ❋ Earnings Growth Potential: High
- ❋ Growth: 24.2%
- ❋ Annual Job Openings: 4,681
- ❋ Self-Employed: 12.8%
- ❋ Part-Time: 12.9%

Set up or set up and operate audio and video equipment, including microphones, sound speakers, video screens, projectors, video monitors, recording equipment, connecting wires and cables, sound and mixing boards, and related electronic equipment for concerts, sports events, meetings and conventions, presentations, and news conferences. May also set up and operate associated spotlights and other custom lighting systems. Notify supervisors when major equipment repairs are needed. Monitor incoming and outgoing pictures and sound feeds to ensure quality; notify directors of any possible problems. Mix and regulate sound inputs and feeds or coordinate audio feeds with television pictures. Install, adjust, and operate electronic equipment used to record, edit, and transmit radio and television programs, cable programs, and motion pictures. Design layouts of audio and video equipment and perform upgrades and maintenance. Perform minor repairs and routine cleaning of audio and video equipment. Diagnose and resolve media system problems in classrooms. Switch sources of video input from one camera or studio to another, from film to live programming, or from network to local programming. Meet with directors and senior members of camera crews to discuss assignments and determine filming sequences, camera movements, and picture composition. Construct and position properties, sets, lighting equipment, and other equipment. Compress, digitize, duplicate, and store audio and video data. Obtain, set up, and load videotapes for scheduled productions or broadcasts. Edit videotapes by erasing and removing portions of programs and adding video or sound as required. Direct and coordinate activities of assistants and other personnel during production. Plan and develop pre-production ideas into outlines, scripts, storyboards, and graphics, using own ideas or specifications of assignments. Maintain inventories of audiotapes and videotapes and related supplies. Determine formats, approaches, content, levels, and media to effectively meet objectives within budgetary constraints, utilizing research, knowledge, and training. Record and edit audio material such as movie soundtracks, using audio recording and editing equipment. Inform users of audiotaping and videotaping service policies and procedures. Obtain and preview musical performance programs prior to events to become familiar with the order and approximate times of pieces. Produce rough and finished graphics and graphic designs. Locate and secure settings, properties, effects, and other production necessities.

GOE—Interest Area/Cluster: 03. Arts and Communication. **Work Group:** 03.09. Media Technology. **Other Jobs in This Work Group:** Broadcast Technicians; Camera Operators, Television, Video, and Motion Picture; Film and Video Editors; Multi-

Media Artists and Animators; Photographers; Radio Operators; Sound Engineering Technicians.

Skills: Installation; Operation and Control; Equipment Maintenance; Troubleshooting; Operation Monitoring; Repairing; Equipment Selection; Technology Design.

Education and Training Programs: Agricultural Communication/Journalism; Photographic and Film/Video Technology/Technician and Assistant; Recording Arts Technology/Technician. **Related Knowledge/Courses:** Computers and Electronics; Telecommunications; Engineering and Technology; Communications and Media; Mechanical Devices; Physics.

Work Environment: Indoors; standing; using hands on objects, tools, or controls.

Automotive Body and Related Repairers

- ❋ Personality Code: R
- ❋ Education/Training Required: Long-term on-the-job training
- ❋ Annual Earnings: $35,690
- ❋ Beginning Wage: $21,480
- ❋ Earnings Growth Potential: Medium
- ❋ Growth: 11.6%
- ❋ Annual Job Openings: 37,469
- ❋ Self-Employed: 14.1%
- ❋ Part-Time: 5.6%

Repair and refinish automotive vehicle bodies and straighten vehicle frames. File, grind, sand, and smooth filled or repaired surfaces, using power tools and hand tools. Sand body areas to be painted and cover bumpers, windows, and trim with masking tape or paper to protect them from the paint. Follow supervisors' instructions as to which parts to restore or replace and how much time a job should take. Remove damaged sections of vehicles, using metal-cutting guns, air grinders, and wrenches, and install replacement parts, using wrenches or welding equipment. Cut and tape plastic separating film to outside repair areas to avoid damaging surrounding surfaces during repair procedure and remove tape and wash surfaces after repairs are complete. Prime and paint repaired surfaces, using paint spray guns and motorized sanders. Inspect repaired vehicles for dimensional accuracy and test-drive them to ensure proper alignment and handling. Mix polyester resins and hardeners to be used in restoring damaged areas. Chain or clamp frames and sections to alignment machines that use hydraulic pressure to align damaged components. Fill small dents that cannot be worked out with plastic or solder. Fit and weld replacement parts into place, using wrenches and welding equipment, and grind down welds to smooth them, using power grinders and other tools. Position dolly blocks against surfaces of dented areas and beat opposite surfaces to remove dents, using hammers. Remove damaged panels and identify the family and properties of the plastic used on a vehicle. Review damage reports, prepare or review repair cost estimates, and plan work to be performed. Remove small pits and dimples in body metal, using pick hammers and punches. Remove upholstery, accessories, electrical window- and seat-operating equipment, and trim to gain access to vehicle bodies and fenders. Clean work areas, using air hoses, to remove damaged material and discarded fiberglass strips used in repair procedures. Adjust or align headlights, wheels, and brake systems. Apply heat to plastic panels, using hot-air welding guns or immersion in hot water, and press the softened panels back into shape by hand. Soak fiberglass matting in resin mixtures and apply layers of matting over repair areas to specified thicknesses.

GOE—Interest Area/Cluster: 13. Manufacturing. **Work Group:** 13.14. Vehicle and Facility Mechanical Work. **Other Jobs in This Work Group:** Aircraft Mechanics and Service Technicians; Aircraft Structure, Surfaces, Rigging, and Systems Assemblers; Automotive Glass Installers and Repairers; Automotive Master Mechanics; Automotive Service Technicians and Mechanics; Automotive Specialty Technicians; Bus and Truck Mechanics and Diesel Engine Specialists; Farm Equipment Mechanics;

Fiberglass Laminators and Fabricators; Mobile Heavy Equipment Mechanics, Except Engines; Motorboat Mechanics; Motorcycle Mechanics; Outdoor Power Equipment and Other Small Engine Mechanics; Rail Car Repairers; Recreational Vehicle Service Technicians; Tire Repairers and Changers.

Skills: Repairing; Installation; Equipment Maintenance; Troubleshooting; Equipment Selection; Management of Financial Resources.

Education and Training Program: Autobody/Collision and Repair Technology/Technician. **Related Knowledge/Courses:** Mechanical Devices; Building and Construction; Chemistry; Production and Processing; Administration and Management; Transportation.

Work Environment: Noisy; contaminants; hazardous equipment; standing; using hands on objects, tools, or controls; repetitive motions.

Automotive Master Mechanics

- ❀ Personality Code: RI
- ❀ Education/Training Required: Postsecondary vocational training
- ❀ Annual Earnings: $34,170
- ❀ Beginning Wage: $19,240
- ❀ Earnings Growth Potential: High
- ❀ Growth: 14.3%
- ❀ Annual Job Openings: 97,350
- ❀ Self-Employed: 16.8%
- ❀ Part-Time: 5.6%

The job openings listed here are shared with Automotive Specialty Technicians.

Repair automobiles, trucks, buses, and other vehicles. Master mechanics repair virtually any part on the vehicle or specialize in the transmission system. Examine vehicles to determine extent of damage or malfunctions. Test-drive vehicles and test components and systems, using equipment such as infrared engine analyzers, compression gauges, and computerized diagnostic devices. Repair, reline, replace, and adjust brakes. Review work orders and discuss work with supervisors. Follow checklists to ensure all important parts are examined, including belts, hoses, steering systems, spark plugs, brake and fuel systems, wheel bearings, and other potentially troublesome areas. Plan work procedures, using charts, technical manuals, and experience. Test and adjust repaired systems to meet manufacturers' performance specifications. Confer with customers to obtain descriptions of vehicle problems and to discuss work to be performed and future repair requirements. Perform routine and scheduled maintenance services such as oil changes, lubrications, and tune-ups. Disassemble units and inspect parts for wear, using micrometers, calipers, and gauges. Overhaul or replace carburetors, blowers, generators, distributors, starters, and pumps. Repair and service air conditioning, heating, engine-cooling, and electrical systems. Repair or replace parts such as pistons, rods, gears, valves, and bearings. Tear down, repair, and rebuild faulty assemblies such as power systems, steering systems, and linkages. Rewire ignition systems, lights, and instrument panels. Repair radiator leaks. Install and repair accessories such as radios, heaters, mirrors, and windshield wipers. Repair manual and automatic transmissions. Repair or replace shock absorbers. Align vehicles' front ends. Rebuild parts such as crankshafts and cylinder blocks. Repair damaged automobile bodies. Replace and adjust headlights.

GOE—Interest Area/Cluster: 13. Manufacturing. **Work Group:** 13.14. Vehicle and Facility Mechanical Work. **Other Jobs in This Work Group:** Aircraft Mechanics and Service Technicians; Aircraft Structure, Surfaces, Rigging, and Systems Assemblers; Automotive Body and Related Repairers; Automotive Glass Installers and Repairers; Automotive Service Technicians and Mechanics; Automotive Specialty Technicians; Bus and Truck Mechanics and Diesel Engine Specialists; Farm Equipment Mechanics; Fiberglass Laminators and Fabricators; Mobile Heavy Equipment Mechanics, Except Engines; Motorboat Mechanics; Motorcycle Mechanics; Outdoor Power Equipment and Other Small Engine Mechanics; Rail Car Repairers; Recreational Vehicle Service Technicians; Tire Repairers and Changers.

Skills: Repairing; Troubleshooting; Installation; Equipment Maintenance; Equipment Selection; Operation Monitoring; Complex Problem Solving; Technology Design.

Education and Training Programs: Automotive Engineering Technology/Technician; Automobile/Automotive Mechanics Technology/Technician; Medium/Heavy Vehicle and Truck Technology/Technician. **Related Knowledge/Courses:** Mechanical Devices; Physics; Computers and Electronics; Engineering and Technology; Chemistry; Public Safety and Security.

Work Environment: Noisy; contaminants; hazardous equipment; minor burns, cuts, bites, or stings; standing; using hands on objects, tools, or controls.

Automotive Service Technicians and Mechanics

See Automotive Master Mechanics (a Realistic job) and Automotive Specialty Technicians (a Realistic job), described separately.

Automotive Specialty Technicians

- ❋ Personality Code: RIC
- ❋ Education/Training Required: Postsecondary vocational training
- ❋ Annual Earnings: $34,170
- ❋ Beginning Wage: $19,240
- ❋ Earnings Growth Potential: High
- ❋ Growth: 14.3%
- ❋ Annual Job Openings: 97,350
- ❋ Self-Employed: 16.8%
- ❋ Part-Time: 5.6%

The job openings listed here are shared with Automotive Master Mechanics.

Repair only one system or component on a vehicle, such as brakes, suspension, or radiator. Examine vehicles, compile estimates of repair costs, and secure customers' approval to perform repairs. Repair, overhaul, and adjust automobile brake systems. Use electronic test equipment to locate and correct malfunctions in fuel, ignition, and emissions control systems. Repair and replace defective ball joint suspensions, brake shoes, and wheel bearings. Inspect and test new vehicles for damage; then record findings so that necessary repairs can be made. Test electronic computer components in automobiles to ensure that they are working properly. Tune automobile engines to ensure proper and efficient functioning. Install and repair air conditioners and service components such as compressors, condensers, and controls. Repair, replace, and adjust defective carburetor parts and gasoline filters. Remove and replace defective mufflers and tailpipes. Repair and replace automobile leaf springs. Rebuild, repair, and test automotive fuel injection units. Align and repair wheels, axles, frames, torsion bars, and steering mechanisms of automobiles, using special alignment equipment and wheel-balancing machines. Repair, install, and adjust hydraulic and electromagnetic automatic lift mechanisms used to raise and lower automobile windows, seats, and tops. Repair and rebuild clutch systems. Convert vehicle fuel systems from gasoline to butane gas operations and repair and service operating butane fuel units.

GOE—Interest Area/Cluster: 13. Manufacturing. **Work Group:** 13.14. Vehicle and Facility Mechanical Work. **Other Jobs in This Work Group:** Aircraft Mechanics and Service Technicians; Aircraft Structure, Surfaces, Rigging, and Systems Assemblers; Automotive Body and Related Repairers; Automotive Glass Installers and Repairers; Automotive Master Mechanics; Automotive Service Technicians and Mechanics; Bus and Truck Mechanics and Diesel Engine Specialists; Farm Equipment Mechanics; Fiberglass Laminators and Fabricators; Mobile Heavy Equipment Mechanics, Except Engines; Motorboat Mechanics; Motorcycle Mechanics; Outdoor Power Equipment and Other Small Engine Mechanics; Rail Car Repairers; Recreational Vehicle Service Technicians; Tire Repairers and Changers.

Skills: Repairing; Troubleshooting; Operation Monitoring; Equipment Maintenance; Installation;

Equipment Selection; Active Learning; Operation and Control.

Education and Training Programs: Automotive Engineering Technology/Technician; Vehicle Emissions Inspection and Maintenance Technology/Technician; Alternative Fuel Vehicle Technology/Technician. **Related Knowledge/Courses:** Mechanical Devices; Physics; Engineering and Technology; Customer and Personal Service; Sales and Marketing; Administration and Management.

Work Environment: Contaminants; cramped work space, awkward positions; minor burns, cuts, bites, or stings; standing; using hands on objects, tools, or controls; bending or twisting the body.

Aviation Inspectors

- ❋ Personality Code: RCI
- ❋ Education/Training Required: Work experience in a related occupation
- ❋ Annual Earnings: $51,440
- ❋ Beginning Wage: $27,340
- ❋ Earnings Growth Potential: High
- ❋ Growth: 16.4%
- ❋ Annual Job Openings: 2,122
- ❋ Self-Employed: 5.9%
- ❋ Part-Time: 3.7%

The job openings listed here are shared with Freight and Cargo Inspectors and with Transportation Vehicle, Equipment, and Systems Inspectors, Except Aviation.

Inspect aircraft, maintenance procedures, air navigational aids, air traffic controls, and communications equipment to ensure conformance with federal safety regulations. Inspect work of aircraft mechanics performing maintenance, modification, or repair and overhaul of aircraft and aircraft mechanical systems to ensure adherence to standards and procedures. Start aircraft and observe gauges, meters, and other instruments to detect evidence of malfunctions. Examine aircraft access plates and doors for security. Examine landing gear, tires, and exteriors of fuselage, wings, and engines for evidence of damage or corrosion and to determine whether repairs are needed. Prepare and maintain detailed repair, inspection, investigation, and certification records and reports. Inspect new, repaired, or modified aircraft to identify damage or defects and to assess airworthiness and conformance to standards, using checklists, hand tools, and test instruments. Examine maintenance records and flight logs to determine if service and maintenance checks and overhauls were performed at prescribed intervals. Recommend replacement, repair, or modification of aircraft equipment. Recommend changes in rules, policies, standards, and regulations based on knowledge of operating conditions, aircraft improvements, and other factors. Issue pilots' licenses to individuals meeting standards. Investigate air accidents and complaints to determine causes. Observe flight activities of pilots to assess flying skills and to ensure conformance to flight and safety regulations. Conduct flight test programs to test equipment, instruments, and systems under a variety of conditions, using both manual and automatic controls. Approve or deny issuance of certificates of airworthiness. Analyze training programs and conduct oral and written examinations to ensure the competency of persons operating, installing, and repairing aircraft equipment. Schedule and coordinate in-flight testing programs with ground crews and air traffic control to ensure availability of ground tracking, equipment monitoring, and related services.

GOE—Interest Area/Cluster: 07. Government and Public Administration. **Work Group:** 07.03. Regulations Enforcement. **Other Jobs in This Work Group:** Agricultural Inspectors; Compliance Officers, Except Agriculture, Construction, Health and Safety, and Transportation; Construction and Building Inspectors; Environmental Compliance Inspectors; Equal Opportunity Representatives and Officers; Financial Examiners; Fire Inspectors; Fish and Game Wardens; Forest Fire Inspectors and Prevention Specialists; Freight and Cargo Inspectors; Government Property Inspectors and Investigators; Immigration and Customs Inspectors; Licensing Examiners and Inspectors; Nuclear Monitoring Technicians; Occupational

Health and Safety Specialists; Occupational Health and Safety Technicians; Tax Examiners, Collectors, and Revenue Agents; Transportation Vehicle, Equipment, and Systems Inspectors, Except Aviation.

Skills: Systems Analysis; Systems Evaluation; Quality Control Analysis; Operation Monitoring; Troubleshooting; Operation and Control; Reading Comprehension; Judgment and Decision Making.

Education and Training Program: Avionics Maintenance Technology/Technician. **Related Knowledge/Courses:** Physics; Mechanical Devices; Transportation; Chemistry; Design; Law and Government.

Work Environment: More often indoors than outdoors; noisy; sitting.

Biological Technicians

- ❋ Personality Code: RIC
- ❋ Education/Training Required: Bachelor's degree
- ❋ Annual Earnings: $37,810
- ❋ Beginning Wage: $24,360
- ❋ Earnings Growth Potential: Medium
- ❋ Growth: 16.0%
- ❋ Annual Job Openings: 15,374
- ❋ Self-Employed: 0.0%
- ❋ Part-Time: 6.2%

Assist biological and medical scientists in laboratories. Set up, operate, and maintain laboratory instruments and equipment; monitor experiments; make observations; and calculate and record results. May analyze organic substances, such as blood, food, and drugs. Keep detailed logs of all work-related activities. Monitor laboratory work to ensure compliance with set standards. Isolate, identify, and prepare specimens for examination. Use computers, computer-interfaced equipment, robotics, or high-technology industrial applications to perform work duties. Conduct research or assist in the conduct of research, including the collection of information and samples such as blood, water, soil,

Realistic–B

plants, and animals. Set up, adjust, calibrate, clean, maintain, and troubleshoot laboratory and field equipment. Provide technical support and services for scientists and engineers working in fields such as agriculture, environmental science, resource management, biology, and health sciences. Clean, maintain, and prepare supplies and work areas. Participate in the research, development, or manufacturing of medicinal and pharmaceutical preparations. Conduct standardized biological, microbiological, or biochemical tests and laboratory analyses to evaluate the quantity or quality of physical or chemical substances in food or other products. Analyze experimental data and interpret results to write reports and summaries of findings. Measure or weigh compounds and solutions for use in testing or animal feed. Monitor and observe experiments, recording production and test data for evaluation by research personnel. Examine animals and specimens to detect the presence of disease or other problems. Conduct or supervise operational programs such as fish hatcheries, greenhouses, and livestock production programs. Feed livestock or laboratory animals.

GOE—Interest Area/Cluster: 08. Health Science. **Work Group:** 08.06. Medical Technology. **Other Jobs in This Work Group:** Cardiovascular Technologists and Technicians; Diagnostic Medical Sonographers; Medical and Clinical Laboratory Technicians; Medical and Clinical Laboratory Technologists; Medical Equipment Preparers; Medical Records and Health Information Technicians; Nuclear Medicine Technologists; Opticians, Dispensing; Orthotists and Prosthetists; Radiologic Technicians; Radiologic Technologists; Radiologic Technologists and Technicians.

Skills: Science; Equipment Maintenance; Quality Control Analysis; Troubleshooting; Mathematics; Active Learning; Technology Design; Learning Strategies.

Education and Training Program: Biology Technician/Biotechnology Laboratory Technician. **Related Knowledge/Courses:** Chemistry; Biology.

Work Environment: Indoors; standing; using hands on objects, tools, or controls; repetitive motions.

Boilermakers

- ❊ Personality Code: RC
- ❊ Education/Training Required: Long-term on-the-job training
- ❊ Annual Earnings: $50,700
- ❊ Beginning Wage: $32,910
- ❊ Earnings Growth Potential: Medium
- ❊ Growth: 14.0%
- ❊ Annual Job Openings: 2,333
- ❊ Self-Employed: 0.2%
- ❊ Part-Time: 2.6%

Construct, assemble, maintain, and repair stationary steam boilers and boiler house auxiliaries. Align structures or plate sections to assemble boiler frame tanks or vats, following blueprints. Work involves use of hand and power tools, plumb bobs, levels, wedges, dogs, or turnbuckles. Assist in testing assembled vessels. Direct cleaning of boilers and boiler furnaces. Inspect and repair boiler fittings, such as safety valves, regulators, automatic-control mechanisms, water columns, and auxiliary machines. Examine boilers, pressure vessels, tanks, and vats to locate defects such as leaks, weak spots, and defective sections so that they can be repaired. Bolt or arc-weld pressure vessel structures and parts together, using wrenches and welding equipment. Inspect assembled vessels and individual components, such as tubes, fittings, valves, controls, and auxiliary mechanisms, to locate any defects. Repair or replace defective pressure vessel parts, such as safety valves and regulators, using torches, jacks, caulking hammers, power saws, threading dies, welding equipment, and metalworking machinery. Attach rigging and signal crane or hoist operators to lift heavy frame and plate sections and other parts into place. Bell, bead with power hammers, or weld pressure vessel tube ends in order to ensure leakproof joints. Lay out plate, sheet steel, or other heavy metal and locate and mark bending and cutting lines, using protractors, compasses, and drawing instruments or templates. Install manholes, handholes, taps, tubes, valves, gauges, and feedwater connections in drums of water tube boilers, using hand tools. Study blueprints to determine locations, relationships, and dimensions of parts. Straighten or reshape bent pressure vessel plates and structure parts, using hammers, jacks, and torches. Shape seams, joints, and irregular edges of pressure vessel sections and structural parts in order to attain specified fit of parts, using cutting torches, hammers, files, and metalworking machines. Position, align, and secure structural parts and related assemblies to boiler frames, tanks, or vats of pressure vessels, following blueprints. Locate and mark reference points for columns or plates on boiler foundations, following blueprints and using straightedges, squares, transits, and measuring instruments. Shape and fabricate parts, such as stacks, uptakes, and chutes, in order to adapt pressure vessels, heat exchangers, and piping to premises, using heavy-metalworking machines such as brakes, rolls, and drill presses. Clean pressure vessel equipment, using scrapers, wire brushes, and cleaning solvents.

GOE—Interest Area/Cluster: 02. Architecture and Construction. **Work Group:** 02.04. Construction Crafts. **Other Jobs in This Work Group:** Brickmasons and Blockmasons; Carpet Installers; Cement Masons and Concrete Finishers; Commercial Divers; Construction Carpenters; Crane and Tower Operators; Drywall and Ceiling Tile Installers; Electricians; Fence Erectors; Floor Layers, Except Carpet, Wood, and Hard Tiles; Floor Sanders and Finishers; Glaziers; Hazardous Materials Removal Workers; Insulation Workers, Floor, Ceiling, and Wall; Insulation Workers, Mechanical; Manufactured Building and Mobile Home Installers; Operating Engineers and Other Construction Equipment Operators; Painters, Construction and Maintenance; Paperhangers; Paving, Surfacing, and Tamping Equipment Operators; Pile-Driver Operators; Pipe Fitters and Steamfitters; Pipelayers; Plasterers and Stucco Masons; Plumbers; Plumbers, Pipefitters, and Steamfitters; Rail-Track

Laying and Maintenance Equipment Operators; Refractory Materials Repairers, Except Brickmasons; Reinforcing Iron and Rebar Workers; Riggers; Roofers; Rough Carpenters; Security and Fire Alarm Systems Installers; Segmental Pavers; Sheet Metal Workers; Stone Cutters and Carvers, Manufacturing; Stonemasons; Structural Iron and Steel Workers; Tapers; Terrazzo Workers and Finishers; Tile and Marble Setters.

Skills: Repairing; Installation; Equipment Maintenance; Operation Monitoring; Mathematics; Troubleshooting; Operation and Control; Equipment Selection.

Education and Training Program: Boilermaking/Boilermaker. **Related Knowledge/Courses:** Building and Construction; Mechanical Devices; Engineering and Technology; Design; Physics; Transportation.

Work Environment: Noisy; very hot or cold; contaminants; minor burns, cuts, bites, or stings; standing; using hands on objects, tools, or controls.

Brickmasons and Blockmasons

- Personality Code: RCI
- Education/Training Required: Long-term on-the-job training
- Annual Earnings: $44,070
- Beginning Wage: $26,370
- Earnings Growth Potential: High
- Growth: 9.7%
- Annual Job Openings: 17,569
- Self-Employed: 24.5%
- Part-Time: 7.9%

Lay and bind building materials, such as brick, structural tile, concrete block, cinderblock, glass block, and terra-cotta block, with mortar and other substances to construct or repair walls, partitions, arches, sewers, and other structures. Construct corners by fastening in plumb position a corner pole or building a corner pyramid of bricks and filling in between the corners, using a line from corner to corner to guide each course, or layer, of brick. Measure distance from reference points and mark guidelines to lay out work, using plumb bobs and levels. Fasten or fuse brick or other building material to structure with wire clamps, anchor holes, torch, or cement. Calculate angles and courses and determine vertical and horizontal alignment of courses. Break or cut bricks, tiles, or blocks to size, using trowel edge, hammer, or power saw. Remove excess mortar with trowels and hand tools and finish mortar joints with jointing tools for a sealed, uniform appearance. Interpret blueprints and drawings to determine specifications and to calculate the materials required. Apply and smooth mortar or other mixture over work surface. Mix specified amounts of sand, clay, dirt, or mortar powder with water to form refractory mixtures. Examine brickwork or structure to determine need for repair. Clean working surface to remove scale, dust, soot, or chips of brick and mortar, using broom, wire brush, or scraper. Lay and align bricks, blocks, or tiles to build or repair structures or high-temperature equipment, such as cupola, kilns, ovens, or furnaces. Remove burned or damaged brick or mortar, using sledgehammer, crowbar, chipping gun, or chisel. Spray or spread refractory material over brickwork to protect against deterioration.

GOE—Interest Area/Cluster: 02. Architecture and Construction. **Work Group:** 02.04. Construction Crafts. **Other Jobs in This Work Group:** Boilermakers; Carpet Installers; Cement Masons and Concrete Finishers; Commercial Divers; Construction Carpenters; Crane and Tower Operators; Drywall and Ceiling Tile Installers; Electricians; Fence Erectors; Floor Layers, Except Carpet, Wood, and Hard Tiles; Floor Sanders and Finishers; Glaziers; Hazardous Materials Removal Workers; Insulation Workers, Floor, Ceiling, and Wall; Insulation Workers, Mechanical; Manufactured Building and Mobile Home Installers; Operating Engineers and Other Construction Equipment Operators; Painters, Construction and Maintenance; Paperhangers; Paving, Surfacing, and Tamping Equipment Operators; Pile-Driver Operators; Pipe Fitters and Steamfitters; Pipelayers; Plasterers and Stucco Masons; Plumbers;

Plumbers, Pipefitters, and Steamfitters; Rail-Track Laying and Maintenance Equipment Operators; Refractory Materials Repairers, Except Brickmasons; Reinforcing Iron and Rebar Workers; Riggers; Roofers; Rough Carpenters; Security and Fire Alarm Systems Installers; Segmental Pavers; Sheet Metal Workers; Stone Cutters and Carvers, Manufacturing; Stonemasons; Structural Iron and Steel Workers; Tapers; Terrazzo Workers and Finishers; Tile and Marble Setters.

Skills: Equipment Maintenance; Mathematics; Installation; Repairing; Technology Design.

Education and Training Program: Mason/Masonry. **Related Knowledge/Courses:** Building and Construction; Design; Mechanical Devices; Production and Processing; Public Safety and Security; Mathematics.

Work Environment: Outdoors; very hot or cold; hazardous equipment; standing; using hands on objects, tools, or controls; bending or twisting the body.

Bus and Truck Mechanics and Diesel Engine Specialists

- ❋ Personality Code: RC
- ❋ Education/Training Required: Postsecondary vocational training
- ❋ Annual Earnings: $38,640
- ❋ Beginning Wage: $25,210
- ❋ Earnings Growth Potential: Low
- ❋ Growth: 11.5%
- ❋ Annual Job Openings: 25,428
- ❋ Self-Employed: 5.8%
- ❋ Part-Time: 2.8%

Diagnose, adjust, repair, or overhaul trucks, buses, and all types of diesel engines. Includes mechanics working primarily with automobile diesel engines. Use hand tools such as screwdrivers, pliers, wrenches, pressure gauges, and precision instruments, as well as power tools such as pneumatic wrenches, lathes, welding equipment, and jacks and hoists. Inspect brake systems, steering mechanisms, wheel bearings, and other important parts to ensure that they are in proper operating condition. Perform routine maintenance such as changing oil, checking batteries, and lubricating equipment and machinery. Adjust and reline brakes, align wheels, tighten bolts and screws, and reassemble equipment. Raise trucks, buses, and heavy parts or equipment, using hydraulic jacks or hoists. Test drive trucks and buses to diagnose malfunctions or to ensure that they are working properly. Inspect, test, and listen to defective equipment to diagnose malfunctions, using test instruments such as handheld computers, motor analyzers, chassis charts, and pressure gauges. Examine and adjust protective guards, loose bolts, and specified safety devices. Inspect and verify dimensions and clearances of parts to ensure conformance to factory specifications. Specialize in repairing and maintaining parts of the engine, such as fuel injection systems. Attach test instruments to equipment and read dials and gauges to diagnose malfunctions. Rewire ignition systems, lights, and instrument panels. Recondition and replace parts, pistons, bearings, gears, and valves. Repair and adjust seats, doors, and windows and install and repair accessories. Inspect, repair, and maintain automotive and mechanical equipment and machinery such as pumps and compressors. Disassemble and overhaul internal combustion engines, pumps, generators, transmissions, clutches, and differential units. Rebuild gas or diesel engines. Align front ends and suspension systems. Operate valve-grinding machines to grind and reset valves.

GOE—Interest Area/Cluster: 13. Manufacturing. **Work Group:** 13.14. Vehicle and Facility Mechanical Work. **Other Jobs in This Work Group:** Aircraft Mechanics and Service Technicians; Aircraft Structure, Surfaces, Rigging, and Systems Assemblers; Automotive Body and Related Repairers; Automotive Glass Installers and Repairers; Automotive Master Mechanics; Automotive Service Technicians and Mechanics; Automotive Specialty Technicians; Farm Equipment Mechanics; Fiberglass Laminators and Fabricators; Mobile Heavy Equipment Mechanics, Except Engines; Motorboat Mechanics; Motorcycle Mechanics; Outdoor Power Equipment and Other

Small Engine Mechanics; Rail Car Repairers; Recreational Vehicle Service Technicians; Tire Repairers and Changers.

Skills: Repairing; Equipment Maintenance; Troubleshooting; Installation; Science; Technology Design; Equipment Selection.

Education and Training Programs: Diesel Mechanics Technology/Technician; Medium/Heavy Vehicle and Truck Technology/Technician. **Related Knowledge/Courses:** Mechanical Devices; Transportation; Public Safety and Security; Physics; Engineering and Technology; Law and Government.

Work Environment: Noisy; very bright or dim lighting; contaminants; hazardous equipment; standing; using hands on objects, tools, or controls.

Bus Drivers, Transit and Intercity

- ❋ Personality Code: RS
- ❋ Education/Training Required: Moderate-term on-the-job training
- ❋ Annual Earnings: $33,160
- ❋ Beginning Wage: $19,660
- ❋ Earnings Growth Potential: High
- ❋ Growth: 12.5%
- ❋ Annual Job Openings: 27,100
- ❋ Self-Employed: 1.3%
- ❋ Part-Time: 34.1%

Drive bus or motor coach, including regular route operations, charters, and private carriage. May assist passengers with baggage. May collect fares or tickets. Inspect vehicles and check gas, oil, and water levels prior to departure. Drive vehicles over specified routes or to specified destinations according to time schedules to transport passengers, complying with traffic regulations. Park vehicles at loading areas so that passengers can board. Assist passengers with baggage and collect tickets or cash fares. Report delays or accidents. Advise passengers to be seated and orderly while on vehicles. Regulate heating, lighting, and ventilating systems for passenger comfort. Load and unload baggage in baggage compartments. Record cash receipts and ticket fares. Make minor repairs to vehicle and change tires.

GOE—Interest Area/Cluster: 16. Transportation, Distribution, and Logistics. **Work Group:** 16.06. Other Services Requiring Driving. **Other Jobs in This Work Group:** Ambulance Drivers and Attendants, Except Emergency Medical Technicians; Bus Drivers, School; Couriers and Messengers; Driver/Sales Workers; Parking Lot Attendants; Postal Service Mail Carriers; Taxi Drivers and Chauffeurs.

Skills: Equipment Maintenance; Operation and Control; Social Perceptiveness; Operation Monitoring; Troubleshooting; Repairing.

Education and Training Program: Truck and Bus Driver/Commercial Vehicle Operation. **Related Knowledge/Courses:** Transportation; Geography; Public Safety and Security; Psychology; Law and Government; Customer and Personal Service.

Work Environment: Outdoors; noisy; contaminants; sitting; using hands on objects, tools, or controls; repetitive motions.

Camera Operators, Television, Video, and Motion Picture

- ❋ Personality Code: RA
- ❋ Education/Training Required: Postsecondary vocational training
- ❋ Annual Earnings: $41,850
- ❋ Beginning Wage: $21,050
- ❋ Earnings Growth Potential: High
- ❋ Growth: 11.5%
- ❋ Annual Job Openings: 3,496
- ❋ Self-Employed: 16.9%
- ❋ Part-Time: 18.9%

Operate television, video, or motion picture camera to photograph images or scenes for various purposes, such as TV broadcasts, advertising, video production, or motion pictures. Operate television or motion picture cameras to record scenes for television broadcasts, advertising, or motion pictures.

Compose and frame each shot, applying the technical aspects of light, lenses, film, filters, and camera settings to achieve the effects sought by directors. Operate zoom lenses, changing images according to specifications and rehearsal instructions. Use cameras in any of several different camera mounts, such as stationary, track-mounted, or crane-mounted. Test, clean, and maintain equipment to ensure proper working condition. Adjust positions and controls of cameras, printers, and related equipment to change focus, exposure, and lighting. Gather and edit raw footage on location to send to television affiliates for broadcast, using electronic news-gathering or film-production equipment. Confer with directors, sound and lighting technicians, electricians, and other crew members to discuss assignments and determine filming sequences, desired effects, camera movements, and lighting requirements. Observe sets or locations for potential problems and to determine filming and lighting requirements. Instruct camera operators regarding camera setups, angles, distances, movement, and variables and cues for starting and stopping filming. Select and assemble cameras, accessories, equipment, and film stock to be used during filming, using knowledge of filming techniques, requirements, and computations. Label and record contents of exposed film and note details on report forms. Read charts and compute ratios to determine variables such as lighting, shutter angles, filter factors, and camera distances. Set up cameras, optical printers, and related equipment to produce photographs and special effects. View films to resolve problems of exposure control, subject and camera movement, changes in subject distance, and related variables. Reload camera magazines with fresh raw film stock. Read and analyze work orders and specifications to determine locations of subject material, work procedures, sequences of operations, and machine setups. Receive raw film stock and maintain film inventories.

GOE—Interest Area/Cluster: 03. Arts and Communication. **Work Group:** 03.09. Media Technology. **Other Jobs in This Work Group:** Audio and Video Equipment Technicians; Broadcast Technicians; Film and Video Editors; Multi-Media Artists and Animators; Photographers; Radio Operators; Sound Engineering Technicians.

Skills: Operation Monitoring; Operation and Control; Equipment Maintenance; Troubleshooting; Equipment Selection; Operations Analysis; Active Listening; Installation.

Education and Training Programs: Radio and Television Broadcasting Technology/Technician; Audiovisual Communications Technologies/Technicians, Other; Cinematography and Film/Video Production. **Related Knowledge/Courses:** Communications and Media; Telecommunications; Computers and Electronics; Engineering and Technology.

Work Environment: More often indoors than outdoors; very bright or dim lighting; standing; using hands on objects, tools, or controls.

Captains, Mates, and Pilots of Water Vessels

See Mates—Ship, Boat, and Barge (a Realistic job), Pilots, Ship (a Realistic job), and Ship and Boat Captains (an Enterprising job), described separately.

Cardiovascular Technologists and Technicians

- ❋ Personality Code: RIS
- ❋ Education/Training Required: Associate degree
- ❋ Annual Earnings: $44,940
- ❋ Beginning Wage: $24,650
- ❋ Earnings Growth Potential: High
- ❋ Growth: 25.5%
- ❋ Annual Job Openings: 3,550
- ❋ Self-Employed: 1.1%
- ❋ Part-Time: 17.3%

Conduct tests on pulmonary or cardiovascular systems of patients for diagnostic purposes. May conduct or assist in electrocardiograms, **cardiac catheterizations, pulmonary-functions, lung capacity, and similar tests.** Monitor patients' blood pressures and heart rates, using electrocardiogram (EKG) equipment during diagnostic and therapeutic procedures to notify physicians if something appears wrong. Explain testing procedures to patients to obtain cooperation and reduce anxiety. Observe gauges, recorders, and video screens of data analysis systems during imaging of cardiovascular systems. Monitor patients' comfort and safety during tests, alerting physicians to abnormalities or changes in patient responses. Obtain and record patients' identities, medical histories, or test results. Attach electrodes to patients' chests, arms, and legs; connect electrodes to leads from electrocardiogram (EKG) machines; and operate EKG machines to obtain readings. Adjust equipment and controls according to physicians' orders or established protocol. Prepare and position patients for testing. Check, test, and maintain cardiology equipment, making minor repairs when necessary, to ensure proper operation. Supervise and train other cardiology technologists and students. Perform general administrative tasks, such as scheduling appointments or ordering supplies and equipment. Maintain a proper sterile field during surgical procedures. Assist physicians in the diagnosis and treatment of cardiac and peripheral vascular treatments, such as implanting pacemakers or assisting with balloon angioplasties to treat blood vessel blockages. Inject contrast medium into patients' blood vessels. Assess cardiac physiology and calculate valve areas from blood flow velocity measurements. Operate diagnostic imaging equipment to produce contrast enhanced radiographs of hearts and cardiovascular systems. Observe ultrasound display screens and listen to signals to record vascular information such as blood pressure, limb volume changes, oxygen saturation, and cerebral circulation. Transcribe, type, and distribute reports of diagnostic procedures for interpretation by physician. Conduct electrocardiogram (EKG), phonocardiogram, echocardiogram, stress testing, or other cardiovascular tests to record patients' cardiac activities, using specialized electronic test equipment, recording devices, and laboratory instruments.

Realistic-C

GOE—Interest Area/Cluster: 08. Health Science. **Work Group:** 08.06. Medical Technology. **Other Jobs in This Work Group:** Biological Technicians; Diagnostic Medical Sonographers; Medical and Clinical Laboratory Technicians; Medical and Clinical Laboratory Technologists; Medical Equipment Preparers; Medical Records and Health Information Technicians; Nuclear Medicine Technologists; Opticians, Dispensing; Orthotists and Prosthetists; Radiologic Technicians; Radiologic Technologists; Radiologic Technologists and Technicians.

Skills: Operation Monitoring; Management of Personnel Resources; Systems Analysis; Quality Control Analysis; Management of Material Resources.

Education and Training Programs: Cardiovascular Technology/Technologist; Electrocardiograph Technology/Technician; Perfusion Technology/Perfusionist; Cardiopulmonary Technology/Technologist. **Related Knowledge/Courses:** Medicine and Dentistry; Biology; Psychology; Customer and Personal Service; Sociology and Anthropology; Chemistry.

Work Environment: Indoors; radiation; disease or infections; standing; walking and running; using hands on objects, tools, or controls.

Carpenters

See Construction Carpenters (a Realistic job) and Rough Carpenters (a Realistic job), described separately.

Cartographers and Photogrammetrists

- ❀ Personality Code: RIC
- ❀ Education/Training Required: Bachelor's degree
- ❀ Annual Earnings: $49,970
- ❀ Beginning Wage: $32,380
- ❀ Earnings Growth Potential: Medium
- ❀ Growth: 20.3%
- ❀ Annual Job Openings: 2,823
- ❀ Self-Employed: 3.4%
- ❀ Part-Time: 4.6%

Collect, analyze, and interpret geographic information provided by geodetic surveys, aerial photographs, and satellite data. Research, study, and prepare maps and other spatial data in digital or graphic form for legal, social, political, educational, and design purposes. May work with Geographic Information Systems (GIS). May design and evaluate algorithms, data structures, and user interfaces for GIS and mapping systems. Identify, scale, and orient geodetic points, elevations, and other planimetric or topographic features, applying standard mathematical formulas. Collect information about specific features of the Earth, using aerial photography and other digital remote sensing techniques. Revise existing maps and charts, making all necessary corrections and adjustments. Compile data required for map preparation, including aerial photographs, survey notes, records, reports, and original maps. Inspect final compositions to ensure completeness and accuracy. Determine map content and layout, as well as production specifications such as scale, size, projection, and colors, and direct production to ensure that specifications are followed. Examine and analyze data from ground surveys, reports, aerial photographs, and satellite images to prepare topographic maps, aerial-photograph mosaics, and related charts. Select aerial photographic and remote sensing techniques and plotting equipment needed to meet required standards of accuracy. Delineate aerial photographic detail such as control points, hydrography, topography, and cultural features, using precision ste- reoplotting apparatus or drafting instruments. Build and update digital databases. Prepare and alter trace maps, charts, tables, detailed drawings, and three- dimensional optical models of terrain, using stereo- scopic plotting and computer graphics equipment. Determine guidelines that specify which source material is acceptable for use. Study legal records to establish boundaries of local, national, and inter- national properties. Travel over photographed areas to observe, identify, record, and verify all relevant features.

GOE—Interest Area/Cluster: 15. Scientific Research, Engineering, and Mathematics. **Work Group:** 15.09. Engineering Technology. **Other Jobs in This Work Group:** Aerospace Engineering and Operations Technicians; Civil Engineering Techni- cians; Electrical and Electronic Engineering Techni- cians; Electrical and Electronics Drafters; Electrical Drafters; Electrical Engineering Technicians; Elec- tro-Mechanical Technicians; Electronic Drafters; Electronics Engineering Technicians; Environmen- tal Engineering Technicians; Mapping Technicians; Mechanical Drafters; Mechanical Engineering Tech- nicians; Surveying and Mapping Technicians; Sur- veying Technicians.

Skills: Science; Technology Design; Mathematics; Active Learning; Troubleshooting; Reading Com- prehension; Operation and Control; Writing.

Education and Training Programs: Survey- ing Technology/Surveying; Cartography. **Related Knowledge/Courses:** Geography; Design; Engi- neering and Technology; Computers and Electron- ics; Production and Processing; Mathematics.

Work Environment: Indoors; sitting; using hands on objects, tools, or controls; repetitive motions.

Cement Masons and Concrete Finishers

- ❀ Personality Code: RE
- ❀ Education/Training Required: Moderate- term on-the-job training
- ❀ Annual Earnings: $33,840
- ❀ Beginning Wage: $21,980
- ❀ Earnings Growth Potential: Medium
- ❀ Growth: 11.4%
- ❀ Annual Job Openings: 34,625
- ❀ Self-Employed: 2.0%
- ❀ Part-Time: 6.0%

Smooth and finish surfaces of poured concrete, such as floors, walks, sidewalks, roads, or curbs, using a variety of hand and power tools. Align forms for sidewalks, curbs, or gutters; patch voids; and use saws to cut expansion joints. Check the forms that hold the concrete to see that they are properly constructed. Set the forms that hold con- crete to the desired pitch and depth and align them. Spread, level, and smooth concrete, using rake, shovel, hand or power trowel, hand or power screed, and float. Mold expansion joints and edges, using edging tools, jointers, and straightedge. Monitor how the wind, heat, or cold affect the curing of the concrete throughout the entire process. Signal truck driver to position truck to facilitate pouring concrete and move chute to direct concrete on forms. Produce rough concrete surface, using broom. Operate power vibrator to compact concrete. Direct the casting of the concrete and supervise laborers who use shovels or special tools to spread it. Mix cement, sand, and water to produce concrete, grout, or slurry, using hoe, trowel, tamper, scraper, or concrete-mixing machine. Cut out damaged areas, drill holes for reinforcing rods, and position reinforcing rods to repair concrete, using power saw and drill. Wet surface to prepare for bonding, fill holes and cracks with grout or slurry, and smooth, using trowel. Wet concrete surface and rub with stone to smooth surface and obtain speci- fied finish. Clean chipped area, using wire brush, and feel and observe surface to determine if it is rough

Realistic–C

or uneven. Apply hardening and sealing compounds to cure surface of concrete and waterproof or restore surface. Chip, scrape, and grind high spots, ridges, and rough projections to finish concrete, using pneumatic chisels, power grinders, or hand tools. Spread roofing paper on surface of foundation and spread concrete onto roofing paper with trowel to form terrazzo base. Build wooden molds and clamp molds around area to be repaired, using hand tools. Sprinkle colored marble or stone chips, powdered steel, or coloring powder over surface to produce prescribed finish. Cut metal division strips and press them into terrazzo base so that top edges form desired design or pattern. Fabricate concrete beams, columns, and panels. Waterproof or restore concrete surfaces, using appropriate compounds.

GOE—Interest Area/Cluster: 02. Architecture and Construction. **Work Group:** 02.04. Construction Crafts. **Other Jobs in This Work Group:** Boilermakers; Brickmasons and Blockmasons; Carpet Installers; Commercial Divers; Construction Carpenters; Crane and Tower Operators; Drywall and Ceiling Tile Installers; Electricians; Fence Erectors; Floor Layers, Except Carpet, Wood, and Hard Tiles; Floor Sanders and Finishers; Glaziers; Hazardous Materials Removal Workers; Insulation Workers, Floor, Ceiling, and Wall; Insulation Workers, Mechanical; Manufactured Building and Mobile Home Installers; Operating Engineers and Other Construction Equipment Operators; Painters, Construction and Maintenance; Paperhangers; Paving, Surfacing, and Tamping Equipment Operators; Pile-Driver Operators; Pipe Fitters and Steamfitters; Pipelayers; Plasterers and Stucco Masons; Plumbers; Plumbers, Pipefitters, and Steamfitters; Rail-Track Laying and Maintenance Equipment Operators; Refractory Materials Repairers, Except Brickmasons; Reinforcing Iron and Rebar Workers; Riggers; Roofers; Rough Carpenters; Security and Fire Alarm Systems Installers; Segmental Pavers; Sheet Metal Workers; Stone Cutters and Carvers, Manufacturing; Stonemasons; Structural Iron and Steel Workers; Tapers; Terrazzo Workers and Finishers; Tile and Marble Setters.

Skills: Mathematics; Installation; Repairing; Equipment Maintenance; Equipment Selection; Coordination.

Education and Training Program: Concrete Finishing/Concrete Finisher. **Related Knowledge/Courses:** Building and Construction; Public Safety and Security; Mechanical Devices; Design; Engineering and Technology.

Work Environment: Outdoors; noisy; hazardous equipment; standing; using hands on objects, tools, or controls; bending or twisting the body.

Civil Drafters

- ❋ Personality Code: RCI
- ❋ Education/Training Required: Postsecondary vocational training
- ❋ Annual Earnings: $43,310
- ❋ Beginning Wage: $27,680
- ❋ Earnings Growth Potential: Medium
- ❋ Growth: 6.1%
- ❋ Annual Job Openings: 16,238
- ❋ Self-Employed: 5.0%
- ❋ Part-Time: 5.9%

The job openings listed here are shared with Architectural Drafters.

Prepare drawings and topographical and relief maps used in civil engineering projects such as highways, bridges, pipelines, flood control projects, and water and sewerage control systems. Produce drawings by using computer-assisted drafting systems (CAD) or drafting machines or by hand, using compasses, dividers, protractors, triangles, and other drafting devices. Draw maps, diagrams, and profiles, using cross-sections and surveys, to represent elevations, topographical contours, subsurface formations, and structures. Draft plans and detailed drawings for structures, installations, and construction projects such as highways, sewage disposal systems, and dikes, working from sketches or notes. Determine the order of work and method of presentation such as orthographic or isometric drawing. Finish and duplicate drawings and documentation packages according to required mediums and specifications for reproduction, using blueprinting, photography, or other duplication methods. Review rough sketches, drawings, specifications, and other engineering data received from civil engineers to ensure that they conform to design concepts. Calculate excavation tonnage and prepare graphs and fill-hauling diagrams for use in earth-moving operations. Supervise and train other technologists, technicians, and drafters. Correlate, interpret, and modify data obtained from topographical surveys, well logs, and geophysical prospecting reports. Determine quality, cost, strength, and quantity of required materials and enter figures on materials lists. Locate and identify symbols located on topographical surveys to denote geological and geophysical formations or oil field installations. Calculate weights, volumes, and stress factors and their implications for technical aspects of designs. Supervise or conduct field surveys, inspections, or technical investigations to obtain data required to revise construction drawings. Explain drawings to production or construction teams and provide adjustments as necessary. Plot characteristics of boreholes for oil and gas wells from photographic subsurface survey recordings and other data, representing depth, degree, and direction of inclination.

GOE—Interest Area/Cluster: 02. Architecture and Construction. **Work Group:** 02.03. Architecture/Construction Engineering Technologies. **Other Jobs in This Work Group:** Architectural and Civil Drafters; Architectural Drafters; Surveyors.

Skills: Programming; Systems Analysis; Mathematics; Quality Control Analysis; Systems Evaluation.

Education and Training Programs: Architectural Technology/Technician; Drafting and Design Technology/Technician, General; CAD/CADD Drafting and/or Design Technology/Technician; Architectural Drafting and Architectural CAD/CADD; Civil Drafting and Civil Engineering CAD/CADD. **Related Knowledge/Courses:** Design; Engineering and Technology; Building and Construction; Geography; Mathematics; Physics.

Work Environment: Indoors; sitting; repetitive motions.

Civil Engineering Technicians

- ❋ Personality Code: RCI
- ❋ Education/Training Required: Associate degree
- ❋ Annual Earnings: $42,580
- ❋ Beginning Wage: $25,390
- ❋ Earnings Growth Potential: High
- ❋ Growth: 10.2%
- ❋ Annual Job Openings: 7,499
- ❋ Self-Employed: 0.9%
- ❋ Part-Time: 5.9%

Apply theory and principles of civil engineering in planning, designing, and overseeing construction and maintenance of structures and facilities under the direction of engineering staff or physical scientists. Calculate dimensions, square footage, profile and component specifications, and material quantities, using calculator or computer. Draft detailed dimensional drawings and design layouts for projects and to ensure conformance to specifications. Analyze proposed site factors and design maps, graphs, tracings, and diagrams to illustrate findings. Read and review project blueprints and structural specifications to determine dimensions of structure or system and material requirements. Prepare reports and document project activities and data. Confer with supervisor to determine project details such as plan preparation, acceptance testing, and evaluation of field conditions. Inspect project site and evaluate contractor work to detect design malfunctions and ensure conformance to design specifications and applicable codes. Plan and conduct field surveys to locate new sites and analyze details of project sites. Develop plans and estimate costs for installation of systems, utilization of facilities, or construction of structures. Report maintenance problems occurring at project site to supervisor and negotiate changes to resolve system conflicts. Conduct materials test and analysis, using tools and equipment and applying engineering knowledge. Respond to public suggestions and complaints. Evaluate facility to determine suitability for occupancy and square footage availability.

GOE—Interest Area/Cluster: 15. Scientific Research, Engineering, and Mathematics. **Work Group:** 15.09. Engineering Technology. **Other Jobs in This Work Group:** Aerospace Engineering and Operations Technicians; Cartographers and Photogrammetrists; Electrical and Electronic Engineering Technicians; Electrical and Electronics Drafters; Electrical Drafters; Electrical Engineering Technicians; Electro-Mechanical Technicians; Electronic Drafters; Electronics Engineering Technicians; Environmental Engineering Technicians; Mapping Technicians; Mechanical Drafters; Mechanical Engineering Technicians; Surveying and Mapping Technicians; Surveying Technicians.

Skills: Mathematics; Science; Operations Analysis; Writing; Complex Problem Solving; Reading Comprehension; Technology Design; Active Learning.

Education and Training Programs: Civil Engineering Technology/Technician; Construction Engineering Technology/Technician. **Related Knowledge/Courses:** Building and Construction; Design; Engineering and Technology; Mathematics; Computers and Electronics; Transportation.

Work Environment: More often indoors than outdoors; sitting.

Civil Engineers

- ❋ Personality Code: RIC
- ❋ Education/Training Required: Bachelor's degree
- ❋ Annual Earnings: $71,710
- ❋ Beginning Wage: $46,420
- ❋ Earnings Growth Potential: Medium
- ❋ Growth: 18.0%
- ❋ Annual Job Openings: 15,979
- ❋ Self-Employed: 4.9%
- ❋ Part-Time: 3.2%

Perform engineering duties in planning, designing, and overseeing construction and maintenance of building structures and facilities such as roads, railroads, airports, bridges, harbors, channels, dams, irrigation projects, pipelines, power plants, water and sewage systems, and waste disposal units. Includes architectural, structural, traffic, ocean, and geo-technical engineers. Manage and direct staff members and the construction, operations, or maintenance activities at project site. Provide technical advice regarding design, construction, or program modifications and structural repairs to industrial and managerial personnel. Inspect project sites to monitor progress and ensure conformance to design specifications and safety or sanitation standards. Estimate quantities and cost of materials, equipment, or labor to determine project feasibility. Test soils and materials to determine the adequacy and strength of foundations, concrete, asphalt, or steel. Compute load and grade requirements, water flow rates, and material stress factors to determine design specifications. Plan and design transportation or hydraulic systems and structures, following construction and government standards and using design software and drawing tools. Analyze survey reports, maps, drawings, blueprints, aerial photography, and other topographical or geologic data to plan projects. Prepare or present public reports on topics such as bid proposals, deeds, environmental impact statements, or property and right-of-way descriptions. Direct or participate in surveying to lay out installations and establish reference points, grades, and elevations to guide construction. Conduct studies of traffic patterns or environmental conditions to identify engineering problems and assess the potential impact of projects.

GOE—Interest Area/Cluster: 15. Scientific Research, Engineering, and Mathematics. **Work Group:** 15.07. Research and Design Engineering. **Other Jobs in This Work Group:** Aerospace Engineers; Biomedical Engineers; Chemical Engineers; Computer Hardware Engineers; Electrical Engineers; Electronics Engineers, Except Computer; Marine Architects; Marine Engineers; Marine Engineers and

Naval Architects; Materials Engineers; Mechanical Engineers; Nuclear Engineers.

Skills: Management of Personnel Resources; Systems Analysis; Systems Evaluation; Management of Material Resources; Management of Financial Resources; Operation Monitoring; Negotiation; Complex Problem Solving.

Education and Training Programs: Civil Engineering, General; Transportation and Highway Engineering; Water Resources Engineering; Civil Engineering, Other. **Related Knowledge/Courses:** Engineering and Technology; Design; Building and Construction; Physics; Transportation; Geography.

Work Environment: More often outdoors than indoors; very hot or cold; contaminants; hazardous equipment; sitting.

Computer Support Specialists

- ❋ Personality Code: RIC
- ❋ Education/Training Required: Associate degree
- ❋ Annual Earnings: $42,400
- ❋ Beginning Wage: $25,950
- ❋ Earnings Growth Potential: Medium
- ❋ Growth: 12.9%
- ❋ Annual Job Openings: 97,334
- ❋ Self-Employed: 1.3%
- ❋ Part-Time: 6.9%

Provide technical assistance to computer system users. Answer questions or resolve computer problems for clients in person, via telephone, or from remote locations. May provide assistance concerning the use of computer hardware and software, including printing, installation, word processing, e-mail, and operating systems. Oversee the daily performance of computer systems. Answer user inquiries regarding computer software or hardware operation to resolve problems. Enter commands and observe system functioning to verify correct operations and detect errors. Set up equipment for employee use, performing or ensuring proper installation of cables, operating systems, or appropriate software. Install and perform minor repairs to hardware, software, or peripheral equipment, following design or installation specifications. Maintain records of daily data communication transactions, problems and remedial actions taken, or installation activities. Read technical manuals, confer with users, or conduct computer diagnostics to investigate and resolve problems or to provide technical assistance and support. Refer major hardware or software problems or defective products to vendors or technicians for service. Develop training materials and procedures or train users in the proper use of hardware or software. Confer with staff, users, and management to establish requirements for new systems or modifications. Prepare evaluations of software or hardware and recommend improvements or upgrades. Read trade magazines and technical manuals or attend conferences and seminars to maintain knowledge of hardware and software. Hire, supervise, and direct workers engaged in special project work, problem solving, monitoring, and installing data communication equipment and software. Inspect equipment and read order sheets to prepare for delivery to users. Modify and customize commercial programs for internal needs. Conduct office automation feasibility studies, including workflow analysis, space design, or cost comparison analysis.

GOE—Interest Area/Cluster: 11. Information Technology. **Work Group:** 11.02. Information Technology Specialties. **Other Jobs in This Work Group:** Computer and Information Scientists, Research; Computer Operators; Computer Programmers; Computer Security Specialists; Computer Software Engineers, Applications; Computer Software Engineers, Systems Software; Computer Systems Analysts; Computer Systems Engineers/Architects; Database Administrators; Network Designers; Network Systems and Data Communications Analysts; Software Quality Assurance Engineers and Testers; Web Administrators; Web Developers.

Skills: Programming; Installation; Systems Analysis; Operation Monitoring; Repairing;

Systems Evaluation; Troubleshooting; Operation and Control.

Education and Training Programs: Agricultural Business Technology; Data Processing and Data Processing Technology/Technician; Computer Hardware Technology/Technician; Computer Software Technology/Technician; Accounting and Computer Science; Medical Office Computer Specialist/Assistant. **Related Knowledge/Courses:** Computers and Electronics; Telecommunications; Engineering and Technology; Clerical Practices; Customer and Personal Service; Communications and Media.

Work Environment: Indoors; noisy; sitting; repetitive motions.

Construction and Building Inspectors

- ❋ Personality Code: RCI
- ❋ Education/Training Required: Work experience in a related occupation
- ❋ Annual Earnings: $48,330
- ❋ Beginning Wage: $30,450
- ❋ Earnings Growth Potential: Medium
- ❋ Growth: 18.2%
- ❋ Annual Job Openings: 12,606
- ❋ Self-Employed: 9.4%
- ❋ Part-Time: 4.6%

Inspect structures using engineering skills to determine structural soundness and compliance with specifications, building codes, and other regulations. Inspections may be general in nature or may be limited to a specific area, such as electrical systems or plumbing. Issue violation notices and stop-work orders, conferring with owners, violators, and authorities to explain regulations and recommend rectifications. Inspect bridges, dams, highways, buildings, wiring, plumbing, electrical circuits, sewers, heating systems, and foundations during and after construction for structural quality, general safety, and conformance to specifications and codes. Approve and sign plans that meet required specifications. Review and interpret plans, blueprints, site layouts, specifications, and construction methods to ensure compliance to legal requirements and safety regulations. Monitor installation of plumbing, wiring, equipment, and appliances to ensure that installation is performed properly and is in compliance with applicable regulations. Inspect and monitor construction sites to ensure adherence to safety standards, building codes, and specifications. Measure dimensions and verify level, alignment, and elevation of structures and fixtures to ensure compliance to building plans and codes. Maintain daily logs and supplement inspection records with photographs. Use survey instruments, metering devices, tape measures, and test equipment such as concrete strength measurers to perform inspections. Train, direct, and supervise other construction inspectors. Issue permits for construction, relocation, demolition, and occupancy. Examine lifting and conveying devices such as elevators, escalators, moving sidewalks, lifts and hoists, inclined railways, ski lifts, and amusement rides to ensure safety and proper functioning. Compute estimates of work completed or of needed renovations or upgrades and approve payment for contractors. Evaluate premises for cleanliness, including proper garbage disposal and lack of vermin infestation.

GOE—Interest Area/Cluster: 07. Government and Public Administration. **Work Group:** 07.03. Regulations Enforcement. **Other Jobs in This Work Group:** Agricultural Inspectors; Aviation Inspectors; Compliance Officers, Except Agriculture, Construction, Health and Safety, and Transportation; Environmental Compliance Inspectors; Equal Opportunity Representatives and Officers; Financial Examiners; Fire Inspectors; Fish and Game Wardens; Forest Fire Inspectors and Prevention Specialists; Freight and Cargo Inspectors; Government Property Inspectors and Investigators; Immigration and Customs Inspectors; Licensing Examiners and Inspectors; Nuclear Monitoring Technicians; Occupational Health and Safety Specialists; Occupational Health and Safety Technicians; Tax Examiners, Collectors, and Revenue Agents; Transportation Vehicle, Equipment, and Systems Inspectors, Except Aviation.

Skills: Quality Control Analysis; Systems Analysis; Systems Evaluation; Management of Personnel Resources; Operation Monitoring.

Education and Training Program: Building/Home/Construction Inspection/Inspector. **Related Knowledge/Courses:** Building and Construction; Engineering and Technology; Design; Physics; Public Safety and Security; Mechanical Devices.

Work Environment: More often outdoors than indoors; noisy; contaminants; hazardous equipment; standing.

Construction Carpenters

- ❋ Personality Code: RCI
- ❋ Education/Training Required: Long-term on-the-job training
- ❋ Annual Earnings: $37,660
- ❋ Beginning Wage: $23,370
- ❋ Earnings Growth Potential: Medium
- ❋ Growth: 10.3%
- ❋ Annual Job Openings: 223,225
- ❋ Self-Employed: 31.8%
- ❋ Part-Time: 6.1%

The job openings listed here are shared with Rough Carpenters.

Construct, erect, install, and repair structures and fixtures of wood, plywood, and wallboard, using carpenter's hand tools and power tools. Measure and mark cutting lines on materials, using ruler, pencil, chalk, and marking gauge. Follow established safety rules and regulations and maintain a safe and clean environment. Verify trueness of structure, using plumb bob and level. Shape or cut materials to specified measurements, using hand tools, machines, or power saw. Study specifications in blueprints, sketches, or building plans to prepare project layout and determine dimensions and materials required. Assemble and fasten materials to make framework or props, using hand tools and wood screws, nails, dowel pins, or glue. Build or repair cabinets, doors, frameworks, floors, and other wooden fixtures used in buildings, using woodworking machines, carpenter's hand tools, and power tools. Erect scaffolding and ladders for assembling structures above ground level. Remove damaged or defective parts or sections of structures and repair or replace, using hand tools. Install structures and fixtures, such as windows, frames, floorings, and trim, or hardware, using carpenter's hand and power tools. Select and order lumber and other required materials. Maintain records, document actions, and present written progress reports. Finish surfaces of woodwork or wallboard in houses and buildings, using paint, hand tools, and paneling. Prepare cost estimates for clients or employers. Arrange for subcontractors to deal with special areas such as heating and electrical wiring work. Inspect ceiling or floor tile, wall coverings, siding, glass, or woodwork to detect broken or damaged structures. Work with or remove hazardous material. Construct forms and chutes for pouring concrete. Cover sub-floors with building paper to keep out moisture and lay hardwood, parquet, and wood-strip-block floors by nailing floors to subfloor or cementing them to mastic or asphalt base. Fill cracks and other defects in plaster or plasterboard and sand patch, using patching plaster, trowel, and sanding tool. Perform minor plumbing, welding, or concrete mixing work. Apply shock-absorbing, sound-deadening, and decorative paneling to ceilings and walls.

GOE—Interest Area/Cluster: 02. Architecture and Construction. **Work Group:** 02.04. Construction Crafts. **Other Jobs in This Work Group:** Boilermakers; Brickmasons and Blockmasons; Carpet Installers; Cement Masons and Concrete Finishers; Commercial Divers; Crane and Tower Operators; Drywall and Ceiling Tile Installers; Electricians; Fence Erectors; Floor Layers, Except Carpet, Wood, and Hard Tiles; Floor Sanders and Finishers; Glaziers; Hazardous Materials Removal Workers; Insulation Workers, Floor, Ceiling, and Wall; Insulation Workers, Mechanical; Manufactured Building and Mobile Home Installers; Operating Engineers and Other Construction Equipment Operators; Painters, Construction and Maintenance; Paperhangers; Paving, Surfacing, and Tamping Equipment Operators;

Realistic-C

Pile-Driver Operators; Pipe Fitters and Steamfitters; Pipelayers; Plasterers and Stucco Masons; Plumbers; Plumbers, Pipefitters, and Steamfitters; Rail-Track Laying and Maintenance Equipment Operators; Refractory Materials Repairers, Except Brickmasons; Reinforcing Iron and Rebar Workers; Riggers; Roofers; Rough Carpenters; Security and Fire Alarm Systems Installers; Segmental Pavers; Sheet Metal Workers; Stone Cutters and Carvers, Manufacturing; Stonemasons; Structural Iron and Steel Workers; Tapers; Terrazzo Workers and Finishers; Tile and Marble Setters.

Skills: Management of Personnel Resources; Management of Material Resources; Management of Financial Resources; Repairing; Equipment Maintenance; Quality Control Analysis; Installation; Mathematics.

Education and Training Program: Carpentry/Carpenter. **Related Knowledge/Courses:** Building and Construction; Mechanical Devices; Design; Engineering and Technology; Production and Processing; Public Safety and Security.

Work Environment: Outdoors; noisy; hazardous equipment; standing; walking and running; using hands on objects, tools, or controls.

Correctional Officers and Jailers

- ❀ Personality Code: REC
- ❀ Education/Training Required: Moderate-term on-the-job training
- ❀ Annual Earnings: $36,970
- ❀ Beginning Wage: $24,820
- ❀ Earnings Growth Potential: Low
- ❀ Growth: 16.9%
- ❀ Annual Job Openings: 56,579
- ❀ Self-Employed: 0.0%
- ❀ Part-Time: 1.8%

Guard inmates in penal or rehabilitative institution in accordance with established regulations and procedures. May guard prisoners in transit between jail, courtroom, prison, or other point. Includes deputy sheriffs and police who spend the majority of their time guarding prisoners in correctional institutions. Conduct head counts to ensure that each prisoner is present. Monitor conduct of prisoners in housing unit or during work or recreational activities according to established policies, regulations, and procedures to prevent escape or violence. Inspect conditions of locks, window bars, grills, doors, and gates at correctional facilities to ensure security and help prevent escapes. Record information such as prisoner identification, charges, and incidences of inmate disturbance and keep daily logs of prisoner activities. Search prisoners and vehicles and conduct shakedowns of cells for valuables and contraband, such as weapons or drugs. Use weapons, handcuffs, and physical force to maintain discipline and order among prisoners. Guard facility entrances to screen visitors. Inspect mail for the presence of contraband. Maintain records of prisoners' identification and charges. Process or book convicted individuals into prison. Settle disputes between inmates. Conduct fire, safety, and sanitation inspections. Provide to supervisors oral and written reports of the quality and quantity of work performed by inmates, inmate disturbances and rule violations, and unusual occurrences. Participate in required job training. Take prisoners into custody and escort to locations within and outside of facility, such as visiting room, courtroom, or airport. Serve meals, distribute commissary items, and dispense prescribed medication to prisoners. Counsel inmates and respond to legitimate questions, concerns, and requests. Drive passenger vehicles and trucks used to transport inmates to other institutions, courtrooms, hospitals, and work sites. Use nondisciplinary tools and equipment such as a computer. Assign duties to inmates, providing instructions as needed. Investigate crimes that have occurred within an institution or assist police in their investigations of crimes and inmates. Issue clothing, tools, and other authorized items to inmates. Arrange daily schedules for prisoners, including library visits, work assignments, family visits, and counseling appointments. Search for and recapture escapees.

GOE—Interest Area/Cluster: 12. Law and Public Safety. **Work Group:** 12.04. Law Enforcement and Public Safety. **Other Jobs in This Work Group:** Bailiffs; Criminal Investigators and Special Agents; Detectives and Criminal Investigators; Fire Investigators; Forensic Science Technicians; Parking Enforcement Workers; Police and Sheriff's Patrol Officers; Police Detectives; Police Identification and Records Officers; Police Patrol Officers; Sheriffs and Deputy Sheriffs; Transit and Railroad Police.

Skills: None met the criteria.

Education and Training Programs: Corrections; Juvenile Corrections; Corrections and Criminal Justice, Other. **Related Knowledge/Courses:** Public Safety and Security; Psychology; Therapy and Counseling; Law and Government; Medicine and Dentistry; Sociology and Anthropology.

Work Environment: More often indoors than outdoors; noisy; contaminants; disease or infections; standing.

Drywall and Ceiling Tile Installers

- Personality Code: RC
- Education/Training Required: Moderate-term on-the-job training
- Annual Earnings: $36,520
- Beginning Wage: $23,480
- Earnings Growth Potential: Medium
- Growth: 7.3%
- Annual Job Openings: 30,945
- Self-Employed: 23.0%
- Part-Time: 6.1%

Apply plasterboard or other wallboard to ceilings or interior walls of buildings. Apply or mount acoustical tiles or blocks, strips, or sheets of shock-absorbing materials to ceilings and walls of buildings to reduce or reflect sound. Materials may be of decorative quality. Includes lathers who fasten wooden, metal, or rockboard lath to walls, ceilings, or partitions of buildings to provide support

base for plaster, fireproofing, or acoustical material. Inspect furrings, mechanical mountings, and masonry surface for plumbness and level, using spirit or water levels. Install metal lath where plaster applications will be exposed to weather or water or for curved or irregular surfaces. Install blanket insulation between studs and tack plastic moisture barriers over insulation. Coordinate work with drywall finishers who cover the seams between drywall panels. Trim rough edges from wallboard to maintain even joints, using knives. Seal joints between ceiling tiles and walls. Scribe and cut edges of tile to fit walls where wall molding is not specified. Read blueprints and other specifications to determine methods of installation, work procedures, and material and tool requirements. Nail channels or wood furring strips to surfaces to provide mounting for tile. Mount tile by using adhesives or by nailing, screwing, stapling, or wire-tying lath directly to structural frameworks. Measure and mark surfaces to lay out work according to blueprints and drawings, using tape measures, straightedges or squares, and marking devices. Hang drywall panels on metal frameworks of walls and ceilings in offices, schools, and other large buildings, using lifts or hoists to adjust panel heights when necessary. Install horizontal and vertical metal or wooden studs to frames so that wallboard can be attached to interior walls. Fasten metal or rockboard lath to the structural framework of walls, ceilings, and partitions of buildings, using nails, screws, staples, or wire-ties. Apply or mount acoustical tile or blocks, strips, or sheets of shock-absorbing materials to ceilings and walls of buildings to reduce reflection of sound or to decorate rooms. Apply cement to backs of tiles and press tiles into place, aligning them with layout marks or joints of previously laid tile. Hang dry lines (stretched string) to wall moldings in order to guide positioning of main runners. Assemble and install metal framing and decorative trim for windows, doorways, and vents. Fit and fasten wallboard or drywall into position on wood or metal frameworks, using glue, nails, or screws.

GOE—Interest Area/Cluster: 02. Architecture and Construction. **Work Group:** 02.04. Construction Crafts. **Other Jobs in This Work Group:**

Boilermakers; Brickmasons and Blockmasons; Carpet Installers; Cement Masons and Concrete Finishers; Commercial Divers; Construction Carpenters; Crane and Tower Operators; Electricians; Fence Erectors; Floor Layers, Except Carpet, Wood, and Hard Tiles; Floor Sanders and Finishers; Glaziers; Hazardous Materials Removal Workers; Insulation Workers, Floor, Ceiling, and Wall; Insulation Workers, Mechanical; Manufactured Building and Mobile Home Installers; Operating Engineers and Other Construction Equipment Operators; Painters, Construction and Maintenance; Paperhangers; Paving, Surfacing, and Tamping Equipment Operators; Pile-Driver Operators; Pipe Fitters and Steamfitters; Pipelayers; Plasterers and Stucco Masons; Plumbers; Plumbers, Pipefitters, and Steamfitters; Rail-Track Laying and Maintenance Equipment Operators; Refractory Materials Repairers, Except Brickmasons; Reinforcing Iron and Rebar Workers; Riggers; Roofers; Rough Carpenters; Security and Fire Alarm Systems Installers; Segmental Pavers; Sheet Metal Workers; Stone Cutters and Carvers, Manufacturing; Stonemasons; Structural Iron and Steel Workers; Tapers; Terrazzo Workers and Finishers; Tile and Marble Setters.

Skills: Installation; Management of Personnel Resources; Management of Material Resources; Management of Financial Resources; Mathematics; Repairing; Science; Equipment Selection.

Education and Training Program: Drywall Installation/Drywaller. **Related Knowledge/Courses:** Building and Construction; Design; Mechanical Devices; Mathematics; Production and Processing; Public Safety and Security.

Work Environment: Indoors; contaminants; hazardous equipment; minor burns, cuts, bites, or stings; standing; using hands on objects, tools, or controls.

Electrical and Electronic Engineering Technicians

See *Electrical Engineering Technicians (a Realistic job) and Electronics Engineering Technicians (a Realistic job), described separately.*

Electrical Engineering Technicians

- ❋ Personality Code: RIC
- ❋ Education/Training Required: Associate degree
- ❋ Annual Earnings: $52,140
- ❋ Beginning Wage: $31,310
- ❋ Earnings Growth Potential: High
- ❋ Growth: 3.6%
- ❋ Annual Job Openings: 12,583
- ❋ Self-Employed: 0.9%
- ❋ Part-Time: 5.9%

The job openings listed here are shared with Electronics Engineering Technicians.

Apply electrical theory and related knowledge to test and modify developmental or operational electrical machinery and electrical control equipment and circuitry in industrial or commercial plants and laboratories. Usually work under direction of engineering staff. Assemble electrical and electronic systems and prototypes according to engineering data and knowledge of electrical principles, using hand tools and measuring instruments. Provide technical assistance and resolution when electrical or engineering problems are encountered before, during, and after construction. Install and maintain electrical control systems and solid state equipment. Modify electrical prototypes, parts, assemblies, and systems to correct functional deviations. Set up and operate test equipment to evaluate performance of developmental parts, assemblies, or systems under simulated operating conditions and record results. Collaborate with electrical engineers and other personnel to identify, define, and solve developmental problems.

Build, calibrate, maintain, troubleshoot, and repair electrical instruments or testing equipment. Analyze and interpret test information to resolve design-related problems. Write commissioning procedures for electrical installations. Prepare project cost and work-time estimates. Evaluate engineering proposals, shop drawings, and design comments for sound electrical engineering practice and conformance with established safety and design criteria and recommend approval or disapproval. Draw or modify diagrams and write engineering specifications to clarify design details and functional criteria of experimental electronics units. Conduct inspections for quality control and assurance programs, reporting findings and recommendations. Prepare contracts and initiate, review, and coordinate modifications to contract specifications and plans throughout the construction process. Plan, schedule, and monitor work of support personnel to assist supervisor. Review existing electrical engineering criteria to identify necessary revisions, deletions, or amendments to outdated material. Perform supervisory duties such as recommending work assignments, approving leaves, and completing performance evaluations. Plan method and sequence of operations for developing and testing experimental electronic and electrical equipment. Visit construction sites to observe conditions impacting design and to identify solutions to technical design problems involving electrical systems equipment that arise during construction.

GOE—Interest Area/Cluster: 15. Scientific Research, Engineering, and Mathematics. **Work Group:** 15.09. Engineering Technology. **Other Jobs in This Work Group:** Aerospace Engineering and Operations Technicians; Cartographers and Photogrammetrists; Civil Engineering Technicians; Electrical and Electronic Engineering Technicians; Electrical and Electronics Drafters; Electrical Drafters; Electro-Mechanical Technicians; Electronic Drafters; Electronics Engineering Technicians; Environmental Engineering Technicians; Mapping Technicians; Mechanical Drafters; Mechanical Engineering Technicians; Surveying and Mapping Technicians; Surveying Technicians.

Skills: Repairing; Installation; Troubleshooting; Science; Operations Analysis; Technology Design; Mathematics; Equipment Maintenance.

Education and Training Programs: Electrical, Electronic, and Communications Engineering Technology/Technician; Telecommunications Technology/Technician; Electrical and Electronic Engineering Technologies/Technicians, Other; Computer Engineering Technology/Technician; Computer Technology/Computer Systems Technology. **Related Knowledge/Courses:** Engineering and Technology; Design; Computers and Electronics; Physics; Mechanical Devices; Telecommunications.

Work Environment: Indoors; noisy; sitting; using hands on objects, tools, or controls.

Electrical Power-Line Installers and Repairers

- ✼ Personality Code: RIC
- ✼ Education/Training Required: Long-term on-the-job training
- ✼ Annual Earnings: $52,570
- ✼ Beginning Wage: $29,780
- ✼ Earnings Growth Potential: High
- ✼ Growth: 7.2%
- ✼ Annual Job Openings: 6,401
- ✼ Self-Employed: 0.6%
- ✼ Part-Time: 1.3%

Install or repair cables or wires used in electrical power or distribution systems. May erect poles and light- or heavy-duty transmission towers. Adhere to safety practices and procedures, such as checking equipment regularly and erecting barriers around work areas. Open switches or attach grounding devices to remove electrical hazards from disturbed or fallen lines or to facilitate repairs. Climb poles or use truck-mounted buckets to access equipment. Place insulating or fireproofing materials over conductors and joints. Install, maintain, and repair electrical distribution and transmission systems, including conduits; cables; wires; and related

Realistic-E

equipment such as transformers, circuit breakers, and switches. Identify defective sectionalizing devices, circuit breakers, fuses, voltage regulators, transformers, switches, relays, or wiring, using wiring diagrams and electrical-testing instruments. Drive vehicles equipped with tools and materials to job sites. Coordinate work assignment preparation and completion with other workers. String wire conductors and cables between poles, towers, trenches, pylons, and buildings, setting lines in place and using winches to adjust tension. Inspect and test power lines and auxiliary equipment to locate and identify problems, using reading and testing instruments. Test conductors according to electrical diagrams and specifications to identify corresponding conductors and to prevent incorrect connections. Replace damaged poles with new poles and straighten the poles. Install watt-hour meters and connect service drops between power lines and consumers' facilities. Attach crossarms, insulators, and auxiliary equipment to poles prior to installing them. Travel in trucks, helicopters, and airplanes to inspect lines for freedom from obstruction and adequacy of insulation. Dig holes, using augers, and set poles, using cranes and power equipment. Trim trees that could be hazardous to the functioning of cables or wires. Splice or solder cables together or to overhead transmission lines, customer service lines, or street light lines, using hand tools, epoxies, or specialized equipment. Cut and peel lead sheathing and insulation from defective or newly installed cables and conduits prior to splicing.

GOE—Interest Area/Cluster: 02. Architecture and Construction. **Work Group:** 02.05. Systems and Equipment Installation, Maintenance, and Repair. **Other Jobs in This Work Group:** Electrical and Electronics Repairers, Powerhouse, Substation, and Relay; Elevator Installers and Repairers; Heating and Air Conditioning Mechanics and Installers; Maintenance and Repair Workers, General; Refrigeration Mechanics and Installers; Telecommunications Equipment Installers and Repairers, Except Line Installers; Telecommunications Line Installers and Repairers.

Skills: Repairing; Installation; Equipment Maintenance; Operation Monitoring; Troubleshooting; Operation and Control; Equipment Selection; Technology Design.

Education and Training Programs: Electrical and Power Transmission Installation/Installer, General; Lineworker; Electrical and Power Transmission Installers, Other. **Related Knowledge/Courses:** Building and Construction; Mechanical Devices; Customer and Personal Service; Engineering and Technology; Transportation; Design.

Work Environment: Outdoors; very hot or cold; high places; hazardous conditions; hazardous equipment; using hands on objects, tools, or controls.

Electricians

- ❀ Personality Code: RIC
- ❀ Education/Training Required: Long-term on-the-job training
- ❀ Annual Earnings: $44,780
- ❀ Beginning Wage: $27,330
- ❀ Earnings Growth Potential: Medium
- ❀ Growth: 7.4%
- ❀ Annual Job Openings: 79,083
- ❀ Self-Employed: 10.7%
- ❀ Part-Time: 2.3%

Install, maintain, and repair electrical wiring, equipment, and fixtures. Ensure that work is in accordance with relevant codes. May install or service street lights, intercom systems, or electrical control systems. Maintain current electrician's license or identification card to meet governmental regulations. Connect wires to circuit breakers, transformers, or other components. Repair or replace wiring, equipment, and fixtures, using hand tools and power tools. Assemble, install, test, and maintain electrical or electronic wiring, equipment, appliances, apparatus, and fixtures, using hand tools and power tools. Test electrical systems and continuity of circuits in electrical wiring, equipment, and fixtures, using testing devices such as ohmmeters, voltmeters, and oscilloscopes, to ensure compatibility and safety of system. Use a variety of tools and equipment such as power construction equipment, measuring devices, power tools, and testing equipment, including oscilloscopes, ammeters, and test lamps. Plan layout and installation of electrical wiring, equipment, and fixtures based on job specifications and local codes. Inspect electrical systems, equipment, and components to identify hazards, defects, and the need for adjustment or repair and to ensure compliance with codes. Direct and train workers to install, maintain, or repair electrical wiring, equipment, and fixtures. Diagnose malfunctioning systems, apparatus, and components, using test equipment and hand tools, to locate the cause of a breakdown and correct the problem. Prepare sketches or follow blueprints to determine the location of wiring and equipment and to ensure conformance to building and safety codes. Install ground leads and connect power cables to equipment such as motors. Work from ladders, scaffolds, and roofs to install, maintain, or repair electrical wiring, equipment, and fixtures. Perform business management duties such as maintaining records and files, preparing reports, and ordering supplies and equipment. Fasten small metal or plastic boxes to walls to house electrical switches or outlets. Place conduit, pipes, or tubing inside designated partitions, walls, or other concealed areas and pull insulated wires or cables through the conduit to complete circuits between boxes. Advise management on whether continued operation of equipment could be hazardous.

GOE—Interest Area/Cluster: 02. Architecture and Construction. **Work Group:** 02.04. Construction Crafts. **Other Jobs in This Work Group:** Boilermakers; Brickmasons and Blockmasons; Carpet Installers; Cement Masons and Concrete Finishers; Commercial Divers; Construction Carpenters; Crane and Tower Operators; Drywall and Ceiling Tile Installers; Fence Erectors; Floor Layers, Except Carpet, Wood, and Hard Tiles; Floor Sanders and Finishers; Glaziers; Hazardous Materials Removal Workers; Insulation Workers, Floor, Ceiling, and Wall; Insulation Workers, Mechanical; Manufactured Building and Mobile Home Installers; Operating Engineers and Other Construction Equipment Operators; Painters, Construction and Maintenance; Paperhangers; Paving, Surfacing, and Tamping Equipment Operators; Pile-Driver Operators; Pipe Fitters and Steamfitters; Pipelayers; Plasterers and Stucco Masons; Plumbers; Plumbers, Pipefitters, and Steamfitters; Rail-Track Laying and Maintenance Equipment Operators; Refractory Materials Repairers, Except Brickmasons; Reinforcing Iron and Rebar Workers; Riggers; Roofers; Rough Carpenters; Security and Fire Alarm Systems Installers; Segmental Pavers; Sheet Metal Workers; Stone Cutters and Carvers, Manufacturing; Stonemasons; Structural Iron and Steel Workers; Tapers; Terrazzo Workers and Finishers; Tile and Marble Setters.

Skills: Repairing; Operation Monitoring; Installation; Equipment Maintenance; Troubleshooting; Operation and Control; Quality Control Analysis.

Education and Training Program: Electrician. **Related Knowledge/Courses:** Building and Construction; Mechanical Devices; Design; Physics; Telecommunications; Engineering and Technology.

Work Environment: Outdoors; noisy; minor burns, cuts, bites, or stings; standing; walking and running; using hands on objects, tools, or controls.

Electronics Engineering Technicians

- ✳ Personality Code: RI
- ✳ Education/Training Required: Associate degree
- ✳ Annual Earnings: $52,140
- ✳ Beginning Wage: $31,310
- ✳ Earnings Growth Potential: High
- ✳ Growth: 3.6%
- ✳ Annual Job Openings: 12,583
- ✳ Self-Employed: 0.9%
- ✳ Part-Time: 5.9%

The job openings listed here are shared with Electrical Engineering Technicians.

Realistic-E

Lay out, build, test, troubleshoot, repair, and modify developmental and production electronic components, parts, equipment, and systems, such as computer equipment, missile control instrumentation, electron tubes, test equipment, and machine tool numerical controls, applying principles and theories of electronics, electrical circuitry, engineering mathematics, electronic and electrical testing, and physics. Usually work under direction of engineering staff. Read blueprints, wiring diagrams, schematic drawings, and engineering instructions for assembling electronics units, applying knowledge of electronic theory and components. Test electronics units, using standard test equipment, and analyze results to evaluate performance and determine need for adjustment. Perform preventative maintenance and calibration of equipment and systems. Assemble, test, and maintain circuitry or electronic components according to engineering instructions, technical manuals, and knowledge of electronics, using hand and power tools. Adjust and replace defective or improperly functioning circuitry and electronics components, using hand tools and soldering iron. Write reports and record data on testing techniques, laboratory equipment, and specifications to assist engineers. Identify and resolve equipment malfunctions, working with manufacturers and field representatives as necessary to procure replacement parts. Provide user applications and engineering support and recommendations for new and existing equipment with regard to installation, upgrades, and enhancement. Maintain system logs and manuals to document testing and operation of equipment. Provide customer support and education, working with users to identify needs, determine sources of problems, and provide information on product use. Maintain working knowledge of state-of-the-art tools or software by reading or by attending conferences, workshops, or other training. Build prototypes from rough sketches or plans. Design basic circuitry and draft sketches for clarification of details and design documentation under engineers' direction, using drafting instruments and computer-aided design (CAD) equipment. Procure parts and maintain inventory and related documentation.

Research equipment and component needs, sources, competitive prices, delivery times, and ongoing operational costs. Write computer or microprocessor software programs. Fabricate parts such as coils, terminal boards, and chassis, using bench lathes, drills, or other machine tools. Develop and upgrade preventative maintenance procedures for components, equipment, parts, and systems.

GOE—Interest Area/Cluster: 15. Scientific Research, Engineering, and Mathematics. **Work Group:** 15.09. Engineering Technology. **Other Jobs in This Work Group:** Aerospace Engineering and Operations Technicians; Cartographers and Photogrammetrists; Civil Engineering Technicians; Electrical and Electronic Engineering Technicians; Electrical and Electronics Drafters; Electrical Drafters; Electrical Engineering Technicians; Electro-Mechanical Technicians; Electronic Drafters; Environmental Engineering Technicians; Mapping Technicians; Mechanical Drafters; Mechanical Engineering Technicians; Surveying and Mapping Technicians; Surveying Technicians.

Skills: Repairing; Troubleshooting; Operation Monitoring; Equipment Maintenance; Systems Analysis; Quality Control Analysis; Systems Evaluation; Operation and Control.

Education and Training Programs: Electrical, Electronic, and Communications Engineering Technology/Technician; Telecommunications Technology/Technician; Electrical and Electronic Engineering Technologies/Technicians, Other; Computer Engineering Technology/Technician. **Related Knowledge/Courses:** Telecommunications; Engineering and Technology; Design; Mechanical Devices; Computers and Electronics; Physics.

Work Environment: Indoors; contaminants; hazardous conditions; hazardous equipment; sitting; using hands on objects, tools, or controls.

Fire Fighters

See Forest Fire Fighters (a Realistic job) and Municipal Fire Fighters (a Realistic job), described separately.

Forest Fire Fighters

- ❋ Personality Code: RS
- ❋ Education/Training Required: Long-term on-the-job training
- ❋ Annual Earnings: $43,170
- ❋ Beginning Wage: $21,530
- ❋ Earnings Growth Potential: Very high
- ❋ Growth: 12.1%
- ❋ Annual Job Openings: 18,887
- ❋ Self-Employed: 0.0%
- ❋ Part-Time: 1.3%

The job openings listed here are shared with Municipal Fire Fighters.

Control and suppress fires in forests or vacant public land. Maintain contact with fire dispatchers at all times to notify them of the need for additional firefighters and supplies or to detail any difficulties encountered. Rescue fire victims and administer emergency medical aid. Collaborate with other firefighters as a member of a firefighting crew. Patrol burned areas after fires to locate and eliminate hot spots that may restart fires. Extinguish flames and embers to suppress fires, using shovels or engine- or hand-driven water or chemical pumps. Fell trees, cut and clear brush, and dig trenches to create firelines, using axes, chain saws, or shovels. Maintain knowledge of current firefighting practices by participating in drills and by attending seminars, conventions, and conferences. Operate pumps connected to high-pressure hoses. Participate in physical training to maintain high levels of physical fitness. Establish water supplies, connect hoses, and direct water onto fires. Maintain fire equipment and firehouse living quarters. Inform and educate the public about fire prevention. Take action to contain any hazardous chemicals that could catch fire, leak, or spill. Organize fire caches, positioning equipment for the most effective response. Transport personnel and cargo to and from fire areas. Participate in fire prevention and inspection programs. Perform forest maintenance and improvement tasks such as cutting brush, planting trees, building trails, and marking timber. Test and maintain tools, equipment, jump gear, and parachutes to ensure readiness for fire-suppression activities. Observe forest areas from fire lookout towers to spot potential problems. Orient self in relation to fire, using compass and map, and collect supplies and equipment dropped by parachute. Serve as fully trained lead helicopter crewmember and as helispot manager. Drop weighted paper streamers from aircraft to determine the speed and direction of the wind at fire sites.

GOE—Interest Area/Cluster: 12. Law and Public Safety. **Work Group:** 12.06. Emergency Responding. **Other Jobs in This Work Group:** Emergency Medical Technicians and Paramedics; Fire Fighters; Municipal Fire Fighters.

Skills: Repairing; Equipment Maintenance; Management of Personnel Resources; Operation Monitoring; Equipment Selection; Operation and Control; Systems Analysis; Operations Analysis.

Education and Training Programs: Fire Science/Firefighting; Fire Protection, Other. **Related Knowledge/Courses:** Geography; Customer and Personal Service; Mechanical Devices; Public Safety and Security; Education and Training; Psychology.

Work Environment: Outdoors; very hot or cold; contaminants; hazardous conditions; minor burns, cuts, bites, or stings; using hands on objects, tools, or controls.

Freight and Cargo Inspectors

- ❋ Personality Code: RC
- ❋ Education/Training Required: Work experience in a related occupation
- ❋ Annual Earnings: $51,440
- ❋ Beginning Wage: $27,340
- ❋ Earnings Growth Potential: High
- ❋ Growth: 16.4%
- ❋ Annual Job Openings: 2,122
- ❋ Self-Employed: 5.9%
- ❋ Part-Time: 3.7%

The job openings listed here are shared with Aviation Inspectors and with Transportation Vehicle, Equipment, and Systems Inspectors, Except Aviation.

Inspect the handling, storage, and stowing of freight and cargoes. Prepare and submit reports after completion of freight shipments. Inspect shipments to ensure that freight is securely braced and blocked. Record details about freight conditions, handling of freight, and any problems encountered. Advise crews in techniques of stowing dangerous and heavy cargo. Observe loading of freight to ensure that crews comply with procedures. Recommend remedial procedures to correct any violations found during inspections. Inspect loaded cargo, cargo lashed to decks or in storage facilities, and cargo handling devices to determine compliance with health and safety regulations and need for maintenance. Measure ships' holds and depths of fuel and water in tanks, using sounding lines and tape measures. Notify workers of any special treatment required for shipments. Direct crews to reload freight or to insert additional bracing or packing as necessary. Check temperatures and humidities of shipping and storage areas to ensure that they are at appropriate levels to protect cargo. Determine cargo transportation capabilities by reading documents that set forth cargo loading and securing procedures, capacities, and stability factors. Read draft markings to determine depths of vessels in water. Issue certificates of compliance for vessels without violations. Write certificates of admeasurement that list details such as designs, lengths, depths, and breadths of vessels, and methods of propulsion. Calculate gross and net tonnage, hold capacities, volumes of stored fuel and water, cargo weights, and ship stability factors, using mathematical formulas. Post warning signs on vehicles containing explosives or flammable or radioactive materials. Measure heights and widths of loads to ensure they will pass over bridges or through tunnels on scheduled routes. Time rolls of ships, using stopwatches. Determine types of licenses and safety equipment required, and compute applicable fees such as tolls and wharfage fees.

GOE—Interest Area/Cluster: 07. Government and Public Administration. **Work Group:** 07.03. Regulations Enforcement. **Other Jobs in This Work Group:** Agricultural Inspectors; Aviation Inspectors; Compliance Officers, Except Agriculture, Construction, Health and Safety, and Transportation; Construction and Building Inspectors; Environmental Compliance Inspectors; Equal Opportunity Representatives and Officers; Financial Examiners; Fire Inspectors; Fish and Game Wardens; Forest Fire Inspectors and Prevention Specialists; Government Property Inspectors and Investigators; Immigration and Customs Inspectors; Licensing Examiners and Inspectors; Nuclear Monitoring Technicians; Occupational Health and Safety Specialists; Occupational Health and Safety Technicians; Tax Examiners, Collectors, and Revenue Agents; Transportation Vehicle, Equipment, and Systems Inspectors, Except Aviation.

Skills: Operation Monitoring; Quality Control Analysis; Science; Mathematics; Writing; Service Orientation; Equipment Selection; Troubleshooting.

Education and Training Programs: No related CIP programs; this job is learned through work experience in a related occupation. **Related Knowledge/Courses:** Transportation; Engineering and Technology; Public Safety and Security; Physics; Geography; Mechanical Devices.

Work Environment: Outdoors; standing; walking and running; using hands on objects, tools, or controls.

Heating and Air Conditioning Mechanics and Installers

❀ Personality Code: RCI
❀ Education/Training Required: Long-term on-the-job training
❀ Annual Earnings: $38,360
❀ Beginning Wage: $24,240
❀ Earnings Growth Potential: Medium
❀ Growth: 8.7%
❀ Annual Job Openings: 29,719
❀ Self-Employed: 12.7%
❀ Part-Time: 3.6%

The job openings listed here are shared with Refrigeration Mechanics and Installers.

Install, service, and repair heating and air conditioning systems in residences and commercial establishments. Obtain and maintain required certifications. Comply with all applicable standards, policies, and procedures, including safety procedures and the maintenance of a clean work area. Repair or replace defective equipment, components, or wiring. Test electrical circuits and components for continuity, using electrical test equipment. Reassemble and test equipment following repairs. Inspect and test system to verify system compliance with plans and specifications and to detect and locate malfunctions. Discuss heating-cooling system malfunctions with users to isolate problems or to verify that malfunctions have been corrected. Test pipe or tubing joints and connections for leaks, using pressure gauge or soap-and-water solution. Record and report all faults, deficiencies, and other unusual occurrences, as well as the time and materials expended on work orders. Adjust system controls to setting recommended by manufacturer to balance system, using hand tools. Recommend, develop, and perform preventive and general maintenance procedures such as cleaning, power-washing, and vacuuming equipment; oiling parts; and changing filters. Lay out and connect electrical wiring between controls and equipment according to wiring diagram, using electrician's hand tools. Install auxiliary components to heating-cooling equipment, such as expansion and discharge valves, air ducts, pipes, blowers, dampers, flues, and stokers, following blueprints. Assist with other work in coordination with repair and maintenance teams. Install, connect, and adjust thermostats, humidistats, and timers, using hand tools. Generate work orders that address deficiencies in need of correction. Join pipes or tubing to equipment and to fuel, water, or refrigerant source to form complete circuit. Assemble, position, and mount heating or cooling equipment, following blueprints. Study blueprints, design specifications, and manufacturers' recommendations to ascertain the configuration of heating or cooling equipment components and to ensure the proper installation of components. Cut and drill holes in floors, walls, and roof to install equipment, using power saws and drills.

GOE—Interest Area/Cluster: 02. Architecture and Construction. **Work Group:** 02.05. Systems and Equipment Installation, Maintenance, and Repair. **Other Jobs in This Work Group:** Electrical and Electronics Repairers, Powerhouse, Substation, and Relay; Electrical Power-Line Installers and Repairers; Elevator Installers and Repairers; Maintenance and Repair Workers, General; Refrigeration Mechanics and Installers; Telecommunications Equipment Installers and Repairers, Except Line Installers; Telecommunications Line Installers and Repairers.

Skills: Repairing; Installation; Equipment Maintenance; Troubleshooting; Systems Evaluation; Science; Systems Analysis; Coordination.

Education and Training Programs: Heating, Air Conditioning, and Refrigeration Technology/Technician (ACH/ACR/ACHR/HRAC/HVAC); Solar Energy Technology/Technician; Heating, Air Conditioning, Ventilation, and Refrigeration Maintenance Technology/Technician. **Related Knowledge/Courses:** Mechanical Devices; Building and Construction; Design; Physics; Engineering and Technology; Sales and Marketing.

Realistic—H

Work Environment: Outdoors; very hot or cold; contaminants; hazardous conditions; minor burns, cuts, bites, or stings; using hands on objects, tools, or controls.

Heating, Air Conditioning, and Refrigeration Mechanics and Installers

See *Heating and Air Conditioning Mechanics and Installers (a Realistic job) and Refrigeration Mechanics and Installers (a Realistic job), described separately.*

Industrial Machinery Mechanics

- ❋ Personality Code: RIC
- ❋ Education/Training Required: Long-term on-the-job training
- ❋ Annual Earnings: $42,350
- ❋ Beginning Wage: $27,650
- ❋ Earnings Growth Potential: Low
- ❋ Growth: 9.0%
- ❋ Annual Job Openings: 23,361
- ❋ Self-Employed: 2.5%
- ❋ Part-Time: 1.7%

Repair, install, adjust, or maintain industrial production and processing machinery or refinery and pipeline distribution systems. Disassemble machinery and equipment to remove parts and make repairs. Repair and replace broken or malfunctioning components of machinery and equipment. Repair and maintain the operating condition of industrial production and processing machinery and equipment. Examine parts for defects such as breakage and excessive wear. Reassemble equipment after completion of inspections, testing, or repairs. Observe and test the operation of machinery and equipment to diagnose malfunctions, using voltmeters and other testing devices. Operate newly repaired machinery and equipment to verify the adequacy of repairs. Clean, lubricate, and adjust parts, equipment, and machinery. Analyze test results, machine error messages, and information obtained from operators to diagnose equipment problems. Record repairs and maintenance performed. Study blueprints and manufacturers' manuals to determine correct installation and operation of machinery. Record parts and materials used, ordering or requisitioning new parts and materials as necessary. Cut and weld metal to repair broken metal parts, fabricate new parts, and assemble new equipment. Demonstrate equipment functions and features to machine operators. Enter codes and instructions to program computer-controlled machinery.

GOE—Interest Area/Cluster: 13. Manufacturing. **Work Group:** 13.13. Machinery Repair. **Other Jobs in This Work Group:** Bicycle Repairers; Control and Valve Installers and Repairers, Except Mechanical Door; Home Appliance Repairers; Locksmiths and Safe Repairers; Maintenance Workers, Machinery; Mechanical Door Repairers; Millwrights; Signal and Track Switch Repairers.

Skills: Installation; Repairing; Equipment Maintenance; Operation Monitoring; Troubleshooting; Technology Design; Equipment Selection; Operation and Control.

Education and Training Programs: Industrial Mechanics and Maintenance Technology; Heavy/Industrial Equipment Maintenance Technologies, Other. **Related Knowledge/Courses:** Mechanical Devices; Engineering and Technology; Building and Construction; Design; Chemistry; Physics.

Work Environment: Noisy; contaminants; hazardous conditions; hazardous equipment; standing; using hands on objects, tools, or controls.

Maintenance and Repair Workers, General

* ❋ Personality Code: RCI
* ❋ Education/Training Required: Moderate-term on-the-job training
* ❋ Annual Earnings: $32,570
* ❋ Beginning Wage: $19,590
* ❋ Earnings Growth Potential: Medium
* ❋ Growth: 10.1%
* ❋ Annual Job Openings: 165,502
* ❋ Self-Employed: 1.5%
* ❋ Part-Time: 5.2%

Perform work involving the skills of two or more maintenance or craft occupations to keep machines, mechanical equipment, or the structure of an establishment in repair. Duties may involve pipe fitting; boiler making; insulating; welding; machining; carpentry; repairing electrical or mechanical equipment; installing, aligning, and balancing new equipment; and repairing buildings, floors, or stairs. Repair or replace defective equipment parts, using hand tools and power tools, and reassemble equipment. Perform routine preventive maintenance to ensure that machines continue to run smoothly, building systems operate efficiently, and the physical condition of buildings does not deteriorate. Inspect drives, motors, and belts; check fluid levels; replace filters; and perform other maintenance actions, following checklists. Use tools ranging from common hand and power tools, such as hammers, hoists, saws, drills, and wrenches, to precision measuring instruments and electrical and electronic testing devices. Assemble, install, or repair wiring, electrical and electronic components, pipe systems and plumbing, machinery, and equipment. Diagnose mechanical problems and determine how to correct them, checking blueprints, repair manuals, and parts catalogs as necessary. Inspect, operate, and test machinery and equipment to diagnose machine malfunctions. Record maintenance and repair work performed and the costs of the work. Clean and lubricate shafts, bearings, gears, and other parts of machinery. Dismantle devices to gain access to and remove defective parts, using hoists, cranes, hand tools, and power tools. Plan and lay out repair work, using diagrams, drawings, blueprints, maintenance manuals, and schematic diagrams. Adjust functional parts of devices and control instruments, using hand tools, levels, plumb bobs, and straightedges. Order parts, supplies, and equipment from catalogs and suppliers or obtain them from storerooms. Paint and repair roofs, windows, doors, floors, woodwork, plaster, drywall, and other parts of building structures. Operate cutting torches or welding equipment to cut or join metal parts. Align and balance new equipment after installation. Inspect used parts to determine changes in dimensional requirements, using rules, calipers, micrometers, and other measuring instruments. Set up and operate machine tools to repair or fabricate machine parts, jigs and fixtures, and tools. Maintain and repair specialized equipment and machinery found in cafeterias, laundries, hospitals, stores, offices, and factories.

GOE—Interest Area/Cluster: 02. Architecture and Construction. **Work Group:** 02.05. Systems and Equipment Installation, Maintenance, and Repair. **Other Jobs in This Work Group:** Electrical and Electronics Repairers, Powerhouse, Substation, and Relay; Electrical Power-Line Installers and Repairers; Elevator Installers and Repairers; Heating and Air Conditioning Mechanics and Installers; Refrigeration Mechanics and Installers; Telecommunications Equipment Installers and Repairers, Except Line Installers; Telecommunications Line Installers and Repairers.

Skills: Equipment Maintenance; Installation; Repairing; Troubleshooting; Operation Monitoring; Operation and Control; Equipment Selection; Technology Design.

Education and Training Program: Building/Construction Site Management/Manager. **Related Knowledge/Courses:** Building and Construction; Mechanical Devices; Design; Physics; Engineering and Technology; Public Safety and Security.

Realistic-M

Work Environment: Indoors; noisy; minor burns, cuts, bites, or stings; standing; walking and running; using hands on objects, tools, or controls.

Mates—Ship, Boat, and Barge

- ❋ Personality Code: ERC
- ❋ Education/Training Required: Work experience in a related occupation
- ❋ Annual Earnings: $57,210
- ❋ Beginning Wage: $29,530
- ❋ Earnings Growth Potential: High
- ❋ Growth: 17.9%
- ❋ Annual Job Openings: 2,665
- ❋ Self-Employed: 6.8%
- ❋ Part-Time: 4.8%

The job openings listed here are shared with Pilots, Ship, and with Ship and Boat Captains.

Supervise and coordinate activities of crew aboard ships, boats, barges, or dredges. Determine geographical position of ship, using lorans, azimuths of celestial bodies, or computers, and use this information to determine the course and speed of the ship. Observe water from ship's masthead to advise on navigational direction. Supervise crews in cleaning and maintaining decks, superstructures, and bridges. Supervise crew members in the repair or replacement of defective gear and equipment. Steer vessels, using navigational devices such as compasses and sextants and navigational aids such as lighthouses and buoys. Inspect equipment such as cargo-handling gear, life-saving equipment, visual-signaling equipment, and fishing, towing, or dredging gear to detect problems. Arrange for ships to be stocked, fueled, and repaired. Assume command of vessel in the event that ship's master becomes incapacitated. Participate in activities related to maintenance of vessel security. Stand watches on vessel during specified periods while vessel is under way. Observe loading and unloading of cargo and equipment to ensure that handling and storage are performed according to specifications.

GOE—Interest Area/Cluster: 16. Transportation, Distribution, and Logistics. **Work Group:** 16.05. Water Vehicle Operation. **Other Jobs in This Work Group:** Captains, Mates, and Pilots of Water Vessels; Dredge Operators; Motorboat Operators; Pilots, Ship; Sailors and Marine Oilers; Ship and Boat Captains.

Skills: Equipment Maintenance; Repairing; Operation and Control; Operation Monitoring; Troubleshooting; Installation; Equipment Selection; Judgment and Decision Making.

Education and Training Programs: Commercial Fishing; Marine Science/Merchant Marine Officer; Marine Transportation, Other. **Related Knowledge/Courses:** Geography; Transportation; Public Safety and Security; Telecommunications; Personnel and Human Resources; Mechanical Devices.

Work Environment: More often outdoors than indoors; very hot or cold; standing; using hands on objects, tools, or controls.

Mechanical Drafters

- ❋ Personality Code: RCI
- ❋ Education/Training Required: Postsecondary vocational training
- ❋ Annual Earnings: $44,740
- ❋ Beginning Wage: $28,540
- ❋ Earnings Growth Potential: Medium
- ❋ Growth: 5.2%
- ❋ Annual Job Openings: 10,902
- ❋ Self-Employed: 5.5%
- ❋ Part-Time: 5.9%

Prepare detailed working diagrams of machinery and mechanical devices, including dimensions, fastening methods, and other engineering information. Develop detailed design drawings and specifications for mechanical equipment, dies, tools, and controls, using computer-assisted drafting (CAD) equipment. Coordinate with and consult other workers to design, lay out, or detail components and systems and to resolve design or other problems. Review and analyze specifications, sketches, drawings, ideas, and related data to assess factors affecting component designs and the procedures and instructions to be followed. Position instructions and comments onto drawings. Compute mathematical formulas to develop and design detailed specifications for components or machinery, using computer-assisted equipment. Modify and revise designs to correct operating deficiencies or to reduce production problems. Design scale or full-size blueprints of specialty items such as furniture and automobile body or chassis components. Check dimensions of materials to be used and assign numbers to the materials. Lay out and draw schematic, orthographic, or angle views to depict functional relationships of components, assemblies, systems, and machines. Confer with customer representatives to review schematics and answer questions pertaining to installation of systems. Draw freehand sketches of designs, trace finished drawings onto designated paper for the reproduction of blueprints, and reproduce working drawings on copy machines. Supervise and train other drafters, technologists, and technicians. Lay out, draw, and reproduce illustrations for reference manuals and technical publications to describe operation and maintenance of mechanical systems. Shade or color drawings to clarify and emphasize details and dimensions or eliminate background, using ink, crayon, airbrush, and overlays.

GOE—Interest Area/Cluster: 15. Scientific Research, Engineering, and Mathematics. **Work Group:** 15.09. Engineering Technology. **Other Jobs in This Work Group:** Aerospace Engineering and Operations Technicians; Cartographers and Photogrammetrists; Civil Engineering Technicians; Electrical and Electronic Engineering Technicians; Electrical and Electronics Drafters; Electrical Drafters; Electrical Engineering Technicians; Electro-Mechanical Technicians; Electronic Drafters; Electronics Engineering Technicians; Environmental Engineering Technicians; Mapping Technicians; Mechanical Engineering Technicians; Surveying and Mapping Technicians; Surveying Technicians.

Skills: Technology Design; Installation; Equipment Selection; Operations Analysis; Quality Control Analysis; Mathematics; Repairing; Science.

Education and Training Program: Mechanical Drafting and Mechanical Drafting CAD/CADD. **Related Knowledge/Courses:** Design; Engineering and Technology; Building and Construction; Physics; Mathematics; English Language.

Work Environment: Indoors; noisy; sitting; using hands on objects, tools, or controls; repetitive motions.

Medical and Clinical Laboratory Technicians

- ✺ Personality Code: RIC
- ✺ Education/Training Required: Associate degree
- ✺ Annual Earnings: $34,270
- ✺ Beginning Wage: $22,670
- ✺ Earnings Growth Potential: Low
- ✺ Growth: 15.0%
- ✺ Annual Job Openings: 10,866
- ✺ Self-Employed: 0.7%
- ✺ Part-Time: 14.3%

Perform routine medical laboratory tests for the diagnosis, treatment, and prevention of disease. May work under the supervision of a medical technologist. Conduct chemical analyses of bodily fluids, such as blood and urine, using microscope or automatic analyzer to detect abnormalities or diseases, and enter findings into computer. Set up, adjust, maintain, and clean medical laboratory equipment. Analyze the results of tests and experiments to ensure conformity to specifications, using special mechanical and electrical devices. Analyze and record test data to issue reports that use charts, graphs and narratives. Conduct blood tests for transfusion purposes and perform blood counts. Perform medical research to further control and cure disease. Obtain specimens, cultivating, isolating, and identifying microorganisms for analysis. Examine cells stained with

Realistic–M

dye to locate abnormalities. Collect blood or tissue samples from patients, observing principles of asepsis to obtain blood sample. Consult with a pathologist to determine a final diagnosis when abnormal cells are found. Inoculate fertilized eggs, broths, or other bacteriological media with organisms. Cut, stain, and mount tissue samples for examination by pathologists. Supervise and instruct other technicians and laboratory assistants. Prepare standard volumetric solutions and reagents to be combined with samples, following standardized formulas or experimental procedures. Prepare vaccines and serums by standard laboratory methods, testing for virus inactivity and sterility. Test raw materials, processes, and finished products to determine quality and quantity of materials or characteristics of a substance.

GOE—Interest Area/Cluster: 08. Health Science. **Work Group:** 08.06. Medical Technology. **Other Jobs in This Work Group:** Biological Technicians; Cardiovascular Technologists and Technicians; Diagnostic Medical Sonographers; Medical and Clinical Laboratory Technologists; Medical Equipment Preparers; Medical Records and Health Information Technicians; Nuclear Medicine Technologists; Opticians, Dispensing; Orthotists and Prosthetists; Radiologic Technicians; Radiologic Technologists; Radiologic Technologists and Technicians.

Skills: Science; Equipment Maintenance; Troubleshooting; Quality Control Analysis; Operation Monitoring; Operation and Control; Monitoring; Installation.

Education and Training Programs: Clinical/Medical Laboratory Assistant; Blood Bank Technology Specialist; Hematology Technology/Technician; Clinical/Medical Laboratory Technician; Histologic Technician. **Related Knowledge/Courses:** Medicine and Dentistry; Therapy and Counseling; Biology; Clerical Practices.

Work Environment: Indoors; disease or infections; standing; walking and running; using hands on objects, tools, or controls.

Mobile Heavy Equipment Mechanics, Except Engines

- ✹ Personality Code: RC
- ✹ Education/Training Required: Long-term on-the-job training
- ✹ Annual Earnings: $41,450
- ✹ Beginning Wage: $27,200
- ✹ Earnings Growth Potential: Low
- ✹ Growth: 12.3%
- ✹ Annual Job Openings: 11,037
- ✹ Self-Employed: 5.0%
- ✹ Part-Time: 2.3%

Diagnose, adjust, repair, or overhaul mobile mechanical, hydraulic, and pneumatic equipment, such as cranes, bulldozers, graders, and conveyors, used in construction, logging, and surface mining. Test mechanical products and equipment after repair or assembly to ensure proper performance and compliance with manufacturers' specifications. Repair and replace damaged or worn parts. Diagnose faults or malfunctions to determine required repairs, using engine diagnostic equipment such as computerized test equipment and calibration devices. Operate and inspect machines or heavy equipment to diagnose defects. Dismantle and reassemble heavy equipment, using hoists and hand tools. Clean, lubricate, and perform other routine maintenance work on equipment and vehicles. Examine parts for damage or excessive wear, using micrometers and gauges. Read and understand operating manuals, blueprints, and technical drawings. Schedule maintenance for industrial machines and equipment and keep equipment service records. Overhaul and test machines or equipment to ensure operating efficiency. Assemble gear systems and align frames and gears. Fit bearings to adjust, repair, or overhaul mobile mechanical, hydraulic, and pneumatic equipment. Weld or solder broken parts and structural members, using electric or gas welders and soldering tools. Clean parts by spraying them with grease solvent or immersing them in tanks of solvent. Adjust, maintain, and repair or replace subassemblies, such as transmissions and crawler heads, using hand tools, jacks, and cranes. Adjust and maintain industrial machinery, using control and regulating devices. Fabricate needed parts or items from sheet metal. Direct workers who are assembling or disassembling equipment or cleaning parts.

GOE—Interest Area/Cluster: 13. Manufacturing. **Work Group:** 13.14. Vehicle and Facility Mechanical Work. **Other Jobs in This Work Group:** Aircraft Mechanics and Service Technicians; Aircraft Structure, Surfaces, Rigging, and Systems Assemblers; Automotive Body and Related Repairers; Automotive Glass Installers and Repairers; Automotive Master Mechanics; Automotive Service Technicians and Mechanics; Automotive Specialty Technicians; Bus and Truck Mechanics and Diesel Engine Specialists; Farm Equipment Mechanics; Fiberglass Laminators and Fabricators; Motorboat Mechanics; Motorcycle Mechanics; Outdoor Power Equipment and Other Small Engine Mechanics; Rail Car Repairers; Recreational Vehicle Service Technicians; Tire Repairers and Changers.

Skills: Installation; Repairing; Equipment Maintenance; Operation Monitoring; Troubleshooting; Operation and Control; Equipment Selection; Technology Design.

Education and Training Programs: Agricultural Mechanics and Equipment/Machine Technology; Heavy Equipment Maintenance Technology/Technician. **Related Knowledge/Courses:** Mechanical Devices; Engineering and Technology; Physics.

Work Environment: Noisy; contaminants; hazardous equipment; minor burns, cuts, bites, or stings; standing; using hands on objects, tools, or controls.

Municipal Fire Fighters

- ❀ Personality Code: RSE
- ❀ Education/Training Required: Long-term on-the-job training
- ❀ Annual Earnings: $43,170
- ❀ Beginning Wage: $21,530
- ❀ Earnings Growth Potential: Very high
- ❀ Growth: 12.1%
- ❀ Annual Job Openings: 18,887
- ❀ Self-Employed: 0.0%
- ❀ Part-Time: 1.3%

The job openings listed here are shared with Forest Fire Fighters.

Control and extinguish municipal fires, protect life and property, and conduct rescue efforts. Administer first aid and cardiopulmonary resuscitation to injured persons. Rescue victims from burning buildings and accident sites. Search burning buildings to locate fire victims. Drive and operate fire fighting vehicles and equipment. Move toward the source of a fire, using knowledge of types of fires, construction design, building materials, and physical layout of properties. Dress with equipment such as fire-resistant clothing and breathing apparatus. Position and climb ladders to gain access to upper levels of buildings or to rescue individuals from burning structures. Take action to contain hazardous chemicals that might catch fire, leak, or spill. Assess fires and situations and report conditions to superiors to receive instructions, using two-way radios. Respond to fire alarms and other calls for assistance, such as automobile and industrial accidents. Operate pumps connected to high-pressure hoses. Select and attach hose nozzles, depending on fire type, and direct streams of water or chemicals onto fires. Create openings in buildings for ventilation or entrance, using axes, chisels, crowbars, electric saws, or core cutters. Inspect fire sites after flames have been extinguished to ensure that there is no further danger. Lay hose lines and connect them to water supplies. Protect property from water and smoke, using waterproof salvage covers, smoke ejectors, and deodorants. Participate in physical training activities to maintain a high level of physical fitness. Salvage property by removing broken glass, pumping out water, and ventilating buildings to remove smoke. Participate in fire drills and demonstrations of fire fighting techniques. Clean and maintain fire stations and fire fighting equipment and apparatus. Collaborate with police to respond to accidents, disasters, and arson investigation calls. Establish firelines to prevent unauthorized persons from entering areas near fires. Inform and educate the public on fire prevention. Inspect buildings for fire hazards and compliance with fire prevention ordinances, testing and checking smoke alarms and fire suppression equipment as necessary.

GOE—Interest Area/Cluster: 12. Law and Public Safety. **Work Group:** 12.06. Emergency Responding. **Other Jobs in This Work Group:** Emergency Medical Technicians and Paramedics; Fire Fighters; Forest Fire Fighters.

Skills: Equipment Maintenance; Equipment Selection; Service Orientation; Operation Monitoring; Science; Social Perceptiveness; Coordination; Complex Problem Solving.

Education and Training Programs: Fire Science/ Firefighting; Fire Protection, Other. **Related Knowledge/Courses:** Medicine and Dentistry; Physics; Customer and Personal Service; Building and Construction; Chemistry; Public Safety and Security.

Work Environment: More often outdoors than indoors; noisy; contaminants; disease or infections; hazardous equipment.

Operating Engineers and Other Construction Equipment Operators

- ❋ Personality Code: RCI
- ❋ Education/Training Required: Moderate-term on-the-job training
- ❋ Annual Earnings: $38,130
- ❋ Beginning Wage: $24,840
- ❋ Earnings Growth Potential: Low
- ❋ Growth: 8.4%
- ❋ Annual Job Openings: 55,468
- ❋ Self-Employed: 5.7%
- ❋ Part-Time: 2.1%

Operate one or several types of power construction equipment, such as motor graders, bulldozers, scrapers, compressors, pumps, derricks, shovels, tractors, or front-end loaders, to excavate, move, and grade earth; erect structures; or pour concrete or other hard-surface pavement. May repair and maintain equipment in addition to other duties. Learn and follow safety regulations. Take actions to avoid potential hazards and obstructions such as utility lines, other equipment, other workers, and falling objects. Adjust handwheels and depress pedals to control attachments such as blades, buckets, scrapers, and swing booms. Start engines; move throttles, switches, and levers; and depress pedals to operate machines such as bulldozers, trench excavators, road graders, and backhoes. Locate underground services, such as pipes and wires, prior to beginning work. Monitor operations to ensure that health and safety standards are met. Align machines, cutterheads, or depth gauge makers with reference stakes and guidelines or ground or position equipment by following hand signals of other workers. Load and move dirt, rocks, equipment, and materials, using trucks, crawler tractors, power cranes, shovels, graders, and related equipment. Drive and maneuver equipment equipped with blades in successive passes over working areas to remove topsoil, vegetation, and rocks and to distribute and level earth or terrain. Coordinate machine actions with other activities, positioning or moving loads in response to hand or audio signals from crew members. Operate tractors and bulldozers to perform such tasks as clearing land, mixing sludge, trimming backfills, and building roadways and parking lots. Repair and maintain equipment, making emergency adjustments or assisting with major repairs as necessary. Check fuel supplies at sites to ensure adequate availability. Connect hydraulic hoses, belts, mechanical linkages, or power takeoff shafts to tractors. Operate loaders to pull out stumps, rip asphalt or concrete, rough-grade properties, bury refuse, or perform general cleanup. Select and fasten bulldozer blades or other attachments to tractors, using hitches. Test atmosphere for adequate oxygen and explosive conditions when working in confined spaces. Operate compactors, scrapers, and rollers to level, compact, and cover refuse at disposal grounds. Talk to clients and study instructions, plans, and diagrams to establish work requirements.

GOE—Interest Area/Cluster: 02. Architecture and Construction. **Work Group:** 02.04. Construction Crafts. **Other Jobs in This Work Group:** Boilermakers; Brickmasons and Blockmasons; Carpet Installers; Cement Masons and Concrete Finishers; Commercial Divers; Construction Carpenters; Crane and Tower Operators; Drywall and Ceiling Tile Installers; Electricians; Fence Erectors; Floor Layers, Except Carpet, Wood, and Hard Tiles; Floor Sanders and Finishers; Glaziers; Hazardous Materials Removal Workers; Insulation Workers, Floor, Ceiling, and Wall; Insulation Workers, Mechanical; Manufactured Building and Mobile Home Installers; Painters, Construction and Maintenance; Paperhangers; Paving, Surfacing, and Tamping Equipment Operators; Pile-Driver Operators; Pipe Fitters and Steamfitters; Pipelayers; Plasterers and Stucco Masons; Plumbers; Plumbers, Pipefitters, and Steamfitters; Rail-Track Laying and Maintenance Equipment Operators; Refractory Materials Repairers, Except Brickmasons; Reinforcing Iron and Rebar Workers; Riggers; Roofers; Rough Carpenters; Security and Fire Alarm Systems Installers; Segmental Pavers; Sheet Metal Workers; Stone Cutters and Carvers, Manufacturing; Stonemasons; Structural Iron and Steel Workers; Tapers; Terrazzo Workers and Finishers; Tile and Marble Setters.

Skills: Equipment Maintenance; Installation; Operation and Control; Operation Monitoring; Repairing; Equipment Selection; Management of Financial Resources; Management of Material Resources.

Education and Training Programs: Construction/Heavy Equipment/Earthmoving Equipment Operation; Mobile Crane Operation/Operator. **Related Knowledge/Courses:** Building and Construction; Mechanical Devices; Engineering and Technology; Design; Production and Processing; Public Safety and Security.

Work Environment: Outdoors; noisy; very hot or cold; contaminants; whole-body vibration; using hands on objects, tools, or controls.

Painters, Construction and Maintenance

* Personality Code: RC
* Education/Training Required: Moderate-term on-the-job training
* Annual Earnings: $32,080
* Beginning Wage: $21,720
* Earnings Growth Potential: Low
* Growth: 11.8%
* Annual Job Openings: 101,140
* Self-Employed: 42.2%
* Part-Time: 9.8%

Paint walls, equipment, buildings, bridges, and other structural surfaces with brushes, rollers, and spray guns. May remove old paint to prepare surfaces before painting. May mix colors or oils to obtain desired color or consistencies. Cover surfaces with dropcloths or masking tape and paper to protect surfaces during painting. Fill cracks, holes, and joints with caulk, putty, plaster, or other fillers, using caulking guns or putty knives. Apply primers or sealers to prepare new surfaces such as bare wood or metal for finish coats. Apply paint, stain, varnish, enamel, and other finishes to equipment, buildings, bridges, and/or other structures, using brushes, spray guns, or rollers. Calculate amounts of required

Realistic-P

materials and estimate costs, based on surface measurements and/or work orders. Read work orders or receive instructions from supervisors or homeowners to determine work requirements. Erect scaffolding and swing gates, or set up ladders, to work above ground level. Remove fixtures such as pictures, door knobs, lamps, and electric switch covers prior to painting. Wash and treat surfaces with oil, turpentine, mildew remover, or other preparations, and sand rough spots to ensure that finishes will adhere properly. Mix and match colors of paint, stain, or varnish with oil and thinning and drying additives to obtain desired colors and consistencies. Remove old finishes by stripping, sanding, wire brushing, burning, or using water and/or abrasive blasting. Select and purchase tools and finishes for surfaces to be covered, considering durability, ease of handling, methods of application, and customers' wishes. Smooth surfaces, using sandpaper, scrapers, brushes, steel wool, and/or sanding machines. Polish final coats to specified finishes. Use special finishing techniques such as sponging, ragging, layering, or faux finishing. Waterproof buildings, using waterproofers and caulking. Cut stencils, and brush and spray lettering and decorations on surfaces. Spray or brush hot plastics or pitch onto surfaces. Bake finishes on painted and enameled articles, using baking ovens.

GOE—Interest Area/Cluster: 02. Architecture and Construction. **Work Group:** 02.04. Construction Crafts. **Other Jobs in This Work Group:** Boilermakers; Brickmasons and Blockmasons; Carpet Installers; Cement Masons and Concrete Finishers; Commercial Divers; Construction Carpenters; Crane and Tower Operators; Drywall and Ceiling Tile Installers; Electricians; Fence Erectors; Floor Layers, Except Carpet, Wood, and Hard Tiles; Floor Sanders and Finishers; Glaziers; Hazardous Materials Removal Workers; Insulation Workers, Floor, Ceiling, and Wall; Insulation Workers, Mechanical; Manufactured Building and Mobile Home Installers; Operating Engineers and Other Construction Equipment Operators; Paperhangers; Paving, Surfacing, and Tamping Equipment Operators; Pile-Driver Operators; Pipe Fitters and Steamfitters; Pipelayers; Plasterers and Stucco Masons; Plumbers; Plumbers,

Pipefitters, and Steamfitters; Rail-Track Laying and Maintenance Equipment Operators; Refractory Materials Repairers, Except Brickmasons; Reinforcing Iron and Rebar Workers; Riggers; Roofers; Rough Carpenters; Security and Fire Alarm Systems Installers; Segmental Pavers; Sheet Metal Workers; Stone Cutters and Carvers, Manufacturing; Stonemasons; Structural Iron and Steel Workers; Tapers; Terrazzo Workers and Finishers; Tile and Marble Setters.

Skills: Equipment Maintenance; Management of Material Resources; Equipment Selection; Repairing; Management of Personnel Resources; Monitoring; Coordination.

Education and Training Program: Painting/Painter and Wall Coverer. **Related Knowledge/Courses:** Building and Construction; Design; Transportation; Customer and Personal Service; Production and Processing; Administration and Management.

Work Environment: Contaminants; standing; climbing ladders, scaffolds, or poles; using hands on objects, tools, or controls; bending or twisting the body; repetitive motions.

Pilots, Ship

- ❋ Personality Code: RCI
- ❋ Education/Training Required: Work experience in a related occupation
- ❋ Annual Earnings: $57,210
- ❋ Beginning Wage: $29,530
- ❋ Earnings Growth Potential: High
- ❋ Growth: 17.9%
- ❋ Annual Job Openings: 2,665
- ❋ Self-Employed: 6.8%
- ❋ Part-Time: 4.8%

The job openings listed here are shared with Mates—Ship, Boat, and Barge, and with Ship and Boat Captains.

Command ships to steer them into and out of harbors, estuaries, straits, and sounds and on rivers, lakes, and bays. Must be licensed by U.S. Coast

Guard with limitations indicating class and tonnage of vessels for which licenses are valid and routes and waters that may be piloted. Maintain and repair boats and equipment. Give directions to crew members who are steering ships. Make nautical maps. Set ships' courses to avoid reefs, outlying shoals, and other hazards, using navigational aids such as lighthouses and buoys. Report to appropriate authorities any violations of federal or state pilotage laws. Relieve crew members on tugs and launches. Provide assistance to vessels approaching or leaving seacoasts, navigating harbors, and docking and undocking. Provide assistance in maritime rescue operations. Prevent ships under their navigational control from engaging in unsafe operations. Operate amphibious craft during troop landings. Maintain ships' logs. Learn to operate new technology systems and procedures, through the use of instruction, simulators, and models. Advise ships' masters on harbor rules and customs procedures. Steer ships into and out of berths or signal tugboat captains to berth and unberth ships. Serve as vessels' docking masters upon arrival at a port and when at a berth. Operate ship-to-shore radios to exchange information needed for ship operations. Consult maps, charts, weather reports, and navigation equipment to determine and direct ship movements. Direct courses and speeds of ships, based on specialized knowledge of local winds, weather, water depths, tides, currents, and hazards. Oversee cargo storage on or below decks.

GOE—Interest Area/Cluster: 16. Transportation, Distribution, and Logistics. **Work Group:** 16.05. Water Vehicle Operation. **Other Jobs in This Work Group:** Captains, Mates, and Pilots of Water Vessels; Dredge Operators; Mates—Ship, Boat, and Barge; Motorboat Operators; Sailors and Marine Oilers; Ship and Boat Captains.

Skills: Operation and Control; Operation Monitoring; Judgment and Decision Making; Management of Personnel Resources; Troubleshooting; Equipment Maintenance; Negotiation; Coordination.

Education and Training Programs: Commercial Fishing; Marine Science/Merchant Marine Officer; Marine Transportation, Other. **Related Knowledge/**

Courses: Transportation; Geography; Public Safety and Security; Telecommunications; Mechanical Devices; Law and Government.

Work Environment: More often indoors than outdoors; more often standing than sitting; keeping or regaining balance; using hands on objects, tools, or controls.

Pipe Fitters and Steamfitters

- ❀ Personality Code: RC
- ❀ Education/Training Required: Long-term on-the-job training
- ❀ Annual Earnings: $44,090
- ❀ Beginning Wage: $26,550
- ❀ Earnings Growth Potential: Medium
- ❀ Growth: 10.6%
- ❀ Annual Job Openings: 68,643
- ❀ Self-Employed: 12.3%
- ❀ Part-Time: 3.4%

The job openings listed here are shared with Plumbers.

Lay out, assemble, install, and maintain pipe systems, pipe supports, and related hydraulic and pneumatic equipment for steam, hot water, heating, cooling, lubricating, sprinkling, and industrial production and processing systems. Cut, thread, and hammer pipe to specifications, using tools such as saws, cutting torches, and pipe threaders and benders. Assemble and secure pipes, tubes, fittings, and related equipment according to specifications by welding, brazing, cementing, soldering, and threading joints. Attach pipes to walls, structures, and fixtures, such as radiators or tanks, using brackets, clamps, tools, or welding equipment. Inspect, examine, and test installed systems and pipelines, using pressure gauge, hydrostatic testing, observation, or other methods. Measure and mark pipes for cutting and threading. Lay out full scale drawings of pipe systems, supports, and related equipment, following blueprints. Plan pipe system layout, installation, or repair according to specifications. Select pipe

Realistic-P

sizes and types and related materials, such as supports, hangers, and hydraulic cylinders, according to specifications. Cut and bore holes in structures such as bulkheads, decks, walls, and mains prior to pipe installation, using hand and power tools. Modify, clean, and maintain pipe systems, units, fittings, and related machines and equipment, following specifications and using hand and power tools. Install automatic controls used to regulate pipe systems. Turn valves to shut off steam, water, or other gases or liquids from pipe sections, using valve keys or wrenches. Remove and replace worn components. Prepare cost estimates for clients. Inspect work sites for obstructions and to ensure that holes will not cause structural weakness. Operate motorized pumps to remove water from flooded manholes, basements, or facility floors. Dip nonferrous piping materials in a mixture of molten tin and lead to obtain a coating that prevents erosion or galvanic and electrolytic action.

GOE—Interest Area/Cluster: 02. Architecture and Construction. **Work Group:** 02.04. Construction Crafts. **Other Jobs in This Work Group:** Boilermakers; Brickmasons and Blockmasons; Carpet Installers; Cement Masons and Concrete Finishers; Commercial Divers; Construction Carpenters; Crane and Tower Operators; Drywall and Ceiling Tile Installers; Electricians; Fence Erectors; Floor Layers, Except Carpet, Wood, and Hard Tiles; Floor Sanders and Finishers; Glaziers; Hazardous Materials Removal Workers; Insulation Workers, Floor, Ceiling, and Wall; Insulation Workers, Mechanical; Manufactured Building and Mobile Home Installers; Operating Engineers and Other Construction Equipment Operators; Painters, Construction and Maintenance; Paperhangers; Paving, Surfacing, and Tamping Equipment Operators; Pile-Driver Operators; Pipelayers; Plasterers and Stucco Masons; Plumbers; Plumbers, Pipefitters, and Steamfitters; Rail-Track Laying and Maintenance Equipment Operators; Refractory Materials Repairers, Except Brickmasons; Reinforcing Iron and Rebar Workers; Riggers; Roofers; Rough Carpenters; Security and Fire Alarm Systems Installers; Segmental Pavers; Sheet Metal Workers; Stone Cutters and Carvers, Manufacturing; Stonemasons; Structural Iron and Steel Workers; Tapers; Terrazzo Workers and Finishers; Tile and Marble Setters.

Skills: Installation; Repairing; Systems Analysis; Management of Personnel Resources; Equipment Maintenance; Operation Monitoring; Operation and Control; Technology Design.

Education and Training Program: Pipefitting/ Pipefitter and Sprinkler Fitter. **Related Knowledge/Courses:** Building and Construction; Design; Mechanical Devices; Engineering and Technology; Economics and Accounting; Transportation.

Work Environment: Outdoors; hazardous equipment; minor burns, cuts, bites, or stings; standing; using hands on objects, tools, or controls; repetitive motions.

Plumbers

* Personality Code: RCI
* Education/Training Required: Long-term on-the-job training
* Annual Earnings: $44,090
* Beginning Wage: $26,550
* Earnings Growth Potential: Medium
* Growth: 10.6%
* Annual Job Openings: 68,643
* Self-Employed: 12.3%
* Part-Time: 3.4%

The job openings listed here are shared with Pipe Fitters and Steamfitters.

Assemble, install, and repair pipes, fittings, and fixtures of heating, water, and drainage systems according to specifications and plumbing codes. Measure, cut, thread, and bend pipe to required angles, using hand and power tools or machines such as pipe cutters, pipe-threading machines, and pipe-bending machines. Study building plans and inspect structures to assess material and equipment needs to establish the sequence of pipe installations and to plan installation around obstructions such as electrical wiring. Locate and mark the position of pipe installations, connections, passage holes, and fixtures in structures, using measuring instruments such as rulers and levels. Assemble pipe sections, tubing, and fittings, using couplings, clamps, screws, bolts, cement, plastic solvent, caulking, or soldering, brazing, and welding equipment. Fill pipes or plumbing fixtures with water or air and observe pressure gauges to detect and locate leaks. Install pipe assemblies, fittings, valves, appliances such as dishwashers and water heaters, and fixtures such as sinks and toilets, using hand and power tools. Direct workers engaged in pipe cutting and preassembly and installation of plumbing systems and components. Cut openings in structures to accommodate pipes and pipe fittings, using hand and power tools. Review blueprints and building codes and specifications to determine work details and procedures. Install underground storm, sanitary, and water piping systems and extend piping to connect fixtures and plumbing to these systems. Repair and maintain plumbing, replacing defective washers, replacing or mending broken pipes, and opening clogged drains. Keep records of assignments and produce detailed work reports. Hang steel supports from ceiling joists to hold pipes in place. Perform complex calculations and planning for special or very large jobs. Clear away debris in renovations. Install oxygen and medical gas in hospitals. Prepare written work cost estimates and negotiate contracts. Use specialized techniques, equipment, or materials, such as performing computer-assisted welding of small pipes or working with the special piping used in microchip fabrication.

GOE—Interest Area/Cluster: 02. Architecture and Construction. **Work Group:** 02.04. Construction Crafts. **Other Jobs in This Work Group:** Boilermakers; Brickmasons and Blockmasons; Carpet Installers; Cement Masons and Concrete Finishers; Commercial Divers; Construction Carpenters; Crane and Tower Operators; Drywall and Ceiling Tile Installers; Electricians; Fence Erectors; Floor Layers, Except Carpet, Wood, and Hard Tiles; Floor Sanders and Finishers; Glaziers; Hazardous Materials Removal Workers; Insulation Workers, Floor, Ceiling, and Wall; Insulation Workers, Mechanical; Manufactured Building and Mobile Home Installers; Operating Engineers and Other Construction Equipment Operators; Painters, Construction and Maintenance; Paperhangers; Paving, Surfacing, and Tamping Equipment Operators; Pile-Driver Operators; Pipe Fitters and Steamfitters; Pipelayers; Plasterers and Stucco Masons; Plumbers, Pipefitters, and Steamfitters; Rail-Track Laying and Maintenance Equipment Operators; Refractory Materials Repairers, Except Brickmasons; Reinforcing Iron and Rebar Workers; Riggers; Roofers; Rough Carpenters; Security and Fire Alarm Systems Installers; Segmental Pavers; Sheet Metal Workers; Stone Cutters and Carvers, Manufacturing; Stonemasons; Structural Iron and Steel Workers; Tapers; Terrazzo Workers and Finishers; Tile and Marble Setters.

Skills: Installation; Quality Control Analysis; Repairing; Operation and Control; Operation Monitoring; Mathematics; Systems Analysis.

Education and Training Programs: Pipefitting/Pipefitter and Sprinkler Fitter; Plumbing Technology/Plumber; Plumbing and Related Water Supply Services, Other. **Related Knowledge/Courses:** Building and Construction; Physics; Mechanical Devices; Design; Engineering and Technology; Customer and Personal Service.

Work Environment: Outdoors; contaminants; cramped work space, awkward positions; hazardous equipment; minor burns, cuts, bites, or stings; using hands on objects, tools, or controls.

Plumbers, Pipefitters, and Steamfitters

See Pipe Fitters and Steamfitters (a Realistic job) and Plumbers (a Realistic job), described separately.

Realistic-P

Radiologic Technicians

❋ Personality Code: RC
❋ Education/Training Required: Associate degree
❋ Annual Earnings: $50,260
❋ Beginning Wage: $33,910
❋ Earnings Growth Potential: Low
❋ Growth: 15.1%
❋ Annual Job Openings: 12,836
❋ Self-Employed: 1.1%
❋ Part-Time: 17.3%

The job openings listed here are shared with Radiologic Technologists.

Maintain and use equipment and supplies necessary to demonstrate portions of the human body on X-ray film or fluoroscopic screen for diagnostic purposes. Use beam-restrictive devices and patient-shielding techniques to minimize radiation exposure to patient and staff. Position X-ray equipment and adjust controls to set exposure factors, such as time and distance. Position patient on examining table and set up and adjust equipment to obtain optimum view of specific body area as requested by physician. Determine patients' X-ray needs by reading requests or instructions from physicians. Make exposures necessary for the requested procedures, rejecting and repeating work that does not meet established standards. Process exposed radiographs, using film processors or computer-generated methods. Explain procedures to patients to reduce anxieties and obtain cooperation. Perform procedures such as linear tomography; mammography; sonograms; joint and cyst aspirations; routine contrast studies; routine fluoroscopy; and examinations of the head, trunk, and extremities under supervision of physician. Prepare and set up X-ray room for patient. Assure that sterile supplies, contrast materials, catheters, and other required equipment are present and in working order, requisitioning materials as necessary. Maintain records of patients examined, examinations performed, views taken, and technical factors used. Provide assistance to physicians or other technologists in the performance of more complex procedures. Monitor equipment operation and report malfunctioning equipment to supervisor. Provide students and other technologists with suggestions of additional views, alternate positioning, or improved techniques to ensure the images produced are of the highest quality. Coordinate work of other technicians or technologists when procedures require more than one person. Assist with on-the-job training of new employees and students and provide input to supervisors regarding training performance. Maintain a current file of examination protocols. Operate mobile X-ray equipment in operating room, in emergency room, or at patient's bedside. Provide assistance in radiopharmaceutical administration, monitoring patients' vital signs and notifying the radiologist of any relevant changes.

GOE—Interest Area/Cluster: 08. Health Science. **Work Group:** 08.06. Medical Technology. **Other Jobs in This Work Group:** Biological Technicians; Cardiovascular Technologists and Technicians; Diagnostic Medical Sonographers; Medical and Clinical Laboratory Technicians; Medical and Clinical Laboratory Technologists; Medical Equipment Preparers; Medical Records and Health Information Technicians; Nuclear Medicine Technologists; Opticians, Dispensing; Orthotists and Prosthetists; Radiologic Technologists; Radiologic Technologists and Technicians.

Skills: Science; Operation Monitoring; Equipment Selection; Operation and Control; Service Orientation; Active Listening; Negotiation; Writing.

Education and Training Programs: Medical Radiologic Technology/Science—Radiation Therapist; Radiologic Technology/Science—Radiographer; Allied Health Diagnostic, Intervention, and Treatment Professions, Other. **Related Knowledge/Courses:** Medicine and Dentistry; Clerical Practices; Psychology; Physics; Biology; Chemistry.

Work Environment: Indoors; radiation; disease or infections; standing; walking and running; using hands on objects, tools, or controls.

Radiologic Technologists

- ❋ Personality Code: RS
- ❋ Education/Training Required: Associate degree
- ❋ Annual Earnings: $50,260
- ❋ Beginning Wage: $33,910
- ❋ Earnings Growth Potential: Low
- ❋ Growth: 15.1%
- ❋ Annual Job Openings: 12,836
- ❋ Self-Employed: 1.1%
- ❋ Part-Time: 17.3%

The job openings listed here are shared with Radiologic Technicians.

Take X rays and Computerized Axial Tomography (CAT or CT) scans or administer nonradioactive materials into patient's bloodstream for diagnostic purposes. Includes technologists who specialize in other modalities such as computed tomography, ultrasound, and magnetic resonance. Use radiation safety measures and protection devices to comply with government regulations and to ensure safety of patients and staff. Review and evaluate developed X rays, videotape, or computer-generated information to determine if images are satisfactory for diagnostic purposes. Position imaging equipment and adjust controls to set exposure times and distances, according to specification of examinations. Explain procedures and observe patients to ensure safety and comfort during scans. Key commands and data into computers to document and specify scan sequences, adjust transmitters and receivers, or photograph certain images. Operate or oversee operation of radiologic and magnetic imaging equipment to produce images of the body for diagnostic purposes. Position and immobilize patients on examining tables. Record, process, and maintain patient data and treatment records, and prepare reports. Take thorough and accurate patient medical histories. Remove and process film. Set up examination rooms, ensuring that all necessary equipment is ready. Monitor patients' conditions and reactions, reporting abnormal signs to physicians. Coordinate work with clerical personnel or other technologists. Provide assistance in dressing or changing seriously ill, injured, or disabled patients. Demonstrate new equipment, procedures, and techniques to staff and provide technical assistance. Collaborate with other medical team members such as physicians and nurses to conduct angiography or special vascular procedures. Prepare and administer oral or injected contrast media to patients. Monitor video displays of areas being scanned and adjust density or contrast to improve picture quality. Operate fluoroscope to aid physicians to view and guide wires or catheters through blood vessels to areas of interest. Assign duties to radiologic staffs to maintain patient flows and achieve production goals. Perform scheduled maintenance and minor emergency repairs on radiographic equipment. Perform administrative duties such as developing departmental operating budgets, coordinating purchases of supplies and equipment, and preparing work schedules.

GOE—Interest Area/Cluster: 08. Health Science. **Work Group:** 08.06. Medical Technology. **Other Jobs in This Work Group:** Biological Technicians; Cardiovascular Technologists and Technicians; Diagnostic Medical Sonographers; Medical and Clinical Laboratory Technicians; Medical and Clinical Laboratory Technologists; Medical Equipment Preparers; Medical Records and Health Information Technicians; Nuclear Medicine Technologists; Opticians, Dispensing; Orthotists and Prosthetists; Radiologic Technicians; Radiologic Technologists and Technicians.

Skills: Operation Monitoring; Operation and Control.

Education and Training Programs: Medical Radiologic Technology/Science—Radiation Therapist; Radiologic Technology/Science—Radiographer; Allied Health Diagnostic, Intervention, and Treatment Professions, Other. **Related Knowledge/Courses:** Medicine and Dentistry; Physics; Customer and Personal Service; Biology; Psychology; Chemistry.

Realistic–R

Work Environment: Indoors; disease or infections; standing; walking and running; using hands on objects, tools, or controls; repetitive motions.

Radiologic Technologists and Technicians

See *Radiologic Technicians (a Realistic job) and Radiologic Technologists (a Realistic job), described separately.*

Refrigeration Mechanics and Installers

- ❀ Personality Code: RCE
- ❀ Education/Training Required: Long-term on-the-job training
- ❀ Annual Earnings: $38,360
- ❀ Beginning Wage: $24,240
- ❀ Earnings Growth Potential: Medium
- ❀ Growth: 8.7%
- ❀ Annual Job Openings: 29,719
- ❀ Self-Employed: 12.7%
- ❀ Part-Time: 3.6%

The job openings listed here are shared with Heating and Air Conditioning Mechanics and Installers.

Install and repair industrial and commercial refrigerating systems. Braze or solder parts to repair defective joints and leaks. Observe and test system operation, using gauges and instruments. Test lines, components, and connections for leaks. Dismantle malfunctioning systems and test components, using electrical, mechanical, and pneumatic testing equipment. Adjust or replace worn or defective mechanisms and parts and reassemble repaired systems. Read blueprints to determine location, size, capacity, and type of components needed to build refrigeration system. Supervise and instruct assistants. Perform mechanical overhauls and refrigerant reclaiming. Install wiring to connect components to an electric power source. Cut, bend, thread, and connect pipe to functional components and water, power, or refrigeration system. Adjust valves according to specifications and charge system with proper type of refrigerant by pumping the specified gas or fluid into the system. Estimate, order, pick up, deliver, and install materials and supplies needed to maintain equipment in good working condition. Install expansion and control valves, using acetylene torches and wrenches. Mount compressor, condenser, and other components in specified locations on frames, using hand tools and acetylene welding equipment. Keep records of repairs and replacements made and causes of malfunctions. Schedule work with customers and initiate work orders, house requisitions, and orders from stock. Lay out reference points for installation of structural and functional components, using measuring instruments. Fabricate and assemble structural and functional components of refrigeration system, using hand tools, power tools, and welding equipment. Lift and align components into position, using hoist or block and tackle. Drill holes and install mounting brackets and hangers into floor and walls of building. Insulate shells and cabinets of systems.

GOE—Interest Area/Cluster: 02. Architecture and Construction. **Work Group:** 02.05. Systems and Equipment Installation, Maintenance, and Repair. **Other Jobs in This Work Group:** Electrical and Electronics Repairers, Powerhouse, Substation, and Relay; Electrical Power-Line Installers and Repairers; Elevator Installers and Repairers; Heating and Air Conditioning Mechanics and Installers; Maintenance and Repair Workers, General; Telecommunications Equipment Installers and Repairers, Except Line Installers; Telecommunications Line Installers and Repairers.

Skills: Installation; Repairing; Equipment Maintenance; Operation Monitoring; Science; Systems Evaluation; Systems Analysis; Troubleshooting.

Education and Training Programs: Heating, Air Conditioning, and Refrigeration Technology/Technician (ACH/ACR/ACHR/HRAC/HVAC); Solar Energy Technology/Technician; Heating, Air Conditioning, Ventilation, and Refrigeration Maintenance

Technology/Technician. **Related Knowledge/ Courses:** Building and Construction; Mechanical Devices; Engineering and Technology; Physics; Chemistry; Design.

Work Environment: Outdoors; very hot or cold; cramped work space, awkward positions; minor burns, cuts, bites, or stings; standing; using hands on objects, tools, or controls.

Roofers

- ❋ Personality Code: RC
- ❋ Education/Training Required: Moderate-term on-the-job training
- ❋ Annual Earnings: $33,240
- ❋ Beginning Wage: $21,290
- ❋ Earnings Growth Potential: Medium
- ❋ Growth: 14.3%
- ❋ Annual Job Openings: 38,398
- ❋ Self-Employed: 20.1%
- ❋ Part-Time: 7.6%

Cover roofs of structures with shingles, slate, asphalt, aluminum, wood, and related materials. May spray roofs, sidings, and walls with material to bind, seal, insulate, or soundproof sections of structures. Install, repair, or replace single-ply roofing systems, using waterproof sheet materials such as modified plastics, elastomeric coatings, or other asphaltic compositions. Apply alternate layers of hot asphalt or tar and roofing paper to roofs, according to specification. Apply gravel or pebbles over top layers of roofs, using rakes or stiff-bristled brooms. Cement or nail flashing strips of metal or shingle over joints to make them watertight. Punch holes in slate, tile, terra cotta, or wooden shingles, using punches and hammers. Hammer and chisel away rough spots or remove them with rubbing bricks to prepare surfaces for waterproofing. Align roofing materials with edges of roofs. Mop or pour hot asphalt or tar onto roof bases. Apply plastic coatings and membranes, fiberglass, or felt over sloped roofs before applying shingles. Install vapor barriers and/or layers of insulation

on the roof decks of flat roofs and seal the seams. Install partially overlapping layers of material over roof insulation surfaces, determining distance of roofing material overlap using chalk lines, gauges on shingling hatchets, or lines on shingles. Inspect problem roofs to determine the best procedures for repairing them. Glaze top layers to make a smooth finish, or embed gravel in the bitumen for rough surfaces. Cut roofing paper to size, using knives, and nail or staple roofing paper to roofs in overlapping strips to form bases for other materials. Cut felt, shingles, and strips of flashing and fit them into angles formed by walls, vents, and intersecting roof surfaces. Cover roofs and exterior walls of structures with slate, asphalt, aluminum, wood, gravel, gypsum, and/or related materials, using brushes, knives, punches, hammers, and other tools. Clean and maintain equipment. Cover exposed nailheads with roofing cement or caulking to prevent water leakage and rust. Waterproof and damp-proof walls, floors, roofs, foundations, and basements by painting or spraying surfaces with waterproof coatings or by attaching waterproofing membranes to surfaces. Spray roofs, sidings, and walls with material to bind, seal, insulate, or soundproof sections of structures, using spray guns, air compressors, and heaters.

GOE—Interest Area/Cluster: 02. Architecture and Construction. **Work Group:** 02.04. Construction Crafts. **Other Jobs in This Work Group:** Boilermakers; Brickmasons and Blockmasons; Carpet Installers; Cement Masons and Concrete Finishers; Commercial Divers; Construction Carpenters; Crane and Tower Operators; Drywall and Ceiling Tile Installers; Electricians; Fence Erectors; Floor Layers, Except Carpet, Wood, and Hard Tiles; Floor Sanders and Finishers; Glaziers; Hazardous Materials Removal Workers; Insulation Workers, Floor, Ceiling, and Wall; Insulation Workers, Mechanical; Manufactured Building and Mobile Home Installers; Operating Engineers and Other Construction Equipment Operators; Painters, Construction and Maintenance; Paperhangers; Paving, Surfacing, and Tamping Equipment Operators; Pile-Driver Operators; Pipe Fitters and Steamfitters; Pipelayers; Plasterers and Stucco Masons; Plumbers; Plumbers,

Realistic-R

Pipefitters, and Steamfitters; Rail-Track Laying and Maintenance Equipment Operators; Refractory Materials Repairers, Except Brickmasons; Reinforcing Iron and Rebar Workers; Riggers; Rough Carpenters; Security and Fire Alarm Systems Installers; Segmental Pavers; Sheet Metal Workers; Stone Cutters and Carvers, Manufacturing; Stonemasons; Structural Iron and Steel Workers; Tapers; Terrazzo Workers and Finishers; Tile and Marble Setters.

Skills: Repairing; Installation; Equipment Maintenance; Operations Analysis; Technology Design; Mathematics; Management of Personnel Resources; Coordination.

Education and Training Program: Roofer. **Related Knowledge/Courses:** Building and Construction; Design; Engineering and Technology; Transportation.

Work Environment: Outdoors; high places; minor burns, cuts, bites, or stings; kneeling, crouching, stooping, or crawling; keeping or regaining balance; using hands on objects, tools, or controls.

Rough Carpenters

- ❋ Personality Code: RCI
- ❋ Education/Training Required: Long-term on-the-job training
- ❋ Annual Earnings: $37,660
- ❋ Beginning Wage: $23,370
- ❋ Earnings Growth Potential: Medium
- ❋ Growth: 10.3%
- ❋ Annual Job Openings: 223,225
- ❋ Self-Employed: 31.8%
- ❋ Part-Time: 6.1%

The job openings listed here are shared with Construction Carpenters.

Build rough wooden structures, such as concrete forms, scaffolds, tunnel, bridge, or sewer supports, billboard signs, and temporary frame shelters, according to sketches, blueprints, or

oral instructions. Study blueprints and diagrams to determine dimensions of structure or form to be constructed. Measure materials or distances, using square, measuring tape, or rule to lay out work. Cut or saw boards, timbers, or plywood to required size, using handsaw, power saw, or woodworking machine. Assemble and fasten material together to construct wood or metal framework of structure, using bolts, nails, or screws. Anchor and brace forms and other structures in place, using nails, bolts, anchor rods, steel cables, planks, wedges, and timbers. Mark cutting lines on materials, using pencil and scriber. Erect forms, framework, scaffolds, hoists, roof supports, or chutes, using hand tools, plumb rule, and level. Install rough door and window frames, subflooring, fixtures, or temporary supports in structures undergoing construction or repair. Examine structural timbers and supports to detect decay and replace timbers as required, using hand tools, nuts, and bolts. Bore boltholes in timber, masonry, or concrete walls, using power drill. Fabricate parts, using woodworking and metalworking machines. Dig or direct digging of post holes and set poles to support structures. Build sleds from logs and timbers for use in hauling camp buildings and machinery through wooded areas. Build chutes for pouring concrete.

GOE—Interest Area/Cluster: 02. Architecture and Construction. **Work Group:** 02.04. Construction Crafts. **Other Jobs in This Work Group:** Boilermakers; Brickmasons and Blockmasons; Carpet Installers; Cement Masons and Concrete Finishers; Commercial Divers; Construction Carpenters; Crane and Tower Operators; Drywall and Ceiling Tile Installers; Electricians; Fence Erectors; Floor Layers, Except Carpet, Wood, and Hard Tiles; Floor Sanders and Finishers; Glaziers; Hazardous Materials Removal Workers; Insulation Workers, Floor, Ceiling, and Wall; Insulation Workers, Mechanical; Manufactured Building and Mobile Home Installers; Operating Engineers and Other Construction Equipment Operators; Painters, Construction and Maintenance; Paperhangers; Paving, Surfacing, and Tamping Equipment Operators; Pile-Driver Operators; Pipe Fitters and Steamfitters; Pipelayers; Plasterers and Stucco Masons; Plumbers; Plumbers,

Pipefitters, and Steamfitters; Rail-Track Laying and Maintenance Equipment Operators; Refractory Materials Repairers, Except Brickmasons; Reinforcing Iron and Rebar Workers; Riggers; Roofers; Security and Fire Alarm Systems Installers; Segmental Pavers; Sheet Metal Workers; Stone Cutters and Carvers, Manufacturing; Stonemasons; Structural Iron and Steel Workers; Tapers; Terrazzo Workers and Finishers; Tile and Marble Setters.

Skills: Repairing; Installation; Management of Personnel Resources; Equipment Selection; Mathematics; Technology Design; Equipment Maintenance; Coordination.

Education and Training Program: Carpentry/Carpenter. **Related Knowledge/Courses:** Building and Construction; Design; Engineering and Technology; Mechanical Devices; Production and Processing; Physics.

Work Environment: Outdoors; noisy; very hot or cold; contaminants; standing; using hands on objects, tools, or controls.

Sailors and Marine Oilers

- ❋ Personality Code: RC
- ❋ Education/Training Required: Short-term on-the-job training
- ❋ Annual Earnings: $32,570
- ❋ Beginning Wage: $19,500
- ❋ Earnings Growth Potential: High
- ❋ Growth: 15.7%
- ❋ Annual Job Openings: 8,600
- ❋ Self-Employed: 0.1%
- ❋ Part-Time: 5.7%

Stand watch to look for obstructions in path of vessels; measure water depths; turn wheels on bridges; or use emergency equipment as directed by captains, mates, or pilots. Break out, rig, overhaul, and store cargo-handling gear, stationary rigging, and running gear. Perform a variety of maintenance tasks to preserve the painted surface

of ships and to maintain line and ship equipment. Must hold government-issued certification and tankerman certification when working aboard liquid-carrying vessels. Provide engineers with assistance in repairing and adjusting machinery. Attach hoses and operate pumps to transfer substances to and from liquid cargo tanks. Give directions to crew members engaged in cleaning wheelhouses and quarterdecks. Load or unload materials from vessels. Lower and man lifeboats when emergencies occur. Participate in shore patrols. Read pressure and temperature gauges or displays and record data in engineering logs. Record in ships' logs data such as weather conditions and distances traveled. Stand by wheels when ships are on automatic pilot and verify accuracy of courses, using magnetic compasses. Steer ships under the direction of commanders or navigating officers or direct helmsmen to steer, following designated courses. Chip and clean rust spots on decks, superstructures, and sides of ships, using wire brushes and hand or air chipping machines. Relay specified signals to other ships, using visual signaling devices such as blinker lights and semaphores. Splice and repair ropes, wire cables, and cordage, using marlinespikes, wirecutters, twine, and hand tools. Paint or varnish decks, superstructures, lifeboats, or sides of ships. Overhaul lifeboats and lifeboat gear and lower or raise lifeboats with winches or falls. Operate, maintain, and repair ship equipment such as winches, cranes, derricks, and weapons systems. Measure depths of water in shallow or unfamiliar waters, using leadlines, and telephone or shout depth information to vessel bridges. Maintain ships' engines under direction of ships' engineering officers. Lubricate machinery, equipment, and engine parts such as gears, shafts, and bearings. Handle lines to moor vessels to wharfs, to tie up vessels to other vessels, or to rig towing lines. Examine machinery to verify specified pressures and lubricant flows. Clean and polish wood trim, brass, and other metal parts. Break out, rig, and stow cargo-handling gear, stationary rigging, and running gear. Stand gangway watches to prevent unauthorized persons from boarding ships in port. Tie barges together into tow units for tugboats to handle, inspecting barges periodically during voyages and disconnecting them when destinations are reached.

GOE—Interest Area/Cluster: 16. Transportation, Distribution, and Logistics. **Work Group:** 16.05. Water Vehicle Operation. **Other Jobs in This Work Group:** Captains, Mates, and Pilots of Water Vessels; Dredge Operators; Mates—Ship, Boat, and Barge; Motorboat Operators; Pilots, Ship; Ship and Boat Captains.

Skills: Repairing; Equipment Maintenance.

Education and Training Program: Marine Transportation Services, Other. **Related Knowledge/Courses:** Mechanical Devices; Transportation; Engineering and Technology; Public Safety and Security; Geography; Production and Processing.

Work Environment: Outdoors; minor burns, cuts, bites, or stings; standing; keeping or regaining balance; using hands on objects, tools, or controls; bending or twisting the body.

Security and Fire Alarm Systems Installers

- ❋ Personality Code: RC
- ❋ Education/Training Required: Postsecondary vocational training
- ❋ Annual Earnings: $35,390
- ❋ Beginning Wage: $22,800
- ❋ Earnings Growth Potential: Medium
- ❋ Growth: 20.2%
- ❋ Annual Job Openings: 5,729
- ❋ Self-Employed: 7.2%
- ❋ Part-Time: 2.7%

Install, program, maintain, and repair security and fire alarm wiring and equipment. Ensure that work is in accordance with relevant codes. Examine systems to locate problems such as loose connections or broken insulation. Test backup batteries, keypad programming, sirens, and all security features in order to ensure proper functioning, and to diagnose malfunctions. Mount and fasten control panels, door and window contacts, sensors, and video cameras, and attach electrical and telephone wiring in order to connect components. Install, maintain, or repair security systems, alarm devices, and related equipment, following blueprints of electrical layouts and building plans. Inspect installation sites and study work orders, building plans, and installation manuals in order to determine materials requirements and installation procedures. Feed cables through access holes, roof spaces, and cavity walls to reach fixture outlets; then position and terminate cables, wires and strapping. Adjust sensitivity of units based on room structures and manufacturers' recommendations, using programming keypads. Test and repair circuits and sensors, following wiring and system specifications. Drill holes for wiring in wall studs, joists, ceilings, and floors. Demonstrate systems for customers, and explain details such as the causes and consequences of false alarms. Consult with clients to assess risks and to determine security requirements. Keep informed of new products and developments. Mount raceways and conduits, and fasten wires to wood framing, using staplers. Prepare documents such as invoices and warranties. Provide customers with cost estimates for equipment installation. Order replacement parts.

GOE—Interest Area/Cluster: 02. Architecture and Construction. **Work Group:** 02.04. Construction Crafts. **Other Jobs in This Work Group:** Boilermakers; Brickmasons and Blockmasons; Carpet Installers; Cement Masons and Concrete Finishers; Commercial Divers; Construction Carpenters; Crane and Tower Operators; Drywall and Ceiling Tile Installers; Electricians; Fence Erectors; Floor Layers, Except Carpet, Wood, and Hard Tiles; Floor Sanders and Finishers; Glaziers; Hazardous Materials Removal Workers; Insulation Workers, Floor, Ceiling, and Wall; Insulation Workers, Mechanical; Manufactured Building and Mobile Home Installers; Operating Engineers and Other Construction Equipment Operators; Painters, Construction and Maintenance; Paperhangers; Paving, Surfacing, and Tamping Equipment Operators; Pile-Driver Operators; Pipe Fitters and Steamfitters; Pipelayers; Plasterers and Stucco Masons; Plumbers; Plumbers,

Pipefitters, and Steamfitters; Rail-Track Laying and Maintenance Equipment Operators; Refractory Materials Repairers, Except Brickmasons; Reinforcing Iron and Rebar Workers; Riggers; Roofers; Rough Carpenters; Segmental Pavers; Sheet Metal Workers; Stone Cutters and Carvers, Manufacturing; Stonemasons; Structural Iron and Steel Workers; Tapers; Terrazzo Workers and Finishers; Tile and Marble Setters.

Skills: Installation; Repairing; Troubleshooting; Equipment Maintenance; Systems Evaluation; Technology Design; Operations Analysis; Programming.

Education and Training Programs: Electrician; Security System Installation, Repair, and Inspection Technology/Technician. **Related Knowledge/Courses:** Telecommunications; Building and Construction; Mechanical Devices; Computers and Electronics; Public Safety and Security; Design.

Work Environment: More often indoors than outdoors; noisy; very hot or cold; standing; using hands on objects, tools, or controls.

Sheet Metal Workers

- ❋ Personality Code: R
- ❋ Education/Training Required: Long-term on-the-job training
- ❋ Annual Earnings: $39,210
- ❋ Beginning Wage: $22,820
- ❋ Earnings Growth Potential: High
- ❋ Growth: 6.7%
- ❋ Annual Job Openings: 31,677
- ❋ Self-Employed: 4.7%
- ❋ Part-Time: 4.2%

Fabricate, assemble, install, and repair sheet metal products and equipment, such as ducts, control boxes, drainpipes, and furnace casings. Work may involve any of the following: setting up and operating fabricating machines to cut, bend, and straighten sheet metal; shaping metal over anvils, blocks, or forms, using hammer; operating soldering and welding equipment to join sheet metal parts; and inspecting, assembling, and smoothing seams and joints of burred surfaces. Determine project requirements, including scope, assembly sequences, and required methods and materials, according to blueprints, drawings, and written or verbal instructions. Lay out, measure, and mark dimensions and reference lines on material such as roofing panels according to drawings or templates, using calculators, scribes, dividers, squares, and rulers. Maneuver completed units into position for installation and anchor the units. Convert blueprints into shop drawings to be followed in the construction and assembly of sheet metal products. Install assemblies such as flashing, pipes, tubes, heating and air conditioning ducts, furnace casings, rain gutters, and downspouts in supportive frameworks. Select gauges and types of sheet metal or non-metallic material according to product specifications. Drill and punch holes in metal for screws, bolts, and rivets. Fasten seams and joints together with welds, bolts, cement, rivets, solder, caulks, metal drive clips, and bonds to assemble components into products or to repair sheet metal items. Fabricate or alter parts at construction sites, using shears, hammers, punches, and drills. Finish parts, using hacksaws and hand, rotary, or squaring shears. Trim, file, grind, deburr, buff, and smooth surfaces, seams, and joints of assembled parts, using hand tools and portable power tools. Maintain equipment, making repairs and modifications when necessary. Shape metal material over anvils, blocks, or other forms, using hand tools. Transport prefabricated parts to construction sites for assembly and installation. Develop and lay out patterns that use materials most efficiently, using computerized metalworking equipment to experiment with different layouts. Inspect individual parts, assemblies, and installations for conformance to specifications and building codes, using measuring instruments such as calipers, scales, and micrometers. Secure metal roof panels in place and interlock and fasten grooved panel edges. Fasten roof panel edges and machine-made molding to structures, nailing or welding pieces into place.

GOE—Interest Area/Cluster: 02. Architecture and Construction. **Work Group:** 02.04. Construction Crafts. **Other Jobs in This Work Group:** Boilermakers; Brickmasons and Blockmasons; Carpet Installers; Cement Masons and Concrete Finishers; Commercial Divers; Construction Carpenters; Crane and Tower Operators; Drywall and Ceiling Tile Installers; Electricians; Fence Erectors; Floor Layers, Except Carpet, Wood, and Hard Tiles; Floor Sanders and Finishers; Glaziers; Hazardous Materials Removal Workers; Insulation Workers, Floor, Ceiling, and Wall; Insulation Workers, Mechanical; Manufactured Building and Mobile Home Installers; Operating Engineers and Other Construction Equipment Operators; Painters, Construction and Maintenance; Paperhangers; Paving, Surfacing, and Tamping Equipment Operators; Pile-Driver Operators; Pipe Fitters and Steamfitters; Pipelayers; Plasterers and Stucco Masons; Plumbers; Plumbers, Pipefitters, and Steamfitters; Rail-Track Laying and Maintenance Equipment Operators; Refractory Materials Repairers, Except Brickmasons; Reinforcing Iron and Rebar Workers; Riggers; Roofers; Rough Carpenters; Security and Fire Alarm Systems Installers; Segmental Pavers; Stone Cutters and Carvers, Manufacturing; Stonemasons; Structural Iron and Steel Workers; Tapers; Terrazzo Workers and Finishers; Tile and Marble Setters.

Skills: Installation; Repairing; Equipment Maintenance; Mathematics; Technology Design; Equipment Selection; Troubleshooting; Coordination.

Education and Training Program: Sheet Metal Technology/Sheetworking. **Related Knowledge/Courses:** Building and Construction; Mechanical Devices; Physics; Design; Production and Processing; Mathematics.

Work Environment: Noisy; contaminants; hazardous equipment; minor burns, cuts, bites, or stings; standing; using hands on objects, tools, or controls.

Surgical Technologists

- ❋ Personality Code: RSC
- ❋ Education/Training Required: Postsecondary vocational training
- ❋ Annual Earnings: $37,540
- ❋ Beginning Wage: $26,650
- ❋ Earnings Growth Potential: Low
- ❋ Growth: 24.5%
- ❋ Annual Job Openings: 15,365
- ❋ Self-Employed: 0.2%
- ❋ Part-Time: 20.8%

Assist in operations under the supervision of surgeons, registered nurses, or other surgical personnel. May help set up operating rooms; prepare and transport patients for surgery; adjust lights and equipment; pass instruments and other supplies to surgeons and surgeons' assistants; hold retractors; cut sutures; and help count sponges, needles, supplies, and instruments. Count sponges, needles, and instruments before and after operations. Maintain a proper sterile field during surgical procedures. Hand instruments and supplies to surgeons and surgeons' assistants, hold retractors and cut sutures, and perform other tasks as directed by surgeons during operations. Prepare patients for surgery, including positioning patients on operating tables and covering them with sterile surgical drapes to prevent exposure. Scrub arms and hands and assist surgical teams to scrub and put on gloves, masks, and surgical clothing. Wash and sterilize equipment, using germicides and sterilizers. Monitor and continually assess operating room conditions, including needs of the patient and surgical team. Prepare dressings or bandages and apply or assist with their application following surgeries. Clean and restock operating rooms, gathering and placing equipment and supplies and arranging instruments according to instructions such as those found on a preference card. Operate, assemble, adjust, or monitor sterilizers, lights, suction machines, and diagnostic equipment to ensure proper operation. Prepare, care for, and dispose of tissue specimens taken for laboratory analysis. Provide technical assistance to surgeons, surgical nurses, and anesthesiologists. Maintain supply of fluids such as plasma, saline, blood, and glucose for use during operations. Maintain files and records of surgical procedures. Observe patients' vital signs to assess physical condition. Order surgical supplies.

GOE—Interest Area/Cluster: 08. Health Science. **Work Group:** 08.02. Medicine and Surgery. **Other Jobs in This Work Group:** Anesthesiologists; Family and General Practitioners; Internists, General; Medical Assistants; Medical Transcriptionists; Obstetricians and Gynecologists; Pediatricians, General; Pharmacists; Pharmacy Aides; Pharmacy Technicians; Physician Assistants; Psychiatrists; Registered Nurses; Surgeons.

Skills: Operation Monitoring; Quality Control Analysis.

Education and Training Programs: Pathology/ Pathologist Assistant; Surgical Technology/Technologist. **Related Knowledge/Courses:** Medicine and Dentistry; Biology; Psychology; Chemistry; Therapy and Counseling; Customer and Personal Service.

Work Environment: Indoors; contaminants; disease or infections; hazardous conditions; standing; using hands on objects, tools, or controls.

Surveying Technicians

- ❀ Personality Code: RC
- ❀ Education/Training Required: Moderate-term on-the-job training
- ❀ Annual Earnings: $33,640
- ❀ Beginning Wage: $20,670
- ❀ Earnings Growth Potential: Medium
- ❀ Growth: 19.4%
- ❀ Annual Job Openings: 8,299
- ❀ Self-Employed: 4.2%
- ❀ Part-Time: 4.5%

The job openings listed here are shared with Mapping Technicians.

Adjust and operate surveying instruments such as theodolite and electronic distance-measuring equipment and compile notes, make sketches, and enter data into computers. Perform calculations to determine Earth curvature corrections, atmospheric impacts on measurements, traverse closures and adjustments, azimuths, level runs, and placement of markers. Record survey measurements and descriptive data using notes, drawings, sketches, and inked tracings. Search for section corners, property irons, and survey points. Position and hold the vertical rods, or targets, that theodolite operators use for sighting to measure angles, distances, and elevations. Lay out grids and determine horizontal and vertical controls. Compare survey computations with applicable standards to determine adequacy of data. Set out and recover stakes, marks, and other monumentation. Conduct surveys to ascertain the locations of natural features and man-made structures on Earth's surface, underground, and underwater, using electronic distance-measuring equipment and other surveying instruments. Direct and supervise work of subordinate members of surveying parties. Compile information necessary to stake projects for construction, using engineering plans. Prepare topographic and contour maps of land surveyed, including site features and other relevant information, such as charts, drawings, and survey notes. Place and hold measuring tapes when electronic distance-measuring equipment is not used. Collect information needed to carry out new surveys using source maps, previous survey data, photographs, computer records, and other relevant information. Operate and manage land-information computer systems, performing tasks such as storing data, making inquiries, and producing plots and reports. Run rods for benches and cross-section elevations. Perform manual labor, such as cutting brush for lines, carrying stakes, rebar, and other heavy items, and stacking rods. Maintain equipment and vehicles used by surveying crews. Provide assistance in the development of methods and procedures for conducting field surveys.

GOE—Interest Area/Cluster: 15. Scientific Research, Engineering, and Mathematics. **Work Group:** 15.09. Engineering Technology. **Other**

Jobs in This Work Group: Aerospace Engineering and Operations Technicians; Cartographers and Photogrammetrists; Civil Engineering Technicians; Electrical and Electronic Engineering Technicians; Electrical and Electronics Drafters; Electrical Drafters; Electrical Engineering Technicians; Electro-Mechanical Technicians; Electronic Drafters; Electronics Engineering Technicians; Environmental Engineering Technicians; Mapping Technicians; Mechanical Drafters; Mechanical Engineering Technicians; Surveying and Mapping Technicians.

Skills: Mathematics; Operation and Control; Management of Personnel Resources; Operation Monitoring; Systems Analysis.

Education and Training Programs: Surveying Technology/Surveying; Cartography. **Related Knowledge/Courses:** Geography; Design; Building and Construction; Mathematics; Law and Government; Engineering and Technology.

Work Environment: Outdoors; very hot or cold; very bright or dim lighting; hazardous equipment; minor burns, cuts, bites, or stings; using hands on objects, tools, or controls.

Surveyors

- ❋ Personality Code: RCI
- ❋ Education/Training Required: Bachelor's degree
- ❋ Annual Earnings: $51,630
- ❋ Beginning Wage: $28,590
- ❋ Earnings Growth Potential: High
- ❋ Growth: 23.7%
- ❋ Annual Job Openings: 14,305
- ❋ Self-Employed: 3.7%
- ❋ Part-Time: 4.6%

Make exact measurements and determine property boundaries. Provide data relevant to the shape, contour, gravitation, location, elevation, or dimension of land or land features on or near Earth's surface for engineering, mapmaking, mining, land evaluation, construction, and other purposes. Verify the accuracy of survey data including measurements and calculations conducted at survey sites. Calculate heights, depths, relative positions, property lines, and other characteristics of terrain. Search legal records, survey records, and land titles to obtain information about property boundaries in areas to be surveyed. Prepare and maintain sketches, maps, reports, and legal descriptions of surveys to describe, certify, and assume liability for work performed. Direct or conduct surveys to establish legal boundaries for properties, based on legal deeds and titles. Prepare or supervise preparation of all data, charts, plots, maps, records, and documents related to surveys. Write descriptions of property boundary surveys for use in deeds, leases, or other legal documents. Compute geodetic measurements and interpret survey data to determine positions, shapes, and elevations of geomorphic and topographic features. Determine longitudes and latitudes of important features and boundaries in survey areas using theodolites, transits, levels, and satellite-based global positioning systems (GPS). Record the results of surveys including the shape, contour, location, elevation, and dimensions of land or land features. Coordinate findings with the work of engineering and architectural personnel, clients, and others concerned with projects. Establish fixed points for use in making maps, using geodetic and engineering instruments. Train assistants and helpers, and direct their work in such activities as performing surveys or drafting maps. Plan and conduct ground surveys designed to establish baselines, elevations, and other geodetic measurements. Adjust surveying instruments to maintain their accuracy. Analyze survey objectives and specifications to prepare survey proposals or to direct others in survey proposal preparation. Develop criteria for survey methods and procedures. Survey bodies of water to determine navigable channels and to secure data for construction of breakwaters, piers, and other marine structures. Conduct research in surveying and mapping methods using knowledge of techniques of photogrammetric map compilation and electronic data processing.

GOE—Interest Area/Cluster: 02. Architecture and Construction. **Work Group:** 02.03. Architecture/Construction Engineering Technologies. **Other Jobs in This Work Group:** Architectural and Civil Drafters; Architectural Drafters; Civil Drafters.

Skills: Operation Monitoring; Management of Personnel Resources; Operation and Control; Repairing.

Education and Training Program: Surveying Technology/Surveying. **Related Knowledge/Courses:** Geography; Design; Building and Construction; History and Archeology; Engineering and Technology; Mathematics.

Work Environment: More often outdoors than indoors; very hot or cold; hazardous equipment; minor burns, cuts, bites, or stings; standing.

Telecommunications Equipment Installers and Repairers, Except Line Installers

- ❈ Personality Code: RIC
- ❈ Education/Training Required: Postsecondary vocational training
- ❈ Annual Earnings: $54,070
- ❈ Beginning Wage: $31,520
- ❈ Earnings Growth Potential: High
- ❈ Growth: 2.5%
- ❈ Annual Job Openings: 13,541
- ❈ Self-Employed: 4.1%
- ❈ Part-Time: 3.1%

Set up, rearrange, or remove switching and dialing equipment used in central offices. Service or repair telephones and other communication equipment on customers' properties. May install equipment in new locations or install wiring and telephone jacks in buildings under construction. Note differences in wire and cable colors so that work can be performed correctly. Test circuits and components of malfunctioning telecommunications equipment to isolate sources of malfunctions, using test meters, circuit diagrams, polarity probes, and other hand tools. Test repaired, newly installed, or updated equipment to ensure that it functions properly and conforms to specifications, using test equipment and observation. Drive crew trucks to and from work areas. Inspect equipment on a regular basis to ensure proper functioning. Repair or replace faulty equipment such as defective and damaged telephones, wires, switching system components, and associated equipment. Remove and remake connections to change circuit layouts, following work orders or diagrams. Demonstrate equipment to customers, explain how it is to be used, and respond to any inquiries or complaints. Analyze test readings, computer printouts, and trouble reports to determine equipment repair needs and required repair methods. Adjust or modify equipment to enhance equipment performance or to respond to customer requests. Remove loose wires and other debris after work is completed. Request support from technical service centers when on-site procedures fail to solve installation or maintenance problems. Communicate with bases, using telephones or two-way radios, to receive instructions or technical advice or to report equipment status. Assemble and install communication equipment such as data and telephone communication lines, wiring, switching equipment, wiring frames, power apparatus, computer systems, and networks. Collaborate with other workers to locate and correct malfunctions. Review manufacturers' instructions, manuals, technical specifications, building permits, and ordinances to determine communication equipment requirements and procedures. Test connections to ensure that power supplies are adequate and that communications links function. Refer to manufacturers' manuals to obtain maintenance instructions pertaining to specific malfunctions. Climb poles and ladders, use truck-mounted booms, and enter areas such as manholes and cable vaults to install, maintain, or inspect equipment.

GOE—Interest Area/Cluster: 02. Architecture and Construction. **Work Group:** 02.05. Systems and Equipment Installation, Maintenance, and Repair. **Other Jobs in This Work Group:** Electrical and Electronics Repairers, Powerhouse, Substation, and

Relay; Electrical Power-Line Installers and Repairers; Elevator Installers and Repairers; Heating and Air Conditioning Mechanics and Installers; Maintenance and Repair Workers, General; Refrigeration Mechanics and Installers; Telecommunications Line Installers and Repairers.

Skills: Installation; Repairing; Troubleshooting; Technology Design; Equipment Selection; Systems Analysis; Quality Control Analysis; Equipment Maintenance.

Education and Training Program: Communications Systems Installation and Repair Technology. **Related Knowledge/Courses:** Telecommunications; Mechanical Devices; Computers and Electronics; Engineering and Technology; Design; Public Safety and Security.

Work Environment: Outdoors; noisy; very hot or cold; contaminants; cramped work space, awkward positions; using hands on objects, tools, or controls.

Telecommunications Line Installers and Repairers

- ❋ Personality Code: RE
- ❋ Education/Training Required: Long-term on-the-job training
- ❋ Annual Earnings: $47,220
- ❋ Beginning Wage: $25,140
- ❋ Earnings Growth Potential: High
- ❋ Growth: 4.6%
- ❋ Annual Job Openings: 14,719
- ❋ Self-Employed: 3.3%
- ❋ Part-Time: 1.9%

String and repair telephone and television cable, including fiber optics and other equipment for transmitting messages or television programming. Travel to customers' premises to install, maintain, and repair audio and visual electronic reception equipment and accessories. Inspect and test lines and cables, recording and analyzing test results, to assess transmission characteristics and locate faults and malfunctions. Splice cables, using hand tools, epoxy, or mechanical equipment. Measure signal strength at utility poles, using electronic test equipment. Set up service for customers, installing, connecting, testing, and adjusting equipment. Place insulation over conductors and seal splices with moisture-proof covering. Access specific areas to string lines and install terminal boxes, auxiliary equipment, and appliances, using bucket trucks, or by climbing poles and ladders or entering tunnels, trenches, or crawl spaces. String cables between structures and lines from poles, towers, or trenches and pull lines to proper tension. Install equipment such as amplifiers and repeaters to maintain the strength of communications transmissions. Lay underground cable directly in trenches or string it through conduits running through trenches. Pull up cable by hand from large reels mounted on trucks; then pull lines through ducts by hand or with winches. Clean and maintain tools and test equipment. Explain cable service to subscribers after installation and collect any installation fees that are due. Compute impedance of wires from poles to houses to determine additional resistance needed for reducing signals to desired levels. Use a variety of construction equipment to complete installations, including digger derricks, trenchers, and cable plows. Dig trenches for underground wires and cables. Dig holes for power poles, using power augers or shovels, set poles in place with cranes, and hoist poles upright, using winches. Fill and tamp holes, using cement, earth, and tamping devices. Participate in the construction and removal of telecommunication towers and associated support structures.

GOE—Interest Area/Cluster: 02. Architecture and Construction. **Work Group:** 02.05. Systems and Equipment Installation, Maintenance, and Repair. **Other Jobs in This Work Group:** Electrical and Electronics Repairers, Powerhouse, Substation, and Relay; Electrical Power-Line Installers and Repairers; Elevator Installers and Repairers; Heating and Air Conditioning Mechanics and Installers; Maintenance and Repair Workers, General; Refrigeration Mechanics and Installers; Telecommunications Equipment Installers and Repairers, Except Line Installers.

Skills: Installation; Troubleshooting; Repairing; Equipment Maintenance; Programming; Technology Design; Quality Control Analysis; Equipment Selection.

Education and Training Program: Communications Systems Installation and Repair Technology. **Related Knowledge/Courses:** Telecommunications; Engineering and Technology; Building and Construction; Customer and Personal Service; Design; Mechanical Devices.

Work Environment: Outdoors; very hot or cold; contaminants; cramped work space, awkward positions; hazardous equipment; using hands on objects, tools, or controls.

Tile and Marble Setters

- ❋ Personality Code: RCA
- ❋ Education/Training Required: Long-term on-the-job training
- ❋ Annual Earnings: $38,720
- ❋ Beginning Wage: $21,890
- ❋ Earnings Growth Potential: High
- ❋ Growth: 15.4%
- ❋ Annual Job Openings: 9,066
- ❋ Self-Employed: 33.8%
- ❋ Part-Time: 7.2%

Apply hard tile, marble, and wood tile to walls, floors, ceilings, and roof decks. Align and straighten tile, using levels, squares, and straightedges. Determine and implement the best layout to achieve a desired pattern. Cut and shape tile to fit around obstacles and into odd spaces and corners, using hand- and power-cutting tools. Finish and dress the joints and wipe excess grout from between tiles, using damp sponge. Apply mortar to tile back, position the tile, and press or tap with trowel handle to affix tile to base. Mix, apply, and spread plaster, concrete, mortar, cement, mastic, glue, or other adhesives to form a bed for the tiles, using brush, trowel, and screed. Prepare cost and labor estimates based on calculations of time and materials needed for project. Measure and mark surfaces to be tiled, following blueprints. Level concrete and allow to dry. Build underbeds and install anchor bolts, wires, and brackets. Prepare surfaces for tiling by attaching lath or waterproof paper or by applying a cement mortar coat onto a metal screen. Study blueprints and examine surface to be covered to determine amount of material needed. Cut, surface, polish, and install marble and granite or install pre-cast terrazzo, granite, or marble units. Install and anchor fixtures in designated positions, using hand tools. Cut tile backing to required size, using shears. Remove any old tile, grout, and adhesive, using chisels and scrapers, and clean the surface carefully. Lay and set mosaic tiles to create decorative wall, mural, and floor designs. Assist customers in selection of tile and grout. Remove and replace cracked or damaged tile. Measure and cut metal lath to size for walls and ceilings, using tin snips. Select and order tile and other items to be installed, such as bathroom accessories, walls, panels, and cabinets, according to specifications. Mix and apply mortar or cement to edges and ends of drain tiles to seal halves and joints. Spread mastic or other adhesive base on roof deck to form base for promenade tile, using serrated spreader. Apply a sealer to make grout stain- and water-resistant. Brush glue onto manila paper on which design has been drawn and position tiles, finished side down, onto paper.

GOE—Interest Area/Cluster: 02. Architecture and Construction. **Work Group:** 02.04. Construction Crafts. **Other Jobs in This Work Group:** Boilermakers; Brickmasons and Blockmasons; Carpet Installers; Cement Masons and Concrete Finishers; Commercial Divers; Construction Carpenters; Crane and Tower Operators; Drywall and Ceiling Tile Installers; Electricians; Fence Erectors; Floor Layers, Except Carpet, Wood, and Hard Tiles; Floor Sanders and Finishers; Glaziers; Hazardous Materials Removal Workers; Insulation Workers, Floor, Ceiling, and Wall; Insulation Workers, Mechanical; Manufactured Building and Mobile Home Installers; Operating Engineers and Other Construction Equipment Operators; Painters, Construction and Maintenance; Paperhangers; Paving, Surfacing, and Tamping Equipment Operators; Pile-Driver

Operators; Pipe Fitters and Steamfitters; Pipelayers; Plasterers and Stucco Masons; Plumbers; Plumbers, Pipefitters, and Steamfitters; Rail-Track Laying and Maintenance Equipment Operators; Refractory Materials Repairers, Except Brickmasons; Reinforcing Iron and Rebar Workers; Riggers; Roofers; Rough Carpenters; Security and Fire Alarm Systems Installers; Segmental Pavers; Sheet Metal Workers; Stone Cutters and Carvers, Manufacturing; Stonemasons; Structural Iron and Steel Workers; Tapers; Terrazzo Workers and Finishers.

Skills: Installation; Management of Financial Resources; Mathematics; Equipment Selection; Technology Design; Management of Material Resources; Social Perceptiveness; Equipment Maintenance.

Education and Training Program: Mason/Masonry. **Related Knowledge/Courses:** Building and Construction; Design; Production and Processing; Economics and Accounting; Administration and Management; Transportation.

Work Environment: Noisy; contaminants; cramped work space, awkward positions; standing; using hands on objects, tools, or controls; bending or twisting the body.

Transportation Inspectors

See *Aviation Inspectors (a Realistic job), Freight and Cargo Inspectors (a Realistic job), and Transportation Vehicle, Equipment, and Systems Inspectors, Except Aviation (a Realistic job), described separately.*

Transportation Vehicle, Equipment, and Systems Inspectors, Except Aviation

* Personality Code: RCI
* Education/Training Required: Work experience in a related occupation
* Annual Earnings: $51,440
* Beginning Wage: $27,340
* Earnings Growth Potential: High
* Growth: 16.4%
* Annual Job Openings: 2,122
* Self-Employed: 5.9%
* Part-Time: 3.7%

The job openings listed here are shared with Aviation Inspectors and with Freight and Cargo Inspectors.

Inspect and monitor transportation equipment, vehicles, or systems to ensure compliance with regulations and safety standards. Conduct vehicle or transportation equipment tests, using diagnostic equipment. Investigate and make recommendations on carrier requests for waiver of federal standards. Prepare reports on investigations or inspections and actions taken. Issue notices and recommend corrective actions when infractions or problems are found. Investigate incidents or violations such as delays, accidents, and equipment failures. Investigate complaints regarding safety violations. Inspect repairs to transportation vehicles and equipment to ensure that repair work was performed properly. Examine transportation vehicles, equipment, or systems to detect damage, wear, or malfunction. Inspect vehicles and other equipment for evidence of abuse, damage, or mechanical malfunction. Examine carrier operating rules, employee qualification guidelines, and carrier training and testing programs for compliance with regulations or safety standards. Inspect vehicles or equipment to ensure compliance with rules, standards, or regulations.

GOE—Interest Area/Cluster: 07. Government and Public Administration. **Work Group:** 07.03.

Regulations Enforcement. **Other Jobs in This Work Group:** Agricultural Inspectors; Aviation Inspectors; Compliance Officers, Except Agriculture, Construction, Health and Safety, and Transportation; Construction and Building Inspectors; Environmental Compliance Inspectors; Equal Opportunity Representatives and Officers; Financial Examiners; Fire Inspectors; Fish and Game Wardens; Forest Fire Inspectors and Prevention Specialists; Freight and Cargo Inspectors; Government Property Inspectors and Investigators; Immigration and Customs Inspectors; Licensing Examiners and Inspectors; Nuclear Monitoring Technicians; Occupational Health and Safety Specialists; Occupational Health and Safety Technicians; Tax Examiners, Collectors, and Revenue Agents.

Skills: Repairing; Equipment Maintenance; Troubleshooting; Installation; Quality Control Analysis; Operation Monitoring; Systems Analysis; Systems Evaluation.

Education and Training Programs: No related CIP programs; this job is learned through work experience in a related occupation. **Related Knowledge/Courses:** Mechanical Devices; Transportation; Public Safety and Security; Engineering and Technology; Administration and Management; Physics.

Work Environment: Outdoors; standing; using hands on objects, tools, or controls.

Truck Drivers, Heavy and Tractor-Trailer

* Personality Code: RC
* Education/Training Required: Moderate-term on-the-job training
* Annual Earnings: $36,220
* Beginning Wage: $23,380
* Earnings Growth Potential: Medium
* Growth: 10.4%
* Annual Job Openings: 279,032
* Self-Employed: 8.8%
* Part-Time: 7.2%

Drive a tractor-trailer combination or a truck with a capacity of at least 26,000 GVW to transport and deliver goods, livestock, or materials in liquid, loose, or packaged form. May be required to unload truck. May require use of automated routing equipment. Requires commercial drivers' license. Follow appropriate safety procedures when transporting dangerous goods. Check vehicles before driving them to ensure that mechanical, safety, and emergency equipment is in good working order. Maintain logs of working hours and of vehicle service and repair status, following applicable state and federal regulations. Obtain receipts or signatures when loads are delivered and collect payment for services when required. Check all load-related documentation to ensure that it is complete and accurate. Maneuver trucks into loading or unloading positions, following signals from loading crew as needed; check that vehicle position is correct and any special loading equipment is properly positioned. Drive trucks with capacities greater than 3 tons, including tractor-trailer combinations, to transport and deliver products, livestock, or other materials. Secure cargo for transport, using ropes, blocks, chain, binders, or covers. Read bills of lading to determine assignment details. Report vehicle defects, accidents, traffic violations, or damage to the vehicles. Read and interpret maps to determine vehicle routes. Couple and uncouple trailers by changing trailer jack positions, connecting or disconnecting air and electrical lines, and manipulating fifth-wheel locks. Collect delivery instructions from appropriate sources, verifying instructions and routes. Drive trucks to weigh stations before and after loading and along routes to document weights and to comply with state regulations. Operate equipment such as truck cab computers, CB radios, and telephones to exchange necessary information with bases, supervisors, or other drivers. Check conditions of trailers after contents have been unloaded to ensure that there has been no damage. Crank trailer landing gear up and down to safely secure vehicles. Wrap goods, using pads, packing paper, and containers, and secure loads to trailer walls, using straps. Perform basic vehicle maintenance tasks such as adding oil, fuel, and radiator fluid or performing minor repairs. Load and unload trucks or help others with loading and unloading, operating any special loading-related equipment on vehicles and using other equipment as necessary.

GOE—Interest Area/Cluster: 16. Transportation, Distribution, and Logistics. **Work Group:** 16.03. Truck Driving. **Other Jobs in This Work Group:** Truck Drivers, Light or Delivery Services.

Skills: Equipment Maintenance; Repairing; Operation Monitoring; Troubleshooting; Operation and Control.

Education and Training Program: Truck and Bus Driver/Commercial Vehicle Operation. **Related Knowledge/Courses:** Transportation; Geography; Public Safety and Security; Law and Government; Mechanical Devices.

Work Environment: Outdoors; very hot or cold; contaminants; sitting; using hands on objects, tools, or controls; repetitive motions.

Water and Liquid Waste Treatment Plant and System Operators

- ❋ Personality Code: RC
- ❋ Education/Training Required: Long-term on-the-job training
- ❋ Annual Earnings: $37,090
- ❋ Beginning Wage: $22,570
- ❋ Earnings Growth Potential: Medium
- ❋ Growth: 13.8%
- ❋ Annual Job Openings: 9,575
- ❋ Self-Employed: 1.3%
- ❋ Part-Time: 3.4%

Operate or control an entire process or system of machines, often through the use of control boards, to transfer or treat water or liquid waste. Add chemicals such as ammonia, chlorine, or lime to disinfect and deodorize water and other liquids. Operate and adjust controls on equipment to purify and clarify water, process or dispose of sewage, and

generate power. Inspect equipment or monitor operating conditions, meters, and gauges to determine load requirements and detect malfunctions. Collect and test water and sewage samples, using test equipment and color analysis standards. Record operational data, personnel attendance, or meter and gauge readings on specified forms. Maintain, repair, and lubricate equipment, using hand tools and power tools. Clean and maintain tanks and filter beds, using hand tools and power tools. Direct and coordinate plant workers engaged in routine operations and maintenance activities.

GOE—Interest Area/Cluster: 13. Manufacturing. **Work Group:** 13.16. Utility Operation and Energy Distribution. **Other Jobs in This Work Group:** Chemical Plant and System Operators; Gas Compressor and Gas Pumping Station Operators; Gas Plant Operators; Nuclear Power Reactor Operators; Petroleum Pump System Operators, Refinery Operators, and Gaugers; Power Distributors and Dispatchers; Power Plant Operators; Ship Engineers; Stationary Engineers and Boiler Operators.

Skills: Operation Monitoring; Operation and Control; Installation; Troubleshooting; Operations Analysis; Management of Material Resources; Equipment Maintenance; Science.

Education and Training Program: Water Quality and Wastewater Treatment Management and Recycling Technology/Technician. **Related Knowledge/Courses:** Biology; Chemistry; Physics; Public Safety and Security; Mechanical Devices; Law and Government.

Work Environment: More often outdoors than indoors; noisy; very hot or cold; contaminants; minor burns, cuts, bites, or stings.

Investigative Occupations

Aerospace Engineers

- ❋ Personality Code: IR
- ❋ Education/Training Required: Bachelor's degree
- ❋ Annual Earnings: $90,930
- ❋ Beginning Wage: $60,760
- ❋ Earnings Growth Potential: Low
- ❋ Growth: 10.2%
- ❋ Annual Job Openings: 6,498
- ❋ Self-Employed: 1.4%
- ❋ Part-Time: 2.6%

Perform a variety of engineering work in designing, constructing, and testing aircraft, missiles, and spacecraft. May conduct basic and applied research to evaluate adaptability of materials and equipment to aircraft design and manufacture. May recommend improvements in testing equipment and techniques. Formulate conceptual design of aeronautical or aerospace products or systems to meet customer requirements. Direct and coordinate activities of engineering or technical personnel designing, fabricating, modifying, or testing aircraft or aerospace products. Develop design criteria for aeronautical or aerospace products or systems, including testing methods, production costs, quality standards, and completion dates. Plan and conduct experimental, environmental, operational, and stress tests on models and prototypes of aircraft and aerospace systems and equipment. Evaluate product data and design from inspections and reports for conformance to engineering principles, customer requirements, and quality standards. Formulate mathematical models or other methods of computer analysis to develop, evaluate, or modify design according to customer engineering requirements. Write technical reports and other documentation, such as handbooks and bulletins, for use by engineering staff, management, and customers.

Analyze project requests and proposals and engineering data to determine feasibility, productibility, cost, and production time of aerospace or aeronautical product. Review performance reports and documentation from customers and field engineers and inspect malfunctioning or damaged products to determine problem. Direct research and development programs. Evaluate and approve selection of vendors by study of past performance and new advertisements. Plan and coordinate activities concerned with investigating and resolving customers' reports of technical problems with aircraft or aerospace vehicles. Maintain records of performance reports for future reference.

GOE—Interest Area/Cluster: 15. Scientific Research, Engineering, and Mathematics. **Work Group:** 15.07. Research and Design Engineering. **Other Jobs in This Work Group:** Biomedical Engineers; Chemical Engineers; Civil Engineers; Computer Hardware Engineers; Electrical Engineers; Electronics Engineers, Except Computer; Marine Architects; Marine Engineers; Marine Engineers and Naval Architects; Materials Engineers; Mechanical Engineers; Nuclear Engineers.

Skills: Science; Systems Evaluation; Systems Analysis; Judgment and Decision Making; Technology Design; Persuasion; Operations Analysis; Management of Personnel Resources.

Education and Training Program: Aerospace, Aeronautical and Astronautical Engineering. **Related Knowledge/Courses:** Engineering and Technology; Physics; Design; Mechanical Devices; Production and Processing; Mathematics.

Work Environment: Indoors; sitting; repetitive motions.

Anesthesiologists

- ❋ Personality Code: IRS
- ❋ Education/Training Required: First professional degree
- ❋ Annual Earnings: More than $145,600
- ❋ Beginning Wage: $118,320
- ❋ Earnings Growth Potential: Cannot be calculated
- ❋ Growth: 14.2%
- ❋ Annual Job Openings: 38,027
- ❋ Self-Employed: 14.7%
- ❋ Part-Time: 8.1%

The job openings listed here are shared with Family and General Practitioners; Internists, General; Obstetricians and Gynecologists; Pediatricians, General; Psychiatrists; and Surgeons.

Administer anesthetics during surgery or other medical procedures. Administer anesthetic or sedation during medical procedures, using local, intravenous, spinal, or caudal methods. Monitor patient before, during, and after anesthesia and counteract adverse reactions or complications. Provide and maintain life support and airway management and help prepare patients for emergency surgery. Record type and amount of anesthesia and patient condition throughout procedure. Examine patient; obtain medical history; and use diagnostic tests to determine risk during surgical, obstetrical, and other medical procedures. Position patient on operating table to maximize patient comfort and surgical accessibility. Decide when patients have recovered or stabilized enough to be sent to another room or ward or to be sent home following outpatient surgery. Coordinate administration of anesthetics with surgeons during operation. Confer with other medical professionals to determine type and method of anesthetic or sedation to render patient insensible to pain. Coordinate and direct work of nurses, medical technicians, and other health-care providers. Order laboratory tests, X rays, and other diagnostic procedures. Diagnose illnesses, using examinations, tests, and reports. Manage anesthesiological services, coordinating them with other medical activities and formulating plans and procedures. Provide medical care and consultation in many settings, prescribing medication and treatment and referring patients for surgery. Inform students and staff of types and methods of anesthesia administration, signs of complications, and emergency methods to counteract reactions. Schedule and maintain use of surgical suite, including operating, wash-up, and waiting rooms and anesthetic and sterilizing equipment. Instruct individuals and groups on ways to preserve health and prevent disease. Conduct medical research to aid in controlling and curing disease, to investigate new medications, and to develop and test new medical techniques.

GOE—Interest Area/Cluster: 08. Health Science. **Work Group:** 08.02. Medicine and Surgery. **Other Jobs in This Work Group:** Family and General Practitioners; Internists, General; Medical Assistants; Medical Transcriptionists; Obstetricians and Gynecologists; Pediatricians, General; Pharmacists; Pharmacy Aides; Pharmacy Technicians; Physician Assistants; Psychiatrists; Registered Nurses; Surgeons; Surgical Technologists.

Skills: Operation Monitoring; Science; Operation and Control; Judgment and Decision Making; Equipment Selection; Monitoring; Equipment Maintenance; Complex Problem Solving.

Education and Training Programs: Anesthesiology; Critical Care Anesthesiology. **Related Knowledge/ Courses:** Medicine and Dentistry; Biology; Chemistry; Psychology; Physics; Therapy and Counseling.

Work Environment: Indoors; contaminants; radiation; disease or infections; standing; using hands on objects, tools, or controls.

Anthropologists

- ❈ Personality Code: IA
- ❈ Education/Training Required: Master's degree
- ❈ Annual Earnings: $53,080
- ❈ Beginning Wage: $31,130
- ❈ Earnings Growth Potential: High
- ❈ Growth: 15.0%
- ❈ Annual Job Openings: 446
- ❈ Self-Employed: 6.1%
- ❈ Part-Time: 20.1%

The job openings listed here are shared with Archeologists.

Research, evaluate, and establish public policy concerning the origins of humans; their physical, social, linguistic, and cultural development; and their behavior, as well as the cultures, organizations, and institutions they have created. Collect information and make judgments through observation, interviews, and the review of documents. Plan and direct research to characterize and compare the economic, demographic, health-care, social, political, linguistic, and religious institutions of distinct cultural groups, communities, and organizations. Write about and present research findings for a variety of specialized and general audiences. Advise government agencies, private organizations, and communities regarding proposed programs, plans, and policies and their potential impacts on cultural institutions, organizations, and communities. Identify culturally-specific beliefs and practices affecting health status and access to services for distinct populations and communities in collaboration with medical and public health officials. Build and use text-based database management systems to support the analysis of detailed first-hand observational records, or "field notes." Develop intervention procedures, utilizing techniques such as individual and focus group interviews, consultations, and participant observation of social interaction. Construct and test data collection methods. Explain the origins and physical, social, or cultural development of humans, including physical attributes, cultural traditions, beliefs, languages, resource management practices, and settlement patterns. Conduct participatory action research in communities and organizations to assess how work is done and to design work systems, technologies, and environments. Train others in the application of ethnographic research methods to solve problems in organizational effectiveness, communications, technology development, policy-making, and program planning. Formulate general rules that describe and predict the development and behavior of cultures and social institutions. Collaborate with economic development planners to decide on the implementation of proposed development policies, plans, and programs based on culturally institutionalized barriers and facilitating circumstances. Create data records for use in describing and analyzing social patterns and processes, using photography, videography, and audio recordings.

GOE—Interest Area/Cluster: 15. Scientific Research, Engineering, and Mathematics. **Work Group:** 15.04. Social Sciences. **Other Jobs in This Work Group:** Anthropologists and Archeologists; Archeologists; Economists; Historians; Industrial-Organizational Psychologists; Political Scientists; School Psychologists; Sociologists.

Skills: Writing; Science; Social Perceptiveness; Complex Problem Solving; Systems Evaluation; Reading Comprehension; Systems Analysis; Active Listening.

Education and Training Programs: Anthropology; Physical Anthropology. **Related Knowledge/Courses:** Sociology and Anthropology; History and Archeology; Foreign Language; Philosophy and Theology; Geography; Biology.

Work Environment: Indoors; sitting.

Anthropologists and Archeologists

See Anthropologists (an Investigative job) and Archeologists (an Investigative job), described separately.

Archeologists

* Personality Code: IRA
* Education/Training Required: Master's degree
* Annual Earnings: $53,080
* Beginning Wage: $31,130
* Earnings Growth Potential: High
* Growth: 15.0%
* Annual Job Openings: 446
* Self-Employed: 6.1%
* Part-Time: 20.1%

The job openings listed here are shared with Anthropologists.

Conduct research to reconstruct record of past human life and culture from human remains, artifacts, architectural features, and structures recovered through excavation, underwater recovery, or other means of discovery. Write, present, and publish reports that record site history, methodology, and artifact analysis results, along with recommendations for conserving and interpreting findings. Compare findings from one site with archeological data from other sites to find similarities or differences. Research, survey, or assess sites of past societies and cultures in search of answers to specific research questions. Study objects and structures recovered by excavation to identify, date, and authenticate them and to interpret their significance. Develop and test theories concerning the origin and development of past cultures. Consult site reports, existing artifacts, and topographic maps to identify archeological sites. Create a grid of each site and draw and update maps of unit profiles, stratum surfaces, features, and findings. Record the exact locations and conditions of artifacts uncovered in diggings or surveys, using drawings and photographs as necessary. Assess archeological sites for resource management, development, or conservation purposes and recommend methods for site protection. Describe artifacts' physical properties or attributes, such as the materials from which artifacts are made and their size, shape, function, and decoration. Teach archeology at colleges and universities.

Collect artifacts made of stone, bone, metal, and other materials, placing them in bags and marking them to show where they were found. Create artifact typologies to organize and make sense of past material cultures. Lead field training sites and train field staff, students, and volunteers in excavation methods. Clean, restore, and preserve artifacts.

GOE—Interest Area/Cluster: 15. Scientific Research, Engineering, and Mathematics. **Work Group:** 15.04. Social Sciences. **Other Jobs in This Work Group:** Anthropologists; Anthropologists and Archeologists; Economists; Historians; Industrial-Organizational Psychologists; Political Scientists; School Psychologists; Sociologists.

Skills: Science; Management of Financial Resources; Writing; Management of Personnel Resources; Reading Comprehension; Active Learning; Management of Material Resources; Critical Thinking.

Education and Training Program: Archeology. **Related Knowledge/Courses:** History and Archeology; Sociology and Anthropology; Geography; Philosophy and Theology; Foreign Language; Biology.

Work Environment: More often indoors than outdoors; sitting; using hands on objects, tools, or controls.

Astronomers

* Personality Code: IAR
* Education/Training Required: Doctoral degree
* Annual Earnings: $99,020
* Beginning Wage: $44,490
* Earnings Growth Potential: Very high
* Growth: 5.6%
* Annual Job Openings: 128
* Self-Employed: 0.4%
* Part-Time: 5.2%

Observe, research, and interpret celestial and astronomical phenomena to increase basic knowledge and apply such information to practical

problems. Study celestial phenomena, using a variety of ground-based and space-borne telescopes and scientific instruments. Analyze research data to determine its significance, using computers. Present research findings at scientific conferences and in papers written for scientific journals. Measure radio, infrared, gamma, and X-ray emissions from extraterrestrial sources. Develop theories based on personal observations or on observations and theories of other astronomers. Raise funds for scientific research. Collaborate with other astronomers to carry out research projects. Develop instrumentation and software for astronomical observation and analysis. Teach astronomy or astrophysics. Develop and modify astronomy-related programs for public presentation. Calculate orbits and determine sizes, shapes, brightness, and motions of different celestial bodies. Direct the operations of a planetarium.

GOE—Interest Area/Cluster: 15. Scientific Research, Engineering, and Mathematics. **Work Group:** 15.02. Physical Sciences. **Other Jobs in This Work Group:** Atmospheric and Space Scientists; Chemists; Geographers; Geoscientists, Except Hydrologists and Geographers; Hydrologists; Materials Scientists; Physicists.

Skills: Science; Programming; Mathematics; Complex Problem Solving; Technology Design; Active Learning; Critical Thinking; Reading Comprehension.

Education and Training Programs: Astronomy; Astrophysics; Planetary Astronomy and Science; Astronomy and Astrophysics, Other. **Related Knowledge/Courses:** Physics; Mathematics; Engineering and Technology; Chemistry; Computers and Electronics; Education and Training.

Work Environment: Indoors; sitting.

Atmospheric and Space Scientists

- ❋ Personality Code: IR
- ❋ Education/Training Required: Bachelor's degree
- ❋ Annual Earnings: $78,390
- ❋ Beginning Wage: $37,030
- ❋ Earnings Growth Potential: Very high
- ❋ Growth: 10.6%
- ❋ Annual Job Openings: 735
- ❋ Self-Employed: 0.0%
- ❋ Part-Time: 5.2%

Investigate atmospheric phenomena and interpret meteorological data gathered by surface and air stations, satellites, and radar to prepare reports and forecasts for public and other uses. Study and interpret data, reports, maps, photographs, and charts to predict long- and short-range weather conditions, using computer models and knowledge of climate theory, physics, and mathematics. Broadcast weather conditions, forecasts, and severe weather warnings to the public via television, radio, and the Internet or provide this information to the news media. Gather data from sources such as surface and upper air stations, satellites, weather bureaus, and radar for use in meteorological reports and forecasts. Prepare forecasts and briefings to meet the needs of industry, business, government, and other groups. Apply meteorological knowledge to problems in areas including agriculture, pollution control, and water management and to issues such as global warming or ozone depletion. Conduct basic or applied meteorological research into the processes and determinants of atmospheric phenomena, weather, and climate. Operate computer graphic equipment to produce weather reports and maps for analysis, distribution, or use in weather broadcasts. Measure wind, temperature, and humidity in the upper atmosphere, using weather balloons. Develop and use weather forecasting tools such as mathematical and computer models. Direct forecasting services at weather stations or at radio or television broadcasting facilities. Research and analyze the impact of industrial projects and pollution on climate, air quality, and weather phenomena. Collect air samples from planes and ships over land and sea to study atmospheric composition. Conduct numerical simulations of climate conditions to understand and predict global and regional weather patterns. Collect and analyze historical climate information such as precipitation and temperature records help predict future weather and climate trends. Consult with agencies, professionals, or researchers regarding the use and interpretation of climatological information. Design and develop new equipment and methods for meteorological data collection, remote sensing, or related applications. Make scientific presentations and publish reports, articles, or texts.

GOE—Interest Area/Cluster: 15. Scientific Research, Engineering, and Mathematics. **Work Group:** 15.02. Physical Sciences. **Other Jobs in This Work Group:** Astronomers; Chemists; Geographers; Geoscientists, Except Hydrologists and Geographers; Hydrologists; Materials Scientists; Physicists.

Skills: Science; Programming; Judgment and Decision Making; Operation Monitoring; Operations Analysis; Technology Design; Quality Control Analysis; Operation and Control.

Education and Training Programs: Atmospheric Sciences and Meteorology, General; Atmospheric Chemistry and Climatology; Atmospheric Physics and Dynamics; Meteorology; Atmospheric Sciences and Meteorology, Other. **Related Knowledge/Courses:** Geography; Physics; Mathematics; Computers and Electronics; Communications and Media; Customer and Personal Service.

Work Environment: Indoors; noisy; sitting; repetitive motions.

Biochemists and Biophysicists

* Personality Code: IAR
* Education/Training Required: Doctoral degree
* Annual Earnings: $79,270
* Beginning Wage: $42,670
* Earnings Growth Potential: High
* Growth: 15.9%
* Annual Job Openings: 1,637
* Self-Employed: 2.5%
* Part-Time: 7.3%

Study the chemical composition and physical principles of living cells and organisms and their electrical and mechanical energy and related phenomena. May conduct research in order to further understanding of the complex chemical combinations and reactions involved in metabolism, reproduction, growth, and heredity. May determine the effects of foods, drugs, serums, hormones, and other substances on tissues and vital processes of living organisms. Design and perform experiments with equipment such as lasers, accelerators, and mass spectrometers. Analyze brain functions, such as learning, thinking, and memory, and analyze the dynamics of seeing and hearing. Share research findings by writing scientific articles and by making presentations at scientific conferences. Develop and test new drugs and medications intended for commercial distribution. Develop methods to process, store, and use foods, drugs, and chemical compounds. Develop new methods to study the mechanisms of biological processes. Examine the molecular and chemical aspects of immune system functioning. Investigate the nature, composition, and expression of genes and research how genetic engineering can impact these processes. Determine the three-dimensional structure of biological macromolecules. Prepare reports and recommendations based upon research outcomes. Design and build laboratory equipment needed for special research projects. Isolate, analyze, and synthesize vitamins, hormones, allergens, minerals, and enzymes and determine their effects on body functions. Research cancer treatment, using radiation and nuclear particles. Research transformations of substances in cells, using atomic isotopes. Study how light is absorbed in processes such as photosynthesis or vision. Analyze foods to determine their nutritional values and the effects of cooking, canning, and processing on these values. Study spatial configurations of submicroscopic molecules such as proteins, using X rays and electron microscopes. Teach and advise undergraduate and graduate students and supervise their research. Investigate the transmission of electrical impulses along nerves and muscles. Research how characteristics of plants and animals are carried through successive generations. Investigate damage to cells and tissues caused by X rays and nuclear particles. Research the chemical effects of substances such as drugs, serums, hormones, and food on tissues and vital processes. Develop and execute tests to detect diseases, genetic disorders, or other abnormalities. Produce pharmaceutically and industrially useful proteins, using recombinant DNA technology.

GOE—Interest Area/Cluster: 15. Scientific Research, Engineering, and Mathematics. **Work Group:** 15.03. Life Sciences. **Other Jobs in This Work Group:** Biologists; Environmental Scientists and Specialists, Including Health; Epidemiologists; Medical Scientists, Except Epidemiologists; Microbiologists.

Skills: Science; Technology Design; Writing; Equipment Selection; Operations Analysis; Reading Comprehension; Troubleshooting; Quality Control Analysis.

Education and Training Programs: Soil Chemistry and Physics; Soil Microbiology; Biophysics; Molecular Biophysics; Biochemistry/Biophysics and Molecular Biology; Cell/Cellular Biology and Anatomical Sciences, Other. **Related Knowledge/Courses:** Biology; Chemistry; Physics; Engineering and Technology; Medicine and Dentistry; Design.

Work Environment: Indoors; sitting; using hands on objects, tools, or controls.

Biomedical Engineers

- ❋ Personality Code: IR
- ❋ Education/Training Required: Bachelor's degree
- ❋ Annual Earnings: $75,440
- ❋ Beginning Wage: $45,910
- ❋ Earnings Growth Potential: Medium
- ❋ Growth: 21.1%
- ❋ Annual Job Openings: 1,804
- ❋ Self-Employed: 0.0%
- ❋ Part-Time: 3.4%

Apply knowledge of engineering, biology, and biomechanical principles to the design, development, and evaluation of biological and health systems and products, such as artificial organs, prostheses, instrumentation, medical information systems, and health management and care delivery systems. Evaluate the safety, efficiency, and effectiveness of biomedical equipment. Install, adjust, maintain, and/or repair biomedical equipment. Advise hospital administrators on the planning, acquisition, and use of medical equipment. Advise and assist in the application of instrumentation in clinical environments. Develop models or computer simulations of human bio-behavioral systems in order to obtain data for measuring or controlling life processes. Research new materials to be used for products such as implanted artificial organs. Design and develop medical diagnostic and clinical instrumentation, equipment, and procedures, utilizing the principles of engineering and bio-behavioral sciences. Conduct research, along with life scientists, chemists, and medical scientists, on the engineering aspects of the biological systems of humans and animals. Teach biomedical engineering or disseminate knowledge about field through writing or consulting. Design and deliver technology to assist people with disabilities. Diagnose and interpret bioelectric data, using signal-processing techniques. Adapt or design computer hardware or software for medical science uses. Analyze new medical procedures in order to forecast likely outcomes. Develop new applications for energy sources, such as using nuclear power for biomedical implants.

GOE—Interest Area/Cluster: 15. Scientific Research, Engineering, and Mathematics. **Work Group:** 15.07. Research and Design Engineering. **Other Jobs in This Work Group:** Aerospace Engineers; Chemical Engineers; Civil Engineers; Computer Hardware Engineers; Electrical Engineers; Electronics Engineers, Except Computer; Marine Architects; Marine Engineers; Marine Engineers and Naval Architects; Materials Engineers; Mechanical Engineers; Nuclear Engineers.

Skills: Technology Design; Science; Installation; Operations Analysis; Quality Control Analysis; Systems Evaluation; Troubleshooting; Management of Material Resources.

Education and Training Program: Biomedical/Medical Engineering. **Related Knowledge/Courses:** Engineering and Technology; Computers and Electronics; Physics; Design; Mechanical Devices; Chemistry.

Work Environment: Indoors; contaminants; disease or infections; hazardous conditions; sitting; using hands on objects, tools, or controls.

Chemical Engineers

- ❀ Personality Code: IR
- ❀ Education/Training Required: Bachelor's degree
- ❀ Annual Earnings: $81,500
- ❀ Beginning Wage: $52,060
- ❀ Earnings Growth Potential: Medium
- ❀ Growth: 7.9%
- ❀ Annual Job Openings: 2,111
- ❀ Self-Employed: 1.9%
- ❀ Part-Time: 3.4%

Design chemical plant equipment and devise processes for manufacturing chemicals and products, such as gasoline, synthetic rubber, plastics, detergents, cement, paper, and pulp, by applying principles and technology of chemistry, physics, and engineering. Perform tests throughout stages of production to determine degree of control over variables, including temperature, density, specific gravity, and pressure. Develop safety procedures to be employed by workers operating equipment or working in close proximity to ongoing chemical reactions. Determine most effective arrangement of operations such as mixing, crushing, heat transfer, distillation, and drying. Prepare estimate of production costs and production progress reports for management. Direct activities of workers who operate or who are engaged in constructing and improving absorption, evaporation, or electromagnetic equipment. Perform laboratory studies of steps in manufacture of new product and test proposed process in small-scale operation such as a pilot plant. Develop processes to separate components of liquids or gases or generate electrical currents by using controlled chemical processes. Conduct research to develop new and improved chemical manufacturing processes. Design measurement and control systems for chemical plants based on data collected in laboratory experiments and in pilot plant operations. Design and plan layout of equipment.

GOE—Interest Area/Cluster: 15. Scientific Research, Engineering, and Mathematics. **Work Group:** 15.07. Research and Design Engineering. **Other Jobs in This Work Group:** Aerospace Engineers; Biomedical Engineers; Civil Engineers; Computer Hardware Engineers; Electrical Engineers; Electronics Engineers, Except Computer; Marine Architects; Marine Engineers; Marine Engineers and Naval Architects; Materials Engineers; Mechanical Engineers; Nuclear Engineers.

Skills: Science; Technology Design; Troubleshooting; Programming; Operations Analysis; Installation; Mathematics; Systems Analysis.

Education and Training Program: Chemical Engineering. **Related Knowledge/Courses:** Engineering and Technology; Chemistry; Physics; Design; Production and Processing; Mathematics.

Work Environment: Indoors; noisy; hazardous conditions; sitting.

Chemists

- ❋ Personality Code: IRC
- ❋ Education/Training Required: Bachelor's degree
- ❋ Annual Earnings: $63,490
- ❋ Beginning Wage: $36,810
- ❋ Earnings Growth Potential: High
- ❋ Growth: 9.1%
- ❋ Annual Job Openings: 9,024
- ❋ Self-Employed: 1.2%
- ❋ Part-Time: 3.9%

Conduct qualitative and quantitative chemical analyses or chemical experiments in laboratories for quality or process control or to develop new products or knowledge. Analyze organic and inorganic compounds to determine chemical and physical properties, composition, structure, relationships, and reactions, utilizing chromatography, spectroscopy, and spectrophotometry techniques. Develop, improve, and customize products, equipment, formulas, processes, and analytical methods. Compile and analyze test information to determine process or equipment operating efficiency and to diagnose malfunctions. Confer with scientists and engineers to conduct analyses of research projects, interpret test results, or develop nonstandard tests. Direct, coordinate, and advise personnel in test procedures for analyzing components and physical properties of materials. Induce changes in composition of substances by introducing heat, light, energy, and chemical catalysts for quantitative and qualitative analysis. Write technical papers and reports and prepare standards and specifications for processes, facilities, products, or tests. Study effects of various methods of processing, preserving, and packaging on composition and properties of foods. Prepare test solutions, compounds, and reagents for laboratory personnel to conduct test.

GOE—Interest Area/Cluster: 15. Scientific Research, Engineering, and Mathematics. **Work Group:** 15.02. Physical Sciences. **Other Jobs in**

This Work Group: Astronomers; Atmospheric and Space Scientists; Geographers; Geoscientists, Except Hydrologists and Geographers; Hydrologists; Materials Scientists; Physicists.

Skills: Science; Quality Control Analysis; Technology Design; Operation Monitoring; Equipment Selection; Management of Material Resources; Management of Financial Resources; Operations Analysis.

Education and Training Programs: Chemistry, General; Analytical Chemistry; Inorganic Chemistry; Organic Chemistry; Physical and Theoretical Chemistry; Polymer Chemistry; Chemical Physics; Chemistry, Other. **Related Knowledge/Courses:** Chemistry; Mathematics; Engineering and Technology; Production and Processing; Computers and Electronics; Law and Government.

Work Environment: Indoors; contaminants; hazardous conditions; standing.

Clinical Psychologists

- ❋ Personality Code: ISA
- ❋ Education/Training Required: Doctoral degree
- ❋ Annual Earnings: $62,210
- ❋ Beginning Wage: $37,300
- ❋ Earnings Growth Potential: High
- ❋ Growth: 15.8%
- ❋ Annual Job Openings: 8,309
- ❋ Self-Employed: 34.2%
- ❋ Part-Time: 24.0%

The job openings listed here are shared with Counseling Psychologists and with School Psychologists.

Diagnose or evaluate mental and emotional disorders of individuals through observation, interview, and psychological tests and formulate and administer programs of treatment. Identify psychological, emotional, or behavioral issues and diagnose disorders, using information obtained from interviews, tests, records, and reference materials. Develop and implement individual treatment plans, specifying type, frequency, intensity, and duration of therapy. Interact with clients to assist them in gaining insight, defining goals, and planning action to achieve effective personal, social, educational, and vocational development and adjustment. Discuss the treatment of problems with clients. Utilize a variety of treatment methods such as psychotherapy, hypnosis, behavior modification, stress reduction therapy, psychodrama, and play therapy. Counsel individuals and groups regarding problems such as stress, substance abuse, and family situations to modify behavior or to improve personal, social, and vocational adjustment. Write reports on clients and maintain required paperwork. Evaluate the effectiveness of counseling or treatments and the accuracy and completeness of diagnoses; then modify plans and diagnoses as necessary. Obtain and study medical, psychological, social, and family histories by interviewing individuals, couples, or families and by reviewing records. Consult reference material such as textbooks, manuals, and journals to identify symptoms, make diagnoses, and develop approaches to treatment. Maintain current knowledge of relevant research. Observe individuals at play, in group interactions, or in other contexts to detect indications of mental deficiency, abnormal behavior, or maladjustment. Select, administer, score, and interpret psychological tests to obtain information on individuals' intelligence, achievements, interests, and personalities. Refer clients to other specialists, institutions, or support services as necessary. Develop, direct, and participate in training programs for staff and students. Provide psychological or administrative services and advice to private firms and community agencies regarding mental health programs or individual cases. Provide occupational, educational, and other information to individuals so that they can make educational and vocational plans.

GOE—Interest Area/Cluster: 10. Human Service. **Work Group:** 10.01. Counseling and Social Work. **Other Jobs in This Work Group:** Child, Family, and School Social Workers; Clinical, Counseling, and School Psychologists; Counseling Psychologists; Marriage and Family Therapists; Medical and Public Health Social Workers; Mental Health and Substance Abuse Social Workers; Mental Health Counselors; Probation Officers and Correctional Treatment Specialists; Rehabilitation Counselors; Residential Advisors; Social and Human Service Assistants; Substance Abuse and Behavioral Disorder Counselors.

Skills: Social Perceptiveness; Service Orientation; Complex Problem Solving; Learning Strategies; Active Listening; Negotiation; Active Learning; Critical Thinking.

Education and Training Programs: Psychology, General; Clinical Psychology; Counseling Psychology; Developmental and Child Psychology; School Psychology; Clinical Child Psychology; Psychoanalysis and Psychotherapy. **Related Knowledge/Courses:** Therapy and Counseling; Psychology; Sociology and Anthropology; Philosophy and Theology; Customer and Personal Service; Medicine and Dentistry.

Work Environment: Indoors; sitting.

Clinical, Counseling, and School Psychologists

See Clinical Psychologists (an Investigative job), Counseling Psychologists (a Social job), and School Psychologists (an Investigative job), described separately.

Computer and Information Scientists, Research

- ❋ Personality Code: IRC
- ❋ Education/Training Required: Doctoral degree
- ❋ Annual Earnings: $97,970
- ❋ Beginning Wage: $55,930
- ❋ Earnings Growth Potential: High
- ❋ Growth: 21.5%
- ❋ Annual Job Openings: 2,901
- ❋ Self-Employed: 5.3%
- ❋ Part-Time: 5.6%

Conduct research into fundamental computer and information science as theorists, designers, or inventors. Solve or develop solutions to problems in the field of computer hardware and software. Analyze problems to develop solutions involving computer hardware and software. Assign or schedule tasks in order to meet work priorities and goals. Evaluate project plans and proposals to assess feasibility issues. Apply theoretical expertise and innovation to create or apply new technology, such as adapting principles for applying computers to new uses. Consult with users, management, vendors, and technicians to determine computing needs and system requirements. Meet with managers, vendors, and others to solicit cooperation and resolve problems. Conduct logical analyses of business, scientific, engineering, and other technical problems, formulating mathematical models of problems for solution by computers. Develop and interpret organizational goals, policies, and procedures. Participate in staffing decisions and direct training of subordinates. Develop performance standards and evaluate work in light of established standards. Design computers and the software that runs them. Maintain network hardware and software, direct network security measures, and monitor networks to ensure availability to system users. Participate in multidisciplinary projects in areas such as virtual reality, human-computer interaction, or robotics. Approve, prepare, monitor, and adjust operational budgets. Direct daily operations of departments, coordinating project activities with other departments.

GOE—Interest Area/Cluster: 11. Information Technology. **Work Group:** 11.02. Information Technology Specialties. **Other Jobs in This Work Group:** Computer Operators; Computer Programmers; Computer Security Specialists; Computer Software Engineers, Applications; Computer Software Engineers, Systems Software; Computer Support Specialists; Computer Systems Analysts; Computer Systems Engineers/Architects; Database Administrators; Network Designers; Network Systems and Data Communications Analysts; Software Quality Assurance Engineers and Testers; Web Administrators; Web Developers.

Skills: Programming; Science; Systems Analysis; Operations Analysis; Technology Design; Active Learning; Complex Problem Solving; Mathematics.

Education and Training Programs: Computer and Information Sciences, General; Artificial Intelligence and Robotics; Information Science/Studies; Computer Systems Analysis/Analyst; Computer Science; Computer and Information Sciences and Support Services, Other; Medical Informatics. **Related Knowledge/Courses:** Computers and Electronics; Telecommunications; Engineering and Technology; Mathematics; Design; Education and Training.

Work Environment: No data available.

Computer Hardware Engineers

- ❋ Personality Code: IRC
- ❋ Education/Training Required: Bachelor's degree
- ❋ Annual Earnings: $91,860
- ❋ Beginning Wage: $55,880
- ❋ Earnings Growth Potential: Medium
- ❋ Growth: 4.6%
- ❋ Annual Job Openings: 3,572
- ❋ Self-Employed: 3.6%
- ❋ Part-Time: 2.7%

Investigative–C

Research, design, develop, and test computer or computer-related equipment for commercial, industrial, military, or scientific use. May supervise the manufacturing and installation of computer or computer-related equipment and components. Update knowledge and skills to keep up with rapid advancements in computer technology. Provide technical support to designers, marketing and sales departments, suppliers, engineers, and other team members throughout the product development and implementation process. Test and verify hardware and support peripherals to ensure that they meet specifications and requirements, analyzing and recording test data. Monitor functioning of equipment and make necessary modifications to ensure system operates in conformance with specifications. Analyze information to determine, recommend, and plan layout, including type of computers and peripheral equipment modifications. Build, test, and modify product prototypes, using working models or theoretical models constructed using computer simulation. Analyze user needs and recommend appropriate hardware. Direct technicians, engineering designers, or other technical support personnel as needed. Confer with engineering staff and consult specifications to evaluate interface between hardware and software and operational and performance requirements of overall system. Select hardware and material, assuring compliance with specifications and product requirements. Store, retrieve, and manipulate data for analysis of system capabilities and requirements. Write detailed functional specifications that document the hardware development process and support hardware introduction. Specify power supply requirements and configuration, drawing on system performance expectations and design specifications. Provide training and support to system designers and users. Assemble and modify existing pieces of equipment to meet special needs. Evaluate factors such as reporting formats required, cost constraints, and need for security restrictions to determine hardware configuration. Design and develop computer hardware and support peripherals, including central processing units (CPUs), support logic, microprocessors, custom integrated circuits, and printers and disk drives. Recommend purchase of equipment to control dust, temperature, and humidity in area of system installation.

GOE—Interest Area/Cluster: 15. Scientific Research, Engineering, and Mathematics. **Work Group:** 15.07. Research and Design Engineering. **Other Jobs in This Work Group:** Aerospace Engineers; Biomedical Engineers; Chemical Engineers; Civil Engineers; Electrical Engineers; Electronics Engineers, Except Computer; Marine Architects; Marine Engineers; Marine Engineers and Naval Architects; Materials Engineers; Mechanical Engineers; Nuclear Engineers.

Skills: Programming; Operations Analysis; Systems Analysis; Systems Evaluation; Troubleshooting; Technology Design; Science; Quality Control Analysis.

Education and Training Programs: Computer Engineering, General; Computer Hardware Engineering. **Related Knowledge/Courses:** Computers and Electronics; Engineering and Technology; Telecommunications; Design; Physics; Communications and Media.

Work Environment: Indoors; sitting.

Computer Security Specialists

- ❋ Personality Code: CIR
- ❋ Education/Training Required: Bachelor's degree
- ❋ Annual Earnings: $64,690
- ❋ Beginning Wage: $39,970
- ❋ Earnings Growth Potential: Medium
- ❋ Growth: 27.0%
- ❋ Annual Job Openings: 37,010
- ❋ Self-Employed: 0.4%
- ❋ Part-Time: 3.1%

The job openings listed here are shared with Network and Computer Systems Administrators.

Plan, coordinate, and implement security measures for information systems to regulate access to computer data files and prevent unauthorized modification, destruction, or disclosure of information. Train users and promote security awareness to ensure system security and to improve server and network efficiency. Develop plans to safeguard computer files against accidental or unauthorized modification, destruction, or disclosure and to meet emergency data processing needs. Confer with users to discuss issues such as computer data access needs, security violations, and programming changes. Monitor current reports of computer viruses to determine when to update virus protection systems. Modify computer security files to incorporate new software, correct errors, or change individual access status. Coordinate implementation of computer system plan with establishment personnel and outside vendors. Monitor use of data files and regulate access to safeguard information in computer files. Perform risk assessments and execute tests of data-processing system to ensure functioning of data-processing activities and security measures. Encrypt data transmissions and erect firewalls to conceal confidential information as it is being transmitted and to keep out tainted digital transfers. Document computer security and emergency measures policies, procedures, and tests. Review violations of computer security procedures and discuss procedures with violators to ensure violations are not repeated. Maintain permanent fleet cryptologic and carry-on direct support systems required in special land, sea surface, and subsurface operations.

GOE—Interest Area/Cluster: 11. Information Technology. **Work Group:** 11.02. Information Technology Specialties. **Other Jobs in This Work Group:** Computer and Information Scientists, Research; Computer Operators; Computer Programmers; Computer Software Engineers, Applications; Computer Software Engineers, Systems Software; Computer Support Specialists; Computer Systems Analysts; Computer Systems Engineers/Architects; Database Administrators; Network Designers; Network Systems and Data Communications Analysts;

Software Quality Assurance Engineers and Testers; Web Administrators; Web Developers.

Skills: Systems Evaluation; Systems Analysis; Operations Analysis; Programming; Installation; Management of Material Resources; Troubleshooting; Management of Financial Resources.

Education and Training Programs: Computer and Information Sciences, General; Information Science/Studies; Computer Systems Analysis/Analyst; Computer Systems Networking and Telecommunications; System Administration/Administrator; System, Networking, and LAN/WAN Management/Manager; Computer and Information Systems Security; Computer and Information Sciences and Support Services, Other. **Related Knowledge/Courses:** Computers and Electronics; Telecommunications; Engineering and Technology; Design; Education and Training; Therapy and Counseling.

Work Environment: Indoors; sitting.

Computer Software Engineers, Applications

- ✷ Personality Code: IRC
- ✷ Education/Training Required: Bachelor's degree
- ✷ Annual Earnings: $83,130
- ✷ Beginning Wage: $52,090
- ✷ Earnings Growth Potential: Medium
- ✷ Growth: 44.6%
- ✷ Annual Job Openings: 58,690
- ✷ Self-Employed: 2.0%
- ✷ Part-Time: 2.6%

Develop, create, and modify general computer applications software or specialized utility programs. Analyze user needs and develop software solutions. Design software or customize software for client use with the aim of optimizing operational efficiency. May analyze and design databases within an application area, working individually

or coordinating database development as part of a team. Confer with systems analysts, engineers, programmers, and others to design system and to obtain information on project limitations and capabilities, performance requirements, and interfaces. Modify existing software to correct errors, allow it to adapt to new hardware, or improve its performance. Analyze user needs and software requirements to determine feasibility of design within time and cost constraints. Consult with customers about software system design and maintenance. Coordinate software system installation and monitor equipment functioning to ensure specifications are met. Design, develop, and modify software systems, using scientific analysis and mathematical models to predict and measure outcome and consequences of design. Develop and direct software system testing and validation procedures, programming, and documentation. Analyze information to determine, recommend, and plan computer specifications and layouts and peripheral equipment modifications. Supervise the work of programmers, technologists, and technicians and other engineering and scientific personnel. Obtain and evaluate information on factors such as reporting formats required, costs, and security needs to determine hardware configuration. Determine system performance standards. Train users to use new or modified equipment. Store, retrieve, and manipulate data for analysis of system capabilities and requirements. Specify power supply requirements and configuration. Recommend purchase of equipment to control dust, temperature, and humidity in area of system installation.

GOE—Interest Area/Cluster: 11. Information Technology. **Work Group:** 11.02. Information Technology Specialties. **Other Jobs in This Work Group:** Computer and Information Scientists, Research; Computer Operators; Computer Programmers; Computer Security Specialists; Computer Software Engineers, Systems Software; Computer Support Specialists; Computer Systems Analysts; Computer Systems Engineers/Architects; Database Administrators; Network Designers; Network Systems and Data Communications Analysts; Software Quality Assurance Engineers and Testers; Web Administrators; Web Developers.

Skills: Programming; Troubleshooting; Technology Design; Systems Analysis; Quality Control Analysis; Operations Analysis; Installation; Complex Problem Solving.

Education and Training Programs: Artificial Intelligence and Robotics; Information Technology; Computer Science; Computer Engineering, General; Computer Software Engineering; Computer Engineering Technologies/Technicians, Other; Bioinformatics; Medical Informatics; Medical Illustration and Informatics, Other. **Related Knowledge/Courses:** Computers and Electronics; Telecommunications; Engineering and Technology; Design; Mathematics; Physics.

Work Environment: Indoors; sitting; using hands on objects, tools, or controls; repetitive motions.

Computer Software Engineers, Systems Software

- ❋ Personality Code: ICR
- ❋ Education/Training Required: Bachelor's degree
- ❋ Annual Earnings: $89,070
- ❋ Beginning Wage: $55,870
- ❋ Earnings Growth Potential: Medium
- ❋ Growth: 28.2%
- ❋ Annual Job Openings: 33,139
- ❋ Self-Employed: 2.1%
- ❋ Part-Time: 2.6%

Research, design, develop, and test operating systems-level software, compilers, and network distribution software for medical, industrial, military, communications, aerospace, business, scientific, and general computing applications. Set operational specifications and formulate and analyze software requirements. Apply principles and techniques of computer science, engineering, and mathematical analysis. Modify existing software to correct errors, to adapt it to new hardware, or to upgrade interfaces and improve performance. Design and develop software systems, using scientific analysis and mathematical models to predict and measure outcome and consequences of design. Consult with engineering staff to evaluate interface between hardware and software, develop specifications and performance requirements, and resolve customer problems. Analyze information to determine, recommend, and plan installation of a new system or modification of an existing system. Develop and direct software system testing and validation procedures. Direct software programming and development of documentation. Consult with customers or other departments on project status, proposals, and technical issues such as software system design and maintenance. Advise customer about, or perform, maintenance of software system. Coordinate installation of software system. Monitor functioning of equipment to ensure system operates in conformance with specifications. Store, retrieve, and manipulate data for analysis of system capabilities and requirements. Confer with data processing and project managers to obtain information on limitations and capabilities for data-processing projects. Prepare reports and correspondence concerning project specifications, activities, and status. Evaluate factors such as reporting formats required, cost constraints, and need for security restrictions to determine hardware configuration. Supervise and assign work to programmers, designers, technologists and technicians, and other engineering and scientific personnel. Train users to use new or modified equipment. Utilize microcontrollers to develop control signals; implement control algorithms; and measure process variables such as temperatures, pressures, and positions. Recommend purchase of equipment to control dust, temperature, and humidity in area of system installation. Specify power supply requirements and configuration.

GOE—Interest Area/Cluster: 11. Information Technology. **Work Group:** 11.02. Information Technology Specialties. **Other Jobs in This Work Group:** Computer and Information Scientists, Research; Computer Operators; Computer Programmers; Computer Security Specialists; Computer Software Engineers, Applications; Computer Support Specialists; Computer Systems Analysts; Computer Systems Engineers/Architects; Database Administrators;

Network Designers; Network Systems and Data Communications Analysts; Software Quality Assurance Engineers and Testers; Web Administrators; Web Developers.

Skills: Programming; Technology Design; Systems Analysis; Troubleshooting; Operations Analysis; Complex Problem Solving; Science; Mathematics.

Education and Training Programs: Artificial Intelligence and Robotics; Information Technology; Information Science/Studies; Computer Science; System, Networking, and LAN/WAN Management/Manager; Computer Engineering, General; Computer Engineering Technologies/Technicians, Other. **Related Knowledge/Courses:** Computers and Electronics; Design; Engineering and Technology; Telecommunications; Mathematics; Communications and Media.

Work Environment: Indoors; sitting; using hands on objects, tools, or controls; repetitive motions.

Computer Systems Analysts

- ✵ Personality Code: ICR
- ✵ Education/Training Required: Bachelor's degree
- ✵ Annual Earnings: $73,090
- ✵ Beginning Wage: $43,930
- ✵ Earnings Growth Potential: Medium
- ✵ Growth: 29.0%
- ✵ Annual Job Openings: 63,166
- ✵ Self-Employed: 5.8%
- ✵ Part-Time: 5.6%

Analyze science, engineering, business, and all other data-processing problems for application to electronic data processing systems. Analyze user requirements, procedures, and problems to automate or improve existing systems and review computer system capabilities, workflow, and scheduling limitations. May analyze or recommend commercially available software. May supervise computer programmers. Provide staff and

Investigative-C

users with assistance solving computer-related problems, such as malfunctions and program problems. Test, maintain, and monitor computer programs and systems, including coordinating the installation of computer programs and systems. Use object-oriented programming languages as well as client and server applications development processes and multimedia and Internet technology. Confer with clients regarding the nature of the information processing or computation needs a computer program is to address. Coordinate and link the computer systems within an organization to increase compatibility and so information can be shared. Consult with management to ensure agreement on system principles. Expand or modify system to serve new purposes or improve workflow. Interview or survey workers, observe job performance, or perform the job to determine what information is processed and how it is processed. Determine computer software or hardware needed to set up or alter system. Train staff and users to work with computer systems and programs. Analyze information processing or computation needs and plan and design computer systems, using techniques such as structured analysis, data modeling, and information engineering. Assess the usefulness of pre-developed application packages and adapt them to a user environment. Define the goals of the system and devise flow charts and diagrams describing logical operational steps of programs. Develop, document, and revise system design procedures, test procedures, and quality standards. Review and analyze computer printouts and performance indicators to locate code problems; correct errors by correcting codes. Recommend new equipment or software packages. Read manuals, periodicals, and technical reports to learn how to develop programs that meet staff and user requirements. Supervise computer programmers or other systems analysts or serve as project leaders for particular systems projects. Utilize the computer in the analysis and solution of business problems such as development of integrated production and inventory control and cost analysis systems.

GOE—Interest Area/Cluster: 11. Information Technology. **Work Group:** 11.02. Information Technology Specialties. **Other Jobs in This Work Group:** Computer and Information Scientists, Research; Computer Operators; Computer Programmers; Computer Security Specialists; Computer Software Engineers, Applications; Computer Software Engineers, Systems Software; Computer Support Specialists; Computer Systems Engineers/Architects; Database Administrators; Network Designers; Network Systems and Data Communications Analysts; Software Quality Assurance Engineers and Testers; Web Administrators; Web Developers.

Skills: Installation; Quality Control Analysis; Technology Design; Programming; Systems Analysis; Troubleshooting; Operations Analysis; Systems Evaluation.

Education and Training Programs: Computer and Information Sciences, General; Information Technology; Computer Systems Analysis/Analyst; Web/Multimedia Management and Webmaster. **Related Knowledge/Courses:** Computers and Electronics; Telecommunications; Design; Customer and Personal Service; Law and Government; Communications and Media.

Work Environment: Indoors; sitting.

Computer Systems Engineers/ Architects

- ❋ Personality Code: IRC
- ❋ Education/Training Required: Bachelor's degree
- ❋ Annual Earnings: $71,510
- ❋ Beginning Wage: $37,600
- ❋ Earnings Growth Potential: High
- ❋ Growth: 15.1%
- ❋ Annual Job Openings: 14,374
- ❋ Self-Employed: 6.6%
- ❋ Part-Time: 5.6%

The job openings listed here are shared with Network Designers, with Software Quality Assurance Engineers and Testers, with Web Administrators, and with Web Developers.

Design and develop solutions to complex applications problems, system administration issues, or network concerns. Perform systems management and integration functions. Communicate with staff or clients to understand specific system requirements. Provide advice on project costs, design concepts, or design changes. Document design specifications, installation instructions, and other system-related information. Verify stability, interoperability, portability, security, or scalability of system architecture. Collaborate with engineers or software developers to select appropriate design solutions or ensure the compatibility of system components. Provide technical guidance or support for the development or troubleshooting of systems. Evaluate current or emerging technologies to consider factors such as cost, portability, compatibility, or usability. Identify system data, hardware, or software components required to meet user needs. Provide guidelines for implementing secure systems to customers or installation teams. Monitor system operation to detect potential problems. Direct the analysis, development, and operation of complete computer systems. Investigate system component suitability for specified purposes and make recommendations regarding component use. Perform ongoing hardware and software maintenance operations, including installing or upgrading hardware or software. Develop or approve project plans, schedules, or budgets. Configure servers to meet functional specifications. Design and conduct hardware or software tests. Define and analyze objectives, scope, issues, or organizational impact of information systems. Develop system engineering, software engineering, system integration, or distributed system architectures. Establish functional or system standards to ensure operational requirements, quality requirements, and design constraints are addressed. Evaluate existing systems to determine effectiveness and suggest changes to meet organizational requirements. Research, test, or verify proper functioning of software patches and fixes. Communicate project information through presentations, technical reports, or white papers. Complete models and simulations, using manual or automated tools, to analyze or predict system performance under different operating conditions.

GOE—Interest Area/Cluster: 11. Information Technology. Work Group: 11.02. Information Technology Specialties. Other Jobs in This Work Group: Computer and Information Scientists, Research; Computer Operators; Computer Programmers; Computer Security Specialists; Computer Software Engineers, Applications; Computer Software Engineers, Systems Software; Computer Support Specialists; Computer Systems Analysts; Database Administrators; Network Designers; Network Systems and Data Communications Analysts; Software Quality Assurance Engineers and Testers; Web Administrators; Web Developers.

Skills: Programming; Systems Evaluation; Technology Design; Systems Analysis; Troubleshooting; Operations Analysis; Installation; Science.

Education and Training Programs: Computer Engineering, General; Computer Software Engineering. Related Knowledge/Courses: Computers and Electronics; Engineering and Technology; Telecommunications; Design; Mathematics; Sales and Marketing.

Work Environment: No data available.

Coroners

- ❋ Personality Code: IRC
- ❋ Education/Training Required: Work experience in a related occupation
- ❋ Annual Earnings: $48,400
- ❋ Beginning Wage: $28,980
- ❋ Earnings Growth Potential: High
- ❋ Growth: 4.9%
- ❋ Annual Job Openings: 15,841
- ❋ Self-Employed: 0.4%
- ❋ Part-Time: 5.0%

The job openings listed here are shared with Environmental Compliance Inspectors, with Equal Opportunity Representatives and Officers, with Government Property Inspectors and Investigators, and with Licensing Examiners and Inspectors.

Investigative-C

Direct activities such as autopsies, pathological and toxicological analyses, and inquests relating to the investigation of deaths occurring within a legal jurisdiction to determine cause of death or to fix responsibility for accidental, violent, or unexplained deaths. Perform medico-legal examinations and autopsies, conducting preliminary examinations of the body in order to identify victims, to locate signs of trauma, and to identify factors that would indicate time of death. Inquire into the cause, manner, and circumstances of human deaths and establish the identities of deceased persons. Direct activities of workers who conduct autopsies, perform pathological and toxicological analyses, and prepare documents for permanent records. Complete death certificates, including the assignment of a cause and manner of death. Observe and record the positions and conditions of bodies and of related evidence. Collect and document any pertinent medical history information. Observe, record, and preserve any objects or personal property related to deaths, including objects such as medication containers and suicide notes. Complete reports and forms required to finalize cases. Remove or supervise removal of bodies from death scenes, using the proper equipment and supplies, and arrange for transportation to morgues. Testify at inquests, hearings, and court trials. Interview persons present at death scenes to obtain information useful in determining the manner of death. Provide information concerning the circumstances of death to relatives of the deceased. Locate and document information regarding the next of kin, including their relationship to the deceased and the status of notification attempts. Confer with officials of public health and law enforcement agencies in order to coordinate interdepartmental activities. Inventory personal effects, such as jewelry or wallets, that are recovered from bodies. Coordinate the release of personal effects to authorized persons and facilitate the disposition of unclaimed corpses and personal effects. Arrange for the next of kin to be notified of deaths. Record the disposition of minor children, as well as details of arrangements made for their care. Collect wills, burial instructions, and other documentation needed for investigations and for handling of the remains. Witness and certify deaths that are the result of a judicial order.

GOE—Interest Area/Cluster: 08. Health Science. **Work Group:** 08.01. Managerial Work in Medical and Health Services. **Other Jobs in This Work Group:** Medical and Health Services Managers.

Skills: Science; Management of Financial Resources; Reading Comprehension; Critical Thinking; Management of Personnel Resources; Speaking; Management of Material Resources; Writing.

Education and Training Program: Public Administration. **Related Knowledge/Courses:** Medicine and Dentistry; Biology; Psychology; Therapy and Counseling; Chemistry; Law and Government.

Work Environment: More often indoors than outdoors; contaminants; disease or infections; hazardous equipment; using hands on objects, tools, or controls.

Dentists, General

- ❋ Personality Code: IRS
- ❋ Education/Training Required: First professional degree
- ❋ Annual Earnings: $137,630
- ❋ Beginning Wage: $71,520
- ❋ Earnings Growth Potential: High
- ❋ Growth: 9.2%
- ❋ Annual Job Openings: 7,106
- ❋ Self-Employed: 36.6%
- ❋ Part-Time: 25.9%

Diagnose and treat diseases, injuries, and malformations of teeth and gums and related oral structures. May treat diseases of nerve, pulp, and other dental tissues affecting vitality of teeth. Use masks, gloves, and safety glasses to protect themselves and their patients from infectious diseases. Administer anesthetics to limit the amount of pain experienced by patients during procedures. Examine teeth, gums, and related tissues, using dental instruments, X rays, and other diagnostic equipment, to evaluate dental health, diagnose diseases or abnormalities, and plan appropriate treatments. Formulate plan of treatment for patient's teeth and mouth tissue. Use air turbine and hand instruments, dental appliances, and surgical implements. Advise and instruct patients regarding preventive dental care, the causes and treatment of dental problems, and oral health-care services. Design, make, and fit prosthodontic appliances such as space maintainers, bridges, and dentures or write fabrication instructions or prescriptions for denturists and dental technicians. Diagnose and treat diseases, injuries, and malformations of teeth, gums, and related oral structures and provide preventive and corrective services. Fill pulp chamber and canal with endodontic materials. Write prescriptions for antibiotics and other medications. Analyze and evaluate dental needs to determine changes and trends in patterns of dental disease. Treat exposure of pulp by pulp capping, removal of pulp from pulp chamber, or root canal, using dental instruments. Eliminate irritating margins of fillings and correct occlusions, using dental instruments. Perform oral and periodontal surgery on the jaw or mouth. Remove diseased tissue, using surgical instruments. Apply fluoride and sealants to teeth. Manage business, employing and supervising staff and handling paperwork and insurance claims. Bleach, clean, or polish teeth to restore natural color. Plan, organize, and maintain dental health programs. Produce and evaluate dental health educational materials.

GOE—Interest Area/Cluster: 08. Health Science. **Work Group:** 08.03. Dentistry. **Other Jobs in This Work Group:** Dental Assistants; Dental Hygienists; Oral and Maxillofacial Surgeons; Orthodontists; Prosthodontists.

Skills: Science; Management of Financial Resources; Management of Material Resources; Equipment Selection; Complex Problem Solving; Reading Comprehension; Service Orientation; Management of Personnel Resources.

Education and Training Programs: Dentistry (DDS, DMD); Dental Clinical Sciences, General (MS, PhD); Advanced General Dentistry (Cert, MS, PhD); Oral Biology and Oral Pathology (MS, PhD); Dental Public Health and Education (Cert, MS/MPH, PhD/DPH); Dental Materials (MS, PhD); Pediatric Dentistry/Pedodontics (Cert, MS, PhD); Dental Public Health Specialty; Pedodontics Specialty. **Related Knowledge/Courses:** Medicine and Dentistry; Biology; Psychology; Chemistry; Personnel and Human Resources; Economics and Accounting.

Work Environment: Indoors; contaminants; radiation; disease or infections; sitting; using hands on objects, tools, or controls.

Diagnostic Medical Sonographers

- ❊ Personality Code: ISR
- ❊ Education/Training Required: Associate degree
- ❊ Annual Earnings: $59,860
- ❊ Beginning Wage: $42,250
- ❊ Earnings Growth Potential: Low
- ❊ Growth: 19.1%
- ❊ Annual Job Openings: 3,211
- ❊ Self-Employed: 1.1%
- ❊ Part-Time: 17.3%

Produce ultrasonic recordings of internal organs for use by physicians. Provide sonograms and oral or written summaries of technical findings to physicians for use in medical diagnosis. Decide which images to include, looking for differences between healthy and pathological areas. Operate ultrasound equipment to produce and record images of the motion, shape, and composition of blood, organs, tissues, and bodily masses such as fluid accumulations. Select appropriate equipment settings and adjust patient positions to obtain the best sites and angles. Observe screens during scans to ensure that images produced are satisfactory for diagnostic purposes, making adjustments to equipment as required. Prepare patients for exams by explaining procedures, transferring them to ultrasound tables, scrubbing skin and applying gel, and positioning them properly. Observe and care for patients throughout examinations to ensure

Investigative–D

their safety and comfort. Obtain and record accurate patient histories, including prior test results and information from physical examinations. Determine whether scope of exams should be extended, based on findings. Maintain records that include patient information; sonographs and interpretations; files of correspondence; publications and regulations; or quality assurance records such as pathology, biopsy, or post-operative reports. Record and store suitable images, using camera unit connected to the ultrasound equipment. Coordinate work with physicians and other health-care team members, including providing assistance during invasive procedures. Perform clerical duties such as scheduling exams and special procedures, keeping records, and archiving computerized images. Perform legal and ethical duties, including preparing safety and accident reports, obtaining written consent from patients to perform invasive procedures, and reporting symptoms of abuse and neglect. Clean, check, and maintain sonographic equipment, submitting maintenance requests or performing minor repairs as necessary. Supervise and train students and other medical sonographers. Maintain stock and supplies, preparing supplies for special examinations and ordering supplies when necessary. Process and code film from procedures and complete appropriate documentation.

GOE—Interest Area/Cluster: 08. Health Science. **Work Group:** 08.06. Medical Technology. **Other Jobs in This Work Group:** Biological Technicians; Cardiovascular Technologists and Technicians; Medical and Clinical Laboratory Technicians; Medical and Clinical Laboratory Technologists; Medical Equipment Preparers; Medical Records and Health Information Technicians; Nuclear Medicine Technologists; Opticians, Dispensing; Orthotists and Prosthetists; Radiologic Technicians; Radiologic Technologists; Radiologic Technologists and Technicians.

Skills: Operation Monitoring; Service Orientation; Systems Analysis; Systems Evaluation.

Education and Training Programs: Diagnostic Medical Sonography/Sonographer and Ultrasound Technician; Allied Health Diagnostic, Intervention,

and Treatment Professions, Other. **Related Knowledge/Courses:** Medicine and Dentistry; Physics; Biology; Psychology; Customer and Personal Service; Clerical Practices.

Work Environment: Indoors; cramped work space, awkward positions; disease or infections; using hands on objects, tools, or controls; bending or twisting the body; repetitive motions.

Electrical Engineers

- ❋ Personality Code: IR
- ❋ Education/Training Required: Bachelor's degree
- ❋ Annual Earnings: $79,240
- ❋ Beginning Wage: $51,220
- ❋ Earnings Growth Potential: Medium
- ❋ Growth: 6.3%
- ❋ Annual Job Openings: 6,806
- ❋ Self-Employed: 2.1%
- ❋ Part-Time: 2.0%

Design, develop, test, or supervise the manufacturing and installation of electrical equipment, components, or systems for commercial, industrial, military, or scientific use. Confer with engineers, customers, and others to discuss existing or potential engineering projects and products. Design, implement, maintain, and improve electrical instruments, equipment, facilities, components, products, and systems for commercial, industrial, and domestic purposes. Operate computer-assisted engineering and design software and equipment to perform engineering tasks. Direct and coordinate manufacturing, construction, installation, maintenance, support, documentation, and testing activities to ensure compliance with specifications, codes, and customer requirements. Perform detailed calculations to compute and establish manufacturing, construction, and installation standards and specifications. Inspect completed installations and observe operations to ensure conformance to design and equipment specifications and compliance with operational and safety standards. Plan and implement research methodology and procedures to apply principles of electrical theory to engineering projects. Prepare specifications for purchase of materials and equipment. Supervise and train project team members as necessary. Investigate and test vendors' and competitors' products. Oversee project production efforts to assure projects are completed satisfactorily, on time, and within budget. Prepare and study technical drawings, specifications of electrical systems, and topographical maps to ensure that installation and operations conform to standards and customer requirements. Investigate customer or public complaints, determine nature and extent of problem, and recommend remedial measures. Plan layout of electric-power-generating plants and distribution lines and stations. Assist in developing capital project programs for new equipment and major repairs. Develop budgets, estimating labor, material, and construction costs. Compile data and write reports regarding existing and potential engineering studies and projects. Collect data relating to commercial and residential development, population, and power system interconnection to determine operating efficiency of electrical systems. Conduct field surveys and study maps, graphs, diagrams, and other data to identify and correct power system problems.

GOE—Interest Area/Cluster: 15. Scientific Research, Engineering, and Mathematics. **Work Group:** 15.07. Research and Design Engineering. **Other Jobs in This Work Group:** Aerospace Engineers; Biomedical Engineers; Chemical Engineers; Civil Engineers; Computer Hardware Engineers; Electronics Engineers, Except Computer; Marine Architects; Marine Engineers; Marine Engineers and Naval Architects; Materials Engineers; Mechanical Engineers; Nuclear Engineers.

Skills: Technology Design; Science; Systems Analysis; Troubleshooting; Systems Evaluation; Equipment Selection; Management of Material Resources; Programming.

Education and Training Program: Electrical, Electronic, and Communications Engineering. **Related Knowledge/Courses:** Engineering and Technology; Design; Physics; Telecommunications; Computers and Electronics; Mathematics.

Work Environment: Indoors; sitting.

Electronics Engineers, Except Computer

- ❋ Personality Code: IR
- ❋ Education/Training Required: Bachelor's degree
- ❋ Annual Earnings: $83,340
- ❋ Beginning Wage: $53,710
- ❋ Earnings Growth Potential: Medium
- ❋ Growth: 3.7%
- ❋ Annual Job Openings: 5,699
- ❋ Self-Employed: 2.2%
- ❋ Part-Time: 2.0%

Research, design, develop, and test electronic components and systems for commercial, industrial, military, or scientific use, utilizing knowledge of electronic theory and materials properties. Design electronic circuits and components for use in fields such as telecommunications, aerospace guidance and propulsion control, acoustics, or instruments and controls. Design electronic components, software, products, or systems for commercial, industrial, medical, military, or scientific applications. Provide technical support and instruction to staff or customers regarding equipment standards, assisting with specific, difficult in-service engineering. Operate computer-assisted engineering and design software and equipment to perform engineering tasks. Analyze system requirements, capacity, cost, and customer needs to determine feasibility of project and develop system plan. Confer with engineers, customers, vendors, or others to discuss existing and potential engineering projects or products. Review and evaluate work of others inside and outside the organization to ensure effectiveness, technical adequacy, and compatibility in the resolution of complex engineering problems. Determine material and equipment needs and order supplies.

Inspect electronic equipment, instruments, products, and systems to ensure conformance to specifications, safety standards, and applicable codes and regulations. Evaluate operational systems, prototypes, and proposals and recommend repair or design modifications based on factors such as environment, service, cost, and system capabilities. Prepare documentation containing information such as confidential descriptions and specifications of proprietary hardware and software, product development and introduction schedules, product costs, and information about product performance weaknesses. Direct and coordinate activities concerned with manufacture, construction, installation, maintenance, operation, and modification of electronic equipment, products, and systems. Develop and perform operational, maintenance, and testing procedures for electronic products, components, equipment, and systems. Plan and develop applications and modifications for electronic properties used in components, products, and systems to improve technical performance. Plan and implement research, methodology, and procedures to apply principles of electronic theory to engineering projects. Prepare engineering sketches and specifications for construction, relocation, and installation of equipment, facilities, products, and systems.

GOE—Interest Area/Cluster: 15. Scientific Research, Engineering, and Mathematics. **Work Group:** 15.07. Research and Design Engineering. **Other Jobs in This Work Group:** Aerospace Engineers; Biomedical Engineers; Chemical Engineers; Civil Engineers; Computer Hardware Engineers; Electrical Engineers; Marine Architects; Marine Engineers; Marine Engineers and Naval Architects; Materials Engineers; Mechanical Engineers; Nuclear Engineers.

Skills: Troubleshooting; Installation; Science; Operations Analysis; Technology Design; Equipment Selection; Systems Evaluation; Quality Control Analysis.

Education and Training Program: Electrical, Electronic, and Communications Engineering. **Related Knowledge/Courses:** Engineering and Technology;

Design; Physics; Computers and Electronics; Telecommunications; Production and Processing.

Work Environment: Indoors; noisy; sitting.

Engineering Teachers, Postsecondary

- ❋ Personality Code: IRS
- ❋ Education/Training Required: Doctoral degree
- ❋ Annual Earnings: $79,510
- ❋ Beginning Wage: $43,090
- ❋ Earnings Growth Potential: High
- ❋ Growth: 22.9%
- ❋ Annual Job Openings: 5,565
- ❋ Self-Employed: 0.4%
- ❋ Part-Time: 27.8%

Teach courses pertaining to the application of physical laws and principles of engineering for the development of machines, materials, instruments, processes, and services. Includes teachers of subjects such as chemical, civil, electrical, industrial, mechanical, mineral, and petroleum engineering. Includes both teachers primarily engaged in teaching and those who do a combination of both teaching and research. Prepare and deliver lectures to undergraduate and/or graduate students on topics such as mechanics, hydraulics, and robotics. Keep abreast of developments in their field by reading current literature, talking with colleagues, and participating in professional conferences. Supervise undergraduate and/or graduate teaching, internship, and research work. Evaluate and grade students' classwork, laboratory work, assignments, and papers. Conduct research in a particular field of knowledge and publish findings in professional journals, books, and/or electronic media. Prepare course materials such as syllabi, homework assignments, and handouts. Compile, administer, and grade examinations or assign this work to others. Write grant proposals to procure external research funding. Supervise students' laboratory work. Initiate, facilitate, and moderate class discussions. Maintain regularly scheduled office hours to advise and assist students. Plan, evaluate, and revise curricula, course content, and course materials and methods of instruction. Advise students on academic and vocational curricula and on career issues. Maintain student attendance records, grades, and other required records. Collaborate with colleagues to address teaching and research issues. Select and obtain materials and supplies such as textbooks and laboratory equipment. Participate in student recruitment, registration, and placement activities. Serve on academic or administrative committees that deal with institutional policies, departmental matters, and academic issues. Perform administrative duties such as serving as department head. Provide professional consulting services to government and/or industry. Compile bibliographies of specialized materials for outside reading assignments. Act as advisers to student organizations. Participate in campus and community events.

GOE—Interest Area/Cluster: 05. Education and Training. **Work Group:** 05.03. Postsecondary and Adult Teaching and Instructing. **Other Jobs in This Work Group:** Adult Literacy, Remedial Education, and GED Teachers and Instructors; Agricultural Sciences Teachers, Postsecondary; Anthropology and Archeology Teachers, Postsecondary; Architecture Teachers, Postsecondary; Area, Ethnic, and Cultural Studies Teachers, Postsecondary; Art, Drama, and Music Teachers, Postsecondary; Atmospheric, Earth, Marine, and Space Sciences Teachers, Postsecondary; Biological Science Teachers, Postsecondary; Business Teachers, Postsecondary; Chemistry Teachers, Postsecondary; Communications Teachers, Postsecondary; Computer Science Teachers, Postsecondary; Criminal Justice and Law Enforcement Teachers, Postsecondary; Economics Teachers, Postsecondary; Education Teachers, Postsecondary; English Language and Literature Teachers, Postsecondary; Environmental Science Teachers, Postsecondary; Farm and Home Management Advisors; Foreign Language and Literature Teachers, Postsecondary; Forestry and Conservation Science Teachers, Postsecondary; Geography Teachers, Postsecondary;

Graduate Teaching Assistants; Health Specialties Teachers, Postsecondary; History Teachers, Postsecondary; Home Economics Teachers, Postsecondary; Law Teachers, Postsecondary; Library Science Teachers, Postsecondary; Mathematical Science Teachers, Postsecondary; Nursing Instructors and Teachers, Postsecondary; Philosophy and Religion Teachers, Postsecondary; Physics Teachers, Postsecondary; Political Science Teachers, Postsecondary; Psychology Teachers, Postsecondary; Recreation and Fitness Studies Teachers, Postsecondary; Self-Enrichment Education Teachers; Social Work Teachers, Postsecondary; Sociology Teachers, Postsecondary; Vocational Education Teachers, Postsecondary.

Skills: Science; Programming; Mathematics; Technology Design; Complex Problem Solving; Management of Financial Resources; Critical Thinking; Operations Analysis.

Education and Training Programs: Teacher Education and Professional Development, Specific Subject Areas, Other; Engineering, General; Aerospace, Aeronautical and Astronautical Engineering; Agricultural/Biological Engineering and Bioengineering; Architectural Engineering; Biomedical/Medical Engineering; Ceramic Sciences and Engineering; Chemical Engineering; Civil Engineering, General; Geotechnical Engineering; Structural Engineering; others. **Related Knowledge/Courses:** Engineering and Technology; Physics; Design; Mathematics; Education and Training; Telecommunications.

Work Environment: Indoors; sitting.

Environmental Engineers

- ❋ Personality Code: IRC
- ❋ Education/Training Required: Bachelor's degree
- ❋ Annual Earnings: $72,350
- ❋ Beginning Wage: $44,090
- ❋ Earnings Growth Potential: Medium
- ❋ Growth: 25.4%
- ❋ Annual Job Openings: 5,003
- ❋ Self-Employed: 2.7%
- ❋ Part-Time: 3.0%

Design, plan, or perform engineering duties in the prevention, control, and remediation of environmental health hazards, using various engineering disciplines. Work may include waste treatment, site remediation, or pollution control technology. Collaborate with environmental scientists, planners, hazardous waste technicians, engineers, and other specialists, and experts in law and business to address environmental problems. Inspect industrial and municipal facilities and programs to evaluate operational effectiveness and ensure compliance with environmental regulations. Prepare, review, and update environmental investigation and recommendation reports. Design and supervise the development of systems processes or equipment for control, management, or remediation of water, air, or soil quality. Provide environmental engineering assistance in network analysis, regulatory analysis, and planning or reviewing database development. Obtain, update, and maintain plans, permits, and standard operating procedures. Provide technical-level support for environmental remediation and litigation projects, including remediation system design and determination of regulatory applicability. Monitor progress of environmental improvement programs. Inform company employees and other interested parties of environmental issues. Advise corporations and government agencies of procedures to follow in cleaning up contaminated sites to protect people and the environment. Develop proposed project objectives and targets, and report to management on progress in attaining them. Request bids from suppliers or consultants. Advise industries and government agencies about environmental policies and standards. Assess the existing or potential environmental impact of land use projects on air, water, and land. Assist in budget implementation, forecasts, and administration. Serve on teams conducting multimedia inspections at complex facilities, providing assistance with planning, quality assurance, safety inspection protocols, and sampling. Coordinate and manage environmental protection programs and projects, assigning and evaluating work. Maintain, write, and revise quality assurance documentation and procedures. Provide administrative support for projects by collecting data, providing project documentation, training staff, and performing other general administrative duties.

GOE—Interest Area/Cluster: 01. Agriculture and Natural Resources. **Work Group:** 01.02. Resource Science/Engineering for Plants, Animals, and the Environment. **Other Jobs in This Work Group:** Agricultural Engineers; Animal Scientists; Conservation Scientists; Foresters; Mining and Geological Engineers, Including Mining Safety Engineers; Petroleum Engineers; Range Managers; Soil and Plant Scientists; Soil and Water Conservationists; Zoologists and Wildlife Biologists.

Skills: Management of Financial Resources; Systems Analysis; Mathematics; Systems Evaluation; Management of Personnel Resources; Writing; Operation Monitoring; Complex Problem Solving.

Education and Training Program: Environmental/Environmental Health Engineering. **Related Knowledge/Courses:** Engineering and Technology; Physics; Design; Chemistry; Building and Construction; Biology.

Work Environment: Indoors; sitting.

Environmental Science and Protection Technicians, Including Health

- ✳ Personality Code: IRC
- ✳ Education/Training Required: Associate degree
- ✳ Annual Earnings: $39,370
- ✳ Beginning Wage: $25,090
- ✳ Earnings Growth Potential: Medium
- ✳ Growth: 28.0%
- ✳ Annual Job Openings: 8,404
- ✳ Self-Employed: 1.5%
- ✳ Part-Time: 19.4%

Perform laboratory and field tests to monitor the environment and investigate sources of pollution, including those that affect health. Under direction of environmental scientists or specialists, may collect samples of gases, soil, water, and other materials for testing and take corrective actions as assigned. Collect samples of gases, soils, water, industrial wastewater, and asbestos products to conduct tests on pollutant levels and identify sources of pollution. Record test data and prepare reports, summaries, and charts that interpret test results. Develop and implement programs for monitoring of environmental pollution and radiation. Discuss test results and analyses with customers. Set up equipment or stations to monitor and collect pollutants from sites such as smokestacks, manufacturing plants, or mechanical equipment. Maintain files, such as hazardous waste databases, chemical usage data, personnel exposure information, and diagrams showing equipment locations. Develop testing procedures or direct activities of workers in laboratory. Prepare samples or photomicrographs for testing and analysis. Calibrate microscopes and test instruments. Examine and analyze material for presence and concentration of contaminants such as asbestos, using variety of microscopes. Calculate amount of pollutant in samples or compute air pollution or gas flow in industrial processes, using chemical and mathematical formulas. Make recommendations to control or eliminate unsafe conditions at workplaces or public facilities. Weigh, analyze, and measure collected sample particles such as lead, coal dust, or rock to determine concentration of pollutants. Provide information and technical and program assistance to government representatives, employers, and the general public on the issues of public health, environmental protection, or workplace safety. Conduct standardized tests to ensure materials and supplies used throughout power supply systems meet processing and safety specifications. Perform statistical analysis of environmental data. Respond to and investigate hazardous conditions or spills or outbreaks of disease or food poisoning, collecting samples for analysis. Determine amounts and kinds of chemicals to use in destroying harmful organisms and removing impurities from purification systems. Inspect sanitary conditions at public facilities. Inspect workplaces to ensure the absence of health and safety hazards such as high noise levels, radiation, or lighting that is too bright or dim.

GOE—Interest Area/Cluster: 01. Agriculture and Natural Resources. **Work Group:** 01.03. Resource Technologies for Plants, Animals, and the Environment. **Other Jobs in This Work Group:** Agricultural and Food Science Technicians; Agricultural Technicians; Food Science Technicians; Food Scientists and Technologists; Geological and Petroleum Technicians; Geological Sample Test Technicians; Geophysical Data Technicians.

Skills: Quality Control Analysis; Systems Analysis; Systems Evaluation; Operation Monitoring; Operation and Control; Science.

Education and Training Programs: Environmental Studies; Environmental Science; Physical Science Technologies/Technicians, Other; Science Technologies/Technicians, Other. **Related Knowledge/Courses:** Biology; Chemistry; Geography; Physics; Computers and Electronics; Building and Construction.

Work Environment: More often indoors than outdoors; noisy; very hot or cold; contaminants; sitting.

Investigative-E

Environmental Scientists and Specialists, Including Health

- ❀ Personality Code: IRC
- ❀ Education/Training Required: Master's degree
- ❀ Annual Earnings: $58,380
- ❀ Beginning Wage: $35,630
- ❀ Earnings Growth Potential: Medium
- ❀ Growth: 25.1%
- ❀ Annual Job Openings: 6,961
- ❀ Self-Employed: 2.2%
- ❀ Part-Time: 5.3%

Conduct research or perform investigation for the purpose of identifying, abating, or eliminating sources of pollutants or hazards that affect either the environment or the health of the population. Using knowledge of various scientific disciplines, may collect, synthesize, study, report, and take action based on data derived from measurements or observations of air, food, soil, water, and other sources. Collect, synthesize, analyze, manage, and report environmental data such as pollution emission measurements, atmospheric monitoring measurements, meteorological and mineralogical information, and soil or water samples. Analyze data to determine validity, quality, and scientific significance, and to interpret correlations between human activities and environmental effects. Communicate scientific and technical information to the public, organizations, or internal audiences through oral briefings, written documents, workshops, conferences, training sessions, or public hearings. Provide scientific and technical guidance, support, coordination, and oversight to governmental agencies, environmental programs, industry, or the public. Process and review environmental permits, licenses, and related materials. Review and implement environmental technical standards, guidelines, policies, and formal regulations that meet all appropriate requirements. Prepare charts or graphs from data samples, providing summary information on the environmental relevance of the data. Determine data collection methods to be employed in research projects and surveys. Investigate and report on accidents affecting the environment. Research sources of pollution to determine their effects on the environment and to develop theories or methods of pollution abatement or control. Provide advice on proper standards and regulations or the development of policies, strategies, and codes of practice for environmental management. Monitor effects of pollution and land degradation, and recommend means of prevention or control. Supervise or train students, environmental technologists, technicians, or other related staff. Evaluate violations or problems discovered during inspections to determine appropriate regulatory actions or to provide advice on the development and prosecution of regulatory cases. Conduct environmental audits and inspections, and investigations of violations. Plan and develop research models, using knowledge of mathematical and statistical concepts. Conduct applied research on environmental topics such as waste control and treatment and pollution abatement methods.

GOE—Interest Area/Cluster: 15. Scientific Research, Engineering, and Mathematics. **Work Group:** 15.03. Life Sciences. **Other Jobs in This Work Group:** Biochemists and Biophysicists; Biologists; Epidemiologists; Medical Scientists, Except Epidemiologists; Microbiologists.

Skills: Science; Systems Analysis; Systems Evaluation; Writing; Reading Comprehension; Management of Personnel Resources; Management of Material Resources; Operation Monitoring.

Education and Training Programs: Environmental Studies; Environmental Science. **Related Knowledge/Courses:** Biology; Geography; Chemistry; Physics; Law and Government; Engineering and Technology.

Work Environment: More often indoors than outdoors; noisy; sitting.

Family and General Practitioners

- ❋ Personality Code: IS
- ❋ Education/Training Required: First professional degree
- ❋ Annual Earnings: More than $145,600
- ❋ Beginning Wage: $67,400
- ❋ Earnings Growth Potential: Cannot be calculated
- ❋ Growth: 14.2%
- ❋ Annual Job Openings: 38,027
- ❋ Self-Employed: 14.7%
- ❋ Part-Time: 8.1%

The job openings listed here are shared with Anesthesiologists; Internists, General; Obstetricians and Gynecologists; Pediatricians, General; Psychiatrists; and Surgeons.

Diagnose, treat, and help prevent diseases and injuries that commonly occur in the general population. Prescribe or administer treatment, therapy, medication, vaccination, and other specialized medical care to treat or prevent illness, disease, or injury. Order, perform, and interpret tests and analyze records, reports, and examination information to diagnose patients' condition. Monitor the patients' conditions and progress and re-evaluate treatments as necessary. Explain procedures and discuss test results or prescribed treatments with patients. Collect, record, and maintain patient information, such as medical history, reports, and examination results. Advise patients and community members concerning diet, activity, hygiene, and disease prevention. Refer patients to medical specialists or other practitioners when necessary. Direct and coordinate activities of nurses, students, assistants, specialists, therapists, and other medical staff. Coordinate work with nurses, social workers, rehabilitation therapists, pharmacists, psychologists, and other healthcare providers. Deliver babies. Operate on patients to remove, repair, or improve functioning of diseased or injured body parts and systems. Plan, implement, or administer health programs or standards in hospital, business, or community for information, prevention, or treatment of injury or illness. Prepare reports for government or management of birth, death, and disease statistics; workforce evaluations; or medical status of individuals. Conduct research to study anatomy and develop or test medications, treatments, or procedures to prevent or control disease or injury.

GOE—Interest Area/Cluster: 08. Health Science. **Work Group:** 08.02. Medicine and Surgery. **Other Jobs in This Work Group:** Anesthesiologists; Internists, General; Medical Assistants; Medical Transcriptionists; Obstetricians and Gynecologists; Pediatricians, General; Pharmacists; Pharmacy Aides; Pharmacy Technicians; Physician Assistants; Psychiatrists; Registered Nurses; Surgeons; Surgical Technologists.

Skills: Science; Social Perceptiveness; Reading Comprehension; Complex Problem Solving; Persuasion; Service Orientation; Management of Financial Resources; Active Learning.

Education and Training Programs: Medicine (MD); Osteopathic Medicine/Osteopathy (DO); Family Medicine. **Related Knowledge/Courses:** Medicine and Dentistry; Biology; Therapy and Counseling; Psychology; Sociology and Anthropology; Chemistry.

Work Environment: Indoors; disease or infections; standing; using hands on objects, tools, or controls.

Forensic Science Technicians

- ❋ Personality Code: IRC
- ❋ Education/Training Required: Bachelor's degree
- ❋ Annual Earnings: $47,680
- ❋ Beginning Wage: $29,170
- ❋ Earnings Growth Potential: Medium
- ❋ Growth: 30.7%
- ❋ Annual Job Openings: 3,074
- ❋ Self-Employed: 1.3%
- ❋ Part-Time: 19.4%

Collect, identify, classify, and analyze physical evidence related to criminal investigations. Perform tests on weapons or substances such as fiber, hair, and tissue to determine significance to investigation. May testify as expert witnesses on evidence or crime laboratory techniques. May serve as specialists in area of expertise, such as ballistics, fingerprinting, handwriting, or biochemistry. Testify in court about investigative and analytical methods and findings. Keep records and prepare reports detailing findings, investigative methods, and laboratory techniques. Interpret laboratory findings and test results to identify and classify substances, materials, and other evidence collected at crime scenes. Operate and maintain laboratory equipment and apparatus. Prepare solutions, reagents, and sample formulations needed for laboratory work. Analyze and classify biological fluids, using DNA typing or serological techniques. Collect evidence from crime scenes, storing it in conditions that preserve its integrity. Identify and quantify drugs and poisons found in biological fluids and tissues, in foods, and at crime scenes. Analyze handwritten and machine-produced textual evidence to decipher altered or obliterated text or to determine authorship, age, or source. Reconstruct crime scenes to determine relationships among pieces of evidence. Examine DNA samples to determine if they match other samples. Collect impressions of dust from surfaces to obtain and identify fingerprints. Analyze gunshot residue and bullet paths to determine how shootings occurred. Visit morgues, examine scenes of crimes, or contact other sources to obtain evidence or information to be used in investigations. Examine physical evidence such as hair, fiber, wood, or soil residues to obtain information about its source and composition. Determine types of bullets used in shooting and whether they were fired from a specific weapon. Examine firearms to determine mechanical condition and legal status, performing restoration work on damaged firearms to obtain information such as serial numbers. Confer with ballistics, fingerprinting, handwriting, document, electronics, medical, chemical, or metallurgical experts concerning evidence and its interpretation. Interpret the pharmacological effects of a drug or a combination of drugs

on an individual. Compare objects such as tools with impression marks to determine whether a specific object is responsible for a specific mark.

GOE—Interest Area/Cluster: 12. Law and Public Safety. **Work Group:** 12.04. Law Enforcement and Public Safety. **Other Jobs in This Work Group:** Bailiffs; Correctional Officers and Jailers; Criminal Investigators and Special Agents; Detectives and Criminal Investigators; Fire Investigators; Parking Enforcement Workers; Police and Sheriff's Patrol Officers; Police Detectives; Police Identification and Records Officers; Police Patrol Officers; Sheriffs and Deputy Sheriffs; Transit and Railroad Police.

Skills: Science; Quality Control Analysis; Troubleshooting; Speaking; Equipment Selection; Active Learning; Reading Comprehension; Monitoring.

Education and Training Program: Forensic Science and Technology. **Related Knowledge/Courses:** Chemistry; Law and Government; Biology; Public Safety and Security; English Language; Clerical Practices.

Work Environment: Indoors; contaminants; disease or infections; hazardous conditions; sitting.

Geoscientists, Except Hydrologists and Geographers

- ❋ Personality Code: IR
- ❋ Education/Training Required: Master's degree
- ❋ Annual Earnings: $75,800
- ❋ Beginning Wage: $41,020
- ❋ Earnings Growth Potential: High
- ❋ Growth: 21.9%
- ❋ Annual Job Openings: 2,471
- ❋ Self-Employed: 2.2%
- ❋ Part-Time: 5.3%

Study the composition, structure, and other physical aspects of the Earth. May use knowledge of geology, physics, and mathematics in exploration for oil, gas, minerals, or underground water

or in waste disposal, land reclamation, or other environmental problems. May study the Earth's internal composition, atmospheres, and oceans and its magnetic, electrical, and gravitational forces. Includes mineralogists, crystallographers, paleontologists, stratigraphers, geodesists, and seismologists. Analyze and interpret geological, geochemical, and geophysical information from sources such as survey data, well logs, bore holes, and aerial photos. Locate and estimate probable natural gas, oil, and mineral ore deposits and underground water resources, using aerial photographs, charts, or research and survey results. Plan and conduct geological, geochemical, and geophysical field studies and surveys, sample collection, or drilling and testing programs used to collect data for research or application. Analyze and interpret geological data, using computer software. Search for and review research articles or environmental, historical, and technical reports. Assess ground and surface water movement to provide advice regarding issues such as waste management, route and site selection, and the restoration of contaminated sites. Prepare geological maps, cross-sectional diagrams, charts, and reports concerning mineral extraction, land use, and resource management, using results of field work and laboratory research. Investigate the composition, structure, and history of the Earth's crust through the collection, examination, measurement, and classification of soils, minerals, rocks, or fossil remains. Conduct geological and geophysical studies to provide information for use in regional development, site selection, and development of public works projects. Measure characteristics of the Earth, such as gravity and magnetic fields, using equipment such as seismographs, gravimeters, torsion balances, and magnetometers. Inspect construction projects to analyze engineering problems, applying geological knowledge and using test equipment and drilling machinery. Design geological mine maps, monitor mine structural integrity, or advise and monitor mining crews. Identify risks for natural disasters such as mud slides, earthquakes, and volcanic eruptions, providing advice on mitigation of potential damage. Advise construction firms and government agencies on dam and road construction, foundation design, or land use and resource management. Test industrial diamonds and abrasives, soil, or rocks to determine their geological characteristics, using optical, X-ray, heat, acid, and precision instruments.

GOE—Interest Area/Cluster: 15. Scientific Research, Engineering, and Mathematics. **Work Group:** 15.02. Physical Sciences. **Other Jobs in This Work Group:** Astronomers; Atmospheric and Space Scientists; Chemists; Geographers; Hydrologists; Materials Scientists; Physicists.

Skills: Systems Analysis; Science; Systems Evaluation; Mathematics; Writing; Operation Monitoring; Speaking.

Education and Training Programs: Geology/Earth Science, General; Geochemistry; Geophysics and Seismology; Paleontology; Geochemistry and Petrology; Oceanography, Chemical and Physical; Geological and Earth Sciences/Geosciences, Other. **Related Knowledge/Courses:** Geography; Engineering and Technology; Physics; Chemistry; Mathematics; Design.

Work Environment: More often indoors than outdoors; sitting.

Hydrologists

- ❋ Personality Code: IR
- ❋ Education/Training Required: Master's degree
- ❋ Annual Earnings: $68,140
- ❋ Beginning Wage: $42,450
- ❋ Earnings Growth Potential: Medium
- ❋ Growth: 24.3%
- ❋ Annual Job Openings: 687
- ❋ Self-Employed: 2.4%
- ❋ Part-Time: 5.3%

Research the distribution, circulation, and physical properties of underground and surface waters; study the form and intensity of precipitation, its rate of infiltration into the soil, its movement

through the earth, and its return to the ocean and atmosphere. Study and document quantities, distribution, disposition, and development of underground and surface waters. Draft final reports describing research results, including illustrations, appendices, maps, and other attachments. Coordinate and supervise the work of professional and technical staff, including research assistants, technologists, and technicians. Prepare hydrogeologic evaluations of known or suspected hazardous waste sites and land treatment and feedlot facilities. Design and conduct scientific hydrogeological investigations to ensure that accurate and appropriate information is available for use in water resource management decisions. Study public water supply issues, including flood and drought risks, water quality, wastewater, and impacts on wetland habitats. Collect and analyze water samples as part of field investigations and/or to validate data from automatic monitors. Apply research findings to help minimize the environmental impacts of pollution, water-borne diseases, erosion, and sedimentation. Measure and graph phenomena such as lake levels, stream flows, and changes in water volumes. Investigate complaints or conflicts related to the alteration of public waters, gathering information, recommending alternatives, informing participants of progress, and preparing draft orders. Develop or modify methods of conducting hydrologic studies. Answer questions and provide technical assistance and information to contractors and/or the public regarding issues such as well drilling, code requirements, hydrology, and geology. Install, maintain, and calibrate instruments such as those that monitor water levels, rainfall, and sediments. Evaluate data and provide recommendations regarding the feasibility of municipal projects such as hydroelectric power plants, irrigation systems, flood warning systems, and waste treatment facilities. Conduct short-term and long-term climate assessments and study storm occurrences. Study and analyze the physical aspects of the Earth in terms of the hydrological components, including atmosphere, hydrosphere, and interior structure. Conduct research and communicate information to promote the conservation and preservation of water resources.

GOE—Interest Area/Cluster: 15. Scientific Research, Engineering, and Mathematics. **Work Group:** 15.02. Physical Sciences. **Other Jobs in This Work Group:** Astronomers; Atmospheric and Space Scientists; Chemists; Geographers; Geoscientists, Except Hydrologists and Geographers; Materials Scientists; Physicists.

Skills: Science; Programming; Management of Financial Resources; Mathematics; Management of Personnel Resources; Complex Problem Solving; Systems Analysis; Management of Material Resources.

Education and Training Programs: Geology/Earth Science, General; Hydrology and Water Resources Science; Oceanography, Chemical and Physical. **Related Knowledge/Courses:** Geography; Physics; Engineering and Technology; Biology; Chemistry; Mathematics.

Work Environment: More often indoors than outdoors; sitting.

Industrial Engineers

- Personality Code: ICE
- Education/Training Required: Bachelor's degree
- Annual Earnings: $71,430
- Beginning Wage: $46,340
- Earnings Growth Potential: Medium
- Growth: 20.3%
- Annual Job Openings: 11,272
- Self-Employed: 0.9%
- Part-Time: 2.0%

Design, develop, test, and evaluate integrated systems for managing industrial production processes, including human work factors, quality control, inventory control, logistics and material flow, cost analysis, and production coordination. Analyze statistical data and product specifications to determine standards and establish quality and reliability objectives of finished product. Develop manufacturing methods, labor utilization standards, and cost analysis systems to promote efficient staff and facility utilization. Recommend methods for improving utilization of personnel, material, and utilities. Plan and establish sequence of operations to fabricate and assemble parts or products and to promote efficient utilization. Apply statistical methods and perform mathematical calculations to determine manufacturing processes, staff requirements, and production standards. Coordinate quality control objectives and activities to resolve production problems, maximize product reliability, and minimize cost. Confer with vendors, staff, and management personnel regarding purchases, procedures, product specifications, manufacturing capabilities, and project status. Draft and design layout of equipment, materials, and workspace to illustrate maximum efficiency, using drafting tools and computer. Review production schedules, engineering specifications, orders, and related information to obtain knowledge of manufacturing methods, procedures, and activities. Communicate with management and user personnel to develop production and design standards. Estimate production cost and effect of product design changes for management review, action, and control. Formulate sampling procedures and designs and develop forms and instructions for recording, evaluating, and reporting quality and reliability data. Record or oversee recording of information to ensure currency of engineering drawings and documentation of production problems. Study operations sequence, material flow, functional statements, organization charts, and project information to determine worker functions and responsibilities. Direct workers engaged in product measurement, inspection, and testing activities to ensure quality control and reliability. Implement methods and procedures for disposition of discrepant material and defective or damaged parts and assess cost and responsibility.

GOE—Interest Area/Cluster: 15. Scientific Research, Engineering, and Mathematics. **Work Group:** 15.08. Industrial and Safety Engineering. **Other Jobs in This Work Group:** Fire-Prevention and Protection Engineers; Health and Safety Engineers, Except Mining Safety Engineers and Inspectors; Industrial Safety and Health Engineers; Product Safety Engineers.

Skills: Equipment Selection; Technology Design; Troubleshooting; Installation; Systems Analysis; Mathematics; Judgment and Decision Making; Negotiation.

Education and Training Program: Industrial Engineering. **Related Knowledge/Courses:** Engineering and Technology; Design; Production and Processing; Mechanical Devices; Physics; Mathematics.

Work Environment: Indoors; noisy; contaminants; hazardous equipment; more often sitting than standing.

Industrial-Organizational Psychologists

- ❋ Personality Code: IEA
- ❋ Education/Training Required: Master's degree
- ❋ Annual Earnings: $80,820
- ❋ Beginning Wage: $38,910
- ❋ Earnings Growth Potential: Very high
- ❋ Growth: 21.3%
- ❋ Annual Job Openings: 118
- ❋ Self-Employed: 39.3%
- ❋ Part-Time: 24.0%

Apply principles of psychology to personnel, administration, management, sales, and marketing problems. Activities may include policy planning; employee screening, training, and development; and organizational development and analysis. May work with management to reorganize the work setting to improve worker productivity. Develop and implement employee selection and placement programs. Analyze job requirements and content to establish criteria for classification, selection, training, and other related personnel functions. Develop interview techniques, rating scales, and psychological tests used to assess skills, abilities, and interests for the purpose of employee selection, placement, and promotion. Advise management concerning personnel, managerial, and marketing policies and practices and their potential effects on organizational effectiveness and efficiency. Analyze data, using statistical methods and applications, to evaluate the outcomes and effectiveness of workplace programs. Assess employee performance. Observe and interview workers to obtain information about the physical, mental, and educational requirements of jobs as well as information about aspects such as job satisfaction. Write reports on research findings and implications to contribute to general knowledge and to suggest potential changes in organizational functioning. Facilitate organizational development and change. Identify training and development needs. Formulate and implement training programs, applying principles of learning and individual differences. Study organizational effectiveness, productivity, and efficiency, including the nature of workplace supervision and leadership. Conduct research studies of physical work environments, organizational structures, communication systems, group interactions, morale, and motivation to assess organizational functioning. Counsel workers about job and career-related issues. Study consumers' reactions to new products and package designs, and to advertising efforts, using surveys and tests. Participate in mediation and dispute resolution.

GOE—Interest Area/Cluster: 15. Scientific Research, Engineering, and Mathematics. **Work Group:** 15.04. Social Sciences. **Other Jobs in This Work Group:** Anthropologists; Anthropologists and Archeologists; Archeologists; Economists; Historians; Political Scientists; School Psychologists; Sociologists.

Skills: Science; Systems Evaluation; Judgment and Decision Making; Writing; Monitoring; Time Management; Coordination; Critical Thinking.

Education and Training Programs: Psychology, General; Industrial and Organizational Psychology. **Related Knowledge/Courses:** Personnel and Human Resources; Psychology; Sociology and Anthropology; Education and Training; Therapy and Counseling; Mathematics.

Work Environment: Indoors; sitting.

Internists, General

- ❋ Personality Code: ISR
- ❋ Education/Training Required: First professional degree
- ❋ Annual Earnings: More than $145,600
- ❋ Beginning Wage: $89,130
- ❋ Earnings Growth Potential: Cannot be calculated
- ❋ Growth: 14.2%
- ❋ Annual Job Openings: 38,027
- ❋ Self-Employed: 14.7%
- ❋ Part-Time: 8.1%

The job openings listed here are shared with Anesthesiologists; Family and General Practitioners; Obstetricians and Gynecologists; Pediatricians, General; Psychiatrists; and Surgeons.

Diagnose and provide non-surgical treatment of diseases and injuries of internal organ systems. Provide care mainly for adults who have a wide range of problems associated with the internal organs. Treat internal disorders, such as hypertension; heart disease; diabetes; and problems of the lung, brain, kidney, and gastrointestinal tract. Analyze records, reports, test results, or examination information to diagnose medical condition of patient. Prescribe or administer medication, therapy, and other specialized medical care to treat or prevent illness, disease, or injury. Provide and manage long-term, comprehensive medical care, including diagnosis and non-surgical treatment of diseases, for adult patients in an office or hospital. Manage and treat common health problems, such as infections, influenza and pneumonia, as well as serious, chronic, and complex illnesses, in adolescents, adults, and the elderly. Monitor patients' conditions and progress and re-evaluate treatments as necessary. Collect, record, and maintain patient information, such as medical history, reports, and examination results. Make diagnoses when different illnesses occur together or in situations where the diagnosis may be obscure. Explain procedures and discuss test results or prescribed treatments with patients. Advise patients and community members concerning diet, activity, hygiene, and disease prevention. Refer patient to medical specialist or other practitioner when necessary. Immunize patients to protect them from preventable diseases. Advise surgeon of a patient's risk status and recommend appropriate intervention to minimize risk. Direct and coordinate activities of nurses, students, assistants, specialists, therapists, and other medical staff. Provide consulting services to other doctors caring for patients with special or difficult problems. Operate on patients to remove, repair, or improve functioning of diseased or injured body parts and systems. Plan, implement, or administer health programs in hospitals, businesses, or communities for prevention and treatment of injuries or illnesses. Conduct research to develop or test medications, treatments, or procedures to prevent or control disease or injury. Prepare government or organizational reports on birth, death, and disease statistics; workforce evaluations; or the medical status of individuals.

GOE—Interest Area/Cluster: 08. Health Science. **Work Group:** 08.02. Medicine and Surgery. **Other Jobs in This Work Group:** Anesthesiologists; Family and General Practitioners; Medical Assistants; Medical Transcriptionists; Obstetricians and Gynecologists; Pediatricians, General; Pharmacists; Pharmacy Aides; Pharmacy Technicians; Physician Assistants; Psychiatrists; Registered Nurses; Surgeons; Surgical Technologists.

Skills: Science; Judgment and Decision Making; Complex Problem Solving; Reading Comprehension; Social Perceptiveness; Service Orientation; Management of Financial Resources; Persuasion.

Education and Training Programs: Cardiology; Critical Care Medicine; Endocrinology and Metabolism; Gastroenterology; Geriatric Medicine; Hematology; Infectious Disease; Internal Medicine; Nephrology; Neurology; Nuclear Medicine; Oncology; Pulmonary Disease; Rheumatology. **Related Knowledge/Courses:** Medicine and Dentistry;

Biology; Therapy and Counseling; Psychology; Chemistry; Education and Training.

Work Environment: Indoors; disease or infections; standing.

Management Analysts

- ✻ Personality Code: IEC
- ✻ Education/Training Required: Work experience plus degree
- ✻ Annual Earnings: $71,150
- ✻ Beginning Wage: $40,860
- ✻ Earnings Growth Potential: High
- ✻ Growth: 21.9%
- ✻ Annual Job Openings: 125,669
- ✻ Self-Employed: 27.0%
- ✻ Part-Time: 13.2%

Conduct organizational studies and evaluations, design systems and procedures, conduct work simplifications and measurement studies, and prepare operations and procedures manuals to assist management in operating more efficiently and effectively. Includes program analysts and management consultants. Gather and organize information on problems or procedures. Analyze data gathered and develop solutions or alternative methods of proceeding. Confer with personnel concerned to ensure successful functioning of newly implemented systems or procedures. Develop and implement records management program for filing, protection, and retrieval of records and assure compliance with program. Review forms and reports and confer with management and users about format, distribution, and purpose and to identify problems and improvements. Document findings of study and prepare recommendations for implementation of new systems, procedures, or organizational changes. Interview personnel and conduct on-site observation to ascertain unit functions; work performed; and methods, equipment, and personnel used. Prepare manuals and train workers in use of new forms, reports, procedures, or equipment according to organizational policy. Design, evaluate, recommend, and approve changes of forms and reports. Plan study of work problems and procedures, such as organizational change, communications, information flow, integrated production methods, inventory control, or cost analysis. Recommend purchase of storage equipment and design area layout to locate equipment in space available.

GOE—Interest Area/Cluster: 04. Business and Administration. **Work Group:** 04.05. Accounting, Auditing, and Analytical Support. **Other Jobs in This Work Group:** Accountants; Accountants and Auditors; Auditors; Budget Analysts; Industrial Engineering Technicians; Logisticians; Operations Research Analysts.

Skills: Operations Analysis; Systems Evaluation; Installation; Management of Financial Resources; Quality Control Analysis; Operation and Control; Systems Analysis; Equipment Maintenance.

Education and Training Programs: Business/Commerce, General; Business Administration and Management, General. **Related Knowledge/Courses:** Personnel and Human Resources; Clerical Practices; Sales and Marketing; Economics and Accounting; Customer and Personal Service; Administration and Management.

Work Environment: Indoors; sitting.

Market Research Analysts

- ❋ Personality Code: IEC
- ❋ Education/Training Required: Bachelor's degree
- ❋ Annual Earnings: $60,300
- ❋ Beginning Wage: $33,310
- ❋ Earnings Growth Potential: High
- ❋ Growth: 20.1%
- ❋ Annual Job Openings: 45,015
- ❋ Self-Employed: 6.6%
- ❋ Part-Time: 12.5%

Research market conditions in local, regional, or national areas to determine potential sales of a product or service. May gather information on competitors, prices, sales, and methods of marketing and distribution. May use survey results to create a marketing campaign based on regional preferences and buying habits. Collect and analyze data on customer demographics, preferences, needs, and buying habits to identify potential markets and factors affecting product demand. Prepare reports of findings, illustrating data graphically and translating complex findings into written text. Measure and assess customer and employee satisfaction. Forecast and track marketing and sales trends, analyzing collected data. Seek and provide information to help companies determine their position in the marketplace. Measure the effectiveness of marketing, advertising, and communications programs and strategies. Conduct research on consumer opinions and marketing strategies, collaborating with marketing professionals, statisticians, pollsters, and other professionals. Attend staff conferences to provide management with information and proposals concerning the promotion, distribution, design, and pricing of company products or services. Gather data on competitors and analyze their prices, sales, and method of marketing and distribution. Monitor industry statistics and follow trends in trade literature. Devise and evaluate methods and procedures for collecting data, such as surveys, opinion polls, or questionnaires, or arrange to obtain existing data. Develop and implement procedures for identifying advertising needs. Direct trained survey interviewers.

GOE—Interest Area/Cluster: 06. Finance and Insurance. **Work Group:** 06.02. Finance/Insurance Investigation and Analysis. **Other Jobs in This Work Group:** Appraisers and Assessors of Real Estate; Appraisers, Real Estate; Assessors; Claims Adjusters, Examiners, and Investigators; Claims Examiners, Property and Casualty Insurance; Cost Estimators; Credit Analysts; Financial Analysts; Insurance Adjusters, Examiners, and Investigators; Insurance Appraisers, Auto Damage; Insurance Underwriters; Loan Counselors; Loan Officers; Survey Researchers.

Skills: Writing; Negotiation; Persuasion; Judgment and Decision Making; Reading Comprehension; Management of Financial Resources; Coordination; Active Listening.

Education and Training Programs: Economics, General; Applied Economics; Econometrics and Quantitative Economics; International Economics; Business/Managerial Economics; Marketing Research. **Related Knowledge/Courses:** Sales and Marketing; Communications and Media; Administration and Management; Economics and Accounting; Clerical Practices; Computers and Electronics.

Work Environment: Indoors; sitting.

Mathematicians

- ❋ Personality Code: ICA
- ❋ Education/Training Required: Doctoral degree
- ❋ Annual Earnings: $90,870
- ❋ Beginning Wage: $51,240
- ❋ Earnings Growth Potential: High
- ❋ Growth: 10.2%
- ❋ Annual Job Openings: 473
- ❋ Self-Employed: 0.0%
- ❋ Part-Time: 5.6%

Conduct research in fundamental mathematics or in application of mathematical techniques to science, management, and other fields. Solve or direct solutions to problems in various fields by mathematical methods. Apply mathematical theories and techniques to the solution of practical problems in business, engineering, the sciences, or other fields. Develop computational methods for solving problems that occur in areas of science and engineering or that come from applications in business or industry. Maintain knowledge in the field by reading professional journals, talking with other mathematicians, and attending professional conferences. Perform computations and apply methods of numerical analysis to data. Develop mathematical or statistical models of phenomena to be used for analysis or for computational simulation. Assemble sets of assumptions and explore the consequences of each set. Address the relationships of quantities, magnitudes, and forms through the use of numbers and symbols. Develop new principles and new relationships between existing mathematical principles to advance mathematical science. Design, analyze, and decipher encryption systems designed to transmit military, political, financial, or law-enforcement-related information in code. Conduct research to extend mathematical knowledge in traditional areas, such as algebra, geometry, probability, and logic.

GOE—Interest Area/Cluster: 15. Scientific Research, Engineering, and Mathematics. **Work Group:** 15.06. Mathematics and Data Analysis. **Other Jobs in This Work Group:** Actuaries; Mathematical Technicians; Social Science Research Assistants; Statistical Assistants; Statisticians.

Skills: Programming; Science; Mathematics; Complex Problem Solving; Operations Analysis; Reading Comprehension; Critical Thinking; Active Learning.

Education and Training Programs: Mathematics, General; Algebra and Number Theory; Analysis and Functional Analysis; Geometry/Geometric Analysis; Topology and Foundations; Mathematics, Other; Applied Mathematics; Computational Mathematics; Applied Mathematics, Other; Mathematical Statistics and Probability; Mathematics and Statistics, Other; Logic. **Related Knowledge/Courses:** Mathematics; Physics; Computers and Electronics; Engineering and Technology; English Language.

Work Environment: Indoors; sitting.

Investigative—M

Mechanical Engineers

- ❋ Personality Code: IRC
- ❋ Education/Training Required: Bachelor's degree
- ❋ Annual Earnings: $72,300
- ❋ Beginning Wage: $46,560
- ❋ Earnings Growth Potential: Medium
- ❋ Growth: 4.2%
- ❋ Annual Job Openings: 12,394
- ❋ Self-Employed: 2.2%
- ❋ Part-Time: 1.9%

Perform engineering duties in planning and designing tools, engines, machines, and other mechanically functioning equipment. Oversee installation, operation, maintenance, and repair of such equipment as centralized heat, gas, water, and steam systems. Read and interpret blueprints, technical drawings, schematics, and computer-generated reports. Confer with engineers and other personnel to implement operating procedures, resolve system malfunctions, and provide technical information. Research and analyze customer design proposals, specifications, manuals, and other data to evaluate the feasibility, cost, and maintenance requirements of designs or applications. Specify system components or direct modification of products to ensure conformance with engineering design and performance specifications. Research, design, evaluate, install, operate, and maintain mechanical products, equipment, systems, and processes to meet requirements, applying knowledge of engineering principles. Investigate equipment failures and difficulties to diagnose faulty operation and to make recommendations to maintenance crew. Assist drafters in developing the structural design of products, using drafting tools or computer-assisted design (CAD) or drafting equipment and software. Provide feedback to design engineers on customer problems and needs. Oversee installation, operation, maintenance, and repair to ensure that machines and equipment are installed and functioning according to specifications. Conduct research that tests and analyzes the feasibility, design, operation, and performance of equipment, components, and systems. Recommend design modifications to eliminate machine or system malfunctions. Develop and test models of alternate designs and processing methods to assess feasibility, operating condition effects, possible new applications, and necessity of modification. Develop, coordinate, and monitor all aspects of production, including selection of manufacturing methods, fabrication, and operation of product designs. Estimate costs and submit bids for engineering, construction, or extraction projects and prepare contract documents. Perform personnel functions such as supervision of production workers, technicians, technologists, and other engineers or design of evaluation programs. Solicit new business and provide technical customer service. Establish and coordinate the maintenance and safety procedures, service schedule, and supply of materials required to maintain machines and equipment in the prescribed condition.

GOE—Interest Area/Cluster: 15. Scientific Research, Engineering, and Mathematics. **Work Group:** 15.07. Research and Design Engineering. **Other Jobs in This Work Group:** Aerospace Engineers; Biomedical Engineers; Chemical Engineers; Civil Engineers; Computer Hardware Engineers; Electrical Engineers; Electronics Engineers, Except Computer; Marine Architects; Marine Engineers; Marine Engineers and Naval Architects; Materials Engineers; Nuclear Engineers.

Skills: Science; Operations Analysis; Installation; Complex Problem Solving; Mathematics; Systems Analysis; Judgment and Decision Making; Coordination.

Education and Training Program: Mechanical Engineering. **Related Knowledge/Courses:** Design; Engineering and Technology; Mechanical Devices; Production and Processing; Physics; Administration and Management.

Work Environment: Indoors; sitting.

Medical and Clinical Laboratory Technologists

- ❋ Personality Code: IRC
- ❋ Education/Training Required: Bachelor's degree
- ❋ Annual Earnings: $51,720
- ❋ Beginning Wage: $35,460
- ❋ Earnings Growth Potential: Low
- ❋ Growth: 12.4%
- ❋ Annual Job Openings: 11,457
- ❋ Self-Employed: 0.7%
- ❋ Part-Time: 14.3%

Perform complex medical laboratory tests for diagnosis, treatment, and prevention of disease. May train or supervise staff. Conduct chemical analysis of bodily fluids, including blood, urine, and spinal fluid, to determine presence of normal and abnormal components. Analyze laboratory findings to check the accuracy of the results. Enter data from analysis of medical tests and clinical results into computer for storage. Operate, calibrate, and maintain equipment used in quantitative and qualitative analysis, such as spectrophotometers, calorimeters, flame photometers, and computer-controlled analyzers. Establish and monitor quality assurance programs and activities to ensure the accuracy of laboratory results. Set up, clean, and maintain laboratory equipment. Provide technical information about test results to physicians, family members, and researchers. Supervise, train, and direct lab assistants, medical and clinical laboratory technicians and technologists, and other medical laboratory workers engaged in laboratory testing. Collect and study blood samples to determine the number of cells, their morphology, or their blood group, blood type, and compatibility for transfusion purposes, using microscopic techniques. Analyze samples of biological material for chemical content or reaction. Cultivate, isolate, and assist in identifying microbial organisms, and perform various tests on these microorganisms. Obtain, cut, stain, and mount biological material on slides for microscopic study and diagnosis, following standard laboratory procedures. Select and prepare specimen and media for cell culture, using aseptic technique and knowledge of medium components and cell requirements. Develop, standardize, evaluate, and modify procedures, techniques, and tests used in the analysis of specimens and in medical laboratory experiments. Harvest cell cultures at optimum time based on knowledge of cell cycle differences and culture conditions. Conduct medical research under direction of microbiologist or biochemist.

GOE—Interest Area/Cluster: 08. Health Science. **Work Group:** 08.06. Medical Technology. **Other Jobs in This Work Group:** Biological Technicians; Cardiovascular Technologists and Technicians; Diagnostic Medical Sonographers; Medical and Clinical Laboratory Technicians; Medical Equipment Preparers; Medical Records and Health Information Technicians; Nuclear Medicine Technologists; Opticians, Dispensing; Orthotists and Prosthetists; Radiologic Technicians; Radiologic Technologists; Radiologic Technologists and Technicians.

Skills: Operation Monitoring; Management of Personnel Resources; Quality Control Analysis.

Education and Training Programs: Cytotechnology/Cytotechnologist; Clinical Laboratory Science/Medical Technology/Technologist; Histologic Technology/Histotechnologist; Cytogenetics/Genetics/Clinical Genetics Technology/Technologist; Renal/Dialysis Technologist/Technician; Clinical/Medical Laboratory Science and Allied Professions, Other. **Related Knowledge/Courses:** Biology; Chemistry; Medicine and Dentistry; Mechanical Devices; Clerical Practices; Mathematics.

Work Environment: Indoors; contaminants; disease or infections; hazardous conditions; using hands on objects, tools, or controls; repetitive motions.

Investigative-M

Medical Scientists, Except Epidemiologists

- ❀ Personality Code: IRA
- ❀ Education/Training Required: Doctoral degree
- ❀ Annual Earnings: $64,200
- ❀ Beginning Wage: $36,730
- ❀ Earnings Growth Potential: High
- ❀ Growth: 20.2%
- ❀ Annual Job Openings: 10,596
- ❀ Self-Employed: 2.0%
- ❀ Part-Time: 5.9%

Conduct research dealing with the understanding of human diseases and the improvement of human health. Engage in clinical investigation or other research, production, technical writing, or related activities. Conduct research to develop methodologies, instrumentation, and procedures for medical application, analyzing data and presenting findings. Plan and direct studies to investigate human or animal disease, preventive methods, and treatments for disease. Follow strict safety procedures when handling toxic materials to avoid contamination. Evaluate effects of drugs, gases, pesticides, parasites, and microorganisms at various levels. Teach principles of medicine and medical and laboratory procedures to physicians, residents, students, and technicians. Prepare and analyze organ, tissue, and cell samples to identify toxicity, bacteria, or microorganisms or to study cell structure. Standardize drug dosages, methods of immunization, and procedures for manufacture of drugs and medicinal compounds. Investigate cause, progress, life cycle, or mode of transmission of diseases or parasites. Confer with health department, industry personnel, physicians, and others to develop health safety standards and public health improvement programs. Study animal and human health and physiological processes. Consult with and advise physicians, educators, researchers, and others regarding medical applications of physics, biology, and chemistry. Use equipment such as atomic absorption spectrometers, electron microscopes, flow cytometers, and chromatography systems.

GOE—Interest Area/Cluster: 15. Scientific Research, Engineering, and Mathematics. **Work Group:** 15.03. Life Sciences. **Other Jobs in This Work Group:** Biochemists and Biophysicists; Biologists; Environmental Scientists and Specialists, Including Health; Epidemiologists; Microbiologists.

Skills: Science; Management of Financial Resources; Judgment and Decision Making; Reading Comprehension; Writing; Time Management; Complex Problem Solving; Active Listening.

Education and Training Programs: Biomedical Sciences, General; Biochemistry; Biophysics; Molecular Biology; Cell/Cellular Biology and Histology; Anatomy; Medical Microbiology and Bacteriology; Immunology; Human/Medical Genetics; Physiology, General; Molecular Physiology; Cell Physiology; Endocrinology; Reproductive Biology; Neurobiology and Neurophysiology; Cardiovascular Science; others. **Related Knowledge/Courses:** Biology; Medicine and Dentistry; Chemistry; Communications and Media; Personnel and Human Resources; Sociology and Anthropology.

Work Environment: Indoors; sitting; using hands on objects, tools, or controls.

Network and Computer Systems Administrators

- ❀ Personality Code: IRC
- ❀ Education/Training Required: Bachelor's degree
- ❀ Annual Earnings: $64,690
- ❀ Beginning Wage: $39,970
- ❀ Earnings Growth Potential: Medium
- ❀ Growth: 27.0%
- ❀ Annual Job Openings: 37,010
- ❀ Self-Employed: 0.4%
- ❀ Part-Time: 3.1%

The job openings listed here are shared with Computer Security Specialists.

Install, configure, and support organizations' local area networks (LANs), wide area networks (WANs), and Internet systems or segments of network systems. Maintain network hardware and software. Monitor networks to ensure network availability to all system users and perform necessary maintenance to support network availability. May supervise other network support and client server specialists and plan, coordinate, and implement network security measures. Maintain and administer computer networks and related computing environments including computer hardware, systems software, applications software, and all configurations. Perform data backups and disaster recovery operations. Diagnose, troubleshoot, and resolve hardware, software, or other network and system problems, and replace defective components when necessary. Plan, coordinate, and implement network security measures to protect data, software, and hardware. Configure, monitor, and maintain e-mail applications or virus protection software. Operate master consoles to monitor the performance of computer systems and networks, and to coordinate computer network access and use. Load computer tapes and disks, and install software and printer paper or forms. Design, configure, and test computer hardware, networking software, and operating system software. Monitor network performance to determine whether adjustments need to be made and to determine where changes will need to be made in the future. Confer with network users about how to solve existing system problems. Research new technologies by attending seminars, reading trade articles, or taking classes, and implement or recommend the implementation of new technologies. Analyze equipment performance records to determine the need for repair or replacement. Implement and provide technical support for voice services and equipment such as private branch exchanges, voice mail systems, and telecom systems. Maintain inventories of parts for emergency repairs. Recommend changes to improve systems and network configurations, and determine hardware or software requirements related to such changes. Gather data pertaining to customer needs, and use the information to identify, predict, interpret, and evaluate system and network requirements. Train people in computer system use. Coordinate with vendors and with company personnel to facilitate purchases. Perform routine network startup and shutdown procedures, and maintain control records. Maintain logs related to network functions, as well as maintenance and repair records.

GOE—Interest Area/Cluster: 11. Information Technology. **Work Group:** 11.01. Managerial Work in Information Technology. **Other Jobs in This Work Group:** Computer and Information Systems Managers.

Skills: Programming; Systems Analysis; Systems Evaluation; Operation Monitoring; Quality Control Analysis; Troubleshooting; Management of Personnel Resources; Operation and Control.

Education and Training Programs: Computer and Information Sciences and Support Services, Other; Computer and Information Sciences, General; Computer and Information Systems Security; Computer Systems Analysis/Analyst; Computer Systems Networking and Telecommunications; Information Science/Studies; System Administration/Administrator; System, Networking, and LAN/WAN Management/Manager. **Related Knowledge/Courses:** Telecommunications; Computers and Electronics; Clerical Practices; Administration and Management; Engineering and Technology.

Work Environment: Indoors; sitting; using hands on objects, tools, or controls; repetitive motions.

Investigative-N

Network Systems and Data Communications Analysts

- ❈ Personality Code: IC
- ❈ Education/Training Required: Bachelor's degree
- ❈ Annual Earnings: $68,220
- ❈ Beginning Wage: $40,100
- ❈ Earnings Growth Potential: High
- ❈ Growth: 53.4%
- ❈ Annual Job Openings: 35,086
- ❈ Self-Employed: 17.5%
- ❈ Part-Time: 8.6%

Analyze, design, test, and evaluate network systems, such as local area networks (LAN); wide area networks (WAN); and Internet, intranet, and other data communications systems. Perform network modeling, analysis, and planning. Research and recommend network and data communications hardware and software. Includes telecommunications specialists who deal with the interfacing of computer and communications equipment. May supervise computer programmers. Maintain needed files by adding and deleting files on the network server and backing up files to guarantee their safety in the event of problems with the network. Monitor system performance and provide security measures, troubleshooting, and maintenance as needed. Assist users to diagnose and solve data communication problems. Set up user accounts, regulating and monitoring file access to ensure confidentiality and proper use. Design and implement systems, network configurations, and network architecture, including hardware and software technology, site locations, and integration of technologies. Maintain the peripherals, such as printers, that are connected to the network. Identify areas of operation that need upgraded equipment such as modems, fiber-optic cables, and telephone wires. Train users in use of equipment. Develop and write procedures for installation, use, and troubleshooting of communications hardware and software. Adapt and modify existing software to meet specific needs. Work with other engineers, systems analysts, programmers, technicians, scientists, and top-level managers in the design, testing, and evaluation of systems. Test and evaluate hardware and software to determine efficiency, reliability, and compatibility with existing system and make purchase recommendations. Read technical manuals and brochures to determine which equipment meets establishment requirements. Consult customers, visit workplaces, or conduct surveys to determine present and future user needs. Visit vendors, attend conferences or training, and study technical journals to keep up with changes in technology.

GOE—Interest Area/Cluster: 11. Information Technology. **Work Group:** 11.02. Information Technology Specialties. **Other Jobs in This Work Group:** Computer and Information Scientists, Research; Computer Operators; Computer Programmers; Computer Security Specialists; Computer Software Engineers, Applications; Computer Software Engineers, Systems Software; Computer Support Specialists; Computer Systems Analysts; Computer Systems Engineers/Architects; Database Administrators; Network Designers; Software Quality Assurance Engineers and Testers; Web Administrators; Web Developers.

Skills: Installation; Technology Design; Troubleshooting; Systems Analysis; Programming; Systems Evaluation; Management of Material Resources; Operations Analysis.

Education and Training Programs: Computer and Information Sciences, General; Information Technology; Computer Systems Analysis/Analyst; Computer Systems Networking and Telecommunications; System, Networking, and LAN/WAN Management/Manager; Computer and Information Systems Security. **Related Knowledge/Courses:** Telecommunications; Computers and Electronics; Customer and Personal Service; Engineering and Technology; Education and Training; Design.

Work Environment: Indoors; sitting.

Nuclear Medicine Technologists

* Personality Code: IRS
* Education/Training Required: Associate degree
* Annual Earnings: $64,670
* Beginning Wage: $47,370
* Earnings Growth Potential: Low
* Growth: 14.8%
* Annual Job Openings: 1,290
* Self-Employed: 1.0%
* Part-Time: 17.3%

Prepare, administer, and measure radioactive isotopes in therapeutic, diagnostic, and tracer studies, using a variety of radioisotope equipment. Prepare stock solutions of radioactive materials and calculate doses to be administered by radiologists. Subject patients to radiation. Execute blood volume, red cell survival, and fat absorption studies, following standard laboratory techniques. Detect and map radiopharmaceuticals in patients' bodies, using a camera to produce photographic or computer images. Administer radiopharmaceuticals or radiation intravenously to detect or treat diseases, using radioisotope equipment, under direction of a physician. Produce computer-generated or film images for interpretation by physicians. Calculate, measure, and record radiation dosages or radiopharmaceuticals received, used, and disposed, using computers and following physicians' prescriptions. Perform quality control checks on laboratory equipment and cameras. Maintain and calibrate radioisotope and laboratory equipment. Dispose of radioactive materials and store radiopharmaceuticals, following radiation safety procedures. Process cardiac function studies, using computers. Prepare stock radiopharmaceuticals, adhering to safety standards that minimize radiation exposure to workers and patients. Record and process results of procedures. Explain test procedures and safety precautions to patients and provide them with assistance during test procedures. Gather information on patients' illnesses and medical histories to guide choices of diagnostic procedures for therapies. Measure glandular activity, blood volume, red cell survival, and radioactivity of patient, using scanners, Geiger counters, scintillation counters, and other laboratory equipment. Train and supervise student or subordinate nuclear medicine technologists. Position radiation fields, radiation beams, and patients to allow for most effective treatment of patients' diseases, using computers. Add radioactive substances to biological specimens such as blood, urine, and feces to determine therapeutic drug or hormone levels. Develop treatment procedures for nuclear medicine treatment programs.

GOE—Interest Area/Cluster: 08. Health Science. **Work Group:** 08.06. Medical Technology. **Other Jobs in This Work Group:** Biological Technicians; Cardiovascular Technologists and Technicians; Diagnostic Medical Sonographers; Medical and Clinical Laboratory Technicians; Medical and Clinical Laboratory Technologists; Medical Equipment Preparers; Medical Records and Health Information Technicians; Opticians, Dispensing; Orthotists and Prosthetists; Radiologic Technicians; Radiologic Technologists; Radiologic Technologists and Technicians.

Skills: Operation Monitoring; Equipment Maintenance; Quality Control Analysis; Systems Analysis; Operation and Control; Systems Evaluation.

Education and Training Programs: Nuclear Medical Technology/Technologist; Radiation Protection/Health Physics Technician. **Related Knowledge/Courses:** Medicine and Dentistry; Biology; Chemistry; Physics; Customer and Personal Service; Therapy and Counseling.

Work Environment: Indoors; contaminants; radiation; disease or infections; standing; using hands on objects, tools, or controls.

Investigative-N

Obstetricians and Gynecologists

- ❀ Personality Code: ISR
- ❀ Education/Training Required: First professional degree
- ❀ Annual Earnings: More than $145,600
- ❀ Beginning Wage: $100,770
- ❀ Earnings Growth Potential: Cannot be calculated
- ❀ Growth: 14.2%
- ❀ Annual Job Openings: 38,027
- ❀ Self-Employed: 14.7%
- ❀ Part-Time: 8.1%

The job openings listed here are shared with Anesthesiologists; Family and General Practitioners; Internists, General; Pediatricians, General; Psychiatrists; and Surgeons.

Diagnose, treat, and help prevent diseases of women, especially those affecting the reproductive system and the process of childbirth. Care for and treat women during prenatal, natal, and postnatal periods. Explain procedures and discuss test results or prescribed treatments with patients. Treat diseases of female organs. Monitor patients' condition and progress and re-evaluate treatments as necessary. Perform cesarean sections or other surgical procedures as needed to preserve patients' health and deliver babies safely. Prescribe or administer therapy, medication, and other specialized medical care to treat or prevent illness, disease, or injury. Analyze records, reports, test results, or examination information to diagnose medical condition of patient. Collect, record, and maintain patient information, such as medical histories, reports, and examination results. Advise patients and community members concerning diet, activity, hygiene, and disease prevention. Refer patient to medical specialist or other practitioner when necessary. Consult with, or provide consulting services to, other physicians. Direct and coordinate activities of nurses, students, assistants, specialists, therapists, and other medical staff. Plan, implement, or administer health programs in hospitals, businesses, or communities for prevention and treatment of injuries or illnesses. Prepare government and organizational reports on birth, death, and disease statistics; workforce evaluations; or the medical status of individuals. Conduct research to develop or test medications, treatments, or procedures to prevent or control disease or injury.

GOE—Interest Area/Cluster: 08. Health Science. **Work Group:** 08.02. Medicine and Surgery. **Other Jobs in This Work Group:** Anesthesiologists; Family and General Practitioners; Internists, General; Medical Assistants; Medical Transcriptionists; Pediatricians, General; Pharmacists; Pharmacy Aides; Pharmacy Technicians; Physician Assistants; Psychiatrists; Registered Nurses; Surgeons; Surgical Technologists.

Skills: Science; Judgment and Decision Making; Reading Comprehension; Complex Problem Solving; Active Learning; Social Perceptiveness; Critical Thinking; Instructing.

Education and Training Programs: Neonatal-Perinatal Medicine; Obstetrics and Gynecology. **Related Knowledge/Courses:** Medicine and Dentistry; Therapy and Counseling; Biology; Psychology; Sociology and Anthropology; Chemistry.

Work Environment: Indoors; disease or infections; standing; using hands on objects, tools, or controls.

Operations Research Analysts

- ❀ Personality Code: ICE
- ❀ Education/Training Required: Master's degree
- ❀ Annual Earnings: $66,950
- ❀ Beginning Wage: $39,760
- ❀ Earnings Growth Potential: High
- ❀ Growth: 10.6%
- ❀ Annual Job Openings: 5,727
- ❀ Self-Employed: 0.2%
- ❀ Part-Time: 5.6%

Formulate and apply mathematical modeling and other optimizing methods, using a computer to develop and interpret information that assists management with decision making, policy formulation, or other managerial functions. May develop related software, service, or products. Frequently concentrates on collecting and analyzing data and developing decision support software. May develop and supply optimal time, cost, or logistics networks for program evaluation, review, or implementation. Formulate mathematical or simulation models of problems, relating constants and variables, restrictions, alternatives, and conflicting objectives and their numerical parameters. Collaborate with others in the organization to ensure successful implementation of chosen problem solutions. Analyze information obtained from management in order to conceptualize and define operational problems. Perform validation and testing of models to ensure adequacy; reformulate models as necessary. Collaborate with senior managers and decision-makers to identify and solve a variety of problems and to clarify management objectives. Define data requirements; then gather and validate information, applying judgment and statistical tests. Study and analyze information about alternative courses of action in order to determine which plan will offer the best outcomes. Prepare management reports defining and evaluating problems and recommending solutions. Break systems into their component parts, assign numerical values to each component, and examine the mathematical relationships between them. Specify manipulative or computational methods to be applied to models. Observe the current system in operation and gather and analyze information about each of the parts of component problems, using a variety of sources. Design, conduct, and evaluate experimental operational models in cases where models cannot be developed from existing data. Develop and apply time and cost networks in order to plan, control, and review large projects. Develop business methods and procedures, including accounting systems, file systems, office systems, logistics systems, and production schedules.

GOE—Interest Area/Cluster: 04. Business and Administration. Work Group: 04.05. Accounting, Auditing, and Analytical Support. Other Jobs in This Work Group: Accountants; Accountants and Auditors; Auditors; Budget Analysts; Industrial Engineering Technicians; Logisticians; Management Analysts.

Skills: Programming; Systems Analysis; Operations Analysis; Science; Mathematics; Systems Evaluation; Complex Problem Solving; Judgment and Decision Making.

Education and Training Programs: Educational Evaluation and Research; Educational Statistics and Research Methods; Operations Research; Management Science, General; Management Sciences and Quantitative Methods, Other. Related Knowledge/Courses: Mathematics; Engineering and Technology; Computers and Electronics; Production and Processing; Economics and Accounting; Administration and Management.

Work Environment: Indoors; sitting.

Optometrists

* Personality Code: ISR
* Education/Training Required: First professional degree
* Annual Earnings: $93,800
* Beginning Wage: $47,980
* Earnings Growth Potential: High
* Growth: 11.3%
* Annual Job Openings: 1,789
* Self-Employed: 25.5%
* Part-Time: 20.8%

Diagnose, manage, and treat conditions and diseases of the human eye and visual system. Examine eyes and visual systems, diagnose problems or impairments, prescribe corrective lenses, and provide treatment. May prescribe therapeutic drugs to treat specific eye conditions. Examine eyes, using observation, instruments, and pharmaceutical agents, to determine visual acuity and perception, focus, and coordination and to diagnose diseases and other abnormalities such as glaucoma or color blindness. Prescribe medications to treat eye diseases if state laws permit. Analyze test results and develop treatment plans. Prescribe, supply, fit, and adjust eyeglasses, contact lenses, and other vision aids. Educate and counsel patients on contact lens care, visual hygiene, lighting arrangements, and safety factors. Remove foreign bodies from eyes. Consult with and refer patients to ophthalmologist or other health care practitioners if additional medical treatment is determined necessary. Provide patients undergoing eye surgeries such as cataract and laser vision correction, with pre- and post-operative care. Prescribe therapeutic procedures to correct or conserve vision. Provide vision therapy and low vision rehabilitation.

GOE—Interest Area/Cluster: 08. Health Science. **Work Group:** 08.04. Health Specialties. **Other Jobs in This Work Group:** Chiropractors; Podiatrists.

Skills: Management of Personnel Resources; Systems Evaluation; Writing; Systems Analysis.

Education and Training Program: Optometry (OD). **Related Knowledge/Courses:** Medicine and Dentistry; Biology; Therapy and Counseling; Physics; Sales and Marketing; Economics and Accounting.

Work Environment: Indoors; disease or infections; sitting; using hands on objects, tools, or controls; repetitive motions.

Orthodontists

* Personality Code: IRS
* Education/Training Required: First professional degree
* Annual Earnings: More than $145,600
* Beginning Wage: $95,740
* Earnings Growth Potential: Cannot be calculated
* Growth: 9.2%
* Annual Job Openings: 479
* Self-Employed: 43.3%
* Part-Time: 25.9%

Examine, diagnose, and treat dental malocclusions and oral cavity anomalies. Design and fabricate appliances to realign teeth and jaws to produce and maintain normal function and to improve appearance. Fit dental appliances in patients' mouths to alter the position and relationship of teeth and jaws and to realign teeth. Study diagnostic records such as medical/dental histories, plaster models of the teeth, photos of a patient's face and teeth, and X rays to develop patient treatment plans. Diagnose teeth and jaw or other dental-facial abnormalities. Examine patients to assess abnormalities of jaw development, tooth position, and other dental-facial structures. Prepare diagnostic and treatment records. Adjust dental appliances periodically to produce and maintain normal function. Provide patients with proposed treatment plans and cost estimates. Instruct dental officers and technical assistants in orthodontic procedures and techniques. Coordinate orthodontic services with other dental and medical services. Design and fabricate appliances, such as space maintainers, retainers, and labial and lingual arch wires.

GOE—Interest Area/Cluster: 08. Health Science. **Work Group:** 08.03. Dentistry. **Other Jobs in This Work Group:** Dental Assistants; Dental Hygienists; Dentists, General; Oral and Maxillofacial Surgeons; Prosthodontists.

Skills: Management of Financial Resources; Equipment Selection; Management of Personnel Resources; Management of Material Resources; Technology Design; Judgment and Decision Making; Operations Analysis; Service Orientation.

Education and Training Programs: Orthodontics/Orthodontology (Cert, MS, PhD); Orthodontics Specialty. **Related Knowledge/Courses:** Medicine and Dentistry; Biology; Sales and Marketing; Economics and Accounting; Personnel and Human Resources; Customer and Personal Service.

Work Environment: Indoors; disease or infections; sitting; using hands on objects, tools, or controls; bending or twisting the body; repetitive motions.

Pediatricians, General

- ❋ Personality Code: IS
- ❋ Education/Training Required: First professional degree
- ❋ Annual Earnings: $140,690
- ❋ Beginning Wage: $67,430
- ❋ Earnings Growth Potential: Very high
- ❋ Growth: 14.2%
- ❋ Annual Job Openings: 38,027
- ❋ Self-Employed: 14.7%
- ❋ Part-Time: 8.1%

The job openings listed here are shared with Anesthesiologists; Family and General Practitioners; Internists, General; Obstetricians and Gynecologists; Psychiatrists; and Surgeons.

Diagnose, treat, and help prevent children's diseases and injuries. Examine patients or order, perform, and interpret diagnostic tests to obtain information on medical condition and determine diagnosis. Examine children regularly to assess their growth and development. Prescribe or administer treatment, therapy, medication, vaccination, and other specialized medical care to treat or prevent illness, disease, or injury in infants and children. Collect, record, and maintain patient information, such as medical history, reports, and examination results. Advise patients, parents or guardians, and community members concerning diet, activity, hygiene, and disease prevention. Treat children who have minor illnesses, acute and chronic health problems, and growth and development concerns. Explain procedures and discuss test results or prescribed treatments with patients and parents or guardians. Monitor patients' condition and progress and re-evaluate treatments as necessary. Plan and execute medical care programs to aid in the mental and physical growth and development of children and adolescents. Refer patient to medical specialist or other practitioner when necessary. Direct and coordinate activities of nurses, students, assistants, specialists, therapists, and other medical staff. Provide consulting services to other physicians. Plan, implement, or administer health programs or standards in hospital, business, or community for information, prevention, or treatment of injury or illness. Operate on patients to remove, repair, or improve functioning of diseased or injured body parts and systems. Conduct research to study anatomy and develop or test medications, treatments, or procedures to prevent or control disease or injury. Prepare reports for government or management of birth, death, and disease statistics; workforce evaluations; or medical status of individuals.

GOE—Interest Area/Cluster: 08. Health Science. **Work Group:** 08.02. Medicine and Surgery. **Other Jobs in This Work Group:** Anesthesiologists; Family and General Practitioners; Internists, General; Medical Assistants; Medical Transcriptionists; Obstetricians and Gynecologists; Pharmacists; Pharmacy Aides; Pharmacy Technicians; Physician Assistants; Psychiatrists; Registered Nurses; Surgeons; Surgical Technologists.

Skills: Science; Social Perceptiveness; Active Learning; Reading Comprehension; Persuasion; Critical Thinking; Management of Financial Resources; Monitoring.

Education and Training Programs: Child/Pediatric Neurology; Family Medicine; Neonatal-Perinatal Medicine; Pediatric Cardiology; Pediatric Endocrinology; Pediatric Hemato-Oncology; Pediatric

Nephrology; Pediatric Orthopedics; Pediatric Surgery; Pediatrics. **Related Knowledge/Courses:** Medicine and Dentistry; Therapy and Counseling; Biology; Psychology; Chemistry; Sociology and Anthropology.

Work Environment: Indoors; disease or infections; standing; using hands on objects, tools, or controls.

Pharmacists

- ❋ Personality Code: ICS
- ❋ Education/Training Required: First professional degree
- ❋ Annual Earnings: $100,480
- ❋ Beginning Wage: $73,010
- ❋ Earnings Growth Potential: Low
- ❋ Growth: 21.7%
- ❋ Annual Job Openings: 16,358
- ❋ Self-Employed: 0.5%
- ❋ Part-Time: 18.1%

Compound and dispense medications, following prescriptions issued by physicians, dentists, or other authorized medical practitioners. Review prescriptions to assure accuracy, to ascertain the needed ingredients, and to evaluate their suitability. Provide information and advice regarding drug interactions, side effects, dosage, and proper medication storage. Analyze prescribing trends to monitor patient compliance and to prevent excessive usage or harmful interactions. Order and purchase pharmaceutical supplies, medical supplies, and drugs, maintaining stock and storing and handling it properly. Maintain records, such as pharmacy files; patient profiles; charge system files; inventories; control records for radioactive nuclei; and registries of poisons, narcotics, and controlled drugs. Provide specialized services to help patients manage conditions such as diabetes, asthma, smoking cessation, or high blood pressure. Advise customers on the selection of medication brands, medical equipment, and health-care supplies. Collaborate with other health-care professionals to plan, monitor, review, and evaluate the quality and effectiveness of drugs and drug regimens, providing advice on drug applications and characteristics. Compound and dispense medications as prescribed by doctors and dentists by calculating, weighing, measuring, and mixing ingredients or oversee these activities. Offer health promotion and prevention activities—for example, training people to use devices such as blood-pressure or diabetes monitors. Refer patients to other health professionals and agencies when appropriate. Prepare sterile solutions and infusions for use in surgical procedures, emergency rooms, or patients' homes. Plan, implement, and maintain procedures for mixing, packaging, and labeling pharmaceuticals according to policy and legal requirements to ensure quality, security, and proper disposal. Assay radiopharmaceuticals, verify rates of disintegration, and calculate the volume required to produce the desired results to ensure proper dosages. Manage pharmacy operations, hiring and supervising staff, performing administrative duties, and buying and selling nonpharmaceutical merchandise. Work in hospitals, clinics, or for health maintenance organizations (HMOs), dispensing prescriptions, serving as a medical team consultant, or specializing in specific drug therapy areas such as oncology or nuclear pharmacotherapy.

GOE—Interest Area/Cluster: 08. Health Science. **Work Group:** 08.02. Medicine and Surgery. **Other Jobs in This Work Group:** Anesthesiologists; Family and General Practitioners; Internists, General; Medical Assistants; Medical Transcriptionists; Obstetricians and Gynecologists; Pediatricians, General; Pharmacy Aides; Pharmacy Technicians; Physician Assistants; Psychiatrists; Registered Nurses; Surgeons; Surgical Technologists.

Skills: Science; Reading Comprehension; Social Perceptiveness; Active Listening; Instructing; Mathematics; Speaking; Critical Thinking.

Education and Training Programs: Pharmacy (PharmD [USA] PharmD, BS/BPharm [Canada]); Pharmacy Administration and Pharmacy Policy and Regulatory Affairs (MS, PhD); Pharmaceutics and Drug Design (MS, PhD); Medicinal and Pharmaceutical Chemistry (MS, PhD); Natural Products

Chemistry and Pharmacognosy (MS, PhD); Clinical and Industrial Drug Development (MS, PhD); Pharmacoeconomics/Pharmaceutical Economics (MS, PhD); Clinical, Hospital, and Managed Care Pharmacy (MS, PhD); others. **Related Knowledge/Courses:** Medicine and Dentistry; Chemistry; Therapy and Counseling; Biology; Psychology; Mathematics.

Work Environment: Indoors; disease or infections; standing; repetitive motions.

Physicists

- ❈ Personality Code: IR
- ❈ Education/Training Required: Doctoral degree
- ❈ Annual Earnings: $96,850
- ❈ Beginning Wage: $51,870
- ❈ Earnings Growth Potential: High
- ❈ Growth: 6.8%
- ❈ Annual Job Openings: 1,302
- ❈ Self-Employed: 0.8%
- ❈ Part-Time: 5.2%

Conduct research into phases of physical phenomena, develop theories and laws on basis of observation and experiments, and devise methods to apply laws and theories to industry and other fields. Perform complex calculations as part of the analysis and evaluation of data, using computers. Describe and express observations and conclusions in mathematical terms. Analyze data from research conducted to detect and measure physical phenomena. Report experimental results by writing papers for scientific journals or by presenting information at scientific conferences. Design computer simulations to model physical data so that it can be better understood. Collaborate with other scientists in the design, development, and testing of experimental, industrial, or medical equipment, instrumentation, and procedures. Direct testing and monitoring of contamination of radioactive equipment, and recording of personnel and plant area radiation exposure data.

Observe the structure and properties of matter, and the transformation and propagation of energy, using equipment such as masers, lasers, and telescopes, in order to explore and identify the basic principles governing these phenomena. Develop theories and laws on the basis of observation and experiments, and apply these theories and laws to problems in areas such as nuclear energy, optics, and aerospace technology. Teach physics to students. Develop manufacturing, assembly, and fabrication processes of lasers, masers, infrared, and other light-emitting and light-sensitive devices. Conduct application evaluations and analyze results in order to determine commercial, industrial, scientific, medical, military, or other uses for electro-optical devices. Develop standards of permissible concentrations of radioisotopes in liquids and gases. Conduct research pertaining to potential environmental impacts of atomic energy-related industrial development in order to determine licensing qualifications. Advise authorities of procedures to be followed in radiation incidents or hazards, and assist in civil defense planning.

GOE—Interest Area/Cluster: 15. Scientific Research, Engineering, and Mathematics. **Work Group:** 15.02. Physical Sciences. **Other Jobs in This Work Group:** Astronomers; Atmospheric and Space Scientists; Chemists; Geographers; Geoscientists, Except Hydrologists and Geographers; Hydrologists; Materials Scientists.

Skills: Programming; Science; Mathematics; Complex Problem Solving; Management of Financial Resources; Systems Analysis; Writing; Critical Thinking.

Education and Training Programs: Astrophysics; Physics, General; Atomic/Molecular Physics; Elementary Particle Physics; Plasma and High-Temperature Physics; Nuclear Physics; Optics/Optical Sciences; Solid State and Low-Temperature Physics; Acoustics; Theoretical and Mathematical Physics; Physics, Other; Health/Medical Physics. **Related Knowledge/Courses:** Physics; Mathematics; Engineering and Technology; Computers and Electronics; English Language; Telecommunications.

Work Environment: Indoors; sitting.

Investigative–P

Podiatrists

- ❈ Personality Code: ISR
- ❈ Education/Training Required: First professional degree
- ❈ Annual Earnings: $110,510
- ❈ Beginning Wage: $45,260
- ❈ Earnings Growth Potential: Very high
- ❈ Growth: 9.5%
- ❈ Annual Job Openings: 648
- ❈ Self-Employed: 23.9%
- ❈ Part-Time: 23.6%

Diagnose and treat diseases and deformities of the human foot. Treat bone, muscle, and joint disorders affecting the feet. Diagnose diseases and deformities of the foot, using medical histories, physical examinations, X rays, and laboratory test results. Prescribe medications, corrective devices, physical therapy, or surgery. Treat conditions such as corns, calluses, ingrown nails, tumors, shortened tendons, bunions, cysts, and abscesses by surgical methods. Advise patients about treatments and foot care techniques necessary for prevention of future problems. Refer patients to physicians when symptoms indicative of systemic disorders, such as arthritis or diabetes, are observed in feet and legs. Correct deformities by means of plaster casts and strapping. Make and fit prosthetic appliances. Perform administrative duties such as hiring employees, ordering supplies, and keeping records. Educate the public about the benefits of foot care through techniques such as speaking engagements, advertising, and other forums. Treat deformities, using mechanical methods, such as whirlpool or paraffin baths, and electrical methods, such as shortwave and low-voltage currents.

GOE—Interest Area/Cluster: 08. Health Science. **Work Group:** 08.04. Health Specialties. **Other Jobs in This Work Group:** Chiropractors; Optometrists.

Skills: Science; Active Listening; Complex Problem Solving; Management of Financial Resources; Reading Comprehension; Equipment Selection; Active Learning; Judgment and Decision Making.

Education and Training Program: Podiatric Medicine/Podiatry (DPM). **Related Knowledge/Courses:** Medicine and Dentistry; Biology; Therapy and Counseling; Sales and Marketing; Chemistry; Psychology.

Work Environment: Indoors; contaminants; disease or infections; sitting; using hands on objects, tools, or controls; repetitive motions.

Political Scientists

- ❈ Personality Code: IAS
- ❈ Education/Training Required: Master's degree
- ❈ Annual Earnings: $91,580
- ❈ Beginning Wage: $37,960
- ❈ Earnings Growth Potential: Very high
- ❈ Growth: 5.3%
- ❈ Annual Job Openings: 318
- ❈ Self-Employed: 7.5%
- ❈ Part-Time: 20.1%

Study the origin, development, and operation of political systems. Research a wide range of subjects, such as relations between the United States and foreign countries, the beliefs and institutions of foreign nations, or the politics of small towns or a major metropolis. May study topics such as public opinion, political decision making, and ideology. May analyze the structure and operation of governments, as well as various political entities. May conduct public opinion surveys, analyze election results, or analyze public documents. Teach political science. Disseminate research results through academic publications, written reports, or public presentations. Identify issues for research and analysis. Develop and test theories, using information from interviews, newspapers, periodicals, case law, historical papers, polls, and/or statistical sources. Maintain current knowledge of government policy decisions. Collect, analyze, and interpret data such as election results and public opinion surveys; report on findings, recommendations, and conclusions. Interpret and analyze policies; public issues; legislation; and the operations of governments, businesses, and organizations. Evaluate programs and policies and make related recommendations to institutions and organizations. Write drafts of legislative proposals and prepare speeches, correspondence, and policy papers for governmental use. Forecast political, economic, and social trends. Consult with and advise government officials, civic bodies, research agencies, the media, political parties, and others concerned with political issues. Provide media commentary and/or criticism related to public policy and political issues and events.

GOE—Interest Area/Cluster: 15. Scientific Research, Engineering, and Mathematics. **Work Group:** 15.04. Social Sciences. **Other Jobs in This Work Group:** Anthropologists; Anthropologists and Archeologists; Archeologists; Economists; Historians; Industrial-Organizational Psychologists; School Psychologists; Sociologists.

Skills: Writing; Reading Comprehension; Critical Thinking; Speaking; Active Learning; Instructing; Complex Problem Solving; Persuasion.

Education and Training Programs: International/Global Studies; Political Science and Government, General; American Government and Politics (United States); Canadian Government and Politics; Political Science and Government, Other. **Related Knowledge/Courses:** History and Archeology; Law and Government; Philosophy and Theology; Sociology and Anthropology; Foreign Language; Geography.

Work Environment: Indoors; sitting.

Prosthodontists

- ❁ Personality Code: IR
- ❁ Education/Training Required: First professional degree
- ❁ Annual Earnings: More than $145,600
- ❁ Beginning Wage: $75,450
- ❁ Earnings Growth Potential: Cannot be calculated
- ❁ Growth: 10.7%
- ❁ Annual Job Openings: 54
- ❁ Self-Employed: 51.3%
- ❁ Part-Time: 25.9%

Construct oral prostheses to replace missing teeth and other oral structures to correct natural and acquired deformation of mouth and jaws; to restore and maintain oral function, such as chewing and speaking; and to improve appearance. Replace missing teeth and associated oral structures with permanent fixtures, such as crowns and bridges, or removable fixtures, such as dentures. Fit prostheses to patients, making any necessary adjustments and modifications. Design and fabricate dental prostheses or supervise dental technicians and laboratory bench workers who construct the devices. Measure and take impressions of patients' jaws and teeth to determine the shape and size of dental prostheses, using face bows, dental articulators, recording devices, and other materials. Collaborate with general dentists, specialists, and other health professionals to develop solutions to dental and oral health concerns. Repair, reline, and/or rebase dentures. Restore function and aesthetics to traumatic injury victims or to individuals with diseases or birth defects. Use bonding technology on the surface of the teeth to change tooth shape or to close gaps. Treat facial pain and jaw joint problems. Place veneers onto teeth to conceal defects. Bleach discolored teeth to brighten and whiten them.

GOE—Interest Area/Cluster: 08. Health Science. **Work Group:** 08.03. Dentistry. **Other Jobs in This Work Group:** Dental Assistants; Dental Hygienists;

Dentists, General; Oral and Maxillofacial Surgeons; Orthodontists.

Skills: Science; Management of Financial Resources; Social Perceptiveness; Equipment Selection; Reading Comprehension; Active Learning; Complex Problem Solving; Technology Design.

Education and Training Programs: Prosthodontics/Prosthodontology (Cert, MS, PhD); Prosthodontics Specialty. **Related Knowledge/Courses:** Medicine and Dentistry; Biology; Chemistry; Psychology; Engineering and Technology; Sales and Marketing.

Work Environment: Indoors; noisy; contaminants; disease or infections; hazardous equipment; using hands on objects, tools, or controls.

Psychiatrists

- ❋ Personality Code: ISA
- ❋ Education/Training Required: First professional degree
- ❋ Annual Earnings: More than $145,600
- ❋ Beginning Wage: $59,090
- ❋ Earnings Growth Potential: Cannot be calculated
- ❋ Growth: 14.2%
- ❋ Annual Job Openings: 38,027
- ❋ Self-Employed: 14.7%
- ❋ Part-Time: 8.1%

The job openings listed here are shared with Anesthesiologists; Family and General Practitioners; Internists, General; Obstetricians and Gynecologists; Pediatricians, General; and Surgeons.

Diagnose, treat, and help prevent disorders of the mind. Prescribe, direct, and administer psychotherapeutic treatments or medications to treat mental, emotional, or behavioral disorders. Analyze and evaluate patient data and test findings to diagnose nature and extent of mental disorders. Collaborate with physicians, psychologists, social workers, psychiatric nurses, or other professionals to discuss treatment plans and progress. Gather and maintain patient information and records, including social and medical histories obtained from patients, relatives, and other professionals. Design individualized care plans, using a variety of treatments. Counsel outpatients and other patients during office visits. Examine or conduct laboratory or diagnostic tests on patients to provide information on general physical conditions and mental disorders. Advise and inform guardians, relatives, and significant others of patients' conditions and treatments. Teach, take continuing education classes, attend conferences and seminars, and conduct research and publish findings to increase understanding of mental, emotional, and behavioral states and disorders. Review and evaluate treatment procedures and outcomes of other psychiatrists and medical professionals. Prepare and submit case reports and summaries to government and mental health agencies. Serve on committees to promote and maintain community mental health services and delivery systems.

GOE—Interest Area/Cluster: 08. Health Science. **Work Group:** 08.02. Medicine and Surgery. **Other Jobs in This Work Group:** Anesthesiologists; Family and General Practitioners; Internists, General; Medical Assistants; Medical Transcriptionists; Obstetricians and Gynecologists; Pediatricians, General; Pharmacists; Pharmacy Aides; Pharmacy Technicians; Physician Assistants; Registered Nurses; Surgeons; Surgical Technologists.

Skills: Social Perceptiveness; Systems Evaluation; Systems Analysis; Active Listening; Writing; Speaking; Reading Comprehension; Judgment and Decision Making.

Education and Training Programs: Child Psychiatry; Psychiatry; Physical Medical and Rehabilitation/Psychiatry. **Related Knowledge/Courses:** Therapy and Counseling; Medicine and Dentistry; Psychology; Biology; Sociology and Anthropology; Philosophy and Theology.

Work Environment: Indoors; disease or infections; sitting.

School Psychologists

- ❀ Personality Code: IS
- ❀ Education/Training Required: Doctoral degree
- ❀ Annual Earnings: $62,210
- ❀ Beginning Wage: $37,300
- ❀ Earnings Growth Potential: High
- ❀ Growth: 15.8%
- ❀ Annual Job Openings: 8,309
- ❀ Self-Employed: 34.2%
- ❀ Part-Time: 24.0%

The job openings listed here are shared with Clinical Psychologists and with Counseling Psychologists.

Investigate processes of learning and teaching and develop psychological principles and techniques applicable to educational problems. Compile and interpret students' test results, along with information from teachers and parents, to diagnose conditions and to help assess eligibility for special services. Report any pertinent information to the proper authorities in cases of child endangerment, neglect, or abuse. Assess an individual child's needs, limitations, and potential, using observation, review of school records, and consultation with parents and school personnel. Select, administer, and score psychological tests. Provide consultation to parents, teachers, administrators, and others on topics such as learning styles and behavior modification techniques. Promote an understanding of child development and its relationship to learning and behavior. Collaborate with other educational professionals to develop teaching strategies and school programs. Counsel children and families to help solve conflicts and problems in learning and adjustment. Develop individualized educational plans in collaboration with teachers and other staff members. Maintain student records, including special education reports, confidential records, records of services provided, and behavioral data. Serve as a resource to help families and schools deal with crises, such as separation and loss. Attend workshops, seminars, or professional meetings to remain informed of new developments in school psychology. Design classes and programs to meet the needs of special students. Refer students and their families to appropriate community agencies for medical, vocational, or social services. Initiate and direct efforts to foster tolerance, understanding, and appreciation of diversity in school communities. Collect and analyze data to evaluate the effectiveness of academic programs and other services, such as behavioral management systems. Provide educational programs on topics such as classroom management, teaching strategies, or parenting skills. Conduct research to generate new knowledge that can be used to address learning and behavior issues.

GOE—Interest Area/Cluster: 15. Scientific Research, Engineering, and Mathematics. **Work Group:** 15.04. Social Sciences. **Other Jobs in This Work Group:** Anthropologists; Anthropologists and Archeologists; Archeologists; Economists; Historians; Industrial-Organizational Psychologists; Political Scientists; Sociologists.

Skills: Social Perceptiveness; Negotiation; Learning Strategies; Persuasion; Writing; Active Listening; Service Orientation; Active Learning.

Education and Training Programs: Educational Assessment, Testing, and Measurement; Psychology, General; Clinical Psychology; Counseling Psychology; Developmental and Child Psychology; School Psychology; Psychoanalysis and Psychotherapy. **Related Knowledge/Courses:** Therapy and Counseling; Psychology; Sociology and Anthropology; Philosophy and Theology; Education and Training; Medicine and Dentistry.

Work Environment: Indoors; sitting.

Investigative-S

Sociologists

- ❀ Personality Code: IAS
- ❀ Education/Training Required: Master's degree
- ❀ Annual Earnings: $61,140
- ❀ Beginning Wage: $36,740
- ❀ Earnings Growth Potential: Medium
- ❀ Growth: 10.0%
- ❀ Annual Job Openings: 403
- ❀ Self-Employed: 0.0%
- ❀ Part-Time: 24.0%

Study human society and social behavior by examining the groups and social institutions that people form, as well as various social, religious, political, and business organizations. May study the behavior and interaction of groups, trace their origin and growth, and analyze the influence of group activities on individual members. Analyze and interpret data in order to increase the understanding of human social behavior. Prepare publications and reports containing research findings. Plan and conduct research to develop and test theories about societal issues such as crime, group relations, poverty, and aging. Collect data about the attitudes, values, and behaviors of people in groups, using observation, interviews, and review of documents. Develop, implement, and evaluate methods of data collection, such as questionnaires or interviews. Teach sociology. Direct work of statistical clerks, statisticians, and others who compile and evaluate research data. Consult with and advise individuals such as administrators, social workers, and legislators regarding social issues and policies, as well as the implications of research findings. Collaborate with research workers in other disciplines. Develop approaches to the solution of groups' problems based on research findings in sociology and related disciplines. Observe group interactions and role affiliations to collect data, identify problems, evaluate progress, and determine the need for additional change. Develop problem intervention procedures, utilizing techniques such as interviews, consultations, role-playing, and participant observation of group interactions.

GOE—Interest Area/Cluster: 15. Scientific Research, Engineering, and Mathematics. **Work Group:** 15.04. Social Sciences. **Other Jobs in This Work Group:** Anthropologists; Anthropologists and Archeologists; Archeologists; Economists; Historians; Industrial-Organizational Psychologists; Political Scientists; School Psychologists.

Skills: Science; Writing; Management of Financial Resources; Reading Comprehension; Critical Thinking; Complex Problem Solving; Mathematics; Active Learning.

Education and Training Programs: Criminology; Demography and Population Studies; Sociology; Urban Studies/Affairs. **Related Knowledge/Courses:** Sociology and Anthropology; Philosophy and Theology; History and Archeology; Psychology; English Language; Mathematics.

Work Environment: Indoors; sitting.

Software Quality Assurance Engineers and Testers

- ❀ Personality Code: ICR
- ❀ Education/Training Required: Associate degree
- ❀ Annual Earnings: $71,510
- ❀ Beginning Wage: $37,600
- ❀ Earnings Growth Potential: High
- ❀ Growth: 15.1%
- ❀ Annual Job Openings: 14,374
- ❀ Self-Employed: 6.6%
- ❀ Part-Time: 5.6%

The job openings listed here are shared with Computer Systems Engineers/Architects, with Network Designers, with Web Administrators, and with Web Developers.

Develop and execute software test plans in order to identify software problems and their causes. Design test plans, scenarios, scripts, or procedures.

Test system modifications to prepare for implementation. Document software defects, using a bug tracking system, and report defects to software developers. Develop testing programs that address areas such as database impacts, software scenarios, regression testing, negative testing, error or bug retests, or usability. Identify, analyze, and document problems with program function, output, online screens, or content. Monitor bug resolution efforts and track successes. Create or maintain databases of known test defects. Plan test schedules or strategies in accordance with project scope or delivery dates. Participate in product design reviews to provide input on functional requirements, product designs, schedules, or potential problems. Review software documentation to ensure technical accuracy, compliance, or completeness, or to mitigate risks. Document test procedures to ensure replicability and compliance with standards. Develop or specify standards, methods, or procedures to determine product quality or release readiness. Update automated test scripts to ensure currency. Investigate customer problems referred by technical support. Install, maintain, or use software testing programs. Provide feedback and recommendations to developers on software usability and functionality. Monitor program performance to ensure efficient and problem-free operations. Install and configure recreations of software production environments to allow testing of software performance. Collaborate with field staff or customers to evaluate or diagnose problems and recommend possible solutions. Conduct software compatibility tests with programs, hardware, operating systems, or network environments. Identify program deviance from standards, and suggest modifications to ensure compliance. Design or develop automated testing tools. Coordinate user or third party testing. Perform initial debugging procedures by reviewing configuration files, logs, or code pieces to determine breakdown sources. Visit beta testing sites to evaluate software performance. Evaluate or recommend software for testing or bug tracking.

GOE—Interest Area/Cluster: 11. Information Technology. **Work Group:** 11.02. Information Technology Specialties. **Other Jobs in This Work Group:** Computer and Information Scientists, Research; Computer Operators; Computer Programmers; Computer Security Specialists; Computer Software Engineers, Applications; Computer Software Engineers, Systems Software; Computer Support Specialists; Computer Systems Analysts; Computer Systems Engineers/Architects; Database Administrators; Network Designers; Network Systems and Data Communications Analysts; Web Administrators; Web Developers.

Skills: Quality Control Analysis; Programming; Systems Analysis; Systems Evaluation; Troubleshooting; Technology Design; Operations Analysis; Writing.

Education and Training Programs: Computer and Information Sciences, General; Information Technology; Information Science/Studies; Computer Science; Computer and Information Sciences and Support Services, Other; Computer Engineering, General; Computer Software Engineering; Computer Engineering Technologies/Technicians, Other. **Related Knowledge/Courses:** Computers and Electronics; Engineering and Technology; Design; English Language; Mathematics; Clerical Practices.

Work Environment: No data available.

Surgeons

- ❋ Personality Code: IRS
- ❋ Education/Training Required: First professional degree
- ❋ Annual Earnings: More than $145,600
- ❋ Beginning Wage: $104,410
- ❋ Earnings Growth Potential: Cannot be calculated
- ❋ Growth: 14.2%
- ❋ Annual Job Openings: 38,027
- ❋ Self-Employed: 14.7%
- ❋ Part-Time: 8.1%

The job openings listed here are shared with Anesthesiologists; Family and General Practitioners; Internists, General; Obstetricians and Gynecologists; Pediatricians, General; and Psychiatrists.

Investigative-S

Treat diseases, injuries, and deformities by invasive methods, such as manual manipulation, or by using instruments and appliances. Analyze patient's medical history, medication allergies, physical condition, and examination results to verify operation's necessity and to determine best procedure. Operate on patients to correct deformities, repair injuries, prevent and treat diseases, or improve or restore patients' functions. Follow established surgical techniques during the operation. Prescribe preoperative and postoperative treatments and procedures, such as sedatives, diets, antibiotics, and preparation and treatment of the patient's operative area. Examine patient to provide information on medical condition and surgical risk. Diagnose bodily disorders and orthopedic conditions and provide treatments, such as medicines and surgeries, in clinics, hospital wards, and operating rooms. Direct and coordinate activities of nurses, assistants, specialists, residents, and other medical staff. Provide consultation and surgical assistance to other physicians and surgeons. Refer patient to medical specialist or other practitioners when necessary. Examine instruments, equipment, and operating room to ensure sterility. Prepare case histories. Manage surgery services, including planning, scheduling and coordination, determination of procedures, and procurement of supplies and equipment. Conduct research to develop and test surgical techniques that can improve operating procedures and outcomes.

GOE—Interest Area/Cluster: 08. Health Science. Work Group: 08.02. Medicine and Surgery. Other Jobs in This Work Group: Anesthesiologists; Family and General Practitioners; Internists, General; Medical Assistants; Medical Transcriptionists; Obstetricians and Gynecologists; Pediatricians, General; Pharmacists; Pharmacy Aides; Pharmacy Technicians; Physician Assistants; Psychiatrists; Registered Nurses; Surgical Technologists.

Skills: Science; Reading Comprehension; Judgment and Decision Making; Complex Problem Solving; Management of Financial Resources; Critical Thinking; Equipment Selection; Technology Design.

Education and Training Programs: Colon and Rectal Surgery; Critical Care Surgery; General Surgery; Hand Surgery; Neurological Surgery/Neurosurgery; Orthopedics/Orthopedic Surgery; Otolaryngology; Pediatric Orthopedics; Pediatric Surgery; Plastic Surgery; Sports Medicine; Thoracic Surgery; Urology; Vascular Surgery; Adult Reconstructive Orthopedics (Orthopedic Surgery); Orthopedic Surgery of the Spine. Related Knowledge/Courses: Medicine and Dentistry; Biology; Therapy and Counseling; Psychology; Chemistry; Customer and Personal Service.

Work Environment: Indoors; contaminants; radiation; disease or infections; standing; using hands on objects, tools, or controls.

Survey Researchers

- Personality Code: ICE
- Education/Training Required: Bachelor's degree
- Annual Earnings: $36,820
- Beginning Wage: $17,240
- Earnings Growth Potential: Very high
- Growth: 15.9%
- Annual Job Openings: 4,959
- Self-Employed: 6.8%
- Part-Time: 12.5%

Design or conduct surveys. May supervise interviewers who conduct the survey in person or over the telephone. May present survey results to client. Prepare and present summaries and analyses of survey data, including tables, graphs, and fact sheets that describe survey techniques and results. Consult with clients in order to identify survey needs and any specific requirements, such as special samples. Analyze data from surveys, old records, and/or case studies, using statistical software programs. Review, classify, and record survey data in preparation for computer analysis. Conduct research in order to gather information about survey topics. Conduct surveys and collect data, using methods such as interviews, questionnaires, focus groups, market analysis surveys, public opinion polls, literature reviews, and file reviews. Collaborate with other researchers in the planning, implementation, and evaluation of surveys. Direct and review the work of staff members, including survey support staff and interviewers who gather survey data. Monitor and evaluate survey progress and performance, using sample disposition reports and response rate calculations. Produce documentation of the questionnaire development process, data collection methods, sampling designs, and decisions related to sample statistical weighting. Determine and specify details of survey projects, including sources of information, procedures to be used, and the design of survey instruments and materials. Support, plan, and coordinate operations for single or multiple surveys. Direct updates and changes in survey implementation and methods. Hire and train recruiters and data collectors. Write training manuals to be used by survey interviewers.

GOE—Interest Area/Cluster: 06. Finance and Insurance. **Work Group:** 06.02. Finance/Insurance Investigation and Analysis. **Other Jobs in This Work Group:** Appraisers and Assessors of Real Estate; Appraisers, Real Estate; Assessors; Claims Adjusters, Examiners, and Investigators; Claims Examiners, Property and Casualty Insurance; Cost Estimators; Credit Analysts; Financial Analysts; Insurance Adjusters, Examiners, and Investigators; Insurance Appraisers, Auto Damage; Insurance Underwriters; Loan Counselors; Loan Officers; Market Research Analysts.

Skills: Management of Financial Resources; Management of Personnel Resources; Time Management; Writing; Persuasion; Mathematics; Complex Problem Solving; Active Learning.

Education and Training Programs: Economics, General; Applied Economics; Business/Managerial Economics; Marketing Research. **Related Knowledge/Courses:** Administration and Management; Sociology and Anthropology; Mathematics;

Economics and Accounting; Personnel and Human Resources; Clerical Practices.

Work Environment: Indoors; noisy; sitting.

Veterinarians

* Personality Code: IR
* Education/Training Required: First professional degree
* Annual Earnings: $75,230
* Beginning Wage: $44,150
* Earnings Growth Potential: High
* Growth: 35.0%
* Annual Job Openings: 5,301
* Self-Employed: 17.1%
* Part-Time: 13.4%

Diagnose and treat diseases and dysfunctions of animals. May engage in a particular function, such as research and development, consultation, administration, technical writing, sale or production of commercial products, or rendering of technical services to commercial firms or other organizations. Includes veterinarians who inspect livestock. Examine animals to detect and determine the nature of diseases or injuries. Treat sick or injured animals by prescribing medication, setting bones, dressing wounds, or performing surgery. Inoculate animals against various diseases such as rabies and distemper. Collect body tissue, feces, blood, urine, or other body fluids for examination and analysis. Operate diagnostic equipment such as radiographic and ultrasound equipment and interpret the resulting images. Advise animal owners regarding sanitary measures, feeding, and general care necessary to promote health of animals. Educate the public about diseases that can be spread from animals to humans. Train and supervise workers who handle and care for animals. Provide care to a wide range of animals or specialize in a particular species, such as horses or exotic birds. Euthanize animals. Establish and conduct quarantine and testing procedures that prevent the spread of diseases to other animals or to humans

Investigative-V

and that comply with applicable government regulations. Conduct postmortem studies and analyses to determine the causes of animals' deaths. Perform administrative duties such as scheduling appointments, accepting payments from clients, and maintaining business records. Drive mobile clinic vans to farms so that health problems can be treated or prevented. Direct the overall operations of animal hospitals, clinics, or mobile services to farms. Specialize in a particular type of treatment such as dentistry, pathology, nutrition, surgery, microbiology, or internal medicine. Inspect and test horses, sheep, poultry, and other animals to detect the presence of communicable diseases. Research diseases to which animals could be susceptible. Plan and execute animal nutrition and reproduction programs. Inspect animal housing facilities to determine their cleanliness and adequacy. Determine the effects of drug therapies, antibiotics, or new surgical techniques by testing them on animals.

GOE—Interest Area/Cluster: 08. Health Science. **Work Group:** 08.05. Animal Care. **Other Jobs in This Work Group:** Animal Breeders; Animal Trainers; Nonfarm Animal Caretakers; Veterinary Assistants and Laboratory Animal Caretakers; Veterinary Technologists and Technicians.

Skills: Science; Management of Financial Resources; Reading Comprehension; Judgment and Decision Making; Complex Problem Solving; Management of Personnel Resources; Equipment Selection; Management of Material Resources.

Education and Training Programs: Veterinary Medicine (DVM); Veterinary Sciences/Veterinary Clinical Sciences, General (Cert, MS, PhD); Veterinary Anatomy (Cert, MS, PhD); Veterinary Physiology (Cert, MS, PhD); Veterinary Microbiology and Immunobiology (Cert, MS, PhD); Veterinary Pathology and Pathobiology (Cert, MS, PhD); Veterinary Toxicology and Pharmacology (Cert, MS, PhD); Large Animal/Food Animal and Equine Surgery and Medicine (Cert, MS, PhD); others. **Related Knowledge/Courses:** Biology; Medicine and Dentistry; Chemistry; Therapy and Counseling; Sales and Marketing; Customer and Personal Service.

Work Environment: Indoors; noisy; contaminants; disease or infections; standing; using hands on objects, tools, or controls.

Artistic Occupations

Adult Literacy, Remedial Education, and GED Teachers and Instructors

The primary personality type for this occupation is Social. Look for the description among the Social jobs.

Advertising and Promotions Managers

The primary personality type for this occupation is Enterprising. Look for the description among the Enterprising jobs.

Anthropologists and Archeologists

The primary personality type for this occupation is Investigative. **See** *Anthropologists (an Investigative job) and Archeologists (an Investigative job), described separately.*

Architects, Except Landscape and Naval

- ❋ Personality Code: AI
- ❋ Education/Training Required: Bachelor's degree
- ❋ Annual Earnings: $67,620
- ❋ Beginning Wage: $40,250
- ❋ Earnings Growth Potential: High
- ❋ Growth: 17.7%
- ❋ Annual Job Openings: 11,324
- ❋ Self-Employed: 20.3%
- ❋ Part-Time: 6.1%

Plan and design structures, such as private residences, office buildings, theaters, factories, and other structural property. Prepare information regarding design, structure specifications, materials, color, equipment, estimated costs, or construction time. Consult with client to determine functional and spatial requirements of structure. Direct activities of workers engaged in preparing drawings and specification documents. Plan layout of project. Prepare contract documents for building contractors. Prepare scale drawings. Integrate engineering element into unified design. Conduct periodic on-site observation of work during construction to monitor compliance with plans. Administer construction contracts. Represent client in obtaining bids and awarding construction contracts. Prepare operating and maintenance manuals, studies, and reports.

GOE—Interest Area/Cluster: 02. Architecture and Construction. **Work Group:** 02.02. Architectural Design. **Other Jobs in This Work Group:** Landscape Architects.

Skills: Operations Analysis; Management of Financial Resources; Complex Problem Solving; Management of Personnel Resources; Coordination; Negotiation; Persuasion; Science.

Education and Training Programs: Architecture (BArch, BA/BS, MArch, MA/MS, PhD); Environmental Design/Architecture; Architectural History and Criticism, General; Architecture and Related Services, Other. **Related Knowledge/Courses:** Building and Construction; Design; Engineering and Technology; Fine Arts; Law and Government; Physics.

Work Environment: Indoors; sitting.

Architectural Drafters

- ❋ Personality Code: ARI
- ❋ Education/Training Required: Postsecondary vocational training
- ❋ Annual Earnings: $43,310
- ❋ Beginning Wage: $27,680
- ❋ Earnings Growth Potential: Medium
- ❋ Growth: 6.1%
- ❋ Annual Job Openings: 16,238
- ❋ Self-Employed: 5.0%
- ❋ Part-Time: 5.9%

The job openings listed here are shared with Civil Drafters.

Prepare detailed drawings of architectural designs and plans for buildings and structures according to specifications provided by architect. Analyze building codes, by-laws, space and site requirements, and other technical documents and reports to determine their effect on architectural designs. Operate computer-aided drafting (CAD) equipment or conventional drafting station to produce designs, working drawings, charts, forms, and records. Coordinate structural, electrical, and mechanical designs and determine a method of presentation to graphically represent building plans. Obtain and assemble data to complete architectural designs, visiting job sites to compile measurements as necessary. Lay out and plan interior room arrangements for commercial buildings, using computer-assisted drafting (CAD) equipment and software. Draw rough and detailed scale plans for foundations, buildings, and structures based on preliminary concepts, sketches, engineering calculations, specification sheets, and other data. Supervise, coordinate, and inspect the work of draftspersons, technicians, and technologists on construction projects. Represent architect on construction site, ensuring builder compliance with design specifications and advising on design corrections under architect's supervision. Check dimensions of materials to be used and assign numbers to lists of materials. Determine procedures and instructions to be followed according to design specifications and quantity of required materials. Analyze technical implications of architect's design concept, calculating weights, volumes, and stress factors. Create freehand drawings and lettering to accompany drawings. Prepare colored drawings of landscape and interior designs for presentation to client. Reproduce drawings on copy machines or trace copies of plans and drawings, using transparent paper or cloth, ink, pencil, and standard drafting instruments. Prepare cost estimates, contracts, bidding documents, and technical reports for specific projects under an architect's supervision. Calculate heat loss and gain of buildings and structures to determine required equipment specifications, following standard procedures. Build landscape, architectural, and display models.

GOE—Interest Area/Cluster: 02. Architecture and Construction. **Work Group:** 02.03. Architecture/Construction Engineering Technologies. **Other Jobs in This Work Group:** Architectural and Civil Drafters; Civil Drafters; Surveyors.

Skills: Operations Analysis; Coordination; Active Learning; Technology Design; Mathematics; Complex Problem Solving; Science; Monitoring.

Education and Training Programs: Architectural Technology/Technician; Drafting and Design Technology/Technician, General; CAD/CADD Drafting and/or Design Technology/Technician; Architectural Drafting and Architectural CAD/CADD; Civil Drafting and Civil Engineering CAD/CADD. **Related Knowledge/Courses:** Design; Building and Construction; Engineering and Technology; Computers and Electronics; Mathematics; Physics.

Work Environment: Indoors; noisy; sitting; using hands on objects, tools, or controls; repetitive motions.

Architecture Teachers, Postsecondary

The primary personality type for this occupation is Social. Look for the description among the Social jobs.

Art Directors

- ❀ Personality Code: AE
- ❀ Education/Training Required: Work experience plus degree
- ❀ Annual Earnings: $72,320
- ❀ Beginning Wage: $39,600
- ❀ Earnings Growth Potential: High
- ❀ Growth: 9.0%
- ❀ Annual Job Openings: 9,719
- ❀ Self-Employed: 59.0%
- ❀ Part-Time: 22.5%

Formulate design concepts and presentation approaches and direct workers engaged in art work, layout design, and copy writing for visual communications media, such as magazines, books, newspapers, and packaging. Formulate basic layout design or presentation approach and specify material details, such as style and size of type, photographs, graphics, animation, video, and sound. Review and approve proofs of printed copy and art and copy materials developed by staff members. Manage own accounts and projects, working within budget and scheduling requirements. Confer with creative, art, copy-writing, or production department heads to discuss client requirements and presentation concepts and to coordinate creative activities. Present final layouts to clients for approval. Confer with clients to determine objectives; budget; background information; and presentation approaches, styles, and techniques. Hire, train, and direct staff members who develop design concepts into art layouts or who prepare layouts for printing. Work with creative directors to develop design solutions. Review illustrative material to determine if it conforms to standards and specifications. Attend photo shoots and printing sessions to ensure that the products needed are obtained. Create custom illustrations or other graphic elements. Mark up, paste, and complete layouts and write typography instructions to prepare materials for typesetting or printing. Negotiate with printers and estimators to determine what services will be performed. Conceptualize and help design interfaces for multimedia games, products, and devices. Prepare detailed storyboards showing sequence and timing of story development for television production.

GOE—Interest Area/Cluster: 03. Arts and Communication. **Work Group:** 03.01. Managerial Work in Arts and Communication. **Other Jobs in This Work Group:** Agents and Business Managers of Artists, Performers, and Athletes; Producers; Producers and Directors; Program Directors; Public Relations Managers; Technical Directors/Managers.

Skills: Operations Analysis; Management of Financial Resources; Coordination; Negotiation; Persuasion; Service Orientation; Systems Evaluation; Management of Personnel Resources.

Education and Training Programs: Graphic Design; Intermedia/Multimedia. **Related Knowledge/Courses:** Fine Arts; Design; Communications and Media; Production and Processing; Computers and Electronics; Administration and Management.

Work Environment: Indoors; sitting; using hands on objects, tools, or controls; repetitive motions.

Art, Drama, and Music Teachers, Postsecondary

The primary personality type for this occupation is Social. Look for the description among the Social jobs.

Astronomers

The primary personality type for this occupation is Investigative. Look for the description among the Investigative jobs.

Biochemists and Biophysicists

The primary personality type for this occupation is Investigative. Look for the description among the Investigative jobs.

Broadcast News Analysts

- ❋ Personality Code: ASE
- ❋ Education/Training Required: Work experience plus degree
- ❋ Annual Earnings: $49,060
- ❋ Beginning Wage: $22,480
- ❋ Earnings Growth Potential: Very high
- ❋ Growth: 6.0%
- ❋ Annual Job Openings: 1,444
- ❋ Self-Employed: 11.1%
- ❋ Part-Time: 17.3%

Analyze, interpret, and broadcast news received from various sources. Analyze and interpret news and information received from various sources in order to be able to broadcast the information. Write commentaries, columns, or scripts, using computers. Examine news items of local, national, and international significance to determine topics to address or obtain assignments from editorial staff members. Coordinate and serve as an anchor on news broadcast programs. Edit news material to ensure that it fits within available time or space. Select material most pertinent to presentation and organize this material into appropriate formats. Gather information and develop perspectives about news subjects through research, interviews, observation, and experience. Present news stories and introduce in-depth videotaped segments or live transmissions from on-the-scene reporters.

GOE—Interest Area/Cluster: 03. Arts and Communication. **Work Group:** 03.03. News, Broadcasting, and Public Relations. **Other Jobs in This Work Group:** Interpreters and Translators; Public Relations Specialists; Reporters and Correspondents.

Skills: Writing; Time Management; Management of Personnel Resources; Speaking; Social Perceptiveness; Reading Comprehension; Operation and Control; Monitoring.

Education and Training Programs: Journalism; Broadcast Journalism; Radio and Television;

Political Communication. **Related Knowledge/Courses:** Communications and Media; Telecommunications; English Language; Geography; Sociology and Anthropology; History and Archeology.

Work Environment: Indoors; noisy; sitting; repetitive motions.

Camera Operators, Television, Video, and Motion Picture

The primary personality type for this occupation is Realistic. Look for the description among the Realistic jobs.

Commercial and Industrial Designers

- ❋ Personality Code: AER
- ❋ Education/Training Required: Bachelor's degree
- ❋ Annual Earnings: $56,550
- ❋ Beginning Wage: $31,400
- ❋ Earnings Growth Potential: High
- ❋ Growth: 7.2%
- ❋ Annual Job Openings: 4,777
- ❋ Self-Employed: 29.8%
- ❋ Part-Time: 16.7%

Develop and design manufactured products, such as cars, home appliances, and children's toys. Combine artistic talent with research on product use, marketing, and materials to create the most functional and appealing product design. Prepare sketches of ideas, detailed drawings, illustrations, artwork, or blueprints, using drafting instruments, paints and brushes, or computer-aided design equipment. Direct and coordinate the fabrication of models or samples and the drafting of working drawings and specification sheets from sketches. Modify and refine designs, using working models, to conform with customer specifications, production limitations, or changes in design trends. Coordinate the look and function of product lines. Confer with engineering, marketing, production, or sales departments, or with customers, to establish and evaluate design concepts for manufactured products. Present designs and reports to customers or design committees for approval and discuss need for modification. Evaluate feasibility of design ideas based on factors such as appearance, safety, function, serviceability, budget, production costs/methods, and market characteristics. Read publications, attend showings, and study competing products and design styles and motifs to obtain perspective and generate design concepts. Research production specifications, costs, production materials, and manufacturing methods and provide cost estimates and itemized production requirements. Design graphic material for use as ornamentation, illustration, or advertising on manufactured materials and packaging or containers. Develop manufacturing procedures and monitor the manufacture of their designs in a factory to improve operations and product quality. Supervise assistants' work throughout the design process. Fabricate models or samples in paper, wood, glass, fabric, plastic, metal, or other materials, using hand or power tools. Investigate product characteristics such as the product's safety and handling qualities; its market appeal; how efficiently it can be produced; and ways of distributing, using, and maintaining it. Develop industrial standards and regulatory guidelines. Participate in new product planning or market research, including studying the potential need for new products. Advise corporations on issues involving corporate image projects or problems.

GOE—Interest Area/Cluster: 03. Arts and Communication. **Work Group:** 03.05. Design. **Other Jobs in This Work Group:** Fashion Designers; Floral Designers; Graphic Designers; Interior Designers; Merchandise Displayers and Window Trimmers; Set and Exhibit Designers.

Skills: Technology Design; Operations Analysis; Quality Control Analysis; Troubleshooting; Equipment Selection; Installation; Mathematics; Systems Evaluation.

Education and Training Programs: Design and Visual Communications, General; Commercial and Advertising Art; Industrial Design; Design and Applied Arts, Other. **Related Knowledge/Courses:** Design; Engineering and Technology; Mathematics; Physics; Mechanical Devices; Production and Processing.

Work Environment: Indoors; sitting; using hands on objects, tools, or controls; repetitive motions.

Communications Teachers, Postsecondary

The primary personality type for this occupation is Social. Look for the description among the Social jobs.

Editors

- ❋ Personality Code: AEC
- ❋ Education/Training Required: Bachelor's degree
- ❋ Annual Earnings: $48,320
- ❋ Beginning Wage: $27,360
- ❋ Earnings Growth Potential: High
- ❋ Growth: 2.3%
- ❋ Annual Job Openings: 20,193
- ❋ Self-Employed: 13.4%
- ❋ Part-Time: 14.6%

Perform variety of editorial duties, such as laying out, indexing, and revising content of written materials, in preparation for final publication. Prepare, rewrite, and edit copy to improve readability or supervise others who do this work. Read copy or proof to detect and correct errors in spelling, punctuation, and syntax. Allocate print space for story text, photos, and illustrations according to space parameters and copy significance, using knowledge of layout principles. Plan the contents of publications according to the publication's style, editorial policy, and publishing requirements. Verify facts, dates, and statistics, using standard reference sources. Review and

Artistic-E

approve proofs submitted by composing room prior to publication production. Develop story or content ideas, considering reader or audience appeal. Oversee publication production, including artwork, layout, computer typesetting, and printing, ensuring adherence to deadlines and budget requirements. Confer with management and editorial staff members regarding placement and emphasis of developing news stories. Assign topics, events, and stories to individual writers or reporters for coverage. Read, evaluate, and edit manuscripts or other materials submitted for publication and confer with authors regarding changes in content, style or organization, or publication. Monitor news-gathering operations to ensure utilization of all news sources, such as press releases, telephone contacts, radio, television, wire services, and other reporters. Meet frequently with artists, typesetters, layout personnel, marketing directors, and production managers to discuss projects and resolve problems. Supervise and coordinate work of reporters and other editors. Make manuscript acceptance or revision recommendations to the publisher. Select local, state, national, and international news items received from wire services based on assessment of items' significance and interest value. Interview and hire writers and reporters or negotiate contracts, royalties, and payments for authors or freelancers. Direct the policies and departments of newspapers, magazines, and other publishing establishments. Arrange for copyright permissions. Read material to determine index items and arrange them alphabetically or topically, indicating page or chapter location.

GOE—Interest Area/Cluster: 03. Arts and Communication. **Work Group:** 03.02. Writing and Editing. **Other Jobs in This Work Group:** Copy Writers; Poets, Lyricists, and Creative Writers; Technical Writers; Writers and Authors.

Skills: Writing; Reading Comprehension; Active Listening; Judgment and Decision Making; Time Management; Critical Thinking; Persuasion; Active Learning.

Education and Training Programs: Mass Communication/Media Studies; Journalism; Broadcast Journalism; Publishing; Communication, Journalism,

and Related Programs, Other; Family and Consumer Sciences/Human Sciences Communication; Creative Writing; Technical and Business Writing; Business/Corporate Communications. **Related Knowledge/Courses:** Communications and Media; History and Archeology; Geography; English Language; Sales and Marketing; Clerical Practices.

Work Environment: Indoors; sitting; using hands on objects, tools, or controls; repetitive motions.

Education Teachers, Postsecondary

The primary personality type for this occupation is Social. Look for the description among the Social jobs.

Elementary School Teachers, Except Special Education

The primary personality type for this occupation is Social. Look for the description among the Social jobs.

English Language and Literature Teachers, Postsecondary

The primary personality type for this occupation is Social. Look for the description among the Social jobs.

Fashion Designers

- ❈ Personality Code: AER
- ❈ Education/Training Required: Associate degree
- ❈ Annual Earnings: $62,810
- ❈ Beginning Wage: $31,340
- ❈ Earnings Growth Potential: Very high
- ❈ Growth: 5.0%
- ❈ Annual Job Openings: 1,968
- ❈ Self-Employed: 23.6%
- ❈ Part-Time: 16.7%

Design clothing and accessories. Create original garments or design garments that follow well-established fashion trends. May develop the line of color and kinds of materials. Examine sample garments on and off models, then modify designs to achieve desired effects. Determine prices for styles. Select materials and production techniques to be used for products. Draw patterns for articles designed, then cut patterns and cut material according to patterns, using measuring instruments and scissors. Design custom clothing and accessories for individuals, retailers, or theatrical, television, or film productions. Attend fashion shows and review garment magazines and manuals to gather information about fashion trends and consumer preferences. Develop a group of products and/or accessories and market them through venues such as boutiques or mail-order catalogs. Test fabrics or oversee testing so that garment-care labels can be created. Visit textile showrooms to keep up to date on the latest fabrics. Sew together sections of material to form mockups or samples of garments or articles, using sewing equipment. Research the styles and periods of clothing needed for film or theatrical productions. Direct and coordinate workers involved in drawing and cutting patterns and constructing samples or finished garments. Purchase new or used clothing and accessory items as needed to complete designs. Provide sample garments to agents and sales representatives and arrange for showings of sample garments at sales meetings or fashion shows. Identify target markets for designs, looking at factors such as age, gender, and socioeconomic status. Read scripts and consult directors and other production staff to develop design concepts and plan productions. Confer with sales and management executives or with clients to discuss design ideas. Collaborate with other designers to coordinate special products and designs. Sketch rough and detailed drawings of apparel or accessories and write specifications such as color schemes, construction, material types, and accessory requirements. Adapt other designers' ideas for the mass market.

GOE—Interest Area/Cluster: 03. Arts and Communication. **Work Group:** 03.05. Design. **Other Jobs in This Work Group:** Commercial and Industrial Designers; Floral Designers; Graphic Designers; Interior Designers; Merchandise Displayers and Window Trimmers; Set and Exhibit Designers.

Skills: Technology Design; Operations Analysis; Quality Control Analysis; Negotiation; Time Management; Systems Evaluation; Mathematics; Active Learning.

Education and Training Programs: Apparel and Textile Manufacture; Textile Science; Fashion and Fabric Consultant; Fashion/Apparel Design. **Related Knowledge/Courses:** Fine Arts; Design; Sales and Marketing; Production and Processing; Communications and Media; Administration and Management.

Work Environment: Indoors; sitting; using hands on objects, tools, or controls.

Film and Video Editors

- ❋ Personality Code: AEI
- ❋ Education/Training Required: Bachelor's degree
- ❋ Annual Earnings: $47,870
- ❋ Beginning Wage: $24,270
- ❋ Earnings Growth Potential: High
- ❋ Growth: 12.7%
- ❋ Annual Job Openings: 2,707
- ❋ Self-Employed: 15.9%
- ❋ Part-Time: 18.9%

Edit motion picture soundtracks, film, and video. Cut shot sequences to different angles at specific points in scenes, making each individual cut as fluid and seamless as possible. Study scripts to become familiar with production concepts and requirements. Edit films and videotapes to insert music, dialogue, and sound effects; to arrange films into sequences; and to correct errors, using editing equipment. Select and combine the most effective shots of each scene to form a logical and smoothly running story. Mark frames where a particular shot or piece of sound is to begin or end. Determine the specific audio and visual effects and music necessary to complete films.

Artistic–F

Verify key numbers and time codes on materials. Organize and string together raw footage into a continuous whole according to scripts or the instructions of directors and producers. Review assembled films or edited videotapes on screens or monitors to determine if corrections are necessary. Program computerized graphic effects. Review footage sequence by sequence to become familiar with it before assembling it into a final product. Set up and operate computer editing systems, electronic titling systems, video switching equipment, and digital video effects units to produce a final product. Record needed sounds or obtain them from sound effects libraries. Confer with producers and directors concerning layout or editing approaches needed to increase dramatic or entertainment value of productions. Manipulate plot, score, sound, and graphics to make the parts into a continuous whole, working closely with people in audio, visual, music, optical, or special effects departments. Supervise and coordinate activities of workers engaged in film editing, assembling, and recording activities. Trim film segments to specified lengths and reassemble segments in sequences that present stories with maximum effect. Develop postproduction models for films. Piece sounds together to develop film soundtracks. Conduct film screenings for directors and members of production staffs. Collaborate with music editors to select appropriate passages of music and develop production scores. Discuss the sound requirements of pictures with sound effects editors.

GOE—Interest Area/Cluster: 03. Arts and Communication. **Work Group:** 03.09. Media Technology. **Other Jobs in This Work Group:** Audio and Video Equipment Technicians; Broadcast Technicians; Camera Operators, Television, Video, and Motion Picture; Multi-Media Artists and Animators; Photographers; Radio Operators; Sound Engineering Technicians.

Skills: Equipment Selection; Operation and Control; Operations Analysis; Equipment Maintenance; Installation; Troubleshooting; Operation Monitoring; Active Learning.

Education and Training Programs: Photojournalism; Radio and Television; Communications Technology/Technician; Radio and Television Broadcasting Technology/Technician; Audiovisual Communications Technologies/Technicians, Other; Cinematography and Film/Video Production. **Related Knowledge/Courses:** Fine Arts; Communications and Media; Design; Computers and Electronics; Telecommunications; English Language.

Work Environment: Indoors; sitting; using hands on objects, tools, or controls; repetitive motions.

Fine Artists, Including Painters, Sculptors, and Illustrators

- ❋ Personality Code: AR
- ❋ Education/Training Required: Long-term on-the-job training
- ❋ Annual Earnings: $42,070
- ❋ Beginning Wage: $18,650
- ❋ Earnings Growth Potential: Very high
- ❋ Growth: 9.9%
- ❋ Annual Job Openings: 3,830
- ❋ Self-Employed: 62.6%
- ❋ Part-Time: 22.5%

Create original artwork, using any of a wide variety of mediums and techniques such as painting and sculpture. Use materials such as pens and ink, watercolors, charcoal, oil, or computer software to create artwork. Integrate and develop visual elements such as line, space, mass, color, and perspective to produce desired effects, such as the illustration of ideas, emotions, or moods. Confer with clients, editors, writers, art directors, and other interested parties regarding the nature and content of artwork to be produced. Submit preliminary or finished artwork or project plans to clients for approval, incorporating changes as necessary. Maintain portfolios of artistic work to demonstrate styles, interests, and abilities. Create finished artwork as decoration or to elucidate or substitute for spoken or written messages. Cut, bend, laminate, arrange, and fasten individual or mixed raw and manufactured materials and products to form works of art. Monitor events, trends, and other circumstances, research specific subject areas, attend art exhibitions, and read art publications to develop ideas and keep current on art-world activities. Study different techniques to learn how to apply them to artistic endeavors. Render drawings, illustrations, and sketches of buildings, manufactured products, or models, working from sketches, blueprints, memory, models, or reference materials. Create sculptures, statues, and other three-dimensional artwork, using abrasives and tools to shape, carve, and fabricate materials such as clay, stone, wood, or metal. Create sketches, profiles, or likenesses of posed subjects or photographs, using any combination of freehand drawing, mechanical assembly kits, and computer imaging. Develop project budgets for approval, estimating time lines and material costs. Study styles, techniques, colors, textures, and materials used in works undergoing restoration to ensure consistency during the restoration process. Shade and fill in sketch outlines and backgrounds, using a variety of media such as water colors, markers, and transparent washes, labeling designated colors when necessary. Collaborate with engineers, mechanics, and other technical experts as necessary to build and install creations.

GOE—Interest Area/Cluster: 03. Arts and Communication. **Work Group:** 03.04. Studio Art. **Other Jobs in This Work Group:** Craft Artists; Potters, Manufacturing.

Skills: Management of Financial Resources; Equipment Selection; Operations Analysis; Repairing; Equipment Maintenance; Installation; Complex Problem Solving; Mathematics.

Education and Training Programs: Visual and Performing Arts, General; Art/Art Studies, General; Fine/Studio Arts, General; Drawing; Painting; Fine Arts and Art Studies, Other. **Related Knowledge/Courses:** Fine Arts; Design; Sales and Marketing; Production and Processing; Economics and Accounting; Communications and Media.

Work Environment: Indoors; contaminants; standing; using hands on objects, tools, or controls; repetitive motions.

Foreign Language and Literature Teachers, Postsecondary

The primary personality type for this occupation is Social. Look for the description among the Social jobs.

Graphic Designers

- ❋ Personality Code: ARE
- ❋ Education/Training Required: Bachelor's degree
- ❋ Annual Earnings: $41,280
- ❋ Beginning Wage: $25,090
- ❋ Earnings Growth Potential: Medium
- ❋ Growth: 9.8%
- ❋ Annual Job Openings: 26,968
- ❋ Self-Employed: 25.3%
- ❋ Part-Time: 16.7%

Design or create graphics to meet specific commercial or promotional needs such as packaging, displays, or logos. May use a variety of media to achieve artistic or decorative effects. Create designs, concepts, and sample layouts based on knowledge of layout principles and esthetic design concepts. Determine size and arrangement of illustrative material and copy and select style and size of type. Confer with clients to discuss and determine layout designs. Develop graphics and layouts for product illustrations, company logos, and Internet Web sites. Review final layouts and suggest improvements as needed. Prepare illustrations or rough sketches of material, discussing them with clients or supervisors and making necessary changes. Use computer software to generate new images. Key information into computer equipment to create layouts for client or supervisor. Maintain archive of images, photos, or previous work products. Prepare notes and instructions for workers who

Artistic-G

assemble and prepare final layouts for printing. Draw and print charts, graphs, illustrations, and other artwork, using computer. Study illustrations and photographs to plan presentations of materials, products, or services. Research new software or design concepts. Mark up, paste, and assemble final layouts to prepare layouts for printer. Produce still and animated graphics for on-air and taped portions of television news broadcasts, using electronic video equipment. Photograph layouts, using cameras, to make layout prints for supervisors or clients. Develop negatives and prints to produce layout photographs, using negative and print developing equipment and tools.

GOE—Interest Area/Cluster: 03. Arts and Communication. **Work Group:** 03.05. Design. **Other Jobs in This Work Group:** Commercial and Industrial Designers; Fashion Designers; Floral Designers; Interior Designers; Merchandise Displayers and Window Trimmers; Set and Exhibit Designers.

Skills: Programming; Systems Analysis.

Education and Training Programs: Agricultural Communication/Journalism; Web Page, Digital/Multimedia and Information Resources Design; Computer Graphics; Design and Visual Communications, General; Commercial and Advertising Art; Industrial Design; Graphic Design. **Related Knowledge/Courses:** Fine Arts; Design; Communications and Media; Sales and Marketing; Sociology and Anthropology; Computers and Electronics.

Work Environment: Indoors; sitting; using hands on objects, tools, or controls; repetitive motions.

Hairdressers, Hairstylists, and Cosmetologists

- ❋ Personality Code: AES
- ❋ Education/Training Required: Postsecondary vocational training
- ❋ Annual Earnings: $22,210
- ❋ Beginning Wage: $14,790
- ❋ Earnings Growth Potential: Low
- ❋ Growth: 12.4%
- ❋ Annual Job Openings: 73,030
- ❋ Self-Employed: 44.5%
- ❋ Part-Time: 31.1%

Provide beauty services, such as shampooing, cutting, coloring, and styling hair and massaging and treating scalp. May also apply makeup, dress wigs, perform hair removal, and provide nail and skin care services. Keep work stations clean and sanitize tools such as scissors and combs. Cut, trim, and shape hair or hairpieces based on customers' instructions, hair type, and facial features, using clippers, scissors, trimmers, and razors. Analyze patrons' hair and other physical features to determine and recommend beauty treatment or suggest hairstyles. Schedule client appointments. Bleach, dye, or tint hair, using applicator or brush. Update and maintain customer information records, such as beauty services provided. Shampoo, rinse, condition, and dry hair and scalp or hairpieces with water, liquid soap, or other solutions. Operate cash registers to receive payments from patrons. Demonstrate and sell hair care products and cosmetics. Apply water, setting, straightening, or waving solutions to hair and use curlers, rollers, hot combs, and curling irons to press and curl hair. Develop new styles and techniques. Comb, brush, and spray hair or wigs to set style. Shape eyebrows and remove facial hair, using depilatory cream, tweezers, electrolysis, or wax. Administer therapeutic medication and advise patron to seek medical treatment for chronic or contagious scalp conditions. Massage and treat scalp for hygienic and remedial purposes, using hands, fingers, or vibrating equipment. Shave, trim, and shape beards and moustaches. Train or supervise other hairstylists, hairdressers, and assistants. Recommend and explain the use of cosmetics, lotions, and creams to soften and lubricate skin and enhance and restore natural appearance. Give facials to patrons, using special compounds such as lotions and creams. Clean, shape, and polish fingernails and toenails, using files and nail polish. Apply artificial fingernails. Attach wigs or hairpieces to model heads and dress wigs and hairpieces according to instructions, samples, sketches, or photographs.

GOE—Interest Area/Cluster: 09. Hospitality, Tourism, and Recreation. **Work Group:** 09.07. Barber and Beauty Services. **Other Jobs in This Work Group:** Barbers; Manicurists and Pedicurists; Shampooers; Skin Care Specialists.

Skills: Science; Operations Analysis; Equipment Selection; Management of Financial Resources; Equipment Maintenance; Learning Strategies; Social Perceptiveness; Management of Material Resources.

Education and Training Programs: Cosmetology/Cosmetologist, General; Electrolysis/Electrology and Electrolysis Technician; Make-Up Artist/Specialist; Hair Styling/Stylist and Hair Design; Permanent Cosmetics/Makeup and Tattooing; Salon/Beauty Salon Management/Manager; Cosmetology, Barber/Styling, and Nail Instructor; Cosmetology and Related Personal Grooming Arts, Other. **Related Knowledge/Courses:** Chemistry; Sales and Marketing; Customer and Personal Service.

Work Environment: Indoors; contaminants; minor burns, cuts, bites, or stings; standing; using hands on objects, tools, or controls; repetitive motions.

Interior Designers

* Personality Code: AE
* Education/Training Required: Associate degree
* Annual Earnings: $43,970
* Beginning Wage: $25,920
* Earnings Growth Potential: High
* Growth: 19.5%
* Annual Job Openings: 8,434
* Self-Employed: 26.3%
* Part-Time: 16.7%

Plan, design, and furnish interiors of residential, commercial, or industrial buildings. Formulate design that is practical, aesthetic, and conducive to intended purposes, such as raising productivity, selling merchandise, or improving lifestyle. May specialize in a particular field, style, or phase of interior design. Estimate material requirements and costs and present design to client for approval. Confer with client to determine factors affecting planning interior environments, such as budget, architectural preferences, and purpose and function. Advise client on interior design factors such as space planning, layout, and utilization of furnishings or equipment and color coordination. Select or design and purchase furnishings, artwork, and accessories. Formulate environmental plan to be practical, esthetic, and conducive to intended purposes such as raising productivity or selling merchandise. Subcontract fabrication, installation, and arrangement of carpeting, fixtures, accessories, draperies, paint and wall coverings, artwork, furniture, and related items. Render design ideas in form of paste-ups or drawings. Plan and design interior environments for boats, planes, buses, trains, and other enclosed spaces.

GOE—Interest Area/Cluster: 03. Arts and Communication. **Work Group:** 03.05. Design. **Other Jobs in This Work Group:** Commercial and Industrial Designers; Fashion Designers; Floral Designers; Graphic Designers; Merchandise Displayers and Window Trimmers; Set and Exhibit Designers.

Skills: Installation; Management of Financial Resources; Persuasion; Operations Analysis; Negotiation; Active Learning; Mathematics; Speaking.

Education and Training Programs: Interior Architecture; Facilities Planning and Management; Textile Science; Interior Design. **Related Knowledge/ Courses:** Design; Sales and Marketing; Building and Construction; Clerical Practices; Fine Arts; Administration and Management.

Work Environment: Indoors; sitting.

Interpreters and Translators

- ❋ Personality Code: AS
- ❋ Education/Training Required: Long-term on-the-job training
- ❋ Annual Earnings: $37,490
- ❋ Beginning Wage: $21,500
- ❋ Earnings Growth Potential: High
- ❋ Growth: 23.6%
- ❋ Annual Job Openings: 6,630
- ❋ Self-Employed: 21.6%
- ❋ Part-Time: 28.5%

Translate or interpret written, oral, or sign language text into another language for others. Follow ethical codes that protect the confidentiality of information. Identify and resolve conflicts related to the meanings of words, concepts, practices, or behaviors. Proofread, edit, and revise translated materials. Translate messages simultaneously or consecutively into specified languages orally or by using hand signs, maintaining message content, context, and style as much as possible. Check translations of technical terms and terminology to ensure that they are accurate and remain consistent throughout translation revisions. Read written materials such as legal documents, scientific works, or news reports and rewrite material into specified languages. Refer to reference materials such as dictionaries, lexicons, encyclopedias, and computerized terminology banks as needed to ensure translation accuracy. Compile terminology and information to be used in translations, including technical terms such as those for legal or medical material. Adapt translations to students' cognitive and grade levels, collaborating with educational team members as necessary. Listen to speakers' statements to determine meanings and to prepare translations, using electronic listening systems as necessary. Check original texts or confer with authors to ensure that translations retain the content, meaning, and feeling of the original material. Compile information about the content and context of information to be translated, as well as details of the groups for whom translation or interpretation is being performed. Discuss translation requirements with clients and determine any fees to be charged for services provided. Adapt software and accompanying technical documents to another language and culture. Educate students, parents, staff, and teachers about the roles and functions of educational interpreters. Train and supervise other translators/interpreters. Travel with or guide tourists who speak another language.

GOE—Interest Area/Cluster: 03. Arts and Communication. **Work Group:** 03.03. News, Broadcasting, and Public Relations. **Other Jobs in This Work Group:** Broadcast News Analysts; Public Relations Specialists; Reporters and Correspondents.

Skills: Social Perceptiveness; Speaking; Active Listening; Writing; Reading Comprehension.

Education and Training Programs: Education/ Teaching of Individuals with Hearing Impairments, Including Deafness; Foreign Languages and Literatures, General; Linguistics; Language Interpretation and Translation; African Languages, Literatures, and Linguistics; East Asian Languages, Literatures, and Linguistics, General; Chinese Language and Literature; Japanese Language and Literature; Korean Language and Literature; Tibetan Language and Literature; others. **Related Knowledge/Courses:** Foreign Language; English Language; Geography; Sociology and Anthropology; Computers and Electronics; Communications and Media.

Work Environment: Indoors; sitting; repetitive motions.

Kindergarten Teachers, Except Special Education

The primary personality type for this occupation is Social. Look for the description among the Social jobs.

Landscape Architects

- ❋ Personality Code: AIR
- ❋ Education/Training Required: Bachelor's degree
- ❋ Annual Earnings: $57,580
- ❋ Beginning Wage: $36,250
- ❋ Earnings Growth Potential: Medium
- ❋ Growth: 16.4%
- ❋ Annual Job Openings: 2,342
- ❋ Self-Employed: 18.5%
- ❋ Part-Time: 6.1%

Plan and design land areas for such projects as parks and other recreational facilities; airports; highways; hospitals; schools; land subdivisions; and commercial, industrial, and residential sites. Prepare site plans, specifications, and cost estimates for land development, coordinating arrangement of existing and proposed land features and structures. Confer with clients, engineering personnel, and architects on overall program. Compile and analyze data on conditions such as location, drainage, and location of structures for environmental reports and landscaping plans. Inspect landscape work to ensure compliance with specifications, approve quality of materials and work, and advise client and construction personnel.

GOE—Interest Area/Cluster: 02. Architecture and Construction. **Work Group:** 02.02. Architectural Design. **Other Jobs in This Work Group:** Architects, Except Landscape and Naval.

Skills: Operations Analysis; Management of Financial Resources; Coordination; Mathematics; Complex Problem Solving; Social Perceptiveness; Persuasion; Writing.

Education and Training Programs: Environmental Design/Architecture; Landscape Architecture (BS, BSLA, BLA, MSLA, MLA, PhD). **Related Knowledge/Courses:** Design; Building and Construction; Geography; Biology; Engineering and Technology; Fine Arts.

Work Environment: More often indoors than outdoors; very hot or cold; hazardous equipment; minor burns, cuts, bites, or stings; sitting.

Makeup Artists, Theatrical and Performance

- ❋ Personality Code: AR
- ❋ Education/Training Required: Postsecondary vocational training
- ❋ Annual Earnings: $35,250
- ❋ Beginning Wage: $15,920
- ❋ Earnings Growth Potential: Very high
- ❋ Growth: 39.8%
- ❋ Annual Job Openings: 392
- ❋ Self-Employed: 39.7%
- ❋ Part-Time: 26.3%

Apply makeup to performers to reflect period, setting, and situation of their role. Confer with stage or motion picture officials and performers in order to determine desired effects. Duplicate work precisely in order to replicate characters' appearances on a daily basis. Establish budgets, and work within budgetary limits. Apply makeup to enhance and/or alter the appearance of people appearing in productions such as movies. Alter or maintain makeup during productions as necessary to compensate for lighting changes or to achieve continuity of effect. Select desired makeup shades from stock, or mix oil, grease, and coloring in order to achieve specific color effects. Cleanse and tone the skin in order to prepare it for makeup application. Assess performers' skin type in order to ensure that makeup will not cause breakouts or skin irritations. Analyze a script, noting events that affect each character's appearance, so that plans can be made for each scene. Requisition or acquire

Artistic-M

needed materials for special effects, including wigs, beards, and special cosmetics. Write makeup sheets and take photos in order to document specific looks and the products that were used to achieve the looks. Examine sketches, photographs, and plaster models in order to obtain desired character image depiction. Attach prostheses to performers and apply makeup in order to create special features or effects such as scars, aging, or illness. Evaluate environmental characteristics such as venue size and lighting plans in order to determine makeup requirements. Design rubber or plastic prostheses that can be used to change performers' appearances. Create character drawings or models, based upon independent research, in order to augment period production files. Advise hairdressers on the hairstyles required for character parts. Study production information such as character descriptions, period settings, and situations in order to determine makeup requirements. Provide performers with makeup removal assistance after performances have been completed. Wash and reset wigs. Demonstrate products to clients, and provide instruction in makeup application.

GOE—Interest Area/Cluster: 03. Arts and Communication. **Work Group:** 03.06. Drama. **Other Jobs in This Work Group:** Actors; Costume Attendants; Directors—Stage, Motion Pictures, Television, and Radio; Public Address System and Other Announcers; Radio and Television Announcers.

Skills: Management of Financial Resources; Equipment Selection; Time Management; Operations Analysis; Management of Material Resources; Management of Personnel Resources; Negotiation; Coordination.

Education and Training Programs: Cosmetology/Cosmetologist, General; Make-Up Artist/Specialist; Permanent Cosmetics/Makeup and Tattooing. **Related Knowledge/Courses:** Fine Arts; Chemistry; Design; Sales and Marketing; Personnel and Human Resources; Psychology.

Work Environment: Indoors; more often standing than sitting; using hands on objects, tools, or controls.

Marriage and Family Therapists

The primary personality type for this occupation is Social. Look for the description among the Social jobs.

Merchandise Displayers and Window Trimmers

- ❋ Personality Code: AER
- ❋ Education/Training Required: Moderate-term on-the-job training
- ❋ Annual Earnings: $24,830
- ❋ Beginning Wage: $16,300
- ❋ Earnings Growth Potential: Low
- ❋ Growth: 10.7%
- ❋ Annual Job Openings: 9,103
- ❋ Self-Employed: 28.6%
- ❋ Part-Time: 16.7%

Plan and erect commercial displays, such as those in windows and interiors of retail stores and at trade exhibitions. Take photographs of displays and signage. Plan and erect commercial displays to entice and appeal to customers. Place prices and descriptive signs on backdrops, fixtures, merchandise, or floor. Change or rotate window displays, interior display areas, and signage to reflect changes in inventory or promotion. Obtain plans from display designers or display managers and discuss their implementation with clients or supervisors. Develop ideas or plans for merchandise displays or window decorations. Consult with advertising and sales staff to determine type of merchandise to be featured and time and place for each display. Arrange properties, furniture, merchandise, backdrops, and other accessories as shown in prepared sketches. Construct or assemble displays and display components from fabric, glass, paper, and plastic according to specifications, using hand tools and woodworking power tools. Collaborate with others to obtain products and other display items. Use computers to produce signage. Dress mannequins for displays. Maintain props and mannequins, inspecting them for imperfections and applying preservative coatings as necessary. Select themes, lighting, colors, and props to be used. Attend training sessions and corporate planning meetings to obtain new ideas for product launches. Instruct sales staff in color-coordination of clothing racks and counter displays. Store, pack, and maintain records of props and display items. Prepare sketches, floor plans, or models of proposed displays. Cut out designs on cardboard, hardboard, and plywood according to motif of event. Install booths, exhibits, displays, carpets, and drapes as guided by floor plan of building and specifications. Install decorations such as flags, banners, festive lights, and bunting on or in building, street, exhibit hall, or booth. Create and enhance mannequin faces by mixing and applying paint and attaching measured eyelash strips, using artist's brush, airbrush, pins, ruler, and scissors.

GOE—Interest Area/Cluster: 03. Arts and Communication. **Work Group:** 03.05. Design. **Other Jobs in This Work Group:** Commercial and Industrial Designers; Fashion Designers; Floral Designers; Graphic Designers; Interior Designers; Set and Exhibit Designers.

Skills: Persuasion; Negotiation; Management of Personnel Resources.

Education and Training Program: Commercial and Advertising Art. **Related Knowledge/Courses:** Sales and Marketing; Design; Administration and Management; Computers and Electronics.

Work Environment: Indoors; contaminants; walking and running; using hands on objects, tools, or controls; bending or twisting the body; repetitive motions.

Middle School Teachers, Except Special and Vocational Education

The primary personality type for this occupation is Social. Look for the description among the Social jobs.

Multi-Media Artists and Animators

- ❋ Personality Code: AI
- ❋ Education/Training Required: Bachelor's degree
- ❋ Annual Earnings: $54,550
- ❋ Beginning Wage: $30,620
- ❋ Earnings Growth Potential: High
- ❋ Growth: 25.8%
- ❋ Annual Job Openings: 13,182
- ❋ Self-Employed: 69.7%
- ❋ Part-Time: 22.5%

Create special effects, animation, or other visual images, using film, video, computers, or other electronic tools and media, for use in products or creations such as computer games, movies, music videos, and commercials. Design complex graphics and animation, using independent judgment, creativity, and computer equipment. Create two-dimensional and three-dimensional images depicting objects in motion or illustrating a process, using computer animation or modeling programs. Make objects or characters appear lifelike by manipulating light, color, texture, shadow, and transparency or manipulating static images to give the illusion of motion. Apply story development, directing, cinematography, and editing to animation to create storyboards that show the flow of the animation and map out key scenes and characters. Assemble, typeset, scan, and produce digital camera-ready art or film negatives and printer's proofs. Script, plan, and create animated narrative sequences under tight deadlines, using computer software and hand-drawing techniques. Create basic designs, drawings, and illustrations for product labels, cartons, direct mail, or television. Create pen-and-paper images to be scanned, edited, colored, textured, or animated by computer. Develop briefings, brochures, multimedia presentations, Web pages, promotional products, technical illustrations, and computer artwork for use in products, technical manuals, literature, newsletters, and slide shows. Use models to simulate the behavior of animated objects in the finished sequence. Create

Artistic-M

and install special effects as required by the script, mixing chemicals and fabricating needed parts from wood, metal, plaster, and clay. Participate in design and production of multimedia campaigns, handling budgeting and scheduling and assisting with such responsibilities as production coordination, background design, and progress tracking. Convert real objects to animated objects through modeling, using techniques such as optical scanning. Implement and maintain configuration control systems.

GOE—Interest Area/Cluster: 03. Arts and Communication. **Work Group:** 03.09. Media Technology. **Other Jobs in This Work Group:** Audio and Video Equipment Technicians; Broadcast Technicians; Camera Operators, Television, Video, and Motion Picture; Film and Video Editors; Photographers; Radio Operators; Sound Engineering Technicians.

Skills: Operations Analysis; Technology Design; Time Management; Judgment and Decision Making; Science; Reading Comprehension; Active Listening; Programming.

Education and Training Programs: Animation, Interactive Technology, Video Graphics and Special Effects; Web Page, Digital/Multimedia and Information Resources Design; Graphic Design; Drawing; Intermedia/Multimedia; Painting; Printmaking. **Related Knowledge/Courses:** Fine Arts; Design; Computers and Electronics; Communications and Media; English Language.

Work Environment: Indoors; sitting; using hands on objects, tools, or controls; repetitive motions.

Music Composers and Arrangers

* Personality Code: AE
* Education/Training Required: Work experience plus degree
* Annual Earnings: $40,150
* Beginning Wage: $16,110
* Earnings Growth Potential: Very high
* Growth: 12.9%
* Annual Job Openings: 8,597
* Self-Employed: 44.7%
* Part-Time: 37.0%

The job openings listed here are shared with Music Directors.

Write and transcribe musical scores. Copy parts from scores for individual performers. Transpose music from one voice or instrument to another to accommodate particular musicians. Use computers and synthesizers to compose, orchestrate, and arrange music. Write changes directly into compositions, or use computer software to make changes. Confer with producers and directors to define the nature and placement of film or television music. Guide musicians during rehearsals, performances, or recording sessions. Study original pieces of music to become familiar with them prior to making any changes. Study films or scripts to determine how musical scores can be used to create desired effects or moods. Write music for commercial mediums, including advertising jingles or film soundtracks. Accept commissions to create music for special occasions. Arrange music composed by others, changing the music to achieve desired effects. Write musical scores for orchestras, bands, choral groups, or individual instrumentalists or vocalists, using knowledge of music theory and of instrumental and vocal capabilities. Score compositions so that they are consistent with instrumental and vocal capabilities such as ranges and keys, using knowledge of music theory. Apply elements of music theory to create musical and tonal structures, including harmonies and melodies. Collaborate with other colleagues such as copyists to complete final scores. Determine voices, instruments, harmonic structures, rhythms, tempos, and tone balances required to achieve the effects desired in musical compositions. Experiment with different sounds and types and pieces of music, using synthesizers and computers as necessary to test and evaluate ideas. Explore and develop musical ideas based on sources such as imagination or sounds in the environment. Rewrite original musical scores in different musical styles by changing rhythms, harmonies, or tempos. Transcribe ideas for musical compositions into musical notation, using instruments, pen and paper, or computers. Create original musical forms, or write within circumscribed musical forms such as sonatas, symphonies, or operas.

GOE—Interest Area/Cluster: 03. Arts and Communication. **Work Group:** 03.07. Music. **Other Jobs in This Work Group:** Music Directors; Music Directors and Composers; Musicians and Singers; Musicians, Instrumental; Singers; Talent Directors.

Skills: Management of Financial Resources; Installation; Equipment Maintenance; Operation and Control; Management of Material Resources; Writing; Technology Design; Operations Analysis.

Education and Training Programs: Religious/Sacred Music; Music Performance, General; Music Theory and Composition; Musicology and Ethnomusicology; Conducting; Voice and Opera; Music Management and Merchandising; Music, Other. **Related Knowledge/Courses:** Fine Arts; Communications and Media; Computers and Electronics; Sales and Marketing; Production and Processing; Design.

Work Environment: Indoors; sitting.

Music Directors

* ❋ Personality Code: AES
* ❋ Education/Training Required: Work experience plus degree
* ❋ Annual Earnings: $40,150
* ❋ Beginning Wage: $16,110
* ❋ Earnings Growth Potential: Very high
* ❋ Growth: 12.9%
* ❋ Annual Job Openings: 8,597
* ❋ Self-Employed: 44.7%
* ❋ Part-Time: 37.0%

The job openings listed here are shared with Music Composers and Arrangers.

Direct and conduct instrumental or vocal performances by musical groups such as orchestras or choirs. Study scores to learn the music in detail, and to develop interpretations. Consider such factors as ensemble size and abilities, availability of scores, and the need for musical variety in order to select music to be performed. Use gestures to shape the music being played, communicating desired tempo, phrasing, tone, color, pitch, volume, and other performance aspects. Engage services of composers to write scores. Plan and implement fund-raising and promotional activities. Coordinate and organize tours, or hire touring companies to arrange concert dates, venues, accommodations, and transportation for longer tours. Confer with clergy to select music for church services. Transcribe musical compositions and melodic lines to adapt them to a particular group, or to create a particular musical style. Audition and select performers for musical presentations. Meet with composers to discuss interpretations of their works. Conduct guest soloists in addition to ensemble members. Collaborate with music librarians to ensure availability of scores. Assign and review staff work in such areas as scoring, arranging, copying music, and vocal coaching. Position members within groups to obtain balance among instrumental or vocal sections. Plan and schedule rehearsals and performances, and arrange details such as locations,

Artistic–M

accompanists, and instrumentalists. Meet with soloists and concertmasters to discuss and prepare for performances. Direct groups at rehearsals and live or recorded performances in order to achieve desired effects such as tonal and harmonic balance, dynamics, rhythm, and tempo. Perform administrative tasks such as applying for grants, developing budgets, negotiating contracts, and designing and printing programs and other promotional materials.

GOE—Interest Area/Cluster: 03. Arts and Communication. **Work Group:** 03.07. Music. **Other Jobs in This Work Group:** Music Composers and Arrangers; Music Directors and Composers; Musicians and Singers; Musicians, Instrumental; Singers; Talent Directors.

Skills: Coordination; Management of Personnel Resources; Social Perceptiveness; Negotiation; Monitoring; Learning Strategies; Persuasion; Instructing.

Education and Training Programs: Religious/Sacred Music; Music Performance, General; Music Theory and Composition; Musicology and Ethnomusicology; Conducting; Voice and Opera; Music Management and Merchandising; Music, Other. **Related Knowledge/Courses:** Fine Arts; Philosophy and Theology; Education and Training; History and Archeology; Communications and Media; Personnel and Human Resources.

Work Environment: Indoors; more often standing than sitting.

Music Directors and Composers

See Music Composers and Arrangers (an Artistic job) and Music Directors (an Artistic job), described separately.

Philosophy and Religion Teachers, Postsecondary

The primary personality type for this occupation is Social. Look for the description among the Social jobs.

Photographers

* Personality Code: AR
* Education/Training Required: Long-term on-the-job training
* Annual Earnings: $27,720
* Beginning Wage: $16,170
* Earnings Growth Potential: High
* Growth: 10.3%
* Annual Job Openings: 16,100
* Self-Employed: 54.3%
* Part-Time: 22.1%

Photograph persons, subjects, merchandise, or other commercial products. May develop negatives and produce finished prints. Take pictures of individuals, families, and small groups, either in studio or on location. Adjust apertures, shutter speeds, and camera focus based on a combination of factors such as lighting, field depth, subject motion, film type, and film speed. Use traditional or digital cameras, along with a variety of equipment such as tripods, filters, and flash attachments. Create artificial light, using flashes and reflectors. Determine desired images and picture composition; select and adjust subjects, equipment, and lighting to achieve desired effects. Scan photographs into computers for editing, storage, and electronic transmission. Test equipment prior to use to ensure that it is in good working order. Review sets of photographs to select the best work. Estimate or measure light levels, distances, and numbers of exposures needed, using measuring devices and formulas. Manipulate and enhance scanned or digital images to create desired effects, using computers and specialized software. Perform maintenance tasks necessary to keep equipment working properly. Perform general office duties such as scheduling appointments, keeping books, and ordering supplies. Consult with clients or advertising staff and study assignments to determine project goals, locations, and equipment needs. Select and assemble equipment and required background properties according to subjects, materials, and conditions. Enhance, retouch, and resize photographs and negatives, using airbrushing and other techniques. Set up, mount, or install photographic equipment and cameras. Produce computer-readable digital images from film, using flatbed scanners and photofinishing laboratories. Develop and print exposed film, using chemicals, touchup tools, and developing and printing equipment, or send film to photofinishing laboratories for processing. Direct activities of workers who are setting up photographic equipment. Employ a variety of specialized photographic materials and techniques, including infrared and ultraviolet films, macro-photography, photogrammetry, and sensitometry. Engage in research to develop new photographic procedures and materials.

GOE—Interest Area/Cluster: 03. Arts and Communication. **Work Group:** 03.09. Media Technology. **Other Jobs in This Work Group:** Audio and Video Equipment Technicians; Broadcast Technicians; Camera Operators, Television, Video, and Motion Picture; Film and Video Editors; Multi-Media Artists and Animators; Radio Operators; Sound Engineering Technicians.

Skills: Persuasion; Equipment Maintenance; Management of Financial Resources; Operation Monitoring; Service Orientation; Equipment Selection; Technology Design; Operations Analysis.

Education and Training Programs: Photojournalism; Visual and Performing Arts, General; Commercial Photography; Photography; Film/Video and Photographic Arts, Other; Art/Art Studies, General. **Related Knowledge/Courses:** Sales and Marketing; Fine Arts; Clerical Practices; Customer and Personal Service; Communications and Media; Production and Processing.

Work Environment: More often indoors than outdoors; sitting; using hands on objects, tools, or controls.

Poets, Lyricists, and Creative Writers

- ❋ Personality Code: AI
- ❋ Education/Training Required: Bachelor's degree
- ❋ Annual Earnings: $50,660
- ❋ Beginning Wage: $26,530
- ❋ Earnings Growth Potential: High
- ❋ Growth: 12.8%
- ❋ Annual Job Openings: 24,023
- ❋ Self-Employed: 65.9%
- ❋ Part-Time: 21.8%

The job openings listed here are shared with Copy Writers.

Create original written works, such as scripts, essays, prose, poetry, or song lyrics, for publication or performance. Revise written material to meet personal standards and to satisfy needs of clients, publishers, directors, or producers. Choose subject matter and suitable form to express personal feelings and experiences or ideas, or to narrate stories or events. Plan project arrangements or outlines, and organize material accordingly. Prepare works in appropriate format for publication, and send them to publishers or producers. Follow appropriate procedures to get copyrights for completed work. Write fiction or nonfiction prose such as short stories, novels, biographies, articles, descriptive or critical analyses, and essays. Develop factors such as themes, plots, characterizations, psychological analyses, historical environments, action, and dialogue, to create material. Confer with clients, editors, publishers, or producers to discuss changes or revisions to written material. Conduct research to obtain factual information and authentic detail, using sources such as newspaper accounts, diaries, and interviews. Write narrative, dramatic, lyric, or other types of poetry for publication. Attend book launches and publicity events, or conduct public readings. Write words to fit musical compositions, including lyrics for operas, musical plays, and choral works. Adapt text

Artistic-P

to accommodate musical requirements of composers and singers. Teach writing classes. Write humorous material for publication, or for performances such as comedy routines, gags, and comedy shows. Collaborate with other writers on specific projects.

GOE—Interest Area/Cluster: 03. Arts and Communication. **Work Group:** 03.02. Writing and Editing. **Other Jobs in This Work Group:** Copy Writers; Editors; Technical Writers; Writers and Authors.

Skills: Writing; Social Perceptiveness; Management of Financial Resources; Persuasion; Active Listening; Reading Comprehension; Speaking; Critical Thinking.

Education and Training Programs: Communication Studies/Speech Communication and Rhetoric; Mass Communication/Media Studies; Family and Consumer Sciences/Human Sciences Communication; English Composition; Creative Writing; Playwriting and Screenwriting. **Related Knowledge/Courses:** Fine Arts; Communications and Media; Philosophy and Theology; Sociology and Anthropology; Sales and Marketing; English Language.

Work Environment: Indoors; sitting; using hands on objects, tools, or controls; repetitive motions.

Political Scientists

The primary personality type for this occupation is Investigative. Look for the description among the Investigative jobs.

Preschool Teachers, Except Special Education

The primary personality type for this occupation is Social. Look for the description among the Social jobs.

Producers and Directors

The primary personality type for this occupation is Investigative. Look for the description among the Investigative jobs.

Public Relations Managers

The primary personality type for this occupation is Enterprising. Look for the description among the Enterprising jobs.

Public Relations Specialists

The primary personality type for this occupation is Enterprising. Look for the description among the Enterprising jobs.

Secondary School Teachers, Except Special and Vocational Education

The primary personality type for this occupation is Social. Look for the description among the Social jobs.

Self-Enrichment Education Teachers

The primary personality type for this occupation is Social. Look for the description among the Social jobs.

Set and Exhibit Designers

* Personality Code: AR
* Education/Training Required: Bachelor's degree
* Annual Earnings: $43,220
* Beginning Wage: $23,600
* Earnings Growth Potential: High
* Growth: 17.8%
* Annual Job Openings: 1,402
* Self-Employed: 29.8%
* Part-Time: 16.7%

Design special exhibits and movie, television, and theater sets. May study scripts, confer with directors, and conduct research to determine

appropriate architectural styles. Examine objects to be included in exhibits to plan where and how to display them. Acquire, or arrange for acquisition of, specimens or graphics required to complete exhibits. Prepare rough drafts and scale working drawings of sets, including floor plans, scenery, and properties to be constructed. Confer with clients and staff to gather information about exhibit space, proposed themes and content, timelines, budgets, materials, and promotion requirements. Estimate set- or exhibit-related costs, including materials, construction, and rental of props or locations. Develop set designs based on evaluation of scripts, budgets, research information, and available locations. Direct and coordinate construction, erection, or decoration activities to ensure that sets or exhibits meet design, budget, and schedule requirements. Inspect installed exhibits for conformance to specifications and satisfactory operation of special effects components. Plan for location-specific issues such as space limitations, traffic flow patterns, and safety concerns. Submit plans for approval and adapt plans to serve intended purposes or to conform to budget or fabrication restrictions. Prepare preliminary renderings of proposed exhibits, including detailed construction, layout, and material specifications and diagrams relating to aspects such as special effects and lighting. Select and purchase lumber and hardware necessary for set construction. Collaborate with those in charge of lighting and sound so that those production aspects can be coordinated with set designs or exhibit layouts. Research architectural and stylistic elements appropriate to the time period to be depicted, consulting experts for information as necessary. Design and produce displays and materials that can be used to decorate windows, interior displays, or event locations such as streets and fairgrounds. Coordinate the removal of sets, props, and exhibits after productions or events are complete. Select set props such as furniture, pictures, lamps, and rugs. Confer with conservators to determine how to handle an exhibit's environmental aspects, such as lighting, temperature, and humidity, so that objects will be protected and exhibits will be enhanced.

GOE—Interest Area/Cluster: 03. Arts and Communication. **Work Group:** 03.05. Design. **Other Jobs in This Work Group:** Commercial and Industrial Designers; Fashion Designers; Floral Designers; Graphic Designers; Interior Designers; Merchandise Displayers and Window Trimmers.

Skills: Installation; Operations Analysis; Persuasion; Management of Material Resources; Equipment Selection; Management of Personnel Resources; Management of Financial Resources; Complex Problem Solving.

Education and Training Programs: Design and Visual Communications, General; Illustration; Design and Applied Arts, Other; Technical Theatre/Theatre Design and Technology. **Related Knowledge/Courses:** Fine Arts; Design; History and Archeology; Communications and Media; Sociology and Anthropology; Computers and Electronics.

Work Environment: Indoors; sitting; using hands on objects, tools, or controls.

Sociologists

The primary personality type for this occupation is Investigative. Look for the description among the Investigative jobs.

Special Education Teachers, Middle School

The primary personality type for this occupation is Social. Look for the description among the Social jobs.

Special Education Teachers, Preschool, Kindergarten, and Elementary School

The primary personality type for this occupation is Social. Look for the description among the Social jobs.

Artistic-S

Substance Abuse and Behavioral Disorder Counselors

The primary personality type for this occupation is Social. Look for the description among the Social jobs.

Technical Writers

- ❋ Personality Code: AIC
- ❋ Education/Training Required: Bachelor's degree
- ❋ Annual Earnings: $60,390
- ❋ Beginning Wage: $36,490
- ❋ Earnings Growth Potential: Medium
- ❋ Growth: 19.5%
- ❋ Annual Job Openings: 7,498
- ❋ Self-Employed: 6.0%
- ❋ Part-Time: 6.5%

Write technical materials, such as equipment manuals, appendices, or operating and maintenance instructions. May assist in layout work. Organize material and complete writing assignment according to set standards regarding order, clarity, conciseness, style, and terminology. Maintain records and files of work and revisions. Edit, standardize, or make changes to material prepared by other writers or establishment personnel. Confer with customer representatives, vendors, plant executives, or publisher to establish technical specifications and to determine subject material to be developed for publication. Review published materials and recommend revisions or changes in scope, format, content, and methods of reproduction and binding. Select photographs, drawings, sketches, diagrams, and charts to illustrate material. Study drawings, specifications, mockups, and product samples to integrate and delineate technology, operating procedure, and production sequence and detail. Interview production and engineering personnel and read journals and other material to become familiar with product technologies and production methods. Observe production, developmental, and experimental activities to determine operating procedure and detail. Arrange for typing, duplication, and distribution of material. Assist in laying out material for publication. Analyze developments in specific field to determine need for revisions in previously published materials and development of new material. Review manufacturer's and trade catalogs, drawings, and other data relative to operation, maintenance, and service of equipment. Draw sketches to illustrate specified materials or assembly sequence.

GOE—Interest Area/Cluster: 03. Arts and Communication. **Work Group:** 03.02. Writing and Editing. **Other Jobs in This Work Group:** Copy Writers; Editors; Poets, Lyricists, and Creative Writers; Writers and Authors.

Skills: Writing; Technology Design; Quality Control Analysis; Active Listening; Operations Analysis; Reading Comprehension; Coordination; Active Learning.

Education and Training Programs: Communication Studies/Speech Communication and Rhetoric; Technical and Business Writing; Business/Corporate Communications. **Related Knowledge/Courses:** Communications and Media; Clerical Practices; English Language; Computers and Electronics; Education and Training; Engineering and Technology.

Work Environment: Indoors; sitting; using hands on objects, tools, or controls; repetitive motions.

Training and Development Specialists

The primary personality type for this occupation is Social. Look for the description among the Social jobs.

Writers and Authors

***See** Copy Writers (an Enterprising job) and Poets, Lyricists, and Creative Writers (an Artistic job), described separately.*

Social Occupations

Adult Literacy, Remedial Education, and GED Teachers and Instructors

❋ Personality Code: SAE
❋ Education/Training Required: Bachelor's degree
❋ Annual Earnings: $44,710
❋ Beginning Wage: $25,310
❋ Earnings Growth Potential: High
❋ Growth: 14.2%
❋ Annual Job Openings: 17,340
❋ Self-Employed: 0.0%
❋ Part-Time: 41.3%

Teach or instruct out-of-school youths and adults in remedial education classes, preparatory classes for the General Educational Development test, literacy, or English as a Second Language. Teaching may or may not take place in a traditional educational institution. Adapt teaching methods and instructional materials to meet students' varying needs, abilities, and interests. Observe and evaluate students' work to determine progress and make suggestions for improvement. Instruct students individually and in groups, using various teaching methods such as lectures, discussions, and demonstrations. Plan and conduct activities for a balanced program of instruction, demonstration, and work time that provides students with opportunities to observe, question, and investigate. Maintain accurate and complete student records as required by laws or administrative policies. Prepare materials and classrooms for class activities. Establish clear objectives for all lessons, units, and projects and communicate those objectives to students. Conduct classes, workshops, and demonstrations to teach principles, techniques, or methods in subjects such as basic English language skills, life skills, and workforce entry skills. Prepare students for further education by encouraging them to explore learning opportunities and to persevere with challenging tasks. Establish and

Social-A

enforce rules for behavior and procedures for maintaining order among the students for whom they are responsible. Provide information, guidance, and preparation for the General Equivalency Diploma (GED) examination. Assign and grade classwork and homework. Observe students to determine qualifications, limitations, abilities, interests, and other individual characteristics. Register, orient, and assess new students according to standards and procedures. Prepare and implement remedial programs for students requiring extra help. Prepare and administer written, oral, and performance tests and issue grades in accordance with performance. Use computers, audiovisual aids, and other equipment and materials to supplement presentations. Prepare objectives and outlines for courses of study, following curriculum guidelines or requirements of states and schools. Guide and counsel students with adjustment or academic problems or special academic interests. Enforce administration policies and rules governing students.

GOE—Interest Area/Cluster: 05. Education and Training. **Work Group:** 05.03. Postsecondary and Adult Teaching and Instructing. **Other Jobs in This Work Group:** Agricultural Sciences Teachers, Postsecondary; Anthropology and Archeology Teachers, Postsecondary; Architecture Teachers, Postsecondary; Area, Ethnic, and Cultural Studies Teachers, Postsecondary; Art, Drama, and Music Teachers, Postsecondary; Atmospheric, Earth, Marine, and Space Sciences Teachers, Postsecondary; Biological Science Teachers, Postsecondary; Business Teachers, Postsecondary; Chemistry Teachers, Postsecondary; Communications Teachers, Postsecondary; Computer Science Teachers, Postsecondary; Criminal Justice and Law Enforcement Teachers, Postsecondary; Economics Teachers, Postsecondary; Education Teachers, Postsecondary; Engineering Teachers, Postsecondary; English Language and Literature Teachers, Postsecondary; Environmental Science Teachers, Postsecondary; Farm and Home Management Advisors; Foreign Language and Literature Teachers, Postsecondary; Forestry and Conservation Science Teachers, Postsecondary; Geography Teachers, Postsecondary; Graduate Teaching Assistants; Health Specialties Teachers, Postsecondary;

History Teachers, Postsecondary; Home Economics Teachers, Postsecondary; Law Teachers, Postsecondary; Library Science Teachers, Postsecondary; Mathematical Science Teachers, Postsecondary; Nursing Instructors and Teachers, Postsecondary; Philosophy and Religion Teachers, Postsecondary; Physics Teachers, Postsecondary; Political Science Teachers, Postsecondary; Psychology Teachers, Postsecondary; Recreation and Fitness Studies Teachers, Postsecondary; Self-Enrichment Education Teachers; Social Work Teachers, Postsecondary; Sociology Teachers, Postsecondary; Vocational Education Teachers, Postsecondary.

Skills: Instructing; Learning Strategies; Social Perceptiveness; Service Orientation; Monitoring; Speaking; Persuasion; Writing.

Education and Training Programs: Bilingual and Multilingual Education; Multicultural Education; Adult and Continuing Education and Teaching; Teaching English as a Second or Foreign Language/ ESL Language Instructor; Teaching French as a Second or Foreign Language; Adult Literacy Tutor/ Instructor; Linguistics of ASL and Other Sign Languages. **Related Knowledge/Courses:** History and Archeology; Sociology and Anthropology; Therapy and Counseling; Geography; Education and Training; English Language.

Work Environment: Indoors; more often standing than sitting.

Agricultural Sciences Teachers, Postsecondary

- ❈ Personality Code: SIR
- ❈ Education/Training Required: Doctoral degree
- ❈ Annual Earnings: $78,460
- ❈ Beginning Wage: $43,050
- ❈ Earnings Growth Potential: High
- ❈ Growth: 22.9%
- ❈ Annual Job Openings: 1,840
- ❈ Self-Employed: 0.4%
- ❈ Part-Time: 27.8%

Teach courses in the agricultural sciences, including agronomy, dairy sciences, fisheries management, horticultural sciences, poultry sciences, range management, and agricultural soil conservation. Prepare course materials such as syllabi, homework assignments, and handouts. Evaluate and grade students' classwork, laboratory work, assignments, and papers. Keep abreast of developments in agriculture by reading current literature, talking with colleagues, and participating in professional conferences. Prepare and deliver lectures to undergraduate and/or graduate students on topics such as crop production, plant genetics, and soil chemistry. Initiate, facilitate, and moderate classroom discussions. Conduct research in a particular field of knowledge and publish findings in professional journals, books, and/ or electronic media. Supervise laboratory sessions and fieldwork and coordinate laboratory operations. Supervise undergraduate and/or graduate teaching, internship, and research work. Compile, administer, and grade examinations or assign this work to others. Advise students on academic and vocational curricula and on career issues. Plan, evaluate, and revise curricula, course content, and course materials and methods of instruction. Maintain student attendance records, grades, and other required records. Write grant proposals to procure external research funding. Collaborate with colleagues to address teaching and research issues. Maintain regularly scheduled office hours in order to advise and assist students.

Participate in student recruitment, registration, and placement activities. Select and obtain materials and supplies such as textbooks and laboratory equipment. Act as advisers to student organizations. Participate in campus and community events. Serve on academic or administrative committees that deal with institutional policies, departmental matters, and academic issues. Provide professional consulting services to government and/or industry. Perform administrative duties such as serving as department head. Compile bibliographies of specialized materials for outside reading assignments.

GOE—Interest Area/Cluster: 05. Education and Training. **Work Group:** 05.03. Postsecondary and Adult Teaching and Instructing. **Other Jobs in This Work Group:** Adult Literacy, Remedial Education, and GED Teachers and Instructors; Anthropology and Archeology Teachers, Postsecondary; Architecture Teachers, Postsecondary; Area, Ethnic, and Cultural Studies Teachers, Postsecondary; Art, Drama, and Music Teachers, Postsecondary; Atmospheric, Earth, Marine, and Space Sciences Teachers, Postsecondary; Biological Science Teachers, Postsecondary; Business Teachers, Postsecondary; Chemistry Teachers, Postsecondary; Communications Teachers, Postsecondary; Computer Science Teachers, Postsecondary; Criminal Justice and Law Enforcement Teachers, Postsecondary; Economics Teachers, Postsecondary; Education Teachers, Postsecondary; Engineering Teachers, Postsecondary; English Language and Literature Teachers, Postsecondary; Environmental Science Teachers, Postsecondary; Farm and Home Management Advisors; Foreign Language and Literature Teachers, Postsecondary; Forestry and Conservation Science Teachers, Postsecondary; Geography Teachers, Postsecondary; Graduate Teaching Assistants; Health Specialties Teachers, Postsecondary; History Teachers, Postsecondary; Home Economics Teachers, Postsecondary; Law Teachers, Postsecondary; Library Science Teachers, Postsecondary; Mathematical Science Teachers, Postsecondary; Nursing Instructors and Teachers, Postsecondary; Philosophy and Religion Teachers, Postsecondary; Physics Teachers, Postsecondary; Political Science Teachers, Postsecondary; Psychology Teachers, Postsecondary;

Recreation and Fitness Studies Teachers, Postsecondary; Self-Enrichment Education Teachers; Social Work Teachers, Postsecondary; Sociology Teachers, Postsecondary; Vocational Education Teachers, Postsecondary.

Skills: Science; Management of Financial Resources; Writing; Reading Comprehension; Instructing; Complex Problem Solving; Active Learning; Mathematics.

Education and Training Programs: Agriculture, General; Agricultural Business and Management, General; Agribusiness/Agricultural Business Operations; Agricultural Economics; Farm/Farm and Ranch Management; Agricultural/Farm Supplies Retailing and Wholesaling; Agricultural Business and Management, Other; Agricultural Mechanization, General; Agricultural Power Machinery Operation; Agricultural Mechanization, Other; others. **Related Knowledge/Courses:** Biology; Food Production; Education and Training; Geography; Chemistry; Communications and Media.

Work Environment: Indoors; sitting.

Anthropology and Archeology Teachers, Postsecondary

- ❋ Personality Code: SI
- ❋ Education/Training Required: Doctoral degree
- ❋ Annual Earnings: $64,530
- ❋ Beginning Wage: $38,840
- ❋ Earnings Growth Potential: Medium
- ❋ Growth: 22.9%
- ❋ Annual Job Openings: 910
- ❋ Self-Employed: 0.4%
- ❋ Part-Time: 27.8%

Teach courses in anthropology or archeology. Conduct research in a particular field of knowledge and publish findings in professional journals, books, and electronic media. Keep abreast of developments in their field by reading current literature, talking with colleagues, and participating in professional conferences. Prepare and deliver lectures to undergraduate and graduate students on topics such as research methods, urban anthropology, and language and culture. Evaluate and grade students' classwork, assignments, and papers. Initiate, facilitate, and moderate classroom discussions. Write grant proposals to procure external research funding. Supervise undergraduate and/or graduate teaching, internship, and research work. Prepare course materials such as syllabi, homework assignments, and handouts. Compile, administer, and grade examinations or assign this work to others. Supervise students' laboratory work or fieldwork. Plan, evaluate, and revise curricula, course content, and course materials and methods of instruction. Advise students on academic and vocational curricula, career issues, and laboratory and field research. Maintain student attendance records, grades, and other required records. Maintain regularly scheduled office hours in order to advise and assist students. Collaborate with colleagues to address teaching and research issues. Compile bibliographies of specialized materials for outside reading assignments. Perform administrative duties such as serving as department head. Select and obtain materials and supplies such as textbooks and laboratory equipment. Serve on academic or administrative committees that deal with institutional policies, departmental matters, and academic issues. Participate in student recruitment, registration, and placement activities. Participate in campus and community events. Provide professional consulting services to government and industry. Act as advisers to student organizations.

GOE—Interest Area/Cluster: 05. Education and Training. **Work Group:** 05.03. Postsecondary and Adult Teaching and Instructing. **Other Jobs in This Work Group:** Adult Literacy, Remedial Education, and GED Teachers and Instructors; Agricultural Sciences Teachers, Postsecondary; Architecture Teachers, Postsecondary; Area, Ethnic, and Cultural Studies Teachers, Postsecondary; Art, Drama, and Music Teachers, Postsecondary; Atmospheric, Earth,

Marine, and Space Sciences Teachers, Postsecondary; Biological Science Teachers, Postsecondary; Business Teachers, Postsecondary; Chemistry Teachers, Postsecondary; Communications Teachers, Postsecondary; Computer Science Teachers, Postsecondary; Criminal Justice and Law Enforcement Teachers, Postsecondary; Economics Teachers, Postsecondary; Education Teachers, Postsecondary; Engineering Teachers, Postsecondary; English Language and Literature Teachers, Postsecondary; Environmental Science Teachers, Postsecondary; Farm and Home Management Advisors; Foreign Language and Literature Teachers, Postsecondary; Forestry and Conservation Science Teachers, Postsecondary; Geography Teachers, Postsecondary; Graduate Teaching Assistants; Health Specialties Teachers, Postsecondary; History Teachers, Postsecondary; Home Economics Teachers, Postsecondary; Law Teachers, Postsecondary; Library Science Teachers, Postsecondary; Mathematical Science Teachers, Postsecondary; Nursing Instructors and Teachers, Postsecondary; Philosophy and Religion Teachers, Postsecondary; Physics Teachers, Postsecondary; Political Science Teachers, Postsecondary; Psychology Teachers, Postsecondary; Recreation and Fitness Studies Teachers, Postsecondary; Self-Enrichment Education Teachers; Social Work Teachers, Postsecondary; Sociology Teachers, Postsecondary; Vocational Education Teachers, Postsecondary.

Skills: Science; Writing; Critical Thinking; Reading Comprehension; Active Learning; Instructing; Management of Financial Resources; Active Listening.

Education and Training Programs: Social Science Teacher Education; Anthropology; Physical Anthropology; Archeology. **Related Knowledge/Courses:** Sociology and Anthropology; History and Archeology; Geography; Foreign Language; Philosophy and Theology; English Language.

Work Environment: Indoors; sitting.

Architecture Teachers, Postsecondary

- ❋ Personality Code: SA
- ❋ Education/Training Required: Doctoral degree
- ❋ Annual Earnings: $68,540
- ❋ Beginning Wage: $41,080
- ❋ Earnings Growth Potential: High
- ❋ Growth: 22.9%
- ❋ Annual Job Openings: 1,044
- ❋ Self-Employed: 0.4%
- ❋ Part-Time: 27.8%

Teach courses in architecture and architectural design, such as architectural environmental design, interior architecture/design, and landscape architecture. Evaluate and grade students' work, including work performed in design studios. Prepare and deliver lectures to undergraduate and/or graduate students on topics such as architectural design methods, aesthetics and design, and structures and materials. Prepare course materials such as syllabi, homework assignments, and handouts. Initiate, facilitate, and moderate classroom discussions. Plan, evaluate, and revise curricula, course content, and course materials and methods of instruction. Keep abreast of developments in their field by reading current literature, talking with colleagues, and participating in professional conferences. Maintain student attendance records, grades, and other required records. Maintain regularly scheduled office hours to advise and assist students. Compile, administer, and grade examinations or assign this work to others. Conduct research in a particular field of knowledge and publish findings in professional journals, books, and/or electronic media. Supervise undergraduate and/or graduate teaching, internship, and research work. Advise students on academic and vocational curricula and on career issues. Collaborate with colleagues to address teaching and research issues. Compile bibliographies of specialized materials for outside reading assignments. Serve on academic or administrative committees that deal with institutional policies, departmental matters, and academic issues. Participate in student recruitment, registration, and placement activities. Select and obtain materials and supplies such as textbooks and laboratory equipment. Write grant proposals to procure external research funding. Provide professional consulting services to government and/or industry. Perform administrative duties such as serving as department head. Act as advisers to student organizations. Participate in campus and community events.

GOE—Interest Area/Cluster: 05. Education and Training. **Work Group:** 05.03. Postsecondary and Adult Teaching and Instructing. **Other Jobs in This Work Group:** Adult Literacy, Remedial Education, and GED Teachers and Instructors; Agricultural Sciences Teachers, Postsecondary; Anthropology and Archeology Teachers, Postsecondary; Area, Ethnic, and Cultural Studies Teachers, Postsecondary; Art, Drama, and Music Teachers, Postsecondary; Atmospheric, Earth, Marine, and Space Sciences Teachers, Postsecondary; Biological Science Teachers, Postsecondary; Business Teachers, Postsecondary; Chemistry Teachers, Postsecondary; Communications Teachers, Postsecondary; Computer Science Teachers, Postsecondary; Criminal Justice and Law Enforcement Teachers, Postsecondary; Economics Teachers, Postsecondary; Education Teachers, Postsecondary; Engineering Teachers, Postsecondary; English Language and Literature Teachers, Postsecondary; Environmental Science Teachers, Postsecondary; Farm and Home Management Advisors; Foreign Language and Literature Teachers, Postsecondary; Forestry and Conservation Science Teachers, Postsecondary; Geography Teachers, Postsecondary; Graduate Teaching Assistants; Health Specialties Teachers, Postsecondary; History Teachers, Postsecondary; Home Economics Teachers, Postsecondary; Law Teachers, Postsecondary; Library Science Teachers, Postsecondary; Mathematical Science Teachers, Postsecondary; Nursing Instructors and Teachers, Postsecondary; Philosophy and Religion Teachers, Postsecondary; Physics Teachers, Postsecondary; Political Science Teachers, Postsecondary; Psychology Teachers, Postsecondary; Recreation and Fitness Studies Teachers, Postsecondary; Self-Enrichment

Education Teachers; Social Work Teachers, Postsecondary; Sociology Teachers, Postsecondary; Vocational Education Teachers, Postsecondary.

Skills: Technology Design; Operations Analysis; Instructing; Writing; Science; Complex Problem Solving; Speaking; Critical Thinking.

Education and Training Programs: Architecture (BArch, BA/BS, MArch, MA/MS, PhD); City/Urban, Community and Regional Planning; Environmental Design/Architecture; Interior Architecture; Landscape Architecture (BS, BSLA, BLA, MSLA, MLA, PhD); Teacher Education and Professional Development, Specific Subject Areas, Other; Architectural Engineering. **Related Knowledge/Courses:** Fine Arts; Design; Building and Construction; History and Archeology; Philosophy and Theology; Geography.

Work Environment: Indoors; sitting.

Art, Drama, and Music Teachers, Postsecondary

- ❋ Personality Code: SA
- ❋ Education/Training Required: Doctoral degree
- ❋ Annual Earnings: $55,190
- ❋ Beginning Wage: $30,340
- ❋ Earnings Growth Potential: High
- ❋ Growth: 22.9%
- ❋ Annual Job Openings: 12,707
- ❋ Self-Employed: 0.4%
- ❋ Part-Time: 27.8%

Teach courses in drama; music; and the arts, including fine and applied art, such as painting and sculpture, or design and crafts. Evaluate and grade students' classwork, performances, projects, assignments, and papers. Explain and demonstrate artistic techniques. Prepare students for performances, exams, or assessments. Prepare and deliver lectures to undergraduate or graduate students on topics such as acting techniques, fundamentals of music, and art history. Organize performance groups and direct their rehearsals. Prepare course materials such as syllabi, homework assignments, and handouts. Initiate, facilitate, and moderate classroom discussions. Keep abreast of developments in their field by reading current literature, talking with colleagues, and participating in professional conferences. Advise students on academic and vocational curricula and on career issues. Maintain student attendance records, grades, and other required records. Conduct research in a particular field of knowledge and publish findings in professional journals, books, or electronic media. Supervise undergraduate and/or graduate teaching, internship, and research work. Plan, evaluate, and revise curricula, course content, and course materials and methods of instruction. Maintain regularly scheduled office hours to advise and assist students. Compile, administer, and grade examinations or assign this work to others. Participate in student recruitment, registration, and placement activities. Select and obtain materials and supplies such as textbooks and performance pieces. Collaborate with colleagues to address teaching and research issues. Serve on academic or administrative committees that deal with institutional policies, departmental matters, and academic issues. Participate in campus and community events. Keep students informed of community events such as plays and concerts. Compile bibliographies of specialized materials for outside reading assignments. Display students' work in schools, galleries, and exhibitions. Perform administrative duties such as serving as department head. Act as advisers to student organizations. Write grant proposals to procure external research funding. Provide professional consulting services to government or industry.

GOE—Interest Area/Cluster: 05. Education and Training. **Work Group:** 05.03. Postsecondary and Adult Teaching and Instructing. **Other Jobs in This Work Group:** Adult Literacy, Remedial Education, and GED Teachers and Instructors; Agricultural Sciences Teachers, Postsecondary; Anthropology and Archeology Teachers, Postsecondary; Architecture Teachers, Postsecondary; Area, Ethnic, and Cultural Studies Teachers, Postsecondary; Atmospheric, Earth, Marine, and Space Sciences Teachers, Postsecondary;

Biological Science Teachers, Postsecondary; Business Teachers, Postsecondary; Chemistry Teachers, Postsecondary; Communications Teachers, Postsecondary; Computer Science Teachers, Postsecondary; Criminal Justice and Law Enforcement Teachers, Postsecondary; Economics Teachers, Postsecondary; Education Teachers, Postsecondary; Engineering Teachers, Postsecondary; English Language and Literature Teachers, Postsecondary; Environmental Science Teachers, Postsecondary; Farm and Home Management Advisors; Foreign Language and Literature Teachers, Postsecondary; Forestry and Conservation Science Teachers, Postsecondary; Geography Teachers, Postsecondary; Graduate Teaching Assistants; Health Specialties Teachers, Postsecondary; History Teachers, Postsecondary; Home Economics Teachers, Postsecondary; Law Teachers, Postsecondary; Library Science Teachers, Postsecondary; Mathematical Science Teachers, Postsecondary; Nursing Instructors and Teachers, Postsecondary; Philosophy and Religion Teachers, Postsecondary; Physics Teachers, Postsecondary; Political Science Teachers, Postsecondary; Psychology Teachers, Postsecondary; Recreation and Fitness Studies Teachers, Postsecondary; Self-Enrichment Education Teachers; Social Work Teachers, Postsecondary; Sociology Teachers, Postsecondary; Vocational Education Teachers, Postsecondary.

Skills: Instructing; Social Perceptiveness; Speaking; Active Listening; Persuasion; Learning Strategies; Critical Thinking; Monitoring.

Education and Training Programs: Visual and Performing Arts, General; Crafts/Craft Design, Folk Art and Artisanry; Dance, General; Design and Visual Communications, General; Industrial Design; Commercial Photography; Fashion/Apparel Design; Interior Design; Graphic Design; Design and Applied Arts, Other; Drama and Dramatics/Theatre Arts, General; Technical Theatre/Theatre Design and Technology; Playwriting and Screenwriting; others. **Related Knowledge/Courses:** Fine Arts; History and Archeology; Philosophy and Theology; Education and Training; Communications and Media; Sociology and Anthropology.

Work Environment: Indoors; noisy; sitting.

Atmospheric, Earth, Marine, and Space Sciences Teachers, Postsecondary

- ❋ Personality Code: SI
- ❋ Education/Training Required: Doctoral degree
- ❋ Annual Earnings: $73,280
- ❋ Beginning Wage: $39,840
- ❋ Earnings Growth Potential: High
- ❋ Growth: 22.9%
- ❋ Annual Job Openings: 1,553
- ❋ Self-Employed: 0.4%
- ❋ Part-Time: 27.8%

Teach courses in the physical sciences, except chemistry and physics. Conduct research in a particular field of knowledge and publish findings in professional journals, books, and/or electronic media. Write grant proposals to procure external research funding. Keep abreast of developments in their field by reading current literature, talking with colleagues, and participating in professional conferences. Supervise undergraduate and/or graduate teaching, internships, and research work. Prepare and deliver lectures to undergraduate and/or graduate students on topics such as structural geology, micrometeorology, and atmospheric thermodynamics. Supervise laboratory work and fieldwork. Evaluate and grade students' classwork, assignments, and papers. Prepare course materials such as syllabi, homework assignments, and handouts. Collaborate with colleagues to address teaching and research issues. Compile, administer, and grade examinations or assign this work to others. Plan, evaluate, and revise curricula, course content, course materials, and methods of instruction. Initiate, facilitate, and moderate classroom discussions. Maintain regularly scheduled office hours to advise and assist students. Advise students on academic and vocational curricula and on career issues. Maintain student attendance records, grades, and other required records. Participate in student recruitment, registration, and placement activities. Perform administrative duties such as serving as department head. Select and obtain materials and supplies such as textbooks and laboratory equipment. Serve on academic or administrative committees that deal with institutional policies, departmental matters, and academic issues. Compile bibliographies of specialized materials for outside reading assignments. Provide professional consulting services to government and/or industry. Act as adviser to student organizations. Participate in campus and community events.

GOE—Interest Area/Cluster: 05. Education and Training. **Work Group:** 05.03. Postsecondary and Adult Teaching and Instructing. **Other Jobs in This Work Group:** Adult Literacy, Remedial Education, and GED Teachers and Instructors; Agricultural Sciences Teachers, Postsecondary; Anthropology and Archeology Teachers, Postsecondary; Architecture Teachers, Postsecondary; Area, Ethnic, and Cultural Studies Teachers, Postsecondary; Art, Drama, and Music Teachers, Postsecondary; Biological Science Teachers, Postsecondary; Business Teachers, Postsecondary; Chemistry Teachers, Postsecondary; Communications Teachers, Postsecondary; Computer Science Teachers, Postsecondary; Criminal Justice and Law Enforcement Teachers, Postsecondary; Economics Teachers, Postsecondary; Education Teachers, Postsecondary; Engineering Teachers, Postsecondary; English Language and Literature Teachers, Postsecondary; Environmental Science Teachers, Postsecondary; Farm and Home Management Advisors; Foreign Language and Literature Teachers, Postsecondary; Forestry and Conservation Science Teachers, Postsecondary; Geography Teachers, Postsecondary; Graduate Teaching Assistants; Health Specialties Teachers, Postsecondary; History Teachers, Postsecondary; Home Economics Teachers, Postsecondary; Law Teachers, Postsecondary; Library Science Teachers, Postsecondary; Mathematical Science Teachers, Postsecondary; Nursing Instructors and Teachers, Postsecondary; Philosophy and Religion Teachers, Postsecondary; Physics Teachers, Postsecondary; Political Science Teachers, Postsecondary; Psychology Teachers, Postsecondary;

Recreation and Fitness Studies Teachers, Postsecondary; Self-Enrichment Education Teachers; Social Work Teachers, Postsecondary; Sociology Teachers, Postsecondary; Vocational Education Teachers, Postsecondary.

Skills: Science; Programming; Mathematics; Management of Financial Resources; Complex Problem Solving; Writing; Active Learning; Reading Comprehension.

Education and Training Programs: Science Teacher Education/General Science Teacher Education; Physics Teacher Education; Astronomy; Astrophysics; Planetary Astronomy and Science; Atmospheric Sciences and Meteorology, General; Atmospheric Chemistry and Climatology; Atmospheric Physics and Dynamics; Meteorology; Atmospheric Sciences and Meteorology, Other; Geology/Earth Science, General; Geochemistry; Geophysics and Seismology; others. **Related Knowledge/Courses:** Physics; Geography; Chemistry; Biology; Mathematics; Education and Training.

Work Environment: Indoors; sitting.

Biological Science Teachers, Postsecondary

- ❋ Personality Code: SI
- ❋ Education/Training Required: Doctoral degree
- ❋ Annual Earnings: $71,780
- ❋ Beginning Wage: $39,100
- ❋ Earnings Growth Potential: High
- ❋ Growth: 22.9%
- ❋ Annual Job Openings: 9,039
- ❋ Self-Employed: 0.4%
- ❋ Part-Time: 27.8%

Teach courses in biological sciences. Prepare and deliver lectures to undergraduate and/or graduate students on topics such as molecular biology, marine biology, and botany. Evaluate and grade students' classwork, laboratory work, assignments, and papers.

Prepare course materials such as syllabi, homework assignments, and handouts. Compile, administer, and grade examinations or assign this work to others. Supervise students' laboratory work. Keep abreast of developments in their field by reading current literature, talking with colleagues, and participating in professional conferences. Maintain student attendance records, grades, and other required records. Initiate, facilitate, and moderate classroom discussions. Plan, evaluate, and revise curricula, course content, course materials, and methods of instruction. Advise students on academic and vocational curricula and on career issues. Maintain regularly scheduled office hours to advise and assist students. Supervise undergraduate and/or graduate teaching, internships, and research work. Select and obtain materials and supplies such as textbooks and laboratory equipment. Collaborate with colleagues to address teaching and research issues. Conduct research in a particular field of knowledge and publish findings in professional journals, books, and/or electronic media. Serve on academic or administrative committees that deal with institutional policies, departmental matters, and academic issues. Participate in student recruitment, registration, and placement activities. Write grant proposals to procure external research funding. Perform administrative duties such as serving as department head. Act as advisers to student organizations. Compile bibliographies of specialized materials for outside reading assignments. Participate in campus and community events. Provide professional consulting services to government and/or industry.

GOE—Interest Area/Cluster: 05. Education and Training. **Work Group:** 05.03. Postsecondary and Adult Teaching and Instructing. **Other Jobs in This Work Group:** Adult Literacy, Remedial Education, and GED Teachers and Instructors; Agricultural Sciences Teachers, Postsecondary; Anthropology and Archeology Teachers, Postsecondary; Architecture Teachers, Postsecondary; Area, Ethnic, and Cultural Studies Teachers, Postsecondary; Art, Drama, and Music Teachers, Postsecondary; Atmospheric, Earth, Marine, and Space Sciences Teachers, Postsecondary; Business Teachers, Postsecondary; Chemistry Teachers, Postsecondary; Communications Teachers, Postsecondary; Computer Science Teachers, Postsecondary; Criminal Justice and Law Enforcement Teachers, Postsecondary; Economics Teachers, Postsecondary; Education Teachers, Postsecondary; Engineering Teachers, Postsecondary; English Language and Literature Teachers, Postsecondary; Environmental Science Teachers, Postsecondary; Farm and Home Management Advisors; Foreign Language and Literature Teachers, Postsecondary; Forestry and Conservation Science Teachers, Postsecondary; Geography Teachers, Postsecondary; Graduate Teaching Assistants; Health Specialties Teachers, Postsecondary; History Teachers, Postsecondary; Home Economics Teachers, Postsecondary; Law Teachers, Postsecondary; Library Science Teachers, Postsecondary; Mathematical Science Teachers, Postsecondary; Nursing Instructors and Teachers, Postsecondary; Philosophy and Religion Teachers, Postsecondary; Physics Teachers, Postsecondary; Political Science Teachers, Postsecondary; Psychology Teachers, Postsecondary; Recreation and Fitness Studies Teachers, Postsecondary; Self-Enrichment Education Teachers; Social Work Teachers, Postsecondary; Sociology Teachers, Postsecondary; Vocational Education Teachers, Postsecondary.

Skills: Science; Instructing; Writing; Reading Comprehension; Learning Strategies; Speaking; Active Learning; Critical Thinking.

Education and Training Programs: Biology/Biological Sciences, General; Biochemistry; Biophysics; Molecular Biology; Radiation Biology/Radiobiology; Botany/Plant Biology; Plant Pathology/Phytopathology; Plant Physiology; Cell/Cellular Biology and Histology; Anatomy; Microbiology, General; Virology; Parasitology; Immunology; Zoology/Animal Biology; Entomology; Animal Physiology; others. **Related Knowledge/Courses:** Biology; Chemistry; Education and Training; Medicine and Dentistry; Physics; Geography.

Work Environment: Indoors; more often sitting than standing.

Business Teachers, Postsecondary

* ❋ Personality Code: SEI
* ❋ Education/Training Required: Doctoral degree
* ❋ Annual Earnings: $64,900
* ❋ Beginning Wage: $32,770
* ❋ Earnings Growth Potential: High
* ❋ Growth: 22.9%
* ❋ Annual Job Openings: 11,643
* ❋ Self-Employed: 0.4%
* ❋ Part-Time: 27.8%

Teach courses in business administration and management, such as accounting, finance, human resources, labor relations, marketing, and operations research. Prepare and deliver lectures to undergraduate and/or graduate students on topics such as financial accounting, principles of marketing, and operations management. Evaluate and grade students' classwork, assignments, and papers. Compile, administer, and grade examinations or assign this work to others. Prepare course materials such as syllabi, homework assignments, and handouts. Maintain student attendance records, grades, and other required records. Initiate, facilitate, and moderate classroom discussions. Plan, evaluate, and revise curricula, course content, and course materials and methods of instruction. Keep abreast of developments in their field by reading current literature, talking with colleagues, and participating in professional organizations and conferences. Maintain regularly scheduled office hours to advise and assist students. Advise students on academic and vocational curricula and on career issues. Select and obtain materials and supplies such as textbooks. Collaborate with colleagues to address teaching and research issues. Collaborate with members of the business community to improve programs, to develop new programs, and to provide student access to learning opportunities such as internships. Participate in student recruitment, registration, and placement activities. Serve on academic or administrative committees that deal with institutional policies, departmental matters, and academic issues. Participate in campus and community events. Compile bibliographies of specialized materials for outside reading assignments. Perform administrative duties such as serving as department head. Supervise undergraduate and/or graduate teaching, internship, and research work. Conduct research in a particular field of knowledge and publish findings in professional journals, books, and/or electronic media. Act as advisers to student organizations. Provide professional consulting services to government and/or industry. Write grant proposals to procure external research funding.

GOE—Interest Area/Cluster: 05. Education and Training. **Work Group:** 05.03. Postsecondary and Adult Teaching and Instructing. **Other Jobs in This Work Group:** Adult Literacy, Remedial Education, and GED Teachers and Instructors; Agricultural Sciences Teachers, Postsecondary; Anthropology and Archeology Teachers, Postsecondary; Architecture Teachers, Postsecondary; Area, Ethnic, and Cultural Studies Teachers, Postsecondary; Art, Drama, and Music Teachers, Postsecondary; Atmospheric, Earth, Marine, and Space Sciences Teachers, Postsecondary; Biological Science Teachers, Postsecondary; Chemistry Teachers, Postsecondary; Communications Teachers, Postsecondary; Computer Science Teachers, Postsecondary; Criminal Justice and Law Enforcement Teachers, Postsecondary; Economics Teachers, Postsecondary; Education Teachers, Postsecondary; Engineering Teachers, Postsecondary; English Language and Literature Teachers, Postsecondary; Environmental Science Teachers, Postsecondary; Farm and Home Management Advisors; Foreign Language and Literature Teachers, Postsecondary; Forestry and Conservation Science Teachers, Postsecondary; Geography Teachers, Postsecondary; Graduate Teaching Assistants; Health Specialties Teachers, Postsecondary; History Teachers, Postsecondary; Home Economics Teachers, Postsecondary; Law Teachers, Postsecondary; Library Science Teachers, Postsecondary; Mathematical Science Teachers, Postsecondary; Nursing Instructors and Teachers, Postsecondary; Philosophy and Religion Teachers, Postsecondary; Physics Teachers, Postsecondary; Political Science Teachers, Postsecondary;

Psychology Teachers, Postsecondary; Recreation and Fitness Studies Teachers, Postsecondary; Self-Enrichment Education Teachers; Social Work Teachers, Postsecondary; Sociology Teachers, Postsecondary; Vocational Education Teachers, Postsecondary.

Skills: Instructing; Learning Strategies; Writing; Monitoring; Speaking; Active Learning; Reading Comprehension; Critical Thinking.

Education and Training Programs: Business Teacher Education; Business/Commerce, General; Business Administration and Management, General; Purchasing, Procurement/Acquisitions and Contracts Management; Logistics and Materials Management; Operations Management and Supervision; Accounting; Business/Corporate Communications; Entrepreneurship/Entrepreneurial Studies; Franchising and Franchise Operations; Finance, General; others. **Related Knowledge/Courses:** Economics and Accounting; Education and Training; Sociology and Anthropology; Sales and Marketing; Philosophy and Theology; English Language.

Work Environment: Indoors; sitting.

Chemistry Teachers, Postsecondary

- ❋ Personality Code: SIR
- ❋ Education/Training Required: Doctoral degree
- ❋ Annual Earnings: $63,870
- ❋ Beginning Wage: $37,810
- ❋ Earnings Growth Potential: High
- ❋ Growth: 22.9%
- ❋ Annual Job Openings: 3,405
- ❋ Self-Employed: 0.4%
- ❋ Part-Time: 27.8%

Teach courses pertaining to the chemical and physical properties and compositional changes of substances. Work may include instruction in the methods of qualitative and quantitative chemical analysis. Includes both teachers primarily engaged in teaching and those who do a combination of both teaching and research. Prepare and deliver lectures to undergraduate and/or graduate students on topics such as organic chemistry, analytical chemistry, and chemical separation. Supervise students' laboratory work. Evaluate and grade students' classwork, laboratory performance, assignments, and papers. Compile, administer, and grade examinations or assign this work to others. Maintain student attendance records, grades, and other required records. Prepare course materials such as syllabi, homework assignments, and handouts. Maintain regularly scheduled office hours to advise and assist students. Plan, evaluate, and revise curricula, course content, course materials, and methods of instruction. Supervise undergraduate and/or graduate teaching, internships, and research work. Keep abreast of developments in the field by reading current literature, talking with colleagues, and participating in professional conferences. Initiate, facilitate, and moderate classroom discussions. Select and obtain materials and supplies such as textbooks and laboratory equipment. Conduct research in a particular field of knowledge and publish findings in professional journals, books, and/or electronic media. Advise students on academic and vocational curricula and on career issues. Collaborate with colleagues to address teaching and research issues. Serve on academic or administrative committees that deal with institutional policies, departmental matters, and academic issues. Write grant proposals to procure external research funding. Participate in student recruitment, registration, and placement activities. Prepare and submit required reports related to instruction. Perform administrative duties such as serving as a department head. Act as advisers to student organizations. Compile bibliographies of specialized materials for outside reading assignments. Participate in campus and community events. Provide professional consulting services to government and/or industry.

GOE—Interest Area/Cluster: 05. Education and Training. **Work Group:** 05.03. Postsecondary and Adult Teaching and Instructing. **Other Jobs in This Work Group:** Adult Literacy, Remedial Education, and GED Teachers and Instructors; Agricultural Sciences Teachers, Postsecondary; Anthropology and

Social–C

Archeology Teachers, Postsecondary; Architecture Teachers, Postsecondary; Area, Ethnic, and Cultural Studies Teachers, Postsecondary; Art, Drama, and Music Teachers, Postsecondary; Atmospheric, Earth, Marine, and Space Sciences Teachers, Postsecondary; Biological Science Teachers, Postsecondary; Business Teachers, Postsecondary; Communications Teachers, Postsecondary; Computer Science Teachers, Postsecondary; Criminal Justice and Law Enforcement Teachers, Postsecondary; Economics Teachers, Postsecondary; Education Teachers, Postsecondary; Engineering Teachers, Postsecondary; English Language and Literature Teachers, Postsecondary; Environmental Science Teachers, Postsecondary; Farm and Home Management Advisors; Foreign Language and Literature Teachers, Postsecondary; Forestry and Conservation Science Teachers, Postsecondary; Geography Teachers, Postsecondary; Graduate Teaching Assistants; Health Specialties Teachers, Postsecondary; History Teachers, Postsecondary; Home Economics Teachers, Postsecondary; Law Teachers, Postsecondary; Library Science Teachers, Postsecondary; Mathematical Science Teachers, Postsecondary; Nursing Instructors and Teachers, Postsecondary; Philosophy and Religion Teachers, Postsecondary; Physics Teachers, Postsecondary; Political Science Teachers, Postsecondary; Psychology Teachers, Postsecondary; Recreation and Fitness Studies Teachers, Postsecondary; Self-Enrichment Education Teachers; Social Work Teachers, Postsecondary; Sociology Teachers, Postsecondary; Vocational Education Teachers, Postsecondary.

Skills: Science; Mathematics; Instructing; Writing; Reading Comprehension; Active Learning; Technology Design; Complex Problem Solving.

Education and Training Programs: Chemistry, General; Analytical Chemistry; Inorganic Chemistry; Organic Chemistry; Physical and Theoretical Chemistry; Polymer Chemistry; Chemical Physics; Chemistry, Other; Geochemistry. **Related Knowledge/Courses:** Chemistry; Biology; Physics; Education and Training; Mathematics; English Language.

Work Environment: Indoors; contaminants; hazardous conditions; sitting.

Communications Teachers, Postsecondary

- ❈ Personality Code: SA
- ❈ Education/Training Required: Doctoral degree
- ❈ Annual Earnings: $54,720
- ❈ Beginning Wage: $29,700
- ❈ Earnings Growth Potential: High
- ❈ Growth: 22.9%
- ❈ Annual Job Openings: 4,074
- ❈ Self-Employed: 0.4%
- ❈ Part-Time: 27.8%

Teach courses in communications, such as organizational communications, public relations, radio/television broadcasting, and journalism. Evaluate and grade students' classwork, assignments, and papers. Prepare course materials such as syllabi, homework assignments, and handouts. Initiate, facilitate, and moderate classroom discussions. Prepare and deliver lectures to undergraduate or graduate students on topics such as public speaking, media criticism, and oral traditions. Compile, administer, and grade examinations or assign this work to others. Maintain student attendance records, grades, and other required records. Plan, evaluate, and revise curricula, course content, and course materials and methods of instruction. Maintain regularly scheduled office hours to advise and assist students. Keep abreast of developments in their field by reading current literature, talking with colleagues, and participating in professional conferences. Advise students on academic and vocational curricula and on career issues. Supervise undergraduate or graduate teaching, internship, and research work. Select and obtain materials and supplies such as textbooks. Collaborate with colleagues to address teaching and research issues. Conduct research in a particular field of knowledge and publish findings in professional journals, books, or electronic media. Participate in student recruitment, registration, and placement activities. Serve on academic or administrative committees that deal with institutional policies, departmental matters, and academic issues. Compile bibliographies of specialized materials for outside reading assignments. Act as advisers to student organizations. Participate in campus and community events. Perform administrative duties such as serving as department head. Write grant proposals to procure external research funding. Provide professional consulting services to government or industry.

GOE—Interest Area/Cluster: 05. Education and Training. **Work Group:** 05.03. Postsecondary and Adult Teaching and Instructing. **Other Jobs in This Work Group:** Adult Literacy, Remedial Education, and GED Teachers and Instructors; Agricultural Sciences Teachers, Postsecondary; Anthropology and Archeology Teachers, Postsecondary; Architecture Teachers, Postsecondary; Area, Ethnic, and Cultural Studies Teachers, Postsecondary; Art, Drama, and Music Teachers, Postsecondary; Atmospheric, Earth, Marine, and Space Sciences Teachers, Postsecondary; Biological Science Teachers, Postsecondary; Business Teachers, Postsecondary; Chemistry Teachers, Postsecondary; Computer Science Teachers, Postsecondary; Criminal Justice and Law Enforcement Teachers, Postsecondary; Economics Teachers, Postsecondary; Education Teachers, Postsecondary; Engineering Teachers, Postsecondary; English Language and Literature Teachers, Postsecondary; Environmental Science Teachers, Postsecondary; Farm and Home Management Advisors; Foreign Language and Literature Teachers, Postsecondary; Forestry and Conservation Science Teachers, Postsecondary; Geography Teachers, Postsecondary; Graduate Teaching Assistants; Health Specialties Teachers, Postsecondary; History Teachers, Postsecondary; Home Economics Teachers, Postsecondary; Law Teachers, Postsecondary; Library Science Teachers, Postsecondary; Mathematical Science Teachers, Postsecondary; Nursing Instructors and Teachers, Postsecondary; Philosophy and Religion Teachers, Postsecondary; Physics Teachers, Postsecondary; Political Science Teachers, Postsecondary; Psychology Teachers, Postsecondary; Recreation and Fitness Studies Teachers, Postsecondary; Self-Enrichment Education Teachers; Social Work Teachers, Postsecondary; Sociology Teachers,

Postsecondary; Vocational Education Teachers, Postsecondary.

Skills: Instructing; Writing; Persuasion; Learning Strategies; Monitoring; Speaking; Social Perceptiveness; Critical Thinking.

Education and Training Programs: Communication Studies/Speech Communication and Rhetoric; Mass Communication/Media Studies; Journalism; Broadcast Journalism; Journalism, Other; Radio and Television; Digital Communication and Media/Multimedia; Public Relations/Image Management; Advertising; Political Communication; Health Communication; Communication, Journalism, and Related Programs, Other. **Related Knowledge/Courses:** Communications and Media; Education and Training; Philosophy and Theology; Sociology and Anthropology; English Language; History and Archeology.

Work Environment: Indoors; sitting.

Computer Science Teachers, Postsecondary

- ❋ Personality Code: SIC
- ❋ Education/Training Required: Doctoral degree
- ❋ Annual Earnings: $62,020
- ❋ Beginning Wage: $33,720
- ❋ Earnings Growth Potential: High
- ❋ Growth: 22.9%
- ❋ Annual Job Openings: 5,820
- ❋ Self-Employed: 0.4%
- ❋ Part-Time: 27.8%

Teach courses in computer science. May specialize in a field of computer science, such as the design and function of computers or operations and research analysis. Evaluate and grade students' classwork, laboratory work, assignments, and papers. Maintain student attendance records, grades, and other required records. Prepare and deliver lectures to undergraduate and/or graduate students on topics such as programming, data structures, and software design. Prepare course materials such as syllabi, homework assignments, and handouts. Compile, administer, and grade examinations or assign this work to others. Keep abreast of developments in their field by reading current literature, talking with colleagues, and participating in professional conferences. Initiate, facilitate, and moderate classroom discussions. Plan, evaluate, and revise curricula, course content, and course materials and methods of instruction. Supervise students' laboratory work. Maintain regularly scheduled office hours to advise and assist students. Select and obtain materials and supplies such as textbooks and laboratory equipment. Advise students on academic and vocational curricula and on career issues. Participate in student recruitment, registration, and placement activities. Collaborate with colleagues to address teaching and research issues. Serve on academic or administrative committees that deal with institutional policies, departmental matters, and academic issues. Act as advisers to student organizations. Supervise undergraduate and/or graduate teaching, internship, and research work. Perform administrative duties such as serving as department head. Conduct research in a particular field of knowledge and publish findings in professional journals, books, and/or electronic media. Direct research of other teachers or of graduate students working for advanced academic degrees. Provide professional consulting services to government and/or industry. Participate in campus and community events. Compile bibliographies of specialized materials for outside reading assignments. Write grant proposals to procure external research funding.

GOE—Interest Area/Cluster: 05. Education and Training. **Work Group:** 05.03. Postsecondary and Adult Teaching and Instructing. **Other Jobs in This Work Group:** Adult Literacy, Remedial Education, and GED Teachers and Instructors; Agricultural Sciences Teachers, Postsecondary; Anthropology and Archeology Teachers, Postsecondary; Architecture Teachers, Postsecondary; Area, Ethnic, and Cultural Studies Teachers, Postsecondary; Art, Drama, and Music Teachers, Postsecondary; Atmospheric, Earth, Marine, and Space Sciences Teachers, Postsecondary; Biological Science Teachers, Postsecondary; Business Teachers, Postsecondary; Chemistry Teachers, Postsecondary; Communications Teachers, Postsecondary; Criminal Justice and Law Enforcement Teachers, Postsecondary; Economics Teachers, Postsecondary; Education Teachers, Postsecondary; Engineering Teachers, Postsecondary; English Language and Literature Teachers, Postsecondary; Environmental Science Teachers, Postsecondary; Farm and Home Management Advisors; Foreign Language and Literature Teachers, Postsecondary; Forestry and Conservation Science Teachers, Postsecondary; Geography Teachers, Postsecondary; Graduate Teaching Assistants; Health Specialties Teachers, Postsecondary; History Teachers, Postsecondary; Home Economics Teachers, Postsecondary; Law Teachers, Postsecondary; Library Science Teachers, Postsecondary; Mathematical Science Teachers, Postsecondary; Nursing Instructors and Teachers, Postsecondary; Philosophy and Religion Teachers, Postsecondary; Physics Teachers, Postsecondary; Political Science Teachers, Postsecondary; Psychology Teachers, Postsecondary; Recreation and Fitness Studies Teachers, Postsecondary; Self-Enrichment Education Teachers; Social Work Teachers, Postsecondary; Sociology Teachers, Postsecondary; Vocational Education Teachers, Postsecondary.

Skills: Programming; Instructing; Operations Analysis; Technology Design; Science; Mathematics; Learning Strategies; Complex Problem Solving.

Education and Training Programs: Computer and Information Sciences, General; Computer Programming/Programmer, General; Information Science/Studies; Computer Systems Analysis/Analyst; Computer Science. **Related Knowledge/Courses:** Computers and Electronics; Education and Training; Telecommunications; Mathematics; Engineering and Technology; English Language.

Work Environment: Indoors; sitting.

Counseling Psychologists

- ❋ Personality Code: SIA
- ❋ Education/Training Required: Doctoral degree
- ❋ Annual Earnings: $62,210
- ❋ Beginning Wage: $37,300
- ❋ Earnings Growth Potential: High
- ❋ Growth: 15.8%
- ❋ Annual Job Openings: 8,309
- ❋ Self-Employed: 34.2%
- ❋ Part-Time: 24.0%

The job openings listed here are shared with Clinical Psychologists and with School Psychologists.

Assess and evaluate individuals' problems through the use of case history, interview, and observation and provide individual or group counseling services to assist individuals in achieving more effective personal, social, educational, and vocational development and adjustment. Collect information about individuals or clients, using interviews, case histories, observational techniques, and other assessment methods. Counsel individuals, groups, or families to help them understand problems, define goals, and develop realistic action plans. Develop therapeutic and treatment plans based on clients' interests, abilities, and needs. Consult with other professionals to discuss therapies, treatments, counseling resources, or techniques and to share occupational information. Analyze data such as interview notes, test results, and reference manuals in order to identify symptoms and to diagnose the nature of clients' problems. Advise clients on how they could be helped by counseling. Evaluate the results of counseling methods to determine the reliability and validity of treatments. Provide consulting services to schools, social service agencies, and businesses. Refer clients to specialists or to other institutions for non-counseling treatment of problems. Select, administer, and interpret psychological tests to assess intelligence, aptitudes, abilities, or interests. Conduct research to develop or improve diagnostic or therapeutic counseling techniques.

GOE—Interest Area/Cluster: 10. Human Service. **Work Group:** 10.01. Counseling and Social Work. **Other Jobs in This Work Group:** Child, Family, and School Social Workers; Clinical Psychologists; Clinical, Counseling, and School Psychologists; Marriage and Family Therapists; Medical and Public Health Social Workers; Mental Health and Substance Abuse Social Workers; Mental Health Counselors; Probation Officers and Correctional Treatment Specialists; Rehabilitation Counselors; Residential Advisors; Social and Human Service Assistants; Substance Abuse and Behavioral Disorder Counselors.

Skills: Social Perceptiveness; Active Listening; Persuasion; Service Orientation; Coordination; Monitoring; Negotiation; Learning Strategies.

Education and Training Programs: Psychology, General; Clinical Psychology; Counseling Psychology; Developmental and Child Psychology; School Psychology; Clinical Child Psychology; Psychoanalysis and Psychotherapy. **Related Knowledge/ Courses:** Therapy and Counseling; Philosophy and Theology; Sociology and Anthropology; Psychology; English Language; Customer and Personal Service.

Work Environment: Indoors; sitting.

Dental Hygienists

- ❋ Personality Code: SRC
- ❋ Education/Training Required: Associate degree
- ❋ Annual Earnings: $64,740
- ❋ Beginning Wage: $42,480
- ❋ Earnings Growth Potential: Low
- ❋ Growth: 30.1%
- ❋ Annual Job Openings: 10,433
- ❋ Self-Employed: 0.1%
- ❋ Part-Time: 58.7%

Clean teeth and examine oral areas, head, and neck for signs of oral disease. May educate patients on oral hygiene, take and develop X rays, or apply fluoride or sealants. Clean calcareous deposits,

Social-D

accretions, and stains from teeth and beneath margins of gums, using dental instruments. Feel and visually examine gums for sores and signs of disease. Chart conditions of decay and disease for diagnosis and treatment by dentist. Feel lymph nodes under patient's chin to detect swelling or tenderness that could indicate presence of oral cancer. Apply fluorides and other cavity-preventing agents to arrest dental decay. Examine gums, using probes, to locate periodontal recessed gums and signs of gum disease. Expose and develop X-ray film. Provide clinical services and health education to improve and maintain oral health of schoolchildren. Remove excess cement from coronal surfaces of teeth. Make impressions for study casts. Place, carve, and finish amalgam restorations. Administer local anesthetic agents. Conduct dental health clinics for community groups to augment services of dentist. Remove sutures and dressings. Place and remove rubber dams, matrices, and temporary restorations.

GOE—Interest Area/Cluster: 08. Health Science. **Work Group:** 08.03. Dentistry. **Other Jobs in This Work Group:** Dental Assistants; Dentists, General; Oral and Maxillofacial Surgeons; Orthodontists; Prosthodontists.

Skills: Science; Active Learning; Reading Comprehension; Time Management; Equipment Selection; Persuasion; Social Perceptiveness; Writing.

Education and Training Program: Dental Hygiene/Hygienist. **Related Knowledge/Courses:** Biology; Medicine and Dentistry; Chemistry; Psychology; Therapy and Counseling; Sales and Marketing.

Work Environment: Indoors; radiation; disease or infections; sitting; using hands on objects, tools, or controls; repetitive motions.

Economics Teachers, Postsecondary

- ❋ Personality Code: SI
- ❋ Education/Training Required: Doctoral degree
- ❋ Annual Earnings: $75,300
- ❋ Beginning Wage: $41,650
- ❋ Earnings Growth Potential: High
- ❋ Growth: 22.9%
- ❋ Annual Job Openings: 2,208
- ❋ Self-Employed: 0.4%
- ❋ Part-Time: 27.8%

Teach courses in economics. Prepare and deliver lectures to undergraduate and/or graduate students on topics such as econometrics, price theory, and macroeconomics. Prepare course materials such as syllabi, homework assignments, and handouts. Evaluate and grade students' classwork, assignments, and papers. Compile, administer, and grade examinations or assign this work to others. Keep abreast of developments in their field by reading current literature, talking with colleagues, and participating in professional conferences. Maintain student attendance records, grades, and other required records. Initiate, facilitate, and moderate classroom discussions. Maintain regularly scheduled office hours in order to advise and assist students. Select and obtain materials and supplies such as textbooks. Plan, evaluate, and revise curricula, course content, and course materials and methods of instruction. Conduct research in a particular field of knowledge and publish findings in professional journals, books, and/or electronic media. Supervise undergraduate and/or graduate teaching, internship, and research work. Advise students on academic and vocational curricula and on career issues. Serve on academic or administrative committees that deal with institutional policies, departmental matters, and academic issues. Collaborate with colleagues to address teaching and research issues. Compile bibliographies of specialized materials for outside reading assignments. Participate in student recruitment, registration, and placement activities. Perform administrative duties such as serving as department head. Write grant proposals to procure external research funding. Participate in campus and community events. Provide professional consulting services to government and/or industry. Act as advisers to student organizations.

GOE—Interest Area/Cluster: 05. Education and Training. **Work Group:** 05.03. Postsecondary and Adult Teaching and Instructing. **Other Jobs in This Work Group:** Adult Literacy, Remedial Education, and GED Teachers and Instructors; Agricultural Sciences Teachers, Postsecondary; Anthropology and Archeology Teachers, Postsecondary; Architecture Teachers, Postsecondary; Area, Ethnic, and Cultural Studies Teachers, Postsecondary; Art, Drama, and Music Teachers, Postsecondary; Atmospheric, Earth, Marine, and Space Sciences Teachers, Postsecondary; Biological Science Teachers, Postsecondary; Business Teachers, Postsecondary; Chemistry Teachers, Postsecondary; Communications Teachers, Postsecondary; Computer Science Teachers, Postsecondary; Criminal Justice and Law Enforcement Teachers, Postsecondary; Education Teachers, Postsecondary; Engineering Teachers, Postsecondary; English Language and Literature Teachers, Postsecondary; Environmental Science Teachers, Postsecondary; Farm and Home Management Advisors; Foreign Language and Literature Teachers, Postsecondary; Forestry and Conservation Science Teachers, Postsecondary; Geography Teachers, Postsecondary; Graduate Teaching Assistants; Health Specialties Teachers, Postsecondary; History Teachers, Postsecondary; Home Economics Teachers, Postsecondary; Law Teachers, Postsecondary; Library Science Teachers, Postsecondary; Mathematical Science Teachers, Postsecondary; Nursing Instructors and Teachers, Postsecondary; Philosophy and Religion Teachers, Postsecondary; Physics Teachers, Postsecondary; Political Science Teachers, Postsecondary; Psychology Teachers, Postsecondary; Recreation and Fitness Studies Teachers, Postsecondary; Self-Enrichment Education Teachers; Social Work Teachers, Postsecondary; Sociology Teachers, Postsecondary; Vocational Education Teachers, Postsecondary.

Skills: Mathematics; Writing; Instructing; Speaking; Reading Comprehension; Critical Thinking; Learning Strategies; Active Learning.

Education and Training Programs: Social Science Teacher Education; Economics, General; Applied Economics; Econometrics and Quantitative Economics; Development Economics and International Development; International Economics; Economics, Other; Business/Managerial Economics. **Related Knowledge/Courses:** Economics and Accounting; History and Archeology; Mathematics; Philosophy and Theology; Education and Training; English Language.

Work Environment: Indoors; sitting.

Education Administrators, Preschool and Child Care Center/Program

- ❋ Personality Code: SEC
- ❋ Education/Training Required: Work experience plus degree
- ❋ Annual Earnings: $38,580
- ❋ Beginning Wage: $25,340
- ❋ Earnings Growth Potential: Low
- ❋ Growth: 23.5%
- ❋ Annual Job Openings: 8,113
- ❋ Self-Employed: 3.4%
- ❋ Part-Time: 8.3%

Plan, direct, or coordinate the academic and non-academic activities of preschool and child care centers or programs. Confer with parents and staff to discuss educational activities and policies and students' behavioral or learning problems. Prepare and maintain attendance, activity, planning, accounting, or personnel reports and records for officials and agencies or direct preparation and maintenance activities. Set educational standards and goals and help establish policies, procedures, and programs to carry them out. Monitor students' progress and provide students and teachers with assistance in resolving any

Social-E

problems. Determine allocations of funds for staff, supplies, materials, and equipment and authorize purchases. Recruit, hire, train, and evaluate primary and supplemental staff and recommend personnel actions for programs and services. Direct and coordinate activities of teachers or administrators at daycare centers, schools, public agencies, or institutions. Plan, direct, and monitor instructional methods and content of educational, vocational, or student activity programs. Review and interpret government codes and develop procedures to meet codes and to ensure facility safety, security, and maintenance. Determine the scope of educational program offerings and prepare drafts of program schedules and descriptions to estimate staffing and facility requirements. Review and evaluate new and current programs to determine their efficiency; effectiveness; and compliance with state, local, and federal regulations, and recommend any necessary modifications. Teach classes or courses or provide direct care to children. Prepare and submit budget requests or grant proposals to solicit program funding. Write articles, manuals, and other publications and assist in the distribution of promotional literature about programs and facilities. Collect and analyze survey data, regulatory information, and demographic and employment trends to forecast enrollment patterns and the need for curriculum changes. Inform businesses, community groups, and governmental agencies about educational needs, available programs, and program policies. Organize and direct committees of specialists, volunteers, and staff to provide technical and advisory assistance for programs.

GOE—Interest Area/Cluster: 05. Education and Training. **Work Group:** 05.01. Managerial Work in Education. **Other Jobs in This Work Group:** Education Administrators, Elementary and Secondary School; Education Administrators, Postsecondary; Instructional Coordinators.

Skills: Management of Financial Resources; Management of Personnel Resources; Management of Material Resources; Learning Strategies; Monitoring; Social Perceptiveness; Negotiation; Persuasion.

Education and Training Programs: Educational Leadership and Administration, General; Educational, Instructional, and Curriculum Supervision; Elementary and Middle School Administration/Principalship; Educational Administration and Supervision, Other. **Related Knowledge/Courses:** Personnel and Human Resources; Education and Training; Clerical Practices; Philosophy and Theology; Therapy and Counseling; Sociology and Anthropology.

Work Environment: Indoors; standing.

Education Teachers, Postsecondary

- ❋ Personality Code: SAI
- ❋ Education/Training Required: Doctoral degree
- ❋ Annual Earnings: $54,220
- ❋ Beginning Wage: $29,060
- ❋ Earnings Growth Potential: High
- ❋ Growth: 22.9%
- ❋ Annual Job Openings: 9,359
- ❋ Self-Employed: 0.4%
- ❋ Part-Time: 27.8%

Teach courses pertaining to education, such as counseling, curriculum, guidance, instruction, teacher education, and teaching English as a second language. Prepare course materials such as syllabi, homework assignments, and handouts. Prepare and deliver lectures to undergraduate and/or graduate students on topics such as children's literature, learning and development, and reading instruction. Initiate, facilitate, and moderate classroom discussions. Evaluate and grade students' classwork, assignments, and papers. Plan, evaluate, and revise curricula, course content, and course materials and methods of instruction. Supervise students' fieldwork, internship, and research work. Keep abreast of developments in their field by reading current literature, talking with colleagues, and participating in professional conferences. Advise students on academic and vocational curricula and on career issues. Maintain regularly scheduled office hours to advise and assist students. Maintain student attendance records, grades, and other required records. Collaborate with colleagues to address teaching and research issues. Compile, administer, and grade examinations or assign this work to others. Conduct research in a particular field of knowledge and publish findings in professional journals, books, or electronic media. Select and obtain materials and supplies such as textbooks. Participate in student recruitment, registration, and placement activities. Advise and instruct teachers employed in school systems by providing activities such as in-service seminars. Serve on academic or administrative committees that deal with institutional policies, departmental matters, and academic issues. Compile bibliographies of specialized materials for outside reading assignments. Write grant proposals to procure external research funding. Participate in campus and community events. Perform administrative duties such as serving as department head. Act as advisers to student organizations. Provide professional consulting services to government and/or industry.

GOE—Interest Area/Cluster: 05. Education and Training. **Work Group:** 05.03. Postsecondary and Adult Teaching and Instructing. **Other Jobs in This Work Group:** Adult Literacy, Remedial Education, and GED Teachers and Instructors; Agricultural Sciences Teachers, Postsecondary; Anthropology and Archeology Teachers, Postsecondary; Architecture Teachers, Postsecondary; Area, Ethnic, and Cultural Studies Teachers, Postsecondary; Art, Drama, and Music Teachers, Postsecondary; Atmospheric, Earth, Marine, and Space Sciences Teachers, Postsecondary; Biological Science Teachers, Postsecondary; Business Teachers, Postsecondary; Chemistry Teachers, Postsecondary; Communications Teachers, Postsecondary; Computer Science Teachers, Postsecondary; Criminal Justice and Law Enforcement Teachers, Postsecondary; Economics Teachers, Postsecondary; Engineering Teachers, Postsecondary; English Language and Literature Teachers, Postsecondary; Environmental Science Teachers, Postsecondary; Farm and Home Management Advisors; Foreign Language and Literature Teachers, Postsecondary; Forestry and Conservation Science Teachers, Postsecondary; Geography Teachers, Postsecondary; Graduate Teaching Assistants; Health Specialties Teachers, Postsecondary; History Teachers, Postsecondary; Home Economics Teachers, Postsecondary; Law Teachers, Postsecondary; Library Science Teachers, Postsecondary; Mathematical Science Teachers, Postsecondary; Nursing Instructors and Teachers, Postsecondary; Philosophy and Religion Teachers, Postsecondary; Physics Teachers, Postsecondary; Political Science Teachers, Postsecondary; Psychology Teachers, Postsecondary; Recreation and Fitness Studies Teachers, Postsecondary; Self-Enrichment Education Teachers; Social Work Teachers, Postsecondary; Sociology Teachers, Postsecondary; Vocational Education Teachers, Postsecondary.

Skills: Learning Strategies; Instructing; Writing; Social Perceptiveness; Speaking; Persuasion; Science; Monitoring.

Education and Training Programs: Education, General; Indian/Native American Education; Social and Philosophical Foundations of Education; Agricultural Teacher Education; Art Teacher Education; Business Teacher Education; Driver and Safety Teacher Education; English/Language Arts Teacher Education; Foreign Language Teacher Education; Health Teacher Education; Family and Consumer Sciences/Home Economics Teacher Education; others. **Related Knowledge/Courses:** Therapy and Counseling; Education and Training; Sociology and Anthropology; Philosophy and Theology; Psychology; English Language.

Work Environment: Indoors; sitting.

Social-E

Elementary School Teachers, Except Special Education

- ❋ Personality Code: SAC
- ❋ Education/Training Required: Bachelor's degree
- ❋ Annual Earnings: $47,330
- ❋ Beginning Wage: $31,480
- ❋ Earnings Growth Potential: Low
- ❋ Growth: 13.6%
- ❋ Annual Job Openings: 181,612
- ❋ Self-Employed: 0.0%
- ❋ Part-Time: 9.5%

Teach pupils in public or private schools at the elementary level basic academic, social, and other formative skills. Establish and enforce rules for behavior and procedures for maintaining order among the students for whom they are responsible. Observe and evaluate students' performance, behavior, social development, and physical health. Prepare materials and classrooms for class activities. Adapt teaching methods and instructional materials to meet students' varying needs and interests. Plan and conduct activities for a balanced program of instruction, demonstration, and work time that provides students with opportunities to observe, question, and investigate. Instruct students individually and in groups, using various teaching methods such as lectures, discussions, and demonstrations. Establish clear objectives for all lessons, units, and projects and communicate those objectives to students. Assign and grade classwork and homework. Read books to entire classes or small groups. Prepare, administer, and grade tests and assignments in order to evaluate students' progress. Confer with parents or guardians, teachers, counselors, and administrators to resolve students' behavioral and academic problems. Meet with parents and guardians to discuss their children's progress and to determine their priorities for their children and their resource needs. Prepare students for later grades by encouraging them to explore learning opportunities and to persevere with challenging tasks. Maintain accurate and complete student records as required by laws, district policies, and administrative regulations. Guide and counsel students with adjustment or academic problems or special academic interests. Prepare and implement remedial programs for students requiring extra help. Prepare objectives and outlines for courses of study, following curriculum guidelines or requirements of states and schools. Provide a variety of materials and resources for children to explore, manipulate, and use, both in learning activities and in imaginative play. Enforce administration policies and rules governing students. Confer with other staff members to plan and schedule lessons promoting learning, following approved curricula.

GOE—Interest Area/Cluster: 05. Education and Training. **Work Group:** 05.02. Preschool, Elementary, and Secondary Teaching and Instructing. **Other Jobs in This Work Group:** Kindergarten Teachers, Except Special Education; Middle School Teachers, Except Special and Vocational Education; Preschool Teachers, Except Special Education; Secondary School Teachers, Except Special and Vocational Education; Special Education Teachers, Middle School; Special Education Teachers, Preschool, Kindergarten, and Elementary School; Special Education Teachers, Secondary School; Teacher Assistants; Vocational Education Teachers, Middle School; Vocational Education Teachers, Secondary School.

Skills: Instructing; Learning Strategies; Monitoring; Social Perceptiveness; Speaking; Persuasion; Writing; Service Orientation.

Education and Training Programs: Elementary Education and Teaching; Teacher Education, Multiple Levels; Montessori Teacher Education. **Related Knowledge/Courses:** Geography; History and Archeology; Sociology and Anthropology; Therapy and Counseling; Philosophy and Theology; Education and Training.

Work Environment: Indoors; noisy; disease or infections; standing.

English Language and Literature Teachers, Postsecondary

- ❋ Personality Code: SAI
- ❋ Education/Training Required: Doctoral degree
- ❋ Annual Earnings: $54,000
- ❋ Beginning Wage: $30,680
- ❋ Earnings Growth Potential: High
- ❋ Growth: 22.9%
- ❋ Annual Job Openings: 10,475
- ❋ Self-Employed: 0.4%
- ❋ Part-Time: 27.8%

Teach courses in English language and literature, including linguistics and comparative literature. Initiate, facilitate, and moderate classroom discussions. Evaluate and grade students' classwork, assignments, and papers. Prepare course materials such as syllabi, homework assignments, and handouts. Prepare and deliver lectures to undergraduate and graduate students on topics such as poetry, novel structure, and translation and adaptation. Maintain student attendance records, grades, and other required records. Plan, evaluate, and revise curricula, course content, and course materials and methods of instruction. Compile, administer, and grade examinations or assign this work to others. Maintain regularly scheduled office hours in order to advise and assist students. Keep abreast of developments in their field by reading current literature, talking with colleagues, and participating in professional conferences. Select and obtain materials and supplies such as textbooks. Advise students on academic and vocational curricula and on career issues. Conduct research in a particular field of knowledge and publish findings in professional journals, books, or electronic media. Collaborate with colleagues to address teaching and research issues. Serve on academic or administrative committees that deal with institutional policies, departmental matters, and academic issues. Participate in campus and community events. Participate in student recruitment, registration, and placement activities. Compile bibliographies of specialized materials for outside reading assignments. Supervise undergraduate and/or graduate teaching, internship, and research work. Provide assistance to students in college writing centers. Perform administrative duties such as serving as department head. Recruit, train, and supervise student writing instructors. Act as advisers to student organizations. Write grant proposals to procure external research funding. Provide professional consulting services to government or industry.

GOE—Interest Area/Cluster: 05. Education and Training. **Work Group:** 05.03. Postsecondary and Adult Teaching and Instructing. **Other Jobs in This Work Group:** Adult Literacy, Remedial Education, and GED Teachers and Instructors; Agricultural Sciences Teachers, Postsecondary; Anthropology and Archeology Teachers, Postsecondary; Architecture Teachers, Postsecondary; Area, Ethnic, and Cultural Studies Teachers, Postsecondary; Art, Drama, and Music Teachers, Postsecondary; Atmospheric, Earth, Marine, and Space Sciences Teachers, Postsecondary; Biological Science Teachers, Postsecondary; Business Teachers, Postsecondary; Chemistry Teachers, Postsecondary; Communications Teachers, Postsecondary; Computer Science Teachers, Postsecondary; Criminal Justice and Law Enforcement Teachers, Postsecondary; Economics Teachers, Postsecondary; Education Teachers, Postsecondary; Engineering Teachers, Postsecondary; Environmental Science Teachers, Postsecondary; Farm and Home Management Advisors; Foreign Language and Literature Teachers, Postsecondary; Forestry and Conservation Science Teachers, Postsecondary; Geography Teachers, Postsecondary; Graduate Teaching Assistants; Health Specialties Teachers, Postsecondary; History Teachers, Postsecondary; Home Economics Teachers, Postsecondary; Law Teachers, Postsecondary; Library Science Teachers, Postsecondary; Mathematical Science Teachers, Postsecondary; Nursing Instructors and Teachers, Postsecondary; Philosophy and Religion Teachers, Postsecondary; Physics Teachers, Postsecondary; Political Science Teachers, Postsecondary; Psychology Teachers, Postsecondary; Recreation and Fitness Studies Teachers, Postsecondary; Self-Enrichment Education Teachers; Social

Social–E

Work Teachers, Postsecondary; Sociology Teachers, Postsecondary; Vocational Education Teachers, Postsecondary.

Skills: Instructing; Writing; Learning Strategies; Social Perceptiveness; Reading Comprehension; Persuasion; Critical Thinking; Active Learning.

Education and Training Programs: Comparative Literature; English Language and Literature, General; English Composition; Creative Writing; American Literature (United States); American Literature (Canadian); English Literature (British and Commonwealth); Technical and Business Writing; English Language and Literature/Letters, Other. **Related Knowledge/Courses:** Philosophy and Theology; English Language; History and Archeology; Education and Training; Fine Arts; Sociology and Anthropology.

Work Environment: Indoors; sitting.

Environmental Science Teachers, Postsecondary

- ✹ Personality Code: SIA
- ✹ Education/Training Required: Doctoral degree
- ✹ Annual Earnings: $64,850
- ✹ Beginning Wage: $35,120
- ✹ Earnings Growth Potential: High
- ✹ Growth: 22.9%
- ✹ Annual Job Openings: 769
- ✹ Self-Employed: 0.4%
- ✹ Part-Time: 27.8%

Teach courses in environmental science. Supervise undergraduate and/or graduate teaching, internship, and research work. Conduct research in a particular field of knowledge and publish findings in professional journals, books, and/or electronic media. Keep abreast of developments in their field by reading current literature, talking with colleagues, and participating in professional conferences. Evaluate and grade students' classwork, laboratory work, assignments, and papers. Write grant proposals to procure external research funding. Supervise students' laboratory work and fieldwork. Prepare course materials such as syllabi, homework assignments, and handouts. Plan, evaluate, and revise curricula, course content, and course materials and methods of instruction. Compile, administer, and grade examinations or assign this work to others. Initiate, facilitate, and moderate classroom discussions. Advise students on academic and vocational curricula and on career issues. Prepare and deliver lectures to undergraduate and/or graduate students on topics such as hazardous waste management, industrial safety, and environmental toxicology. Maintain student attendance records, grades, and other required records. Select and obtain materials and supplies such as textbooks and laboratory equipment. Maintain regularly scheduled office hours in order to advise and assist students. Collaborate with colleagues to address teaching and research issues. Perform administrative duties such as serving as department head. Participate in student recruitment, registration, and placement activities. Provide professional consulting services to government and/or industry. Serve on academic or administrative committees that deal with institutional policies, departmental matters, and academic issues. Compile bibliographies of specialized materials for outside reading assignments. Participate in campus and community events. Act as advisers to student organizations.

GOE—Interest Area/Cluster: 05. Education and Training. **Work Group:** 05.03. Postsecondary and Adult Teaching and Instructing. **Other Jobs in This Work Group:** Adult Literacy, Remedial Education, and GED Teachers and Instructors; Agricultural Sciences Teachers, Postsecondary; Anthropology and Archeology Teachers, Postsecondary; Architecture Teachers, Postsecondary; Area, Ethnic, and Cultural Studies Teachers, Postsecondary; Art, Drama, and Music Teachers, Postsecondary; Atmospheric, Earth, Marine, and Space Sciences Teachers, Postsecondary; Biological Science Teachers, Postsecondary; Business Teachers, Postsecondary; Chemistry Teachers, Postsecondary; Communications Teachers, Postsecondary; Computer Science Teachers, Postsecondary;

Criminal Justice and Law Enforcement Teachers, Postsecondary; Economics Teachers, Postsecondary; Education Teachers, Postsecondary; Engineering Teachers, Postsecondary; English Language and Literature Teachers, Postsecondary; Farm and Home Management Advisors; Foreign Language and Literature Teachers, Postsecondary; Forestry and Conservation Science Teachers, Postsecondary; Geography Teachers, Postsecondary; Graduate Teaching Assistants; Health Specialties Teachers, Postsecondary; History Teachers, Postsecondary; Home Economics Teachers, Postsecondary; Law Teachers, Postsecondary; Library Science Teachers, Postsecondary; Mathematical Science Teachers, Postsecondary; Nursing Instructors and Teachers, Postsecondary; Philosophy and Religion Teachers, Postsecondary; Physics Teachers, Postsecondary; Political Science Teachers, Postsecondary; Psychology Teachers, Postsecondary; Recreation and Fitness Studies Teachers, Postsecondary; Self-Enrichment Education Teachers; Social Work Teachers, Postsecondary; Sociology Teachers, Postsecondary; Vocational Education Teachers, Postsecondary.

Skills: Science; Writing; Reading Comprehension; Instructing; Mathematics; Management of Financial Resources; Programming; Critical Thinking.

Education and Training Programs: Environmental Studies; Environmental Science; Science Teacher Education/General Science Teacher Education. **Related Knowledge/Courses:** Biology; Geography; Chemistry; Education and Training; Physics; History and Archeology.

Work Environment: Indoors; sitting.

Equal Opportunity Representatives and Officers

- Personality Code: SEC
- Education/Training Required: Long-term on-the-job training
- Annual Earnings: $48,400
- Beginning Wage: $28,980
- Earnings Growth Potential: High
- Growth: 4.9%
- Annual Job Openings: 15,841
- Self-Employed: 0.4%
- Part-Time: 5.0%

The job openings listed here are shared with Coroners, with Environmental Compliance Inspectors, with Government Property Inspectors and Investigators, and with Licensing Examiners and Inspectors.

Monitor and evaluate compliance with equal opportunity laws, guidelines, and policies to ensure that employment practices and contracting arrangements give equal opportunity without regard to race, religion, color, national origin, sex, age, or disability. Investigate employment practices and alleged violations of laws to document and correct discriminatory factors. Interpret civil rights laws and equal opportunity regulations for individuals and employers. Study equal opportunity complaints to clarify issues. Meet with persons involved in equal opportunity complaints to verify case information and to arbitrate and settle disputes. Coordinate, monitor, and revise complaint procedures to ensure timely processing and review of complaints. Prepare reports of selection, survey, and other statistics, and recommendations for corrective action. Conduct surveys and evaluate findings to determine whether systematic discrimination exists. Develop guidelines for nondiscriminatory employment practices and monitor their implementation and impact. Review company contracts to determine actions required to meet governmental equal opportunity provisions. Counsel newly hired members of minority and disadvantaged groups, informing them about details of civil rights

Social–E

laws. Provide information, technical assistance, and training to supervisors, managers, and employees on topics such as employee supervision, hiring, grievance procedures, and staff development. Verify that all job descriptions are submitted for review and approval and that descriptions meet regulatory standards. Act as liaisons between minority placement agencies and employers or between job search committees and other equal opportunity administrators. Consult with community representatives to develop technical assistance agreements in accordance with governmental regulations. Meet with job search committees or coordinators to explain the role of the equal opportunity coordinator, to provide resources for advertising, and to explain expectations for future contacts. Participate in the recruitment of employees through job fairs, career days, and advertising plans.

GOE—Interest Area/Cluster: 07. Government and Public Administration. **Work Group:** 07.03. Regulations Enforcement. **Other Jobs in This Work Group:** Agricultural Inspectors; Aviation Inspectors; Compliance Officers, Except Agriculture, Construction, Health and Safety, and Transportation; Construction and Building Inspectors; Environmental Compliance Inspectors; Financial Examiners; Fire Inspectors; Fish and Game Wardens; Forest Fire Inspectors and Prevention Specialists; Freight and Cargo Inspectors; Government Property Inspectors and Investigators; Immigration and Customs Inspectors; Licensing Examiners and Inspectors; Nuclear Monitoring Technicians; Occupational Health and Safety Specialists; Occupational Health and Safety Technicians; Tax Examiners, Collectors, and Revenue Agents; Transportation Vehicle, Equipment, and Systems Inspectors, Except Aviation.

Skills: Negotiation; Persuasion; Social Perceptiveness; Service Orientation; Complex Problem Solving; Judgment and Decision Making; Active Listening; Writing.

Education and Training Program: Public Administration and Social Service Professions, Other. **Related Knowledge/Courses:** Law and Government; Personnel and Human Resources; Clerical

Practices; English Language; Customer and Personal Service; Administration and Management.

Work Environment: Indoors; sitting; repetitive motions.

Fitness Trainers and Aerobics Instructors

* Personality Code: SRE
* Education/Training Required: Postsecondary vocational training
* Annual Earnings: $27,680
* Beginning Wage: $15,550
* Earnings Growth Potential: High
* Growth: 26.8%
* Annual Job Openings: 51,235
* Self-Employed: 7.6%
* Part-Time: 38.2%

Instruct or coach groups or individuals in exercise activities and the fundamentals of sports. Demonstrate techniques and methods of participation. Observe participants and inform them of corrective measures necessary to improve their skills. Explain and enforce safety rules and regulations governing sports, recreational activities, and the use of exercise equipment. Offer alternatives during classes to accommodate different levels of fitness. Plan routines, choose appropriate music, and choose different movements for each set of muscles, depending on participants' capabilities and limitations. Observe participants and inform them of corrective measures necessary for skill improvement. Teach proper breathing techniques used during physical exertion. Teach and demonstrate use of gymnastic and training equipment such as trampolines and weights. Instruct participants in maintaining exertion levels to maximize benefits from exercise routines. Maintain fitness equipment. Conduct therapeutic, recreational, or athletic activities. Monitor participants' progress and adapt programs as needed. Evaluate individuals' abilities, needs, and physical conditions and develop suitable training programs to meet any special requirements. Plan physical education programs to promote development of participants' physical attributes and social skills. Provide students with information and resources regarding nutrition, weight control, and lifestyle issues. Administer emergency first aid, wrap injuries, treat minor chronic disabilities, or refer injured persons to physicians. Advise clients about proper clothing and shoes. Wrap ankles, fingers, wrists, or other body parts with synthetic skin, gauze, or adhesive tape to support muscles and ligaments. Teach individual and team sports to participants through instruction and demonstration, utilizing knowledge of sports techniques and of participants' physical capabilities. Promote health clubs through membership sales and record member information. Organize, lead, and referee indoor and outdoor games such as volleyball, baseball, and basketball. Maintain equipment inventories and select, store, or issue equipment as needed. Organize and conduct competitions and tournaments. Advise participants in use of heat or ultraviolet treatments and hot baths. Massage body parts to relieve soreness, strains, and bruises.

GOE—Interest Area/Cluster: 05. Education and Training. **Work Group:** 05.06. Counseling, Health, and Fitness Education. **Other Jobs in This Work Group:** Educational, Vocational, and School Counselors; Health Educators.

Skills: Instructing; Equipment Selection; Monitoring; Service Orientation; Coordination; Science; Social Perceptiveness; Time Management.

Education and Training Programs: Physical Education Teaching and Coaching; Health and Physical Education, General; Sport and Fitness Administration/Management. **Related Knowledge/Courses:** Customer and Personal Service; Psychology; Sociology and Anthropology; Education and Training; Sales and Marketing; Personnel and Human Resources.

Work Environment: Indoors; standing; walking and running; repetitive motions.

Foreign Language and Literature Teachers, Postsecondary

* Personality Code: SAI
* Education/Training Required: Doctoral degree
* Annual Earnings: $53,610
* Beginning Wage: $30,590
* Earnings Growth Potential: High
* Growth: 22.9%
* Annual Job Openings: 4,317
* Self-Employed: 0.4%
* Part-Time: 27.8%

Teach courses in foreign (i.e., other than English) languages and literature. Evaluate and grade students' classwork, assignments, and papers. Prepare course materials such as syllabi, homework assignments, and handouts. Initiate, facilitate, and moderate classroom discussions. Maintain student attendance records, grades, and other required records. Compile, administer, and grade examinations or assign this work to others. Plan, evaluate, and revise curricula, course content, and course materials and methods of instruction. Prepare and deliver lectures to undergraduate and graduate students on topics such as how to speak and write a foreign language and the cultural aspects of areas where a particular language is used. Maintain regularly scheduled office hours to advise and assist students. Select and obtain materials and supplies such as textbooks. Keep abreast of developments in their field by reading current literature, talking with colleagues, and participating in professional organizations and activities. Advise students on academic and vocational curricula and on career issues. Conduct research in a particular field of knowledge and publish findings in scholarly journals, books, and/or electronic media. Collaborate with colleagues to address teaching and research issues. Serve on academic or administrative committees that deal with institutional policies, departmental matters, and academic issues. Participate in student recruitment, registration, and placement activities. Compile bibliographies of specialized materials for outside reading assignments. Participate in campus and community events. Act as advisers to student organizations. Perform administrative duties such as serving as department head. Supervise undergraduate and graduate teaching, internship, and research work. Write grant proposals to procure external research funding. Provide professional consulting services to government or industry.

GOE—Interest Area/Cluster: 05. Education and Training. **Work Group:** 05.03. Postsecondary and Adult Teaching and Instructing. **Other Jobs in This Work Group:** Adult Literacy, Remedial Education, and GED Teachers and Instructors; Agricultural Sciences Teachers, Postsecondary; Anthropology and Archeology Teachers, Postsecondary; Architecture Teachers, Postsecondary; Area, Ethnic, and Cultural Studies Teachers, Postsecondary; Art, Drama, and Music Teachers, Postsecondary; Atmospheric, Earth, Marine, and Space Sciences Teachers, Postsecondary; Biological Science Teachers, Postsecondary; Business Teachers, Postsecondary; Chemistry Teachers, Postsecondary; Communications Teachers, Postsecondary; Computer Science Teachers, Postsecondary; Criminal Justice and Law Enforcement Teachers, Postsecondary; Economics Teachers, Postsecondary; Education Teachers, Postsecondary; Engineering Teachers, Postsecondary; English Language and Literature Teachers, Postsecondary; Environmental Science Teachers, Postsecondary; Farm and Home Management Advisors; Forestry and Conservation Science Teachers, Postsecondary; Geography Teachers, Postsecondary; Graduate Teaching Assistants; Health Specialties Teachers, Postsecondary; History Teachers, Postsecondary; Home Economics Teachers, Postsecondary; Law Teachers, Postsecondary; Library Science Teachers, Postsecondary; Mathematical Science Teachers, Postsecondary; Nursing Instructors and Teachers, Postsecondary; Philosophy and Religion Teachers, Postsecondary; Physics Teachers, Postsecondary; Political Science Teachers, Postsecondary; Psychology Teachers, Postsecondary; Recreation and Fitness Studies Teachers, Postsecondary; Self-Enrichment Education Teachers; Social Work Teachers, Postsecondary; Sociology Teachers, Postsecondary; Vocational Education Teachers, Postsecondary.

Skills: Learning Strategies; Instructing; Writing; Reading Comprehension; Speaking; Persuasion; Social Perceptiveness; Critical Thinking.

Education and Training Programs: Latin Teacher Education; Foreign Languages and Literatures, General; Linguistics; Language Interpretation and Translation; African Languages, Literatures, and Linguistics; East Asian Languages, Literatures, and Linguistics, General; Chinese Language and Literature; Japanese Language and Literature; Korean Language and Literature; Tibetan Language and Literature; others. **Related Knowledge/Courses:** Foreign Language; Philosophy and Theology; History and Archeology; Sociology and Anthropology; Geography; English Language.

Work Environment: Indoors; sitting.

Graduate Teaching Assistants

- ❋ Personality Code: SC
- ❋ Education/Training Required: Bachelor's degree
- ❋ Annual Earnings: $28,060
- ❋ Beginning Wage: $15,660
- ❋ Earnings Growth Potential: High
- ❋ Growth: 22.9%
- ❋ Annual Job Openings: 20,601
- ❋ Self-Employed: 0.4%
- ❋ Part-Time: 27.8%

Assist department chairperson, faculty members, or other professional staff members in colleges or universities by performing teaching or teaching-related duties such as teaching lower-level courses, developing teaching materials, preparing and giving examinations, and grading examinations or papers. Graduate assistants must be enrolled in graduate school programs. Graduate assistants who primarily perform non-teaching duties such as laboratory research, should be

reported in the occupational category related to the work performed. Lead discussion sections, tutorials, and laboratory sections. Evaluate and grade examinations, assignments, and papers, and record grades. Return assignments to students in accordance with established deadlines. Schedule and maintain regular office hours to meet with students. Inform students of the procedures for completing and submitting class work such as lab reports. Prepare and proctor examinations. Notify instructors of errors or problems with assignments. Meet with supervisors to discuss students' grades, and to complete required grade-related paperwork. Copy and distribute classroom materials. Demonstrate use of laboratory equipment, and enforce laboratory rules. Teach undergraduate level courses. Complete laboratory projects prior to assigning them to students so that any needed modifications can be made. Develop teaching materials such as syllabi, visual aids, answer keys, supplementary notes, and course websites. Provide assistance to faculty members or staff with laboratory or field research. Arrange for supervisors to conduct teaching observations; meet with supervisors to receive feedback about teaching performance. Attend lectures given by the instructors whom they are assisting. Order or obtain materials needed for classes. Provide instructors with assistance in the use of audiovisual equipment. Assist faculty members or staff with student conferences.

GOE—Interest Area/Cluster: 05. Education and Training. **Work Group:** 05.03. Postsecondary and Adult Teaching and Instructing. **Other Jobs in This Work Group:** Adult Literacy, Remedial Education, and GED Teachers and Instructors; Agricultural Sciences Teachers, Postsecondary; Anthropology and Archeology Teachers, Postsecondary; Architecture Teachers, Postsecondary; Area, Ethnic, and Cultural Studies Teachers, Postsecondary; Art, Drama, and Music Teachers, Postsecondary; Atmospheric, Earth, Marine, and Space Sciences Teachers, Postsecondary; Biological Science Teachers, Postsecondary; Business Teachers, Postsecondary; Chemistry Teachers, Postsecondary; Communications Teachers, Postsecondary; Computer Science Teachers, Postsecondary; Criminal Justice and Law Enforcement Teachers, Postsecondary; Economics Teachers, Postsecondary; Education Teachers, Postsecondary; Engineering Teachers, Postsecondary; English Language and Literature Teachers, Postsecondary; Environmental Science Teachers, Postsecondary; Farm and Home Management Advisors; Foreign Language and Literature Teachers, Postsecondary; Forestry and Conservation Science Teachers, Postsecondary; Geography Teachers, Postsecondary; Health Specialties Teachers, Postsecondary; History Teachers, Postsecondary; Home Economics Teachers, Postsecondary; Law Teachers, Postsecondary; Library Science Teachers, Postsecondary; Mathematical Science Teachers, Postsecondary; Nursing Instructors and Teachers, Postsecondary; Philosophy and Religion Teachers, Postsecondary; Physics Teachers, Postsecondary; Political Science Teachers, Postsecondary; Psychology Teachers, Postsecondary; Recreation and Fitness Studies Teachers, Postsecondary; Self-Enrichment Education Teachers; Social Work Teachers, Postsecondary; Sociology Teachers, Postsecondary; Vocational Education Teachers, Postsecondary.

Skills: Learning Strategies; Instructing; Social Perceptiveness; Reading Comprehension; Writing; Speaking; Time Management; Active Learning.

Education and Training Program: Education, General. **Related Knowledge/Courses:** Sociology and Anthropology; Education and Training; English Language; Philosophy and Theology; Communications and Media; Psychology.

Work Environment: Indoors; sitting.

Health Educators

- ❀ Personality Code: SE
- ❀ Education/Training Required: Bachelor's degree
- ❀ Annual Earnings: $42,920
- ❀ Beginning Wage: $25,340
- ❀ Earnings Growth Potential: High
- ❀ Growth: 26.2%
- ❀ Annual Job Openings: 13,707
- ❀ Self-Employed: 0.1%
- ❀ Part-Time: 12.0%

Promote, maintain, and improve individual and community health by assisting individuals and communities to adopt healthy behaviors. Collect and analyze data to identify community needs prior to planning, implementing, monitoring, and evaluating programs designed to encourage healthy lifestyles, policies, and environments. May also serve as a resource to assist individuals, other professionals, or the community and may administer fiscal resources for health education programs. Document activities, recording information such as the numbers of applications completed, presentations conducted, and persons assisted. Develop and present health education and promotion programs such as training workshops, conferences, and school or community presentations. Develop and maintain cooperative working relationships with agencies and organizations interested in public health care. Prepare and distribute health education materials, including reports; bulletins; and visual aids such as films, videotapes, photographs, and posters. Develop operational plans and policies necessary to achieve health education objectives and services. Collaborate with health specialists and civic groups to determine community health needs and the availability of services and to develop goals for meeting needs. Maintain databases, mailing lists, telephone networks, and other information to facilitate the functioning of health education programs. Supervise professional and technical staff in implementing health programs, objectives, and goals. Design and conduct evaluations and diagnostic studies to assess the quality and performance of health education programs. Provide program information to the public by preparing and presenting press releases, conducting media campaigns, and/or maintaining program-related Web sites. Develop, prepare, and coordinate grant applications and grant-related activities to obtain funding for health education programs and related work. Provide guidance to agencies and organizations in the assessment of health education needs and in the development and delivery of health education programs. Develop and maintain health education libraries to provide resources for staff and community agencies. Develop, conduct, or coordinate health needs assessments and other public health surveys.

GOE—Interest Area/Cluster: 05. Education and Training. **Work Group:** 05.06. Counseling, Health, and Fitness Education. **Other Jobs in This Work Group:** Educational, Vocational, and School Counselors; Fitness Trainers and Aerobics Instructors.

Skills: Service Orientation; Social Perceptiveness; Monitoring; Learning Strategies; Instructing; Speaking; Coordination; Active Learning.

Education and Training Programs: Health Communication; Community Health Services/Liaison/Counseling; Public Health Education and Promotion; Maternal and Child Health; International Public Health/International Health; Bioethics/Medical Ethics. **Related Knowledge/Courses:** Sociology and Anthropology; Customer and Personal Service; Education and Training; Personnel and Human Resources; Psychology; Therapy and Counseling.

Work Environment: Indoors; disease or infections; sitting; using hands on objects, tools, or controls.

Health Specialties Teachers, Postsecondary

❋ Personality Code: SI
❋ Education/Training Required: Doctoral degree
❋ Annual Earnings: $80,700
❋ Beginning Wage: $37,890
❋ Earnings Growth Potential: Very high
❋ Growth: 22.9%
❋ Annual Job Openings: 19,617
❋ Self-Employed: 0.4%
❋ Part-Time: 27.8%

Teach courses in health specialties, such as veterinary medicine, dentistry, pharmacy, therapy, laboratory technology, and public health. Initiate, facilitate, and moderate classroom discussions. Keep abreast of developments in their field by reading current literature, talking with colleagues, and participating in professional conferences. Compile, administer, and grade examinations or assign this work to others. Evaluate and grade students' classwork, assignments, and papers. Prepare course materials such as syllabi, homework assignments, and handouts. Prepare and deliver lectures to undergraduate or graduate students on topics such as public health, stress management, and worksite health promotion. Plan, evaluate, and revise curricula, course content, and course materials and methods of instruction. Supervise undergraduate or graduate teaching, internship, and research work. Conduct research in a particular field of knowledge and publish findings in professional journals, books, or electronic media. Collaborate with colleagues to address teaching and research issues. Supervise laboratory sessions. Maintain student attendance records, grades, and other required records. Maintain regularly scheduled office hours in order to advise and assist students. Advise students on academic and vocational curricula and on career issues. Participate in student recruitment, registration, and placement activities. Write grant proposals to procure external research funding. Serve on academic or administrative committees that deal with institutional policies, departmental matters, and academic issues. Select and obtain materials and supplies such as textbooks and laboratory equipment. Act as advisers to student organizations. Perform administrative duties such as serving as department head. Compile bibliographies of specialized materials for outside reading assignments. Provide professional consulting services to government and industry. Participate in campus and community events.

GOE—Interest Area/Cluster: 05. Education and Training. **Work Group:** 05.03. Postsecondary and Adult Teaching and Instructing. **Other Jobs in This Work Group:** Adult Literacy, Remedial Education, and GED Teachers and Instructors; Agricultural Sciences Teachers, Postsecondary; Anthropology and Archeology Teachers, Postsecondary; Architecture Teachers, Postsecondary; Area, Ethnic, and Cultural Studies Teachers, Postsecondary; Art, Drama, and Music Teachers, Postsecondary; Atmospheric, Earth, Marine, and Space Sciences Teachers, Postsecondary; Biological Science Teachers, Postsecondary; Business Teachers, Postsecondary; Chemistry Teachers, Postsecondary; Communications Teachers, Postsecondary; Computer Science Teachers, Postsecondary; Criminal Justice and Law Enforcement Teachers, Postsecondary; Economics Teachers, Postsecondary; Education Teachers, Postsecondary; Engineering Teachers, Postsecondary; English Language and Literature Teachers, Postsecondary; Environmental Science Teachers, Postsecondary; Farm and Home Management Advisors; Foreign Language and Literature Teachers, Postsecondary; Forestry and Conservation Science Teachers, Postsecondary; Geography Teachers, Postsecondary; Graduate Teaching Assistants; History Teachers, Postsecondary; Home Economics Teachers, Postsecondary; Law Teachers, Postsecondary; Library Science Teachers, Postsecondary; Mathematical Science Teachers, Postsecondary; Nursing Instructors and Teachers, Postsecondary; Philosophy and Religion Teachers, Postsecondary; Physics Teachers, Postsecondary; Political Science Teachers, Postsecondary; Psychology Teachers, Postsecondary; Recreation and Fitness Studies Teachers, Postsecondary; Self-Enrichment Education Teachers; Social Work Teachers, Postsecondary; Sociology

Social–H

Teachers, Postsecondary; Vocational Education Teachers, Postsecondary.

Skills: Science; Instructing; Writing; Reading Comprehension; Learning Strategies; Complex Problem Solving; Critical Thinking; Speaking.

Education and Training Programs: Health Occupations Teacher Education; Biostatistics; Epidemiology; Chiropractic (DC); Communication Disorders, General; Audiology/Audiologist and Hearing Sciences; Speech-Language Pathology/Pathologist; Audiology/Audiologist and Speech-Language Pathology/Pathologist; Dentistry (DDS, DMD); Dental Clinical Sciences, General (MS, PhD); Dental Assisting/Assistant; Dental Hygiene/Hygienist; others. **Related Knowledge/Courses:** Biology; Medicine and Dentistry; Education and Training; Therapy and Counseling; Sociology and Anthropology; Psychology.

Work Environment: Indoors; sitting.

History Teachers, Postsecondary

- ❋ Personality Code: SIA
- ❋ Education/Training Required: Doctoral degree
- ❋ Annual Earnings: $59,160
- ❋ Beginning Wage: $33,540
- ❋ Earnings Growth Potential: High
- ❋ Growth: 22.9%
- ❋ Annual Job Openings: 3,570
- ❋ Self-Employed: 0.4%
- ❋ Part-Time: 27.8%

Teach courses in human history and historiography. Prepare and deliver lectures to undergraduate and/or graduate students on topics such as ancient history, postwar civilizations, and the history of third-world countries. Evaluate and grade students' classwork, assignments, and papers. Prepare course materials such as syllabi, homework assignments, and handouts. Compile, administer, and grade examinations or assign this work to others. Initiate, facilitate, and moderate classroom discussions. Keep abreast of developments in their field by reading current literature, talking with colleagues, and participating in professional conferences. Plan, evaluate, and revise curricula, course content, and course materials and methods of instruction. Maintain student attendance records, grades, and other required records. Maintain regularly scheduled office hours to advise and assist students. Conduct research in a particular field of knowledge and publish findings in professional journals, books, or electronic media. Select and obtain materials and supplies such as textbooks. Advise students on academic and vocational curricula and on career issues. Collaborate with colleagues to address teaching and research issues. Serve on academic or administrative committees that deal with institutional policies, departmental matters, and academic issues. Participate in campus and community events. Act as advisers to student organizations. Participate in student recruitment, registration, and placement activities. Compile bibliographies of specialized materials for outside reading assignments. Supervise undergraduate and graduate teaching, internship, and research work. Perform administrative duties such as serving as department head. Write grant proposals to procure external research funding. Provide professional consulting services to government, educational institutions, and industry.

GOE—Interest Area/Cluster: 05. Education and Training. **Work Group:** 05.03. Postsecondary and Adult Teaching and Instructing. **Other Jobs in This Work Group:** Adult Literacy, Remedial Education, and GED Teachers and Instructors; Agricultural Sciences Teachers, Postsecondary; Anthropology and Archeology Teachers, Postsecondary; Architecture Teachers, Postsecondary; Area, Ethnic, and Cultural Studies Teachers, Postsecondary; Art, Drama, and Music Teachers, Postsecondary; Atmospheric, Earth, Marine, and Space Sciences Teachers, Postsecondary; Biological Science Teachers, Postsecondary; Business Teachers, Postsecondary; Chemistry Teachers, Postsecondary; Communications Teachers, Postsecondary; Computer Science Teachers, Postsecondary; Criminal Justice and Law Enforcement Teachers, Postsecondary; Economics Teachers, Postsecondary; Education Teachers, Postsecondary; Engineering

Teachers, Postsecondary; English Language and Literature Teachers, Postsecondary; Environmental Science Teachers, Postsecondary; Farm and Home Management Advisors; Foreign Language and Literature Teachers, Postsecondary; Forestry and Conservation Science Teachers, Postsecondary; Geography Teachers, Postsecondary; Graduate Teaching Assistants; Health Specialties Teachers, Postsecondary; Home Economics Teachers, Postsecondary; Law Teachers, Postsecondary; Library Science Teachers, Postsecondary; Mathematical Science Teachers, Postsecondary; Nursing Instructors and Teachers, Postsecondary; Philosophy and Religion Teachers, Postsecondary; Physics Teachers, Postsecondary; Political Science Teachers, Postsecondary; Psychology Teachers, Postsecondary; Recreation and Fitness Studies Teachers, Postsecondary; Self-Enrichment Education Teachers; Social Work Teachers, Postsecondary; Sociology Teachers, Postsecondary; Vocational Education Teachers, Postsecondary.

Skills: Writing; Instructing; Learning Strategies; Reading Comprehension; Speaking; Persuasion; Critical Thinking; Active Learning.

Education and Training Programs: History, General; American History (United States); European History; History and Philosophy of Science and Technology; Public/Applied History and Archival Administration; Asian History; Canadian History; History, Other. **Related Knowledge/Courses:** History and Archeology; Philosophy and Theology; Geography; Sociology and Anthropology; Education and Training; English Language.

Work Environment: Indoors; sitting.

Instructional Coordinators

- ❋ Personality Code: SIE
- ❋ Education/Training Required: Master's degree
- ❋ Annual Earnings: $55,270
- ❋ Beginning Wage: $30,580
- ❋ Earnings Growth Potential: High
- ❋ Growth: 22.5%
- ❋ Annual Job Openings: 21,294
- ❋ Self-Employed: 3.1%
- ❋ Part-Time: 19.7%

Develop instructional material, coordinate educational content, and incorporate current technology in specialized fields that provide guidelines to educators and instructors for developing curricula and conducting courses. Conduct or participate in workshops, committees, and conferences designed to promote the intellectual, social, and physical welfare of students. Plan and conduct teacher training programs and conferences dealing with new classroom procedures, instructional materials and equipment, and teaching aids. Advise teaching and administrative staff in curriculum development, use of materials and equipment, and implementation of state and federal programs and procedures. Recommend, order, or authorize purchase of instructional materials, supplies, equipment, and visual aids designed to meet student educational needs and district standards. Interpret and enforce provisions of state education codes and rules and regulations of state education boards. Confer with members of educational committees and advisory groups to obtain knowledge of subject areas and to relate curriculum materials to specific subjects, individual student needs, and occupational areas. Organize production and design of curriculum materials. Research, evaluate, and prepare recommendations on curricula, instructional methods, and materials for school systems. Observe work of teaching staff to evaluate performance and to recommend changes that could strengthen teaching skills. Develop instructional materials to be used by educators and instructors. Prepare grant proposals,

Social-I

budgets, and program policies and goals or assist in their preparation. Develop tests, questionnaires, and procedures that measure the effectiveness of curricula and use these tools to determine whether program objectives are being met. Update the content of educational programs to ensure that students are being trained with equipment and processes that are technologically current. Address public audiences to explain program objectives and to elicit support. Advise and teach students. Prepare or approve manuals, guidelines, and reports on state educational policies and practices for distribution to school districts. Develop classroom-based and distance-learning training courses, using needs assessments and skill level analyses. Inspect instructional equipment to determine if repairs are needed and authorize necessary repairs.

GOE—Interest Area/Cluster: 05. Education and Training. **Work Group:** 05.01. Managerial Work in Education. **Other Jobs in This Work Group:** Education Administrators, Elementary and Secondary School; Education Administrators, Postsecondary; Education Administrators, Preschool and Child Care Center/Program.

Skills: Management of Financial Resources; Learning Strategies; Monitoring; Social Perceptiveness; Coordination; Time Management; Management of Personnel Resources; Persuasion.

Education and Training Programs: Curriculum and Instruction; Educational/Instructional Media Design; International and Comparative Education. **Related Knowledge/Courses:** Education and Training; Sociology and Anthropology; English Language; Personnel and Human Resources; Communications and Media; Psychology.

Work Environment: Indoors; sitting.

Kindergarten Teachers, Except Special Education

* Personality Code: SA
* Education/Training Required: Bachelor's degree
* Annual Earnings: $45,120
* Beginning Wage: $29,300
* Earnings Growth Potential: Medium
* Growth: 16.3%
* Annual Job Openings: 27,603
* Self-Employed: 1.1%
* Part-Time: 25.1%

Teach elemental natural and social science, personal hygiene, music, art, and literature to children from 4 to 6 years old. Promote physical, mental, and social development. May be required to hold state certification. Teach basic skills such as color, shape, number, and letter recognition; personal hygiene; and social skills. Establish and enforce rules for behavior and policies and procedures to maintain order among students. Observe and evaluate children's performance, behavior, social development, and physical health. Instruct students individually and in groups, adapting teaching methods to meet students' varying needs and interests. Read books to entire classes or to small groups. Demonstrate activities to children. Provide a variety of materials and resources for children to explore, manipulate, and use, both in learning activities and in imaginative play. Plan and conduct activities for a balanced program of instruction, demonstration, and work time that provides students with opportunities to observe, question, and investigate. Confer with parents or guardians, other teachers, counselors, and administrators to resolve students' behavioral and academic problems. Prepare children for later grades by encouraging them to explore learning opportunities and to persevere with challenging tasks. Establish clear objectives for all lessons, units, and projects and communicate those objectives to children. Prepare and implement remedial programs for students requiring extra help. Meet with parents and guardians to discuss their children's progress and to determine their priorities for their children and their resource needs. Prepare objectives and outlines for courses of study, following curriculum guidelines or requirements of states and schools. Organize and lead activities designed to promote physical, mental, and social development such as games, arts and crafts, music, and storytelling. Guide and counsel students with adjustment or academic problems or special academic interests. Identify children showing signs of emotional, developmental, or health-related problems and discuss them with supervisors, parents or guardians, and child development specialists. Instruct and monitor students in the use and care of equipment and materials to prevent injuries and damage. Assimilate arriving children to the school environment by greeting them, helping them remove outerwear, and selecting activities of interest to them.

GOE—Interest Area/Cluster: 05. Education and Training. **Work Group:** 05.02. Preschool, Elementary, and Secondary Teaching and Instructing. **Other Jobs in This Work Group:** Elementary School Teachers, Except Special Education; Middle School Teachers, Except Special and Vocational Education; Preschool Teachers, Except Special Education; Secondary School Teachers, Except Special and Vocational Education; Special Education Teachers, Middle School; Special Education Teachers, Preschool, Kindergarten, and Elementary School; Special Education Teachers, Secondary School; Teacher Assistants; Vocational Education Teachers, Middle School; Vocational Education Teachers, Secondary School.

Skills: Learning Strategies; Instructing; Monitoring; Social Perceptiveness; Writing; Time Management; Coordination; Speaking.

Education and Training Programs: Montessori Teacher Education; Waldorf/Steiner Teacher Education; Kindergarten/Preschool Education and Teaching; Early Childhood Education and Teaching. **Related Knowledge/Courses:** History and Archeology; Geography; Sociology and Anthropology; Philosophy and Theology; Psychology; Education and Training.

Work Environment: Indoors; disease or infections; standing.

Law Teachers, Postsecondary

- ❋ Personality Code: SIE
- ❋ Education/Training Required: First professional degree
- ❋ Annual Earnings: $87,730
- ❋ Beginning Wage: $39,670
- ❋ Earnings Growth Potential: Very high
- ❋ Growth: 22.9%
- ❋ Annual Job Openings: 2,169
- ❋ Self-Employed: 0.4%
- ❋ Part-Time: 27.8%

Teach courses in law. Evaluate and grade students' classwork, assignments, papers, and oral presentations. Compile, administer, and grade examinations or assign this work to others. Prepare and deliver lectures to undergraduate or graduate students on topics such as civil procedure, contracts, and torts. Initiate, facilitate, and moderate classroom discussions. Prepare course materials such as syllabi, homework assignments, and handouts. Keep abreast of developments in their field by reading current literature, talking with colleagues, and participating in professional conferences. Plan, evaluate, and revise curricula, course content, and course materials and methods of instruction. Maintain regularly scheduled office hours to advise and assist students. Conduct research in a particular field of knowledge and publish findings in professional journals, books, or electronic media. Advise students on academic and vocational curricula and on career issues. Supervise undergraduate and/or graduate teaching, internship, and research work. Select and obtain materials and supplies such as textbooks. Maintain student attendance records, grades, and other required records. Serve on academic or administrative committees that deal with institutional policies, departmental matters, and academic issues. Perform administrative duties such as serving as department head. Collaborate with colleagues to address teaching and research issues.

Social-L

Participate in student recruitment, registration, and placement activities. Compile bibliographies of specialized materials for outside reading assignments. Participate in campus and community events. Act as advisers to student organizations. Assign cases for students to hear and try. Provide professional consulting services to government or industry. Write grant proposals to procure external research funding.

GOE—Interest Area/Cluster: 05. Education and Training. **Work Group:** 05.03. Postsecondary and Adult Teaching and Instructing. **Other Jobs in This Work Group:** Adult Literacy, Remedial Education, and GED Teachers and Instructors; Agricultural Sciences Teachers, Postsecondary; Anthropology and Archeology Teachers, Postsecondary; Architecture Teachers, Postsecondary; Area, Ethnic, and Cultural Studies Teachers, Postsecondary; Art, Drama, and Music Teachers, Postsecondary; Atmospheric, Earth, Marine, and Space Sciences Teachers, Postsecondary; Biological Science Teachers, Postsecondary; Business Teachers, Postsecondary; Chemistry Teachers, Postsecondary; Communications Teachers, Postsecondary; Computer Science Teachers, Postsecondary; Criminal Justice and Law Enforcement Teachers, Postsecondary; Economics Teachers, Postsecondary; Education Teachers, Postsecondary; Engineering Teachers, Postsecondary; English Language and Literature Teachers, Postsecondary; Environmental Science Teachers, Postsecondary; Farm and Home Management Advisors; Foreign Language and Literature Teachers, Postsecondary; Forestry and Conservation Science Teachers, Postsecondary; Geography Teachers, Postsecondary; Graduate Teaching Assistants; Health Specialties Teachers, Postsecondary; History Teachers, Postsecondary; Home Economics Teachers, Postsecondary; Library Science Teachers, Postsecondary; Mathematical Science Teachers, Postsecondary; Nursing Instructors and Teachers, Postsecondary; Philosophy and Religion Teachers, Postsecondary; Physics Teachers, Postsecondary; Political Science Teachers, Postsecondary; Psychology Teachers, Postsecondary; Recreation and Fitness Studies Teachers, Postsecondary; Self-Enrichment Education Teachers; Social Work Teachers, Postsecondary; Sociology Teachers, Postsecondary; Vocational Education Teachers, Postsecondary.

Skills: Instructing; Critical Thinking; Writing; Reading Comprehension; Persuasion; Speaking; Active Listening; Learning Strategies.

Education and Training Programs: Legal Studies, General; Law (LL.B., J.D.). **Related Knowledge/Courses:** Law and Government; English Language; History and Archeology; Education and Training; Philosophy and Theology; Communications and Media.

Work Environment: Indoors; sitting.

Marriage and Family Therapists

* Personality Code: SAI
* Education/Training Required: Master's degree
* Annual Earnings: $43,600
* Beginning Wage: $26,080
* Earnings Growth Potential: High
* Growth: 29.8%
* Annual Job Openings: 5,953
* Self-Employed: 6.2%
* Part-Time: 15.4%

Diagnose and treat mental and emotional disorders, whether cognitive, affective, or behavioral, within the context of marriage and family systems. Apply psychotherapeutic and family systems theories and techniques in the delivery of professional services to individuals, couples, and families for the purpose of treating such diagnosed nervous and mental disorders. Ask questions that will help clients identify their feelings and behaviors. Counsel clients on concerns such as unsatisfactory relationships, divorce and separation, child rearing, home management, and financial difficulties. Encourage individuals and family members to develop and use skills and strategies for confronting their problems in a constructive manner. Maintain case files that include activities, progress notes, evaluations, and recommendations. Collect information about clients, using techniques such as testing, interviewing, discussion, and observation. Develop and implement individualized treatment plans addressing family relationship problems. Determine whether clients should be counseled or referred to other specialists in such fields as medicine, psychiatry, and legal aid. Confer with clients in order to develop plans for post-treatment activities. Confer with other counselors to analyze individual cases and to coordinate counseling services. Follow up on results of counseling programs and clients' adjustments to determine effectiveness of programs. Provide instructions to clients on how to obtain help with legal, financial, and other personal issues. Contact doctors, schools, social workers, juvenile counselors, law enforcement personnel, and others to gather information in order to make recommendations to courts for the resolution of child custody or visitation disputes. Provide public education and consultation to other professionals or groups regarding counseling services, issues, and methods. Supervise other counselors, social service staff, and assistants. Provide family counseling and treatment services to inmates participating in substance abuse programs. Write evaluations of parents and children for use by courts deciding divorce and custody cases, testifying in court if necessary.

GOE—Interest Area/Cluster: 10. Human Service. **Work Group:** 10.01. Counseling and Social Work. **Other Jobs in This Work Group:** Child, Family, and School Social Workers; Clinical Psychologists; Clinical, Counseling, and School Psychologists; Counseling Psychologists; Medical and Public Health Social Workers; Mental Health and Substance Abuse Social Workers; Mental Health Counselors; Probation Officers and Correctional Treatment Specialists; Rehabilitation Counselors; Residential Advisors; Social and Human Service Assistants; Substance Abuse and Behavioral Disorder Counselors.

Skills: Social Perceptiveness; Negotiation; Active Listening; Persuasion; Service Orientation; Monitoring; Judgment and Decision Making; Writing.

Education and Training Programs: Social Work; Marriage and Family Therapy/Counseling; Clinical Pastoral Counseling/Patient Counseling. **Related Knowledge/Courses:** Therapy and Counseling; Psychology; Philosophy and Theology; Sociology and Anthropology; Medicine and Dentistry; Customer and Personal Service.

Work Environment: Indoors; sitting.

Mathematical Science Teachers, Postsecondary

- ❋ Personality Code: SIA
- ❋ Education/Training Required: Doctoral degree
- ❋ Annual Earnings: $58,560
- ❋ Beginning Wage: $32,690
- ❋ Earnings Growth Potential: High
- ❋ Growth: 22.9%
- ❋ Annual Job Openings: 7,663
- ❋ Self-Employed: 0.4%
- ❋ Part-Time: 27.8%

Teach courses pertaining to mathematical concepts, statistics, and actuarial science and to the application of original and standardized mathematical techniques in solving specific problems and situations. Evaluate and grade students' classwork, assignments, and papers. Compile, administer, and grade examinations or assign this work to others. Prepare and deliver lectures to undergraduate and/ or graduate students on topics such as linear algebra, differential equations, and discrete mathematics. Prepare course materials such as syllabi, homework assignments, and handouts. Maintain student attendance records, grades, and other required records. Maintain regularly scheduled office hours to advise and assist students. Plan, evaluate, and revise curricula, course content, and course materials and methods of instruction. Initiate, facilitate, and moderate classroom discussions. Select and obtain materials and supplies such as textbooks. Keep abreast of developments in their field by reading current literature, talking with colleagues, and participating in professional conferences. Advise students on academic and vocational curricula and on career issues. Collaborate with colleagues to address teaching and research issues. Serve on academic or administrative committees that deal with institutional policies, departmental matters, and academic issues. Participate in student recruitment, registration, and placement activities. Perform administrative duties such as serving as department head. Conduct research in a particular field of knowledge and publish findings in books, professional journals, and/or electronic media. Supervise undergraduate and/or graduate teaching, internship, and research work. Act as advisers to student organizations. Participate in campus and community events. Write grant proposals to procure external research funding. Compile bibliographies of specialized materials for outside reading assignments. Provide professional consulting services to government and/or industry.

GOE—Interest Area/Cluster: 05. Education and Training. **Work Group:** 05.03. Postsecondary and Adult Teaching and Instructing. **Other Jobs in This Work Group:** Adult Literacy, Remedial Education, and GED Teachers and Instructors; Agricultural Sciences Teachers, Postsecondary; Anthropology and Archeology Teachers, Postsecondary; Architecture Teachers, Postsecondary; Area, Ethnic, and Cultural Studies Teachers, Postsecondary; Art, Drama, and Music Teachers, Postsecondary; Atmospheric, Earth, Marine, and Space Sciences Teachers, Postsecondary; Biological Science Teachers, Postsecondary; Business Teachers, Postsecondary; Chemistry Teachers, Postsecondary; Communications Teachers, Postsecondary; Computer Science Teachers, Postsecondary; Criminal Justice and Law Enforcement Teachers, Postsecondary; Economics Teachers, Postsecondary; Education Teachers, Postsecondary; Engineering Teachers, Postsecondary; English Language and Literature Teachers, Postsecondary; Environmental Science Teachers, Postsecondary; Farm and Home Management Advisors; Foreign Language and Literature Teachers, Postsecondary; Forestry and Conservation Science Teachers, Postsecondary; Geography Teachers, Postsecondary; Graduate Teaching Assistants; Health Specialties Teachers, Postsecondary; History Teachers, Postsecondary; Home Economics Teachers, Postsecondary; Law Teachers, Postsecondary; Library Science Teachers, Postsecondary; Nursing Instructors and Teachers, Postsecondary; Philosophy and Religion Teachers, Postsecondary; Physics Teachers, Postsecondary; Political Science Teachers, Postsecondary; Psychology Teachers, Postsecondary; Recreation and Fitness Studies Teachers, Postsecondary; Self-Enrichment Education Teachers; Social Work Teachers, Postsecondary; Sociology Teachers, Postsecondary; Vocational Education Teachers, Postsecondary.

Skills: Mathematics; Instructing; Science; Learning Strategies; Critical Thinking; Complex Problem Solving; Speaking; Reading Comprehension.

Education and Training Programs: Mathematics, General; Algebra and Number Theory; Analysis and Functional Analysis; Geometry/Geometric Analysis; Topology and Foundations; Mathematics, Other; Applied Mathematics; Statistics, General; Mathematical Statistics and Probability; Mathematics and Statistics, Other; Logic; Business Statistics. **Related Knowledge/Courses:** Mathematics; Education and Training; Physics; Computers and Electronics; English Language; Communications and Media.

Work Environment: Indoors; more often standing than sitting.

Medical and Public Health Social Workers

* Personality Code: SI
* Education/Training Required: Bachelor's degree
* Annual Earnings: $44,670
* Beginning Wage: $28,160
* Earnings Growth Potential: Medium
* Growth: 24.2%
* Annual Job Openings: 16,429
* Self-Employed: 2.6%
* Part-Time: 9.4%

Provide persons, families, or vulnerable populations with the psychosocial support needed to cope with chronic, acute, or terminal illnesses such as Alzheimer's, cancer, or AIDS. Services include advising family caregivers, providing patient education and counseling, and making necessary referrals for other social services. Advocate for clients or patients to resolve crises. Collaborate with other professionals to evaluate patients' medical or physical condition and to assess client needs. Refer patients, clients, or families to community resources to assist in recovery from mental or physical illnesses and to provide access to services such as financial assistance, legal aid, housing, job placement, or education. Counsel clients and patients in individual and group sessions to help them overcome dependencies, recover from illnesses, and adjust to life. Use consultation data and social work experience to plan and coordinate client or patient care and rehabilitation, following through to ensure service efficacy. Plan discharge from care facility to home or other care facility. Organize support groups or counsel family members to assist them in understanding, dealing with, and supporting clients or patients. Modify treatment plans to comply with changes in clients' statuses. Monitor, evaluate, and record client progress according to measurable goals described in treatment and care plans. Identify environmental impediments to client or patient progress through interviews and review of patient records. Supervise and direct other workers providing services to clients or patients. Develop or advise on social policy and assist in community development. Investigate child abuse or neglect cases and take authorized protective action when necessary. Oversee Medicaid- and Medicare-related paperwork and recordkeeping in hospitals. Plan and conduct programs to combat social problems, prevent substance abuse, or improve community health and counseling services. Conduct social research to advance knowledge in the social work field.

GOE—Interest Area/Cluster: 10. Human Service. Work Group: 10.01. Counseling and Social Work. Other Jobs in This Work Group: Child, Family, and School Social Workers; Clinical Psychologists; Clinical, Counseling, and School Psychologists; Counseling Psychologists; Marriage and Family Therapists; Mental Health and Substance Abuse Social Workers; Mental Health Counselors; Probation Officers and Correctional Treatment Specialists; Rehabilitation Counselors; Residential Advisors; Social and Human Service Assistants; Substance Abuse and Behavioral Disorder Counselors.

Skills: Social Perceptiveness; Systems Evaluation; Service Orientation; Systems Analysis; Negotiation; Speaking; Writing.

Education and Training Program: Clinical/Medical Social Work. Related Knowledge/Courses: Therapy and Counseling; Sociology and Anthropology; Psychology; Philosophy and Theology; Customer and Personal Service; Medicine and Dentistry.

Work Environment: Indoors; noisy; disease or infections; sitting.

Medical Assistants

- ❋ Personality Code: SCR
- ❋ Education/Training Required: Moderate-term on-the-job training
- ❋ Annual Earnings: $27,430
- ❋ Beginning Wage: $19,850
- ❋ Earnings Growth Potential: Low
- ❋ Growth: 35.4%
- ❋ Annual Job Openings: 92,977
- ❋ Self-Employed: 0.0%
- ❋ Part-Time: 23.2%

Perform administrative and certain clinical duties under the direction of physicians. Administrative duties may include scheduling appointments, maintaining medical records, billing, and coding for insurance purposes. Clinical duties may include taking and recording vital signs and medical histories, preparing patients for examination, drawing blood, and administering medications as directed by physician. Record patients' medical history, vital statistics, and information such as test results in medical records. Prepare treatment rooms for patient examinations, keeping the rooms neat and clean. Interview patients to obtain medical information and measure their vital signs, weights, and heights. Authorize drug refills and provide prescription information to pharmacies. Clean and sterilize instruments and dispose of contaminated supplies. Prepare and administer medications as directed by a physician. Show patients to examination rooms and prepare them for the physician. Explain treatment procedures, medications, diets, and physicians' instructions to patients. Help physicians examine and treat patients, handing them instruments and materials or performing such tasks as giving injections or removing sutures. Collect blood, tissue, or other laboratory specimens, log the specimens, and prepare them for testing. Perform routine laboratory tests and sample analyses. Contact medical facilities or departments to schedule patients for tests or admission. Operate X-ray, electrocardiogram (EKG), and other equipment to administer routine diagnostic tests. Change dressings on wounds. Set up medical laboratory equipment. Perform general office duties such as answering telephones, taking dictation, or completing insurance forms. Greet and log in patients arriving at office or clinic. Schedule appointments for patients. Inventory and order medical, lab, or office supplies and equipment. Keep financial records and perform other bookkeeping duties, such as handling credit and collections and mailing monthly statements to patients.

GOE—Interest Area/Cluster: 08. Health Science. **Work Group:** 08.02. Medicine and Surgery. **Other Jobs in This Work Group:** Anesthesiologists; Family and General Practitioners; Internists, General; Medical Transcriptionists; Obstetricians and Gynecologists; Pediatricians, General; Pharmacists; Pharmacy Aides; Pharmacy Technicians; Physician Assistants; Psychiatrists; Registered Nurses; Surgeons; Surgical Technologists.

Skill: Systems Analysis.

Education and Training Programs: Medical Office Management/Administration; Medical Office Assistant/Specialist; Medical Reception/Receptionist; Medical Insurance Coding Specialist/Coder;

Medical Administrative/Executive Assistant and Medical Secretary; Medical/Clinical Assistant; Anesthesiologist Assistant; Chiropractic Assistant/Technician; Allied Health and Medical Assisting Services, Other; Optomeric Technician/Assistant; others. **Related Knowledge/Courses:** Medicine and Dentistry; Clerical Practices; Psychology; Therapy and Counseling; Customer and Personal Service; Public Safety and Security.

Work Environment: Indoors; disease or infections; standing; walking and running; using hands on objects, tools, or controls.

Mental Health and Substance Abuse Social Workers

* Personality Code: SIA
* Education/Training Required: Master's degree
* Annual Earnings: $36,640
* Beginning Wage: $23,820
* Earnings Growth Potential: Medium
* Growth: 29.9%
* Annual Job Openings: 17,289
* Self-Employed: 2.8%
* Part-Time: 9.4%

Assess and treat individuals with mental, emotional, or substance abuse problems, including abuse of alcohol, tobacco, and/or other drugs. Activities may include individual and group therapy, crisis intervention, case management, client advocacy, prevention, and education. Counsel clients in individual and group sessions to assist them in dealing with substance abuse, mental and physical illness, poverty, unemployment, or physical abuse. Interview clients, review records, and confer with other professionals to evaluate mental or physical condition of client or patient. Collaborate with counselors, physicians, and nurses to plan and coordinate treatment, drawing on social work experience and patient needs. Monitor, evaluate, and record client progress with respect to treatment goals. Refer patient, client, or family to community resources for housing or treatment to assist in recovery from mental or physical illness, following through to ensure service efficacy. Counsel and aid family members to assist them in understanding, dealing with, and supporting the client or patient. Modify treatment plans according to changes in client status. Plan and conduct programs to prevent substance abuse, to combat social problems, or to improve health and counseling services in community. Supervise and direct other workers who provide services to clients or patients. Develop or advise on social policy and assist in community development. Conduct social research to advance knowledge in the social work field.

GOE—Interest Area/Cluster: 10. Human Service. **Work Group:** 10.01. Counseling and Social Work. **Other Jobs in This Work Group:** Child, Family, and School Social Workers; Clinical Psychologists; Clinical, Counseling, and School Psychologists; Counseling Psychologists; Marriage and Family Therapists; Medical and Public Health Social Workers; Mental Health Counselors; Probation Officers and Correctional Treatment Specialists; Rehabilitation Counselors; Residential Advisors; Social and Human Service Assistants; Substance Abuse and Behavioral Disorder Counselors.

Skills: Social Perceptiveness; Service Orientation; Negotiation; Judgment and Decision Making; Active Listening; Persuasion; Complex Problem Solving; Writing.

Education and Training Program: Clinical/Medical Social Work. **Related Knowledge/Courses:** Psychology; Therapy and Counseling; Sociology and Anthropology; Customer and Personal Service.

Work Environment: Indoors; noisy; sitting.

Mental Health Counselors

- Personality Code: SIA
- Education/Training Required: Master's degree
- Annual Earnings: $36,000
- Beginning Wage: $22,900
- Earnings Growth Potential: Medium
- Growth: 30.0%
- Annual Job Openings: 24,103
- Self-Employed: 6.1%
- Part-Time: 15.4%

Counsel with emphasis on prevention. Work with individuals and groups to promote optimum mental health. May help individuals deal with addictions and substance abuse; family, parenting, and marital problems; suicide; stress management; problems with self-esteem; and issues associated with aging and mental and emotional health. Maintain confidentiality of records relating to clients' treatment. Guide clients in the development of skills and strategies for dealing with their problems. Encourage clients to express their feelings and discuss what is happening in their lives and help them to develop insight into themselves and their relationships. Prepare and maintain all required treatment records and reports. Counsel clients and patients, individually and in group sessions, to assist in overcoming dependencies, adjusting to life, and making changes. Collect information about clients through interviews, observation, and tests. Act as client advocates to coordinate required services or to resolve emergency problems in crisis situations. Develop and implement treatment plans based on clinical experience and knowledge. Collaborate with other staff members to perform clinical assessments and develop treatment plans. Evaluate clients' physical or mental condition based on review of client information. Meet with families, probation officers, police, and other interested parties to exchange necessary information during the treatment process. Refer patients, clients, or family members to community resources or to specialists as necessary. Evaluate the effectiveness of counseling programs and clients' progress in resolving identified problems and moving towards defined objectives. Counsel family members to assist them in understanding, dealing with, and supporting clients or patients. Plan, organize, and lead structured programs of counseling, work, study, recreation, and social activities for clients. Modify treatment activities and approaches as needed to comply with changes in clients' status. Learn about new developments in their field by reading professional literature, attending courses and seminars, and establishing and maintaining contact with other social service agencies. Discuss with individual patients their plans for life after leaving therapy. Gather information about community mental health needs and resources that could be used in conjunction with therapy. Monitor clients' use of medications. Supervise other counselors, social service staff, and assistants.

GOE—Interest Area/Cluster: 10. Human Service. **Work Group:** 10.01. Counseling and Social Work. **Other Jobs in This Work Group:** Child, Family, and School Social Workers; Clinical Psychologists; Clinical, Counseling, and School Psychologists; Counseling Psychologists; Marriage and Family Therapists; Medical and Public Health Social Workers; Mental Health and Substance Abuse Social Workers; Probation Officers and Correctional Treatment Specialists; Rehabilitation Counselors; Residential Advisors; Social and Human Service Assistants; Substance Abuse and Behavioral Disorder Counselors.

Skills: Social Perceptiveness; Service Orientation; Negotiation; Active Listening; Persuasion; Learning Strategies; Speaking; Critical Thinking.

Education and Training Programs: Substance Abuse/Addiction Counseling; Clinical/Medical Social Work; Mental Health Counseling/Counselor; Mental and Social Health Services and Allied Professions, Other. **Related Knowledge/Courses:** Therapy and Counseling; Psychology; Sociology and Anthropology; Philosophy and Theology; Medicine and Dentistry; Law and Government.

Work Environment: Indoors; noisy; sitting.

Middle School Teachers, Except Special and Vocational Education

- ❋ Personality Code: SA
- ❋ Education/Training Required: Bachelor's degree
- ❋ Annual Earnings: $47,900
- ❋ Beginning Wage: $32,630
- ❋ Earnings Growth Potential: Low
- ❋ Growth: 11.2%
- ❋ Annual Job Openings: 75,270
- ❋ Self-Employed: 0.0%
- ❋ Part-Time: 9.5%

Teach students in public or private schools in one or more subjects at the middle, intermediate, or junior high level, which falls between elementary and senior high school as defined by applicable state laws and regulations. Establish and enforce rules for behavior and procedures for maintaining order among the students for whom they are responsible. Adapt teaching methods and instructional materials to meet students' varying needs and interests. Instruct through lectures, discussions, and demonstrations in one or more subjects such as English, mathematics, or social studies. Prepare, administer, and grade tests and assignments to evaluate students' progress. Establish clear objectives for all lessons, units, and projects and communicate these objectives to students. Plan and conduct activities for a balanced program of instruction, demonstration, and work time that provides students with opportunities to observe, question, and investigate. Maintain accurate, complete, and correct student records as required by laws, district policies, and administrative regulations. Observe and evaluate students' performance, behavior, social development, and physical health. Assign lessons and correct homework. Prepare materials and classrooms for class activities. Enforce all administration policies and rules governing students. Confer with parents or guardians, other teachers, counselors, and administrators to resolve students' behavioral and academic problems. Prepare students for later grades by encouraging them to explore learning opportunities and to persevere with challenging tasks. Prepare objectives and outlines for courses of study, following curriculum guidelines or requirements of states and schools. Guide and counsel students with adjustment or academic problems or special academic interests. Meet with parents and guardians to discuss their children's progress and to determine their priorities for their children and their resource needs. Meet with other professionals to discuss individual students' needs and progress. Prepare and implement remedial programs for students requiring extra help. Prepare for assigned classes and show written evidence of preparation upon request of immediate supervisors. Instruct and monitor students in the use and care of equipment and materials to prevent injury and damage.

GOE—Interest Area/Cluster: 05. Education and Training. **Work Group:** 05.02. Preschool, Elementary, and Secondary Teaching and Instructing. **Other Jobs in This Work Group:** Elementary School Teachers, Except Special Education; Kindergarten Teachers, Except Special Education; Preschool Teachers, Except Special Education; Secondary School Teachers, Except Special and Vocational Education; Special Education Teachers, Middle School; Special Education Teachers, Preschool, Kindergarten, and Elementary School; Special Education Teachers, Secondary School; Teacher Assistants; Vocational Education Teachers, Middle School; Vocational Education Teachers, Secondary School.

Skills: Learning Strategies; Instructing; Monitoring; Social Perceptiveness; Time Management; Persuasion; Negotiation; Speaking.

Education and Training Programs: Junior High/Intermediate/Middle School Education and Teaching; Montessori Teacher Education; Waldorf/Steiner Teacher Education; Art Teacher Education; English/Language Arts Teacher Education; Foreign Language Teacher Education; Health Teacher Education; Family and Consumer Sciences/Home Economics Teacher Education; Technology Teacher Education/Industrial Arts Teacher Education; Mathematics Teacher Education; others. **Related Knowledge/Courses:** Sociology and Anthropology; History and

Archeology; Philosophy and Theology; Education and Training; Geography; Therapy and Counseling.

Work Environment: Indoors; noisy; standing.

Nursing Instructors and Teachers, Postsecondary

- ❋ Personality Code: SI
- ❋ Education/Training Required: Doctoral degree
- ❋ Annual Earnings: $57,500
- ❋ Beginning Wage: $36,020
- ❋ Earnings Growth Potential: Medium
- ❋ Growth: 22.9%
- ❋ Annual Job Openings: 7,337
- ❋ Self-Employed: 0.4%
- ❋ Part-Time: 27.8%

Demonstrate and teach patient care in classroom and clinical units to nursing students. Includes both teachers primarily engaged in teaching and those who do a combination of both teaching and research. Initiate, facilitate, and moderate classroom discussions. Prepare and deliver lectures to undergraduate or graduate students on topics such as pharmacology, mental health nursing, and community health-care practices. Keep abreast of developments in their field by reading current literature, talking with colleagues, and participating in professional conferences. Prepare course materials such as syllabi, homework assignments, and handouts. Supervise students' laboratory and clinical work. Evaluate and grade students' classwork, laboratory and clinic work, assignments, and papers. Collaborate with colleagues to address teaching and research issues. Plan, evaluate, and revise curricula, course content, and course materials and methods of instruction. Assess clinical education needs and patient and client teaching needs, utilizing a variety of methods. Compile, administer, and grade examinations or assign this work to others. Advise students on academic and vocational curricula and on career issues. Maintain student attendance records, grades, and other required records.

Maintain regularly scheduled office hours to advise and assist students. Supervise undergraduate or graduate teaching, internship, and research work. Conduct research in a particular field of knowledge and publish findings in professional journals, books, and/or electronic media. Participate in student recruitment, registration, and placement activities. Serve on academic or administrative committees that deal with institutional policies, departmental matters, and academic issues. Coordinate training programs with area universities, clinics, hospitals, health agencies, and/or vocational schools. Compile bibliographies of specialized materials for outside reading assignments. Select and obtain materials and supplies such as textbooks and laboratory equipment. Participate in campus and community events. Write grant proposals to procure external research funding. Act as advisers to student organizations. Demonstrate patient care in clinical units of hospitals. Perform administrative duties such as serving as department head.

GOE—Interest Area/Cluster: 05. Education and Training. **Work Group:** 05.03. Postsecondary and Adult Teaching and Instructing. **Other Jobs in This Work Group:** Adult Literacy, Remedial Education, and GED Teachers and Instructors; Agricultural Sciences Teachers, Postsecondary; Anthropology and Archeology Teachers, Postsecondary; Architecture Teachers, Postsecondary; Area, Ethnic, and Cultural Studies Teachers, Postsecondary; Art, Drama, and Music Teachers, Postsecondary; Atmospheric, Earth, Marine, and Space Sciences Teachers, Postsecondary; Biological Science Teachers, Postsecondary; Business Teachers, Postsecondary; Chemistry Teachers, Postsecondary; Communications Teachers, Postsecondary; Computer Science Teachers, Postsecondary; Criminal Justice and Law Enforcement Teachers, Postsecondary; Economics Teachers, Postsecondary; Education Teachers, Postsecondary; Engineering Teachers, Postsecondary; English Language and Literature Teachers, Postsecondary; Environmental Science Teachers, Postsecondary; Farm and Home Management Advisors; Foreign Language and Literature Teachers, Postsecondary; Forestry and Conservation Science Teachers, Postsecondary; Geography Teachers, Postsecondary; Graduate Teaching Assistants; Health Specialties Teachers, Postsecondary; History Teachers, Postsecondary; Home Economics Teachers, Postsecondary; Law Teachers, Postsecondary; Library Science Teachers, Postsecondary; Mathematical Science Teachers, Postsecondary; Philosophy and Religion Teachers, Postsecondary; Physics Teachers, Postsecondary; Political Science Teachers, Postsecondary; Psychology Teachers, Postsecondary; Recreation and Fitness Studies Teachers, Postsecondary; Self-Enrichment Education Teachers; Social Work Teachers, Postsecondary; Sociology Teachers, Postsecondary; Vocational Education Teachers, Postsecondary.

Skills: Science; Instructing; Writing; Social Perceptiveness; Reading Comprehension; Learning Strategies; Service Orientation; Critical Thinking.

Education and Training Programs: Pre-Nursing Studies; Nursing—Registered Nurse Training (RN, ASN, BSN, MSN); Adult Health Nurse/Nursing; Nurse Anesthetist; Family Practice Nurse/Nurse Practitioner; Maternal/Child Health and Neonatal Nurse/Nursing; Nurse Midwife/Nursing Midwifery; Nursing Science (MS, PhD); Pediatric Nurse/Nursing; Psychiatric/Mental Health Nurse/Nursing; Public Health/Community Nurse/Nursing; others. **Related Knowledge/Courses:** Therapy and Counseling; Biology; Sociology and Anthropology; Medicine and Dentistry; Philosophy and Theology; Psychology.

Work Environment: Indoors; disease or infections; sitting.

Occupational Therapists

- ❋ Personality Code: SI
- ❋ Education/Training Required: Master's degree
- ❋ Annual Earnings: $63,790
- ❋ Beginning Wage: $42,330
- ❋ Earnings Growth Potential: Low
- ❋ Growth: 23.1%
- ❋ Annual Job Openings: 8,338
- ❋ Self-Employed: 8.6%
- ❋ Part-Time: 29.8%

Assess, plan, organize, and participate in rehabilitative programs that help restore vocational, homemaking, and daily living skills, as well as general independence, to disabled persons. Plan, organize, and conduct occupational therapy programs in hospital, institutional, or community settings to help rehabilitate those impaired because of illness, injury, or psychological or developmental problems. Test and evaluate patients' physical and mental abilities and analyze medical data to determine realistic rehabilitation goals for patients. Select activities that will help individuals learn work and life-management skills within limits of their mental and physical capabilities. Evaluate patients' progress and prepare reports that detail progress. Complete and maintain necessary records. Train caregivers to provide for the needs of patients during and after therapies. Recommend changes in patients' work or living environments, consistent with their needs and capabilities. Develop and participate in health promotion programs, group activities, or discussions to promote client health, facilitate social adjustment, alleviate stress, and prevent physical or mental disability. Consult with rehabilitation team to select activity programs and coordinate occupational therapy with other therapeutic activities. Plan and implement programs and social activities to help patients learn work and school skills and adjust to handicaps. Design and create, or requisition, special supplies and equipment such as splints, braces and computer-aided adaptive equipment. Conduct research in occupational therapy. Provide training and supervision in therapy techniques and objectives for students and nurses and other medical staff. Help clients improve decision making, abstract reasoning, memory, sequencing, coordination, and perceptual skills, using computer programs. Advise on health risks in the workplace and on health-related transition to retirement. Lay out materials such as puzzles, scissors, and eating utensils for use in therapy, and clean and repair these tools after therapy sessions. Provide patients with assistance in locating and holding jobs.

GOE—Interest Area/Cluster: 08. Health Science. **Work Group:** 08.07. Medical Therapy. **Other Jobs in This Work Group:** Audiologists; Massage Therapists; Occupational Therapist Aides; Occupational Therapist Assistants; Physical Therapist Aides; Physical Therapist Assistants; Physical Therapists; Radiation Therapists; Recreational Therapists; Respiratory Therapists; Respiratory Therapy Technicians; Speech-Language Pathologists.

Skills: Systems Evaluation; Systems Analysis; Social Perceptiveness; Judgment and Decision Making; Service Orientation; Persuasion; Management of Personnel Resources; Complex Problem Solving.

Education and Training Program: Occupational Therapy/Therapist. **Related Knowledge/Courses:** Therapy and Counseling; Psychology; Sociology and Anthropology; Medicine and Dentistry; Biology; Education and Training.

Work Environment: Indoors; disease or infections; standing.

Social–O

Philosophy and Religion Teachers, Postsecondary

- ❋ Personality Code: SAI
- ❋ Education/Training Required: Doctoral degree
- ❋ Annual Earnings: $56,380
- ❋ Beginning Wage: $32,640
- ❋ Earnings Growth Potential: High
- ❋ Growth: 22.9%
- ❋ Annual Job Openings: 3,120
- ❋ Self-Employed: 0.4%
- ❋ Part-Time: 27.8%

Teach courses in philosophy, religion, and theology. Evaluate and grade students' classwork, assignments, and papers. Initiate, facilitate, and moderate classroom discussions. Prepare and deliver lectures to undergraduate and graduate students on topics such as ethics, logic, and contemporary religious thought. Prepare course materials such as syllabi, homework assignments, and handouts. Compile, administer, and grade examinations or assign this work to others. Keep abreast of developments in their field by reading current literature, talking with colleagues, and participating in professional conferences. Maintain student attendance records, grades, and other required records. Plan, evaluate, and revise curricula, course content, and course materials and methods of instruction. Maintain regularly scheduled office hours to advise and assist students. Select and obtain materials and supplies such as textbooks. Advise students on academic and vocational curricula and on career issues. Conduct research in a particular field of knowledge and publish findings in professional journals, books, or electronic media. Perform administrative duties such as serving as department head. Serve on academic or administrative committees that deal with institutional policies, departmental matters, and academic issues. Collaborate with colleagues to address teaching and research issues. Participate in campus and community events. Participate in student recruitment, registration, and placement activities. Compile bibliographies of specialized materials for outside reading assignments. Supervise undergraduate and graduate teaching, internship, and research work. Act as advisers to student organizations. Write grant proposals to procure external research funding. Provide professional consulting services to government or industry.

GOE—Interest Area/Cluster: 05. Education and Training. **Work Group:** 05.03. Postsecondary and Adult Teaching and Instructing. **Other Jobs in This Work Group:** Adult Literacy, Remedial Education, and GED Teachers and Instructors; Agricultural Sciences Teachers, Postsecondary; Anthropology and Archeology Teachers, Postsecondary; Architecture Teachers, Postsecondary; Area, Ethnic, and Cultural Studies Teachers, Postsecondary; Art, Drama, and Music Teachers, Postsecondary; Atmospheric, Earth, Marine, and Space Sciences Teachers, Postsecondary; Biological Science Teachers, Postsecondary; Business Teachers, Postsecondary; Chemistry Teachers, Postsecondary; Communications Teachers, Postsecondary; Computer Science Teachers, Postsecondary; Criminal Justice and Law Enforcement Teachers, Postsecondary; Economics Teachers, Postsecondary; Education Teachers, Postsecondary; Engineering Teachers, Postsecondary; English Language and Literature Teachers, Postsecondary; Environmental Science Teachers, Postsecondary; Farm and Home Management Advisors; Foreign Language and Literature Teachers, Postsecondary; Forestry and Conservation Science Teachers, Postsecondary; Geography Teachers, Postsecondary; Graduate Teaching Assistants; Health Specialties Teachers, Postsecondary; History Teachers, Postsecondary; Home Economics Teachers, Postsecondary; Law Teachers, Postsecondary; Library Science Teachers, Postsecondary; Mathematical Science Teachers, Postsecondary; Nursing Instructors and Teachers, Postsecondary; Physics Teachers, Postsecondary; Political Science Teachers, Postsecondary; Psychology Teachers, Postsecondary; Recreation and Fitness Studies Teachers, Postsecondary; Self-Enrichment Education Teachers; Social Work Teachers, Postsecondary; Sociology Teachers, Postsecondary; Vocational Education Teachers, Postsecondary.

Skills: Writing; Instructing; Reading Comprehension; Critical Thinking; Speaking; Learning Strategies; Social Perceptiveness; Persuasion.

Education and Training Programs: Philosophy; Ethics; Philosophy, Other; Religion/Religious Studies; Buddhist Studies; Christian Studies; Hindu Studies; Philosophy and Religious Studies, Other; Bible/Biblical Studies; Missions/Missionary Studies and Missiology; Religious Education; Religious/Sacred Music; Theology/Theological Studies; Divinity/Ministry (BD, MDiv.); Pre-Theology/Pre-Ministerial Studies; others. **Related Knowledge/Courses:** Philosophy and Theology; History and Archeology; Sociology and Anthropology; Foreign Language; English Language; Education and Training.

Work Environment: Indoors; sitting.

Physical Therapist Assistants

- ❀ Personality Code: SRI
- ❀ Education/Training Required: Associate degree
- ❀ Annual Earnings: $44,130
- ❀ Beginning Wage: $27,800
- ❀ Earnings Growth Potential: Medium
- ❀ Growth: 32.4%
- ❀ Annual Job Openings: 5,957
- ❀ Self-Employed: 0.2%
- ❀ Part-Time: 27.1%

Assist physical therapists in providing physical therapy treatments and procedures. May, in accordance with state laws, assist in the development of treatment plans, carry out routine functions, document the progress of treatment, and modify specific treatments in accordance with patient status and within the scope of treatment plans established by physical therapists. Generally requires formal training. Instruct, motivate, safeguard, and assist patients as they practice exercises and functional activities. Observe patients during treatments to compile and evaluate data on their responses and progress, and provide results to physical therapists in person or through progress notes. Confer with physical therapy staffs or others to discuss and evaluate patient information for planning, modifying, and coordinating treatment. Transport patients to and from treatment areas, lifting and transferring them according to positioning requirements. Secure patients into or onto therapy equipment. Administer active and passive manual therapeutic exercises, therapeutic massages, aquatic physical therapy, and heat, light, sound, and electrical modality treatments such as ultrasound. Communicate with or instruct caregivers and family members on patient therapeutic activities and treatment plans. Measure patients' ranges-of-joint motion, body parts, and vital signs to determine effects of treatments or for patient evaluations. Monitor operation of equipment and record use of equipment and administration of treatment. Fit patients for orthopedic braces, prostheses, and supportive devices such as crutches. Train patients in the use of orthopedic braces, prostheses, or supportive devices. Clean work areas and check and store equipment after treatments. Assist patients to dress, undress, or put on and remove supportive devices such as braces, splints, and slings. Attend or conduct continuing education courses, seminars, or in-service activities. Perform clerical duties such as taking inventory, ordering supplies, answering telephones, taking messages, and filling out forms. Prepare treatment areas and electrotherapy equipment for use by physiotherapists. Administer traction to relieve neck and back pain, using intermittent and static traction equipment. Perform postural drainage, percussions and vibrations, and teach deep breathing exercises to treat respiratory conditions.

GOE—Interest Area/Cluster: 08. Health Science. **Work Group:** 08.07. Medical Therapy. **Other Jobs in This Work Group:** Audiologists; Massage Therapists; Occupational Therapist Aides; Occupational Therapist Assistants; Occupational Therapists; Physical Therapist Aides; Physical Therapists; Radiation Therapists; Recreational Therapists; Respiratory Therapists; Respiratory Therapy Technicians; Speech-Language Pathologists.

Skill: Service Orientation.

Social-P

Education and Training Program: Physical Therapist Assistant. **Related Knowledge/Courses:** Therapy and Counseling; Medicine and Dentistry; Psychology; Biology; Customer and Personal Service; Education and Training.

Work Environment: Indoors; disease or infections; standing; walking and running; using hands on objects, tools, or controls; bending or twisting the body.

Physical Therapists

- ❋ Personality Code: SIR
- ❋ Education/Training Required: Master's degree
- ❋ Annual Earnings: $69,760
- ❋ Beginning Wage: $48,530
- ❋ Earnings Growth Potential: Low
- ❋ Growth: 27.1%
- ❋ Annual Job Openings: 12,072
- ❋ Self-Employed: 8.4%
- ❋ Part-Time: 22.7%

Assess, plan, organize, and participate in rehabilitative programs that improve mobility, relieve pain, increase strength, and decrease or prevent deformity of patients suffering from disease or injury. Perform and document initial exams, evaluating data to identify problems and determine diagnoses prior to interventions. Plan, prepare, and carry out individually designed programs of physical treatment to maintain, improve, or restore physical functioning, alleviate pain, and prevent physical dysfunction in patients. Record prognoses, treatments, responses, and progresses in patients' charts or enter information into computers. Identify and document goals, anticipated progresses, and plans for reevaluation. Evaluate effects of treatments at various stages and adjust treatments to achieve maximum benefits. Administer manual exercises, massages, or traction to help relieve pain, increase patient strength, or decrease or prevent deformity or crippling. Test and measure patients' strength, motor development and function, sensory perception, functional capacity, and respiratory

and circulatory efficiency and record data. Instruct patients and families in treatment procedures to be continued at home. Confer with patients, medical practitioners, and appropriate others to plan, implement, and assess intervention programs. Review physicians' referrals and patients' medical records to help determine diagnoses and physical therapy treatments required. Obtain patients' informed consent to proposed interventions. Discharge patients from physical therapy when goals or projected outcomes have been attained, and provide for appropriate follow-up care or referrals. Provide information to patients about proposed interventions, material risks, and expected benefits and any reasonable alternatives. Inform patients when diagnoses reveal findings outside the scope of physical therapy to treat and refer to appropriate practitioners. Direct, supervise, assess, and communicate with supportive personnel. Provide educational information about physical therapy and physical therapists, injury prevention, ergonomics, and ways to promote health. Refer clients to community resources and services. Administer treatment involving application of physical agents, using equipment, moist packs, ultraviolet and infrared lamps, and ultrasound machines.

GOE—Interest Area/Cluster: 08. Health Science. **Work Group:** 08.07. Medical Therapy. **Other Jobs in This Work Group:** Audiologists; Massage Therapists; Occupational Therapist Aides; Occupational Therapist Assistants; Occupational Therapists; Physical Therapist Aides; Physical Therapist Assistants; Radiation Therapists; Recreational Therapists; Respiratory Therapists; Respiratory Therapy Technicians; Speech-Language Pathologists.

Skills: Management of Personnel Resources; Systems Analysis; Social Perceptiveness; Complex Problem Solving; Systems Evaluation; Judgment and Decision Making; Monitoring; Speaking.

Education and Training Programs: Physical Therapy/Therapist; Kinesiotherapy/Kinesiotherapist. **Related Knowledge/Courses:** Therapy and Counseling; Medicine and Dentistry; Psychology; Education and Training; Biology; Customer and Personal Service.

Work Environment: Indoors; contaminants; disease or infections; standing; walking and running; bending or twisting the body.

Physician Assistants

- ❋ Personality Code: SIR
- ❋ Education/Training Required: Master's degree
- ❋ Annual Earnings: $78,450
- ❋ Beginning Wage: $46,750
- ❋ Earnings Growth Potential: High
- ❋ Growth: 27.0%
- ❋ Annual Job Openings: 7,147
- ❋ Self-Employed: 1.8%
- ❋ Part-Time: 15.6%

Under the supervision of physicians, provide health-care services typically performed by a physician. Conduct complete physicals, provide treatment, and counsel patients. May, in some cases, prescribe medication. Must graduate from an accredited educational program for physician assistants. Examine patients to obtain information about their physical conditions. Obtain, compile, and record patient medical data, including health history, progress notes, and results of physical examinations. Interpret diagnostic test results for deviations from normal. Make tentative diagnoses and decisions about management and treatment of patients. Prescribe therapy or medication with physician approval. Administer or order diagnostic tests, such as X-ray, electrocardiogram, and laboratory tests. Instruct and counsel patients about prescribed therapeutic regimens, normal growth and development, family planning, emotional problems of daily living, and health maintenance. Perform therapeutic procedures such as injections, immunizations, suturing and wound care, and infection management. Provide physicians with assistance during surgery or complicated medical procedures. Visit and observe patients on hospital rounds or house calls, updating charts, ordering therapy, and reporting back to physicians. Supervise and coordinate activities of technicians

and technical assistants. Order medical and laboratory supplies and equipment.

GOE—Interest Area/Cluster: 08. Health Science. **Work Group:** 08.02. Medicine and Surgery. **Other Jobs in This Work Group:** Anesthesiologists; Family and General Practitioners; Internists, General; Medical Assistants; Medical Transcriptionists; Obstetricians and Gynecologists; Pediatricians, General; Pharmacists; Pharmacy Aides; Pharmacy Technicians; Psychiatrists; Registered Nurses; Surgeons; Surgical Technologists.

Skills: Social Perceptiveness; Systems Analysis; Systems Evaluation; Persuasion; Complex Problem Solving; Reading Comprehension; Service Orientation; Speaking.

Education and Training Program: Physician Assistant. **Related Knowledge/Courses:** Medicine and Dentistry; Biology; Therapy and Counseling; Psychology; Chemistry; Sociology and Anthropology.

Work Environment: Indoors; disease or infections; standing.

Physics Teachers, Postsecondary

- ❋ Personality Code: SI
- ❋ Education/Training Required: Doctoral degree
- ❋ Annual Earnings: $70,090
- ❋ Beginning Wage: $40,580
- ❋ Earnings Growth Potential: High
- ❋ Growth: 22.9%
- ❋ Annual Job Openings: 2,155
- ❋ Self-Employed: 0.4%
- ❋ Part-Time: 27.8%

Teach courses pertaining to the laws of matter and energy. Includes both teachers primarily engaged in teaching and those who do a combination of both teaching and research. Evaluate and grade students' classwork, laboratory work, assignments, and papers. Prepare and deliver lectures to undergraduate and/or graduate students on topics such as quantum mechanics, particle physics, and optics. Compile, administer, and grade examinations or assign this work to others. Maintain student attendance records, grades, and other required records. Supervise students' laboratory work. Prepare course materials such as syllabi, homework assignments, and handouts. Maintain regularly scheduled office hours to advise and assist students. Supervise undergraduate and/or graduate teaching, internship, and research work. Keep abreast of developments in their field by reading current literature, talking with colleagues, and participating in professional conferences. Plan, evaluate, and revise curricula, course content, and course materials and methods of instruction. Initiate, facilitate, and moderate classroom discussions. Conduct research in a particular field of knowledge and publish findings in professional journals, books, and/or electronic media. Advise students on academic and vocational curricula and on career issues. Select and obtain materials and supplies such as textbooks and laboratory equipment. Collaborate with colleagues to address teaching and research issues. Participate in student recruitment, registration, and placement activities. Serve on academic or administrative committees that deal with institutional policies, departmental matters, and academic issues. Write grant proposals to procure external research funding. Perform administrative duties such as serving as department head. Act as advisers to student organizations. Provide professional consulting services to government and/or industry. Compile bibliographies of specialized materials for outside reading assignments. Participate in campus and community events.

GOE—Interest Area/Cluster: 05. Education and Training. **Work Group:** 05.03. Postsecondary and Adult Teaching and Instructing. **Other Jobs in This Work Group:** Adult Literacy, Remedial Education, and GED Teachers and Instructors; Agricultural Sciences Teachers, Postsecondary; Anthropology and Archeology Teachers, Postsecondary; Architecture Teachers, Postsecondary; Area, Ethnic, and Cultural Studies Teachers, Postsecondary; Art, Drama, and Music Teachers, Postsecondary; Atmospheric, Earth, Marine, and Space Sciences Teachers, Postsecondary; Biological Science Teachers, Postsecondary; Business Teachers, Postsecondary; Chemistry Teachers, Postsecondary; Communications Teachers, Postsecondary; Computer Science Teachers, Postsecondary; Criminal Justice and Law Enforcement Teachers, Postsecondary; Economics Teachers, Postsecondary; Education Teachers, Postsecondary; Engineering Teachers, Postsecondary; English Language and Literature Teachers, Postsecondary; Environmental Science Teachers, Postsecondary; Farm and Home Management Advisors; Foreign Language and Literature Teachers, Postsecondary; Forestry and Conservation Science Teachers, Postsecondary; Geography Teachers, Postsecondary; Graduate Teaching Assistants; Health Specialties Teachers, Postsecondary; History Teachers, Postsecondary; Home Economics Teachers, Postsecondary; Law Teachers, Postsecondary; Library Science Teachers, Postsecondary; Mathematical Science Teachers, Postsecondary; Nursing Instructors and Teachers, Postsecondary; Philosophy and Religion Teachers, Postsecondary; Political Science Teachers, Postsecondary; Psychology Teachers, Postsecondary; Recreation and Fitness Studies Teachers, Postsecondary; Self-Enrichment Education Teachers; Social Work Teachers, Postsecondary; Sociology Teachers, Postsecondary; Vocational Education Teachers, Postsecondary.

Skills: Science; Programming; Mathematics; Instructing; Writing; Reading Comprehension; Learning Strategies; Critical Thinking.

Education and Training Programs: Physics, General; Atomic/Molecular Physics; Elementary Particle Physics; Plasma and High-Temperature Physics; Nuclear Physics; Optics/Optical Sciences; Solid State and Low-Temperature Physics; Acoustics; Theoretical and Mathematical Physics; Physics, Other. **Related Knowledge/Courses:** Physics; Mathematics; Chemistry; Engineering and Technology; Education and Training; Computers and Electronics.

Work Environment: Indoors; sitting.

Political Science Teachers, Postsecondary

* Personality Code: SEA
* Education/Training Required: Doctoral degree
* Annual Earnings: $63,100
* Beginning Wage: $35,600
* Earnings Growth Potential: High
* Growth: 22.9%
* Annual Job Openings: 2,435
* Self-Employed: 0.4%
* Part-Time: 27.8%

Teach courses in political science, international affairs, and international relations. Initiate, facilitate, and moderate classroom discussions. Prepare and deliver lectures to undergraduate or graduate students on topics such as classical political thought, international relations, and democracy and citizenship. Evaluate and grade students' classwork, assignments, and papers. Compile, administer, and grade examinations or assign this work to others. Prepare course materials such as syllabi, homework assignments, and handouts. Keep abreast of developments in their field by reading current literature, talking with colleagues, and participating in professional conferences. Plan, evaluate, and revise curricula, course content, and course materials and methods of instruction. Maintain student attendance records, grades, and other required records. Maintain regularly scheduled office hours in order to advise and assist students. Advise students on academic and vocational curricula and on career issues. Select and obtain materials and supplies such as textbooks. Conduct research in a particular field of knowledge and publish findings in professional journals, books, and electronic media. Supervise undergraduate and graduate teaching, internship, and research work. Collaborate with colleagues to address teaching and research issues. Serve on academic or administrative committees that deal with institutional policies, departmental matters, and academic issues. Participate in student recruitment, registration, and placement activities. Participate in campus and community events. Compile bibliographies of specialized materials for outside reading assignments. Act as advisers to student organizations. Perform administrative duties such as serving as department head. Write grant proposals to procure external research funding. Provide professional consulting services to government and industry.

GOE—Interest Area/Cluster: 05. Education and Training. **Work Group:** 05.03. Postsecondary and Adult Teaching and Instructing. **Other Jobs in This Work Group:** Adult Literacy, Remedial Education, and GED Teachers and Instructors; Agricultural Sciences Teachers, Postsecondary; Anthropology and Archeology Teachers, Postsecondary; Architecture Teachers, Postsecondary; Area, Ethnic, and Cultural Studies Teachers, Postsecondary; Art, Drama, and Music Teachers, Postsecondary; Atmospheric, Earth, Marine, and Space Sciences Teachers, Postsecondary; Biological Science Teachers, Postsecondary; Business Teachers, Postsecondary; Chemistry Teachers, Postsecondary; Communications Teachers, Postsecondary; Computer Science Teachers, Postsecondary; Criminal Justice and Law Enforcement Teachers, Postsecondary; Economics Teachers, Postsecondary; Education Teachers, Postsecondary; Engineering Teachers, Postsecondary; English Language and Literature Teachers, Postsecondary; Environmental Science Teachers, Postsecondary; Farm and Home Management Advisors; Foreign Language and Literature Teachers, Postsecondary; Forestry and Conservation Science Teachers, Postsecondary; Geography Teachers, Postsecondary; Graduate Teaching Assistants; Health Specialties Teachers, Postsecondary; History Teachers, Postsecondary; Home Economics Teachers, Postsecondary; Law Teachers, Postsecondary; Library Science Teachers, Postsecondary; Mathematical Science Teachers, Postsecondary; Nursing Instructors and Teachers, Postsecondary; Philosophy and Religion Teachers, Postsecondary; Physics Teachers, Postsecondary; Psychology Teachers, Postsecondary; Recreation and Fitness Studies Teachers, Postsecondary; Self-Enrichment Education Teachers; Social Work Teachers, Postsecondary; Sociology Teachers, Postsecondary; Vocational Education Teachers, Postsecondary.

Social–P

Skills: Writing; Instructing; Reading Comprehension; Learning Strategies; Persuasion; Critical Thinking; Speaking; Active Learning.

Education and Training Programs: Social Science Teacher Education; Political Science and Government, General; American Government and Politics (United States); Political Science and Government, Other. **Related Knowledge/Courses:** History and Archeology; Philosophy and Theology; Sociology and Anthropology; Geography; Law and Government; English Language.

Work Environment: Indoors; sitting.

Preschool Teachers, Except Special Education

- ❋ Personality Code: SA
- ❋ Education/Training Required: Postsecondary vocational training
- ❋ Annual Earnings: $23,130
- ❋ Beginning Wage: $15,380
- ❋ Earnings Growth Potential: Low
- ❋ Growth: 26.3%
- ❋ Annual Job Openings: 78,172
- ❋ Self-Employed: 1.1%
- ❋ Part-Time: 25.1%

Instruct children (normally up to 5 years of age) in activities designed to promote social, physical, and intellectual growth needed for primary school in preschool, day care center, or other child development facility. May be required to hold state certification. Provide a variety of materials and resources for children to explore, manipulate, and use, both in learning activities and in imaginative play. Attend to children's basic needs by feeding them, dressing them, and changing their diapers. Establish and enforce rules for behavior and procedures for maintaining order. Read books to entire classes or to small groups. Teach basic skills such as color, shape, number, and letter recognition; personal hygiene; and social skills. Organize and lead activities designed to promote physical, mental, and social development, such as games, arts and crafts, music, storytelling, and field trips. Observe and evaluate children's performance, behavior, social development, and physical health. Meet with parents and guardians to discuss their children's progress and needs, determine their priorities for their children, and suggest ways that they can promote learning and development. Identify children showing signs of emotional, developmental, or health-related problems and discuss them with supervisors, parents or guardians, and child development specialists. Enforce all administration policies and rules governing students. Prepare materials and classrooms for class activities. Serve meals and snacks in accordance with nutritional guidelines. Teach proper eating habits and personal hygiene. Assimilate arriving children to the school environment by greeting them, helping them remove outerwear, and selecting activities of interest to them. Adapt teaching methods and instructional materials to meet students' varying needs and interests. Establish clear objectives for all lessons, units, and projects and communicate those objectives to children. Demonstrate activities to children. Arrange indoor and outdoor space to facilitate creative play, motor-skill activities, and safety. Plan and conduct activities for a balanced program of instruction, demonstration, and work time that provides students with opportunities to observe, question, and investigate. Maintain accurate and complete student records as required by laws, district policies, and administrative regulations.

GOE—Interest Area/Cluster: 05. Education and Training. **Work Group:** 05.02. Preschool, Elementary, and Secondary Teaching and Instructing. **Other Jobs in This Work Group:** Elementary School Teachers, Except Special Education; Kindergarten Teachers, Except Special Education; Middle School Teachers, Except Special and Vocational Education; Secondary School Teachers, Except Special and Vocational Education; Special Education Teachers, Middle School; Special Education Teachers, Preschool, Kindergarten, and Elementary School; Special Education Teachers, Secondary School; Teacher Assistants; Vocational Education Teachers,

Middle School; Vocational Education Teachers, Secondary School.

Skills: Learning Strategies; Social Perceptiveness; Writing; Negotiation.

Education and Training Programs: Montessori Teacher Education; Early Childhood Education and Teaching; Child Care and Support Services Management. **Related Knowledge/Courses:** Philosophy and Theology; Sociology and Anthropology; Psychology; Customer and Personal Service; Education and Training.

Work Environment: Indoors; standing; walking and running; bending or twisting the body.

Psychology Teachers, Postsecondary

- ❋ Personality Code: SIA
- ❋ Education/Training Required: Doctoral degree
- ❋ Annual Earnings: $60,610
- ❋ Beginning Wage: $34,030
- ❋ Earnings Growth Potential: High
- ❋ Growth: 22.9%
- ❋ Annual Job Openings: 5,261
- ❋ Self-Employed: 0.4%
- ❋ Part-Time: 27.8%

Teach courses in psychology, such as child, clinical, and developmental psychology, and psychological counseling. Prepare and deliver lectures to undergraduate and/or graduate students on topics such as abnormal psychology, cognitive processes, and work motivation. Evaluate and grade students' classwork, laboratory work, assignments, and papers. Initiate, facilitate, and moderate classroom discussions. Compile, administer, and grade examinations or assign this work to others. Keep abreast of developments in their field by reading current literature, talking with colleagues, and participating in professional conferences. Prepare course materials such as syllabi, homework assignments, and handouts. Plan, evaluate, and revise curricula, course content, and course materials and methods of instruction. Maintain student attendance records, grades, and other required records. Supervise undergraduate and/or graduate teaching, internship, and research work. Maintain regularly scheduled office hours to advise and assist students. Conduct research in a particular field of knowledge and publish findings in professional journals, books, and electronic media. Advise students on academic and vocational curricula and on career issues. Select and obtain materials and supplies such as textbooks. Collaborate with colleagues to address teaching and research issues. Serve on academic or administrative committees that deal with institutional policies, departmental matters, and academic issues. Compile bibliographies of specialized materials for outside reading assignments. Participate in student recruitment, registration, and placement activities. Supervise students' laboratory work. Perform administrative duties such as serving as department head. Act as advisers to student organizations. Write grant proposals to procure external research funding. Participate in campus and community events. Provide professional consulting services to government and industry.

GOE—Interest Area/Cluster: 05. Education and Training. **Work Group:** 05.03. Postsecondary and Adult Teaching and Instructing. **Other Jobs in This Work Group:** Adult Literacy, Remedial Education, and GED Teachers and Instructors; Agricultural Sciences Teachers, Postsecondary; Anthropology and Archeology Teachers, Postsecondary; Architecture Teachers, Postsecondary; Area, Ethnic, and Cultural Studies Teachers, Postsecondary; Art, Drama, and Music Teachers, Postsecondary; Atmospheric, Earth, Marine, and Space Sciences Teachers, Postsecondary; Biological Science Teachers, Postsecondary; Business Teachers, Postsecondary; Chemistry Teachers, Postsecondary; Communications Teachers, Postsecondary; Computer Science Teachers, Postsecondary; Criminal Justice and Law Enforcement Teachers, Postsecondary; Economics Teachers, Postsecondary; Education Teachers, Postsecondary; Engineering Teachers, Postsecondary; English Language and Literature Teachers, Postsecondary; Environmental

Social-P

Science Teachers, Postsecondary; Farm and Home Management Advisors; Foreign Language and Literature Teachers, Postsecondary; Forestry and Conservation Science Teachers, Postsecondary; Geography Teachers, Postsecondary; Graduate Teaching Assistants; Health Specialties Teachers, Postsecondary; History Teachers, Postsecondary; Home Economics Teachers, Postsecondary; Law Teachers, Postsecondary; Library Science Teachers, Postsecondary; Mathematical Science Teachers, Postsecondary; Nursing Instructors and Teachers, Postsecondary; Philosophy and Religion Teachers, Postsecondary; Physics Teachers, Postsecondary; Political Science Teachers, Postsecondary; Recreation and Fitness Studies Teachers, Postsecondary; Self-Enrichment Education Teachers; Social Work Teachers, Postsecondary; Sociology Teachers, Postsecondary; Vocational Education Teachers, Postsecondary.

Skills: Science; Learning Strategies; Instructing; Social Perceptiveness; Writing; Reading Comprehension; Critical Thinking; Active Learning.

Education and Training Programs: Social Science Teacher Education; Psychology Teacher Education; Psychology, General; Clinical Psychology; Cognitive Psychology and Psycholinguistics; Community Psychology; Comparative Psychology; Counseling Psychology; Developmental and Child Psychology; Experimental Psychology; Industrial and Organizational Psychology; Personality Psychology; Physiological Psychology/Psychobiology; others. **Related Knowledge/Courses:** Therapy and Counseling; Psychology; Sociology and Anthropology; Philosophy and Theology; Education and Training; English Language.

Work Environment: Indoors; sitting.

Radiation Therapists

* Personality Code: SRC
* Education/Training Required: Associate degree
* Annual Earnings: $70,010
* Beginning Wage: $46,580
* Earnings Growth Potential: Low
* Growth: 24.8%
* Annual Job Openings: 1,461
* Self-Employed: 0.0%
* Part-Time: 10.3%

Provide radiation therapy to patients as prescribed by radiologists according to established practices and standards. Duties may include reviewing prescriptions and diagnoses; acting as liaisons with physicians and supportive care personnel; preparing equipment such as immobilization, treatment, and protection devices; and maintaining records, reports, and files. May assist in dosimetry procedures and tumor localization. Position patients for treatment with accuracy according to prescription. Administer prescribed doses of radiation to specific body parts, using radiation therapy equipment according to established practices and standards. Check radiation therapy equipment to ensure proper operation. Review prescriptions, diagnoses, patient charts, and identification. Follow principles of radiation protection for patients, radiation therapists, and others. Maintain records, reports, and files as required, including such information as radiation dosages, equipment settings, and patients' reactions. Conduct most treatment sessions independently, in accordance with long-term treatment plans and under general direction of patients' physicians. Enter data into computers and set controls to operate and adjust equipment and regulate dosages. Observe and reassure patients during treatments and report unusual reactions to physicians or turn equipment off if unexpected adverse reactions occur. Calculate actual treatment dosages delivered during each session. Check for side effects such as skin irritation, nausea, and hair loss to assess patients' reaction to treatment. Prepare and construct equipment such as immobilization, treatment, and protection devices. Educate, prepare, and reassure patients and their families by answering questions, providing physical assistance, and reinforcing physicians' advice regarding treatment reactions and post-treatment care. Provide assistance to other health care personnel during dosimetry procedures and tumor localization. Help physicians, radiation oncologists, and clinical physicists to prepare physical and technical aspects of radiation treatment plans, using information about patient conditions and anatomies. Photograph treated areas of patients and process film. Act as liaisons with medical physicists and supportive care personnel. Train and supervise student or subordinate radiotherapy technologists. Implement appropriate follow-up care plans. Assist in the preparation of sealed radioactive materials such as cobalt, radium, cesium, and isotopes for use in radiation treatments. Store, sterilize, or prepare the special applicators containing the radioactive substances implanted by physicians.

GOE—Interest Area/Cluster: 08. Health Science. **Work Group:** 08.07. Medical Therapy. **Other Jobs in This Work Group:** Audiologists; Massage Therapists; Occupational Therapist Aides; Occupational Therapist Assistants; Occupational Therapists; Physical Therapist Aides; Physical Therapist Assistants; Physical Therapists; Recreational Therapists; Respiratory Therapists; Respiratory Therapy Technicians; Speech-Language Pathologists.

Skills: Operation Monitoring; Operation and Control; Quality Control Analysis.

Education and Training Program: Medical Radiologic Technology/Science—Radiation Therapist. **Related Knowledge/Courses:** Medicine and Dentistry; Biology; Physics; Psychology; Philosophy and Theology; Therapy and Counseling.

Work Environment: Indoors; disease or infections; standing; walking and running; using hands on objects, tools, or controls; repetitive motions.

Recreation and Fitness Studies Teachers, Postsecondary

* Personality Code: S
* Education/Training Required: Doctoral degree
* Annual Earnings: $52,170
* Beginning Wage: $26,790
* Earnings Growth Potential: High
* Growth: 22.9%
* Annual Job Openings: 3,010
* Self-Employed: 0.4%
* Part-Time: 27.8%

Teach courses pertaining to recreation, leisure, and fitness studies, including exercise physiology and facilities management. Evaluate and grade students' classwork, assignments, and papers. Maintain student attendance records, grades, and other required records. Prepare and deliver lectures to undergraduate and graduate students on topics such as anatomy, therapeutic recreation, and conditioning theory. Prepare course materials such as syllabi, homework assignments, and handouts. Maintain regularly scheduled office hours to advise and assist students. Compile, administer, and grade examinations or assign this work to others. Plan, evaluate, and revise curricula, course content, and course materials and methods of instruction. Initiate, facilitate, and moderate classroom discussions. Keep abreast of developments in their field by reading current literature, talking with colleagues, and participating in professional conferences. Advise students on academic and vocational curricula and on career issues. Participate in student recruitment, registration, and placement activities. Collaborate with colleagues to address teaching and research issues. Select and obtain materials and supplies such as textbooks. Participate in campus and community events. Serve on academic or administrative committees that deal with institutional policies, departmental matters, and academic issues. Compile bibliographies of specialized materials for outside reading assignments. Supervise undergraduate or graduate teaching, internship, and

Social-R

research work. Perform administrative duties such as serving as department heads. Prepare students to act as sports coaches. Conduct research in a particular field of knowledge and publish findings in professional journals, books, or electronic media. Act as advisers to student organizations. Write grant proposals to procure external research funding. Provide professional consulting services to government or industry.

GOE—Interest Area/Cluster: 05. Education and Training. **Work Group:** 05.03. Postsecondary and Adult Teaching and Instructing. **Other Jobs in This Work Group:** Adult Literacy, Remedial Education, and GED Teachers and Instructors; Agricultural Sciences Teachers, Postsecondary; Anthropology and Archeology Teachers, Postsecondary; Architecture Teachers, Postsecondary; Area, Ethnic, and Cultural Studies Teachers, Postsecondary; Art, Drama, and Music Teachers, Postsecondary; Atmospheric, Earth, Marine, and Space Sciences Teachers, Postsecondary; Biological Science Teachers, Postsecondary; Business Teachers, Postsecondary; Chemistry Teachers, Postsecondary; Communications Teachers, Postsecondary; Computer Science Teachers, Postsecondary; Criminal Justice and Law Enforcement Teachers, Postsecondary; Economics Teachers, Postsecondary; Education Teachers, Postsecondary; Engineering Teachers, Postsecondary; English Language and Literature Teachers, Postsecondary; Environmental Science Teachers, Postsecondary; Farm and Home Management Advisors; Foreign Language and Literature Teachers, Postsecondary; Forestry and Conservation Science Teachers, Postsecondary; Geography Teachers, Postsecondary; Graduate Teaching Assistants; Health Specialties Teachers, Postsecondary; History Teachers, Postsecondary; Home Economics Teachers, Postsecondary; Law Teachers, Postsecondary; Library Science Teachers, Postsecondary; Mathematical Science Teachers, Postsecondary; Nursing Instructors and Teachers, Postsecondary; Philosophy and Religion Teachers, Postsecondary; Physics Teachers, Postsecondary; Political Science Teachers, Postsecondary; Psychology Teachers, Postsecondary; Self-Enrichment Education Teachers; Social Work Teachers, Postsecondary; Sociology Teachers,

Postsecondary; Vocational Education Teachers, Postsecondary.

Skills: Instructing; Learning Strategies; Science; Social Perceptiveness; Persuasion; Time Management; Management of Financial Resources; Writing.

Education and Training Programs: Parks, Recreation and Leisure Studies; Health and Physical Education, General; Sport and Fitness Administration/Management. **Related Knowledge/Courses:** Education and Training; Philosophy and Theology; Psychology; Therapy and Counseling; Medicine and Dentistry; Sociology and Anthropology.

Work Environment: More often indoors than outdoors; standing.

Registered Nurses

- ❋ Personality Code: SIC
- ❋ Education/Training Required: Associate degree
- ❋ Annual Earnings: $60,010
- ❋ Beginning Wage: $42,020
- ❋ Earnings Growth Potential: Low
- ❋ Growth: 23.5%
- ❋ Annual Job Openings: 233,499
- ❋ Self-Employed: 0.8%
- ❋ Part-Time: 21.8%

Assess patient health problems and needs, develop and implement nursing care plans, and maintain medical records. Administer nursing care to ill, injured, convalescent, or disabled patients. May advise patients on health maintenance and disease prevention or provide case management. Licensing or registration required. Includes advance practice nurses such as nurse practitioners, clinical nurse specialists, certified nurse midwives, and certified registered nurse anesthetists. Advanced practice nursing is practiced by RNs who have specialized formal, post-basic education and who function in highly autonomous and specialized roles. Monitor, record, and report symptoms and changes in patients' conditions. Maintain accurate, detailed reports and records. Record patients' medical information and vital signs. Order, interpret, and evaluate diagnostic tests to identify and assess patients' conditions. Modify patient treatment plans as indicated by patients' responses and conditions. Direct and supervise less skilled nursing or healthcare personnel or supervise particular units. Consult and coordinate with health care team members to assess, plan, implement and evaluate patient care plans. Monitor all aspects of patient care, including diet and physical activity. Instruct individuals, families, and other groups on topics such as health education, disease prevention, and childbirth, and develop health improvement programs. Prepare patients for, and assist with, examinations and treatments. Assess the needs of individuals, families, or communities, including assessment of individuals' home or work environments to identify potential health or safety problems. Provide health care, first aid, immunizations, and assistance in convalescence and rehabilitation in locations such as schools, hospitals, and industry. Prepare rooms, sterile instruments, equipment, and supplies, and ensure that stock of supplies is maintained. Inform physicians of patients' conditions during anesthesia. Administer local, inhalation, intravenous, and other anesthetics. Perform physical examinations, make tentative diagnoses, and treat patients en route to hospitals or at disaster site triage centers. Observe nurses and visit patients to ensure proper nursing care. Conduct specified laboratory tests. Direct and coordinate infection control programs, advising and consulting with specified personnel about necessary precautions. Prescribe or recommend drugs, medical devices, or other forms of treatment such as physical therapy, inhalation therapy, or related therapeutic procedures. Perform administrative and managerial functions such as taking responsibility for a unit's staff, budget, planning, and long-range goals. Hand items to surgeons during operations.

GOE—Interest Area/Cluster: 08. Health Science. **Work Group:** 08.02. Medicine and Surgery. **Other Jobs in This Work Group:** Anesthesiologists; Family and General Practitioners; Internists, General;

Medical Assistants; Medical Transcriptionists; Obstetricians and Gynecologists; Pediatricians, General; Pharmacists; Pharmacy Aides; Pharmacy Technicians; Physician Assistants; Psychiatrists; Surgeons; Surgical Technologists.

Skills: Negotiation; Systems Analysis; Operation Monitoring; Service Orientation; Systems Evaluation.

Education and Training Programs: Nursing—Registered Nurse Training (RN, ASN, BSN, MSN); Adult Health Nurse/Nursing; Nurse Anesthetist; Family Practice Nurse/Nurse Practitioner; Maternal/Child Health and Neonatal Nurse/Nursing; Nurse Midwife/Nursing Midwifery; Nursing Science (MS, PhD); Pediatric Nurse/Nursing; Psychiatric/Mental Health Nurse/Nursing; Public Health/Community Nurse/Nursing; others. **Related Knowledge/Courses:** Medicine and Dentistry; Psychology; Therapy and Counseling; Biology; Philosophy and Theology; Sociology and Anthropology.

Work Environment: Indoors; noisy; contaminants; disease or infections; standing; using hands on objects, tools, or controls.

Rehabilitation Counselors

- ❋ Personality Code: SI
- ❋ Education/Training Required: Master's degree
- ❋ Annual Earnings: $29,630
- ❋ Beginning Wage: $19,610
- ❋ Earnings Growth Potential: Low
- ❋ Growth: 23.0%
- ❋ Annual Job Openings: 32,081
- ❋ Self-Employed: 5.9%
- ❋ Part-Time: 15.4%

Counsel individuals to maximize the independence and employability of persons coping with personal, social, and vocational difficulties that result from birth defects, illness, disease, accidents, or the stress of daily life. Coordinate

Social-R

activities for residents of care and treatment facilities. **Assess client needs and design and implement rehabilitation programs that may include personal and vocational counseling, training, and job placement.** Monitor and record clients' progress in order to ensure that goals and objectives are met. Confer with clients to discuss their options and goals so that rehabilitation programs and plans for accessing needed services can be developed. Prepare and maintain records and case files, including documentation such as clients' personal and eligibility information, services provided, narratives of client contacts, and relevant correspondence. Arrange for physical, mental, academic, vocational, and other evaluations to obtain information for assessing clients' needs and developing rehabilitation plans. Analyze information from interviews, educational and medical records, consultation with other professionals, and diagnostic evaluations to assess clients' abilities, needs, and eligibility for services. Develop rehabilitation plans that fit clients' aptitudes, education levels, physical abilities, and career goals. Maintain close contact with clients during job training and placements to resolve problems and evaluate placement adequacy. Locate barriers to client employment, such as inaccessible work sites, inflexible schedules, and transportation problems, and work with clients to develop strategies for overcoming these barriers. Develop and maintain relationships with community referral sources such as schools and community groups. Arrange for on-site job coaching or assistive devices such as specially equipped wheelchairs in order to help clients adapt to work or school environments. Confer with physicians, psychologists, occupational therapists, and other professionals to develop and implement client rehabilitation programs. Develop diagnostic procedures for determining clients' needs. Participate in job development and placement programs, contacting prospective employers, placing clients in jobs, and evaluating the success of placements. Collaborate with clients' families to implement rehabilitation plans that include behavioral, residential, social, and/or employment goals. Collaborate with community agencies to establish facilities and programs to assist persons with disabilities.

GOE—Interest Area/Cluster: 10. Human Service. **Work Group:** 10.01. Counseling and Social Work. **Other Jobs in This Work Group:** Child, Family, and School Social Workers; Clinical Psychologists; Clinical, Counseling, and School Psychologists; Counseling Psychologists; Marriage and Family Therapists; Medical and Public Health Social Workers; Mental Health and Substance Abuse Social Workers; Mental Health Counselors; Probation Officers and Correctional Treatment Specialists; Residential Advisors; Social and Human Service Assistants; Substance Abuse and Behavioral Disorder Counselors.

Skills: Management of Financial Resources; Social Perceptiveness; Writing; Service Orientation; Monitoring; Coordination; Speaking; Judgment and Decision Making.

Education and Training Programs: Vocational Rehabilitation Counseling/Counselor; Assistive/Augmentative Technology and Rehabiliation Engineering. **Related Knowledge/Courses:** Therapy and Counseling; Psychology; Philosophy and Theology; Education and Training; Personnel and Human Resources; Sociology and Anthropology.

Work Environment: More often indoors than outdoors; sitting; walking and running.

Secondary School Teachers, Except Special and Vocational Education

- ❋ Personality Code: SAE
- ❋ Education/Training Required: Bachelor's degree
- ❋ Annual Earnings: $49,420
- ❋ Beginning Wage: $32,920
- ❋ Earnings Growth Potential: Low
- ❋ Growth: 5.6%
- ❋ Annual Job Openings: 93,166
- ❋ Self-Employed: 0.0%
- ❋ Part-Time: 7.8%

Instruct students in secondary public or private schools in one or more subjects at the secondary

level, such as English, mathematics, or social studies. May be designated according to subject matter specialty, such as typing instructors, commercial teachers, or English teachers. Establish and enforce rules for behavior and procedures for maintaining order among the students for whom they are responsible. Instruct through lectures, discussions, and demonstrations in one or more subjects such as English, mathematics, or social studies. Establish clear objectives for all lessons, units, and projects and communicate those objectives to students. Prepare, administer, and grade tests and assignments to evaluate students' progress. Prepare materials and classrooms for class activities. Adapt teaching methods and instructional materials to meet students' varying needs and interests. Assign and grade classwork and homework. Maintain accurate and complete student records as required by laws, district policies, and administrative regulations. Enforce all administration policies and rules governing students. Observe and evaluate students' performance, behavior, social development, and physical health. Plan and conduct activities for a balanced program of instruction, demonstration, and work time that provides students with opportunities to observe, question, and investigate. Prepare students for later grades by encouraging them to explore learning opportunities and to persevere with challenging tasks. Guide and counsel students with adjustment and/or academic problems or special academic interests. Instruct and monitor students in the use and care of equipment and materials to prevent injuries and damage. Prepare for assigned classes and show written evidence of preparation upon request of immediate supervisors. Meet with parents and guardians to discuss their children's progress and to determine their priorities for their children and their resource needs. Confer with parents or guardians, other teachers, counselors, and administrators in order to resolve students' behavioral and academic problems. Use computers, audiovisual aids, and other equipment and materials to supplement presentations. Prepare objectives and outlines for courses of study, following curriculum guidelines or requirements of states and schools. Meet with other professionals to discuss individual students' needs and progress.

GOE—Interest Area/Cluster: 05. Education and Training. **Work Group:** 05.02. Preschool, Elementary, and Secondary Teaching and Instructing. **Other Jobs in This Work Group:** Elementary School Teachers, Except Special Education; Kindergarten Teachers, Except Special Education; Middle School Teachers, Except Special and Vocational Education; Preschool Teachers, Except Special Education; Special Education Teachers, Middle School; Special Education Teachers, Preschool, Kindergarten, and Elementary School; Special Education Teachers, Secondary School; Teacher Assistants; Vocational Education Teachers, Middle School; Vocational Education Teachers, Secondary School.

Skills: Learning Strategies; Social Perceptiveness; Persuasion; Monitoring; Instructing; Time Management; Negotiation; Service Orientation.

Education and Training Programs: Junior High/Intermediate/Middle School Education and Teaching; Secondary Education and Teaching; Teacher Education, Multiple Levels; Waldorf/Steiner Teacher Education; Agricultural Teacher Education; Art Teacher Education; Business Teacher Education; Driver and Safety Teacher Education; English/Language Arts Teacher Education; Foreign Language Teacher Education; Health Teacher Education; others. **Related Knowledge/Courses:** History and Archeology; Philosophy and Theology; Sociology and Anthropology; Education and Training; Geography; Therapy and Counseling.

Work Environment: Indoors; noisy; standing.

Self-Enrichment Education Teachers

- ❋ Personality Code: SAE
- ❋ Education/Training Required: Work experience in a related occupation
- ❋ Annual Earnings: $34,580
- ❋ Beginning Wage: $18,530
- ❋ Earnings Growth Potential: High
- ❋ Growth: 23.1%
- ❋ Annual Job Openings: 64,449
- ❋ Self-Employed: 21.5%
- ❋ Part-Time: 41.3%

Teach or instruct courses other than those that normally lead to an occupational objective or degree. Courses may include self-improvement, nonvocational, and nonacademic subjects. Teaching may or may not take place in a traditional educational institution. Adapt teaching methods and instructional materials to meet students' varying needs and interests. Conduct classes, workshops, and demonstrations and provide individual instruction to teach topics and skills such as cooking, dancing, writing, physical fitness, photography, personal finance, and flying. Monitor students' performance to make suggestions for improvement and to ensure that they satisfy course standards, training requirements, and objectives. Observe students to determine qualifications, limitations, abilities, interests, and other individual characteristics. Instruct students individually and in groups, using various teaching methods such as lectures, discussions, and demonstrations. Establish clear objectives for all lessons, units, and projects and communicate those objectives to students. Instruct and monitor students in use and care of equipment and materials to prevent injury and damage. Prepare students for further development by encouraging them to explore learning opportunities and to persevere with challenging tasks. Prepare materials and classrooms for class activities. Enforce policies and rules governing students. Plan and conduct activities for a balanced program of instruction, demonstration, and work time that provides students with opportunities to observe, question, and investigate. Prepare instructional program objectives, outlines, and lesson plans. Maintain accurate and complete student records as required by administrative policy. Participate in publicity planning and student recruitment. Plan and supervise class projects, field trips, visits by guest speakers, contests, or other experiential activities and guide students in learning from those activities. Attend professional meetings, conferences, and workshops in order to maintain and improve professional competence. Meet with other instructors to discuss individual students and their progress. Confer with other teachers and professionals to plan and schedule lessons promoting learning and development. Attend staff meetings and serve on committees as required. Prepare and administer written, oral, and performance tests and issue grades in accordance with performance.

GOE—Interest Area/Cluster: 05. Education and Training. **Work Group:** 05.03. Postsecondary and Adult Teaching and Instructing. **Other Jobs in This Work Group:** Adult Literacy, Remedial Education, and GED Teachers and Instructors; Agricultural Sciences Teachers, Postsecondary; Anthropology and Archeology Teachers, Postsecondary; Architecture Teachers, Postsecondary; Area, Ethnic, and Cultural Studies Teachers, Postsecondary; Art, Drama, and Music Teachers, Postsecondary; Atmospheric, Earth, Marine, and Space Sciences Teachers, Postsecondary; Biological Science Teachers, Postsecondary; Business Teachers, Postsecondary; Chemistry Teachers, Postsecondary; Communications Teachers, Postsecondary; Computer Science Teachers, Postsecondary; Criminal Justice and Law Enforcement Teachers, Postsecondary; Economics Teachers, Postsecondary; Education Teachers, Postsecondary; Engineering Teachers, Postsecondary; English Language and Literature Teachers, Postsecondary; Environmental Science Teachers, Postsecondary; Farm and Home Management Advisors; Foreign Language and Literature Teachers, Postsecondary; Forestry and Conservation Science Teachers, Postsecondary; Geography Teachers, Postsecondary; Graduate Teaching Assistants; Health Specialties Teachers, Postsecondary; History Teachers, Postsecondary; Home Economics

Teachers, Postsecondary; Law Teachers, Postsecondary; Library Science Teachers, Postsecondary; Mathematical Science Teachers, Postsecondary; Nursing Instructors and Teachers, Postsecondary; Philosophy and Religion Teachers, Postsecondary; Physics Teachers, Postsecondary; Political Science Teachers, Postsecondary; Psychology Teachers, Postsecondary; Recreation and Fitness Studies Teachers, Postsecondary; Social Work Teachers, Postsecondary; Sociology Teachers, Postsecondary; Vocational Education Teachers, Postsecondary.

Skills: Instructing; Learning Strategies; Social Perceptiveness; Service Orientation; Monitoring; Speaking; Persuasion; Time Management.

Education and Training Program: Adult and Continuing Education and Teaching. **Related Knowledge/Courses:** Fine Arts; Education and Training; Psychology; Customer and Personal Service; Sales and Marketing; Administration and Management.

Work Environment: Indoors; standing.

Sociology Teachers, Postsecondary

- ❋ Personality Code: SIA
- ❋ Education/Training Required: Doctoral degree
- ❋ Annual Earnings: $58,160
- ❋ Beginning Wage: $31,310
- ❋ Earnings Growth Potential: High
- ❋ Growth: 22.9%
- ❋ Annual Job Openings: 2,774
- ❋ Self-Employed: 0.4%
- ❋ Part-Time: 27.8%

Teach courses in sociology. Evaluate and grade students' classwork, assignments, and papers. Prepare and deliver lectures to undergraduate and graduate students on topics such as race and ethnic relations, measurement and data collection, and workplace social relations. Initiate, facilitate, and moderate classroom discussions. Prepare course materials such as syllabi, homework assignments, and handouts.

Compile, administer, and grade examinations or assign this work to others. Keep abreast of developments in their field by reading current literature, talking with colleagues, and participating in professional conferences. Maintain student attendance records, grades, and other required records. Maintain regularly scheduled office hours in order to advise and assist students. Plan, evaluate, and revise curricula, course content, and course materials and methods of instruction. Advise students on academic and vocational curricula and on career issues. Collaborate with colleagues to address teaching and research issues. Conduct research in a particular field of knowledge and publish findings in professional journals, books, or electronic media. Select and obtain materials and supplies such as textbooks and laboratory equipment. Supervise undergraduate and graduate teaching, internship, and research work. Serve on academic or administrative committees that deal with institutional policies, departmental matters, and academic issues. Participate in student recruitment, registration, and placement activities. Perform administrative duties such as serving as department head. Supervise students' laboratory work and fieldwork. Write grant proposals to procure external research funding. Act as advisers to student organizations. Compile bibliographies of specialized materials for outside reading assignments. Participate in campus and community events. Provide professional consulting services to government and industry.

GOE—Interest Area/Cluster: 05. Education and Training. **Work Group:** 05.03. Postsecondary and Adult Teaching and Instructing. **Other Jobs in This Work Group:** Adult Literacy, Remedial Education, and GED Teachers and Instructors; Agricultural Sciences Teachers, Postsecondary; Anthropology and Archeology Teachers, Postsecondary; Architecture Teachers, Postsecondary; Area, Ethnic, and Cultural Studies Teachers, Postsecondary; Art, Drama, and Music Teachers, Postsecondary; Atmospheric, Earth, Marine, and Space Sciences Teachers, Postsecondary; Biological Science Teachers, Postsecondary; Business Teachers, Postsecondary; Chemistry Teachers, Postsecondary; Communications Teachers, Postsecondary; Computer Science Teachers, Postsecondary;

Criminal Justice and Law Enforcement Teachers, Postsecondary; Economics Teachers, Postsecondary; Education Teachers, Postsecondary; Engineering Teachers, Postsecondary; English Language and Literature Teachers, Postsecondary; Environmental Science Teachers, Postsecondary; Farm and Home Management Advisors; Foreign Language and Literature Teachers, Postsecondary; Forestry and Conservation Science Teachers, Postsecondary; Geography Teachers, Postsecondary; Graduate Teaching Assistants; Health Specialties Teachers, Postsecondary; History Teachers, Postsecondary; Home Economics Teachers, Postsecondary; Law Teachers, Postsecondary; Library Science Teachers, Postsecondary; Mathematical Science Teachers, Postsecondary; Nursing Instructors and Teachers, Postsecondary; Philosophy and Religion Teachers, Postsecondary; Physics Teachers, Postsecondary; Political Science Teachers, Postsecondary; Psychology Teachers, Postsecondary; Recreation and Fitness Studies Teachers, Postsecondary; Self-Enrichment Education Teachers; Social Work Teachers, Postsecondary; Vocational Education Teachers, Postsecondary.

Skills: Science; Instructing; Writing; Learning Strategies; Social Perceptiveness; Critical Thinking; Reading Comprehension; Speaking.

Education and Training Programs: Social Science Teacher Education; Sociology. **Related Knowledge/Courses:** Sociology and Anthropology; Philosophy and Theology; History and Archeology; Education and Training; English Language; Geography.

Work Environment: Indoors; sitting.

Special Education Teachers, Middle School

* Personality Code: SA
* Education/Training Required: Bachelor's degree
* Annual Earnings: $48,940
* Beginning Wage: $33,690
* Earnings Growth Potential: Low
* Growth: 15.8%
* Annual Job Openings: 8,846
* Self-Employed: 0.3%
* Part-Time: 9.6%

Teach middle school subjects to educationally and physically handicapped students. Includes teachers who specialize and work with audibly and visually handicapped students and those who teach basic academic and life processes skills to the mentally impaired. Establish and enforce rules for behavior and policies and procedures to maintain order among students. Maintain accurate and complete student records and prepare reports on children and activities as required by laws, district policies, and administrative regulations. Prepare materials and classrooms for class activities. Confer with parents, administrators, testing specialists, social workers, and professionals to develop individual educational plans designed to promote students' educational, physical, and social development. Develop and implement strategies to meet the needs of students with a variety of handicapping conditions. Teach socially acceptable behavior, employing techniques such as behavior modification and positive reinforcement. Modify the general education curriculum for special-needs students based upon a variety of instructional techniques and instructional technology. Employ special educational strategies and techniques during instruction to improve the development of sensory- and perceptual-motor skills, language, cognition, and memory. Confer with parents or guardians, other teachers, counselors, and administrators to resolve students' behavioral and academic problems. Instruct through lectures, discussions, and demonstrations in one or more subjects such as English, mathematics, or social studies. Coordinate placement of students with special needs into mainstream classes. Meet with parents and guardians to discuss their children's progress and to determine their priorities for their children and their resource needs. Guide and counsel students with adjustment or academic problems or special academic interests. Prepare, administer, and grade tests and assignments to evaluate students' progress. Observe and evaluate students' performance, behavior, social development, and physical health. Establish clear objectives for all lessons, units, and projects and communicate those objectives to students. Teach students personal development skills such as goal setting, independence, and self-advocacy. Plan and conduct activities for a balanced program of instruction, demonstration, and work time that provides students with opportunities to observe, question, and investigate.

GOE—Interest Area/Cluster: 05. Education and Training. **Work Group:** 05.02. Preschool, Elementary, and Secondary Teaching and Instructing. **Other Jobs in This Work Group:** Elementary School Teachers, Except Special Education; Kindergarten Teachers, Except Special Education; Middle School Teachers, Except Special and Vocational Education; Preschool Teachers, Except Special Education; Secondary School Teachers, Except Special and Vocational Education; Special Education Teachers, Preschool, Kindergarten, and Elementary School; Special Education Teachers, Secondary School; Teacher Assistants; Vocational Education Teachers, Middle School; Vocational Education Teachers, Secondary School.

Skills: Learning Strategies; Social Perceptiveness; Instructing; Monitoring; Persuasion; Writing; Negotiation; Time Management.

Education and Training Programs: Special Education and Teaching, General; Education/Teaching of the Gifted and Talented; Education/Teaching of Individuals Who are Developmentally Delayed; Education/Teaching of Individuals in Early Childhood Special Education Programs. **Related Knowledge/Courses:** Geography; History and Archeology;

Psychology; Therapy and Counseling; Sociology and Anthropology; Education and Training.

Work Environment: Indoors; noisy; standing.

Special Education Teachers, Preschool, Kindergarten, and Elementary School

- ❋ Personality Code: SA
- ❋ Education/Training Required: Bachelor's degree
- ❋ Annual Earnings: $48,350
- ❋ Beginning Wage: $32,700
- ❋ Earnings Growth Potential: Low
- ❋ Growth: 19.6%
- ❋ Annual Job Openings: 20,049
- ❋ Self-Employed: 0.3%
- ❋ Part-Time: 9.6%

Teach elementary and preschool school subjects to educationally and physically handicapped students. Includes teachers who specialize and work with audibly and visually handicapped students and those who teach basic academic and life processes skills to the mentally impaired. Instruct students in academic subjects, using a variety of techniques such as phonetics, multisensory learning, and repetition to reinforce learning and to meet students' varying needs and interests. Employ special educational strategies and techniques during instruction to improve the development of sensory- and perceptual-motor skills, language, cognition, and memory. Teach socially acceptable behavior, employing techniques such as behavior modification and positive reinforcement. Modify the general education curriculum for special-needs students based upon a variety of instructional techniques and technologies. Meet with parents and guardians to discuss their children's progress and to determine their priorities for their children and their resource needs. Plan and conduct activities for a balanced program of instruction, demonstration, and work time that provides students with opportunities to observe, question, and investigate.

Establish and enforce rules for behavior and policies and procedures to maintain order among the students for whom they are responsible. Confer with parents, administrators, testing specialists, social workers, and professionals to develop individual educational plans designed to promote students' educational, physical, and social development. Maintain accurate and complete student records and prepare reports on children and activities as required by laws, district policies, and administrative regulations. Establish clear objectives for all lessons, units, and projects and communicate those objectives to students. Develop and implement strategies to meet the needs of students with a variety of handicapping conditions. Prepare classrooms for class activities and provide a variety of materials and resources for children to explore, manipulate, and use, both in learning activities and imaginative play. Confer with parents or guardians, teachers, counselors, and administrators to resolve students' behavioral and academic problems. Observe and evaluate students' performance, behavior, social development, and physical health. Teach students personal development skills such as goal setting, independence, and self-advocacy.

GOE—Interest Area/Cluster: 05. Education and Training. **Work Group:** 05.02. Preschool, Elementary, and Secondary Teaching and Instructing. **Other Jobs in This Work Group:** Elementary School Teachers, Except Special Education; Kindergarten Teachers, Except Special Education; Middle School Teachers, Except Special and Vocational Education; Preschool Teachers, Except Special Education; Secondary School Teachers, Except Special and Vocational Education; Special Education Teachers, Middle School; Special Education Teachers, Secondary School; Teacher Assistants; Vocational Education Teachers, Middle School; Vocational Education Teachers, Secondary School.

Skills: Learning Strategies; Instructing; Social Perceptiveness; Monitoring; Negotiation; Time Management; Coordination; Writing.

Education and Training Programs: Special Education and Teaching, General; Education/Teaching of Individuals with Hearing Impairments, Including

Deafness; Education/Teaching of the Gifted and Talented; Education/Teaching of Individuals with Emotional Disturbances; Education/Teaching of Individuals with Mental Retardation; Education/Teaching of Individuals with Multiple Disabilities; Education/Teaching of Individuals with Orthopedic and Other Physical Health Impairments; others. **Related Knowledge/Courses:** Psychology; History and Archeology; Therapy and Counseling; Geography; Philosophy and Theology; Sociology and Anthropology.

Work Environment: Indoors; noisy; standing.

Substance Abuse and Behavioral Disorder Counselors

- ❋ Personality Code: SAI
- ❋ Education/Training Required: Bachelor's degree
- ❋ Annual Earnings: $35,580
- ❋ Beginning Wage: $23,780
- ❋ Earnings Growth Potential: Low
- ❋ Growth: 34.3%
- ❋ Annual Job Openings: 20,821
- ❋ Self-Employed: 5.8%
- ❋ Part-Time: 15.4%

Counsel and advise individuals with alcohol; tobacco; drug; or other problems, such as gambling and eating disorders. May counsel individuals, families, or groups or engage in prevention programs. Counsel clients and patients individually and in group sessions to assist in overcoming dependencies, adjusting to life, and making changes. Complete and maintain accurate records and reports regarding the patients' histories and progress, services provided, and other required information. Develop client treatment plans based on research, clinical experience, and client histories. Review and evaluate clients' progress in relation to measurable goals described in treatment and care plans. Interview clients, review records, and confer with other professionals to evaluate individuals' mental and physical condition and to determine their suitability for participation in a specific program. Intervene as advocate for clients or patients to resolve emergency problems in crisis situations. Provide clients or family members with information about addiction issues and about available services and programs, making appropriate referrals when necessary. Modify treatment plans to comply with changes in client status. Coordinate counseling efforts with mental health professionals and other health professionals such as doctors, nurses, and social workers. Attend training sessions to increase knowledge and skills. Plan and implement follow-up and aftercare programs for clients to be discharged from treatment programs. Conduct chemical dependency program orientation sessions. Counsel family members to assist them in understanding, dealing with, and supporting clients or patients. Participate in case conferences and staff meetings. Act as liaisons between clients and medical staff. Coordinate activities with courts, probation officers, community services, and other post-treatment agencies. Confer with family members or others close to clients to keep them informed of treatment planning and progress. Instruct others in program methods, procedures, and functions. Follow progress of discharged patients to determine effectiveness of treatments. Develop, implement, and evaluate public education, prevention, and health promotion programs, working in collaboration with organizations, institutions, and communities.

GOE—Interest Area/Cluster: 10. Human Service. **Work Group:** 10.01. Counseling and Social Work. **Other Jobs in This Work Group:** Child, Family, and School Social Workers; Clinical Psychologists; Clinical, Counseling, and School Psychologists; Counseling Psychologists; Marriage and Family Therapists; Medical and Public Health Social Workers; Mental Health and Substance Abuse Social Workers; Mental Health Counselors; Probation Officers and Correctional Treatment Specialists; Rehabilitation Counselors; Residential Advisors; Social and Human Service Assistants.

Skills: Social Perceptiveness; Persuasion; Service Orientation; Negotiation; Active Listening; Learning Strategies; Writing; Complex Problem Solving.

Education and Training Programs: Substance Abuse/Addiction Counseling; Clinical/Medical Social Work; Mental and Social Health Services and Allied Professions, Other. **Related Knowledge/Courses:** Therapy and Counseling; Psychology; Sociology and Anthropology; Philosophy and Theology; Customer and Personal Service; Education and Training.

Work Environment: Indoors; disease or infections; sitting.

Training and Development Specialists

- ✸ Personality Code: SAC
- ✸ Education/Training Required: Work experience plus degree
- ✸ Annual Earnings: $49,630
- ✸ Beginning Wage: $28,600
- ✸ Earnings Growth Potential: High
- ✸ Growth: 18.3%
- ✸ Annual Job Openings: 35,862
- ✸ Self-Employed: 2.3%
- ✸ Part-Time: 7.6%

Conduct training and development programs for employees. Monitor, evaluate and record training activities and program effectiveness. Offer specific training programs to help workers maintain or improve job skills. Assess training needs through surveys, interviews with employees, focus groups, or consultation with managers, instructors, or customer representatives. Develop alternative training methods if expected improvements are not seen. Organize and develop, or obtain, training procedure manuals and guides and course materials such as handouts and visual materials. Present information, using a variety of instructional techniques and formats such as role playing, simulations, team exercises, group discussions, videos, and lectures. Evaluate training materials prepared by instructors, such as outlines, text, and handouts. Design, plan, organize, and direct orientation and training for employees or customers of

Social–T

industrial or commercial establishments. Monitor training costs to ensure budget is not exceeded, and prepare budget reports to justify expenditures. Select and assign instructors to conduct training. Schedule classes based on availability of classrooms, equipment, and instructors. Keep up with developments in their individual areas of expertise by reading current journals, books, and magazine articles. Supervise instructors, evaluate instructor performances, and refer instructors to classes for skill development. Coordinate recruitment and placement of training program participants. Attend meetings and seminars to obtain information for use in training programs, or to inform management of training program statuses. Negotiate contracts with clients, including desired training outcomes, fees, and expenses. Devise programs to develop executive potential among employees in lower-level positions. Screen, hire, and assign workers to positions based on qualifications. Refer trainees to employer relations representatives, to locations offering job placement assistance, or to appropriate social services agencies if warranted.

GOE—Interest Area/Cluster: 04. Business and Administration. **Work Group:** 04.03. Human Resources Support. **Other Jobs in This Work Group:** Compensation, Benefits, and Job Analysis Specialists; Employment Interviewers; Employment, Recruitment, and Placement Specialists; Personnel Recruiters.

Skills: Systems Evaluation; Systems Analysis; Learning Strategies; Management of Personnel Resources; Management of Financial Resources; Instructing; Negotiation; Writing.

Education and Training Programs: Human Resources Management/Personnel Administration, General; Organizational Behavior Studies. **Related Knowledge/Courses:** Education and Training; Sociology and Anthropology; Sales and Marketing; Clerical Practices; Personnel and Human Resources; Psychology.

Work Environment: Indoors; noisy; standing; repetitive motions.

Vocational Education Teachers, Postsecondary

- ❋ Personality Code: SR
- ❋ Education/Training Required: Work experience in a related occupation
- ❋ Annual Earnings: $45,850
- ❋ Beginning Wage: $26,380
- ❋ Earnings Growth Potential: High
- ❋ Growth: 22.9%
- ❋ Annual Job Openings: 19,313
- ❋ Self-Employed: 0.4%
- ❋ Part-Time: 27.8%

Teach or instruct vocational or occupational subjects at the postsecondary level (but at less than the baccalaureate) to students who have graduated or left high school. Includes correspondence school instructors; industrial, commercial, and government training instructors; and adult education teachers and instructors who prepare persons to operate industrial machinery and equipment and transportation and communications equipment. Teaching may take place in public or private schools whose primary business is education or in a school associated with an organization whose primary business is other than education. Supervise and monitor students' use of tools and equipment. Observe and evaluate students' work to determine progress, provide feedback, and make suggestions for improvement. Present lectures and conduct discussions to increase students' knowledge and competence, using visual aids such as graphs, charts, videotapes, and slides. Administer oral, written, or performance tests to measure progress and to evaluate training effectiveness. Prepare reports and maintain records such as student grades, attendance rolls, and training activity details. Supervise independent or group projects, field placements, laboratory work, or other training. Determine training needs of students or workers. Provide individualized instruction and tutorial or remedial instruction. Conduct on-the-job training, classes, or training sessions to teach and demonstrate principles, techniques, procedures, and methods of designated subjects. Develop curricula and plan course content and methods of instruction. Prepare outlines of instructional programs and training schedules and establish course goals. Integrate academic and vocational curricula so that students can obtain a variety of skills. Develop teaching aids such as instructional software, multimedia visual aids, or study materials. Select and assemble books, materials, supplies, and equipment for training, courses, or projects. Advise students on course selection, career decisions, and other academic and vocational concerns. Participate in conferences, seminars, and training sessions to keep abreast of developments in the field and integrate relevant information into training programs. Serve on faculty and school committees concerned with budgeting, curriculum revision, and course and diploma requirements. Review enrollment applications and correspond with applicants to obtain additional information. Arrange for lectures by experts in designated fields.

GOE—Interest Area/Cluster: 05. Education and Training. **Work Group:** 05.03. Postsecondary and Adult Teaching and Instructing. **Other Jobs in This Work Group:** Adult Literacy, Remedial Education, and GED Teachers and Instructors; Agricultural Sciences Teachers, Postsecondary; Anthropology and Archeology Teachers, Postsecondary; Architecture Teachers, Postsecondary; Area, Ethnic, and Cultural Studies Teachers, Postsecondary; Art, Drama, and Music Teachers, Postsecondary; Atmospheric, Earth, Marine, and Space Sciences Teachers, Postsecondary; Biological Science Teachers, Postsecondary; Business Teachers, Postsecondary; Chemistry Teachers, Postsecondary; Communications Teachers, Postsecondary; Computer Science Teachers, Postsecondary; Criminal Justice and Law Enforcement Teachers, Postsecondary; Economics Teachers, Postsecondary; Education Teachers, Postsecondary; Engineering Teachers, Postsecondary; English Language and Literature Teachers, Postsecondary; Environmental Science Teachers, Postsecondary; Farm and Home Management Advisors; Foreign Language and Literature Teachers, Postsecondary; Forestry and Conservation Science Teachers, Postsecondary; Geography Teachers, Postsecondary; Graduate

Teaching Assistants; Health Specialties Teachers, Postsecondary; History Teachers, Postsecondary; Home Economics Teachers, Postsecondary; Law Teachers, Postsecondary; Library Science Teachers, Postsecondary; Mathematical Science Teachers, Postsecondary; Nursing Instructors and Teachers, Postsecondary; Philosophy and Religion Teachers, Postsecondary; Physics Teachers, Postsecondary; Political Science Teachers, Postsecondary; Psychology Teachers, Postsecondary; Recreation and Fitness Studies Teachers, Postsecondary; Self-Enrichment Education Teachers; Social Work Teachers, Postsecondary; Sociology Teachers, Postsecondary; Teachers, Postsecondary.

Skills: Instructing; Learning Strategies; Social Perceptiveness; Service Orientation; Speaking; Time Management; Science; Writing.

Education and Training Programs: Agricultural Teacher Education; Business Teacher Education; Technology Teacher Education/Industrial Arts Teacher Education; Sales and Marketing Operations/Marketing and Distribution Teacher Education; Technical Teacher Education; Trade and Industrial Teacher Education; Health Occupations Teacher Education; Teacher Education and Professional Development, Specific Subject Areas, Other. **Related Knowledge/Courses:** Education and Training; Psychology; Therapy and Counseling; Computers and Electronics; Sales and Marketing; Design.

Work Environment: Indoors; standing; using hands on objects, tools, or controls.

Enterprising Occupations

Administrative Services Managers

- ❋ Personality Code: EC
- ❋ Education/Training Required: Work experience plus degree
- ❋ Annual Earnings: $70,990
- ❋ Beginning Wage: $36,000
- ❋ Earnings Growth Potential: High
- ❋ Growth: 11.7%
- ❋ Annual Job Openings: 19,513
- ❋ Self-Employed: 0.6%
- ❋ Part-Time: 4.7%

Plan, direct, or coordinate supportive services of an organization, such as recordkeeping, mail distribution, telephone operator/receptionist, and other office support services. May oversee facilities planning and maintenance and custodial operations. Monitor the facility to ensure that it remains safe, secure, and well-maintained. Direct or coordinate the supportive services department of a business, agency, or organization. Set goals and deadlines for the department. Prepare and review operational reports and schedules to ensure accuracy and efficiency. Analyze internal processes and recommend and implement procedural or policy changes to improve operations such as supply changes or the disposal of records. Acquire, distribute, and store supplies. Plan, administer, and control budgets for contracts, equipment, and supplies. Oversee construction and renovation projects to improve efficiency and to ensure that facilities meet environmental, health, and security standards and comply with government regulations. Hire and terminate clerical and administrative personnel. Oversee the maintenance and repair of machinery, equipment, and electrical and mechanical systems. Manage leasing of facility space. Participate in architectural and engineering planning and design, including space

and installation management. Conduct classes to teach procedures to staff. Dispose of, or oversee the disposal of, surplus or unclaimed property.

GOE—Interest Area/Cluster: 04. Business and Administration. **Work Group:** 04.02. Managerial Work in Business Detail. **Other Jobs in This Work Group:** First-Line Supervisors/Managers of Housekeeping and Janitorial Workers; First-Line Supervisors/Managers of Office and Administrative Support Workers; Meeting and Convention Planners.

Skills: Management of Financial Resources; Management of Personnel Resources; Programming; Service Orientation; Coordination; Monitoring; Writing; Speaking.

Education and Training Programs: Public Administration; Medical/Health Management and Clinical Assistant/Specialist; Business/Commerce, General; Business Administration and Management, General; Purchasing, Procurement/Acquisitions and Contracts Management; Transportation/Transportation Management. **Related Knowledge/Courses:** Personnel and Human Resources; Clerical Practices; Economics and Accounting; Administration and Management; Customer and Personal Service; Law and Government.

Work Environment: Indoors; more often standing than sitting.

Advertising and Promotions Managers

- ❋ Personality Code: EAC
- ❋ Education/Training Required: Work experience plus degree
- ❋ Annual Earnings: $78,250
- ❋ Beginning Wage: $38,400
- ❋ Earnings Growth Potential: Very high
- ❋ Growth: 6.2%
- ❋ Annual Job Openings: 2,955
- ❋ Self-Employed: 13.4%
- ❋ Part-Time: 4.8%

Plan and direct advertising policies and programs or produce collateral materials, such as posters, contests, coupons, or giveaways, to create extra interest in the purchase of a product or service for a department, for an entire organization, or on an account basis. Prepare budgets and submit estimates for program costs as part of campaign plan development. Plan and prepare advertising and promotional material to increase sales of products or services, working with customers, company officials, sales departments, and advertising agencies. Assist with annual budget development. Inspect layouts and advertising copy and edit scripts, audiotapes and videotapes, and other promotional material for adherence to specifications. Coordinate activities of departments, such as sales, graphic arts, media, finance, and research. Prepare and negotiate advertising and sales contracts. Identify and develop contacts for promotional campaigns and industry programs that meet identified buyer targets, such as dealers, distributors, or consumers. Gather and organize information to plan advertising campaigns. Confer with department heads or staff to discuss topics such as contracts, selection of advertising media, or product to be advertised. Confer with clients to provide marketing or technical advice. Monitor and analyze sales promotion results to determine cost-effectiveness of promotion campaigns. Read trade journals and professional literature to stay informed on trends, innovations, and changes that affect media planning. Formulate plans to extend business with established accounts and to transact business as agent for advertising accounts. Provide presentation and product demonstration support during the introduction of new products and services to field staff and customers. Direct, motivate, and monitor the mobilization of a campaign team to advance campaign goals. Plan and execute advertising policies and strategies for organizations. Track program budgets and expenses and campaign response rates to evaluate each campaign based on program objectives and industry norms. Assemble and communicate with a strong, diverse coalition of organizations or public figures, securing their cooperation, support, and action to further campaign goals. Train and direct workers engaged in developing and producing advertisements. Coordinate with the media to disseminate advertising.

GOE—Interest Area/Cluster: 14. Retail and Wholesale Sales and Service. Work Group: 14.01. Managerial Work in Retail/Wholesale Sales and Service. Other Jobs in This Work Group: First-Line Supervisors/Managers of Non-Retail Sales Workers; First-Line Supervisors/Managers of Retail Sales Workers; Funeral Directors; Marketing Managers; Property, Real Estate, and Community Association Managers; Purchasing Managers; Sales Managers.

Skills: Management of Financial Resources; Service Orientation; Persuasion; Negotiation; Time Management; Coordination; Management of Personnel Resources; Judgment and Decision Making.

Education and Training Programs: Public Relations/Image Management; Advertising; Marketing/Marketing Management, General. Related Knowledge/Courses: Sales and Marketing; Fine Arts; Design; Production and Processing; Communications and Media; Clerical Practices.

Work Environment: Sitting; repetitive motions.

Advertising Sales Agents

* Personality Code: ECA
* Education/Training Required: Moderate-term on-the-job training
* Annual Earnings: $42,820
* Beginning Wage: $22,390
* Earnings Growth Potential: High
* Growth: 20.3%
* Annual Job Openings: 29,233
* Self-Employed: 5.6%
* Part-Time: 10.2%

Sell or solicit advertising, including graphic art, advertising space in publications, custom-made signs, or TV and radio advertising time. May obtain leases for outdoor advertising sites or persuade retailer to use sales promotion display items.

Prepare and deliver sales presentations to new and existing customers to sell new advertising programs and to protect and increase existing advertising. Explain to customers how specific types of advertising will help promote their products or services in the most effective way possible. Maintain assigned account bases while developing new accounts. Process all correspondence and paperwork related to accounts. Deliver advertising or illustration proofs to customers for approval. Draw up contracts for advertising work and collect payments due. Locate and contact potential clients to offer advertising services. Provide clients with estimates of the costs of advertising products or services. Recommend appropriate sizes and formats for advertising, depending on medium being used. Inform customers of available options for advertisement artwork and provide samples. Obtain and study information about clients' products, needs, problems, advertising history, and business practices to offer effective sales presentations and appropriate product assistance. Determine advertising medium to be used and prepare sample advertisements within the selected medium for presentation to customers. Consult with company officials, sales departments, and advertising agencies to develop promotional plans. Prepare promotional plans, sales literature, media kits, and sales contracts, using computer. Identify new advertising markets and propose products to serve them. Write copy as part of layout. Attend sales meetings, industry trade shows, and training seminars to gather information, promote products, expand network of contacts, and increase knowledge. Gather all relevant material for bid processes and coordinate bidding and contract approval. Arrange for commercial taping sessions and accompany clients to sessions. Write sales outlines for use by staff.

GOE—Interest Area/Cluster: 14. Retail and Wholesale Sales and Service. **Work Group:** 14.03. General Sales. **Other Jobs in This Work Group:** Insurance Sales Agents; Personal Financial Advisors; Sales Agents, Financial Services; Sales Agents, Securities and Commodities.

Skills: Negotiation; Management of Financial Resources; Persuasion; Speaking; Social Perceptiveness; Complex Problem Solving; Writing; Service Orientation.

Education and Training Program: Advertising. **Related Knowledge/Courses:** Sales and Marketing; Economics and Accounting; Communications and Media; Customer and Personal Service; English Language; Transportation.

Work Environment: More often outdoors than indoors; standing.

Air Traffic Controllers

- ❋ Personality Code: EC
- ❋ Education/Training Required: Long-term on-the-job training
- ❋ Annual Earnings: $112,930
- ❋ Beginning Wage: $47,290
- ❋ Earnings Growth Potential: Very high
- ❋ Growth: 10.2%
- ❋ Annual Job Openings: 1,213
- ❋ Self-Employed: 0.0%
- ❋ Part-Time: 2.1%

Control air traffic on and within vicinity of airport and movement of air traffic between altitude sectors and control centers according to established procedures and policies. Authorize, regulate, and control commercial airline flights according to government or company regulations to expedite and ensure flight safety. Issue landing and take-off authorizations and instructions. Monitor and direct the movement of aircraft within an assigned airspace and on the ground at airports to minimize delays and maximize safety. Monitor aircraft within a specific airspace, using radar, computer equipment, and visual references. Inform pilots about nearby planes as well as potentially hazardous conditions such as weather, speed and direction of wind, and visibility problems. Provide flight path changes or directions to emergency landing fields for pilots traveling in bad weather or in emergency situations. Alert airport emergency services in cases of emergency and when aircraft experience difficulties. Direct pilots to runways when space is available or direct them to maintain a traffic pattern until there is space for them to land. Transfer control of departing flights to traffic control centers and accept control of arriving flights. Direct ground traffic, including taxiing aircraft, maintenance and baggage vehicles, and airport workers. Determine the timing and procedures for flight vector changes. Maintain radio and telephone contact with adjacent control towers, terminal control units, and other area control centers in order to coordinate aircraft movement. Contact pilots by radio to provide meteorological, navigational, and other information. Initiate and coordinate searches for missing aircraft. Check conditions and traffic at different altitudes in response to pilots' requests for altitude changes. Relay to control centers air traffic information such as courses, altitudes, and expected arrival times. Compile information about flights from flight plans, pilot reports, radar, and observations. Inspect, adjust, and control radio equipment and airport lights. Conduct preflight briefings on weather conditions, suggested routes, altitudes, indications of turbulence, and other flight safety information. Analyze factors such as weather reports, fuel requirements, and maps in order to determine air routes. Organize flight plans and traffic management plans to prepare for planes about to enter assigned airspace.

GOE—Interest Area/Cluster: 03. Arts and Communication. **Work Group:** 03.10. Communications Technology. **Other Jobs in This Work Group:** Airfield Operations Specialists; Dispatchers, Except Police, Fire, and Ambulance; Police, Fire, and Ambulance Dispatchers; Telephone Operators.

Skills: Operation and Control; Operation Monitoring; Coordination; Complex Problem Solving; Active Listening; Instructing; Judgment and Decision Making; Monitoring.

Education and Training Program: Air Traffic Controller Training. **Related Knowledge/Courses:** Transportation; Geography; Telecommunications;

Public Safety and Security; Physics; Education and Training.

Work Environment: Indoors; noisy; sitting; using hands on objects, tools, or controls; repetitive motions.

Appraisers, Real Estate

- ❋ Personality Code: ECR
- ❋ Education/Training Required: Bachelor's degree
- ❋ Annual Earnings: $46,130
- ❋ Beginning Wage: $25,110
- ❋ Earnings Growth Potential: High
- ❋ Growth: 16.9%
- ❋ Annual Job Openings: 6,493
- ❋ Self-Employed: 32.7%
- ❋ Part-Time: 8.4%

The job openings listed here are shared with Assessors.

Appraise real property to determine its value for purchase, sales, investment, mortgage, or loan purposes. Prepare written reports that estimate property values, outline methods by which the estimations were made, and meet appraisal standards. Compute final estimation of property values, taking into account such factors as depreciation, replacement costs, value comparisons of similar properties, and income potential. Search public records for transactions such as sales, leases, and assessments. Inspect properties to evaluate construction, condition, special features, and functional design and to take property measurements. Photograph interiors and exteriors of properties in order to assist in estimating property value, substantiate findings, and complete appraisal reports. Evaluate land and neighborhoods where properties are situated, considering locations and trends or impending changes that could influence future values. Obtain county land values and sales information about nearby properties in order to aid in establishment of property values. Verify legal descriptions of properties by comparing them to county records. Check building codes and zoning bylaws in order to determine any effects on the properties being appraised. Estimate building replacement costs, using building valuation manuals and professional cost estimators. Examine income records and operating costs of income properties. Interview persons familiar with properties and immediate surroundings, such as contractors, homeowners, and realtors, in order to obtain pertinent information. Examine the type and location of nearby services such as shopping centers, schools, parks, and other neighborhood features in order to evaluate their impact on property values. Draw land diagrams that will be used in appraisal reports to support findings. Testify in court as to the value of a piece of real estate property.

GOE—Interest Area/Cluster: 06. Finance and Insurance. **Work Group:** 06.02. Finance/Insurance Investigation and Analysis. **Other Jobs in This Work Group:** Appraisers and Assessors of Real Estate; Assessors; Claims Adjusters, Examiners, and Investigators; Claims Examiners, Property and Casualty Insurance; Cost Estimators; Credit Analysts; Financial Analysts; Insurance Adjusters, Examiners, and Investigators; Insurance Appraisers, Auto Damage; Insurance Underwriters; Loan Counselors; Loan Officers; Market Research Analysts; Survey Researchers.

Skills: Mathematics; Writing; Critical Thinking; Management of Financial Resources; Equipment Selection; Complex Problem Solving; Speaking; Technology Design.

Education and Training Program: Real Estate. **Related Knowledge/Courses:** Building and Construction; Economics and Accounting; Geography; Clerical Practices; Law and Government; Sales and Marketing.

Work Environment: More often outdoors than indoors; sitting.

Chief Executives

- ❋ Personality Code: EC
- ❋ Education/Training Required: Work experience plus degree
- ❋ Annual Earnings: More than $145,600
- ❋ Beginning Wage: $64,530
- ❋ Earnings Growth Potential: Cannot be calculated
- ❋ Growth: 2.0%
- ❋ Annual Job Openings: 21,209
- ❋ Self-Employed: 22.0%
- ❋ Part-Time: 5.5%

Determine and formulate policies and provide the overall direction of companies or private and public sector organizations within the guidelines set up by a board of directors or similar governing body. Plan, direct, or coordinate operational activities at the highest level of management with the help of subordinate executives and staff managers. Direct and coordinate an organization's financial and budget activities in order to fund operations, maximize investments, and increase efficiency. Confer with board members, organization officials, and staff members to discuss issues, coordinate activities, and resolve problems. Analyze operations to evaluate performance of a company and its staff in meeting objectives and to determine areas of potential cost reduction, program improvement, or policy change. Direct, plan, and implement policies, objectives, and activities of organizations or businesses in order to ensure continuing operations, to maximize returns on investments, and to increase productivity. Prepare budgets for approval, including those for funding and implementation of programs. Direct and coordinate activities of businesses or departments concerned with production, pricing, sales, and/or distribution of products. Negotiate or approve contracts and agreements with suppliers, distributors, federal and state agencies, and other organizational entities. Review reports submitted by staff members in order to recommend approval or to suggest changes. Appoint department heads or managers and assign or delegate responsibilities to them. Direct human resources activities, including the approval of human resource plans and activities, the selection of directors and other high-level staff, and establishment and organization of major departments. Preside over or serve on boards of directors, management committees, or other governing boards. Prepare and present reports concerning activities, expenses, budgets, government statutes and rulings, and other items affecting businesses or program services. Establish departmental responsibilities and coordinate functions among departments and sites. Implement corrective action plans to solve organizational or departmental problems. Coordinate the development and implementation of budgetary control systems, recordkeeping systems, and other administrative control processes. Direct non-merchandising departments such as advertising, purchasing, credit, and accounting. Deliver speeches, write articles, and present information at meetings or conventions in order to promote services, exchange ideas, and accomplish objectives.

GOE—Interest Area/Cluster: 04. Business and Administration. **Work Group:** 04.01. Managerial Work in General Business. **Other Jobs in This Work Group:** Compensation and Benefits Managers; General and Operations Managers; Human Resources Managers; Training and Development Managers.

Skills: Management of Financial Resources; Management of Material Resources; Judgment and Decision Making; Negotiation; Management of Personnel Resources; Systems Evaluation; Coordination; Operations Analysis.

Education and Training Programs: Business Administration/Management; Business/Commerce, General; Entrepreneurship/Entrepreneurial Studies; International Business/Trade/Commerce; International Relations and Affairs; Public Administration; Public Administration and Services, Other; Public Policy Analysis; Transportation/Transportation Management. **Related Knowledge/Courses:** Economics and Accounting; Administration and Management; Sales and Marketing; Personnel and Human Resources; Law and Government; Medicine and Dentistry.

Work Environment: Indoors; sitting.

Compensation and Benefits Managers

- ✸ Personality Code: ECS
- ✸ Education/Training Required: Work experience plus degree
- ✸ Annual Earnings: $81,410
- ✸ Beginning Wage: $46,050
- ✸ Earnings Growth Potential: High
- ✸ Growth: 12.0%
- ✸ Annual Job Openings: 6,121
- ✸ Self-Employed: 1.4%
- ✸ Part-Time: 2.7%

Plan, direct, or coordinate compensation and benefits activities and staff of an organization. Design, evaluate, and modify benefits policies to ensure that programs are current, competitive, and in compliance with legal requirements. Analyze compensation policies, government regulations, and prevailing wage rates to develop competitive compensation plans. Fulfill all reporting requirements of all relevant government rules and regulations, including the Employee Retirement Income Security Act (ERISA). Direct preparation and distribution of written and verbal information to inform employees of benefits, compensation, and personnel policies. Administer, direct, and review employee benefit programs, including the integration of benefit programs following mergers and acquisitions. Plan, direct, supervise, and coordinate work activities of subordinates and staff relating to employment, compensation, labor relations, and employee relations. Identify and implement benefits to increase the quality of life for employees by working with brokers and researching benefits issues. Manage the design and development of tools to assist employees in benefits selection and to guide managers through compensation decisions. Prepare detailed job descriptions and classification systems and define job levels and families in partnership with other managers. Prepare budgets for personnel operations. Formulate policies, procedures,

Enterprising—C

and programs for recruitment, testing, placement, classification, orientation, benefits and compensation, and labor and industrial relations. Mediate between benefits providers and employees, such as by assisting in handling employees' benefits-related questions or taking suggestions. Develop methods to improve employment policies, processes, and practices and recommend changes to management. Study legislation, arbitration decisions, and collective bargaining contracts to assess industry trends. Maintain records and compile statistical reports concerning personnel-related data such as hires, transfers, performance appraisals, and absenteeism rates. Negotiate bargaining agreements. Conduct exit interviews to identify reasons for employee termination. Plan and conduct new employee orientations to foster positive attitude toward organizational objectives.

GOE—Interest Area/Cluster: 04. Business and Administration. **Work Group:** 04.01. Managerial Work in General Business. **Other Jobs in This Work Group:** Chief Executives; General and Operations Managers; Human Resources Managers; Training and Development Managers.

Skills: Management of Financial Resources; Management of Personnel Resources; Systems Analysis; Systems Evaluation; Negotiation; Writing; Persuasion; Judgment and Decision Making.

Education and Training Programs: Human Resources Management/Personnel Administration, General; Labor and Industrial Relations. **Related Knowledge/Courses:** Personnel and Human Resources; Economics and Accounting; Administration and Management; Mathematics; Law and Government; Communications and Media.

Work Environment: Indoors; sitting.

Computer and Information Systems Managers

- ❈ Personality Code: ECI
- ❈ Education/Training Required: Work experience plus degree
- ❈ Annual Earnings: $108,070
- ❈ Beginning Wage: $65,760
- ❈ Earnings Growth Potential: Medium
- ❈ Growth: 16.4%
- ❈ Annual Job Openings: 30,887
- ❈ Self-Employed: 1.4%
- ❈ Part-Time: 2.1%

Plan, direct, or coordinate activities in such fields as electronic data processing, information systems, systems analysis, and computer programming. Review project plans to plan and coordinate project activity. Manage backup, security, and user help systems. Develop and interpret organizational goals, policies, and procedures. Develop computer information resources, providing for data security and control, strategic computing, and disaster recovery. Consult with users, management, vendors, and technicians to assess computing needs and system requirements. Stay abreast of advances in technology. Meet with department heads, managers, supervisors, vendors, and others to solicit cooperation and resolve problems. Provide users with technical support for computer problems. Recruit, hire, train, and supervise staff or participate in staffing decisions. Evaluate data processing proposals to assess project feasibility and requirements. Review and approve all systems charts and programs prior to their implementation. Control operational budget and expenditures. Direct daily operations of department, analyzing workflow, establishing priorities, developing standards, and setting deadlines. Assign and review the work of systems analysts, programmers, and other computer-related workers. Evaluate the organization's technology use and needs and recommend improvements such as hardware and software upgrades. Prepare and review operational reports or project progress reports. Purchase necessary equipment.

GOE—Interest Area/Cluster: 11. Information Technology. **Work Group:** 11.01. Managerial Work in Information Technology. **Other Jobs in This Work Group:** Network and Computer Systems Administrators.

Skills: Programming; Systems Analysis; Management of Financial Resources; Systems Evaluation; Management of Material Resources; Management of Personnel Resources; Operation Monitoring; Quality Control Analysis.

Education and Training Programs: Computer and Information Sciences, General; Information Science/Studies; Computer Science; System Administration/Administrator; Operations Management and Supervision; Management Information Systems, General; Information Resources Management/CIO Training; Knowledge Management. **Related Knowledge/Courses:** Telecommunications; Computers and Electronics; Economics and Accounting; Personnel and Human Resources; Production and Processing; Administration and Management.

Work Environment: Indoors; noisy; sitting; using hands on objects, tools, or controls; repetitive motions.

Construction Managers

- ❋ Personality Code: ERC
- ❋ Education/Training Required: Bachelor's degree
- ❋ Annual Earnings: $76,230
- ❋ Beginning Wage: $44,630
- ❋ Earnings Growth Potential: High
- ❋ Growth: 15.7%
- ❋ Annual Job Openings: 44,158
- ❋ Self-Employed: 56.3%
- ❋ Part-Time: 4.9%

Plan, direct, coordinate, or budget, usually through subordinate supervisory personnel, activities concerned with the construction and maintenance of structures, facilities, and systems.

Participate in the conceptual development of a construction project and oversee its organization, scheduling, and implementation. Schedule the project in logical steps and budget time required to meet deadlines. Confer with supervisory personnel, owners, contractors, and design professionals to discuss and resolve matters such as work procedures, complaints, and construction problems. Prepare contracts and negotiate revisions, changes, and additions to contractual agreements with architects, consultants, clients, suppliers, and subcontractors. Prepare and submit budget estimates and progress and cost tracking reports. Interpret and explain plans and contract terms to administrative staff, workers, and clients, representing the owner or developer. Plan, organize, and direct activities concerned with the construction and maintenance of structures, facilities, and systems. Take actions to deal with the results of delays, bad weather, or emergencies at construction sites. Inspect and review projects to monitor compliance with building and safety codes and other regulations. Study job specifications to determine appropriate construction methods. Select, contract, and oversee workers who complete specific pieces of the project such as painting or plumbing. Obtain all necessary permits and licenses. Direct and supervise workers. Develop and implement quality control programs. Investigate damage, accidents, or delays at construction sites to ensure that proper procedures are being carried out. Determine labor requirements and dispatch workers to construction sites. Evaluate construction methods and determine cost-effectiveness of plans, using computers. Requisition supplies and materials to complete construction projects. Direct acquisition of land for construction projects.

GOE—Interest Area/Cluster: 02. Architecture and Construction. **Work Group:** 02.01. Managerial Work in Architecture and Construction. **Other Jobs in This Work Group:** No other jobs in this group.

Skills: Management of Financial Resources; Management of Material Resources; Management of Personnel Resources; Systems Analysis; Systems Evaluation; Negotiation; Persuasion; Monitoring.

Education and Training Programs: Construction Engineering Technology/Technician; Business/Commerce, General; Business Administration and Management, General; Operations Management and Supervision; Construction Management. **Related Knowledge/Courses:** Building and Construction; Design; Engineering and Technology; Mechanical Devices; Administration and Management; Personnel and Human Resources.

Work Environment: Indoors; noisy; sitting.

Copy Writers

❋ Personality Code: EA
❋ Education/Training Required: Bachelor's degree
❋ Annual Earnings: $50,660
❋ Beginning Wage: $26,530
❋ Earnings Growth Potential: High
❋ Growth: 12.8%
❋ Annual Job Openings: 24,023
❋ Self-Employed: 65.9%
❋ Part-Time: 21.8%

The job openings listed here are shared with Poets, Lyricists, and Creative Writers.

Write advertising copy for use by publication or broadcast media to promote sale of goods and services. Write advertising copy for use by publication, broadcast, or Internet media to promote the sale of goods and services. Present drafts and ideas to clients. Discuss with the client the product, advertising themes and methods, and any changes that should be made in advertising copy. Consult with sales, media, and marketing representatives to obtain information on product or service and discuss style and length of advertising copy. Vary language and tone of messages based on product and medium. Edit or rewrite existing copy as necessary and submit copy for approval by supervisor. Write to customers in their terms and on their level so that the advertiser's sales message is more readily received. Write articles; bulletins; sales letters; speeches; and other related informative, marketing, and promotional material. Invent names for products and write the slogans that appear on packaging, brochures, and other promotional material. Review advertising trends, consumer surveys, and other data regarding marketing of goods and services to determine the best way to promote products. Develop advertising campaigns for a wide range of clients, working with an advertising agency's creative director and art director to determine the best way to present advertising information. Conduct research and interviews to determine which of a product's selling features should be promoted.

GOE—Interest Area/Cluster: 03. Arts and Communication. **Work Group:** 03.02. Writing and Editing. **Other Jobs in This Work Group:** Editors; Poets, Lyricists, and Creative Writers; Technical Writers; Writers and Authors.

Skills: Persuasion; Technology Design; Equipment Selection; Quality Control Analysis; Time Management; Writing; Active Listening; Negotiation.

Education and Training Programs: Communication Studies/Speech Communication and Rhetoric; Mass Communication/Media Studies; Journalism; Broadcast Journalism; Communication, Journalism, and Related Programs, Other; English Composition. **Related Knowledge/Courses:** Communications and Media; Sales and Marketing; Sociology and Anthropology; English Language; Computers and Electronics; Psychology.

Work Environment: Indoors; sitting; using hands on objects, tools, or controls; repetitive motions.

Criminal Investigators and Special Agents

- Personality Code: EI
- Education/Training Required: Work experience in a related occupation
- Annual Earnings: $59,930
- Beginning Wage: $35,600
- Earnings Growth Potential: High
- Growth: 17.3%
- Annual Job Openings: 14,746
- Self-Employed: 0.3%
- Part-Time: 2.2%

The job openings listed here are shared with Immigration and Customs Inspectors, with Police Detectives, and with Police Identification and Records Officers.

Investigate alleged or suspected criminal violations of federal, state, or local laws to determine if evidence is sufficient to recommend prosecution. Record evidence and documents, using equipment such as cameras and photocopy machines. Obtain and verify evidence by interviewing and observing suspects and witnesses or by analyzing records. Examine records to locate links in chains of evidence or information. Prepare reports that detail investigation findings. Determine scope, timing, and direction of investigations. Collaborate with other offices and agencies to exchange information and coordinate activities. Testify before grand juries concerning criminal activity investigations. Analyze evidence in laboratories or in the field. Investigate organized crime, public corruption, financial crime, copyright infringement, civil rights violations, bank robbery, extortion, kidnapping, and other violations of federal or state statutes. Identify case issues and evidence needed, based on analysis of charges, complaints, or allegations of law violations. Obtain and use search and arrest warrants. Serve subpoenas or other official papers. Collaborate with other authorities on activities such as surveillance, transcription, and research. Develop relationships with informants to obtain information related to cases. Search for and collect evidence such as fingerprints, using investigative equipment. Collect and record physical information about arrested suspects, including fingerprints, height and weight measurements, and photographs. Compare crime scene fingerprints with those from suspects or fingerprint files to identify perpetrators, using computers. Administer counter-terrorism and counter-narcotics reward programs. Provide protection for individuals such as government leaders, political candidates, and visiting foreign dignitaries. Perform undercover assignments and maintain surveillance, including monitoring authorized wiretaps. Manage security programs designed to protect personnel, facilities, and information. Issue security clearances.

GOE—Interest Area/Cluster: 12. Law and Public Safety. **Work Group:** 12.04. Law Enforcement and Public Safety. **Other Jobs in This Work Group:** Bailiffs; Correctional Officers and Jailers; Detectives and Criminal Investigators; Fire Investigators; Forensic Science Technicians; Parking Enforcement Workers; Police and Sheriff's Patrol Officers; Police Detectives; Police Identification and Records Officers; Police Patrol Officers; Sheriffs and Deputy Sheriffs; Transit and Railroad Police.

Skills: Negotiation; Operations Analysis; Programming; Judgment and Decision Making; Service Orientation; Complex Problem Solving; Equipment Selection; Persuasion.

Education and Training Programs: Criminal Justice/Police Science; Criminalistics and Criminal Science. **Related Knowledge/Courses:** Law and Government; Psychology; Geography; Public Safety and Security; Clerical Practices; Telecommunications.

Work Environment: More often outdoors than indoors; noisy; very hot or cold; standing.

Customer Service Representatives

- ❋ Personality Code: ESC
- ❋ Education/Training Required: Moderate-term on-the-job training
- ❋ Annual Earnings: $29,040
- ❋ Beginning Wage: $18,490
- ❋ Earnings Growth Potential: Medium
- ❋ Growth: 24.8%
- ❋ Annual Job Openings: 600,937
- ❋ Self-Employed: 0.4%
- ❋ Part-Time: 16.5%

Interact with customers to provide information in response to inquiries about products and services and to handle and resolve complaints. Confer with customers by telephone or in person to provide information about products and services, to take orders or cancel accounts, or to obtain details of complaints. Keep records of customer interactions and transactions, recording details of inquiries, complaints, and comments, as well as actions taken. Resolve customers' service or billing complaints by performing activities such as exchanging merchandise, refunding money, and adjusting bills. Check to ensure that appropriate changes were made to resolve customers' problems. Contact customers to respond to inquiries or to notify them of claim investigation results and any planned adjustments. Refer unresolved customer grievances to designated departments for further investigation. Determine charges for services requested, collect deposits or payments, or arrange for billing. Complete contract forms, prepare change of address records, and issue service discontinuance orders, using computers. Obtain and examine all relevant information to assess validity of complaints and to determine possible causes, such as extreme weather conditions, that could increase utility bills. Solicit sale of new or additional services or products. Review insurance policy terms to determine whether a particular loss is covered by insurance. Review claims adjustments with dealers, examining parts claimed to be defective and approving or disapproving dealers' claims. Compare disputed merchandise with original

requisitions and information from invoices and prepare invoices for returned goods. Order tests that could determine the causes of product malfunctions. Recommend improvements in products, packaging, shipping, service, or billing methods and procedures to prevent future problems.

GOE—Interest Area/Cluster: 14. Retail and Wholesale Sales and Service. **Work Group:** 14.06. Customer Service. **Other Jobs in This Work Group:** Cashiers; Counter and Rental Clerks; Gaming Cage Workers; Gaming Change Persons and Booth Cashiers; Order Clerks; Receptionists and Information Clerks.

Skills: Service Orientation; Monitoring; Reading Comprehension; Active Listening; Social Perceptiveness.

Education and Training Programs: Customer Service Support/Call Center/Teleservice Operation; Receptionist. **Related Knowledge/Courses:** Customer and Personal Service; Clerical Practices; Sales and Marketing.

Work Environment: Indoors; sitting; using hands on objects, tools, or controls; repetitive motions.

Demonstrators and Product Promoters

- ❋ Personality Code: ECR
- ❋ Education/Training Required: Moderate-term on-the-job training
- ❋ Annual Earnings: $22,570
- ❋ Beginning Wage: $16,440
- ❋ Earnings Growth Potential: Low
- ❋ Growth: 18.0%
- ❋ Annual Job Openings: 32,779
- ❋ Self-Employed: 20.8%
- ❋ Part-Time: 56.1%

Demonstrate merchandise and answer questions for the purpose of creating public interest in buying the product. May sell demonstrated merchandise. Demonstrate and explain products, methods, or services in order to persuade customers to purchase products or utilize services. Learn about competitors' products and consumers' interests and concerns in order to answer questions and provide more complete information. Recommend product or service improvements to employers. Train demonstrators to present a company's products or services. Give tours of plants where specific products are made. Develop lists of prospective clients from sources such as newspaper items, company records, local merchants, and customers. Contact businesses and civic establishments to arrange to exhibit and sell merchandise. Visit trade shows, stores, community organizations, and other venues to demonstrate products or services and to answer questions from potential customers. Write articles and pamphlets about products. Transport, assemble, and disassemble materials used in presentations. Instruct customers in alteration of products. Collect fees or accept donations. Identify interested and qualified customers in order to provide them with additional information. Work as part of a team of demonstrators to accommodate large crowds. Wear costumes or sign boards and walk in public to promote merchandise, services, or events. Provide product information, using lectures, films, charts, and/or slide shows. Prepare and alter presentation contents to target specific audiences. Keep areas neat while working and return items to correct locations following demonstrations. Record and report demonstration-related information such as the number of questions asked by the audience and the number of coupons distributed. Research and investigate products to be presented to prepare for demonstrations. Sell products being promoted and keep records of sales. Set up and arrange displays and demonstration areas to attract the attention of prospective customers. Stock shelves with products. Suggest specific product purchases to meet customers' needs. Provide product samples, coupons, informational brochures, and other incentives to persuade people to buy products. Practice demonstrations to ensure that they will run smoothly.

GOE—Interest Area/Cluster: 14. Retail and Wholesale Sales and Service. **Work Group:** 14.04. Personal Soliciting. **Other Jobs in This Work Group:** Door-To-Door Sales Workers, News and Street Vendors, and Related Workers; Models; Telemarketers.

Skill: Persuasion.

Education and Training Program: Retailing and Retail Operations. **Related Knowledge/Courses:** Sales and Marketing; Customer and Personal Service.

Work Environment: More often indoors than outdoors; standing; walking and running; using hands on objects, tools, or controls.

Detectives and Criminal Investigators

See Criminal Investigators and Special Agents (an Enterprising job), Immigration and Customs Inspectors (a Conventional job), Police Detectives (an Enterprising job), and Police Identification and Records Officers (a Conventional job), described separately.

Directors, Religious Activities and Education

- ❋ Personality Code: ESC
- ❋ Education/Training Required: Bachelor's degree
- ❋ Annual Earnings: $35,370
- ❋ Beginning Wage: $19,850
- ❋ Earnings Growth Potential: High
- ❋ Growth: 19.7%
- ❋ Annual Job Openings: 11,463
- ❋ Self-Employed: 0.0%
- ❋ Part-Time: 25.2%

Direct and coordinate activities of their chosen denominational groups to meet religious needs of students. Plan, direct, or coordinate church school programs designed to promote religious education among church membership. May provide counseling and guidance relative to marital, health, financial, and religious problems. Analyze

Enterprising-D

member participation and changes in congregation emphasis to determine needs for religious education. Collaborate with other ministry members to establish goals and objectives for religious education programs and to develop ways to encourage program participation. Interpret religious education activities to the public through speaking, leading discussions, and writing articles for local and national publications. Implement program plans by ordering needed materials, scheduling speakers, reserving spaces, and handling other administrative details. Confer with clergy members, congregation officials, and congregation organizations to encourage support of and participation in religious education activities. Develop and direct study courses and religious education programs within congregations. Locate and distribute resources such as periodicals and curricula in order to enhance the effectiveness of educational programs. Visit congregation members' homes, or arrange for pastoral visits, in order to provide information and resources regarding religious education programs. Identify and recruit potential volunteer workers. Participate in denominational activities aimed at goals such as promoting interfaith understanding or providing aid to new or small congregations. Publicize programs through sources such as newsletters, bulletins, and mailings. Counsel individuals regarding interpersonal, health, financial, and religious problems. Attend workshops, seminars, and conferences to obtain program ideas, information, and resources. Analyze revenue and program cost data to determine budget priorities. Train and supervise religious education instructional staffs. Select appropriate curricula and class structures for educational programs. Schedule special events such as camps, conferences, meetings, seminars, and retreats. Plan and conduct conferences dealing with the interpretation of religious ideas and convictions.

GOE—Interest Area/Cluster: 10. Human Service. **Work Group:** 10.02. Religious Work. **Other Jobs in This Work Group:** Clergy.

Skills: Management of Personnel Resources; Social Perceptiveness; Negotiation; Speaking; Management

of Financial Resources; Service Orientation; Coordination; Management of Material Resources.

Education and Training Programs: Bible/Biblical Studies; Missions/Missionary Studies and Missiology; Religious Education; Youth Ministry. **Related Knowledge/Courses:** Philosophy and Theology; Education and Training; Therapy and Counseling; Sales and Marketing; History and Archeology; Economics and Accounting.

Work Environment: Indoors; sitting.

Directors—Stage, Motion Pictures, Television, and Radio

* Personality Code: EA
* Education/Training Required: Work experience plus degree
* Annual Earnings: $61,090
* Beginning Wage: $28,980
* Earnings Growth Potential: Very high
* Growth: 11.1%
* Annual Job Openings: 8,992
* Self-Employed: 29.5%
* Part-Time: 9.0%

The job openings listed here are shared with Producers, with Program Directors, with Talent Directors, and with Technical Directors/Managers.

Interpret script, conduct rehearsals, and direct activities of cast and technical crew for stage, motion pictures, television, or radio programs. Direct live broadcasts, films and recordings, or non-broadcast programming for public entertainment or education. Supervise and coordinate the work of camera, lighting, design, and sound crew members. Study and research scripts to determine how they should be directed. Cut and edit film or tape to integrate component parts into desired sequences. Collaborate with film and sound editors during the post-production process as films are edited and soundtracks are added. Confer with technical directors, managers, crew members, and writers to discuss details of production, such as photography, script, music, sets, and costumes. Plan details such as framing, composition, camera movement, sound, and actor movement for each shot or scene. Communicate to actors the approach, characterization, and movement needed for each scene in such a way that rehearsals and takes are minimized. Establish pace of programs and sequences of scenes according to time requirements and cast and set accessibility. Choose settings and locations for films and determine how scenes will be shot in these settings. Identify and approve equipment and elements required for productions, such as scenery, lights, props, costumes, choreography, and music. Compile scripts, program notes, and other material related to productions. Perform producers' duties such as securing financial backing, establishing and administering budgets, and recruiting cast and crew. Select plays or scripts for production and determine how material should be interpreted and performed. Compile cue words and phrases; cue announcers, cast members, and technicians during performances. Consult with writers, producers, or actors about script changes or "workshop" scripts, through rehearsal with writers and actors, to create final drafts. Collaborate with producers to hire crew members such as art directors, cinematographers, and costumer designers. Review film daily to check on work in progress and to plan for future filming. Interpret stage-set diagrams to determine stage layouts and supervise placement of equipment and scenery. Hold auditions for parts or negotiate contracts with actors determined suitable for specific roles, working in conjunction with producers.

GOE—Interest Area/Cluster: 03. Arts and Communication. **Work Group:** 03.06. Drama. **Other Jobs in This Work Group:** Actors; Costume Attendants; Makeup Artists, Theatrical and Performance; Public Address System and Other Announcers; Radio and Television Announcers.

Skills: Management of Personnel Resources; Time Management; Judgment and Decision Making; Operations Analysis; Equipment Selection; Active Listening; Speaking; Critical Thinking.

Education and Training Programs: Radio and Television; Drama and Dramatics/Theatre Arts, General; Directing and Theatrical Production; Theatre/Theatre Arts Management; Dramatic/Theatre Arts and Stagecraft, Other; Film/Cinema Studies; Cinematography and Film/Video Production. **Related Knowledge/Courses:** Communications and Media; Telecommunications; Fine Arts; Geography; Computers and Electronics; Education and Training.

Work Environment: More often indoors than outdoors; noisy; sitting; using hands on objects, tools, or controls.

Education Administrators, Elementary and Secondary School

* Personality Code: ESC
* Education/Training Required: Work experience plus degree
* Annual Earnings: $80,580
* Beginning Wage: $52,940
* Earnings Growth Potential: Low
* Growth: 7.6%
* Annual Job Openings: 27,143
* Self-Employed: 3.3%
* Part-Time: 8.3%

Plan, direct, or coordinate the academic, clerical, or auxiliary activities of public or private elementary or secondary-level schools. Review and approve new programs or recommend modifications to existing programs, submitting program proposals for school board approval as necessary. Prepare, maintain, or oversee the preparation and maintenance of attendance, activity, planning, or personnel reports and records. Confer with parents and staff to discuss educational activities, policies, and student behavioral or learning problems. Prepare and submit budget requests and recommendations or grant proposals to solicit program funding. Direct and coordinate school maintenance services and the use of school facilities. Counsel and provide guidance to

Enterprising—E

students regarding personal, academic, vocational, or behavioral issues. Organize and direct committees of specialists, volunteers, and staff to provide technical and advisory assistance for programs. Teach classes or courses to students. Advocate for new schools to be built or for existing facilities to be repaired or remodeled. Plan and develop instructional methods and content for educational, vocational, or student activity programs. Develop partnerships with businesses, communities, and other organizations to help meet identified educational needs and to provide school-to-work programs. Direct and coordinate activities of teachers, administrators, and support staff at schools, public agencies, and institutions. Evaluate curricula, teaching methods, and programs to determine their effectiveness, efficiency, and utilization and to ensure that school activities comply with federal, state, and local regulations. Set educational standards and goals and help establish policies and procedures to carry them out. Recruit, hire, train, and evaluate primary and supplemental staff. Enforce discipline and attendance rules. Observe teaching methods and examine learning materials to evaluate and standardize curricula and teaching techniques and to determine areas where improvement is needed. Establish, coordinate, and oversee particular programs across school districts, such as programs to evaluate student academic achievement. Review and interpret government codes and develop programs to ensure adherence to codes and facility safety, security, and maintenance.

GOE—Interest Area/Cluster: 05. Education and Training. **Work Group:** 05.01. Managerial Work in Education. **Other Jobs in This Work Group:** Education Administrators, Postsecondary; Education Administrators, Preschool and Child Care Center/Program; Instructional Coordinators.

Skills: Management of Personnel Resources; Management of Financial Resources; Negotiation; Learning Strategies; Monitoring; Management of Material Resources; Systems Evaluation; Social Perceptiveness.

Education and Training Programs: Educational Leadership and Administration, General; Educational, Instructional, and Curriculum Supervision;

Elementary and Middle School Administration/Principalship; Secondary School Administration/Principalship; Educational Administration and Supervision, Other. **Related Knowledge/Courses:** Therapy and Counseling; Education and Training; Personnel and Human Resources; Psychology; Sociology and Anthropology; History and Archeology.

Work Environment: Indoors; standing.

Education Administrators, Postsecondary

- ❋ Personality Code: ECS
- ❋ Education/Training Required: Work experience plus degree
- ❋ Annual Earnings: $75,780
- ❋ Beginning Wage: $41,910
- ❋ Earnings Growth Potential: High
- ❋ Growth: 14.2%
- ❋ Annual Job Openings: 17,121
- ❋ Self-Employed: 3.3%
- ❋ Part-Time: 8.3%

Plan, direct, or coordinate research, instructional, student administration and services, and other educational activities at postsecondary institutions, including universities, colleges, and junior and community colleges. Recruit, hire, train, and terminate departmental personnel. Plan, administer, and control budgets; maintain financial records; and produce financial reports. Represent institutions at community and campus events, in meetings with other institution personnel, and during accreditation processes. Participate in faculty and college committee activities. Provide assistance to faculty and staff in duties such as teaching classes, conducting orientation programs, issuing transcripts, and scheduling events. Establish operational policies and procedures and make any necessary modifications, based on analysis of operations, demographics, and other research information. Confer with other academic staff to explain and formulate admission requirements and course credit policies. Appoint individuals to faculty positions and evaluate their performance. Direct activities of administrative departments such as admissions, registration, and career services. Develop curricula and recommend curricula revisions and additions. Determine course schedules and coordinate teaching assignments and room assignments to ensure optimum use of buildings and equipment. Consult with government regulatory and licensing agencies to ensure the institution's conformance with applicable standards. Direct, coordinate, and evaluate the activities of personnel engaged in administering academic institutions, departments, and/or alumni organizations. Teach courses within their department. Participate in student recruitment, selection, and admission, making admissions recommendations when required to do so. Review student misconduct reports requiring disciplinary action and counsel students regarding such reports. Supervise coaches. Assess and collect tuition and fees. Direct scholarship, fellowship, and loan programs, performing activities such as selecting recipients and distributing aid. Coordinate the production and dissemination of university publications such as course catalogs and class schedules. Review registration statistics and consult with faculty officials to develop registration policies. Audit the financial status of student organizations and facility accounts.

GOE—Interest Area/Cluster: 05. Education and Training. **Work Group:** 05.01. Managerial Work in Education. **Other Jobs in This Work Group:** Education Administrators, Elementary and Secondary School; Education Administrators, Preschool and Child Care Center/Program; Instructional Coordinators.

Skills: Management of Financial Resources; Management of Personnel Resources; Systems Evaluation; Persuasion; Monitoring; Judgment and Decision Making; Management of Material Resources; Operations Analysis.

Education and Training Programs: Educational Leadership and Administration, General; Educational, Instructional, and Curriculum Supervision; Higher Education/Higher Education Administration; Community College Education; Educational

Administration and Supervision, Other. **Related Knowledge/Courses:** Personnel and Human Resources; Education and Training; Sociology and Anthropology; Administration and Management; Philosophy and Theology; English Language.

Work Environment: Indoors; sitting.

Employment Interviewers

- ❋ Personality Code: ESC
- ❋ Education/Training Required: Bachelor's degree
- ❋ Annual Earnings: $44,380
- ❋ Beginning Wage: $27,340
- ❋ Earnings Growth Potential: Medium
- ❋ Growth: 18.4%
- ❋ Annual Job Openings: 33,588
- ❋ Self-Employed: 2.1%
- ❋ Part-Time: 7.6%

The job openings listed here are shared with Personnel Recruiters.

Interview job applicants in employment office and refer them to prospective employers for consideration. Search application files, notify selected applicants of job openings, and refer qualified applicants to prospective employers. Contact employers to verify referral results. Record and evaluate various pertinent data. Inform applicants of job openings and details such as duties and responsibilities, compensation, benefits, schedules, working conditions, and promotion opportunities. Interview job applicants to match their qualifications with employers' needs, recording and evaluating applicant experience, education, training, and skills. Review employment applications and job orders to match applicants with job requirements, using manual or computerized file searches. Select qualified applicants or refer them to employers according to organization policy. Perform reference and background checks on applicants. Maintain records of applicants not selected for employment. Instruct job applicants

Enterprising—E

in presenting a positive image by providing help with resume writing, personal appearance, and interview techniques. Refer applicants to services such as vocational counseling, literacy or language instruction, transportation assistance, vocational training, and child care. Contact employers to solicit orders for job vacancies, determining their requirements and recording relevant data such as job descriptions. Conduct workshops and demonstrate the use of job listings to assist applicants with skill building. Search for and recruit applicants for open positions through campus job fairs and advertisements. Provide background information on organizations with which interviews are scheduled. Administer assessment tests to identify skill-building needs. Conduct or arrange for skill, intelligence, or psychological testing of applicants and current employees. Hire workers and place them with employers needing temporary help. Evaluate selection and testing techniques by conducting research or follow-up activities and conferring with management and supervisory personnel.

GOE—Interest Area/Cluster: 04. Business and Administration. **Work Group:** 04.03. Human Resources Support. **Other Jobs in This Work Group:** Compensation, Benefits, and Job Analysis Specialists; Employment, Recruitment, and Placement Specialists; Personnel Recruiters; Training and Development Specialists.

Skills: Management of Personnel Resources; Service Orientation; Social Perceptiveness; Persuasion; Negotiation; Writing; Speaking; Instructing.

Education and Training Programs: Human Resources Management/Personnel Administration, General; Labor and Industrial Relations. **Related Knowledge/Courses:** Foreign Language; Clerical Practices; Personnel and Human Resources; Sales and Marketing; Customer and Personal Service; English Language.

Work Environment: Indoors; sitting; repetitive motions.

Employment, Recruitment, and Placement Specialists

See Employment Interviewers (an Enterprising job) and Personnel Recruiters (an Enterprising job), described separately.

Engineering Managers

- ❋ Personality Code: ERI
- ❋ Education/Training Required: Work experience plus degree
- ❋ Annual Earnings: $111,020
- ❋ Beginning Wage: $70,640
- ❋ Earnings Growth Potential: Medium
- ❋ Growth: 7.3%
- ❋ Annual Job Openings: 7,404
- ❋ Self-Employed: 0.0%
- ❋ Part-Time: 2.0%

Plan, direct, or coordinate activities or research and development in such fields as architecture and engineering. Coordinate and direct projects, making detailed plans to accomplish goals and directing the integration of technical activities. Consult or negotiate with clients to prepare project specifications. Present and explain proposals, reports, and findings to clients. Direct, review, and approve product design and changes. Recruit employees, assign, direct, and evaluate their work, and oversee the development and maintenance of staff competence. Perform administrative functions such as reviewing and writing reports, approving expenditures, enforcing rules, and making decisions about the purchase of materials or services. Prepare budgets, bids, and contracts, and direct the negotiation of research contracts. Analyze technology, resource needs, and market demand, to plan and assess the feasibility of projects. Confer with management, production, and marketing staff to discuss project specifications and procedures. Review and recommend or approve contracts and cost estimates. Develop and implement policies, standards, and procedures for the engineering and technical work performed in the department, service, laboratory, or firm. Plan and direct the installation, testing, operation, maintenance, and repair of facilities and equipment. Administer highway planning, construction, and maintenance. Confer with and report to officials and the public to provide information and solicit support for projects. Set scientific and technical goals within broad outlines provided by top management. Direct the engineering of water control, treatment, and distribution projects. Plan, direct, and coordinate survey work with other staff activities, certifying survey work, and writing land legal descriptions.

GOE—Interest Area/Cluster: 15. Scientific Research, Engineering, and Mathematics. **Work Group:** 15.01. Managerial Work in Scientific Research, Engineering, and Mathematics. **Other Jobs in This Work Group:** Natural Sciences Managers.

Skills: Management of Financial Resources; Management of Personnel Resources; Systems Analysis; Management of Material Resources; Systems Evaluation; Negotiation; Mathematics; Writing.

Education and Training Programs: Architecture (BArch, BA/BS, MArch, MA/MS, PhD); City/Urban, Community and Regional Planning; Environmental Design/Architecture; Interior Architecture; Landscape Architecture (BS, BSLA, BLA, MSLA, MLA, PhD); Engineering, General; Aerospace, Aeronautical and Astronautical Engineering; Agricultural/Biological Engineering and Bioengineering; Architectural Engineering; Biomedical/Medical Engineering; others. **Related Knowledge/Courses:** Engineering and Technology; Design; Physics; Building and Construction; Computers and Electronics; Mathematics.

Work Environment: Indoors; noisy; sitting.

Financial Managers

See Financial Managers, Branch or Department (an Enterprising job) and Treasurers and Controllers (a Conventional job), described separately.

Financial Managers, Branch or Department

- ❊ Personality Code: EC
- ❊ Education/Training Required: Work experience plus degree
- ❊ Annual Earnings: $95,310
- ❊ Beginning Wage: $51,910
- ❊ Earnings Growth Potential: High
- ❊ Growth: 12.6%
- ❊ Annual Job Openings: 57,589
- ❊ Self-Employed: 4.6%
- ❊ Part-Time: 4.2%

The job openings listed here are shared with Treasurers and Controllers.

Direct and coordinate financial activities of workers in a branch, office, or department of an establishment, such as branch bank, brokerage firm, risk and insurance department, or credit department. Establish and maintain relationships with individual and business customers and provide assistance with problems these customers may encounter. Examine, evaluate, and process loan applications. Plan, direct, and coordinate the activities of workers in branches, offices, or departments of such establishments as branch banks, brokerage firms, risk and insurance departments, or credit departments. Oversee the flow of cash and financial instruments. Recruit staff members and oversee training programs. Network within communities to find and attract new business. Approve or reject, or coordinate the approval and rejection of, lines of credit and commercial, real estate, and personal loans. Prepare financial and regulatory reports required by laws, regulations, and boards of directors. Establish procedures for custody and control of assets, records, loan collateral, and securities in order to ensure safekeeping. Review collection reports to determine the status of collections and the amounts of outstanding balances. Prepare operational and risk reports for management analysis. Evaluate financial reporting systems, accounting and collection procedures, and investment activities and

Enterprising-F

make recommendations for changes to procedures, operating systems, budgets, and other financial control functions. Plan, direct, and coordinate risk and insurance programs of establishments to control risks and losses. Submit delinquent accounts to attorneys or outside agencies for collection. Communicate with stockholders and other investors to provide information and to raise capital. Evaluate data pertaining to costs in order to plan budgets. Analyze and classify risks and investments to determine their potential impacts on companies. Review reports of securities transactions and price lists in order to analyze market conditions. Develop and analyze information to assess the current and future financial status of firms. Direct insurance negotiations, select insurance brokers and carriers, and place insurance.

GOE—Interest Area/Cluster: 06. Finance and Insurance. **Work Group:** 06.01. Managerial Work in Finance and Insurance. **Other Jobs in This Work Group:** Financial Managers; Treasurers and Controllers.

Skills: Management of Personnel Resources; Management of Financial Resources; Service Orientation; Time Management; Persuasion; Negotiation; Instructing; Systems Evaluation.

Education and Training Programs: Accounting and Finance; Finance, General; International Finance; Public Finance; Credit Management; Finance and Financial Management Services, Other. **Related Knowledge/Courses:** Economics and Accounting; Sales and Marketing; Personnel and Human Resources; Clerical Practices; Customer and Personal Service; Mathematics.

Work Environment: Indoors; sitting.

First-Line Supervisors/Managers of Construction Trades and Extraction Workers

- ❀ Personality Code: ERC
- ❀ Education/Training Required: Work experience in a related occupation
- ❀ Annual Earnings: $55,950
- ❀ Beginning Wage: $34,870
- ❀ Earnings Growth Potential: Medium
- ❀ Growth: 9.1%
- ❀ Annual Job Openings: 82,923
- ❀ Self-Employed: 24.4%
- ❀ Part-Time: 3.0%

Directly supervise and coordinate activities of construction or extraction workers. Examine and inspect work progress, equipment, and construction sites to verify safety and to ensure that specifications are met. Read specifications such as blueprints to determine construction requirements and to plan procedures. Estimate material and worker requirements to complete jobs. Supervise, coordinate, and schedule the activities of construction or extractive workers. Confer with managerial and technical personnel, other departments, and contractors in order to resolve problems and to coordinate activities. Coordinate work activities with other construction project activities. Locate, measure, and mark site locations and placement of structures and equipment, using measuring and marking equipment. Order or requisition materials and supplies. Record information such as personnel, production, and operational data on specified forms and reports. Assign work to employees, based on material and worker requirements of specific jobs. Provide assistance to workers engaged in construction or extraction activities, using hand tools and equipment. Train workers in construction methods, operation of equipment, safety procedures, and company policies. Analyze worker and production problems and recommend solutions such as improving production methods or implementing motivational plans. Arrange for repairs of equipment and machinery. Suggest or initiate personnel actions such as promotions, transfers, and hires.

GOE—Interest Area/Cluster: 01. Agriculture and Natural Resources. **Work Group:** 01.01. Managerial Work in Agriculture and Natural Resources. **Other Jobs in This Work Group:** Aquacultural Managers; Crop and Livestock Managers; Farm Labor Contractors; Farm, Ranch, and Other Agricultural Managers; Farmers and Ranchers; First-Line Supervisors/Managers of Agricultural Crop and Horticultural Workers; First-Line Supervisors/Managers of Animal Husbandry and Animal Care Workers; First-Line Supervisors/Managers of Aquacultural Workers; First-Line Supervisors/Managers of Farming, Fishing, and Forestry Workers; First-Line Supervisors/Managers of Landscaping, Lawn Service, and Groundskeeping Workers; First-Line Supervisors/Managers of Logging Workers; Nursery and Greenhouse Managers; Park Naturalists; Purchasing Agents and Buyers, Farm Products.

Skills: Management of Material Resources; Installation; Equipment Maintenance; Repairing; Coordination; Equipment Selection; Management of Personnel Resources; Mathematics.

Education and Training Programs: Blasting/Blaster; Building/Construction Finishing, Management, and Inspection, Other; Building/Construction Site Management/Manager; Building/Construction Trades, Other; Building/Home/Construction Inspection/Inspector; Building/property Maintenance and Management; Carpentry/Carpenter; Concrete Finishing/Concrete Finisher; Drywall Installation/Drywaller; others. **Related Knowledge/Courses:** Building and Construction; Mechanical Devices; Design; Engineering and Technology; Production and Processing; Administration and Management.

Work Environment: Outdoors; noisy; very hot or cold; contaminants; hazardous equipment; standing.

First-Line Supervisors/Managers of Food Preparation and Serving Workers

- ✳ Personality Code: ECR
- ✳ Education/Training Required: Work experience in a related occupation
- ✳ Annual Earnings: $28,040
- ✳ Beginning Wage: $17,920
- ✳ Earnings Growth Potential: Medium
- ✳ Growth: 11.3%
- ✳ Annual Job Openings: 154,175
- ✳ Self-Employed: 4.1%
- ✳ Part-Time: 14.5%

Supervise workers engaged in preparing and serving food. Compile and balance cash receipts at the end of the day or shift. Resolve customer complaints regarding food service. Inspect supplies, equipment, and work areas to ensure efficient service and conformance to standards. Train workers in food preparation and in service, sanitation, and safety procedures. Control inventories of food, equipment, smallware, and liquor and report shortages to designated personnel. Observe and evaluate workers and work procedures to ensure quality standards and service. Assign duties, responsibilities, and workstations to employees in accordance with work requirements. Estimate ingredients and supplies required to prepare a recipe. Perform personnel actions such as hiring and firing staff, consulting with other managers as necessary. Analyze operational problems, such as theft and wastage, and establish procedures to alleviate these problems. Specify food portions and courses, production and time sequences, and workstation and equipment arrangements. Recommend measures for improving work procedures and worker performance to increase service quality and enhance job safety. Greet and seat guests and present menus and wine lists. Present bills and accept payments. Forecast staff, equipment, and supply requirements based on a master menu. Record production and operational data on specified forms. Perform serving duties such

Enterprising-F

as carving meat, preparing flambé dishes, or serving wine and liquor. Purchase or requisition supplies and equipment needed to ensure quality and timely delivery of services. Collaborate with other personnel to plan menus, serving arrangements, and related details. Supervise and check the assembly of regular and special diet trays and the delivery of food trolleys to hospital patients. Schedule parties and take reservations. Develop departmental objectives, budgets, policies, procedures, and strategies. Develop equipment maintenance schedules and arrange for repairs. Evaluate new products for usefulness and suitability.

GOE—Interest Area/Cluster: 09. Hospitality, Tourism, and Recreation. **Work Group:** 09.01. Managerial Work in Hospitality and Tourism. **Other Jobs in This Work Group:** First-Line Supervisors/Managers of Personal Service Workers; Food Service Managers; Gaming Managers; Gaming Supervisors; Lodging Managers.

Skills: Equipment Maintenance; Management of Financial Resources; Management of Personnel Resources; Operation Monitoring; Management of Material Resources; Monitoring.

Education and Training Programs: Cooking and Related Culinary Arts, General; Restaurant, Culinary, and Catering Management/Manager; Foodservice Systems Administration/Management. **Related Knowledge/Courses:** Food Production; Administration and Management; Customer and Personal Service; Economics and Accounting; Sales and Marketing; Production and Processing.

Work Environment: Indoors; minor burns, cuts, bites, or stings; standing; walking and running; using hands on objects, tools, or controls; repetitive motions.

First-Line Supervisors/Managers of Housekeeping and Janitorial Workers

- ❀ Personality Code: ECR
- ❀ Education/Training Required: Work experience in a related occupation
- ❀ Annual Earnings: $32,850
- ❀ Beginning Wage: $20,650
- ❀ Earnings Growth Potential: Medium
- ❀ Growth: 12.7%
- ❀ Annual Job Openings: 30,613
- ❀ Self-Employed: 30.7%
- ❀ Part-Time: 10.8%

Supervise work activities of cleaning personnel in hotels, hospitals, offices, and other establishments. Direct activities for stopping the spread of infections in facilities such as hospitals. Inspect work performed to ensure that it meets specifications and established standards. Plan and prepare employee work schedules. Perform or assist with cleaning duties as necessary. Investigate complaints about service and equipment and take corrective action. Coordinate activities with other departments to ensure that services are provided in an efficient and timely manner. Check equipment to ensure that it is in working order. Inspect and evaluate the physical condition of facilities to determine the type of work required. Select the most suitable cleaning materials for different types of linens, furniture, flooring, and surfaces. Instruct staff in work policies and procedures and the use and maintenance of equipment. Issue supplies and equipment to workers. Forecast necessary levels of staffing and stock at different times to facilitate effective scheduling and ordering. Inventory stock to ensure that supplies and equipment are available in adequate amounts. Evaluate employee performance and recommend personnel actions such as promotions, transfers, and dismissals. Confer with staff to resolve performance and personnel problems and to discuss company policies. Establish and implement operational standards and procedures for the departments they supervise. Recommend or arrange for additional services such as painting, repair work, renovations, and the replacement of furnishings and equipment. Select and order or purchase new equipment, supplies, and furnishings. Recommend changes that could improve service and increase operational efficiency. Maintain required records of work hours, budgets, payrolls, and other information. Screen job applicants and hire new employees. Supervise in-house services such as laundries, maintenance and repair, dry cleaning, and valet services. Advise managers, desk clerks, or admitting personnel of rooms ready for occupancy. Perform financial tasks such as estimating costs and preparing and managing budgets. Prepare activity and personnel reports and reports containing information such as occupancy, hours worked, facility usage, work performed, and departmental expenses.

GOE—Interest Area/Cluster: 04. Business and Administration. **Work Group:** 04.02. Managerial Work in Business Detail. **Other Jobs in This Work Group:** Administrative Services Managers; First-Line Supervisors/Managers of Office and Administrative Support Workers; Meeting and Convention Planners.

Skills: Management of Personnel Resources; Monitoring; Equipment Maintenance; Equipment Selection; Service Orientation; Writing; Systems Evaluation; Science.

Education and Training Programs: No related CIP programs; this job is learned through work experience in a related occupation. **Related Knowledge/Courses:** Chemistry; Building and Construction; Public Safety and Security; Physics; Mechanical Devices; Administration and Management.

Work Environment: Indoors; contaminants; disease or infections; standing; walking and running.

First-Line Supervisors/Managers of Landscaping, Lawn Service, and Groundskeeping Workers

❋ Personality Code: ERC
❋ Education/Training Required: Work experience in a related occupation
❋ Annual Earnings: $38,720
❋ Beginning Wage: $25,270
❋ Earnings Growth Potential: Low
❋ Growth: 17.6%
❋ Annual Job Openings: 18,956
❋ Self-Employed: 44.1%
❋ Part-Time: 6.1%

Plan, organize, direct, or coordinate activities of workers engaged in landscaping or groundskeeping activities such as planting and maintaining ornamental trees, shrubs, flowers, and lawns and applying fertilizers, pesticides, and other chemicals, according to contract specifications. May also coordinate activities of workers engaged in terracing hillsides, building retaining walls, constructing pathways, installing patios, and similar activities in following a landscape design plan. Work may involve reviewing contracts to ascertain service, machine, and work force requirements; answering inquiries from potential customers regarding methods, material, and price ranges; and preparing estimates according to labor, material, and machine costs. Establish and enforce operating procedures and work standards that will ensure adequate performance and personnel safety. Inspect completed work to ensure conformance to specifications, standards, and contract requirements. Direct activities of workers who perform duties such as landscaping, cultivating lawns, or pruning trees and shrubs. Schedule work for crews depending on work priorities, crew and equipment availability, and weather conditions. Plant and maintain vegetation through activities such as mulching, fertilizing, watering, mowing, and pruning. Monitor project activities to ensure that instructions are

Enterprising–F

followed, deadlines are met, and schedules are maintained. Train workers in tasks such as transplanting and pruning trees and shrubs, finishing cement, using equipment, and caring for turf. Provide workers with assistance in performing duties as necessary to meet deadlines. Inventory supplies of tools, equipment, and materials to ensure that sufficient supplies are available and items are in usable condition. Confer with other supervisors to coordinate work activities with those of other departments or units. Perform personnel-related activities such as hiring workers, evaluating staff performance, and taking disciplinary actions when performance problems occur. Direct or perform mixing and application of fertilizers, insecticides, herbicides, and fungicides. Review contracts or work assignments to determine service, machine, and workforce requirements for jobs. Maintain required records such as personnel information and project records. Prepare and maintain required records such as work activity and personnel reports. Order the performance of corrective work when problems occur, and recommend procedural changes to avoid such problems. Identify diseases and pests affecting landscaping, and order appropriate treatments. Investigate work-related complaints in order to verify problems, and to determine responses. Direct and assist workers engaged in the maintenance and repair of equipment such as power tools and motorized equipment. Install and maintain landscaped areas, performing tasks such as removing snow, pouring cement curbs, and repairing sidewalks.

GOE—Interest Area/Cluster: 01. Agriculture and Natural Resources. **Work Group:** 01.01. Managerial Work in Agriculture and Natural Resources. **Other Jobs in This Work Group:** Aquacultural Managers; Crop and Livestock Managers; Farm Labor Contractors; Farm, Ranch, and Other Agricultural Managers; Farmers and Ranchers; First-Line Supervisors/Managers of Agricultural Crop and Horticultural Workers; First-Line Supervisors/Managers of Animal Husbandry and Animal Care Workers; First-Line Supervisors/Managers of Aquacultural Workers; First-Line Supervisors/Managers of Construction Trades and Extraction Workers; First-Line Supervisors/Managers of Farming, Fishing, and Forestry Workers; First-Line Supervisors/Managers of Logging Workers; Nursery and Greenhouse Managers; Park Naturalists; Purchasing Agents and Buyers, Farm Products.

Skills: Repairing; Equipment Maintenance; Systems Analysis; Operations Analysis; Management of Personnel Resources; Equipment Selection; Monitoring; Operation and Control.

Education and Training Programs: Ornamental Horticulture; Landscaping and Groundskeeping; Turf and Turfgrass Management. **Related Knowledge/Courses:** Mechanical Devices; Building and Construction; Biology; Design; Chemistry; Education and Training.

Work Environment: Outdoors; noisy; very hot or cold; contaminants; minor burns, cuts, bites, or stings; standing.

First-Line Supervisors/Managers of Non-Retail Sales Workers

* Personality Code: ECS
* Education/Training Required: Work experience in a related occupation
* Annual Earnings: $67,020
* Beginning Wage: $36,120
* Earnings Growth Potential: High
* Growth: 3.7%
* Annual Job Openings: 48,883
* Self-Employed: 45.4%
* Part-Time: 5.3%

Directly supervise and coordinate activities of sales workers other than retail sales workers. May perform duties such as budgeting, accounting, and personnel work in addition to supervisory duties. Listen to and resolve customer complaints regarding services, products, or personnel. Monitor sales staff performance to ensure that goals are met. Hire, train, and evaluate personnel. Confer with company officials to develop methods and procedures to increase sales, expand markets, and promote business. Direct and supervise employees engaged in sales, inventory-taking, reconciling cash receipts, or performing specific services such as pumping gasoline for customers. Provide staff with assistance in performing difficult or complicated duties. Plan and prepare work schedules and assign employees to specific duties. Attend company meetings to exchange product information and coordinate work activities with other departments. Prepare sales and inventory reports for management and budget departments. Formulate pricing policies on merchandise according to profitability requirements. Examine merchandise to ensure correct pricing and display and ensure that it functions as advertised. Analyze details of sales territories to assess their growth potential and to set quotas. Visit retailers and sales representatives to promote products and gather information. Keep records pertaining to purchases, sales, and requisitions. Coordinate sales promotion activities and prepare merchandise displays and advertising copy. Prepare rental or lease agreements, specifying charges and payment procedures for use of machinery, tools, or other items. Inventory stock and reorder when inventories drop to specified levels. Examine products purchased for resale or received for storage to determine product condition.

GOE—Interest Area/Cluster: 14. Retail and Wholesale Sales and Service. **Work Group:** 14.01. Managerial Work in Retail/Wholesale Sales and Service. **Other Jobs in This Work Group:** Advertising and Promotions Managers; First-Line Supervisors/Managers of Retail Sales Workers; Funeral Directors; Marketing Managers; Property, Real Estate, and Community Association Managers; Purchasing Managers; Sales Managers.

Skills: Management of Personnel Resources; Negotiation; Persuasion; Time Management; Social Perceptiveness; Operations Analysis; Monitoring; Judgment and Decision Making.

Education and Training Programs: General Merchandising, Sales, and Related Marketing Operations, Other; Special Products Marketing Operations; Specialized Merchandising, Sales, and Related Marketing Operations, Other; Business, Management,

Marketing, and Related Support Services, Other. **Related Knowledge/Courses:** Sales and Marketing; Economics and Accounting; Personnel and Human Resources; Administration and Management; Mathematics; Education and Training.

Work Environment: Indoors; noisy.

First-Line Supervisors/Managers of Office and Administrative Support Workers

- ❋ Personality Code: ECS
- ❋ Education/Training Required: Work experience in a related occupation
- ❋ Annual Earnings: $44,650
- ❋ Beginning Wage: $27,190
- ❋ Earnings Growth Potential: Medium
- ❋ Growth: 5.8%
- ❋ Annual Job Openings: 138,420
- ❋ Self-Employed: 1.6%
- ❋ Part-Time: 7.9%

Supervise and coordinate the activities of clerical and administrative support workers. Resolve customer complaints and answer customers' questions regarding policies and procedures. Supervise the work of office, administrative, or customer service employees to ensure adherence to quality standards, deadlines, and proper procedures, correcting errors or problems. Provide employees with guidance in handling difficult or complex problems and in resolving escalated complaints or disputes. Implement corporate and departmental policies, procedures, and service standards in conjunction with management. Discuss job performance problems with employees to identify causes and issues and to work on resolving problems. Train and instruct employees in job duties and company policies or arrange for training to be provided. Evaluate employees' job performance and conformance to regulations and recommend appropriate personnel action. Recruit, interview, and select employees. Review records and reports pertaining to activities such as production, payroll, and shipping to verify details, monitor work activities, and evaluate performance. Interpret and communicate work procedures and company policies to staff. Prepare and issue work schedules, deadlines, and duty assignments of office or administrative staff. Maintain records pertaining to inventory, personnel, orders, supplies, and machine maintenance. Compute figures such as balances, totals, and commissions. Research, compile, and prepare reports, manuals, correspondence, and other information required by management or governmental agencies. Coordinate activities with other supervisory personnel and with other work units or departments. Analyze financial activities of establishments or departments and provide input into budget planning and preparation processes. Develop or update procedures, policies, and standards. Make recommendations to management concerning such issues as staffing decisions and procedural changes. Consult with managers and other personnel to resolve problems in areas such as equipment performance, output quality, and work schedules. Participate in the work of subordinates to facilitate productivity or to overcome difficult aspects of work.

GOE—Interest Area/Cluster: 04. Business and Administration. **Work Group:** 04.02. Managerial Work in Business Detail. **Other Jobs in This Work Group:** Administrative Services Managers; First-Line Supervisors/Managers of Housekeeping and Janitorial Workers; Meeting and Convention Planners.

Skills: Management of Personnel Resources; Management of Financial Resources; Negotiation; Management of Material Resources; Monitoring; Service Orientation; Persuasion; Judgment and Decision Making.

Education and Training Programs: No related CIP programs; this job is learned through work experience in a related occupation. **Related Knowledge/Courses:** Clerical Practices; Economics and Accounting; Administration and Management; Personnel and Human Resources; Customer and Personal Service; Education and Training.

Work Environment: Indoors; noisy; sitting.

First-Line Supervisors/Managers of Personal Service Workers

- ❋ Personality Code: ECS
- ❋ Education/Training Required: Work experience in a related occupation
- ❋ Annual Earnings: $33,900
- ❋ Beginning Wage: $20,820
- ❋ Earnings Growth Potential: Medium
- ❋ Growth: 15.5%
- ❋ Annual Job Openings: 37,555
- ❋ Self-Employed: 38.6%
- ❋ Part-Time: 15.8%

Supervise and coordinate activities of personal service workers such as flight attendants, hairdressers, or caddies. Requisition necessary supplies, equipment, and services. Inform workers about interests and special needs of specific groups. Participate in continuing education to stay abreast of industry trends and developments. Meet with managers and other supervisors to stay informed of changes affecting operations. Collaborate with staff members to plan and develop programs of events, schedules of activities, or menus. Train workers in proper operational procedures and functions, and explain company policies. Furnish customers with information on events and activities. Resolve customer complaints regarding worker performance and services rendered. Analyze and record personnel and operational data, and write related activity reports. Observe and evaluate workers' appearance and performance to ensure quality service and compliance with specifications. Inspect work areas and operating equipment to ensure conformance to established standards in areas such as cleanliness and maintenance. Direct and coordinate the activities of workers such as flight attendants, hotel staff, or hair stylists. Assign work schedules, following work requirements, to ensure quality and timely delivery of service. Apply customer/guest feedback to service improvement efforts. Direct marketing, advertising, and other customer recruitment efforts. Take disciplinary action to address performance problems. Recruit and hire staff members.

GOE—Interest Area/Cluster: 09. Hospitality, Tourism, and Recreation. **Work Group:** 09.01. Managerial Work in Hospitality and Tourism. **Other Jobs in This Work Group:** First-Line Supervisors/Managers of Food Preparation and Serving Workers; Food Service Managers; Gaming Managers; Gaming Supervisors; Lodging Managers.

Skills: Management of Personnel Resources; Social Perceptiveness; Service Orientation; Learning Strategies; Coordination; Judgment and Decision Making; Writing; Time Management.

Education and Training Program: Personal and Culinary Services, Other. **Related Knowledge/Courses:** Psychology; Therapy and Counseling; Education and Training; Philosophy and Theology; Medicine and Dentistry; Public Safety and Security.

Work Environment: Indoors; more often standing than sitting.

First-Line Supervisors/Managers of Police and Detectives

❋ Personality Code: ESC
❋ Education/Training Required: Work experience in a related occupation
❋ Annual Earnings: $72,620
❋ Beginning Wage: $43,720
❋ Earnings Growth Potential: Medium
❋ Growth: 9.2%
❋ Annual Job Openings: 9,373
❋ Self-Employed: 0.0%
❋ Part-Time: 0.8%

Supervise and coordinate activities of members of police force. Supervise and coordinate the investigation of criminal cases, offering guidance and expertise to investigators, and ensuring that procedures are conducted in accordance with laws and regulations. Maintain logs, prepare reports, and direct the preparation, handling, and maintenance of departmental records. Explain police operations to subordinates to assist them in performing their job duties.

Cooperate with court personnel and officials from other law enforcement agencies and testify in court as necessary. Review contents of written orders to ensure adherence to legal requirements. Investigate and resolve personnel problems within organization and charges of misconduct against staff. Direct collection, preparation, and handling of evidence and personal property of prisoners. Inform personnel of changes in regulations and policies, implications of new or amended laws, and new techniques of police work. Train staff in proper police work procedures. Monitor and evaluate the job performance of subordinates, and authorize promotions and transfers. Prepare work schedules and assign duties to subordinates. Conduct raids and order detention of witnesses and suspects for questioning. Discipline staff for violation of departmental rules and regulations. Develop, implement, and revise departmental policies and procedures. Inspect facilities, supplies, vehicles, and equipment to ensure conformance to standards. Requisition and issue equipment and supplies. Meet with civic, educational, and community groups to develop community programs and events, and to discuss law enforcement subjects. Prepare news releases and respond to police correspondence. Prepare budgets and manage expenditures of department funds. Direct release or transfer of prisoners.

GOE—Interest Area/Cluster: 12. Law and Public Safety. **Work Group:** 12.01. Managerial Work in Law and Public Safety. **Other Jobs in This Work Group:** Emergency Management Specialists; First-Line Supervisors/Managers of Correctional Officers; First-Line Supervisors/Managers of Fire Fighting and Prevention Workers; Forest Fire Fighting and Prevention Supervisors; Municipal Fire Fighting and Prevention Supervisors.

Skills: Management of Personnel Resources; Systems Analysis; Negotiation; Systems Evaluation; Operation Monitoring; Writing; Social Perceptiveness; Persuasion.

Education and Training Programs: Corrections; Criminal Justice/Law Enforcement Administration; Criminal Justice/Safety Studies. **Related Knowledge/Courses:** Public Safety and Security; Law and

Enterprising—F

Government; Psychology; Sociology and Anthropology; Therapy and Counseling; Personnel and Human Resources.

Work Environment: More often outdoors than indoors; very hot or cold; very bright or dim lighting; hazardous equipment; sitting.

Flight Attendants

- ❋ Personality Code: ESC
- ❋ Education/Training Required: Long-term on-the-job training
- ❋ Annual Earnings: $61,120
- ❋ Beginning Wage: $28,880
- ❋ Earnings Growth Potential: Very high
- ❋ Growth: 10.6%
- ❋ Annual Job Openings: 10,773
- ❋ Self-Employed: 0.0%
- ❋ Part-Time: 24.9%

Provide personal services to ensure the safety and comfort of airline passengers during flight. Greet passengers, verify tickets, explain use of safety equipment, and serve food or beverages. Direct and assist passengers in the event of an emergency, such as directing passengers to evacuate a plane following an emergency landing. Announce and demonstrate safety and emergency procedures such as the use of oxygen masks, seat belts, and life jackets. Walk aisles of planes to verify that passengers have complied with federal regulations prior to takeoffs and landings. Verify that first aid kits and other emergency equipment, including fire extinguishers and oxygen bottles, are in working order. Administer first aid to passengers in distress. Attend preflight briefings concerning weather, altitudes, routes, emergency procedures, crew coordination, lengths of flights, food and beverage services offered, and numbers of passengers. Prepare passengers and aircraft for landing, following procedures. Determine special assistance needs of passengers such as small children, the elderly, or disabled persons. Check to ensure that food, beverages, blankets, reading material, emergency equipment,

and other supplies are aboard and are in adequate supply. Reassure passengers when situations such as turbulence are encountered. Announce flight delays and descent preparations. Inspect passenger tickets to verify information and to obtain destination information. Answer passengers' questions about flights, aircraft, weather, travel routes and services, arrival times, and schedules. Assist passengers while entering or disembarking the aircraft. Inspect and clean cabins, checking for any problems and making sure that cabins are in order. Greet passengers boarding aircraft and direct them to assigned seats. Conduct periodic trips through the cabin to ensure passenger comfort and to distribute reading material, headphones, pillows, playing cards, and blankets. Take inventory of headsets, alcoholic beverages, and money collected. Operate audio and video systems. Assist passengers in placing carry-on luggage in overhead, garment, or under-seat storage. Prepare reports showing places of departure and destination, passenger ticket numbers, meal and beverage inventories, the conditions of cabin equipment, and any problems encountered by passengers.

GOE—Interest Area/Cluster: 09. Hospitality, Tourism, and Recreation. **Work Group:** 09.03. Hospitality and Travel Services. **Other Jobs in This Work Group:** Baggage Porters and Bellhops; Concierges; Hotel, Motel, and Resort Desk Clerks; Janitors and Cleaners, Except Maids and Housekeeping Cleaners; Maids and Housekeeping Cleaners; Reservation and Transportation Ticket Agents and Travel Clerks; Tour Guides and Escorts; Transportation Attendants, Except Flight Attendants and Baggage Porters; Travel Agents; Travel Guides.

Skills: Service Orientation; Social Perceptiveness; Reading Comprehension; Critical Thinking.

Education and Training Program: Airline Flight Attendant. **Related Knowledge/Courses:** Customer and Personal Service; Psychology; Geography; Transportation; Philosophy and Theology; Public Safety and Security.

Work Environment: Indoors; noisy; contaminants; disease or infections; high places; standing.

Food Service Managers

* Personality Code: ECR
* Education/Training Required: Work experience in a related occupation
* Annual Earnings: $44,570
* Beginning Wage: $28,240
* Earnings Growth Potential: Medium
* Growth: 5.0%
* Annual Job Openings: 59,302
* Self-Employed: 44.8%
* Part-Time: 8.0%

Plan, direct, or coordinate activities of an organization or department that serves food and beverages. Monitor compliance with health and fire regulations regarding food preparation and serving and building maintenance for lodging and dining facilities. Monitor food preparation methods, portion sizes, and garnishing and presentation of food to ensure that food is prepared and presented in an acceptable manner. Count money and make bank deposits. Investigate and resolve complaints regarding food quality, service, or accommodations. Coordinate assignments of cooking personnel to ensure economical use of food and timely preparation. Schedule and receive food and beverage deliveries, checking delivery contents to verify product quality and quantity. Monitor budgets and payroll records and review financial transactions to ensure that expenditures are authorized and budgeted. Schedule staff hours and assign duties. Maintain food and equipment inventories and keep inventory records. Establish standards for personnel performance and customer service. Perform some food preparation or service tasks such as cooking, clearing tables, and serving food and drinks, when necessary. Plan menus and food utilization based on anticipated number of guests, nutritional value, palatability, popularity, and costs. Keep records required by government agencies regarding sanitation and, when appropriate, food subsidies. Test cooked food by tasting and smelling it to ensure palatability and flavor conformity. Organize and direct worker training programs, resolve personnel problems, hire new staff, and evaluate employee performance in dining and lodging facilities. Order and purchase equipment and supplies. Review work procedures and operational problems to determine ways to improve service, performance, or safety. Assess staffing needs and recruit staff, using methods such as newspaper advertisements or attendance at job fairs. Arrange for equipment maintenance and repairs and coordinate a variety of services such as waste removal and pest control. Record the number, type, and cost of items sold to determine which items may be unpopular or less profitable. Review menus and analyze recipes to determine labor and overhead costs and assign prices to menu items.

GOE—Interest Area/Cluster: 09. Hospitality, Tourism, and Recreation. **Work Group:** 09.01. Managerial Work in Hospitality and Tourism. **Other Jobs in This Work Group:** First-Line Supervisors/Managers of Food Preparation and Serving Workers; First-Line Supervisors/Managers of Personal Service Workers; Gaming Managers; Gaming Supervisors; Lodging Managers.

Skills: Management of Financial Resources; Management of Personnel Resources; Systems Evaluation; Management of Material Resources; Systems Analysis; Negotiation; Service Orientation; Persuasion.

Education and Training Programs: Restaurant, Culinary, and Catering Management/Manager; Hospitality Administration/Management, General; Hotel/Motel Administration/Management; Restaurant/Food Services Management. **Related Knowledge/Courses:** Food Production; Sales and Marketing; Personnel and Human Resources; Production and Processing; Education and Training; Administration and Management.

Work Environment: Indoors; very hot or cold; standing; walking and running; using hands on objects, tools, or controls; repetitive motions.

Gaming Managers

- ❊ Personality Code: EC
- ❊ Education/Training Required: Work experience in a related occupation
- ❊ Annual Earnings: $64,410
- ❊ Beginning Wage: $36,740
- ❊ Earnings Growth Potential: High
- ❊ Growth: 24.4%
- ❊ Annual Job Openings: 549
- ❊ Self-Employed: 16.3%
- ❊ Part-Time: 4.5%

Plan, organize, direct, control, or coordinate gaming operations in a casino. Formulate gaming policies for their area of responsibility. Resolve customer complaints regarding problems such as payout errors. Remove suspected cheaters, such as card counters and other players who may have systems that shift the odds of winning to their favor. Maintain familiarity with all games used at a facility, as well as strategies and tricks employed in those games. Train new workers and evaluate their performance. Circulate among gaming tables to ensure that operations are conducted properly, that dealers follow house rules, and that players are not cheating. Explain and interpret house rules, such as game rules and betting limits. Monitor staffing levels to ensure that games and tables are adequately staffed for each shift, arranging for staff rotations and breaks and locating substitute employees as necessary. Interview and hire workers. Prepare work schedules and station assignments and keep attendance records. Direct the distribution of complimentary hotel rooms, meals, and other discounts or free items given to players based on their length of play and betting totals. Establish policies on issues such as the type of gambling offered and the odds, the extension of credit, and the serving of food and beverages. Track supplies of money to tables and perform any required paperwork. Set and maintain a bank and table limit for each game. Monitor credit extended to players. Review operational expenses, budget estimates, betting accounts, and collection reports for accuracy. Record, collect, and pay off bets,

issuing receipts as necessary. Direct workers compiling summary sheets that show wager amounts and payoffs for races and events. Notify board attendants of table vacancies so that waiting patrons can play.

GOE—Interest Area/Cluster: 09. Hospitality, Tourism, and Recreation. **Work Group:** 09.01. Managerial Work in Hospitality and Tourism. **Other Jobs in This Work Group:** First-Line Supervisors/Managers of Food Preparation and Serving Workers; First-Line Supervisors/Managers of Personal Service Workers; Food Service Managers; Gaming Supervisors; Lodging Managers.

Skills: Management of Personnel Resources; Management of Financial Resources; Systems Evaluation; Service Orientation; Negotiation; Operations Analysis; Social Perceptiveness; Mathematics.

Education and Training Program: Personal and Culinary Services, Other. **Related Knowledge/Courses:** Sales and Marketing; Personnel and Human Resources; Customer and Personal Service; Administration and Management; Economics and Accounting; Mathematics.

Work Environment: Indoors; noisy; contaminants; standing; walking and running.

Gaming Supervisors

- ❊ Personality Code: EC
- ❊ Education/Training Required: Work experience in a related occupation
- ❊ Annual Earnings: $42,980
- ❊ Beginning Wage: $26,310
- ❊ Earnings Growth Potential: Medium
- ❊ Growth: 23.4%
- ❊ Annual Job Openings: 4,602
- ❊ Self-Employed: 29.2%
- ❊ Part-Time: 12.8%

Supervise gaming operations and personnel in an assigned area. Circulate among tables and observe operations. Ensure that stations and games are covered for each shift. May explain and interpret

operating rules of house to patrons. **May plan and organize activities and create friendly atmosphere for guests in hotels/casinos. May adjust service complaints.** Monitor game operations to ensure that house rules are followed, that tribal, state, and federal regulations are adhered to, and that employees provide prompt and courteous service. Observe gamblers' behavior for signs of cheating such as marking, switching, or counting cards; notify security staff of suspected cheating. Maintain familiarity with the games at a facility and with strategies and tricks used by cheaters at such games. Perform paperwork required for monetary transactions. Resolve customer and employee complaints. Greet customers and ask about the quality of service they are receiving. Establish and maintain banks and table limits for each game. Report customer-related incidents occurring in gaming areas to supervisors. Monitor stations and games and move dealers from game to game to ensure adequate staffing. Explain and interpret house rules, such as game rules and betting limits, for patrons. Supervise the distribution of complimentary meals, hotel rooms, discounts, and other items given to players based on length of play and amount bet. Evaluate workers' performance and prepare written performance evaluations. Monitor patrons for signs of compulsive gambling, offering assistance if necessary. Record, issue receipts for, and pay off bets. Monitor and verify the counting, wrapping, weighing, and distribution of currency and coins. Direct workers compiling summary sheets for each race or event to record amounts wagered and amounts to be paid to winners. Determine how many gaming tables to open each day and schedule staff accordingly. Establish policies on types of gambling offered, odds, and extension of credit. Interview, hire, and train workers. Provide fire protection and first-aid assistance when necessary. Review operational expenses, budget estimates, betting accounts, and collection reports for accuracy.

GOE—Interest Area/Cluster: 09. Hospitality, Tourism, and Recreation. **Work Group:** 09.01. Managerial Work in Hospitality and Tourism. **Other Jobs in This Work Group:** First-Line Supervisors/ Managers of Food Preparation and Serving Workers; First-Line Supervisors/Managers of Personal Service Workers; Food Service Managers; Gaming Managers; Lodging Managers.

Skills: Management of Personnel Resources; Instructing; Service Orientation; Monitoring; Social Perceptiveness; Mathematics; Critical Thinking; Judgment and Decision Making.

Education and Training Program: Personal and Culinary Services, Other. **Related Knowledge/ Courses:** Customer and Personal Service; Psychology; Mathematics; Law and Government; Sales and Marketing; Personnel and Human Resources.

Work Environment: Indoors; noisy; contaminants; standing; walking and running.

General and Operations Managers

- ❋ Personality Code: ECS
- ❋ Education/Training Required: Work experience plus degree
- ❋ Annual Earnings: $88,700
- ❋ Beginning Wage: $43,990
- ❋ Earnings Growth Potential: Very high
- ❋ Growth: 1.5%
- ❋ Annual Job Openings: 112,072
- ❋ Self-Employed: 0.9%
- ❋ Part-Time: 3.2%

Plan, direct, or coordinate the operations of companies or public and private sector organizations. Duties and responsibilities include formulating policies, managing daily operations, and planning the use of materials and human resources, but are too diverse and general in nature to be classified in any one functional area of management or administration, such as personnel, purchasing, or administrative services. Includes owners and managers who head small business establishments whose duties are primarily managerial. Oversee activities directly related to making products or providing services. Direct and coordinate activities of businesses or departments concerned with the production, pricing, sales, or distribution of products. Review financial statements, sales and activity reports, and other performance data to measure productivity and goal achievement and to determine areas needing cost reduction and program improvement. Manage staff, preparing work schedules and assigning specific duties. Direct and coordinate organization's financial and budget activities to fund operations, maximize investments, and increase efficiency. Establish and implement departmental policies, goals, objectives, and procedures, conferring with board members, organization officials, and staff members as necessary. Determine staffing requirements, and interview, hire, and train new employees, or oversee those personnel processes. Plan and direct activities such as sales promotions, coordinating with other department heads as required. Determine goods and services to be sold, and set prices and credit terms based on forecasts of customer demand. Monitor businesses and agencies to ensure that they efficiently and effectively provide needed services while staying within budgetary limits. Locate, select, and procure merchandise for resale, representing management in purchase negotiations. Perform sales floor work such as greeting and assisting customers, stocking shelves, and taking inventory. Manage the movement of goods into and out of production facilities. Develop and implement product marketing strategies including advertising campaigns and sales promotions. Recommend locations for new facilities or oversee the remodeling of current facilities. Direct non-merchandising departments of businesses such as advertising and purchasing. Plan store layouts, and design displays.

GOE—Interest Area/Cluster: 04. Business and Administration. **Work Group:** 04.01. Managerial Work in General Business. **Other Jobs in This Work Group:** Chief Executives; Compensation and Benefits Managers; Human Resources Managers; Training and Development Managers.

Skills: Management of Financial Resources; Management of Material Resources; Systems Analysis; Management of Personnel Resources; Systems

Evaluation; Negotiation; Persuasion; Operation Monitoring.

Education and Training Programs: Public Administration; Business/Commerce, General; Business Administration and Management, General; Entrepreneurship/Entrepreneurial Studies; International Business/Trade/Commerce. **Related Knowledge/Courses:** Economics and Accounting; Personnel and Human Resources; Administration and Management; Sales and Marketing; Clerical Practices; Building and Construction.

Work Environment: Indoors; noisy; standing; walking and running.

Insurance Sales Agents

- ❋ Personality Code: ECS
- ❋ Education/Training Required: Bachelor's degree
- ❋ Annual Earnings: $44,110
- ❋ Beginning Wage: $25,230
- ❋ Earnings Growth Potential: High
- ❋ Growth: 12.9%
- ❋ Annual Job Openings: 64,162
- ❋ Self-Employed: 25.5%
- ❋ Part-Time: 9.8%

Sell life, property, casualty, health, automotive, or other types of insurance. May refer clients to independent brokers, work as independent broker, or be employed by an insurance company. Call on policyholders to deliver and explain policy, to analyze insurance program and suggest additions or changes, or to change beneficiaries. Calculate premiums and establish payment method. Customize insurance programs to suit individual customers, often covering a variety of risks. Sell various types of insurance policies to businesses and individuals on behalf of insurance companies, including automobile, fire, life, property, medical, and dental insurance or specialized policies such as marine, farm/crop, and medical malpractice. Interview prospective clients to obtain data about their financial resources and needs and the physical condition of the person or property to be insured and to discuss any existing coverage. Seek out new clients and develop clientele by networking to find new customers and generate lists of prospective clients. Explain features, advantages, and disadvantages of various policies to promote sale of insurance plans. Contact underwriter and submit forms to obtain binder coverage. Ensure that policy requirements are fulfilled, including any necessary medical examinations and the completion of appropriate forms. Confer with clients to obtain and provide information when claims are made on a policy. Perform administrative tasks, such as maintaining records and handling policy renewals. Select company that offers type of coverage requested by client to underwrite policy. Monitor insurance claims to ensure that they are settled equitably for both the client and the insurer. Develop marketing strategies to compete with other individuals or companies who sell insurance. Attend meetings, seminars, and programs to learn about new products and services, learn new skills, and receive technical assistance in developing new accounts. Inspect property, examining its general condition, type of construction, age, and other characteristics, to decide if it is a good insurance risk. Install bookkeeping systems and resolve system problems. Plan and oversee incorporation of insurance program into bookkeeping system of company. Explain necessary bookkeeping requirements for customer to implement and provide group insurance program.

GOE—Interest Area/Cluster: 06. Finance and Insurance. **Work Group:** 06.05. Finance/Insurance Sales and Support. **Other Jobs in This Work Group:** Advertising Sales Agents; Personal Financial Advisors; Sales Agents, Financial Services; Sales Agents, Securities and Commodities; Securities, Commodities, and Financial Services Sales Agents.

Skills: Persuasion; Judgment and Decision Making; Time Management; Negotiation; Service Orientation; Speaking; Active Listening; Social Perceptiveness.

Education and Training Program: Insurance. **Related Knowledge/Courses:** Sales and Marketing; Economics and Accounting; Customer and Personal Service; Computers and Electronics; Clerical Practices; Law and Government.

Work Environment: Indoors; sitting.

Lawyers

- ❋ Personality Code: EI
- ❋ Education/Training Required: First professional degree
- ❋ Annual Earnings: $106,120
- ❋ Beginning Wage: $52,280
- ❋ Earnings Growth Potential: Very high
- ❋ Growth: 11.0%
- ❋ Annual Job Openings: 49,445
- ❋ Self-Employed: 26.7%
- ❋ Part-Time: 5.9%

Represent clients in criminal and civil litigation and other legal proceedings, draw up legal documents, and manage or advise clients on legal transactions. May specialize in a single area or may practice broadly in many areas of law. Advise clients concerning business transactions, claim liability, advisability of prosecuting or defending lawsuits, or legal rights and obligations. Interpret laws, rulings, and regulations for individuals and businesses. Analyze the probable outcomes of cases, using knowledge of legal precedents. Present and summarize cases to judges and juries. Gather evidence to formulate defense or to initiate legal actions by such means as interviewing clients and witnesses to ascertain the facts of a case. Evaluate findings and develop strategies and arguments in preparation for presentation of cases. Represent clients in court or before government agencies. Examine legal data to determine advisability of defending or prosecuting lawsuit. Select jurors, argue motions, meet with judges, and question witnesses during the course of a trial. Present evidence to defend clients or prosecute defendants in criminal or civil litigation. Study Constitution, statutes, decisions, regulations, and ordinances of quasi-judicial bodies to determine ramifications for cases. Prepare and draft legal documents, such as wills, deeds, patent applications, mortgages, leases, and contracts. Prepare legal briefs and opinions and file appeals in state and federal courts of appeal. Negotiate settlements of civil disputes. Confer with colleagues with specialties in appropriate areas of legal issue to establish and verify bases for legal proceedings. Search for and examine public and other legal records to write opinions or establish ownership. Supervise legal assistants. Perform administrative and management functions related to the practice of law. Act as agent, trustee, guardian, or executor for businesses or individuals. Probate wills and represent and advise executors and administrators of estates. Help develop federal and state programs, draft and interpret laws and legislation, and establish enforcement procedures. Work in environmental law, representing public interest groups, waste disposal companies, or construction firms in their dealings with state and federal agencies.

GOE—Interest Area/Cluster: 12. Law and Public Safety. **Work Group:** 12.02. Legal Practice and Justice Administration. **Other Jobs in This Work Group:** Administrative Law Judges, Adjudicators, and Hearing Officers; Arbitrators, Mediators, and Conciliators; Judges, Magistrate Judges, and Magistrates.

Skills: Persuasion; Negotiation; Writing; Judgment and Decision Making; Critical Thinking; Reading Comprehension; Speaking; Active Listening.

Education and Training Programs: Law (LL.B., J.D.); Advanced Legal Research/Studies, General (LL.M., M.C.L., M.L.I., M.S.L., J.S.D./S.J.D.); Programs for Foreign Lawyers (LL.M., M.C.L.); American/U.S. Law/Legal Studies/Jurisprudence (LL.M., M.C.J., J.S.D./S.J.D.); Canadian Law/Legal Studies/Jurisprudence (LL.M., M.C.J., J.S.D./S.J.D.); Banking, Corporate, Finance, and Securities Law (LL.M., J.S.D./S.J.D.); Comparative Law (LL.M., M.C.L., J.S.D./S.J.D.); others. **Related Knowledge/Courses:** Law and Government; English Language; Personnel and Human Resources;

Economics and Accounting; Psychology; Administration and Management.

Work Environment: Indoors; sitting.

Logisticians

- ❋ Personality Code: EC
- ❋ Education/Training Required: Bachelor's degree
- ❋ Annual Earnings: $64,250
- ❋ Beginning Wage: $38,280
- ❋ Earnings Growth Potential: High
- ❋ Growth: 17.3%
- ❋ Annual Job Openings: 9,671
- ❋ Self-Employed: 1.5%
- ❋ Part-Time: 3.6%

Analyze and coordinate the logistical functions of a firm or organization. Responsible for the entire life cycle of a product, including acquisition, distribution, internal allocation, delivery, and final disposal of resources. Maintain and develop positive business relationships with a customer's key personnel involved in or directly relevant to a logistics activity. Develop an understanding of customers' needs and take actions to ensure that such needs are met. Direct availability and allocation of materials, supplies, and finished products. Collaborate with other departments as necessary to meet customer requirements, to take advantage of sales opportunities, or, in the case of shortages, to minimize negative impacts on a business. Protect and control proprietary materials. Review logistics performance with customers against targets, benchmarks, and service agreements. Develop and implement technical project management tools such as plans, schedules, and responsibility and compliance matrices. Direct team activities, establishing task priorities, scheduling and tracking work assignments, providing guidance, and ensuring the availability of resources. Report project plans, progress, and results. Direct and support the compilation and analysis of technical source data necessary for product development. Explain proposed solutions to customers, management, or other interested parties through written proposals and oral presentations. Provide project management services, including the provision and analysis of technical data. Develop proposals that include documentation for estimates. Plan, organize, and execute logistics support activities such as maintenance planning, repair analysis, and test equipment recommendations. Participate in the assessment and review of design alternatives and design change proposal impacts. Support the development of training materials and technical manuals. Stay informed of logistics technology advances and apply appropriate technology in order to improve logistics processes. Redesign the movement of goods in order to maximize value and minimize costs. Manage subcontractor activities, reviewing proposals, developing performance specifications, and serving as liaisons between subcontractors and organizations. Manage the logistical aspects of product life cycles, including coordination or provisioning of samples and the minimization of obsolescence.

GOE—Interest Area/Cluster: 04. Business and Administration. **Work Group:** 04.05. Accounting, Auditing, and Analytical Support. **Other Jobs in This Work Group:** Accountants; Accountants and Auditors; Auditors; Budget Analysts; Industrial Engineering Technicians; Management Analysts; Operations Research Analysts.

Skills: Management of Financial Resources; Management of Material Resources; Systems Analysis; Operations Analysis; Management of Personnel Resources; Service Orientation; Persuasion; Technology Design.

Education and Training Programs: Logistics and Materials Management; Operations Management and Supervision; Transportation/Transportation Management. **Related Knowledge/Courses:** Telecommunications; Geography; Computers and Electronics; Administration and Management; Economics and Accounting; Public Safety and Security.

Work Environment: Indoors; sitting.

Marketing Managers

* Personality Code: EC
* Education/Training Required: Work experience plus degree
* Annual Earnings: $104,400
* Beginning Wage: $53,520
* Earnings Growth Potential: High
* Growth: 14.4%
* Annual Job Openings: 20,189
* Self-Employed: 2.3%
* Part-Time: 4.1%

Determine the demand for products and services offered by firms and their competitors, and identify potential customers. Develop pricing strategies with the goal of maximizing firms' profits or shares of the market while ensuring that firms' customers are satisfied. Oversee product development or monitor trends that indicate the need for new products and services. Formulate, direct, and coordinate marketing activities and policies to promote products and services, working with advertising and promotion managers. Identify, develop, and evaluate marketing strategies, based on knowledge of establishment objectives, market characteristics, and cost and markup factors. Direct the hiring, training, and performance evaluations of marketing and sales staff and oversee their daily activities. Evaluate the financial aspects of product development, such as budgets, expenditures, research and development appropriations, and return-on-investment and profit-loss projections. Develop pricing strategies, balancing firm objectives and customer satisfaction. Compile lists describing product or service offerings. Initiate market research studies and analyze their findings. Use sales forecasting and strategic planning to ensure the sale and profitability of products, lines, or services, analyzing business developments and monitoring market trends. Coordinate and participate in promotional activities and trade shows, working with developers, advertisers, and production managers, to market products and services. Consult with buying personnel to gain advice

Enterprising-M

regarding the types of products or services expected to be in demand. Conduct economic and commercial surveys to identify potential markets for products and services. Select products and accessories to be displayed at trade or special production shows. Negotiate contracts with vendors and distributors to manage product distribution, establishing distribution networks and developing distribution strategies. Consult with product development personnel on product specifications such as design, color, and packaging. Advise businesses and other groups on local, national, and international factors affecting the buying and selling of products and services. Confer with legal staff to resolve problems such as copyright infringement and royalty sharing with outside producers and distributors.

GOE—Interest Area/Cluster: 14. Retail and Wholesale Sales and Service. **Work Group:** 14.01. Managerial Work in Retail/Wholesale Sales and Service. **Other Jobs in This Work Group:** Advertising and Promotions Managers; First-Line Supervisors/Managers of Non-Retail Sales Workers; First-Line Supervisors/Managers of Retail Sales Workers; Funeral Directors; Property, Real Estate, and Community Association Managers; Purchasing Managers; Sales Managers.

Skills: Management of Personnel Resources; Systems Analysis; Systems Evaluation; Persuasion; Negotiation; Management of Financial Resources; Writing; Social Perceptiveness.

Education and Training Programs: Consumer Merchandising/Retailing Management; Apparel and Textile Marketing Management; Marketing/Marketing Management, General; Marketing Research; International Marketing; Marketing, Other. **Related Knowledge/Courses:** Sales and Marketing; Personnel and Human Resources; Customer and Personal Service; Communications and Media; Sociology and Anthropology; Economics and Accounting.

Work Environment: Indoors; sitting.

Medical and Health Services Managers

* ❋ Personality Code: ECS
* ❋ Education/Training Required: Work experience plus degree
* ❋ Annual Earnings: $76,990
* ❋ Beginning Wage: $46,860
* ❋ Earnings Growth Potential: Medium
* ❋ Growth: 16.4%
* ❋ Annual Job Openings: 31,877
* ❋ Self-Employed: 8.2%
* ❋ Part-Time: 5.5%

Plan, direct, or coordinate medicine and health services in hospitals, clinics, managed care organizations, public health agencies, or similar organizations. Conduct and administer fiscal operations, including accounting, planning budgets, authorizing expenditures, establishing rates for services, and coordinating financial reporting. Direct, supervise, and evaluate work activities of medical, nursing, technical, clerical, service, maintenance, and other personnel. Maintain communication between governing boards, medical staff, and department heads by attending board meetings and coordinating interdepartmental functioning. Review and analyze facility activities and data to aid planning and cash and risk management and to improve service utilization. Plan, implement, and administer programs and services in a health-care or medical facility, including personnel administration, training, and coordination of medical, nursing, and physical plant staff. Direct or conduct recruitment, hiring, and training of personnel. Establish work schedules and assignments for staff, according to workload, space, and equipment availability. Maintain awareness of advances in medicine, computerized diagnostic and treatment equipment, data processing technology, government regulations, health insurance changes, and financing options. Monitor the use of diagnostic services, inpatient beds, facilities, and staff to ensure effective use of resources and assess the need for additional staff, equipment, and services. Develop and maintain computerized record management systems to store and process data such as personnel activities and information and to produce reports. Establish and evaluative objectives and evaluative operational criteria for units they manage. Prepare activity reports to inform management of the status and implementation plans of programs, services, and quality initiatives. Inspect facilities and recommend building or equipment modifications to ensure emergency readiness and compliance to access, safety, and sanitation regulations. Develop and implement organizational policies and procedures for the facility or medical unit. Manage change in integrated health care delivery systems such as work restructuring, technological innovations, and shifts in the focus of care.

GOE—Interest Area/Cluster: 08. Health Science. **Work Group:** 08.01. Managerial Work in Medical and Health Services. **Other Jobs in This Work Group:** Coroners.

Skills: Management of Financial Resources; Management of Personnel Resources; Systems Analysis; Systems Evaluation; Management of Material Resources; Negotiation; Persuasion; Monitoring.

Education and Training Programs: Health/Health Care Administration/Management; Hospital and Health Care Facilities Administration/Management; Health Unit Manager/Ward Supervisor; Health Information/Medical Records Administration/Administrator; Medical Staff Services Technology/Technician; Health and Medical Administrative Services, Other; Nursing Administration (MSN, MS, PhD); Public Health, General (MPH, DPH); Community Health and Preventive Medicine; others. **Related Knowledge/Courses:** Economics and Accounting; Personnel and Human Resources; Administration and Management; Sales and Marketing; Medicine and Dentistry; Law and Government.

Work Environment: Indoors; noisy; disease or infections; sitting.

Meeting and Convention Planners

- ❋ Personality Code: ECS
- ❋ Education/Training Required: Bachelor's degree
- ❋ Annual Earnings: $43,530
- ❋ Beginning Wage: $26,880
- ❋ Earnings Growth Potential: Medium
- ❋ Growth: 19.9%
- ❋ Annual Job Openings: 8,318
- ❋ Self-Employed: 5.6%
- ❋ Part-Time: 13.8%

Coordinate activities of staff and convention personnel to make arrangements for group meetings and conventions. Monitor event activities to ensure compliance with applicable regulations and laws, satisfaction of participants, and resolution of any problems that arise. Confer with staffs at chosen event sites to coordinate details. Inspect event facilities to ensure that they conform to customer requirements. Coordinate services for events, such as accommodation and transportation for participants, facilities, catering, signage, displays, special needs requirements, printing, and event security. Consult with customers to determine objectives and requirements for events such as meetings, conferences, and conventions. Meet with sponsors and organizing committees to plan scope and format of events, to establish and monitor budgets, or to review administrative procedures and event progress. Review event bills for accuracy, and approve payments. Evaluate and select providers of services according to customer requirements. Arrange the availability of audio-visual equipment, transportation, displays, and other event needs. Plan and develop programs, agendas, budgets, and services according to customer requirements. Negotiate contracts with such service providers and suppliers as hotels, convention centers, and speakers. Maintain records of event aspects, including financial details. Conduct post-event evaluations to determine how future events could be improved. Organize registration of event participants. Hire, train, and supervise volunteers and support staff required for events. Read

Enterprising–M

trade publications, attend seminars, and consult with other meeting professionals to keep abreast of meeting management standards and trends. Direct administrative details such as financial operations, dissemination of promotional materials, and responses to inquiries. Promote conference, convention, and trade show services by performing tasks such as meeting with professional and trade associations and producing brochures and other publications. Develop event topics and choose featured speakers. Obtain permits from fire and health departments to erect displays and exhibits and serve food at events. Design and implement efforts to publicize events and promote sponsorships.

GOE—Interest Area/Cluster: 04. Business and Administration. **Work Group:** 04.02. Managerial Work in Business Detail. **Other Jobs in This Work Group:** Administrative Services Managers; First-Line Supervisors/Managers of Housekeeping and Janitorial Workers; First-Line Supervisors/Managers of Office and Administrative Support Workers.

Skills: Management of Financial Resources; Systems Evaluation; Management of Material Resources; Systems Analysis; Negotiation; Management of Personnel Resources; Service Orientation; Coordination.

Education and Training Program: Selling Skills and Sales Operations. **Related Knowledge/Courses:** Sales and Marketing; Clerical Practices; Customer and Personal Service; English Language; Economics and Accounting; Administration and Management.

Work Environment: Indoors; sitting.

Natural Sciences Managers

- ❀ Personality Code: EI
- ❀ Education/Training Required: Work experience plus degree
- ❀ Annual Earnings: $104,040
- ❀ Beginning Wage: $62,880
- ❀ Earnings Growth Potential: Medium
- ❀ Growth: 11.4%
- ❀ Annual Job Openings: 3,661
- ❀ Self-Employed: 0.6%
- ❀ Part-Time: 4.4%

Plan, direct, or coordinate activities in such fields as life sciences, physical sciences, mathematics, and statistics and research and development in these fields. Confer with scientists, engineers, regulators, and others to plan and review projects and to provide technical assistance. Develop client relationships and communicate with clients to explain proposals, present research findings, establish specifications, or discuss project status. Plan and direct research, development, and production activities. Prepare project proposals. Design and coordinate successive phases of problem analysis, solution proposals, and testing. Review project activities and prepare and review research, testing, and operational reports. Hire, supervise, and evaluate engineers, technicians, researchers, and other staff. Determine scientific and technical goals within broad outlines provided by top management and make detailed plans to accomplish these goals. Develop and implement policies, standards, and procedures for the architectural, scientific, and technical work performed to ensure regulatory compliance and operations enhancement. Develop innovative technology and train staff for its implementation. Provide for stewardship of plant and animal resources and habitats, studying land use; monitoring animal populations; and providing shelter, resources, and medical treatment for animals. Conduct own research in field of expertise. Recruit personnel and oversee the development and maintenance of staff competence. Advise and assist in obtaining patents or meeting other legal requirements. Prepare and administer budget, approve and review expenditures, and prepare financial reports. Make presentations at professional meetings to further knowledge in the field.

GOE—Interest Area/Cluster: 15. Scientific Research, Engineering, and Mathematics. **Work Group:** 15.01. Managerial Work in Scientific Research, Engineering, and Mathematics. **Other Jobs in This Work Group:** Engineering Managers.

Skills: Science; Mathematics; Active Learning; Reading Comprehension; Writing; Management of Personnel Resources; Complex Problem Solving; Critical Thinking.

Education and Training Programs: Operations Research; Biology/Biological Sciences, General; Biochemistry; Biophysics; Molecular Biology; Radiation Biology/Radiobiology; Botany/Plant Biology; Plant Pathology/Phytopathology; Plant Physiology; Botany/Plant Biology, Other; Cell/Cellular Biology and Histology; Anatomy; Cell/Cellular Biology and Anatomical Sciences, Other; Microbiology, General; others. **Related Knowledge/Courses:** Biology; Chemistry; Engineering and Technology; Law and Government; Administration and Management; Physics.

Work Environment: Indoors; noisy; sitting.

Personal Financial Advisors

- ✸ Personality Code: ECS
- ✸ Education/Training Required: Bachelor's degree
- ✸ Annual Earnings: $67,660
- ✸ Beginning Wage: $33,100
- ✸ Earnings Growth Potential: Very high
- ✸ Growth: 41.0%
- ✸ Annual Job Openings: 17,114
- ✸ Self-Employed: 30.9%
- ✸ Part-Time: 7.7%

Advise clients on financial plans, using knowledge of tax and investment strategies, securities, insurance, pension plans, and real estate. Duties include assessing clients' assets, liabilities, cash flows, insurance coverages, tax statuses, and financial objectives to establish investment strategies. Prepare and interpret for clients information such as investment performance reports, financial document summaries, and income projections. Recommend strategies clients can use to achieve their financial goals and objectives, including specific recommendations in such areas as cash management, insurance coverage, and investment planning. Build and maintain client bases, keeping current client plans up-to-date and recruiting new clients on an ongoing basis. Devise debt liquidation plans that include payoff priorities and timelines. Implement financial planning recommendations, or refer clients to someone who can assist them with plan implementation. Interview clients to determine their current incomes, expenses, insurance coverages, tax statuses, financial objectives, risk tolerances, and other information needed to develop financial plans. Monitor financial market trends to ensure that plans are effective, and to identify any necessary updates. Explain and document for clients the types of services that are to be provided, and the responsibilities to be taken by personal financial advisors. Explain to individuals and groups the details of financial assistance available to college and university students, such as loans, grants, and scholarships. Guide clients in the gathering of information such as bank account records, income tax returns, life and disability insurance records, pension plan information, and wills. Analyze financial information obtained from clients to determine strategies for meeting clients' financial objectives. Meet with clients' other advisors, including attorneys, accountants, trust officers, and investment bankers, to fully understand clients' financial goals and circumstances. Answer clients' questions about the purposes and details of financial plans and strategies. Open accounts for clients, and disburse funds from account to creditors as agents for clients. Authorize release of financial aid funds to students. Participate in the selection of candidates for specific financial aid awards. Research and investigate available investment opportunities to determine whether they fit into financial plans.

GOE—Interest Area/Cluster: 06. Finance and Insurance. **Work Group:** 06.05. Finance/Insurance Sales and Support. **Other Jobs in This Work Group:** Advertising Sales Agents; Insurance Sales Agents; Sales Agents, Financial Services; Sales Agents, Securities and Commodities; Securities, Commodities, and Financial Services Sales Agents.

Skills: Management of Financial Resources; Persuasion; Mathematics; Speaking; Complex Problem Solving; Active Listening; Service Orientation; Judgment and Decision Making.

Education and Training Programs: Finance, General; Financial Planning and Services. **Related Knowledge/Courses:** Economics and Accounting; Sales and Marketing; Law and Government; Customer and Personal Service; Mathematics; Computers and Electronics.

Work Environment: Indoors; sitting.

Personnel Recruiters

- ✳ Personality Code: ESC
- ✳ Education/Training Required: Bachelor's degree
- ✳ Annual Earnings: $44,380
- ✳ Beginning Wage: $27,340
- ✳ Earnings Growth Potential: Medium
- ✳ Growth: 18.4%
- ✳ Annual Job Openings: 33,588
- ✳ Self-Employed: 2.1%
- ✳ Part-Time: 7.6%

The job openings listed here are shared with Employment Interviewers.

Seek out, interview, and screen applicants to fill existing and future job openings and promote career opportunities within an organization. Establish and maintain relationships with hiring managers to stay abreast of current and future hiring and business needs. Interview applicants to obtain information on work history, training, education, and job skills. Maintain current knowledge of Equal Employment Opportunity (EEO) and affirmative action guidelines and laws, such as the Americans with Disabilities Act (ADA). Perform searches for qualified candidates according to relevant job criteria, using computer databases, networking, Internet recruiting resources, cold calls, media, recruiting firms, and employee referrals. Prepare and maintain employment records. Contact applicants to inform them of employment possibilities, consideration, and selection. Inform potential applicants about facilities, operations, benefits, and job or career opportunities in organizations. Screen and refer applicants to hiring personnel in the organization, making hiring recommendations when appropriate. Arrange for interviews and provide travel arrangements as necessary. Advise managers and employees on staffing policies and procedures. Review and evaluate applicant qualifications or eligibility for specified licensing according to established guidelines and designated licensing codes. Hire applicants and authorize paperwork assigning them to positions. Conduct reference and background checks on applicants. Evaluate recruitment and selection criteria to ensure conformance to professional, statistical, and testing standards, recommending revision as needed. Recruit applicants for open positions, arranging job fairs with college campus representatives. Advise management on organizing, preparing, and implementing recruiting and retention programs. Supervise personnel clerks performing filing, typing, and recordkeeping duties. Project yearly recruitment expenditures for budgetary consideration and control. Serve on selection and examination boards to evaluate applicants according to test scores, contacting promising candidates for interviews. Address civic and social groups and attend conferences to disseminate information concerning possible job openings and career opportunities.

GOE—Interest Area/Cluster: 04. Business and Administration. **Work Group:** 04.03. Human Resources Support. **Other Jobs in This Work Group:** Compensation, Benefits, and Job Analysis Specialists; Employment Interviewers; Employment,

Recruitment, and Placement Specialists; Training and Development Specialists.

Skills: Management of Personnel Resources; Negotiation; Persuasion; Management of Financial Resources; Service Orientation; Judgment and Decision Making; Monitoring; Active Listening.

Education and Training Programs: Human Resources Management/Personnel Administration, General; Labor and Industrial Relations. **Related Knowledge/Courses:** Personnel and Human Resources; Clerical Practices; Sales and Marketing; Education and Training; Administration and Management; Communications and Media.

Work Environment: Indoors; sitting.

Police and Sheriff's Patrol Officers

See Police Patrol Officers (a Realistic job) and Sheriffs *and Deputy Sheriffs (a Enterprising job), described separately.*

Police Detectives

- ❋ Personality Code: EI
- ❋ Education/Training Required: Work experience in a related occupation
- ❋ Annual Earnings: $59,930
- ❋ Beginning Wage: $35,600
- ❋ Earnings Growth Potential: High
- ❋ Growth: 17.3%
- ❋ Annual Job Openings: 14,746
- ❋ Self-Employed: 0.3%
- ❋ Part-Time: 2.2%

The job openings listed here are shared with Criminal Investigators and Special Agents, with Immigration and Customs Inspectors, and with Police Identification and Records Officers.

Conduct investigations to prevent crimes or solve criminal cases. Provide testimony as witnesses in court. Secure deceased bodies and obtain evidence from them, preventing bystanders from tampering with bodies prior to medical examiners' arrival. Examine crime scenes to obtain clues and evidence such as loose hairs, fibers, clothing, or weapons. Obtain evidence from suspects. Record progress of investigations, maintain informational files on suspects, and submit reports to commanding officers or magistrates to authorize warrants. Check victims for signs of life such as breathing and pulse. Prepare charges or responses to charges, or information for court cases, according to formalized procedures. Obtain facts or statements from complainants, witnesses, and accused persons and record interviews, using recording devices. Prepare and serve search and arrest warrants. Note, mark, and photograph locations of objects found such as footprints, tire tracks, bullets, and bloodstains, and take measurements of each scene. Question individuals or observe persons and establishments to confirm information given to patrol officers. Preserve, process, and analyze items of evidence obtained from crime scenes and suspects, placing them in proper containers and destroying evidence no longer needed. Secure persons at scenes, keeping witnesses from conversing or leaving scenes before investigators arrive. Take photographs from all angles of relevant parts of crime scenes, including entrance and exit routes and streets and intersections. Analyze completed police reports to determine what additional information and investigative work is needed. Obtain summary of incidents from officers in charge at crime scenes, taking care to avoid disturbing evidence. Provide information to lab personnel concerning the source of each item of evidence and tests to be performed. Examine records and governmental agency files to find identifying data about suspects. Block or rope off scenes and check perimeters to ensure that scenes are completely secured. Summon medical help for injured individuals and alert medical personnel to take statements from them. Observe and photograph narcotic purchase transactions to compile evidence and protect undercover investigators.

GOE—Interest Area/Cluster: 12. Law and Public Safety. **Work Group:** 12.04. Law Enforcement and Public Safety. **Other Jobs in This Work Group:**

Enterprising–P

Bailiffs; Correctional Officers and Jailers; Criminal Investigators and Special Agents; Detectives and Criminal Investigators; Fire Investigators; Forensic Science Technicians; Parking Enforcement Workers; Police and Sheriff's Patrol Officers; Police Identification and Records Officers; Police Patrol Officers; Sheriffs and Deputy Sheriffs; Transit and Railroad Police.

Skills: Persuasion; Systems Analysis; Social Perceptiveness; Systems Evaluation; Complex Problem Solving; Critical Thinking; Negotiation; Active Listening.

Education and Training Programs: Criminal Justice/Police Science; Criminalistics and Criminal Science. **Related Knowledge/Courses:** Public Safety and Security; Law and Government; Psychology; Therapy and Counseling; Customer and Personal Service; Philosophy and Theology.

Work Environment: More often indoors than outdoors; very hot or cold; sitting.

Producers

- ❋ Personality Code: EA
- ❋ Education/Training Required: Work experience plus degree
- ❋ Annual Earnings: $61,090
- ❋ Beginning Wage: $28,980
- ❋ Earnings Growth Potential: Very high
- ❋ Growth: 11.1%
- ❋ Annual Job Openings: 8,992
- ❋ Self-Employed: 29.5%
- ❋ Part-Time: 9.0%

The job openings listed here are shared with Directors—Stage, Motion Pictures, Television, and Radio; Program Directors; Talent Directors; and Technical Directors/Managers.

Plan and coordinate various aspects of radio, television, stage, or motion picture production, such as selecting script; coordinating writing, directing, and editing; and arranging financing. Coordinate the activities of writers, directors, managers, and other personnel throughout the production process. Monitor post-production processes to ensure accurate completion of all details. Perform management activities such as budgeting, scheduling, planning, and marketing. Determine production size, content, and budget, establishing details such as production schedules and management policies. Compose and edit scripts or provide screenwriters with story outlines from which scripts can be written. Conduct meetings with staff to discuss production progress and to ensure production objectives are attained. Resolve personnel problems that arise during the production process by acting as liaisons between dissenting parties when necessary. Produce shows for special occasions, such as holidays or testimonials. Edit and write news stories from information collected by reporters. Write and submit proposals to bid on contracts for projects. Hire directors, principal cast members, and key production staff members. Arrange financing for productions. Select plays, scripts, books, or ideas to be produced. Review film, recordings, or rehearsals to ensure conformance to production and broadcast standards. Perform administrative duties such as preparing operational reports, distributing rehearsal call sheets and script copies, and arranging for rehearsal quarters. Obtain and distribute costumes, props, music, and studio equipment needed to complete productions. Negotiate contracts with artistic personnel, often in accordance with collective bargaining agreements. Maintain knowledge of minimum wages and working conditions established by unions or associations of actors and technicians. Plan and coordinate the production of musical recordings, selecting music and directing performers. Negotiate with parties, including independent producers and the distributors and broadcasters who will be handling completed productions. Develop marketing plans for finished products, collaborating with sales associates to supervise product distribution. Determine and direct the content of radio programming.

GOE—Interest Area/Cluster: 03. Arts and Communication. **Work Group:** 03.01. Managerial Work in Arts and Communication. **Other Jobs in This Work Group:** Agents and Business Managers of Artists, Performers, and Athletes; Art Directors; Producers and Directors; Program Directors; Public Relations Managers; Technical Directors/Managers.

Skills: Monitoring; Writing; Management of Financial Resources; Management of Personnel Resources; Negotiation; Coordination; Equipment Selection; Speaking.

Education and Training Programs: Radio and Television; Drama and Dramatics/Theatre Arts, General; Directing and Theatrical Production; Theatre/Theatre Arts Management; Dramatic/Theatre Arts and Stagecraft, Other; Film/Cinema Studies; Cinematography and Film/Video Production. **Related Knowledge/Courses:** Communications and Media; Fine Arts; Clerical Practices; Sales and Marketing; Telecommunications; English Language.

Work Environment: Indoors; sitting.

Producers and Directors

See Directors—Stage, Motion Pictures, Television, and Radio (an Enterprising job), Producers (an Enterprising job), Program Directors (an Enterprising job), Talent Directors (an Enterprising job), and Technical Directors/Managers (an Enterprising job), described separately.

Program Directors

- ❋ Personality Code: ECA
- ❋ Education/Training Required: Work experience plus degree
- ❋ Annual Earnings: $61,090
- ❋ Beginning Wage: $28,980
- ❋ Earnings Growth Potential: Very high
- ❋ Growth: 11.1%
- ❋ Annual Job Openings: 8,992
- ❋ Self-Employed: 29.5%
- ❋ Part-Time: 9.0%

The job openings listed here are shared with Directors—Stage, Motion Pictures, Television, and Radio; Producers; Talent Directors; and Technical Directors/Managers.

Direct and coordinate activities of personnel engaged in preparation of radio or television station program schedules and programs such as sports or news. Plan and schedule programming and event coverage based on broadcast length; time availability; and other factors such as community needs, ratings data, and viewer demographics. Monitor and review programming to ensure that schedules are met, guidelines are adhered to, and performances are of adequate quality. Direct and coordinate activities of personnel engaged in broadcast news, sports, or programming. Check completed program logs for accuracy and conformance with FCC rules and regulations and resolve program log inaccuracies. Establish work schedules and assign work to staff members. Coordinate activities between departments such as news and programming. Perform personnel duties such as hiring staff and evaluating work performance. Evaluate new and existing programming for suitability and to assess the need for changes, using information such as audience surveys and feedback. Develop budgets for programming and broadcasting activities and monitor expenditures to ensure that they remain within budgetary limits. Confer with directors and production staff to discuss issues such as production and casting problems, budgets, policies, and news coverage. Select, acquire, and maintain programs, music, films, and other needed materials and obtain legal clearances for their use as necessary. Monitor network transmissions for advisories concerning daily program schedules, program content, special feeds, or program changes. Develop promotions for current programs and specials. Prepare copy and edit tape so that material is ready for broadcasting. Develop ideas for programs and features that a station could produce. Participate in the planning and execution of fundraising activities. Review information about programs and schedules to ensure accuracy and provide such information to local media outlets as necessary. Read news, read or record public service and promotional announcements, and otherwise participate as a member of an on-air shift as required. Operate and maintain on-air and production audio equipment. Direct setup of remote facilities and install or cancel programs at remote stations.

GOE—Interest Area/Cluster: 03. Arts and Communication. **Work Group:** 03.01. Managerial Work in Arts and Communication. **Other Jobs in This Work Group:** Agents and Business Managers of Artists, Performers, and Athletes; Art Directors; Producers; Producers and Directors; Public Relations Managers; Technical Directors/Managers.

Skills: Operations Analysis; Management of Financial Resources; Management of Personnel Resources; Coordination; Writing; Time Management; Equipment Selection; Monitoring.

Education and Training Programs: Radio and Television; Drama and Dramatics/Theatre Arts, General; Directing and Theatrical Production; Theatre/Theatre Arts Management; Dramatic/Theatre Arts and Stagecraft, Other; Film/Cinema Studies; Cinematography and Film/Video Production. **Related Knowledge/Courses:** Telecommunications; Communications and Media; Computers and Electronics; Clerical Practices; Personnel and Human Resources; Engineering and Technology.

Work Environment: Indoors; noisy; sitting.

Property, Real Estate, and Community Association Managers

* Personality Code: EC
* Education/Training Required: Bachelor's degree
* Annual Earnings: $43,670
* Beginning Wage: $20,800
* Earnings Growth Potential: Very high
* Growth: 15.1%
* Annual Job Openings: 49,916
* Self-Employed: 50.9%
* Part-Time: 16.1%

Plan, direct, or coordinate selling, buying, leasing, or governance activities of commercial, industrial, or residential real estate properties. Meet with prospective tenants to show properties, explain terms of occupancy, and provide information about local areas. Direct collection of monthly assessments; rental fees; and deposits and payment of insurance premiums, mortgage, taxes, and incurred operating expenses. Inspect grounds, facilities, and equipment routinely to determine necessity of repairs or maintenance. Investigate complaints, disturbances, and violations and resolve problems, following management rules and regulations. Manage and oversee operations, maintenance, administration, and improvement of commercial, industrial, or residential properties. Plan, schedule, and coordinate general maintenance, major repairs, and remodeling or construction projects for commercial or residential properties. Negotiate the sale, lease, or development of property and complete or review appropriate documents and forms. Maintain records of sales, rental or usage activity, special permits issued, maintenance and operating costs, or property availability. Determine and certify the eligibility of prospective tenants, following government regulations. Prepare detailed budgets and financial reports for properties. Direct and coordinate the activities of staff and contract personnel and evaluate their performance. Maintain contact with insurance carriers, fire and police departments, and other agencies to ensure protection and compliance with codes and regulations. Market vacant space to prospective tenants through leasing agents, advertising, or other methods. Solicit and analyze bids from contractors for repairs, renovations, and maintenance. Review rents to ensure that they are in line with rental markets. Prepare and administer contracts for provision of property services such as cleaning, maintenance, and security services. Purchase building and maintenance supplies, equipment, or furniture. Act as liaisons between on-site managers or tenants and owners. Confer regularly with community association members to ensure their needs are being met. Meet with boards of directors and committees to discuss and resolve legal and environmental issues or disputes between neighbors.

GOE—Interest Area/Cluster: 14. Retail and Wholesale Sales and Service. **Work Group:** 14.01. Managerial Work in Retail/Wholesale Sales and Service. **Other Jobs in This Work Group:** Advertising and Promotions Managers; First-Line Supervisors/ Managers of Non-Retail Sales Workers; First-Line Supervisors/Managers of Retail Sales Workers; Funeral Directors; Marketing Managers; Purchasing Managers; Sales Managers.

Skills: Management of Financial Resources; Management of Personnel Resources; Management of Material Resources; Time Management; Repairing; Judgment and Decision Making; Installation; Coordination.

Education and Training Program: Real Estate. **Related Knowledge/Courses:** Sales and Marketing; Clerical Practices; Economics and Accounting; Administration and Management; Customer and Personal Service; Building and Construction.

Work Environment: More often indoors than outdoors; sitting.

Public Relations Managers

- ✱ Personality Code: EA
- ✱ Education/Training Required: Work experience plus degree
- ✱ Annual Earnings: $86,470
- ✱ Beginning Wage: $44,870
- ✱ Earnings Growth Potential: High
- ✱ Growth: 16.9%
- ✱ Annual Job Openings: 5,781
- ✱ Self-Employed: 1.7%
- ✱ Part-Time: 5.4%

Plan and direct public relations programs designed to create and maintain a favorable public image for employer or client or, if engaged in fundraising, plan and direct activities to solicit and maintain funds for special projects and non-profit organizations. Identify main client groups and audiences and determine the best way to communicate publicity information to them. Write interesting and effective press releases, prepare information for media kits, and develop and maintain company Internet or intranet Web pages. Develop and maintain the company's corporate image and identity, which includes the use of logos and signage. Manage communications budgets. Manage special events such as sponsorship of races, parties introducing new products, or other activities the firm supports to gain public attention through the media without advertising directly. Draft speeches for company executives and arrange interviews and other forms of contact for them. Assign, supervise, and review the activities of public relations staff. Evaluate advertising and promotion programs for compatibility with public relations efforts. Establish and maintain effective working relationships with local and municipal government officials and media representatives. Confer with labor relations managers to develop internal communications that keep employees informed of company activities. Direct activities of external agencies, establishments, and departments that develop and implement communication strategies and information programs. Formulate policies and procedures related to public information programs, working with public relations executives. Respond to requests for information about employers' activities or status. Establish goals for soliciting funds, develop policies for collection and safeguarding of contributions, and coordinate disbursement of funds. Facilitate consumer relations or the relationship between parts of the company such as the managers and employees or different branch offices. Maintain company archives. Manage in-house communication courses. Produce films and other video products, regulate their distribution, and operate film library. Observe and report on social, economic, and political trends that might affect employers.

GOE—Interest Area/Cluster: 03. Arts and Communication. **Work Group:** 03.01. Managerial Work in Arts and Communication. **Other Jobs in This Work Group:** Agents and Business Managers of Artists, Performers, and Athletes; Art Directors; Producers; Producers and Directors; Program Directors; Technical Directors/Managers.

Skills: Management of Financial Resources; Monitoring; Social Perceptiveness; Writing; Service Orientation; Operations Analysis; Speaking; Persuasion.

Education and Training Program: Public Relations/Image Management. **Related Knowledge/Courses:** Sales and Marketing; Economics and Accounting; Foreign Language; Law and Government; Education and Training; English Language.

Work Environment: Indoors; sitting.

Public Relations Specialists

- ❋ Personality Code: EAS
- ❋ Education/Training Required: Bachelor's degree
- ❋ Annual Earnings: $49,800
- ❋ Beginning Wage: $29,580
- ❋ Earnings Growth Potential: High
- ❋ Growth: 17.6%
- ❋ Annual Job Openings: 51,216
- ❋ Self-Employed: 4.9%
- ❋ Part-Time: 13.9%

Engage in promoting or creating good will for individuals, groups, or organizations by writing or selecting favorable publicity material and releasing it through various communications media. May prepare and arrange displays and make speeches. Prepare or edit organizational publications for internal and external audiences, including employee newsletters and stockholders' reports. Respond to requests for information from the media or designate another appropriate spokesperson or information source. Establish and maintain cooperative relationships with representatives of community, consumer, employee, and public interest groups. Plan and direct development and communication of informational programs to maintain favorable public and stockholder perceptions of an organization's accomplishments and agenda. Confer with production and support personnel to produce or coordinate production of advertisements and promotions. Arrange public appearances, lectures, contests, or exhibits for clients to increase product and service awareness and to promote goodwill. Study the objectives, promotional policies, and needs of organizations to develop public relations strategies that will influence public opinion or promote ideas, products, and services. Consult with advertising agencies or staff to arrange promotional campaigns in all types of media for products, organizations, or individuals. Confer with other managers to identify trends and key group interests and concerns or to provide advice on business decisions. Coach client representatives in effective communication with the public and with employees. Prepare and deliver speeches to further public relations objectives. Purchase advertising space and time as required to promote client's product or agenda. Plan and conduct market and public opinion research to test products or determine potential for product success, communicating results to client or management.

GOE—Interest Area/Cluster: 03. Arts and Communication. **Work Group:** 03.03. News, Broadcasting, and Public Relations. **Other Jobs in This Work Group:** Broadcast News Analysts; Interpreters and Translators; Reporters and Correspondents.

Skills: Service Orientation; Management of Financial Resources; Persuasion; Writing; Negotiation; Social Perceptiveness; Judgment and Decision Making; Monitoring.

Education and Training Programs: Communication Studies/Speech Communication and Rhetoric; Public Relations/Image Management; Political Communication; Health Communication; Family and Consumer Sciences/Human Sciences Communication. **Related Knowledge/Courses:** Sales and Marketing; Communications and Media; Customer and Personal Service; Sociology and Anthropology; Clerical Practices; Administration and Management.

Work Environment: Indoors; sitting.

Real Estate Brokers

- ❋ Personality Code: EC
- ❋ Education/Training Required: Work experience in a related occupation
- ❋ Annual Earnings: $58,860
- ❋ Beginning Wage: $25,990
- ❋ Earnings Growth Potential: Very high
- ❋ Growth: 11.1%
- ❋ Annual Job Openings: 18,689
- ❋ Self-Employed: 63.5%
- ❋ Part-Time: 15.5%

Operate real estate office or work for commercial real estate firm, overseeing real estate transactions. Other duties usually include selling real estate or renting properties and arranging loans. Sell, for a fee, real estate owned by others. Obtain agreements from property owners to place properties for sale with real estate firms. Monitor fulfillment of purchase contract terms to ensure that they are handled in a timely manner. Compare a property with similar properties that have recently sold to determine its competitive market price. Act as an intermediary in negotiations between buyers and sellers over property prices and settlement details and during the closing of sales. Generate lists of properties for sale, their locations and descriptions, and available financing options, using computers. Maintain knowledge of real estate law; local economies; fair housing laws; and types of available mortgages, financing options, and government programs. Check work completed by loan officers, attorneys, and other professionals to ensure that it is performed properly. Arrange for financing of property purchases. Appraise property values, assessing income potential when relevant. Maintain awareness of current income tax regulations, local zoning, building and tax laws, and growth possibilities of the area where a property is located. Manage and operate real estate offices, handling associated business details. Supervise agents who handle real estate transactions. Rent properties or manage rental properties. Arrange for title searches of properties being sold. Give buyers virtual tours of properties in which they are interested, using computers. Review property details to ensure that environmental regulations are met. Develop, sell, or lease property used for industry or manufacturing. Maintain working knowledge of various factors that determine a farm's capacity to produce, including agricultural variables and proximity to market centers and transportation facilities.

GOE—Interest Area/Cluster: 14. Retail and Wholesale Sales and Service. **Work Group:** 14.03. General Sales. **Other Jobs in This Work Group:** Parts Salespersons; Real Estate Sales Agents; Retail Salespersons; Sales Representatives, Wholesale and Manufacturing, Except Technical and Scientific Products; Service Station Attendants.

Skills: Management of Financial Resources; Negotiation; Mathematics; Judgment and Decision Making; Active Listening; Persuasion; Service Orientation; Complex Problem Solving.

Education and Training Program: Real Estate. **Related Knowledge/Courses:** Sales and Marketing; Law and Government; Building and Construction; Customer and Personal Service; Personnel and Human Resources; Economics and Accounting.

Work Environment: More often indoors than outdoors; sitting.

Real Estate Sales Agents

- ❋ Personality Code: EC
- ❋ Education/Training Required: Postsecondary vocational training
- ❋ Annual Earnings: $40,600
- ❋ Beginning Wage: $20,930
- ❋ Earnings Growth Potential: High
- ❋ Growth: 10.6%
- ❋ Annual Job Openings: 61,232
- ❋ Self-Employed: 60.2%
- ❋ Part-Time: 15.5%

Rent, buy, or sell property for clients. Perform duties such as studying property listings,

Enterprising-R

interviewing prospective clients, accompanying clients to property site, discussing conditions of sale, and drawing up real estate contracts. Includes agents who represent buyer. Present purchase offers to sellers for consideration. Confer with escrow companies, lenders, home inspectors, and pest control operators to ensure that terms and conditions of purchase agreements are met before closing dates. Interview clients to determine what kinds of properties they are seeking. Prepare documents such as representation contracts, purchase agreements, closing statements, deeds, and leases. Coordinate property closings, overseeing signing of documents and disbursement of funds. Act as an intermediary in negotiations between buyers and sellers, generally representing one or the other. Promote sales of properties through advertisements, open houses, and participation in multiple listing services. Compare a property with similar properties that have recently sold to determine its competitive market price. Coordinate appointments to show homes to prospective buyers. Generate lists of properties that are compatible with buyers' needs and financial resources. Display commercial, industrial, agricultural, and residential properties to clients and explain their features. Arrange for title searches to determine whether clients have clear property titles. Review plans for new construction with clients, enumerating and recommending available options and features. Answer clients' questions regarding construction work, financing, maintenance, repairs, and appraisals. Accompany buyers during visits to and inspections of property, advising them on the suitability and value of the homes they are visiting. Inspect condition of premises and arrange for necessary maintenance or notify owners of maintenance needs. Advise sellers on how to make homes more appealing to potential buyers. Arrange meetings between buyers and sellers when details of transactions need to be negotiated. Advise clients on market conditions, prices, mortgages, legal requirements, and related matters. Evaluate mortgage options to help clients obtain financing at the best prevailing rates and terms. Review property listings, trade journals, and relevant literature and attend conventions, seminars, and staff and association meetings to remain knowledgeable about real estate markets.

GOE—Interest Area/Cluster: 14. Retail and Wholesale Sales and Service. **Work Group:** 14.03. General Sales. **Other Jobs in This Work Group:** Parts Salespersons; Real Estate Brokers; Retail Salespersons; Sales Representatives, Wholesale and Manufacturing, Except Technical and Scientific Products; Service Station Attendants.

Skills: Negotiation; Service Orientation; Coordination; Speaking; Management of Financial Resources; Writing; Time Management; Mathematics.

Education and Training Program: Real Estate. **Related Knowledge/Courses:** Sales and Marketing; Clerical Practices; Law and Government; Customer and Personal Service; Economics and Accounting; Building and Construction.

Work Environment: More often indoors than outdoors; sitting.

Sales Agents, Financial Services

- ✳ Personality Code: EC
- ✳ Education/Training Required: Bachelor's degree
- ✳ Annual Earnings: $68,430
- ✳ Beginning Wage: $30,890
- ✳ Earnings Growth Potential: Very high
- ✳ Growth: 24.8%
- ✳ Annual Job Openings: 47,750
- ✳ Self-Employed: 17.7%
- ✳ Part-Time: 6.9%

The job openings listed here are shared with Sales Agents, Securities and Commodities.

Sell financial services such as loan, tax, and securities counseling to customers of financial institutions and business establishments. Determine customers' financial services needs and prepare proposals to sell services that address these needs. Contact prospective customers to present information and explain available services. Sell services and equipment, such as trusts, investments, and check processing services. Prepare forms or agreements to complete sales. Develop prospects from current commercial customers, referral leads, and sales and trade meetings. Review business trends in order to advise customers regarding expected fluctuations. Make presentations on financial services to groups to attract new clients. Evaluate costs and revenue of agreements to determine continued profitability.

GOE—Interest Area/Cluster: 06. Finance and Insurance. **Work Group:** 06.05. Finance/Insurance Sales and Support. **Other Jobs in This Work Group:** Advertising Sales Agents; Insurance Sales Agents; Personal Financial Advisors; Sales Agents, Securities and Commodities; Securities, Commodities, and Financial Services Sales Agents.

Skills: Persuasion; Management of Financial Resources; Service Orientation; Negotiation; Operations Analysis; Monitoring; Speaking; Judgment and Decision Making.

Education and Training Programs: Financial Planning and Services; Investments and Securities; Business and Personal/Financial Services Marketing Operations. **Related Knowledge/Courses:** Sales and Marketing; Economics and Accounting; Customer and Personal Service; Law and Government; Mathematics; Personnel and Human Resources.

Work Environment: Indoors; sitting.

Sales Agents, Securities and Commodities

- ❋ Personality Code: EC
- ❋ Education/Training Required: Bachelor's degree
- ❋ Annual Earnings: $68,430
- ❋ Beginning Wage: $30,890
- ❋ Earnings Growth Potential: Very high
- ❋ Growth: 24.8%
- ❋ Annual Job Openings: 47,750
- ❋ Self-Employed: 17.7%
- ❋ Part-Time: 6.9%

The job openings listed here are shared with Sales Agents, Financial Services.

Buy and sell securities in investment and trading firms and develop and implement financial plans for individuals, businesses, and organizations. Complete sales order tickets and submit for processing of client requested transactions. Interview clients to determine clients' assets, liabilities, cash flow, insurance coverage, tax status, and financial objectives. Record transactions accurately and keep clients informed about transactions. Develop financial plans based on analysis of clients' financial status and discuss financial options with clients. Review all securities transactions to ensure accuracy of information and ensure that trades conform to regulations of governing agencies. Offer advice on the purchase or sale of particular securities. Relay buy or sell orders to securities exchanges or to firm trading departments. Identify potential clients, using advertising campaigns, mailing lists, and personal contacts. Review financial periodicals, stock and bond reports, business publications, and other material to identify potential investments for clients and to keep abreast of trends affecting market conditions. Contact prospective customers to determine customer needs, present information, and explain available services. Prepare documents needed to implement plans selected by clients. Analyze market conditions to determine optimum times to execute securities transactions. Explain stock market terms and trading practices to clients. Inform and advise concerned parties regarding fluctuations and securities transactions affecting plans or accounts. Calculate costs for billings and commissions purposes. Supply the latest price quotes on any security, as well as information on the activities and financial positions of the corporations issuing these securities. Prepare financial reports to monitor client or corporate finances. Read corporate reports and calculate ratios to determine best prospects for profit on stock purchases and to monitor client accounts.

GOE—Interest Area/Cluster: 06. Finance and Insurance. **Work Group:** 06.05. Finance/Insurance Sales and Support. **Other Jobs in This Work**

Group: Advertising Sales Agents; Insurance Sales Agents; Personal Financial Advisors; Sales Agents, Financial Services; Securities, Commodities, and Financial Services Sales Agents.

Skills: Management of Financial Resources; Persuasion; Social Perceptiveness; Negotiation; Judgment and Decision Making; Service Orientation; Speaking; Time Management.

Education and Training Programs: Financial Planning and Services; Investments and Securities. **Related Knowledge/Courses:** Economics and Accounting; Customer and Personal Service; Sales and Marketing; Clerical Practices; Law and Government; Mathematics.

Work Environment: Indoors; sitting.

Sales Engineers

- ❋ Personality Code: ERI
- ❋ Education/Training Required: Bachelor's degree
- ❋ Annual Earnings: $80,270
- ❋ Beginning Wage: $48,290
- ❋ Earnings Growth Potential: Medium
- ❋ Growth: 8.5%
- ❋ Annual Job Openings: 7,371
- ❋ Self-Employed: 0.0%
- ❋ Part-Time: 2.0%

Sell business goods or services, the selling of which requires a technical background equivalent to a baccalaureate degree in engineering. Plan and modify product configurations to meet customer needs. Confer with customers and engineers to assess equipment needs and to determine system requirements. Collaborate with sales teams to understand customer requirements, to promote the sale of company products, and to provide sales support. Secure and renew orders and arrange delivery. Develop, present, or respond to proposals for specific customer requirements, including request for proposal responses and industry-specific solutions. Sell products requiring extensive technical expertise and support for installation and use, such as material handling equipment, numerical-control machinery, and computer systems. Diagnose problems with installed equipment. Prepare and deliver technical presentations that explain products or services to customers and prospective customers. Recommend improved materials or machinery to customers, documenting how such changes will lower costs or increase production. Provide technical and non-technical support and services to clients or other staff members regarding the use, operation, and maintenance of equipment. Research and identify potential customers for products or services. Visit prospective buyers at commercial, industrial, or other establishments to show samples or catalogs and to inform them about product pricing, availability, and advantages. Create sales or service contracts for products or services. Arrange for demonstrations or trial installations of equipment. Keep informed on industry news and trends; products; services; competitors; relevant information about legacy, existing, and emerging technologies; and the latest product-line developments. Attend company training seminars to become familiar with product lines. Provide information needed for the development of custom-made machinery. Develop sales plans to introduce products in new markets. Write technical documentation for products. Identify resale opportunities and support them to achieve sales plans. Document account activities, generate reports, and keep records of business transactions with customers and suppliers.

GOE—Interest Area/Cluster: 14. Retail and Wholesale Sales and Service. **Work Group:** 14.02. Technical Sales. **Other Jobs in This Work Group:** Sales Representatives, Wholesale and Manufacturing, Technical and Scientific Products.

Skills: Operations Analysis; Science; Systems Evaluation; Technology Design; Programming; Installation; Equipment Selection; Mathematics.

Education and Training Programs: Aerospace Engineering; Agricultural Engineering; Chemical Engineering; Computer Engineering; Construction Engineering; Electrical, Electronic, and

Communications Engineering; Environmental Engineering; Forest Engineering; Industrial Engineering; Manufacturing Engineering; Materials Engineering; Mechanical Engineering; Metallurgical Engineering; Mining and Mineral Engineering; Nuclear Engineering; Petroleum Engineering; Transportation and Highway Engineering; Water Resources Engineering; others. **Related Knowledge/Courses:** Sales and Marketing; Engineering and Technology; Design; Physics; Computers and Electronics; Customer and Personal Service.

Work Environment: Indoors; sitting; repetitive motions.

Sales Managers

- ❀ Personality Code: EC
- ❀ Education/Training Required: Work experience plus degree
- ❀ Annual Earnings: $94,910
- ❀ Beginning Wage: $45,860
- ❀ Earnings Growth Potential: Very high
- ❀ Growth: 10.2%
- ❀ Annual Job Openings: 36,392
- ❀ Self-Employed: 2.2%
- ❀ Part-Time: 4.1%

Direct the actual distribution or movement of products or services to customers. Coordinate sales distribution by establishing sales territories, quotas, and goals, and establish training programs for sales representatives. Analyze sales statistics gathered by staff to determine sales potential and inventory requirements and monitor the preferences of customers. Resolve customer complaints regarding sales and service. Oversee regional and local sales managers and their staffs. Plan and direct staffing, training, and performance evaluations to develop and control sales and service programs. Determine price schedules and discount rates. Review operational records and reports to project sales and determine profitability. Monitor customer preferences to determine focus of sales efforts.

Prepare budgets and approve budget expenditures. Confer or consult with department heads to plan advertising services and to secure information on equipment and customer specifications. Direct and coordinate activities involving sales of manufactured products, services, commodities, real estate, or other subjects of sale. Confer with potential customers regarding equipment needs and advise customers on types of equipment to purchase. Direct foreign sales and service outlets of an organization. Advise dealers and distributors on policies and operating procedures to ensure functional effectiveness of businesses. Visit franchised dealers to stimulate interest in establishment or expansion of leasing programs. Direct clerical staff to keep records of export correspondence, bid requests, and credit collections, and to maintain current information on tariffs, licenses, and restrictions. Direct, coordinate, and review activities in sales and service accounting and recordkeeping, and in receiving and shipping operations. Assess marketing potential of new and existing store locations, considering statistics and expenditures. Represent company at trade association meetings to promote products.

GOE—Interest Area/Cluster: 14. Retail and Wholesale Sales and Service. **Work Group:** 14.01. Managerial Work in Retail/Wholesale Sales and Service. **Other Jobs in This Work Group:** Advertising and Promotions Managers; First-Line Supervisors/Managers of Non-Retail Sales Workers; First-Line Supervisors/Managers of Retail Sales Workers; Funeral Directors; Marketing Managers; Property, Real Estate, and Community Association Managers; Purchasing Managers.

Skills: Management of Personnel Resources; Systems Analysis; Management of Financial Resources; Persuasion; Negotiation; Systems Evaluation; Social Perceptiveness; Speaking.

Education and Training Programs: Consumer Merchandising/Retailing Management; Business/Commerce, General; Business Administration and Management, General; Marketing/Marketing Management, General; Marketing, Other. **Related Knowledge/Courses:** Sales and Marketing; Personnel and Human Resources; Economics and

Accounting; Administration and Management; Customer and Personal Service; Psychology.

Work Environment: Indoors; sitting.

Sales Representatives, Wholesale and Manufacturing, Technical and Scientific Products

❋ Personality Code: EC
❋ Education/Training Required: Work experience in a related occupation
❋ Annual Earnings: $68,270
❋ Beginning Wage: $35,090
❋ Earnings Growth Potential: High
❋ Growth: 12.4%
❋ Annual Job Openings: 43,469
❋ Self-Employed: 4.2%
❋ Part-Time: 6.7%

Sell goods for wholesalers or manufacturers where technical or scientific knowledge is required in such areas as biology, engineering, chemistry, and electronics, normally obtained from at least 2 years of postsecondary education. Contact new and existing customers to discuss their needs, and to explain how these needs could be met by specific products and services. Answer customers' questions about products, prices, availability, product uses, and credit terms. Quote prices, credit terms, and other bid specifications. Emphasize product features based on analyses of customers' needs, and on technical knowledge of product capabilities and limitations. Negotiate prices and terms of sales and service agreements. Maintain customer records, using automated systems. Identify prospective customers by using business directories, following leads from existing clients, participating in organizations and clubs, and attending trade shows and conferences. Prepare sales contracts for orders obtained, and submit orders for processing. Select the correct products or assist customers in making product selections, based on customers' needs, product specifications, and applicable regulations. Collaborate with colleagues to exchange information such as selling strategies and marketing information. Prepare sales presentations and proposals that explain product specifications and applications. Provide customers with ongoing technical support. Demonstrate and explain the operation and use of products. Inform customers of estimated delivery schedules, service contracts, warranties, or other information pertaining to purchased products. Attend sales and trade meetings, and read related publications in order to obtain information about market conditions, business trends, and industry developments. Visit establishments to evaluate needs and to promote product or service sales. Complete expense reports, sales reports, and other paperwork. Initiate sales campaigns and follow marketing plan guidelines in order to meet sales and production expectations. Recommend ways for customers to alter product usage in order to improve production. Complete product and development training as required. Provide feedback to companys' product design teams so that products can be tailored to clients' needs. Arrange for installation and test-operation of machinery.

GOE—Interest Area/Cluster: 14. Retail and Wholesale Sales and Service. **Work Group:** 14.02. Technical Sales. **Other Jobs in This Work Group:** Sales Engineers.

Skills: Persuasion; Negotiation; Science; Management of Financial Resources; Service Orientation; Coordination; Operations Analysis; Social Perceptiveness.

Education and Training Programs: Selling Skills and Sales Operations; Business, Management, Marketing, and Related Support Services. **Related Knowledge/Courses:** Sales and Marketing; Customer and Personal Service; Production and Processing; Administration and Management; Computers and Electronics; Transportation.

Work Environment: Indoors; sitting.

Securities, Commodities, and Financial Services Sales Agents

See Sales Agents, Financial Services (an Enterprising job) and Sales Agents, Securities and Commodities (an Enterprising job), described separately.

Sheriffs and Deputy Sheriffs

* Personality Code: ERS
* Education/Training Required: Long-term on-the-job training
* Annual Earnings: $49,630
* Beginning Wage: $28,820
* Earnings Growth Potential: High
* Growth: 10.8%
* Annual Job Openings: 37,842
* Self-Employed: 0.0%
* Part-Time: 1.1%

The job openings listed here are shared with Police Patrol Officers.

Enforce law and order in rural or unincorporated districts or serve legal processes of courts. May patrol courthouse, guard court or grand jury, or escort defendants. Drive vehicles or patrol specific areas to detect law violators, issue citations, and make arrests. Investigate illegal or suspicious activities. Verify that the proper legal charges have been made against law offenders. Execute arrest warrants, locating and taking persons into custody. Record daily activities and submit logs and other related reports and paperwork to appropriate authorities. Patrol and guard courthouses, grand jury rooms, or assigned areas to provide security, enforce laws, maintain order, and arrest violators. Notify patrol units to take violators into custody or to provide needed assistance or medical aid. Place people in protective custody. Serve statements of claims, subpoenas, summonses, jury summonses, orders to pay alimony, and other court orders. Take control of accident scenes to maintain traffic flow, to assist accident victims, and

to investigate causes. Question individuals entering secured areas to determine their business, directing and rerouting individuals as necessary. Transport or escort prisoners and defendants en route to courtrooms, prisons or jails, attorneys' offices, or medical facilities. Locate and confiscate real or personal property, as directed by court order. Manage jail operations and tend to jail inmates.

GOE—Interest Area/Cluster: 12. Law and Public Safety. **Work Group:** 12.04. Law Enforcement and Public Safety. **Other Jobs in This Work Group:** Bailiffs; Correctional Officers and Jailers; Criminal Investigators and Special Agents; Detectives and Criminal Investigators; Fire Investigators; Forensic Science Technicians; Parking Enforcement Workers; Police and Sheriff's Patrol Officers; Police Detectives; Police Identification and Records Officers; Police Patrol Officers; Transit and Railroad Police.

Skills: Negotiation; Persuasion; Social Perceptiveness; Service Orientation; Equipment Selection; Complex Problem Solving; Judgment and Decision Making; Coordination.

Education and Training Programs: Criminal Justice/Police Science; Criminalistics and Criminal Science. **Related Knowledge/Courses:** Public Safety and Security; Law and Government; Telecommunications; Psychology; Therapy and Counseling; Philosophy and Theology.

Work Environment: More often outdoors than indoors; very hot or cold; contaminants; disease or infections; sitting.

Ship and Boat Captains

* Personality Code: ER
* Education/Training Required: Work experience in a related occupation
* Annual Earnings: $57,210
* Beginning Wage: $29,530
* Earnings Growth Potential: High
* Growth: 17.9%
* Annual Job Openings: 2,665
* Self-Employed: 6.8%
* Part-Time: 4.8%

The job openings listed here are shared with Mates— Ship, Boat, and Barge, and with Pilots, Ship.

Command vessels in oceans, bays, lakes, rivers, and coastal waters. Assign watches and living quarters to crew members. Sort logs, form log booms, and salvage lost logs. Perform various marine duties such as checking for oil spills or other pollutants around ports and harbors, and patrolling beaches. Contact buyers to sell cargo such as fish. Tow and maneuver barges, or signal for tugboats to tow barges to destinations. Signal passing vessels, using whistles, flashing lights, flags, and radios. Resolve questions or problems with customs officials. Read gauges to verify sufficient levels of hydraulic fluid, air pressure, and oxygen. Purchase supplies and equipment. Measure depths of water, using depth-measuring equipment. Maintain boats and equipment on board, such as engines, winches, navigational systems, fire extinguishers, and life preservers. Collect fares from customers, or signal ferryboat helpers to collect fares. Arrange for ships to be fueled, restocked with supplies, and/or repaired. Signal crew members or deckhands to rig tow lines, open or close gates and ramps, and pull guard chains across entries. Maintain records of daily activities, personnel reports, ship positions and movements, ports of call, weather and sea conditions, pollution control efforts, and/or cargo and passenger statuses. Inspect vessels to ensure efficient and safe operation of vessels and equipment, and conformance to regulations. Direct and coordinate crew members or workers performing activities such as loading and unloading cargo, steering vessels, operating engines, and operating, maintaining, and repairing ship equipment. Compute positions, set courses, and determine speeds by using charts, area plotting sheets, compasses, sextants, and knowledge of local conditions. Calculate sightings of land, using electronic sounding devices, and following contour lines on charts. Monitor the loading and discharging of cargo or passengers. Interview and hire crew members. Steer and operate vessels, using radios, depth finders, radars, lights, buoys, and lighthouses.

GOE—Interest Area/Cluster: 16. Transportation, Distribution, and Logistics. **Work Group:** 16.05. Water Vehicle Operation. **Other Jobs in This Work Group:** Captains, Mates, and Pilots of Water Vessels; Dredge Operators; Mates—Ship, Boat, and Barge; Motorboat Operators; Pilots, Ship; Sailors and Marine Oilers.

Skills: Operation and Control; Operation Monitoring; Equipment Maintenance; Judgment and Decision Making; Troubleshooting; Management of Personnel Resources; Repairing; Management of Material Resources.

Education and Training Programs: Commercial Fishing; Marine Science/Merchant Marine Officer; Marine Transportation, Other. **Related Knowledge/Courses:** Transportation; Geography; Public Safety and Security; Telecommunications; Psychology; Mechanical Devices.

Work Environment: Outdoors; standing; using hands on objects, tools, or controls; repetitive motions.

Social and Community Service Managers

- ❋ Personality Code: ES
- ❋ Education/Training Required: Bachelor's degree
- ❋ Annual Earnings: $54,530
- ❋ Beginning Wage: $32,480
- ❋ Earnings Growth Potential: High
- ❋ Growth: 24.7%
- ❋ Annual Job Openings: 23,788
- ❋ Self-Employed: 5.9%
- ❋ Part-Time: 11.6%

Plan, organize, or coordinate the activities of a social service program or community outreach organization. Oversee the program or organization's budget and policies regarding participant involvement, program requirements, and benefits. Work may involve directing social workers, counselors, or probation officers. Establish and maintain relationships with other agencies and organizations in community to meet community needs and to ensure that services are not duplicated. Prepare and maintain records and reports, such as budgets, personnel records, or training manuals. Direct activities of professional and technical staff members and volunteers. Evaluate the work of staff and volunteers to ensure that programs are of appropriate quality and that resources are used effectively. Establish and oversee administrative procedures to meet objectives set by boards of directors or senior management. Participate in the determination of organizational policies regarding such issues as participant eligibility, program requirements, and program benefits. Research and analyze member or community needs to determine program directions and goals. Speak to community groups to explain and interpret agency purposes, programs, and policies. Recruit, interview, and hire or sign up volunteers and staff. Represent organizations in relations with governmental and media institutions. Plan and administer budgets for programs, equipment, and support services. Analyze proposed legislation, regulations, or rule changes to determine how agency services could be impacted. Act as consultants to agency staff and other community programs regarding the interpretation of program-related federal, state, and county regulations and policies. Implement and evaluate staff training programs. Direct fundraising activities and the preparation of public relations materials.

GOE—Interest Area/Cluster: 07. Government and Public Administration. **Work Group:** 07.01. Managerial Work in Government and Public Administration. **Other Jobs in This Work Group:** No other jobs in this group.

Skills: Social Perceptiveness; Management of Personnel Resources; Service Orientation; Systems Evaluation; Negotiation; Persuasion; Monitoring; Writing.

Education and Training Programs: Human Services, General; Community Organization and Advocacy; Public Administration; Business/Commerce, General; Business Administration and Management, General; Non-Profit/Public/Organizational Management; Entrepreneurship/Entrepreneurial Studies; Business, Management, Marketing, and Related Support Services, Other. **Related Knowledge/Courses:** Sociology and Anthropology; Therapy and Counseling; Psychology; Philosophy and Theology; Clerical Practices; Education and Training.

Work Environment: Indoors; noisy; sitting.

Talent Directors

- ❋ Personality Code: EA
- ❋ Education/Training Required: Long-term on-the-job training
- ❋ Annual Earnings: $61,090
- ❋ Beginning Wage: $28,980
- ❋ Earnings Growth Potential: Very high
- ❋ Growth: 11.1%
- ❋ Annual Job Openings: 8,992
- ❋ Self-Employed: 29.5%
- ❋ Part-Time: 9.0%

The job openings listed here are shared with Directors— Stage, Motion Pictures, Television, and Radio; Producers; Program Directors; and Technical Directors/Managers.

Audition and interview performers to select most appropriate talent for parts in stage, television, radio, or motion picture productions. Review performer information such as photos, resumes, voice tapes, videos, and union membership, in order to decide whom to audition for parts. Read scripts and confer with producers in order to determine the types and numbers of performers required for a given production. Select performers for roles or submit lists of suitable performers to producers or directors for final selection. Audition and interview performers in order to match their attributes to specific roles or to increase the pool of available acting talent. Maintain talent files that include information such as performers' specialties, past performances, and availability. Prepare actors for auditions by providing scripts and information about roles and casting requirements. Serve as liaisons between directors, actors, and agents. Attend or view productions in order to maintain knowledge of available actors. Negotiate contract agreements with performers, with agents, or between performers and agents or production companies. Contact agents and actors in order to provide notification of audition and performance opportunities and to set up audition times. Hire and supervise workers who help locate people with specified attributes and talents. Arrange for and/or design screen tests or auditions for prospective performers. Locate performers or extras for crowd and background scenes, and stand-ins or photo doubles for actors, by direct contact or through agents.

GOE—Interest Area/Cluster: 03. Arts and Communication. **Work Group:** 03.07. Music. **Other Jobs in This Work Group:** Music Composers and Arrangers; Music Directors; Music Directors and Composers; Musicians and Singers; Musicians, Instrumental; Singers.

Skills: Management of Financial Resources; Management of Personnel Resources; Persuasion; Social Perceptiveness; Negotiation; Judgment and Decision Making; Time Management; Management of Material Resources.

Education and Training Programs: Radio and Television; Drama and Dramatics/Theatre Arts, General; Directing and Theatrical Production; Theatre/ Theatre Arts Management; Dramatic/Theatre Arts and Stagecraft, Other; Film/Cinema Studies; Cinematography and Film/Video Production. **Related Knowledge/Courses:** Fine Arts; Communications and Media; Clerical Practices; Computers and Electronics; Sales and Marketing; Telecommunications.

Work Environment: Indoors; noisy; sitting.

Technical Directors/Managers

- ❋ Personality Code: ERC
- ❋ Education/Training Required: Long-term on-the-job training
- ❋ Annual Earnings: $61,090
- ❋ Beginning Wage: $28,980
- ❋ Earnings Growth Potential: Very high
- ❋ Growth: 11.1%
- ❋ Annual Job Openings: 8,992
- ❋ Self-Employed: 29.5%
- ❋ Part-Time: 9.0%

The job openings listed here are shared with Directors— Stage, Motion Pictures, Television, and Radio; Producers; Program Directors; and Talent Directors.

Coordinate activities of technical departments, such as taping, editing, engineering, and maintenance, to produce radio or television programs. Direct technical aspects of newscasts and other productions, checking and switching between video sources and taking responsibility for the on-air product, including camera shots and graphics. Test equipment to ensure proper operation. Monitor broadcasts to ensure that programs conform to station or network policies and regulations. Observe pictures through monitors and direct camera and video staff concerning shading and composition. Act as liaisons between engineering and production departments. Supervise and assign duties to workers engaged in technical control and production of radio and television programs. Schedule use of studio and editing facilities for producers and engineering and maintenance staff. Confer with operations directors to formulate and maintain fair and attainable technical policies for programs. Operate equipment to produce programs or broadcast live programs from remote locations. Train workers in use of equipment such as switchers, cameras, monitors, microphones, and lights. Switch between video sources in a studio or on multi-camera remotes, using equipment such as switchers, video slide projectors, and video effects generators. Set up and execute video transitions and special effects such as fades, dissolves, cuts, keys, and supers, using computers to manipulate pictures as necessary. Collaborate with promotions directors to produce on-air station promotions. Discuss filter options, lens choices, and the visual effects of objects being filmed with photography directors and video operators. Follow instructions from production managers and directors during productions, such as commands for camera cuts, effects, graphics, and takes.

GOE—Interest Area/Cluster: 03. Arts and Communication. **Work Group:** 03.01. Managerial Work in Arts and Communication. **Other Jobs in This Work Group:** Agents and Business Managers of Artists, Performers, and Athletes; Art Directors; Producers; Producers and Directors; Program Directors; Public Relations Managers.

Skills: Operation and Control; Operation Monitoring; Monitoring; Systems Analysis; Equipment Selection; Troubleshooting; Installation; Time Management.

Education and Training Programs: Radio and Television; Drama and Dramatics/Theatre Arts, General; Directing and Theatrical Production; Theatre/Theatre Arts Management; Dramatic/Theatre Arts and Stagecraft, Other; Film/Cinema Studies; Cinematography and Film/Video Production. **Related Knowledge/Courses:** Communications and Media; Telecommunications; Computers and Electronics;

Philosophy and Theology; Engineering and Technology; Sales and Marketing.

Work Environment: Indoors; noisy; sitting; using hands on objects, tools, or controls.

Training and Development Managers

- ❋ Personality Code: ES
- ❋ Education/Training Required: Work experience plus degree
- ❋ Annual Earnings: $84,340
- ❋ Beginning Wage: $46,450
- ❋ Earnings Growth Potential: High
- ❋ Growth: 15.6%
- ❋ Annual Job Openings: 3,759
- ❋ Self-Employed: 1.6%
- ❋ Part-Time: 2.7%

Plan, direct, or coordinate the training and development activities and staff of organizations. Prepare training budgets for departments or organizations. Evaluate instructor performances and the effectiveness of training programs, providing recommendations for improvements. Analyze training needs to develop new training programs or modify and improve existing programs. Conduct or arrange for ongoing technical training and personal development classes for staff members. Plan, develop, and provide training and staff development programs, using knowledge of the effectiveness of methods such as classroom training, demonstrations, on-the-job training, meetings, conferences, and workshops. Conduct orientation sessions and arrange on-the-job training for new hires. Confer with management and conduct surveys to identify training needs based on projected production processes, changes, and other factors. Train instructors and supervisors in techniques and skills for training and dealing with employees. Develop and organize training manuals, multimedia visual aids, and other educational materials. Develop testing and evaluation procedures. Review and evaluate training and apprenticeship programs for compliance with government standards. Coordinate established courses with technical and professional courses provided by community schools and designate training procedures.

GOE—Interest Area/Cluster: 04. Business and Administration. **Work Group:** 04.01. Managerial Work in General Business. **Other Jobs in This Work Group:** Chief Executives; Compensation and Benefits Managers; General and Operations Managers; Human Resources Managers.

Skills: Systems Evaluation; Management of Financial Resources; Systems Analysis; Management of Personnel Resources; Negotiation; Persuasion; Learning Strategies; Service Orientation.

Education and Training Programs: Human Resources Management/Personnel Administration, General; Human Resources Development. **Related Knowledge/Courses:** Education and Training; Personnel and Human Resources; Sociology and Anthropology; Sales and Marketing; Therapy and Counseling; English Language.

Work Environment: Indoors; sitting; using hands on objects, tools, or controls.

Conventional Occupations

Accountants

- ❋ Personality Code: CE
- ❋ Education/Training Required: Bachelor's degree
- ❋ Annual Earnings: $57,060
- ❋ Beginning Wage: $35,570
- ❋ Earnings Growth Potential: Medium
- ❋ Growth: 17.7%
- ❋ Annual Job Openings: 134,463
- ❋ Self-Employed: 9.5%
- ❋ Part-Time: 9.3%

The job openings listed here are shared with Auditors.

Analyze financial information and prepare financial reports to determine or maintain record of assets, liabilities, profit and loss, tax liability, or other financial activities within an organization. Prepare, examine, or analyze accounting records, financial statements, or other financial reports to assess accuracy, completeness, and conformance to reporting and procedural standards. Compute taxes owed and prepare tax returns, ensuring compliance with payment, reporting, or other tax requirements. Analyze business operations, trends, costs, revenues, financial commitments, and obligations to project future revenues and expenses or to provide advice. Report to management regarding the finances of establishment. Establish tables of accounts and assign entries to proper accounts. Develop, maintain, and analyze budgets, preparing periodic reports that compare budgeted costs to actual costs. Develop, implement, modify, and document recordkeeping and accounting systems, making use of current computer technology. Prepare forms and manuals for accounting and bookkeeping personnel and direct their work activities. Survey operations to ascertain accounting needs and to recommend, develop, or maintain solutions to business and financial problems. Work as

Internal Revenue Service (IRS) agents. Advise management about issues such as resource utilization, tax strategies, and the assumptions underlying budget forecasts. Provide internal and external auditing services for businesses or individuals. Advise clients in areas such as compensation, employee healthcare benefits, the design of accounting or data processing systems, or long-range tax or estate plans. Investigate bankruptcies and other complex financial transactions and prepare reports summarizing the findings. Represent clients before taxing authorities and provide support during litigation involving financial issues. Appraise, evaluate, and inventory real property and equipment, recording information such as the description, value, and location of property. Maintain or examine the records of government agencies. Serve as bankruptcy trustees or business valuators.

GOE—Interest Area/Cluster: 04. Business and Administration. **Work Group:** 04.05. Accounting, Auditing, and Analytical Support. **Other Jobs in This Work Group:** Accountants and Auditors; Auditors; Budget Analysts; Industrial Engineering Technicians; Logisticians; Management Analysts; Operations Research Analysts.

Skills: Management of Financial Resources; Systems Analysis; Systems Evaluation; Operations Analysis; Judgment and Decision Making; Programming; Mathematics; Time Management.

Education and Training Programs: Accounting and Computer Science; Accounting; Accounting and Finance; Accounting and Business/Management. **Related Knowledge/Courses:** Economics and Accounting; Clerical Practices; Mathematics; Law and Government; Computers and Electronics; Personnel and Human Resources.

Work Environment: Indoors; sitting.

Accountants and Auditors

See *Accountants (a Conventional job) and Auditors (a Conventional job), described separately.*

Actuaries

- ❋ Personality Code: CIE
- ❋ Education/Training Required: Work experience plus degree
- ❋ Annual Earnings: $85,690
- ❋ Beginning Wage: $48,750
- ❋ Earnings Growth Potential: High
- ❋ Growth: 23.7%
- ❋ Annual Job Openings: 3,245
- ❋ Self-Employed: 0.0%
- ❋ Part-Time: 5.9%

Analyze statistical data, such as mortality, accident, sickness, disability, and retirement rates, and construct probability tables to forecast risk and liability for payment of future benefits. May ascertain premium rates required and cash reserves necessary to ensure payment of future benefits. Ascertain premium rates required and cash reserves and liabilities necessary to ensure payment of future benefits. Analyze statistical information to estimate mortality, accident, sickness, disability, and retirement rates. Design, review, and help administer insurance, annuity, and pension plans, determining financial soundness and calculating premiums. Collaborate with programmers, underwriters, accountants, claims experts, and senior management to help companies develop plans for new lines of business or for improving existing business. Determine or help determine company policy and explain complex technical matters to company executives, government officials, shareholders, policyholders, or the public. Testify before public agencies on proposed legislation affecting businesses. Provide advice to clients on a contract basis, working as a consultant. Testify in court as expert witness or to provide legal evidence on matters such as the value of potential lifetime earnings of a person who is disabled or killed in an accident. Construct probability tables for events such as fires, natural disasters, and unemployment, based on analysis of statistical data and other pertinent information. Determine policy contract provisions for each type of insurance. Manage credit and help price corporate security offerings. Provide expertise to help financial institutions manage risks and maximize returns associated with investment products or credit offerings. Determine equitable basis for distributing surplus earnings under participating insurance and annuity contracts in mutual companies. Explain changes in contract provisions to customers.

GOE—Interest Area/Cluster: 15. Scientific Research, Engineering, and Mathematics. **Work Group:** 15.06. Mathematics and Data Analysis. **Other Jobs in This Work Group:** Mathematical Technicians; Mathematicians; Social Science Research Assistants; Statistical Assistants; Statisticians.

Skills: Programming; Mathematics; Operations Analysis; Complex Problem Solving; Active Learning; Quality Control Analysis; Troubleshooting; Critical Thinking.

Education and Training Program: Actuarial Science. **Related Knowledge/Courses:** Mathematics; Economics and Accounting; Sales and Marketing; Computers and Electronics; Personnel and Human Resources; Law and Government.

Work Environment: Indoors; sitting; using hands on objects, tools, or controls; repetitive motions.

Appraisers and Assessors of Real Estate

See Appraisers, Real Estate (an Enterprising job) and Assessors (a Conventional job), described separately.

Archivists

- ❋ Personality Code: CI
- ❋ Education/Training Required: Master's degree
- ❋ Annual Earnings: $43,110
- ❋ Beginning Wage: $26,330
- ❋ Earnings Growth Potential: Medium
- ❋ Growth: 14.4%
- ❋ Annual Job Openings: 795
- ❋ Self-Employed: 1.3%
- ❋ Part-Time: 18.4%

Appraise, edit, and direct safekeeping of permanent records and historically valuable documents. Participate in research activities based on archival materials. Create and maintain accessible, retrievable computer archives and databases, incorporating current advances in electric information storage technology. Organize archival records and develop classification systems to facilitate access to archival materials. Authenticate and appraise historical documents and archival materials. Provide reference services and assistance for users needing archival materials. Direct activities of workers who assist in arranging, cataloguing, exhibiting, and maintaining collections of valuable materials. Prepare archival records, such as document descriptions, to allow easy access to information. Preserve records, documents, and objects, copying records to film, videotape, audiotape, disk, or computer formats as necessary. Establish and administer policy guidelines concerning public access and use of materials. Locate new materials and direct their acquisition and display. Research and record the origins and historical significance of archival materials. Specialize in an area of history or technology, researching topics or items relevant to collections to determine what should be retained or acquired. Coordinate educational and public outreach programs such as tours, workshops, lectures, and classes. Select and edit documents for publication and display, applying knowledge of subject, literary expression, and presentation techniques.

GOE—Interest Area/Cluster: 05. Education and Training. **Work Group:** 05.05. Archival and Museum Services. **Other Jobs in This Work Group:** Audio-Visual Collections Specialists; Curators; Museum Technicians and Conservators.

Skills: Programming; Writing; Operations Analysis; Reading Comprehension; Quality Control Analysis; Persuasion; Judgment and Decision Making; Active Listening.

Education and Training Programs: Historic Preservation and Conservation; Cultural Resource Management and Policy Analysis; Historic Preservation and Conservation, Other; Museology/Museum Studies; Art History, Criticism and Conservation; Public/Applied History and Archival Administration; Historic Preservation and Conservation; Cultural Resource Management and Policy Analysis; Historic Preservation and Conservation, Other; Museology/Museum Studies; Art History, Criticism and Conservation; Public/Applied History and Archival Administration; Library Science/Librarianship. **Related Knowledge/Courses:** Clerical Practices; History and Archeology; Computers and Electronics; English Language; Administration and Management; Customer and Personal Service.

Work Environment: Indoors; sitting.

Assessors

- ❋ Personality Code: CEI
- ❋ Education/Training Required: Bachelor's degree
- ❋ Annual Earnings: $46,130
- ❋ Beginning Wage: $25,110
- ❋ Earnings Growth Potential: High
- ❋ Growth: 16.9%
- ❋ Annual Job Openings: 6,493
- ❋ Self-Employed: 32.7%
- ❋ Part-Time: 8.4%

The job openings listed here are shared with Appraisers, Real Estate.

Appraise real and personal property to determine its fair value. May assess taxes in accordance with prescribed schedules. Determine taxability and value of properties, using methods such as field inspection, structural measurement, calculation, sales analysis, market trend studies, and income and expense analysis. Inspect new construction and major improvements to existing structures to determine values. Explain assessed values to property owners and defend appealed assessments at public hearings. Inspect properties, considering factors such as market value, location, and building or replacement costs to determine appraisal value. Prepare and maintain current data on each parcel assessed, including maps of boundaries, inventories of land and structures, property characteristics, and any applicable exemptions. Identify the ownership of each piece of taxable property. Conduct regular reviews of property within jurisdictions to determine changes in property due to construction or demolition. Complete and maintain assessment rolls that show the assessed values and status of all property in a municipality. Issue notices of assessments and taxes. Review information about transfers of property to ensure its accuracy, checking basic information on buyers, sellers, and sales prices and making corrections as necessary. Maintain familiarity with aspects of local real estate markets. Analyze trends in sales prices, construction costs, and rents to assess property values or determine the accuracy of assessments. Approve applications for property tax exemptions or deductions. Establish uniform and equitable systems for assessing all classes and kinds of property. Write and submit appraisal and tax reports for public record. Serve on assessment review boards. Hire staff members. Provide sales analyses to be used for equalization of school aid. Calculate tax bills for properties by multiplying assessed values by jurisdiction tax rates.

GOE—Interest Area/Cluster: 06. Finance and Insurance. **Work Group:** 06.02. Finance/Insurance Investigation and Analysis. **Other Jobs in This Work Group:** Appraisers and Assessors of Real Estate; Appraisers, Real Estate; Claims Adjusters, Examiners, and Investigators; Claims Examiners, Property and Casualty Insurance; Cost Estimators; Credit Analysts; Financial Analysts; Insurance Adjusters, Examiners, and Investigators; Insurance Appraisers, Auto Damage; Insurance Underwriters; Loan Counselors; Loan Officers; Market Research Analysts; Survey Researchers.

Skills: Mathematics; Systems Analysis; Speaking; Negotiation; Systems Evaluation; Active Listening; Management of Financial Resources; Persuasion.

Education and Training Program: Real Estate. **Related Knowledge/Courses:** Building and Construction; Clerical Practices; Law and Government; Mathematics; Geography; Economics and Accounting.

Work Environment: More often indoors than outdoors; sitting; using hands on objects, tools, or controls; repetitive motions.

Auditors

- ❋ Personality Code: CEI
- ❋ Education/Training Required: Bachelor's degree
- ❋ Annual Earnings: $57,060
- ❋ Beginning Wage: $35,570
- ❋ Earnings Growth Potential: Medium
- ❋ Growth: 17.7%
- ❋ Annual Job Openings: 134,463
- ❋ Self-Employed: 9.5%
- ❋ Part-Time: 9.3%

The job openings listed here are shared with Accountants.

Examine and analyze accounting records to determine financial status of establishment and prepare financial reports concerning operating procedures. Collect and analyze data to detect deficient controls; duplicated effort; extravagance; fraud; or non-compliance with laws, regulations, and management policies. Prepare detailed reports on audit findings. Supervise auditing of establishments and determine scope of investigation required. Report to management about asset utilization and audit results and recommend changes in operations and financial activities. Inspect account books and accounting systems for efficiency, effectiveness, and use of accepted accounting procedures to record transactions. Examine records and interview workers to ensure recording of transactions and compliance with laws and regulations. Examine and evaluate financial and information systems, recommending controls to ensure system reliability and data integrity. Review data about material assets, net worth, liabilities, capital stock, surplus, income, and expenditures. Confer with company officials about financial and regulatory matters. Examine whether the organization's objectives are reflected in its management activities and whether employees understand the objectives. Prepare, analyze, and verify annual reports, financial statements, and other records, using accepted accounting and statistical procedures to assess financial condition and facilitate financial planning. Inspect cash on hand, notes receivable and payable, negotiable securities, and canceled checks to confirm records are accurate. Examine inventory to verify journal and ledger entries. Direct activities of personnel engaged in filing, recording, compiling, and transmitting financial records. Conduct pre-implementation audits to determine whether systems and programs under development will work as planned. Audit payroll and personnel records to determine unemployment insurance premiums, workers' compensation coverage, liabilities, and compliance with tax laws. Evaluate taxpayer finances to determine tax liability, using knowledge of interest and discount rates, annuities, valuation of stocks and bonds, and amortization valuation of depletable assets. Review taxpayer accounts and conduct audits on-site, by correspondence, or by summoning taxpayers to office.

GOE—Interest Area/Cluster: 04. Business and Administration. **Work Group:** 04.05. Accounting, Auditing, and Analytical Support. **Other Jobs in This Work Group:** Accountants; Accountants and Auditors; Budget Analysts; Industrial Engineering Technicians; Logisticians; Management Analysts; Operations Research Analysts.

Skills: Systems Analysis; Systems Evaluation.

Education and Training Programs: Accounting and Computer Science; Accounting; Auditing; Accounting and Finance; Accounting and Business/Management. **Related Knowledge/Courses:** Economics and Accounting; Administration and Management; Personnel and Human Resources; Computers and Electronics; Law and Government; English Language.

Work Environment: Indoors; noisy; sitting; using hands on objects, tools, or controls; repetitive motions.

Bill and Account Collectors

- ❋ Personality Code: CE
- ❋ Education/Training Required: Short-term on-the-job training
- ❋ Annual Earnings: $29,990
- ❋ Beginning Wage: $20,630
- ❋ Earnings Growth Potential: Low
- ❋ Growth: 22.9%
- ❋ Annual Job Openings: 118,709
- ❋ Self-Employed: 1.0%
- ❋ Part-Time: 10.7%

Locate and notify customers of delinquent accounts by mail, telephone, or personal visit to solicit payment. Duties include receiving payment and posting amount to customer's account, preparing statements to credit department if customer fails to respond, initiating repossession proceedings or service disconnection, and keeping records of collection and status of accounts. Receive payments and post amounts paid to customer accounts. Locate and monitor overdue accounts, using computers and a variety of automated systems. Record information about financial status of customers and status of collection efforts. Locate and notify customers of delinquent accounts by mail, telephone, or personal visits to solicit payment. Confer with customers by telephone or in person to determine reasons for overdue payments and to review the terms of sales, service, or credit contracts. Advise customers of necessary actions and strategies for debt repayment. Persuade customers to pay amounts due on credit accounts, damage claims, or nonpayable checks or to return merchandise. Sort and file correspondence and perform miscellaneous clerical duties such as answering correspondence and writing reports. Perform various administrative functions for assigned accounts, such as recording address changes and purging the records of deceased customers. Arrange for debt repayment or establish repayment schedules based on customers' financial situations. Negotiate credit extensions when necessary. Trace delinquent customers to new addresses by inquiring at post offices, telephone companies, or credit bureaus or through the questioning of neighbors. Notify credit departments, order merchandise repossession or service disconnection, and turn over account records to attorneys when customers fail to respond to collection attempts. Drive vehicles to visit customers, return merchandise to creditors, or deliver bills.

GOE—Interest Area/Cluster: 06. Finance and Insurance. **Work Group:** 06.04. Finance/Insurance Customer Service. **Other Jobs in This Work Group:** Loan Interviewers and Clerks; New Accounts Clerks; Tellers.

Skills: Management of Financial Resources; Speaking; Management of Personnel Resources; Social Perceptiveness; Operations Analysis; Time Management; Service Orientation; Judgment and Decision Making.

Education and Training Program: Banking and Financial Support Services. **Related Knowledge/Courses:** Clerical Practices; Economics and Accounting; Law and Government; Customer and Personal Service; Computers and Electronics; Personnel and Human Resources.

Work Environment: Indoors; sitting; using hands on objects, tools, or controls; repetitive motions.

Billing and Posting Clerks and Machine Operators

See Billing, Cost, and Rate Clerks (a Conventional job), Billing, Posting, and Calculating Machine Operators (a Conventional job), and Statement Clerks (a Conventional job), described separately.

Billing, Cost, and Rate Clerks

* Personality Code: CE
* Education/Training Required: Moderate-term on-the-job training
* Annual Earnings: $29,970
* Beginning Wage: $20,930
* Earnings Growth Potential: Low
* Growth: 4.4%
* Annual Job Openings: 81,885
* Self-Employed: 1.6%
* Part-Time: 14.3%

The job openings listed here are shared with Billing, Posting, and Calculating Machine Operators and with Statement Clerks.

Compile data, compute fees and charges, and prepare invoices for billing purposes. Duties include computing costs and calculating rates for goods, services, and shipment of goods; posting data; and keeping other relevant records. May involve use of computer or typewriter, calculator, and adding and bookkeeping machines. Verify accuracy of billing data and revise any errors. Operate typing, adding, calculating, and billing machines. Prepare itemized statements, bills, or invoices and record amounts due for items purchased or services rendered. Review documents such as purchase orders, sales tickets, charge slips, or hospital records to compute fees and charges due. Perform bookkeeping work, including posting data and keeping other records concerning costs of goods and services and the shipment of goods. Keep records of invoices and support documents. Resolve discrepancies in accounting records. Type billing documents, shipping labels, credit memorandums, and credit forms, using typewriters or computers. Contact customers to obtain or relay account information. Compute credit terms, discounts, shipment charges, and rates for goods and services to complete billing documents. Answer mail and telephone inquiries regarding rates, routing, and procedures. Track accumulated hours and dollar amounts charged to each client job to calculate client fees for professional services such as legal and accounting services. Review compiled data on operating costs and revenues to set rates. Compile reports of cost factors, such as labor, production, storage, and equipment. Consult sources such as rate books, manuals, and insurance company representatives to determine specific charges and information such as rules, regulations, and government tax and tariff information. Update manuals when rates, rules, or regulations are amended. Estimate market value of products or services.

GOE—Interest Area/Cluster: 04. Business and Administration. **Work Group:** 04.06. Mathematical Clerical Support. **Other Jobs in This Work Group:** Billing and Posting Clerks and Machine Operators; Bookkeeping, Accounting, and Auditing Clerks; Brokerage Clerks; Payroll and Timekeeping Clerks; Statement Clerks; Tax Preparers.

Skills: Writing; Active Listening; Service Orientation; Reading Comprehension; Instructing; Speaking; Social Perceptiveness.

Education and Training Program: Accounting Technology/Technician and Bookkeeping. **Related Knowledge/Courses:** Clerical Practices; Economics and Accounting; Computers and Electronics; Mathematics.

Work Environment: Indoors; sitting.

Billing, Posting, and Calculating Machine Operators

- ❀ Personality Code: CRE
- ❀ Education/Training Required: Moderate-term on-the-job training
- ❀ Annual Earnings: $29,970
- ❀ Beginning Wage: $20,930
- ❀ Earnings Growth Potential: Low
- ❀ Growth: 4.4%
- ❀ Annual Job Openings: 81,885
- ❀ Self-Employed: 1.6%
- ❀ Part-Time: 14.3%

The job openings listed here are shared with Billing, Cost, and Rate Clerks and with Statement Clerks.

Operate machines that automatically perform mathematical processes, such as addition, subtraction, multiplication, and division, to calculate and record billing, accounting, statistical, and other numerical data. Duties include operating special billing machines to prepare statements, bills, and invoices and operating bookkeeping machines to copy and post data, make computations, and compile records of transactions. Enter into machines all information needed for bill generation. Train other calculating machine operators and review their work. Operate special billing machines to prepare statements, bills, and invoices. Operate bookkeeping machines to copy and post data, make computations, and compile records of transactions. Reconcile and post receipts for cash received by various departments. Prepare transmittal reports for changes to assessment and tax rolls; redemption file changes; and warrants, deposits, and invoices. Encode and add amounts of transaction documents, such as checks or money orders, using encoding machines. Balance and reconcile batch control totals with source documents or computer listings to locate errors, encode correct amounts, or prepare correction records. Compute payroll and retirement amounts, applying knowledge of payroll deductions, actuarial tables, disability factors, and survivor allowances.

Conventional–B

Maintain ledgers and registers, posting charges and refunds to individual funds and computing and verifying balances. Compute monies due on personal and real property, inventories, redemption payments, and other amounts, applying specialized knowledge of tax rates, formulas, interest rates, and other relevant information. Verify and post to ledgers purchase orders, reports of goods received, invoices, paid vouchers, and other information. Assign purchase order numbers to invoices, requisitions, and formal and informal bids. Verify completeness and accuracy of original documents such as business property statements, tax rolls, invoices, bonds and coupons, and redemption certificates. Bundle sorted documents to prepare those drawn on other banks for collection. Transcribe data from office records, using specified forms, billing machines, and transcribing machines. Sort and list items for proof or collection. Send completed bills to billing clerks for information verification. Transfer data from machines, such as encoding machines, to computers. Sort and microfilm transaction documents, such as checks, using sorting machines. Observe operation of sorters to locate documents that machines cannot read and manually record amounts of these documents.

GOE—Interest Area/Cluster: 04. Business and Administration. **Work Group:** 04.08. Clerical Machine Operation. **Other Jobs in This Work Group:** Data Entry Keyers; Mail Clerks and Mail Machine Operators, Except Postal Service; Office Machine Operators, Except Computer; Switchboard Operators, Including Answering Service; Word Processors and Typists.

Skills: Speaking; Active Listening; Writing.

Education and Training Program: Accounting Technology/Technician and Bookkeeping. **Related Knowledge/Courses:** Economics and Accounting; Clerical Practices; Personnel and Human Resources.

Work Environment: Indoors; noisy; contaminants; sitting; using hands on objects, tools, or controls; repetitive motions.

Bookkeeping, Accounting, and Auditing Clerks

- ❋ Personality Code: CE
- ❋ Education/Training Required: Moderate-term on-the-job training
- ❋ Annual Earnings: $31,560
- ❋ Beginning Wage: $20,310
- ❋ Earnings Growth Potential: Medium
- ❋ Growth: 12.5%
- ❋ Annual Job Openings: 286,854
- ❋ Self-Employed: 6.6%
- ❋ Part-Time: 24.8%

Compute, classify, and record numerical data to keep financial records complete. Perform any combination of routine calculating, posting, and verifying duties to obtain primary financial data for use in maintaining accounting records. May also check the accuracy of figures, calculations, and postings pertaining to business transactions recorded by other workers. Operate computers programmed with accounting software to record, store, and analyze information. Check figures, postings, and documents for correct entry, mathematical accuracy, and proper codes. Comply with federal, state, and company policies, procedures, and regulations. Debit, credit, and total accounts on computer spreadsheets and databases, using specialized accounting software. Classify, record, and summarize numerical and financial data to compile and keep financial records, using journals and ledgers or computers. Calculate, prepare, and issue bills, invoices, account statements, and other financial statements according to established procedures. Code documents according to company procedures. Compile statistical, financial, accounting, or auditing reports and tables pertaining to such matters as cash receipts, expenditures, accounts payable and receivable, and profits and losses. Operate 10-key calculators, typewriters, and copy machines to perform calculations and produce documents. Access computerized financial information to answer general questions as well as those related to specific accounts. Reconcile or note and report discrepancies found in records. Perform financial calculations such as amounts due, interest charges, balances, discounts, equity, and principal. Perform general office duties such as filing, answering telephones, and handling routine correspondence. Prepare bank deposits by compiling data from cashiers; verifying and balancing receipts; and sending cash, checks, or other forms of payment to banks. Receive, record, and bank cash, checks, and vouchers. Calculate and prepare checks for utilities, taxes, and other payments. Compare computer printouts to manually maintained journals to determine if they match. Reconcile records of bank transactions. Prepare trial balances of books. Monitor status of loans and accounts to ensure that payments are up to date. Transfer details from separate journals to general ledgers or data-processing sheets. Compile budget data and documents based on estimated revenues and expenses and previous budgets. Calculate costs of materials, overhead, and other expenses, based on estimates, quotations, and price lists.

GOE—Interest Area/Cluster: 04. Business and Administration. **Work Group:** 04.06. Mathematical Clerical Support. **Other Jobs in This Work Group:** Billing and Posting Clerks and Machine Operators; Billing, Cost, and Rate Clerks; Brokerage Clerks; Payroll and Timekeeping Clerks; Statement Clerks; Tax Preparers.

Skills: Management of Financial Resources; Mathematics; Time Management.

Education and Training Programs: Accounting Technology/Technician and Bookkeeping; Accounting and Related Services, Other. **Related Knowledge/Courses:** Clerical Practices; Economics and Accounting; Mathematics; Computers and Electronics.

Work Environment: Indoors; sitting; repetitive motions.

Brokerage Clerks

- ❋ Personality Code: CE
- ❋ Education/Training Required: Moderate-term on-the-job training
- ❋ Annual Earnings: $37,360
- ❋ Beginning Wage: $25,710
- ❋ Earnings Growth Potential: Low
- ❋ Growth: 20.0%
- ❋ Annual Job Openings: 10,826
- ❋ Self-Employed: 0.0%
- ❋ Part-Time: 19.4%

Perform clerical duties involving the purchase or sale of securities. Duties include writing orders for stock purchases and sales, computing transfer taxes, verifying stock transactions, accepting and delivering securities, tracking stock price fluctuations, computing equity, distributing dividends, and keeping records of daily transactions and holdings. Correspond with customers and confer with co-workers to answer inquiries, discuss market fluctuations, and resolve account problems. Record and document security transactions, such as purchases, sales, conversions, redemptions, and payments, using computers, accounting ledgers, and certificate records. Schedule and coordinate transfer and delivery of security certificates between companies, departments, and customers. Prepare forms, such as receipts, withdrawal orders, transmittal papers, and transfer confirmations, based on transaction requests from stockholders. File, type, and operate standard office machines. Monitor daily stock prices and compute fluctuations to determine the need for additional collateral to secure loans. Prepare reports summarizing daily transactions and earnings for individual customer accounts. Compute total holdings, dividends, interest, transfer taxes, brokerage fees, and commissions and allocate appropriate payments to customers. Verify ownership and transaction information and dividend distribution instructions to ensure conformance with governmental regulations, using stock records and reports.

Conventional-B

GOE—Interest Area/Cluster: 04. Business and Administration. **Work Group:** 04.06. Mathematical Clerical Support. **Other Jobs in This Work Group:** Billing and Posting Clerks and Machine Operators; Billing, Cost, and Rate Clerks; Bookkeeping, Accounting, and Auditing Clerks; Payroll and Time-keeping Clerks; Statement Clerks; Tax Preparers.

Skills: Service Orientation; Mathematics; Speaking; Active Listening; Systems Evaluation.

Education and Training Program: Accounting Technology/Technician and Bookkeeping. **Related Knowledge/Courses:** Economics and Accounting; Clerical Practices; Customer and Personal Service; Sales and Marketing; Computers and Electronics; Mathematics.

Work Environment: Indoors; sitting; repetitive motions.

Budget Analysts

- ❋ Personality Code: CEI
- ❋ Education/Training Required: Bachelor's degree
- ❋ Annual Earnings: $63,440
- ❋ Beginning Wage: $41,440
- ❋ Earnings Growth Potential: Low
- ❋ Growth: 7.1%
- ❋ Annual Job Openings: 6,423
- ❋ Self-Employed: 0.0%
- ❋ Part-Time: 3.2%

Examine budget estimates for completeness, accuracy, and conformance with procedures and regulations. Analyze budgeting and accounting reports for the purpose of maintaining expenditure controls. Direct the preparation of regular and special budget reports. Consult with managers to ensure that budget adjustments are made in accordance with program changes. Match appropriations for specific programs with appropriations for broader programs, including items for emergency funds. Provide advice and technical assistance with cost

analysis, fiscal allocation, and budget preparation. Summarize budgets and submit recommendations for the approval or disapproval of funds requests. Seek new ways to improve efficiency and increase profits. Review operating budgets to analyze trends affecting budget needs. Perform cost-benefit analyses to compare operating programs, review financial requests, or explore alternative financing methods. Interpret budget directives and establish policies for carrying out directives. Compile and analyze accounting records and other data to determine the financial resources required to implement a program. Testify before examining and fund-granting authorities, clarifying and promoting the proposed budgets.

GOE—Interest Area/Cluster: 04. Business and Administration. **Work Group:** 04.05. Accounting, Auditing, and Analytical Support. **Other Jobs in This Work Group:** Accountants; Accountants and Auditors; Auditors; Industrial Engineering Technicians; Logisticians; Management Analysts; Operations Research Analysts.

Skills: Management of Financial Resources; Systems Analysis; Systems Evaluation; Mathematics; Judgment and Decision Making; Persuasion.

Education and Training Programs: Accounting; Finance, General. **Related Knowledge/Courses:** Economics and Accounting; Clerical Practices; Administration and Management; Mathematics; Personnel and Human Resources; Computers and Electronics.

Work Environment: Indoors; sitting.

Cargo and Freight Agents

* Personality Code: CER
* Education/Training Required: Moderate-term on-the-job training
* Annual Earnings: $37,060
* Beginning Wage: $22,720
* Earnings Growth Potential: Medium
* Growth: 16.5%
* Annual Job Openings: 9,967
* Self-Employed: 1.1%
* Part-Time: 6.1%

Expedite and route movement of incoming and outgoing cargo and freight shipments in airline, train, and trucking terminals and shipping docks. Take orders from customers and arrange pickup of freight and cargo for delivery to loading platform. Prepare and examine bills of lading to determine shipping charges and tariffs. Negotiate and arrange transport of goods with shipping or freight companies. Notify consignees, passengers, or customers of the arrival of freight or baggage and arrange for delivery. Advise clients on transportation and payment methods. Prepare manifests showing baggage, mail, and freight weights and number of passengers on airplanes and transmit data to destinations. Determine method of shipment and prepare bills of lading, invoices, and other shipping documents. Check import/export documentation to determine cargo contents and classify goods into different fee or tariff groups, using a tariff coding system. Estimate freight or postal rates and record shipment costs and weights. Enter shipping information into a computer by hand or by using a hand-held scanner that reads bar codes on goods. Retrieve stored items and trace lost shipments as necessary. Pack goods for shipping, using tools such as staplers, strapping machines, and hammers. Direct delivery trucks to shipping doors or designated marshalling areas and help load and unload goods safely. Inspect and count items received and check them against invoices or other documents, recording shortages and rejecting damaged goods. Install straps, braces, and padding to loads to prevent shifting or damage during shipment. Keep records of all goods shipped, received, and stored. Coordinate and supervise activities of workers engaged in packing and shipping merchandise. Arrange insurance coverage for goods. Direct or participate in cargo loading to ensure completeness of load and even distribution of weight. Open cargo containers and unwrap contents, using steel cutters, crowbars, or other hand tools. Attach address labels, identification codes, and shipping instructions to containers. Contact vendors or claims adjustment departments to resolve problems with shipments or contact service depots to arrange for repairs. Route received goods to first available flight or to appropriate storage areas or departments, using forklifts, handtrucks, or other equipment. Maintain a supply of packing materials.

GOE—Interest Area/Cluster: 16. Transportation, Distribution, and Logistics. **Work Group:** 16.07. Transportation Support Work. **Other Jobs in This Work Group:** Bridge and Lock Tenders; Cleaners of Vehicles and Equipment; Laborers and Freight, Stock, and Material Movers, Hand; Railroad Brake, Signal, and Switch Operators; Traffic Technicians.

Skills: Negotiation; Instructing; Writing; Service Orientation; Monitoring; Speaking; Learning Strategies.

Education and Training Program: General Office Occupations and Clerical Services. **Related Knowledge/Courses:** Transportation; Geography; Customer and Personal Service; Clerical Practices; Computers and Electronics; Administration and Management.

Work Environment: Indoors; sitting; repetitive motions.

Claims Adjusters, Examiners, and Investigators

See Claims Examiners, Property and Casualty Insurance (a Conventional job) and Insurance Adjusters, Examiners, and Investigators (a Conventional job), described separately.

Claims Examiners, Property and Casualty Insurance

- ❋ Personality Code: CE
- ❋ Education/Training Required: Long-term on-the-job training
- ❋ Annual Earnings: $53,560
- ❋ Beginning Wage: $33,010
- ❋ Earnings Growth Potential: Medium
- ❋ Growth: 8.9%
- ❋ Annual Job Openings: 22,024
- ❋ Self-Employed: 3.5%
- ❋ Part-Time: 4.0%

The job openings listed here are shared with Insurance Adjusters, Examiners, and Investigators.

Review settled insurance claims to determine that payments and settlements have been made in accordance with company practices and procedures. Report overpayments, underpayments, and other irregularities. Confer with legal counsel on claims requiring litigation. Investigate, evaluate, and settle claims, applying technical knowledge and human relations skills to effect fair and prompt disposal of cases and to contribute to a reduced loss ratio. Pay and process claims within designated authority level. Adjust reserves or provide reserve recommendations to ensure that reserve activities are consistent with corporate policies. Enter claim payments, reserves, and new claims on computer system, inputting concise yet sufficient file documentation. Resolve complex severe exposure claims, using high-service-oriented file handling. Maintain claim files such as records of settled claims and an inventory of claims requiring detailed analysis. Verify and analyze data used in settling claims to ensure that claims are valid and that settlements are made according to company practices and procedures. Examine claims investigated by insurance adjusters, further investigating questionable claims to determine whether to authorize payments. Present cases and participate in their discussion at claim committee meetings. Contact or interview claimants, doctors, medical specialists, or employers to get additional information. Confer with legal counsel on claims requiring litigation. Report overpayments, underpayments, and other irregularities. Communicate with reinsurance brokers to obtain information necessary for processing claims. Supervise claims adjusters to ensure that adjusters have followed proper methods. Conduct detailed bill reviews to implement sound litigation management and expense control. Prepare reports to be submitted to company's data-processing department.

GOE—Interest Area/Cluster: 06. Finance and Insurance. **Work Group:** 06.02. Finance/Insurance Investigation and Analysis. **Other Jobs in This Work Group:** Appraisers and Assessors of Real Estate; Appraisers, Real Estate; Assessors; Claims Adjusters, Examiners, and Investigators; Cost Estimators; Credit Analysts; Financial Analysts; Insurance Adjusters, Examiners, and Investigators; Insurance Appraisers, Auto Damage; Insurance Underwriters; Loan Counselors; Loan Officers; Market Research Analysts; Survey Researchers.

Skills: Judgment and Decision Making; Writing; Persuasion; Negotiation; Reading Comprehension; Critical Thinking; Instructing; Active Listening.

Education and Training Program: Health/Medical Claims Examiner. **Related Knowledge/Courses:** Customer and Personal Service; Medicine and Dentistry; Clerical Practices; Law and Government; Computers and Electronics; English Language.

Work Environment: Indoors; sitting; using hands on objects, tools, or controls; repetitive motions.

Compensation, Benefits, and Job Analysis Specialists

* Personality Code: CE
* Education/Training Required: Bachelor's degree
* Annual Earnings: $52,180
* Beginning Wage: $33,450
* Earnings Growth Potential: Medium
* Growth: 18.4%
* Annual Job Openings: 18,761
* Self-Employed: 2.1%
* Part-Time: 7.6%

Conduct programs of compensation and benefits and job analysis for employer. May specialize in specific areas, such as position classification and pension programs. Evaluate job positions, determining classification, exempt or non-exempt status, and salary. Ensure company compliance with federal and state laws, including reporting requirements. Advise managers and employees on state and federal employment regulations, collective agreements, benefit and compensation policies, personnel procedures, and classification programs. Plan, develop, evaluate, improve, and communicate methods and techniques for selecting, promoting, compensating, evaluating, and training workers. Provide advice on the resolution of classification and salary complaints. Prepare occupational classifications, job descriptions, and salary scales. Assist in preparing and maintaining personnel records and handbooks. Prepare reports such as organization and flow charts and career path reports to summarize job analysis and evaluation and compensation analysis information. Administer employee insurance, pension, and savings plans, working with insurance brokers and plan carriers. Negotiate collective agreements on behalf of employers or workers and mediate labor disputes and grievances. Develop, implement, administer, and evaluate personnel and labor relations programs, including performance appraisal, affirmative action, and employment equity programs. Perform multifactor data and cost analyses that may be used in areas such as support of collective bargaining agreements. Research employee benefit and health and safety practices and recommend changes or modifications to existing policies. Analyze organizational, occupational, and industrial data to facilitate organizational functions and provide technical information to business, industry, and government. Advise staff of individuals' qualifications. Assess need for and develop job analysis instruments and materials. Review occupational data on Alien Employment Certification Applications to determine the appropriate occupational title and code; provide local offices with information about immigration and occupations. Research job and worker requirements, structural and functional relationships among jobs and occupations, and occupational trends.

GOE—Interest Area/Cluster: 04. Business and Administration. **Work Group:** 04.03. Human Resources Support. **Other Jobs in This Work Group:** Employment Interviewers; Employment, Recruitment, and Placement Specialists; Personnel Recruiters; Training and Development Specialists.

Skills: Service Orientation; Judgment and Decision Making; Management of Financial Resources; Persuasion; Active Listening; Negotiation; Monitoring; Coordination.

Education and Training Programs: Human Resources Management/Personnel Administration, General; Labor and Industrial Relations. **Related Knowledge/Courses:** Personnel and Human Resources; Clerical Practices; Customer and Personal Service; English Language; Administration and Management; Law and Government.

Work Environment: Indoors; noisy; sitting; using hands on objects, tools, or controls; repetitive motions.

Conventional–C

Compliance Officers, Except Agriculture, Construction, Health and Safety, and Transportation

See *Coroners (an Investigative job), Environmental Compliance Inspectors (a Conventional job), Equal Opportunity Representatives and Officers (a Social job), Government Property Inspectors and Investigators (a Conventional job), and Licensing Examiners and Inspectors (a Conventional job), described separately.*

Computer Specialists, All Other

See *Computer Systems Engineers/Architects (an Investigative job), Network Designers (a Conventional job), Software Quality Assurance Engineers and Testers (an Investigative job), Web Administrators (a Conventional job), and Web Developers (a Conventional job), described separately.*

Cost Estimators

- ❋ Personality Code: CE
- ❋ Education/Training Required: Bachelor's degree
- ❋ Annual Earnings: $54,920
- ❋ Beginning Wage: $32,470
- ❋ Earnings Growth Potential: High
- ❋ Growth: 18.5%
- ❋ Annual Job Openings: 38,379
- ❋ Self-Employed: 1.1%
- ❋ Part-Time: 5.8%

Prepare cost estimates for product manufacturing, construction projects, or services to aid management in bidding on or determining prices of products or services. May specialize according to particular service performed or type of product manufactured. Consult with clients, vendors, personnel in other departments, or construction foremen to discuss and formulate estimates and resolve issues. Analyze blueprints and other documentation to prepare time, cost, materials, and labor estimates. Prepare estimates for use in selecting vendors or subcontractors. Confer with engineers, architects, owners, contractors, and subcontractors on changes and adjustments to cost estimates. Prepare estimates used by management for purposes such as planning, organizing, and scheduling work. Prepare cost and expenditure statements and other necessary documentation at regular intervals for the duration of the project. Assess cost-effectiveness of products, projects, or services, tracking actual costs relative to bids as projects develop. Set up cost-monitoring and cost-reporting systems and procedures. Conduct special studies to develop and establish standard hour and related cost data or to effect cost reductions. Review material and labor requirements to decide whether it is more cost-effective to produce or purchase components. Prepare and maintain a directory of suppliers, contractors, and subcontractors. Establish and maintain tendering processes and conduct negotiations. Visit sites and record information about access, drainage and topography, and availability of services such as water and electricity.

GOE—Interest Area/Cluster: 06. Finance and Insurance. **Work Group:** 06.02. Finance/Insurance Investigation and Analysis. **Other Jobs in This Work Group:** Appraisers and Assessors of Real Estate; Appraisers, Real Estate; Assessors; Claims Adjusters, Examiners, and Investigators; Claims Examiners, Property and Casualty Insurance; Credit Analysts; Financial Analysts; Insurance Adjusters, Examiners, and Investigators; Insurance Appraisers, Auto Damage; Insurance Underwriters; Loan Counselors; Loan Officers; Market Research Analysts; Survey Researchers.

Skills: Systems Analysis; Management of Financial Resources; Mathematics; Systems Evaluation; Writing; Negotiation.

Education and Training Programs: Materials Engineering; Mechanical Engineering; Construction Engineering; Manufacturing Engineering; Construction Engineering Technology/Technician; Business/Commerce, General; Business Administration and Management, General. **Related Knowledge/**

Courses: Engineering and Technology; Mathematics; Economics and Accounting; Building and Construction; Design; Computers and Electronics.

Work Environment: Indoors; contaminants; sitting.

Court Clerks

- ✸ Personality Code: CER
- ✸ Education/Training Required: Short-term on-the-job training
- ✸ Annual Earnings: $32,330
- ✸ Beginning Wage: $21,050
- ✸ Earnings Growth Potential: Low
- ✸ Growth: 8.8%
- ✸ Annual Job Openings: 16,163
- ✸ Self-Employed: 2.7%
- ✸ Part-Time: 9.6%

The job openings listed here are shared with License Clerks and with Municipal Clerks.

Perform clerical duties in court of law; prepare docket of cases to be called; secure information for judges; and contact witnesses, attorneys, and litigants to obtain information for court. Prepare dockets or calendars of cases to be called, using typewriters or computers. Record case dispositions, court orders, and arrangements made for payment of court fees. Answer inquiries from the general public regarding judicial procedures, court appearances, trial dates, adjournments, outstanding warrants, summonses, subpoenas, witness fees, and payment of fines. Prepare and issue orders of the court, including probation orders, release documentation, sentencing information, and summonses. Prepare documents recording the outcomes of court proceedings. Instruct parties about timing of court appearances. Explain procedures or forms to parties in cases or to the general public. Search files and contact witnesses, attorneys, and litigants to obtain information for the court. Follow procedures to secure courtrooms and exhibits such as money, drugs, and weapons. Amend indictments when necessary and endorse indictments with pertinent information. Read charges and related information to the court and, if necessary, record defendants' pleas. Swear in jury members, interpreters, witnesses, and defendants. Collect court fees or fines and record amounts collected. Direct support staff in handling of paperwork processed by clerks' offices. Examine legal documents submitted to courts for adherence to laws or court procedures. Prepare and mark all applicable court exhibits and evidence. Record court proceedings, using recording equipment, or record minutes of court proceedings, using stenotype machines or shorthand. Prepare courtrooms with paper, pens, water, easels, and electronic equipment and ensure that recording equipment is working. Conduct roll calls and poll jurors. Meet with judges, lawyers, parole officers, police, and social agency officials to coordinate the functions of the court. Open courts, calling them to order and announcing judges.

GOE—Interest Area/Cluster: 07. Government and Public Administration. **Work Group:** 07.04. Public Administration Clerical Support. **Other Jobs in This Work Group:** Court Reporters; Court, Municipal, and License Clerks; License Clerks; Municipal Clerks.

Skills: Active Listening; Writing; Instructing; Service Orientation; Coordination.

Education and Training Program: General Office Occupations and Clerical Services. **Related Knowledge/Courses:** Clerical Practices; Law and Government; Computers and Electronics.

Work Environment: Indoors; noisy; sitting; using hands on objects, tools, or controls; repetitive motions.

Conventional–C

Court Reporters

- ❋ Personality Code: CE
- ❋ Education/Training Required: Postsecondary vocational training
- ❋ Annual Earnings: $45,330
- ❋ Beginning Wage: $23,810
- ❋ Earnings Growth Potential: High
- ❋ Growth: 24.5%
- ❋ Annual Job Openings: 2,620
- ❋ Self-Employed: 7.9%
- ❋ Part-Time: 13.6%

Use verbatim methods and equipment to capture, store, retrieve, and transcribe pretrial and trial proceedings or other information. Includes stenocaptioners who operate computerized stenographic captioning equipment to provide captions of live or prerecorded broadcasts for hearing-impaired viewers. Take notes in shorthand or use a stenotype or shorthand machine that prints letters on a paper tape. Provide transcripts of proceedings upon request of judges, lawyers, or the public. Record verbatim proceedings of courts, legislative assemblies, committee meetings, and other proceedings, using computerized recording equipment, electronic stenograph machines, or stenomasks. Transcribe recorded proceedings in accordance with established formats. Ask speakers to clarify inaudible statements. File a legible transcript of records of a court case with the court clerk's office. File and store shorthand notes of court session. Respond to requests during court sessions to read portions of the proceedings already recorded. Record depositions and other proceedings for attorneys. Verify accuracy of transcripts by checking copies against original records of proceedings and accuracy of rulings by checking with judges. Record symbols on computer disks or CD-ROM; then translate and display them as text in computer-aided transcription process.

GOE—Interest Area/Cluster: 07. Government and Public Administration. **Work Group:** 07.04. Public Administration Clerical Support. **Other Jobs in This**

Work Group: Court Clerks; Court, Municipal, and License Clerks; License Clerks; Municipal Clerks.

Skills: Reading Comprehension; Active Listening; Equipment Selection; Operation and Control; Equipment Maintenance; Operation Monitoring; Operations Analysis; Installation.

Education and Training Program: Court Reporting/Court Reporter Training. **Related Knowledge/Courses:** Clerical Practices; English Language; Law and Government; Computers and Electronics; Production and Processing; Customer and Personal Service.

Work Environment: Indoors; noisy; sitting; using hands on objects, tools, or controls; repetitive motions.

Court, Municipal, and License Clerks

See Court Clerks (a Conventional job), License Clerks (a Conventional job), and Municipal Clerks (a Conventional job), described separately.

Database Administrators

- ❋ Personality Code: CI
- ❋ Education/Training Required: Bachelor's degree
- ❋ Annual Earnings: $67,250
- ❋ Beginning Wage: $38,890
- ❋ Earnings Growth Potential: High
- ❋ Growth: 28.6%
- ❋ Annual Job Openings: 8,258
- ❋ Self-Employed: 1.3%
- ❋ Part-Time: 5.3%

Coordinate changes to computer databases. Test and implement the databases, applying knowledge of database management systems. May plan, coordinate, and implement security measures to safeguard computer databases. Test programs or databases, correct errors, and make necessary modifications. Modify existing databases and database management systems or direct programmers and analysts to make changes. Plan, coordinate, and implement security measures to safeguard information in computer files against accidental or unauthorized damage, modification, or disclosure. Work as part of project teams to coordinate database development and determine project scope and limitations. Write and code logical and physical database descriptions and specify identifiers of database to management system or direct others in coding descriptions. Train users and answer questions. Specify users and user access levels for each segment of databases. Approve, schedule, plan, and supervise the installation and testing of new products and improvements to computer systems such as the installation of new databases. Review project requests describing database user needs to estimate time and cost required to accomplish project. Develop standards and guidelines to guide the use and acquisition of software and to protect vulnerable information. Review procedures in database management system manuals for making changes to database. Develop methods for integrating different products so they work properly together such as customizing commercial databases to fit specific needs. Develop data models describing data elements and how they are used, following procedures and using pen, template, or computer software. Select and enter codes to monitor database performances and to create production databases. Establish and calculate optimum values for database parameters, using manuals and calculators. Revise company definition of data as defined in data dictionary. Review workflow charts developed by programmer analysts to understand tasks computer will perform, such as updating records. Identify and evaluate industry trends in database systems to serve as a source of information and advice for upper management.

GOE—Interest Area/Cluster: 11. Information Technology. Work Group: 11.02. Information Technology Specialties. Other Jobs in This Work Group: Computer and Information Scientists, Research; Computer Operators; Computer Programmers; Computer Security Specialists; Computer Software

Engineers, Applications; Computer Software Engineers, Systems Software; Computer Support Specialists; Computer Systems Analysts; Computer Systems Engineers/Architects; Network Designers; Network Systems and Data Communications Analysts; Software Quality Assurance Engineers and Testers; Web Administrators; Web Developers.

Skills: Programming; Systems Analysis; Systems Evaluation.

Education and Training Programs: Computer and Information Sciences, General; Computer Systems Analysis/Analyst; Data Modeling/Warehousing and Database Administration; Computer and Information Systems Security; Management Information Systems, General. Related Knowledge/Courses: Computers and Electronics; Telecommunications; Clerical Practices; Communications and Media; Engineering and Technology; Mathematics.

Work Environment: Indoors; noisy; sitting; using hands on objects, tools, or controls; repetitive motions.

Dental Assistants

* Personality Code: CRS
* Education/Training Required: Moderate-term on-the-job training
* Annual Earnings: $31,550
* Beginning Wage: $21,550
* Earnings Growth Potential: Low
* Growth: 29.2%
* Annual Job Openings: 29,482
* Self-Employed: 0.0%
* Part-Time: 35.7%

Assist dentist, set up patient and equipment, and keep records. Prepare patient, sterilize and disinfect instruments, set up instrument trays, prepare materials, and assist dentist during dental procedures. Expose dental diagnostic X rays. Record treatment information in patient records. Take and record medical and dental histories and vital signs of patients.

Provide postoperative instructions prescribed by dentist. Assist dentist in management of medical and dental emergencies. Pour, trim, and polish study casts. Instruct patients in oral hygiene and plaque control programs. Make preliminary impressions for study casts and occlusal registrations for mounting study casts. Clean and polish removable appliances. Clean teeth, using dental instruments. Apply protective coating of fluoride to teeth. Fabricate temporary restorations and custom impressions from preliminary impressions. Schedule appointments, prepare bills, and receive payment for dental services; complete insurance forms; and maintain records, manually or using computer.

GOE—Interest Area/Cluster: 08. Health Science. **Work Group:** 08.03. Dentistry. **Other Jobs in This Work Group:** Dental Hygienists; Dentists, General; Oral and Maxillofacial Surgeons; Orthodontists; Prosthodontists.

Skills: Equipment Maintenance; Operation and Control; Social Perceptiveness; Management of Material Resources; Operation Monitoring; Equipment Selection; Installation; Repairing.

Education and Training Program: Dental Assisting/Assistant. **Related Knowledge/Courses:** Medicine and Dentistry; Chemistry; Clerical Practices; Customer and Personal Service; Psychology.

Work Environment: Indoors; contaminants; disease or infections; using hands on objects, tools, or controls; bending or twisting the body; repetitive motions.

Dispatchers, Except Police, Fire, and Ambulance

- ❋ Personality Code: CRE
- ❋ Education/Training Required: Moderate-term on-the-job training
- ❋ Annual Earnings: $33,140
- ❋ Beginning Wage: $20,410
- ❋ Earnings Growth Potential: Medium
- ❋ Growth: 1.5%
- ❋ Annual Job Openings: 29,793
- ❋ Self-Employed: 1.1%
- ❋ Part-Time: 6.3%

Schedule and dispatch workers, work crews, equipment, or service vehicles for conveyance of materials, freight, or passengers or for normal installation, service, or emergency repairs rendered outside the place of business. Duties may include using radio, telephone, or computer to transmit assignments and compiling statistics and reports on work progress. Schedule and dispatch workers, work crews, equipment, or service vehicles to appropriate locations according to customer requests, specifications, or needs, using radios or telephones. Arrange for necessary repairs to restore service and schedules. Relay work orders, messages, and information to or from work crews, supervisors, and field inspectors, using telephones or two-way radios. Confer with customers or supervising personnel to address questions, problems, and requests for service or equipment. Prepare daily work and run schedules. Receive or prepare work orders. Oversee all communications within specifically assigned territories. Monitor personnel or equipment locations and utilization to coordinate service and schedules. Record and maintain files and records of customer requests, work or services performed, charges, expenses, inventory, and other dispatch information. Determine types or amounts of equipment, vehicles, materials, or personnel required according to work orders or specifications. Advise personnel about traffic problems such as construction areas, accidents, congestion, weather conditions, and other hazards. Ensure timely and efficient movement of trains according to train orders and schedules. Order supplies and equipment and issue them to personnel.

GOE—Interest Area/Cluster: 03. Arts and Communication. **Work Group:** 03.10. Communications Technology. **Other Jobs in This Work Group:** Air Traffic Controllers; Airfield Operations Specialists; Police, Fire, and Ambulance Dispatchers; Telephone Operators.

Skills: Operations Analysis; Service Orientation; Systems Evaluation; Management of Personnel Resources; Troubleshooting; Systems Analysis; Judgment and Decision Making; Critical Thinking.

Education and Training Program: Logistics and Materials Management. **Related Knowledge/Courses:** Transportation; Clerical Practices; Public Safety and Security; Communications and Media.

Work Environment: Indoors; noisy; sitting; using hands on objects, tools, or controls; repetitive motions.

Environmental Compliance Inspectors

- ❋ Personality Code: CIR
- ❋ Education/Training Required: Long-term on-the-job training
- ❋ Annual Earnings: $48,400
- ❋ Beginning Wage: $28,980
- ❋ Earnings Growth Potential: High
- ❋ Growth: 4.9%
- ❋ Annual Job Openings: 15,841
- ❋ Self-Employed: 0.4%
- ❋ Part-Time: 5.0%

The job openings listed here are shared with Coroners, with Equal Opportunity Representatives and Officers, with Government Property Inspectors and Investigators, and with Licensing Examiners and Inspectors.

Inspect and investigate sources of pollution to protect the public and environment and ensure conformance with federal, state, and local regulations and ordinances. Determine the nature of code violations and actions to be taken, and issue written notices of violation; participate in enforcement hearings as necessary. Examine permits, licenses, applications, and records to ensure compliance with licensing requirements. Prepare, organize, and maintain inspection records. Interview individuals to determine the nature of suspected violations and to obtain evidence of violations. Prepare written, oral, tabular, and graphic reports summarizing requirements and regulations, including enforcement and chain of custody documentation. Monitor follow-up actions in cases where violations were found, and review compliance monitoring reports. Investigate complaints and suspected violations regarding illegal dumping, pollution, pesticides, product quality, or labeling laws. Inspect waste pretreatment, treatment, and disposal facilities and systems for conformance to federal, state, or local regulations. Inform individuals and groups of pollution control regulations and inspection findings, and explain how problems can be corrected. Determine sampling locations and methods, and collect water or wastewater samples for analysis, preserving samples with appropriate containers and preservation methods. Verify that hazardous chemicals are handled, stored, and disposed of in accordance with regulations. Research and keep informed of pertinent information and developments in areas such as EPA laws and regulations. Determine which sites and violation reports to investigate, and coordinate compliance and enforcement activities with other government agencies. Observe and record field conditions, gathering, interpreting, and reporting data such as flow meter readings and chemical levels. Learn and observe proper safety precautions, rules, regulations, and practices so that unsafe conditions can be recognized and proper safety protocols implemented. Evaluate label information for accuracy and conformance to regulatory requirements. Inform health professionals, property owners, and the public about harmful properties and related problems of water pollution and contaminated wastewater.

Conventional—E

GOE—Interest Area/Cluster: 07. Government and Public Administration. **Work Group:** 07.03. Regulations Enforcement. **Other Jobs in This Work Group:** Agricultural Inspectors; Aviation Inspectors; Compliance Officers, Except Agriculture, Construction, Health and Safety, and Transportation; Construction and Building Inspectors; Equal Opportunity Representatives and Officers; Financial Examiners; Fire Inspectors; Fish and Game Wardens; Forest Fire Inspectors and Prevention Specialists; Freight and Cargo Inspectors; Government Property Inspectors and Investigators; Immigration and Customs Inspectors; Licensing Examiners and Inspectors; Nuclear Monitoring Technicians; Occupational Health and Safety Specialists; Occupational Health and Safety Technicians; Tax Examiners, Collectors, and Revenue Agents; Transportation Vehicle, Equipment, and Systems Inspectors, Except Aviation.

Skills: Science; Negotiation; Writing; Reading Comprehension; Mathematics; Active Listening; Persuasion; Operation Monitoring.

Education and Training Program: Natural Resources Management and Policy, Other. **Related Knowledge/Courses:** Biology; Chemistry; Law and Government; Geography; Physics; Engineering and Technology.

Work Environment: More often indoors than outdoors; contaminants; sitting.

Executive Secretaries and Administrative Assistants

- ❋ Personality Code: CE
- ❋ Education/Training Required: Work experience in a related occupation
- ❋ Annual Earnings: $38,640
- ❋ Beginning Wage: $26,060
- ❋ Earnings Growth Potential: Low
- ❋ Growth: 14.8%
- ❋ Annual Job Openings: 235,314
- ❋ Self-Employed: 1.4%
- ❋ Part-Time: 18.9%

Provide high-level administrative support by conducting research; preparing statistical reports; handling information requests; and performing clerical functions such as preparing correspondence, receiving visitors, arranging conference calls, and scheduling meetings. May also train and supervise lower-level clerical staff. Manage and maintain executives' schedules. Prepare invoices, reports, memos, letters, financial statements, and other documents, using word-processing, spreadsheet, database, or presentation software. Open, sort, and distribute incoming correspondence, including faxes and e-mail. Read and analyze incoming memos, submissions, and reports to determine their significance and plan their distribution. File and retrieve corporate documents, records, and reports. Greet visitors and determine whether they should be given access to specific individuals. Prepare responses to correspondence containing routine inquiries. Perform general office duties such as ordering supplies, maintaining records management systems, and performing basic bookkeeping work. Prepare agendas and make arrangements for committee, board, and other meetings. Make travel arrangements for executives. Conduct research, compile data, and prepare papers for consideration and presentation by executives, committees, and boards of directors. Compile, transcribe, and distribute minutes of meetings. Attend meetings to record minutes. Coordinate and direct office services, such as records and budget preparation, personnel, and housekeeping, to aid executives. Meet with individuals, special-interest groups, and others on behalf of executives, committees, and boards of directors. Set up and oversee administrative policies and procedures for offices or organizations. Supervise and train other clerical staff. Review operating practices and procedures to determine whether improvements can be made in areas such as workflow, reporting procedures, or expenditures. Interpret administrative and operating policies and procedures for employees.

GOE—Interest Area/Cluster: 04. Business and Administration. **Work Group:** 04.04. Secretarial Support. **Other Jobs in This Work Group:** Legal

Secretaries; Medical Secretaries; Secretaries, Except Legal, Medical, and Executive.

Skills: Writing; Active Listening; Speaking; Management of Financial Resources.

Education and Training Programs: Medical Administrative/Executive Assistant and Medical Secretary; Administrative Assistant and Secretarial Science, General; Executive Assistant/Executive Secretary. **Related Knowledge/Courses:** Clerical Practices; Customer and Personal Service; English Language; Computers and Electronics; Communications and Media; Personnel and Human Resources.

Work Environment: Indoors; sitting; repetitive motions.

Financial Analysts

- ❋ Personality Code: CIE
- ❋ Education/Training Required: Bachelor's degree
- ❋ Annual Earnings: $70,400
- ❋ Beginning Wage: $42,280
- ❋ Earnings Growth Potential: Medium
- ❋ Growth: 33.8%
- ❋ Annual Job Openings: 29,317
- ❋ Self-Employed: 8.3%
- ❋ Part-Time: 7.1%

Conduct quantitative analyses of information affecting investment programs of public or private institutions. Assemble spreadsheets and draw charts and graphs used to illustrate technical reports, using computer. Analyze financial information to produce forecasts of business, industry, and economic conditions for use in making investment decisions. Maintain knowledge and stay abreast of developments in the fields of industrial technology, business, finance, and economic theory. Interpret data affecting investment programs, such as price, yield, stability, future trends in investment risks, and economic influences. Monitor fundamental economic, industrial, and corporate developments through the analysis of information obtained from financial publications and services, investment banking firms, government agencies, trade publications, company sources, and personal interviews. Recommend investments and investment timing to companies, investment firm staff, or the investing public. Determine the prices at which securities should be syndicated and offered to the public. Prepare plans of action for investment based on financial analyses. Evaluate and compare the relative quality of various securities in a given industry. Present oral and written reports on general economic trends, individual corporations, and entire industries. Contact brokers and purchase investments for companies according to company policy. Collaborate with investment bankers to attract new corporate clients to securities firms.

GOE—Interest Area/Cluster: 06. Finance and Insurance. **Work Group:** 06.02. Finance/Insurance Investigation and Analysis. **Other Jobs in This Work Group:** Appraisers and Assessors of Real Estate; Appraisers, Real Estate; Assessors; Claims Adjusters, Examiners, and Investigators; Claims Examiners, Property and Casualty Insurance; Cost Estimators; Credit Analysts; Insurance Adjusters, Examiners, and Investigators; Insurance Appraisers, Auto Damage; Insurance Underwriters; Loan Counselors; Loan Officers; Market Research Analysts; Survey Researchers.

Skills: Management of Financial Resources; Judgment and Decision Making; Mathematics; Systems Evaluation; Programming; Complex Problem Solving; Operations Analysis; Systems Analysis.

Education and Training Programs: Accounting and Finance; Accounting and Business/Management; Finance, General. **Related Knowledge/Courses:** Economics and Accounting; Mathematics; Law and Government; Clerical Practices; English Language; Administration and Management.

Work Environment: Indoors; sitting.

Government Property Inspectors and Investigators

- ✹ Personality Code: CER
- ✹ Education/Training Required: Long-term on-the-job training
- ✹ Annual Earnings: $48,400
- ✹ Beginning Wage: $28,980
- ✹ Earnings Growth Potential: High
- ✹ Growth: 4.9%
- ✹ Annual Job Openings: 15,841
- ✹ Self-Employed: 0.4%
- ✹ Part-Time: 5.0%

The job openings listed here are shared with Coroners, with Environmental Compliance Inspectors, with Equal Opportunity Representatives and Officers, and with Licensing Examiners and Inspectors.

Investigate or inspect government property to ensure compliance with contract agreements and government regulations. Prepare correspondence, reports of inspections or investigations, and recommendations for action. Inspect government-owned equipment and materials in the possession of private contractors to ensure compliance with contracts and regulations and to prevent misuse. Examine records, reports, and documents to establish facts and detect discrepancies. Inspect manufactured or processed products to ensure compliance with contract specifications and legal requirements. Locate and interview plaintiffs, witnesses, or representatives of business or government to gather facts relevant to inspections or alleged violations. Recommend legal or administrative action to protect government property. Submit samples of products to government laboratories for testing as required. Coordinate with and assist law enforcement agencies in matters of mutual concern. Testify in court or at administrative proceedings concerning findings of investigations. Collect, identify, evaluate, and preserve case evidence. Monitor investigations of suspected offenders to ensure that they are conducted in accordance with constitutional requirements. Investigate applications for special licenses or permits, as well as alleged violations of licenses or permits.

GOE—Interest Area/Cluster: 07. Government and Public Administration. **Work Group:** 07.03. Regulations Enforcement. **Other Jobs in This Work Group:** Agricultural Inspectors; Aviation Inspectors; Compliance Officers, Except Agriculture, Construction, Health and Safety, and Transportation; Construction and Building Inspectors; Environmental Compliance Inspectors; Equal Opportunity Representatives and Officers; Financial Examiners; Fire Inspectors; Fish and Game Wardens; Forest Fire Inspectors and Prevention Specialists; Freight and Cargo Inspectors; Immigration and Customs Inspectors; Licensing Examiners and Inspectors; Nuclear Monitoring Technicians; Occupational Health and Safety Specialists; Occupational Health and Safety Technicians; Tax Examiners, Collectors, and Revenue Agents; Transportation Vehicle, Equipment, and Systems Inspectors, Except Aviation.

Skills: Quality Control Analysis; Technology Design; Science; Troubleshooting; Equipment Selection; Coordination; Operation and Control; Service Orientation.

Education and Training Program: Building/Home/Construction Inspection/Inspector. **Related Knowledge/Courses:** Building and Construction; Engineering and Technology; Public Safety and Security; Mechanical Devices; Computers and Electronics; Transportation.

Work Environment: Indoors; more often standing than sitting; walking and running; using hands on objects, tools, or controls.

Human Resources Assistants, Except Payroll and Timekeeping

* ❋ Personality Code: CES
* ❋ Education/Training Required: Short-term on-the-job training
* ❋ Annual Earnings: $34,970
* ❋ Beginning Wage: $23,750
* ❋ Earnings Growth Potential: Low
* ❋ Growth: 11.3%
* ❋ Annual Job Openings: 18,647
* ❋ Self-Employed: 0.0%
* ❋ Part-Time: 9.3%

Compile and keep personnel records. Record data for each employee, such as address, weekly earnings, absences, amount of sales or production, supervisory reports on ability, and date of and reason for termination. Compile and type reports from employment records. File employment records. Search employee files and furnish information to authorized persons. Explain company personnel policies, benefits, and procedures to employees or job applicants. Process, verify, and maintain documentation relating to personnel activities such as staffing, recruitment, training, grievances, performance evaluations, and classifications. Record data for each employee, including such information as addresses, weekly earnings, absences, amount of sales or production, supervisory reports on performance, and dates of and reasons for terminations. Process and review employment applications to evaluate qualifications or eligibility of applicants. Answer questions regarding examinations, eligibility, salaries, benefits, and other pertinent information. Examine employee files to answer inquiries and provide information for personnel actions. Gather personnel records from other departments or employees. Search employee files to obtain information for authorized persons and organizations such as credit bureaus and finance companies. Interview job applicants to obtain and verify information used to screen and evaluate them. Request information from law enforcement officials, previous employers, and other references to determine applicants' employment acceptability. Compile and prepare reports and documents pertaining to personnel activities. Inform job applicants of their acceptance or rejection of employment. Select applicants meeting specified job requirements and refer them to hiring personnel. Arrange for in-house and external training activities. Arrange for advertising or posting of job vacancies and notify eligible workers of position availability. Provide assistance in administering employee benefit programs and worker's compensation plans. Prepare badges, passes, and identification cards and perform other security-related duties. Administer and score applicant and employee aptitude, personality, and interest assessment instruments.

GOE—Interest Area/Cluster: 04. Business and Administration. **Work Group:** 04.07. Records and Materials Processing. **Other Jobs in This Work Group:** Correspondence Clerks; File Clerks; Marking Clerks; Meter Readers, Utilities; Office Clerks, General; Order Fillers, Wholesale and Retail Sales; Postal Service Clerks; Postal Service Mail Sorters, Processors, and Processing Machine Operators; Procurement Clerks; Production, Planning, and Expediting Clerks; Shipping, Receiving, and Traffic Clerks; Stock Clerks and Order Fillers; Stock Clerks, Sales Floor; Stock Clerks—Stockroom, Warehouse, or Storage Yard; Weighers, Measurers, Checkers, and Samplers, Recordkeeping.

Skills: Writing; Active Listening; Management of Personnel Resources.

Education and Training Program: General Office Occupations and Clerical Services. **Related Knowledge/Courses:** Clerical Practices; Personnel and Human Resources; Customer and Personal Service; Computers and Electronics; Economics and Accounting; Sociology and Anthropology.

Work Environment: Indoors; noisy; sitting.

Conventional–H

Immigration and Customs Inspectors

- ❋ Personality Code: CER
- ❋ Education/Training Required: Work experience in a related occupation
- ❋ Annual Earnings: $59,930
- ❋ Beginning Wage: $35,600
- ❋ Earnings Growth Potential: High
- ❋ Growth: 17.3%
- ❋ Annual Job Openings: 14,746
- ❋ Self-Employed: 0.3%
- ❋ Part-Time: 2.2%

The job openings listed here are shared with Criminal Investigators and Special Agents, with Police Detectives, and with Police Identification and Records Officers.

Investigate and inspect persons, common carriers, goods, and merchandise arriving in or departing from the United States or moving between states to detect violations of immigration and customs laws and regulations. Examine immigration applications, visas, and passports and interview persons to determine eligibility for admission, residence, and travel in U.S. Detain persons found to be in violation of customs or immigration laws and arrange for legal action such as deportation. Locate and seize contraband or undeclared merchandise and vehicles, aircraft, or boats that contain such merchandise. Interpret and explain laws and regulations to travelers, prospective immigrants, shippers, and manufacturers. Inspect cargo, baggage, and personal articles entering or leaving U.S. for compliance with revenue laws and U.S. Customs Service regulations. Record and report job-related activities, findings, transactions, violations, discrepancies, and decisions. Institute civil and criminal prosecutions and cooperate with other law enforcement agencies in the investigation and prosecution of those in violation of immigration or customs laws. Testify regarding decisions at immigration appeals or in federal court. Determine duty and taxes to be paid on goods. Collect samples of merchandise for examination, appraisal, or testing. Investigate applications for duty refunds and petition for remission or mitigation of penalties when warranted.

GOE—Interest Area/Cluster: 07. Government and Public Administration. **Work Group:** 07.03. Regulations Enforcement. **Other Jobs in This Work Group:** Agricultural Inspectors; Aviation Inspectors; Compliance Officers, Except Agriculture, Construction, Health and Safety, and Transportation; Construction and Building Inspectors; Environmental Compliance Inspectors; Equal Opportunity Representatives and Officers; Financial Examiners; Fire Inspectors; Fish and Game Wardens; Forest Fire Inspectors and Prevention Specialists; Freight and Cargo Inspectors; Government Property Inspectors and Investigators; Licensing Examiners and Inspectors; Nuclear Monitoring Technicians; Occupational Health and Safety Specialists; Occupational Health and Safety Technicians; Tax Examiners, Collectors, and Revenue Agents; Transportation Vehicle, Equipment, and Systems Inspectors, Except Aviation.

Skills: Persuasion; Operations Analysis; Equipment Selection; Negotiation; Speaking; Social Perceptiveness; Active Listening; Judgment and Decision Making.

Education and Training Programs: Criminal Justice/Police Science; Criminalistics and Criminal Science. **Related Knowledge/Courses:** Public Safety and Security; Law and Government; Foreign Language; Geography; Customer and Personal Service; Philosophy and Theology.

Work Environment: More often outdoors than indoors; noisy; contaminants; radiation; hazardous equipment.

Insurance Adjusters, Examiners, and Investigators

❀ Personality Code: CE
❀ Education/Training Required: Long-term on-the-job training
❀ Annual Earnings: $53,560
❀ Beginning Wage: $33,010
❀ Earnings Growth Potential: Medium
❀ Growth: 8.9%
❀ Annual Job Openings: 22,024
❀ Self-Employed: 3.5%
❀ Part-Time: 4.0%

The job openings listed here are shared with Claims Examiners, Property and Casualty Insurance.

Investigate, analyze, and determine the extent of insurance company's liability concerning personal, casualty, or property loss or damages and attempt to effect settlement with claimants. Correspond with or interview medical specialists, agents, witnesses, or claimants to compile information. Calculate benefit payments and approve payment of claims within a certain monetary limit. Interview or correspond with claimant and witnesses, consult police and hospital records, and inspect property damage to determine extent of liability. Investigate and assess damage to property. Examine claims forms and other records to determine insurance coverage. Analyze information gathered by investigation and report findings and recommendations. Negotiate claim settlements and recommend litigation when settlement cannot be negotiated. Collect evidence to support contested claims in court. Prepare report of findings of investigation. Interview or correspond with agents and claimants to correct errors or omissions and to investigate questionable claims. Refer questionable claims to investigator or claims adjuster for investigation or settlement. Examine titles to property to determine validity and act as company agent in transactions with property owners. Obtain credit information from banks and other credit services. Communicate with former associates to verify employment record and to obtain background information regarding persons or businesses applying for credit.

GOE—Interest Area/Cluster: 06. Finance and Insurance. **Work Group:** 06.02. Finance/Insurance Investigation and Analysis. **Other Jobs in This Work Group:** Appraisers and Assessors of Real Estate; Appraisers, Real Estate; Assessors; Claims Adjusters, Examiners, and Investigators; Claims Examiners, Property and Casualty Insurance; Cost Estimators; Credit Analysts; Financial Analysts; Insurance Appraisers, Auto Damage; Insurance Underwriters; Loan Counselors; Loan Officers; Market Research Analysts; Survey Researchers.

Skills: Negotiation; Persuasion; Judgment and Decision Making; Time Management; Management of Financial Resources; Reading Comprehension; Writing; Critical Thinking.

Education and Training Program: Insurance. **Related Knowledge/Courses:** Customer and Personal Service; Clerical Practices; Computers and Electronics; Law and Government; Medicine and Dentistry; Therapy and Counseling.

Work Environment: Indoors; noisy; sitting; using hands on objects, tools, or controls; repetitive motions.

Insurance Appraisers, Auto Damage

❀ Personality Code: CRE
❀ Education/Training Required: Postsecondary vocational training
❀ Annual Earnings: $51,500
❀ Beginning Wage: $35,750
❀ Earnings Growth Potential: Low
❀ Growth: 12.5%
❀ Annual Job Openings: 1,030
❀ Self-Employed: 4.1%
❀ Part-Time: 4.0%

Appraise automobile or other vehicle damage to determine cost of repair for insurance claim

Conventional-I

settlement and seek agreement with automotive repair shop on cost of repair. Prepare insurance forms to indicate repair cost or cost estimates and recommendations. Estimate parts and labor to repair damage, using standard automotive labor and parts-cost manuals and knowledge of automotive repair. Review repair-cost estimates with automobile-repair shop to secure agreement on cost of repairs. Examine damaged vehicle to determine extent of structural, body, mechanical, electrical, or interior damage. Evaluate practicality of repair as opposed to payment of market value of vehicle before accident. Determine salvage value on total-loss vehicle. Prepare insurance forms to indicate repair-cost estimates and recommendations. Arrange to have damage appraised by another appraiser to resolve disagreement with shop on repair cost.

GOE—Interest Area/Cluster: 06. Finance and Insurance. **Work Group:** 06.02. Finance/Insurance Investigation and Analysis. **Other Jobs in This Work Group:** Appraisers and Assessors of Real Estate; Appraisers, Real Estate; Assessors; Claims Adjusters, Examiners, and Investigators; Claims Examiners, Property and Casualty Insurance; Cost Estimators; Credit Analysts; Financial Analysts; Insurance Adjusters, Examiners, and Investigators; Insurance Underwriters; Loan Counselors; Loan Officers; Market Research Analysts; Survey Researchers.

Skills: Negotiation; Service Orientation; Persuasion; Judgment and Decision Making; Active Listening; Time Management; Equipment Selection; Speaking.

Education and Training Program: Insurance. **Related Knowledge/Courses:** Customer and Personal Service; Law and Government; Medicine and Dentistry; Computers and Electronics; Transportation; Telecommunications.

Work Environment: More often indoors than outdoors; noisy; very hot or cold; contaminants; sitting.

Insurance Claims and Policy Processing Clerks

See *Insurance Claims Clerks (a Conventional job) and Insurance Policy Processing Clerks (a Conventional job), described separately.*

Insurance Claims Clerks

- ❋ Personality Code: CE
- ❋ Education/Training Required: Moderate-term on-the-job training
- ❋ Annual Earnings: $32,040
- ❋ Beginning Wage: $21,950
- ❋ Earnings Growth Potential: Low
- ❋ Growth: –1.3%
- ❋ Annual Job Openings: 42,246
- ❋ Self-Employed: 0.4%
- ❋ Part-Time: 9.7%

The job openings listed here are shared with Insurance Policy Processing Clerks.

Obtain information from insured or designated persons for purpose of settling claim with insurance carrier. Review insurance policy to determine coverage. Prepare and review insurance-claim forms and related documents for completeness. Provide customer service, such as giving limited instructions on how to proceed with claims or providing referrals to auto repair facilities or local contractors. Organize and work with detailed office or warehouse records, using computers to enter, access, search, and retrieve data. Post or attach information to claim file. Pay small claims. Transmit claims for payment or further investigation. Contact insured or other involved persons to obtain missing information. Calculate amount of claim. Apply insurance rating systems.

GOE—Interest Area/Cluster: 06. Finance and Insurance. **Work Group:** 06.03. Finance/Insurance Records Processing. **Other Jobs in This Work Group:** Credit Authorizers; Credit Authorizers,

Checkers, and Clerks; Credit Checkers; Insurance Claims and Policy Processing Clerks; Insurance Policy Processing Clerks; Proofreaders and Copy Markers.

Skill: Service Orientation.

Education and Training Program: General Office Occupations and Clerical Services. **Related Knowledge/Courses:** Clerical Practices; Customer and Personal Service; Computers and Electronics; Economics and Accounting.

Work Environment: Indoors; sitting; repetitive motions.

Insurance Policy Processing Clerks

- ❈ Personality Code: CE
- ❈ Education/Training Required: Moderate-term on-the-job training
- ❈ Annual Earnings: $32,040
- ❈ Beginning Wage: $21,950
- ❈ Earnings Growth Potential: Low
- ❈ Growth: –1.3%
- ❈ Annual Job Openings: 42,246
- ❈ Self-Employed: 0.4%
- ❈ Part-Time: 9.7%

The job openings listed here are shared with Insurance Claims Clerks.

Process applications for, changes to, reinstatement of, and cancellation of insurance policies. Modify, update, and process existing policies and claims to reflect any change in beneficiary, amount of coverage, or type of insurance. Process and record new insurance policies and claims. Review and verify data, such as age, name, address, and principal sum and value of property, on insurance applications and policies. Organize and work with detailed office or warehouse records, maintaining files for each policyholder, including policies that are to be reinstated or cancelled. Examine letters from policyholders or agents, original insurance applications, and other company documents to determine whether changes are needed and effects of changes. Correspond with insured or agent to obtain information or inform them of account status or changes. Transcribe data to worksheets and enter data into computer for use in preparing documents and adjusting accounts. Notify insurance agent and accounting department of policy cancellation. Interview clients and take their calls to provide customer service and obtain information on claims. Compare information from application to criteria for policy reinstatement and approve reinstatement when criteria are met. Process, prepare, and submit business or government forms, such as submitting applications for coverage to insurance carriers. Collect initial premiums and issue receipts. Calculate premiums, refunds, commissions, adjustments, and new reserve requirements, using insurance rate standards. Obtain computer printout of policy cancellations or retrieve cancellation cards from file. Compose business correspondence for supervisors, managers, and professionals. Check computations of interest accrued, premiums due, and settlement surrender on loan values.

GOE—Interest Area/Cluster: 06. Finance and Insurance. **Work Group:** 06.03. Finance/Insurance Records Processing. **Other Jobs in This Work Group:** Credit Authorizers; Credit Authorizers, Checkers, and Clerks; Credit Checkers; Insurance Claims and Policy Processing Clerks; Insurance Claims Clerks; Proofreaders and Copy Markers.

Skill: Critical Thinking.

Education and Training Program: General Office Occupations and Clerical Services. **Related Knowledge/Courses:** Clerical Practices; Customer and Personal Service; Computers and Electronics; Economics and Accounting; Sales and Marketing; Production and Processing.

Work Environment: Sitting; repetitive motions.

Conventional-I

Insurance Underwriters

- ❀ Personality Code: CEI
- ❀ Education/Training Required: Bachelor's degree
- ❀ Annual Earnings: $54,530
- ❀ Beginning Wage: $33,550
- ❀ Earnings Growth Potential: Medium
- ❀ Growth: 6.3%
- ❀ Annual Job Openings: 6,880
- ❀ Self-Employed: 0.0%
- ❀ Part-Time: 3.6%

Review individual applications for insurance to evaluate degree of risk involved and determine acceptance of applications. Examine documents to determine degree of risk from such factors as applicant financial standing and value and condition of property. Decline excessive risks. Write to field representatives, medical personnel, and others to obtain further information, quote rates, or explain company underwriting policies. Evaluate possibility of losses due to catastrophe or excessive insurance. Decrease value of policy when risk is substandard and specify applicable endorsements or apply rating to ensure safe profitable distribution of risks, using reference materials. Review company records to determine amount of insurance in force on single risk or group of closely related risks. Authorize reinsurance of policy when risk is high.

GOE—Interest Area/Cluster: 06. Finance and Insurance. **Work Group:** 06.02. Finance/Insurance Investigation and Analysis. **Other Jobs in This Work Group:** Appraisers and Assessors of Real Estate; Appraisers, Real Estate; Assessors; Claims Adjusters, Examiners, and Investigators; Claims Examiners, Property and Casualty Insurance; Cost Estimators; Credit Analysts; Financial Analysts; Insurance Adjusters, Examiners, and Investigators; Insurance Appraisers, Auto Damage; Loan Counselors; Loan Officers; Market Research Analysts; Survey Researchers.

Skills: Writing; Service Orientation; Speaking; Active Listening; Learning Strategies; Active Learning; Monitoring; Persuasion.

Education and Training Program: Insurance. **Related Knowledge/Courses:** Clerical Practices; Customer and Personal Service; Sales and Marketing; Economics and Accounting; Law and Government; Computers and Electronics.

Work Environment: Indoors; sitting; using hands on objects, tools, or controls; repetitive motions.

Interviewers, Except Eligibility and Loan

- ❀ Personality Code: CES
- ❀ Education/Training Required: Short-term on-the-job training
- ❀ Annual Earnings: $27,320
- ❀ Beginning Wage: $17,960
- ❀ Earnings Growth Potential: Low
- ❀ Growth: 9.5%
- ❀ Annual Job Openings: 54,060
- ❀ Self-Employed: 0.8%
- ❀ Part-Time: 23.4%

Interview persons by telephone, by mail, in person, or by other means for the purpose of completing forms, applications, or questionnaires. Ask specific questions, record answers, and assist persons with completing form. May sort, classify, and file forms. Ask questions in accordance with instructions to obtain various specified information such as person's name, address, age, religious preference, and state of residency. Identify and resolve inconsistencies in interviewees' responses by means of appropriate questioning or explanation. Compile, record, and code results and data from interview or survey, using computer or specified form. Review data obtained from interview for completeness and accuracy. Contact individuals to be interviewed at home, place of business, or field location by telephone, by mail, or in person. Assist individuals in filling out applications or questionnaires. Ensure payment for services by verifying benefits with the person's insurance provider or working out financing options. Identify and report problems in obtaining valid data. Explain survey objectives and procedures to interviewees and interpret survey questions to help interviewees' comprehension. Perform patient services, such as answering the telephone and assisting patients with financial and medical questions. Prepare reports to provide answers in response to specific problems. Locate and list addresses and households. Perform other office duties as needed, such as telemarketing and customer service inquiries, billing patients, and receiving payments. Meet with supervisor daily to submit completed assignments and discuss progress. Collect and analyze data, such as studying old records; tallying the number of outpatients entering each day or week; or participating in federal, state, or local population surveys as a census enumerator.

GOE—Interest Area/Cluster: 10. Human Service. **Work Group:** 10.04. Client Interviewing. **Other Jobs in This Work Group:** Eligibility Interviewers, Government Programs.

Skills: Service Orientation; Speaking.

Education and Training Program: Receptionist. **Related Knowledge/Courses:** Therapy and Counseling; Sales and Marketing; Customer and Personal Service; Psychology; Medicine and Dentistry; Education and Training.

Work Environment: Indoors; sitting; using hands on objects, tools, or controls; repetitive motions.

Legal Secretaries

- ❋ Personality Code: CE
- ❋ Education/Training Required: Associate degree
- ❋ Annual Earnings: $38,810
- ❋ Beginning Wage: $24,380
- ❋ Earnings Growth Potential: Medium
- ❋ Growth: 11.7%
- ❋ Annual Job Openings: 38,682
- ❋ Self-Employed: 1.4%
- ❋ Part-Time: 18.9%

Perform secretarial duties, utilizing legal terminology, procedures, and documents. Prepare legal papers and correspondence, such as summonses, complaints, motions, and subpoenas. May also assist with legal research. Prepare and process legal documents and papers, such as summonses, subpoenas, complaints, appeals, motions, and pretrial agreements. Mail, fax, or arrange for delivery of legal correspondence to clients, witnesses, and court officials. Receive and place telephone calls. Schedule and make appointments. Make photocopies of correspondence, documents, and other printed matter. Organize and maintain law libraries, documents, and case files. Assist attorneys in collecting information such as employment, medical, and other records. Attend legal meetings, such as client interviews, hearings, or depositions, and take notes. Draft and type office memos. Review legal publications and perform database searches to identify laws and court decisions relevant to pending cases. Submit articles and information from searches to attorneys for review and approval for use. Complete various forms such as accident reports, trial and courtroom requests, and applications for clients.

GOE—Interest Area/Cluster: 04. Business and Administration. **Work Group:** 04.04. Secretarial Support. **Other Jobs in This Work Group:** Executive Secretaries and Administrative Assistants; Medical Secretaries; Secretaries, Except Legal, Medical, and Executive.

Conventional–L

Skills: Writing; Reading Comprehension; Time Management; Social Perceptiveness; Judgment and Decision Making; Operation and Control; Active Listening; Speaking.

Education and Training Program: Legal Administrative Assistant/Secretary. **Related Knowledge/ Courses:** Clerical Practices; Law and Government; Economics and Accounting; Computers and Electronics; Customer and Personal Service.

Work Environment: Indoors; sitting; repetitive motions.

Librarians

- ❀ Personality Code: CSE
- ❀ Education/Training Required: Master's degree
- ❀ Annual Earnings: $50,970
- ❀ Beginning Wage: $31,960
- ❀ Earnings Growth Potential: Medium
- ❀ Growth: 3.6%
- ❀ Annual Job Openings: 18,945
- ❀ Self-Employed: 0.6%
- ❀ Part-Time: 21.2%

Administer libraries and perform related library services. Work in a variety of settings, including public libraries, schools, colleges and universities, museums, corporations, government agencies, law firms, non-profit organizations, and health-care providers. Tasks may include selecting, acquiring, cataloguing, classifying, circulating, and maintaining library materials and furnishing reference, bibliographical, and readers' advisory services. May perform in-depth, strategic research and synthesize, analyze, edit, and filter information. May set up or work with databases and information systems to catalogue and access information. Search standard reference materials, including online sources and the Internet, to answer patrons' reference questions. Analyze patrons' requests to determine needed information and assist in furnishing or locating that information. Teach library patrons to search for information by using databases. Keep records of circulation and materials. Supervise budgeting, planning, and personnel activities. Check books in and out of the library. Explain use of library facilities, resources, equipment, and services and provide information about library policies. Review and evaluate resource material, such as book reviews and catalogs, to select and order print, audio-visual, and electronic resources. Code, classify, and catalog books, publications, films, audiovisual aids, and other library materials based on subject matter or standard library classification systems. Locate unusual or unique information in response to specific requests. Direct and train library staff in duties such as receiving, shelving, researching, cataloging, and equipment use. Respond to customer complaints, taking action as necessary. Organize collections of books, publications, documents, audiovisual aids, and other reference materials for convenient access. Develop library policies and procedures. Evaluate materials to determine outdated or unused items to be discarded. Develop information access aids such as indexes and annotated bibliographies, Web pages, electronic pathfinders, and online tutorials. Plan and deliver client-centered programs and services such as special services for corporate clients, storytelling for children, newsletters, or programs for special groups. Compile lists of books, periodicals, articles, and audiovisual materials on particular subjects. Arrange for interlibrary loans of materials not available in a particular library. Assemble and arrange display materials. Confer with teachers, parents, and community organizations to develop, plan, and conduct programs in reading, viewing, and communication skills. Compile lists of overdue materials and notify borrowers that their materials are overdue.

GOE—Interest Area/Cluster: 05. Education and Training. **Work Group:** 05.04. Library Services. **Other Jobs in This Work Group:** Library Assistants, Clerical; Library Technicians.

Skills: Management of Financial Resources; Management of Material Resources; Learning Strategies; Equipment Selection; Service Orientation; Systems Evaluation; Persuasion; Monitoring.

Education and Training Programs: School Librarian/School Library Media Specialist; Library Science/Librarianship; Library Science, Other. **Related Knowledge/Courses:** Communications and Media; Clerical Practices; Customer and Personal Service; Personnel and Human Resources; English Language; Computers and Electronics.

Work Environment: Indoors; sitting; using hands on objects, tools, or controls; repetitive motions.

License Clerks

- ❋ Personality Code: CE
- ❋ Education/Training Required: Short-term on-the-job training
- ❋ Annual Earnings: $32,330
- ❋ Beginning Wage: $21,050
- ❋ Earnings Growth Potential: Low
- ❋ Growth: 8.8%
- ❋ Annual Job Openings: 16,163
- ❋ Self-Employed: 2.7%
- ❋ Part-Time: 9.6%

The job openings listed here are shared with Court Clerks and with Municipal Clerks.

Issue licenses or permits to qualified applicants. Obtain necessary information, record data, advise applicants on requirements, collect fees, and issue licenses. May conduct oral, written, visual, or performance testing. Collect prescribed fees for licenses. Code information on license applications for entry into computers. Evaluate information on applications to verify completeness and accuracy and to determine whether applicants are qualified to obtain desired licenses. Answer questions and provide advice to the public regarding licensing policies, procedures, and regulations. Maintain records of applications made and licensing fees collected. Question applicants to obtain required information, such as name, address, and age, and record data on prescribed forms. Update operational records and licensing information, using computer terminals. Inform customers by mail or telephone of additional steps they need to take to obtain licenses. Perform routine data entry and other office support activities, including creating, sorting, photocopying, distributing, and filing documents. Stock counters with adequate supplies of forms, film, licenses, and other required materials. Enforce canine licensing regulations, contacting non-compliant owners in person or by mail to inform them of the required regulations and potential enforcement actions. Assemble photographs with printed license information to produce completed documents. Prepare bank deposits and take them to banks. Operate specialized photographic equipment to obtain photographs for drivers' licenses and photo identification cards. Instruct customers in the completion of drivers' license application forms and other forms such as voter registration cards and organ donor forms. Conduct and score oral, visual, written, or performance tests to determine applicant qualifications and notify applicants of their scores. Send by mail drivers' licenses to out-of-county or out-of-state applicants. Perform record checks on past and current licensees as required by investigations. Respond to correspondence from insurance companies regarding the licensure of agents, brokers, and adjusters. Prepare lists of overdue accounts and license suspensions and issuances. Train other workers and coordinate their work as necessary.

GOE—Interest Area/Cluster: 07. Government and Public Administration. **Work Group:** 07.04. Public Administration Clerical Support. **Other Jobs in This Work Group:** Court Clerks; Court Reporters; Court, Municipal, and License Clerks; Municipal Clerks.

Skills: Reading Comprehension; Service Orientation; Instructing; Active Listening.

Education and Training Program: General Office Occupations and Clerical Services. **Related Knowledge/Courses:** Clerical Practices; Customer and Personal Service; Law and Government; Computers and Electronics.

Work Environment: Indoors; noisy; sitting; using hands on objects, tools, or controls; repetitive motions.

Licensing Examiners and Inspectors

- ❀ Personality Code: CE
- ❀ Education/Training Required: Long-term on-the-job training
- ❀ Annual Earnings: $48,400
- ❀ Beginning Wage: $28,980
- ❀ Earnings Growth Potential: High
- ❀ Growth: 4.9%
- ❀ Annual Job Openings: 15,841
- ❀ Self-Employed: 0.4%
- ❀ Part-Time: 5.0%

The job openings listed here are shared with Coroners, with Environmental Compliance Inspectors, with Equal Opportunity Representatives and Officers, and with Government Property Inspectors and Investigators.

Examine, evaluate, and investigate eligibility for, conformity with, or liability under licenses or permits. Issue licenses to individuals meeting standards. Evaluate applications, records, and documents in order to gather information about eligibility or liability issues. Administer oral, written, road, or flight tests to license applicants. Score tests and observe equipment operation and control in order to rate ability of applicants. Advise licensees and other individuals or groups concerning licensing, permit, or passport regulations. Warn violators of infractions or penalties. Prepare reports of activities, evaluations, recommendations, and decisions. Prepare correspondence to inform concerned parties of licensing decisions and of appeals processes. Confer with and interview officials, technical or professional specialists, and applicants, in order to obtain information or to clarify facts relevant to licensing decisions. Report law or regulation violations to appropriate boards and agencies. Visit establishments to verify that valid licenses and permits are displayed, and that licensing standards are being upheld. **GOE—Interest Area/Cluster:** 07. Government and Public Administration. **Work Group:** 07.03.

Regulations Enforcement. **Other Jobs in This Work Group:** Agricultural Inspectors; Aviation Inspectors; Compliance Officers, Except Agriculture, Construction, Health and Safety, and Transportation; Construction and Building Inspectors; Environmental Compliance Inspectors; Equal Opportunity Representatives and Officers; Financial Examiners; Fire Inspectors; Fish and Game Wardens; Forest Fire Inspectors and Prevention Specialists; Freight and Cargo Inspectors; Government Property Inspectors and Investigators; Immigration and Customs Inspectors; Nuclear Monitoring Technicians; Occupational Health and Safety Specialists; Occupational Health and Safety Technicians; Tax Examiners, Collectors, and Revenue Agents; Transportation Vehicle, Equipment, and Systems Inspectors, Except Aviation.

Skills: Speaking; Service Orientation; Judgment and Decision Making; Active Listening; Reading Comprehension.

Education and Training Program: Public Administration and Social Service Professions, Other. **Related Knowledge/Courses:** Clerical Practices; Customer and Personal Service; Law and Government; Foreign Language; Psychology; Public Safety and Security.

Work Environment: More often indoors than outdoors; contaminants; sitting; using hands on objects, tools, or controls; repetitive motions.

Loan Interviewers and Clerks

- ❀ Personality Code: CE
- ❀ Education/Training Required: Short-term on-the-job training
- ❀ Annual Earnings: $31,680
- ❀ Beginning Wage: $21,070
- ❀ Earnings Growth Potential: Low
- ❀ Growth: –0.9%
- ❀ Annual Job Openings: 40,217
- ❀ Self-Employed: 2.5%
- ❀ Part-Time: 6.3%

Interview loan applicants to elicit information, investigate applicants' backgrounds and verify references, prepare loan request papers, and forward findings, reports, and documents to appraisal department. Review loan papers to ensure completeness and complete transactions between loan establishment, borrowers, and sellers upon approval of loan. Verify and examine information and accuracy of loan application and closing documents. Interview loan applicants in order to obtain personal and financial data, and to assist in completing applications. Assemble and compile documents for loan closings, such as title abstracts, insurance forms, loan forms, and tax receipts. Answer questions and advise customers regarding loans and transactions. Contact customers by mail, telephone, or in person concerning acceptance or rejection of applications. Record applications for loan and credit, loan information, and disbursements of funds, using computers. Prepare and type loan applications, closing documents, legal documents, letters, forms, government notices, and checks, using computers. Present loan and repayment schedules to customers. Calculate, review, and correct errors on interest, principal, payment, and closing costs, using computers or calculators. Check value of customer collateral to be held as loan security. Contact credit bureaus, employers, and other sources in order to check applicants' credit and personal references. File and maintain loan records. Schedule and conduct closings of mortgage transactions. Accept payment on accounts. Submit loan applications with recommendation for underwriting approval. Order property insurance or mortgage insurance policies in order to ensure protection against loss on mortgaged property. Review customer accounts in order to determine whether payments are made on time and that other loan terms are being followed. Establish credit limits and grant extensions of credit on overdue accounts.

GOE—Interest Area/Cluster: 06. Finance and Insurance. **Work Group:** 06.04. Finance/Insurance Customer Service. **Other Jobs in This Work Group:** Bill and Account Collectors; New Accounts Clerks; Tellers.

Skills: Service Orientation; Learning Strategies; Mathematics; Time Management; Speaking; Writing; Persuasion; Operations Analysis.

Education and Training Program: Banking and Financial Support Services. **Related Knowledge/ Courses:** Economics and Accounting; Clerical Practices; Mathematics; Customer and Personal Service; Law and Government.

Work Environment: Indoors; sitting.

Loan Officers

- ❋ Personality Code: CES
- ❋ Education/Training Required: Bachelor's degree
- ❋ Annual Earnings: $53,000
- ❋ Beginning Wage: $30,340
- ❋ Earnings Growth Potential: High
- ❋ Growth: 11.5%
- ❋ Annual Job Openings: 54,237
- ❋ Self-Employed: 2.9%
- ❋ Part-Time: 6.6%

Evaluate, authorize, or recommend approval of commercial, real estate, or credit loans. Advise borrowers on financial status and methods of payments. Includes mortgage loan officers and agents, collection analysts, loan servicing officers, and loan underwriters. Meet with applicants to obtain information for loan applications and to answer questions about the process. Approve loans within specified limits and refer loan applications outside those limits to management for approval. Analyze applicants' financial status, credit, and property evaluations to determine feasibility of granting loans. Explain to customers the different types of loans and credit options that are available, as well as the terms of those services. Obtain and compile copies of loan applicants' credit histories, corporate financial statements, and other financial information. Review and update credit and loan files. Review loan agreements to ensure that they are complete and accurate according to policy. Compute payment schedules. Stay abreast of new types of loans and other financial services and products to better meet customers' needs. Submit applications to credit analysts for verification and recommendation. Handle customer complaints and take appropriate action to resolve them. Work with clients to identify their financial goals and to find ways of reaching those goals. Confer with underwriters to aid in resolving mortgage application problems. Negotiate payment arrangements with customers who have delinquent loans. Market bank products to individuals and firms, promoting bank services that may meet customers' needs. Supervise loan personnel. Set credit policies, credit lines, procedures, and standards in conjunction with senior managers. Provide special services such as investment banking for clients with more specialized needs. Analyze potential loan markets and develop referral networks to locate prospects for loans. Prepare reports to send to customers whose accounts are delinquent and forward irreconcilable accounts for collector action. Arrange for maintenance and liquidation of delinquent properties. Interview, hire, and train new employees. Petition courts to transfer titles and deeds of collateral to banks.

GOE—Interest Area/Cluster: 06. Finance and Insurance. **Work Group:** 06.02. Finance/Insurance Investigation and Analysis. **Other Jobs in This Work Group:** Appraisers and Assessors of Real Estate; Appraisers, Real Estate; Assessors; Claims Adjusters, Examiners, and Investigators; Claims Examiners, Property and Casualty Insurance; Cost Estimators; Credit Analysts; Financial Analysts; Insurance Adjusters, Examiners, and Investigators; Insurance Appraisers, Auto Damage; Insurance Underwriters; Loan Counselors; Market Research Analysts; Survey Researchers.

Skills: Persuasion; Social Perceptiveness; Service Orientation; Complex Problem Solving; Negotiation; Instructing; Speaking; Judgment and Decision Making.

Education and Training Programs: Finance, General; Credit Management. **Related Knowledge/Courses:** Economics and Accounting; Sales and Marketing; Law and Government; English Language; Mathematics; Customer and Personal Service.

Work Environment: Indoors; sitting; repetitive motions.

Mapping Technicians

- ❋ Personality Code: CR
- ❋ Education/Training Required: Moderate-term on-the-job training
- ❋ Annual Earnings: $33,640
- ❋ Beginning Wage: $20,670
- ❋ Earnings Growth Potential: Medium
- ❋ Growth: 19.4%
- ❋ Annual Job Openings: 8,299
- ❋ Self-Employed: 4.2%
- ❋ Part-Time: 4.5%

The job openings listed here are shared with Surveying Technicians.

Calculate mapmaking information from field notes and draw and verify accuracy of topographical maps. Check all layers of maps to ensure accuracy, identifying and marking errors and making corrections. Determine scales, line sizes, and colors to be used for hard copies of computerized maps, using plotters. Monitor mapping work and the updating of maps to ensure accuracy, the inclusion of new and/or changed information, and compliance with rules and regulations. Identify and compile database information to create maps in response to requests. Produce and update overlay maps to show information boundaries, water locations, and topographic features on various base maps and at different scales. Trace contours and topographic details to generate maps that denote specific land and property locations and geographic attributes. Lay out and match aerial photographs in sequences in which they were taken and identify any areas missing from photographs. Compare topographical features and contour lines with images from aerial photographs, old maps, and other reference materials to verify the accuracy of their identification. Compute and measure scaled distances between reference points to establish relative positions of adjoining prints and enable the creation of photographic mosaics. Research resources such as survey maps and legal descriptions to verify property lines and to obtain information needed for mapping. Form three-dimensional images of aerial photographs taken from different locations, using mathematical techniques and plotting instruments. Enter GPS data, legal deeds, field notes, and land survey reports into GIS workstations so that information can be transformed into graphic land descriptions such as maps and drawings. Analyze aerial photographs to detect and interpret significant military, industrial, resource, or topographical data. Redraw and correct maps, such as revising parcel maps to reflect tax code area changes, using information from official records and surveys. Train staff members in duties such as tax mapping, the use of computerized mapping equipment, and the interpretation of source documents.

GOE—Interest Area/Cluster: 15. Scientific Research, Engineering, and Mathematics. **Work Group:** 15.09. Engineering Technology. **Other Jobs in This Work Group:** Aerospace Engineering and Operations Technicians; Cartographers and Photogrammetrists; Civil Engineering Technicians; Electrical and Electronic Engineering Technicians; Electrical and Electronics Drafters; Electrical Drafters; Electrical Engineering Technicians; Electro-Mechanical Technicians; Electronic Drafters; Electronics Engineering Technicians; Environmental Engineering Technicians; Mechanical Drafters; Mechanical Engineering Technicians; Surveying and Mapping Technicians; Surveying Technicians.

Skills: Technology Design; Operations Analysis; Programming; Quality Control Analysis; Science; Troubleshooting; Mathematics; Complex Problem Solving.

Education and Training Programs: Surveying Technology/Surveying; Cartography. **Related Knowledge/Courses:** Geography; Design; Computers and Electronics; Engineering and Technology; Mathematics; Clerical Practices.

Work Environment: Indoors; sitting; using hands on objects, tools, or controls; repetitive motions.

Medical Records and Health Information Technicians

* Personality Code: CE
* Education/Training Required: Associate degree
* Annual Earnings: $29,290
* Beginning Wage: $19,690
* Earnings Growth Potential: Low
* Growth: 17.8%
* Annual Job Openings: 39,048
* Self-Employed: 0.2%
* Part-Time: 12.5%

Compile, process, and maintain medical records of hospital and clinic patients in a manner consistent with medical, administrative, ethical, legal, and regulatory requirements of the health-care system. Process, maintain, compile, and report patient information for health requirements and standards. Protect the security of medical records to ensure that confidentiality is maintained. Review records for completeness, accuracy, and compliance with regulations. Retrieve patient medical records for physicians, technicians, or other medical personnel. Release information to persons and agencies according to regulations. Plan, develop, maintain, and operate a variety of health record indexes and storage and retrieval systems to collect, classify, store, and analyze information. Enter data such as demographic characteristics, history and extent of disease, diagnostic procedures, and treatment into computer. Process and prepare business and government forms. Compile and maintain patients' medical records to document condition and treatment and to provide data for research or cost control and care improvement efforts. Process patient admission and discharge documents. Assign the patient to diagnosis-related groups (DRGs), using appropriate computer software. Transcribe medical reports. Identify, compile, abstract, and code patient data, using standard

Conventional–M

classification systems. Resolve or clarify codes and diagnoses with conflicting, missing, or unclear information by consulting with doctors or others or by participating in the coding team's regular meetings. Compile medical care and census data for statistical reports on diseases treated, surgeries performed, or use of hospital beds. Post medical insurance billings. Train medical records staff. Prepare statistical reports, narrative reports, and graphic presentations of information such as tumor registry data for use by hospital staff, researchers, or other users. Manage the department and supervise clerical workers, directing and controlling activities of personnel in the medical records department. Develop in-service educational materials. Consult classification manuals to locate information about disease processes.

GOE—Interest Area/Cluster: 08. Health Science. **Work Group:** 08.06. Medical Technology. **Other Jobs in This Work Group:** Biological Technicians; Cardiovascular Technologists and Technicians; Diagnostic Medical Sonographers; Medical and Clinical Laboratory Technicians; Medical and Clinical Laboratory Technologists; Medical Equipment Preparers; Nuclear Medicine Technologists; Opticians, Dispensing; Orthotists and Prosthetists; Radiologic Technicians; Radiologic Technologists; Radiologic Technologists and Technicians.

Skill: Systems Analysis.

Education and Training Programs: Health Information/Medical Records Technology/Technician; Medical Insurance Coding Specialist/Coder. **Related Knowledge/Courses:** Clerical Practices; Law and Government; Customer and Personal Service.

Work Environment: Indoors; noisy; sitting; using hands on objects, tools, or controls; repetitive motions.

Medical Secretaries

* Personality Code: CS
* Education/Training Required: Moderate-term on-the-job training
* Annual Earnings: $28,950
* Beginning Wage: $20,260
* Earnings Growth Potential: Low
* Growth: 16.7%
* Annual Job Openings: 60,659
* Self-Employed: 1.3%
* Part-Time: 18.9%

Perform secretarial duties, using specific knowledge of medical terminology and hospital, clinical, or laboratory procedures. Answer telephones and direct calls to appropriate staff. Schedule and confirm patient diagnostic appointments, surgeries, and medical consultations. Greet visitors, ascertain purpose of visit, and direct them to appropriate staff. Operate office equipment, such as voice mail messaging systems, and use word processing, spreadsheet, and other software applications to prepare reports, invoices, financial statements, letters, case histories, and medical records. Complete insurance and other claim forms. Interview patients to complete documents, case histories, and forms such as intake and insurance forms. Receive and route messages and documents such as laboratory results to appropriate staff. Compile and record medical charts, reports, and correspondence, using typewriter or personal computer. Transmit correspondence and medical records by mail, e-mail, or fax. Maintain medical records, technical library documents, and correspondence files. Perform various clerical and administrative functions, such as ordering and maintaining an inventory of supplies. Perform bookkeeping duties, such as credits and collections, preparing and sending financial statements and bills, and keeping financial records. Transcribe recorded messages and practitioners' diagnoses and recommendations into patients' medical records. Arrange hospital admissions for patients. Prepare correspondence and assist physicians or medical scientists with preparation of reports, speeches, articles, and conference proceedings.

GOE—Interest Area/Cluster: 04. Business and Administration. **Work Group:** 04.04. Secretarial Support. **Other Jobs in This Work Group:** Executive Secretaries and Administrative Assistants; Legal Secretaries; Secretaries, Except Legal, Medical, and Executive.

Skills: None met the criteria.

Education and Training Programs: Medical Office Assistant/Specialist; Medical Insurance Specialist/ Medical Biller; Medical Administrative/Executive Assistant and Medical Secretary. **Related Knowledge/Courses:** Clerical Practices; Medicine and Dentistry; Customer and Personal Service; Computers and Electronics; Economics and Accounting.

Work Environment: Noisy; disease or infections; sitting; using hands on objects, tools, or controls.

Medical Transcriptionists

- ❋ Personality Code: CR
- ❋ Education/Training Required: Postsecondary vocational training
- ❋ Annual Earnings: $31,250
- ❋ Beginning Wage: $22,160
- ❋ Earnings Growth Potential: Low
- ❋ Growth: 13.5%
- ❋ Annual Job Openings: 18,080
- ❋ Self-Employed: 9.7%
- ❋ Part-Time: 23.2%

Use transcribing machines with headset and foot pedal to listen to recordings by physicians and other health-care professionals dictating a variety of medical reports, such as emergency room visits, diagnostic imaging studies, operations, chart reviews, and final summaries. Transcribe dictated reports and translate medical jargon and abbreviations into their expanded forms. Edit as necessary and return reports in either printed or electronic form to the dictator for review and signature or correction. Transcribe dictation for a variety of medical reports such as patient histories, physical examinations, emergency room visits, operations, chart reviews, consultation, or discharge summaries. Review and edit transcribed reports or dictated material for spelling, grammar, clarity, consistency, and proper medical terminology. Distinguish between homonyms and recognize inconsistencies and mistakes in medical terms, referring to dictionaries; drug references; and other sources on anatomy, physiology, and medicine. Return dictated reports in printed or electronic form for physicians' review, signature, and corrections and for inclusion in patients' medical records. Translate medical jargon and abbreviations into their expanded forms to ensure the accuracy of patient and health-care facility records. Take dictation, using either shorthand or a stenotype machine or using headsets and transcribing machines; then convert dictated materials or rough notes to written form. Identify mistakes in reports and check with doctors to obtain the correct information. Perform data entry and data retrieval services, providing data for inclusion in medical records and for transmission to physicians. Produce medical reports, correspondence, records, patient-care information, statistics, medical research, and administrative material. Answer inquiries concerning the progress of medical cases within the limits of confidentiality laws. Set up and maintain medical files and databases, including records such as X-ray, lab, and procedure reports; medical histories; diagnostic workups; admission and discharge summaries; and clinical resumes. Perform a variety of clerical and office tasks, such as handling incoming and outgoing mail, completing and submitting insurance claims, typing, filing, and operating office machines. Decide which information should be included or excluded in reports. Receive patients, schedule appointments, and maintain patient records. Receive and screen telephone calls and visitors.

GOE—Interest Area/Cluster: 08. Health Science. **Work Group:** 08.02. Medicine and Surgery. **Other Jobs in This Work Group:** Anesthesiologists; Family and General Practitioners; Internists, General;

Medical Assistants; Obstetricians and Gynecologists; Pediatricians, General; Pharmacists; Pharmacy Aides; Pharmacy Technicians; Physician Assistants; Psychiatrists; Registered Nurses; Surgeons; Surgical Technologists.

Skills: Active Listening; Reading Comprehension; Time Management.

Education and Training Program: Medical Transcription/Transcriptionist. **Related Knowledge/ Courses:** Clerical Practices; English Language; Medicine and Dentistry; Computers and Electronics.

Work Environment: Indoors; sitting; using hands on objects, tools, or controls; repetitive motions.

Municipal Clerks

- ❀ Personality Code: CE
- ❀ Education/Training Required: Short-term on-the-job training
- ❀ Annual Earnings: $32,330
- ❀ Beginning Wage: $21,050
- ❀ Earnings Growth Potential: Low
- ❀ Growth: 8.8%
- ❀ Annual Job Openings: 16,163
- ❀ Self-Employed: 2.7%
- ❀ Part-Time: 9.6%

The job openings listed here are shared with Court Clerks and with License Clerks.

Draft agendas and bylaws for town or city council, record minutes of council meetings, answer official correspondence, keep fiscal records and accounts, and prepare reports on civic needs. Participate in the administration of municipal elections, including preparation and distribution of ballots, appointment and training of election officers, and tabulation and certification of results. Record and edit the minutes of meetings; then distribute them to appropriate officials and staff members. Plan and direct the maintenance, filing, safekeeping, and computerization of all municipal documents. Issue public

notification of all official activities and meetings. Maintain and update documents such as municipal codes and city charters. Prepare meeting agendas and packets of related information. Prepare ordinances, resolutions, and proclamations so that they can be executed, recorded, archived, and distributed. Respond to requests for information from the public, other municipalities, state officials, and state and federal legislative offices. Maintain fiscal records and accounts. Perform budgeting duties, including assisting in budget preparation, expenditure review, and budget administration. Perform general office duties such as taking and transcribing dictation, typing and proofreading correspondence, distributing and filing official forms, and scheduling appointments. Coordinate and maintain office-tracking systems for correspondence and follow-up actions. Research information in the municipal archives upon request of public officials and private citizens. Perform contract administration duties, assisting with bid openings and the awarding of contracts. Collaborate with other staff to assist in the development and implementation of goals, objectives, policies, and priorities. Represent municipalities at community events and serve as liaisons on community committees. Serve as a notary of the public. Issue various permits and licenses, including marriage, fishing, hunting, and dog licenses, and collect appropriate fees. Provide assistance to persons with disabilities in reaching less-accessible areas of municipal facilities. Process claims against the municipality, maintaining files and log of claims, and coordinate claim response and handling with municipal claims administrators.

GOE—Interest Area/Cluster: 07. Government and Public Administration. **Work Group:** 07.04. Public Administration Clerical Support. **Other Jobs in This Work Group:** Court Clerks; Court Reporters; Court, Municipal, and License Clerks; License Clerks.

Skills: Service Orientation; Management of Financial Resources; Writing; Social Perceptiveness; Active Listening; Operations Analysis; Persuasion; Management of Personnel Resources.

Education and Training Program: General Office Occupations and Clerical Services. **Related Knowledge/Courses:** Clerical Practices; Law and Government; Economics and Accounting; English Language; Personnel and Human Resources; Administration and Management.

Work Environment: Indoors; sitting.

Network Designers

- ❈ Personality Code: CIR
- ❈ Education/Training Required: Bachelor's degree
- ❈ Annual Earnings: $71,510
- ❈ Beginning Wage: $37,600
- ❈ Earnings Growth Potential: High
- ❈ Growth: 15.1%
- ❈ Annual Job Openings: 14,374
- ❈ Self-Employed: 6.6%
- ❈ Part-Time: 5.6%

The job openings listed here are shared with Computer Systems Engineers/Architects, with Software Quality Assurance Engineers and Testers, with Web Administrators, and with Web Developers.

Determine user requirements and design specifications for computer networks. Plan and implement network upgrades. Develop network-related documentation. Design, build, or operate equipment configuration prototypes, including network hardware, software, servers, or server operation systems. Coordinate network operations, maintenance, repairs, or upgrades. Adjust network sizes to meet volume or capacity demands. Communicate with vendors to gather information about products, to alert them to future needs, to resolve problems, or to address system maintenance issues. Coordinate installation of new equipment. Coordinate network or design activities with designers of associated networks. Design, organize, and deliver product awareness, skills transfer, and product education sessions for staff and suppliers. Determine specific network hardware or software requirements, such as platforms, interfaces, bandwidths, or routine schemas. Develop disaster recovery plans. Communicate with customers, sales staff, or marketing staff to determine customer needs. Explain design specifications to integration or test engineers. Develop plans or budgets for network equipment replacement. Prepare design presentations and proposals for staff or customers. Supervise engineers and other staff in the design or implementation of network solutions. Use network computer-aided design (CAD) software packages to optimize network designs. Develop or maintain project reporting systems. Participate in network technology upgrade or expansion projects, including installation of hardware and software and integration testing. Research and test new or modified hardware or software products to determine performance and interoperability. Develop and implement solutions for network problems. Prepare or monitor project schedules, budgets, or cost control systems. Monitor and analyze network performance and data input/output reports to detect problems, identify inefficient use of computer resources, or perform capacity planning. Evaluate network designs to determine whether customer requirements are met efficiently and effectively. Estimate time and materials needed to complete projects. Develop or recommend network security measures, such as firewalls, network security audits, or automated security probes.

GOE—Interest Area/Cluster: 11. Information Technology. **Work Group:** 11.02. Information Technology Specialties. **Other Jobs in This Work Group:** Computer and Information Scientists, Research; Computer Operators; Computer Programmers; Computer Security Specialists; Computer Software Engineers, Applications; Computer Software Engineers, Systems Software; Computer Support Specialists; Computer Systems Analysts; Computer Systems Engineers/Architects; Database Administrators; Network Systems and Data Communications Analysts; Software Quality Assurance Engineers and Testers; Web Administrators; Web Developers.

Skills: No data available.

Education and Training Programs: Computer and Information Sciences, General; Computer Science; Computer Systems Networking and Telecommunications; Computer Engineering, General; Computer Software Engineering. **Related Knowledge/Courses:** No data available.

Work Environment: No data available.

Occupational Health and Safety Technicians

- ❀ Personality Code: CR
- ❀ Education/Training Required: Bachelor's degree
- ❀ Annual Earnings: $44,020
- ❀ Beginning Wage: $25,280
- ❀ Earnings Growth Potential: High
- ❀ Growth: 14.6%
- ❀ Annual Job Openings: 886
- ❀ Self-Employed: 0.0%
- ❀ Part-Time: 8.0%

Collect data on work environments for analysis by occupational health and safety specialists. Implement and conduct evaluation of programs designed to limit chemical, physical, biological, and ergonomic risks to workers. Maintain all required records and documentation. Supply, operate, and maintain personal protective equipment. Verify that safety equipment such as hearing protection and respirators is available to employees, and monitor their use of such equipment to ensure proper fit and use. Evaluate situations where a worker has refused to work on the grounds that danger or potential harm exists, and determine how such situations should be handled. Prepare and calibrate equipment used to collect and analyze samples. Test workplaces for environmental hazards such as exposure to radiation, chemical and biological hazards, and excessive noise. Prepare and review specifications and orders for the purchase of safety equipment, ensuring that proper features are present and that items conform to health and safety standards. Report the results of environmental contaminant analyses, and recommend corrective measures to be applied. Review physicians' reports, and conduct worker studies in order to determine whether specific instances of disease or illness are job-related. Examine credentials, licenses, or permits to ensure compliance with licensing requirements. Conduct fire drills, and inspect fire suppression systems and portable fire systems to ensure that they are in working order. Educate the public about health issues, and enforce health legislation in order to prevent diseases, to promote health, and to help people understand health protection procedures and regulations. Provide consultation to organizations or agencies on the application of safety principles, practices, and techniques in the workplace. Conduct interviews to obtain information and evidence regarding communicable diseases or violations of health and sanitation regulations. Review records and reports concerning laboratory results, staffing, floor plans, fire inspections, and sanitation in order to gather information for the development and enforcement of safety activities. Prepare documents to be used in legal proceedings, testifying in such proceedings when necessary. Plan emergency response drills. Maintain logbooks of daily activities, including areas visited and activities performed.

GOE—Interest Area/Cluster: 07. Government and Public Administration. **Work Group:** 07.03. Regulations Enforcement. **Other Jobs in This Work Group:** Agricultural Inspectors; Aviation Inspectors; Compliance Officers, Except Agriculture, Construction, Health and Safety, and Transportation; Construction and Building Inspectors; Environmental Compliance Inspectors; Equal Opportunity Representatives and Officers; Financial Examiners; Fire Inspectors; Fish and Game Wardens; Forest Fire Inspectors and Prevention Specialists; Freight and Cargo Inspectors; Government Property Inspectors and Investigators; Immigration and Customs Inspectors; Licensing Examiners and Inspectors; Nuclear Monitoring Technicians; Occupational Health and Safety Specialists; Tax Examiners, Collectors, and Revenue Agents; Transportation Vehicle, Equipment, and Systems Inspectors, Except Aviation.

Skills: Science; Persuasion; Operations Analysis; Technology Design; Negotiation; Mathematics; Equipment Selection; Operation Monitoring.

Education and Training Programs: Radiation Protection/Health Physics Technician; Environmental Health; Occupational Health and Industrial Hygiene. **Related Knowledge/Courses:** Building and Construction; Chemistry; Public Safety and Security; Engineering and Technology; Physics; Education and Training.

Work Environment: More often outdoors than indoors; noisy; hazardous conditions; hazardous equipment; standing.

Office Clerks, General

- ❋ Personality Code: CER
- ❋ Education/Training Required: Short-term on-the-job training
- ❋ Annual Earnings: $24,460
- ❋ Beginning Wage: $15,490
- ❋ Earnings Growth Potential: Medium
- ❋ Growth: 12.6%
- ❋ Annual Job Openings: 765,803
- ❋ Self-Employed: 0.7%
- ❋ Part-Time: 26.0%

Perform duties too varied and diverse to be classified in any specific office clerical occupation requiring limited knowledge of office management systems and procedures. Clerical duties may be assigned in accordance with the office procedures of individual establishments and may include a combination of answering telephones, bookkeeping, typing or word processing, stenography, office machine operation, and filing. Collect, count, and disburse money; do basic bookkeeping; and complete banking transactions. Communicate with customers, employees, and other individuals to answer questions, disseminate or explain information, take orders, and address complaints. Answer telephones, direct calls, and take messages. Compile, copy, sort, and file records of office activities, business transactions, and other activities. Complete and mail bills, contracts, policies, invoices, or checks. Operate office machines such as photocopiers and scanners, facsimile machines, voice mail systems, and personal computers. Compute, record, and proofread data and other information, such as records or reports. Maintain and update filing, inventory, mailing, and database systems, either manually or using a computer. Open, sort, and route incoming mail; answer correspondence; and prepare outgoing mail. Review files, records, and other documents to obtain information to respond to requests. Deliver messages and run errands. Inventory and order materials, supplies, and services. Complete work schedules, manage calendars, and arrange appointments. Process and prepare documents such as business or government forms and expense reports. Monitor and direct the work of lower-level clerks. Type, format, proofread, and edit correspondence and other documents from notes or dictating machines, using computers or typewriters. Count, weigh, measure, or organize materials. Train other staff members to perform work activities, such as using computer applications. Prepare meeting agendas, attend meetings, and record and transcribe minutes. Troubleshoot problems involving office equipment, such as computer hardware and software. Make travel arrangements for office personnel.

GOE—Interest Area/Cluster: 04. Business and Administration. **Work Group:** 04.07. Records and Materials Processing. **Other Jobs in This Work Group:** Correspondence Clerks; File Clerks; Human Resources Assistants, Except Payroll and Timekeeping; Marking Clerks; Meter Readers, Utilities; Order Fillers, Wholesale and Retail Sales; Postal Service Clerks; Postal Service Mail Sorters, Processors, and Processing Machine Operators; Procurement Clerks; Production, Planning, and Expediting Clerks; Shipping, Receiving, and Traffic Clerks; Stock Clerks and Order Fillers; Stock Clerks, Sales Floor; Stock Clerks—Stockroom, Warehouse, or Storage Yard; Weighers, Measurers, Checkers, and Samplers, Recordkeeping.

Skills: None met the criteria.

Conventional-O

Education and Training Program: General Office Occupations and Clerical Services. **Related Knowledge/Courses:** Clerical Practices; Economics and Accounting; Customer and Personal Service; Personnel and Human Resources; Mathematics; Computers and Electronics.

Work Environment: Indoors; sitting; using hands on objects, tools, or controls.

Paralegals and Legal Assistants

- ❉ Personality Code: CIE
- ❉ Education/Training Required: Associate degree
- ❉ Annual Earnings: $44,990
- ❉ Beginning Wage: $28,360
- ❉ Earnings Growth Potential: Medium
- ❉ Growth: 22.2%
- ❉ Annual Job Openings: 22,756
- ❉ Self-Employed: 2.2%
- ❉ Part-Time: 11.0%

Assist lawyers by researching legal precedent, investigating facts, or preparing legal documents. Conduct research to support a legal proceeding, to formulate a defense, or to initiate legal action. Prepare legal documents, including briefs, pleadings, appeals, wills, contracts, and real estate closing statements. Prepare affidavits or other documents, maintain document file, and file pleadings with court clerk. Gather and analyze research data, such as statutes; decisions; and legal articles, codes, and documents. Investigate facts and law of cases to determine causes of action and to prepare cases. Call upon witnesses to testify at hearing. Direct and coordinate law office activity, including delivery of subpoenas. Arbitrate disputes between parties and assist in real estate closing process. Keep and monitor legal volumes to ensure that law library is up to date. Appraise and inventory real and personal property for estate planning.

GOE—Interest Area/Cluster: 12. Law and Public Safety. **Work Group:** 12.03. Legal Support. **Other**

Jobs in This Work Group: Law Clerks; Title Examiners, Abstractors, and Searchers.

Skills: Writing; Active Listening; Speaking; Time Management; Reading Comprehension; Monitoring.

Education and Training Program: Legal Assistant/Paralegal Training. **Related Knowledge/Courses:** Clerical Practices; Law and Government; Computers and Electronics; Personnel and Human Resources; English Language; Customer and Personal Service.

Work Environment: Indoors; sitting; repetitive motions.

Pharmacy Technicians

- ❉ Personality Code: CR
- ❉ Education/Training Required: Moderate-term on-the-job training
- ❉ Annual Earnings: $26,720
- ❉ Beginning Wage: $18,520
- ❉ Earnings Growth Potential: Low
- ❉ Growth: 32.0%
- ❉ Annual Job Openings: 54,453
- ❉ Self-Employed: 0.2%
- ❉ Part-Time: 20.8%

Prepare medications under the direction of a pharmacist. May measure, mix, count out, label, and record amounts and dosages of medications. Receive written prescription or refill requests and verify that information is complete and accurate. Maintain proper storage and security conditions for drugs. Answer telephones, responding to questions or requests. Fill bottles with prescribed medications and type and affix labels. Assist customers by answering simple questions, locating items, or referring them to the pharmacist for medication information. Price and file prescriptions that have been filled. Clean and help maintain equipment and work areas and sterilize glassware according to prescribed methods. Establish and maintain patient profiles, including lists of medications taken by individual patients.

Order, label, and count stock of medications, chemicals, and supplies and enter inventory data into computer. Receive and store incoming supplies, verify quantities against invoices, and inform supervisors of stock needs and shortages. Transfer medication from vials to the appropriate number of sterile disposable syringes, using aseptic techniques. Under pharmacist supervision, add measured drugs or nutrients to intravenous solutions under sterile conditions to prepare intravenous (IV) packs. Supply and monitor robotic machines that dispense medicine into containers and label the containers. Prepare and process medical insurance claim forms and records. Mix pharmaceutical preparations according to written prescriptions. Operate cash registers to accept payment from customers. Compute charges for medication and equipment dispensed to hospital patients and enter data in computer. Deliver medications and pharmaceutical supplies to patients, nursing stations, or surgery. Price stock and mark items for sale. Maintain and merchandise home health-care products and services.

GOE—Interest Area/Cluster: 08. Health Science. **Work Group:** 08.02. Medicine and Surgery. **Other Jobs in This Work Group:** Anesthesiologists; Family and General Practitioners; Internists, General; Medical Assistants; Medical Transcriptionists; Obstetricians and Gynecologists; Pediatricians, General; Pharmacists; Pharmacy Aides; Physician Assistants; Psychiatrists; Registered Nurses; Surgeons; Surgical Technologists.

Skills: Service Orientation; Active Listening; Instructing; Mathematics; Speaking; Active Learning; Troubleshooting; Writing.

Education and Training Program: Pharmacy Technician/Assistant. **Related Knowledge/Courses:** Medicine and Dentistry; Chemistry; Customer and Personal Service; Mathematics; Clerical Practices.

Work Environment: Indoors; standing; using hands on objects, tools, or controls; repetitive motions.

Police Identification and Records Officers

- ❋ Personality Code: CRI
- ❋ Education/Training Required: Work experience in a related occupation
- ❋ Annual Earnings: $59,930
- ❋ Beginning Wage: $35,600
- ❋ Earnings Growth Potential: High
- ❋ Growth: 17.3%
- ❋ Annual Job Openings: 14,746
- ❋ Self-Employed: 0.3%
- ❋ Part-Time: 2.2%

The job openings listed here are shared with Criminal Investigators and Special Agents, with Immigration and Customs Inspectors, and with Police Detectives.

Collect evidence at crime scene, classify and identify fingerprints, and photograph evidence for use in criminal and civil cases. Photograph crime or accident scenes for evidence records. Analyze and process evidence at crime scenes and in the laboratory, wearing protective equipment and using powders and chemicals. Look for trace evidence, such as fingerprints, hairs, fibers, or shoe impressions, using alternative light sources when necessary. Dust selected areas of crime scene and lift latent fingerprints, adhering to proper preservation procedures. Testify in court and present evidence. Package, store, and retrieve evidence. Serve as technical advisor and coordinate with other law enforcement workers to exchange information on crime scene collection activities. Perform emergency work during off-hours. Submit evidence to supervisors. Process film and prints from crime or accident scenes. Identify, classify, and file fingerprints, using systems such as the Henry Classification system.

GOE—Interest Area/Cluster: 12. Law and Public Safety. **Work Group:** 12.04. Law Enforcement and Public Safety. **Other Jobs in This Work Group:** Bailiffs; Correctional Officers and Jailers; Criminal Investigators and Special Agents; Detectives and

Conventional-P

Criminal Investigators; Fire Investigators; Forensic Science Technicians; Parking Enforcement Workers; Police and Sheriff's Patrol Officers; Police Detectives; Police Patrol Officers; Sheriffs and Deputy Sheriffs; Transit and Railroad Police.

Skills: Persuasion; Judgment and Decision Making; Negotiation; Service Orientation; Social Perceptiveness; Critical Thinking; Speaking; Science.

Education and Training Programs: Criminal Justice/Police Science; Criminalistics and Criminal Science. **Related Knowledge/Courses:** Law and Government; Public Safety and Security; Telecommunications; Customer and Personal Service; Psychology; Computers and Electronics.

Work Environment: More often outdoors than indoors; noisy; very hot or cold; contaminants; using hands on objects, tools, or controls.

Police, Fire, and Ambulance Dispatchers

- ❋ Personality Code: CRE
- ❋ Education/Training Required: Moderate-term on-the-job training
- ❋ Annual Earnings: $32,660
- ❋ Beginning Wage: $20,910
- ❋ Earnings Growth Potential: Medium
- ❋ Growth: 13.6%
- ❋ Annual Job Openings: 17,628
- ❋ Self-Employed: 1.2%
- ❋ Part-Time: 6.3%

Receive complaints from public concerning crimes and police emergencies. Broadcast orders to police patrol units in vicinity of complaint to investigate. Operate radio, telephone, or computer equipment to receive reports of fires and medical emergencies and relay information or orders to proper officials. Question callers about their locations and the nature of their problems to determine types of response needed. Receive incoming telephone or alarm system calls regarding emergency and nonemergency police and fire service, emergency ambulance service, information, and after-hours calls for departments within a city. Determine response requirements and relative priorities of situations and dispatch units in accordance with established procedures. Record details of calls, dispatches, and messages. Enter, update, and retrieve information from teletype networks and computerized data systems regarding such things as wanted persons, stolen property, vehicle registration, and stolen vehicles. Maintain access to and security of highly sensitive materials. Relay information and messages to and from emergency sites, to law enforcement agencies, and to all other individuals or groups requiring notification. Scan status charts and computer screens and contact emergency response field units to determine emergency units available for dispatch. Observe alarm registers and scan maps to determine whether a specific emergency is in the dispatch service area. Maintain files of information relating to emergency calls such as personnel rosters, and emergency call-out and pager files. Monitor various radio frequencies such as those used by public works departments, school security, and civil defense to keep apprised of developing situations. Learn material and pass required tests for certification. Read and effectively interpret small-scale maps and information from a computer screen to determine locations and provide directions. Answer routine inquiries and refer calls not requiring dispatches to appropriate departments and agencies. Test and adjust communication and alarm systems and report malfunctions to maintenance units. Provide emergency medical instructions to callers. Monitor alarm systems to detect emergencies such as fires and illegal entry into establishments. Operate and maintain mobile dispatch vehicles and equipment.

GOE—Interest Area/Cluster: 03. Arts and Communication. **Work Group:** 03.10. Communications Technology. **Other Jobs in This Work Group:** Air Traffic Controllers; Airfield Operations Specialists; Dispatchers, Except Police, Fire, and Ambulance; Telephone Operators.

Skills: Negotiation; Operation Monitoring.

Related Knowledge/Courses: Telecommunications; Customer and Personal Service; Clerical Practices; Law and Government; Psychology; Public Safety and Security.

Work Environment: Indoors; noisy; sitting; using hands on objects, tools, or controls; repetitive motions.

Postal Service Mail Carriers

- ❋ Personality Code: CR
- ❋ Education/Training Required: Short-term on-the-job training
- ❋ Annual Earnings: $44,500
- ❋ Beginning Wage: $34,990
- ❋ Earnings Growth Potential: Very low
- ❋ Growth: 1.0%
- ❋ Annual Job Openings: 16,710
- ❋ Self-Employed: 0.0%
- ❋ Part-Time: 7.1%

Sort mail for delivery. Deliver mail on established routes by vehicle or on foot. Obtain signed receipts for registered, certified, and insured mail; collect associated charges; and complete any necessary paperwork. Sort mail for delivery, arranging it in delivery sequence. Deliver mail to residences and business establishments along specified routes by walking and/or driving, using a combination of satchels, carts, cars, and small trucks. Return to the post office with mail collected from homes, businesses, and public mailboxes. Turn in money and receipts collected along mail routes. Sign for cash-on-delivery and registered mail before leaving post offices. Record address changes and redirect mail for those addresses. Hold mail for customers who are away from delivery locations. Bundle mail in preparation for delivery or transportation to relay boxes. Leave notices telling patrons where to collect mail that could not be delivered. Meet schedules for the collection and return of mail. Return incorrectly addressed mail to senders. Maintain accurate records of deliveries. Answer customers' questions about postal services

and regulations. Provide customers with change of address cards and other forms. Report any unusual circumstances concerning mail delivery, including the condition of street letter boxes. Register, certify, and insure parcels and letters. Travel to post offices to pick up the mail for routes and/or pick up mail from postal relay boxes. Enter change of address orders into computers that process forwarding address stickers. Complete forms that notify publishers of address changes. Sell stamps and money orders.

GOE—Interest Area/Cluster: 16. Transportation, Distribution, and Logistics. **Work Group:** 16.06. Other Services Requiring Driving. **Other Jobs in This Work Group:** Ambulance Drivers and Attendants, Except Emergency Medical Technicians; Bus Drivers, School; Bus Drivers, Transit and Intercity; Couriers and Messengers; Driver/Sales Workers; Parking Lot Attendants; Taxi Drivers and Chauffeurs.

Skills: None met the criteria.

Education and Training Program: General Office Occupations and Clerical Services. **Related Knowledge/Courses:** Transportation; Public Safety and Security.

Work Environment: Outdoors; very hot or cold; contaminants; standing; using hands on objects, tools, or controls; repetitive motions.

Production, Planning, and Expediting Clerks

- ❋ Personality Code: CE
- ❋ Education/Training Required: Moderate-term on-the-job training
- ❋ Annual Earnings: $39,690
- ❋ Beginning Wage: $24,520
- ❋ Earnings Growth Potential: Medium
- ❋ Growth: 4.2%
- ❋ Annual Job Openings: 52,735
- ❋ Self-Employed: 1.4%
- ❋ Part-Time: 6.7%

Conventional-P

Coordinate and expedite the flow of work and materials within or between departments of an establishment according to production schedules.inventory levels, costs, and production problems. Examine documents, materials, and products, and monitor work processes to assess completeness, accuracy, and conformance to standards and specifications. Review documents such as production schedules, work orders, and staffing tables to determine personnel and materials requirements, and material priorities. Revise production schedules when required due to design changes, labor or material shortages, backlogs, or other interruptions, collaborating with management, marketing, sales, production, and engineering. Confer with department supervisors and other personnel to assess progress and discuss needed changes. Confer with establishment personnel, vendors, and customers to coordinate production and shipping activities, and to resolve complaints or eliminate delays. Record production data, including volume produced, consumption of raw materials, and quality control measures. Requisition and maintain inventories of materials and supplies necessary to meet production demands. Calculate figures such as required amounts of labor and materials, manufacturing costs, and wages, using pricing schedules, adding machines, calculators, or computers. Distribute production schedules and work orders to departments. Compile information such as production rates and progress, materials inventories, materials used, and customer information, so that status reports can be completed. Arrange for delivery, assembly, and distribution of supplies and parts to expedite flow of materials and meet production schedules. Contact suppliers to verify shipment details. Maintain files such as maintenance records, bills of lading, and cost reports. Plan production commitments and timetables for business units, specific programs, and/or jobs, using sales forecasts. Establish and prepare product construction directions and locations; information on required tools, materials, and equipment; numbers of workers needed; and cost projections. Compile and prepare documentation related to production sequences, transportation, personnel schedules, and purchase, maintenance, and repair orders.

Provide documentation and information to account for delays, difficulties, and changes to cost estimates.

GOE—Interest Area/Cluster: 04. Business and Administration. **Work Group:** 04.07. Records and Materials Processing. **Other Jobs in This Work Group:** Correspondence Clerks; File Clerks; Human Resources Assistants, Except Payroll and Timekeeping; Marking Clerks; Meter Readers, Utilities; Office Clerks, General; Order Fillers, Wholesale and Retail Sales; Postal Service Clerks; Postal Service Mail Sorters, Processors, and Processing Machine Operators; Procurement Clerks; Shipping, Receiving, and Traffic Clerks; Stock Clerks and Order Fillers; Stock Clerks, Sales Floor; Stock Clerks—Stockroom, Warehouse, or Storage Yard; Weighers, Measurers, Checkers, and Samplers, Recordkeeping.

Skills: Management of Material Resources; Operations Analysis; Management of Financial Resources; Systems Evaluation; Negotiation; Mathematics; Coordination; Persuasion.

Education and Training Program: Parts, Warehousing, and Inventory Management Operations. **Related Knowledge/Courses:** Production and Processing; Clerical Practices; Computers and Electronics; Administration and Management; Mathematics; Customer and Personal Service.

Work Environment: Indoors; noisy; contaminants; sitting.

Purchasing Agents, Except Wholesale, Retail, and Farm Products

- ❋ Personality Code: CE
- ❋ Education/Training Required: Long-term on-the-job training
- ❋ Annual Earnings: $52,460
- ❋ Beginning Wage: $32,580
- ❋ Earnings Growth Potential: Medium
- ❋ Growth: 0.1%
- ❋ Annual Job Openings: 22,349
- ❋ Self-Employed: 1.6%
- ❋ Part-Time: 3.8%

Purchase machinery, equipment, tools, parts, supplies, or services necessary for the operation of an establishment. Purchase raw or semi-finished materials for manufacturing. Purchase the highest-quality merchandise at the lowest possible price and in correct amounts. Prepare purchase orders, solicit bid proposals, and review requisitions for goods and services. Research and evaluate suppliers based on price, quality, selection, service, support, availability, reliability, production and distribution capabilities, and the supplier's reputation and history. Analyze price proposals, financial reports, and other data and information to determine reasonable prices. Monitor and follow applicable laws and regulations. Negotiate, or renegotiate, and administer contracts with suppliers, vendors, and other representatives. Monitor shipments to ensure that goods come in on time and trace shipments and follow up undelivered goods in the event of problems. Confer with staff, users, and vendors to discuss defective or unacceptable goods or services and determine corrective action. Evaluate and monitor contract performance to ensure compliance with contractual obligations and to determine need for changes. Maintain and review computerized or manual records of items purchased, costs, delivery, product performance, and inventories. Review catalogs, industry periodicals, directories, trade journals, and Internet sites and consult with other department personnel to locate necessary goods and services. Study sales records and inventory levels of current stock to develop strategic purchasing programs that facilitate employee access to supplies. Interview vendors and visit suppliers' plants and distribution centers to examine and learn about products, services, and prices. Arrange the payment of duty and freight charges. Hire, train, and/or supervise purchasing clerks, buyers, and expediters. Write and review product specifications, maintaining a working technical knowledge of the goods or services to be purchased. Monitor changes affecting supply and demand, tracking market conditions, price trends, or futures markets. Formulate policies and procedures for bid proposals and procurement of goods and services. Attend meetings, trade shows, conferences, conventions, and seminars to network with people in other purchasing departments.

GOE—Interest Area/Cluster: 14. Retail and Wholesale Sales and Service. **Work Group:** 14.05. Purchasing. **Other Jobs in This Work Group:** Wholesale and Retail Buyers, Except Farm Products.

Skills: Operations Analysis; Management of Financial Resources; Management of Material Resources; Mathematics; Writing; Management of Personnel Resources; Speaking; Judgment and Decision Making.

Education and Training Programs: Sales, Distribution, and Marketing Operations, General; Merchandising and Buying Operations. **Related Knowledge/Courses:** Clerical Practices; Economics and Accounting; Production and Processing; Administration and Management; Computers and Electronics; Communications and Media.

Work Environment: Indoors; sitting; using hands on objects, tools, or controls; repetitive motions.

Conventional-P

Receptionists and Information Clerks

- ❋ Personality Code: CES
- ❋ Education/Training Required: Short-term on-the-job training
- ❋ Annual Earnings: $23,710
- ❋ Beginning Wage: $16,290
- ❋ Earnings Growth Potential: Low
- ❋ Growth: 17.2%
- ❋ Annual Job Openings: 334,124
- ❋ Self-Employed: 1.4%
- ❋ Part-Time: 31.7%

Answer inquiries and obtain information for general public, customers, visitors, and other interested parties. Provide information regarding activities conducted at establishment and location of departments, offices, and employees within organization. Operate telephone switchboard to answer, screen, and forward calls, providing information, taking messages, and scheduling appointments. Receive payment and record receipts for services. Perform administrative support tasks such as proofreading, transcribing handwritten information, and operating calculators or computers to work with pay records, invoices, balance sheets, and other documents. Greet persons entering establishment, determine nature and purpose of visit, and direct or escort them to specific destinations. Hear and resolve complaints from customers and public. File and maintain records. Transmit information or documents to customers, using computer, mail, or facsimile machine. Schedule appointments and maintain and update appointment calendars. Analyze data to determine answers to questions from customers or members of the public. Provide information about establishment such as location of departments or offices, employees within the organization, or services provided. Keep a current record of staff members' whereabouts and availability. Collect, sort, distribute, and prepare mail, messages, and courier deliveries. Calculate and quote rates for tours, stocks, insurance policies, or other products and services. Take orders for merchandise or materials and send them to the proper departments to be filled. Process and prepare memos, correspondence, travel vouchers, or other documents. Schedule space and equipment for special programs and prepare lists of participants. Enroll individuals to participate in programs and notify them of their acceptance. Conduct tours or deliver talks describing features of public facility such as a historic site or national park. Perform duties such as taking care of plants and straightening magazines to maintain lobby or reception area.

GOE—Interest Area/Cluster: 14. Retail and Wholesale Sales and Service. **Work Group:** 14.06. Customer Service. **Other Jobs in This Work Group:** Cashiers; Counter and Rental Clerks; Customer Service Representatives; Gaming Cage Workers; Gaming Change Persons and Booth Cashiers; Order Clerks.

Skills: Active Listening; Service Orientation; Writing; Social Perceptiveness; Reading Comprehension.

Education and Training Programs: Health Unit Coordinator/Ward Clerk; Medical Reception/Receptionist; Receptionist; General Office Occupations and Clerical Services. **Related Knowledge/Courses:** Clerical Practices; Customer and Personal Service; Computers and Electronics.

Work Environment: Indoors; sitting; repetitive motions.

Sales Representatives, Wholesale and Manufacturing, Except Technical and Scientific Products

- ❈ Personality Code: CE
- ❈ Education/Training Required: Work experience in a related occupation
- ❈ Annual Earnings: $50,750
- ❈ Beginning Wage: $26,490
- ❈ Earnings Growth Potential: High
- ❈ Growth: 8.4%
- ❈ Annual Job Openings: 156,215
- ❈ Self-Employed: 4.0%
- ❈ Part-Time: 6.7%

Sell goods for wholesalers or manufacturers to businesses or groups of individuals. Work requires substantial knowledge of items sold. Answer customers' questions about products, prices, availability, product uses, and credit terms. Recommend products to customers based on customers' needs and interests. Contact regular and prospective customers to demonstrate products, explain product features, and solicit orders. Estimate or quote prices, credit or contract terms, warranties, and delivery dates. Consult with clients after sales or contract signings to resolve problems and to provide ongoing support. Prepare drawings, estimates, and bids that meet specific customer needs. Provide customers with product samples and catalogs. Identify prospective customers by using business directories, following leads from existing clients, participating in organizations and clubs, and attending trade shows and conferences. Arrange and direct delivery and installation of products and equipment. Monitor market conditions; product innovations; and competitors' products, prices, and sales. Negotiate details of contracts and payments and prepare sales contracts and order forms. Perform administrative duties, such as preparing sales budgets and reports, keeping sales records, and filing expense account reports. Obtain credit information about prospective customers. Forward orders to manufacturers. Check stock levels and reorder merchandise as necessary. Plan, assemble, and stock product displays in retail stores or make recommendations to retailers regarding product displays, promotional programs, and advertising. Negotiate with retail merchants to improve product exposure such as shelf positioning and advertising. Train customers' employees to operate and maintain new equipment. Buy products from manufacturers or brokerage firms and distribute them to wholesale and retail clients.

GOE—Interest Area/Cluster: 14. Retail and Wholesale Sales and Service. **Work Group:** 14.03. General Sales. **Other Jobs in This Work Group:** Parts Salespersons; Real Estate Brokers; Real Estate Sales Agents; Retail Salespersons; Service Station Attendants.

Skills: Negotiation; Persuasion; Service Orientation; Management of Financial Resources; Operations Analysis; Time Management; Speaking; Installation.

Education and Training Programs: Insurance; Sales, Distribution, and Marketing Operations, General; General Merchandising, Sales, and Related Marketing Operations, Other; Fashion Merchandising; Apparel and Accessories Marketing Operations; Special Products Marketing Operations; Specialized Merchandising, Sales, and Related Marketing Operations, Other; Business, Management, Marketing, and Related Support Services, Other. **Related Knowledge/Courses:** Sales and Marketing; Economics and Accounting; Customer and Personal Service; Transportation; Mathematics; Administration and Management.

Work Environment: Outdoors; noisy; contaminants; more often standing than sitting; walking and running.

Conventional-S

Secretaries, Except Legal, Medical, and Executive

❋ Personality Code: CE
❋ Education/Training Required: Moderate-term on-the-job training
❋ Annual Earnings: $28,220
❋ Beginning Wage: $17,920
❋ Earnings Growth Potential: Medium
❋ Growth: 1.2%
❋ Annual Job Openings: 239,630
❋ Self-Employed: 1.4%
❋ Part-Time: 18.9%

Perform routine clerical and administrative functions such as drafting correspondence, scheduling appointments, organizing and maintaining paper and electronic files, or providing information to callers. Operate office equipment such as fax machines, copiers, and phone systems and use computers for spreadsheet, word-processing, database management, and other applications. Answer telephones and give information to callers, take messages, or transfer calls to appropriate individuals. Greet visitors and callers, handle their inquiries, and direct them to the appropriate persons according to their needs. Set up and maintain paper and electronic filing systems for records, correspondence, and other material. Locate and attach appropriate files to incoming correspondence requiring replies. Open, read, route, and distribute incoming mail and other material and prepare answers to routine letters. Complete forms in accordance with company procedures. Make copies of correspondence and other printed material. Review work done by others to check for correct spelling and grammar, ensure that company format policies are followed, and recommend revisions. Compose, type, and distribute meeting notes, routine correspondence, and reports. Learn to operate new office technologies as they are developed and implemented. Maintain scheduling and event calendars. Schedule and confirm appointments for clients, customers, or supervisors. Manage projects and contribute to committee and team work.

Mail newsletters, promotional material, and other information. Order and dispense supplies. Conduct searches to find needed information, using such sources as the Internet. Provide services to customers, such as order placement and account information. Collect and disburse funds from cash accounts and keep records of collections and disbursements. Prepare and mail checks. Establish work procedures and schedules and keep track of the daily work of clerical staff. Coordinate conferences and meetings. Take dictation in shorthand or by machine and transcribe information. Arrange conferences, meetings, and travel reservations for office personnel. Operate electronic mail systems and coordinate the flow of information both internally and with other organizations. Supervise other clerical staff and provide training and orientation to new staff.

GOE—Interest Area/Cluster: 04. Business and Administration. **Work Group:** 04.04. Secretarial Support. **Other Jobs in This Work Group:** Executive Secretaries and Administrative Assistants; Legal Secretaries; Medical Secretaries.

Skill: Writing.

Education and Training Programs: Administrative Assistant and Secretarial Science, General; Executive Assistant/Executive Secretary. **Related Knowledge/Courses:** Clerical Practices; Customer and Personal Service; Computers and Electronics; Economics and Accounting; English Language; Personnel and Human Resources.

Work Environment: Indoors; sitting; repetitive motions.

Shipping, Receiving, and Traffic Clerks

- ❋ Personality Code: CRE
- ❋ Education/Training Required: Short-term on-the-job training
- ❋ Annual Earnings: $26,990
- ❋ Beginning Wage: $17,390
- ❋ Earnings Growth Potential: Medium
- ❋ Growth: 3.7%
- ❋ Annual Job Openings: 138,967
- ❋ Self-Employed: 0.2%
- ❋ Part-Time: 8.9%

Verify and keep records on incoming and outgoing shipments. Prepare items for shipment. Examine contents and compare with records such as manifests, invoices, or orders to verify accuracy of incoming or outgoing shipment. Prepare documents such as work orders, bills of lading, and shipping orders to route materials. Determine shipping method for materials, using knowledge of shipping procedures, routes, and rates. Record shipment data such as weight, charges, space availability, and damages and discrepancies for reporting, accounting, and recordkeeping purposes. Contact carrier representative to make arrangements and to issue instructions for shipping and delivery of materials. Confer and correspond with establishment representatives to rectify problems such as damages, shortages, and nonconformance to specifications. Requisition and store shipping materials and supplies to maintain inventory of stock. Deliver or route materials to departments, using work devices such as handtruck, conveyor, or sorting bins. Compute amounts such as space available and shipping, storage, and demurrage charges, using calculator or price list. Pack, seal, label, and affix postage to prepare materials for shipping, using work devices such as hand tools, power tools, and postage meter.

GOE—Interest Area/Cluster: 04. Business and Administration. **Work Group:** 04.07. Records and Materials Processing. **Other Jobs in This Work Group:** Correspondence Clerks; File Clerks; Human Resources Assistants, Except Payroll and Timekeeping; Marking Clerks; Meter Readers, Utilities; Office Clerks, General; Order Fillers, Wholesale and Retail Sales; Postal Service Clerks; Postal Service Mail Sorters, Processors, and Processing Machine Operators; Procurement Clerks; Production, Planning, and Expediting Clerks; Stock Clerks and Order Fillers; Stock Clerks, Sales Floor; Stock Clerks—Stockroom, Warehouse, or Storage Yard; Weighers, Measurers, Checkers, and Samplers, Recordkeeping.

Skills: Mathematics; Learning Strategies; Management of Financial Resources; Writing; Speaking; Negotiation; Social Perceptiveness; Time Management.

Education and Training Programs: General Office Occupations and Clerical Services; Traffic, Customs, and Transportation Clerk/Technician. **Related Knowledge/Courses:** Clerical Practices; Production and Processing; Transportation; Computers and Electronics; Education and Training; Public Safety and Security.

Work Environment: Indoors; noisy; contaminants; sitting; walking and running; using hands on objects, tools, or controls.

Social and Human Service Assistants

- ❋ Personality Code: CSE
- ❋ Education/Training Required: Moderate-term on-the-job training
- ❋ Annual Earnings: $26,630
- ❋ Beginning Wage: $17,350
- ❋ Earnings Growth Potential: Low
- ❋ Growth: 33.6%
- ❋ Annual Job Openings: 80,142
- ❋ Self-Employed: 0.1%
- ❋ Part-Time: 12.0%

Assist professionals from a wide variety of fields such as psychology, rehabilitation, or social work to provide client services, as well as support for

families. May assist clients in identifying available benefits and social and community services and help clients obtain them. May assist social workers with developing, organizing, and conducting programs to prevent and resolve problems relevant to substance abuse, human relationships, rehabilitation, or adult daycare. Keep records and prepare reports for owner or management concerning visits with clients. Submit reports and review reports or problems with superior. Interview individuals and family members to compile information on social, educational, criminal, institutional, or drug histories. Provide information and refer individuals to public or private agencies or community services for assistance. Consult with supervisors concerning programs for individual families. Advise clients regarding food stamps, child care, food, money management, sanitation, or housekeeping. Oversee day-to-day group activities of residents in institution. Visit individuals in homes or attend group meetings to provide information on agency services, requirements, and procedures. Monitor free, supplementary meal program to ensure cleanliness of facility and that eligibility guidelines are met for persons receiving meals. Meet with youth groups to acquaint them with consequences of delinquent acts. Assist in planning of food budgets, using charts and sample budgets. Transport and accompany clients to shopping areas or to appointments, using automobiles. Assist in locating housing for displaced individuals. Observe and discuss meal preparation and suggest alternate methods of food preparation. Observe clients' food selections and recommend alternative economical and nutritional food choices. Explain rules established by owner or management, such as sanitation and maintenance requirements or parking regulations. Care for children in clients' homes during clients' appointments. Inform tenants of facilities such as laundries and playgrounds. Assist clients with preparation of forms such as tax or rent forms. Demonstrate use and care of equipment for tenants' use.

GOE—Interest Area/Cluster: 10. Human Service. **Work Group:** 10.01. Counseling and Social Work. **Other Jobs in This Work Group:** Child, Family, and School Social Workers; Clinical Psychologists; Clinical, Counseling, and School Psychologists; Counseling Psychologists; Marriage and Family Therapists; Medical and Public Health Social Workers; Mental Health and Substance Abuse Social Workers; Mental Health Counselors; Probation Officers and Correctional Treatment Specialists; Rehabilitation Counselors; Residential Advisors; Substance Abuse and Behavioral Disorder Counselors.

Skill: Negotiation.

Education and Training Program: Mental and Social Health Services and Allied Professions, Other. **Related Knowledge/Courses:** Therapy and Counseling; Philosophy and Theology; Psychology; Customer and Personal Service; Sociology and Anthropology; Clerical Practices.

Work Environment: Indoors; noisy; sitting.

Statement Clerks

- ❋ Personality Code: CES
- ❋ Education/Training Required: Moderate-term on-the-job training
- ❋ Annual Earnings: $29,970
- ❋ Beginning Wage: $20,930
- ❋ Earnings Growth Potential: Low
- ❋ Growth: 4.4%
- ❋ Annual Job Openings: 81,885
- ❋ Self-Employed: 1.6%
- ❋ Part-Time: 14.3%

The job openings listed here are shared with Billing, Cost, and Rate Clerks and with Billing, Posting, and Calculating Machine Operators.

Prepare and distribute bank statements to customers, answer inquiries, and reconcile discrepancies in records and accounts. Encode and cancel checks, using bank machines. Take orders for imprinted checks. Compare previously prepared bank statements with canceled checks and reconcile discrepancies. Verify signatures and required information on checks. Post stop-payment notices to prevent payment of protested checks. Maintain files of canceled checks and customers' signatures. Match statements with batches of canceled checks by account numbers. Weigh envelopes containing statements to determine correct postage and affix postage, using stamps or metering equipment. Load machines with statements, cancelled checks, and envelopes to prepare statements for distribution to customers or stuff envelopes by hand. Retrieve checks returned to customers in error, adjusting customer accounts and answering inquiries about errors as necessary. Route statements for mailing or over-the-counter delivery to customers. Monitor equipment to ensure proper operation. Fix minor problems, such as equipment jams, and notify repair personnel of major equipment problems.

GOE—Interest Area/Cluster: 04. Business and Administration. **Work Group:** 04.06. Mathematical Clerical Support. **Other Jobs in This Work Group:** Billing and Posting Clerks and Machine Operators; Billing, Cost, and Rate Clerks; Bookkeeping, Accounting, and Auditing Clerks; Brokerage Clerks; Payroll and Timekeeping Clerks; Tax Preparers.

Skills: None met the criteria.

Education and Training Program: Accounting Technology/Technician and Bookkeeping. **Related Knowledge/Courses:** Economics and Accounting; Clerical Practices; Administration and Management.

Work Environment: Indoors; sitting; repetitive motions.

Statisticians

- ❋ Personality Code: CI
- ❋ Education/Training Required: Master's degree
- ❋ Annual Earnings: $69,900
- ❋ Beginning Wage: $38,140
- ❋ Earnings Growth Potential: High
- ❋ Growth: 8.5%
- ❋ Annual Job Openings: 3,433
- ❋ Self-Employed: 6.0%
- ❋ Part-Time: 13.1%

Engage in the development of mathematical theory or apply statistical theory and methods to collect, organize, interpret, and summarize numerical data to provide usable information. May specialize in fields such as bio-statistics, agricultural statistics, business statistics, economic statistics, or other fields. Report results of statistical analyses, including information in the form of graphs, charts, and tables. Process large amounts of data for statistical modeling and graphic analysis, using computers. Identify relationships and trends in data, as well as any factors that could affect the results of research. Analyze and interpret statistical data in order to identify significant differences in relationships among sources of information. Prepare data for processing by organizing information, checking for any inaccuracies, and adjusting and weighting the raw data. Evaluate the statistical methods and procedures used to obtain data in order to ensure validity, applicability, efficiency, and accuracy. Evaluate sources of information in order to determine any limitations in terms of reliability or usability. Plan data collection methods for specific projects and determine the types and sizes of sample groups to be used. Design research projects that apply valid scientific techniques and utilize information obtained from baselines or historical data in order to structure uncompromised and efficient analyses. Develop an understanding of fields to which statistical methods are to be applied in order to determine whether methods and results are appropriate. Supervise and provide instructions

Conventional–S

for workers collecting and tabulating data. Apply sampling techniques or utilize complete enumeration bases in order to determine and define groups to be surveyed. Adapt statistical methods in order to solve specific problems in many fields, such as economics, biology, and engineering. Develop and test experimental designs, sampling techniques, and analytical methods. Examine theories, such as those of probability and inference, in order to discover mathematical bases for new or improved methods of obtaining and evaluating numerical data.

GOE—Interest Area/Cluster: 15. Scientific Research, Engineering, and Mathematics. **Work Group:** 15.06. Mathematics and Data Analysis. **Other Jobs in This Work Group:** Actuaries; Mathematical Technicians; Mathematicians; Social Science Research Assistants; Statistical Assistants.

Skills: Programming; Science; Mathematics; Writing; Active Learning; Negotiation; Complex Problem Solving; Operations Analysis.

Education and Training Programs: Biostatistics; Mathematics, General; Applied Mathematics; Statistics, General; Mathematical Statistics and Probability; Statistics, Other; Business Statistics. **Related Knowledge/Courses:** Mathematics; Computers and Electronics; English Language; Law and Government; Education and Training.

Work Environment: Indoors; sitting; using hands on objects, tools, or controls; repetitive motions.

Surveying and Mapping Technicians

See Mapping Technicians (a Conventional job) and Surveying Technicians (a Realistic job), described separately.

Tellers

* Personality Code: CE
* Education/Training Required: Short-term on-the-job training
* Annual Earnings: $22,920
* Beginning Wage: $17,360
* Earnings Growth Potential: Very low
* Growth: 13.5%
* Annual Job Openings: 146,077
* Self-Employed: 0.0%
* Part-Time: 27.1%

Receive and pay out money. Keep records of money and negotiable instruments involved in a financial institution's various transactions. Balance currency, coin, and checks in cash drawers at ends of shifts and calculate daily transactions, using computers, calculators, or adding machines. Cash checks and pay out money after verifying that signatures are correct, that written and numerical amounts agree, and that accounts have sufficient funds. Receive checks and cash for deposit, verify amounts, and check accuracy of deposit slips. Examine checks for endorsements and to verify other information such as dates, bank names, identification of the persons receiving payments, and the legality of the documents. Enter customers' transactions into computers to record transactions and issue computer-generated receipts. Count currency, coins, and checks received, by hand or using currency-counting machine, to prepare them for deposit or shipment to branch banks or the Federal Reserve Bank. Identify transaction mistakes when debits and credits do not balance. Prepare and verify cashier's checks. Arrange monies received in cash boxes and coin dispensers according to denomination. Process transactions such as term deposits, retirement savings plan contributions, automated teller transactions, night deposits, and mail deposits. Receive mortgage, loan, or public utility bill payments, verifying payment dates and amounts due. Resolve problems or discrepancies concerning customers' accounts. Explain, promote, or sell products or services such as travelers' checks, savings bonds, money orders, and cashier's checks, using computerized information about customers to tailor recommendations. Perform clerical tasks such as typing, filing, and microfilm photography. Monitor bank vaults to ensure cash balances are correct. Order a supply of cash to meet daily needs. Sort and file deposit slips and checks. Receive and count daily inventories of cash, drafts, and travelers' checks. Process and maintain records of customer loans. Count, verify, and post armored car deposits. Carry out special services for customers, such as ordering bank cards and checks. Compute financial fees, interest, and service charges. Obtain and process information required for the provision of services, such as opening accounts, savings plans, and purchasing bonds.

GOE—Interest Area/Cluster: 06. Finance and Insurance. **Work Group:** 06.04. Finance/Insurance Customer Service. **Other Jobs in This Work Group:** Bill and Account Collectors; Loan Interviewers and Clerks; New Accounts Clerks.

Skills: Service Orientation; Mathematics.

Education and Training Program: Banking and Financial Support Services. **Related Knowledge/Courses:** Customer and Personal Service; Sales and Marketing; English Language; Clerical Practices.

Work Environment: Indoors; more often standing than sitting; using hands on objects, tools, or controls; repetitive motions.

Treasurers and Controllers

* Personality Code: CE
* Education/Training Required: Work experience plus degree
* Annual Earnings: $95,310
* Beginning Wage: $51,910
* Earnings Growth Potential: High
* Growth: 12.6%
* Annual Job Openings: 57,589
* Self-Employed: 4.6%
* Part-Time: 4.2%

The job openings listed here are shared with Financial Managers, Branch or Department.

Direct financial activities, such as planning, procurement, and investments, for all or part of an organization. Prepare and file annual tax returns or prepare financial information so that outside accountants can complete tax returns. Prepare or direct preparation of financial statements, business activity reports, financial position forecasts, annual budgets, and/or reports required by regulatory agencies. Supervise employees performing financial reporting, accounting, billing, collections, payroll, and budgeting duties. Delegate authority for the receipt, disbursement, banking, protection, and custody of funds, securities, and financial instruments. Maintain current knowledge of organizational policies and procedures, federal and state policies and directives, and current accounting standards. Conduct or coordinate audits of company accounts and financial transactions to ensure compliance with state and federal requirements and statutes. Receive and record requests for disbursements; authorize disbursements in accordance with policies and procedures. Monitor financial activities and details such as reserve levels to ensure that all legal and regulatory requirements are met. Monitor and evaluate the performance of accounting and other financial staff; recommend and implement personnel actions such as promotions and dismissals. Develop and maintain relationships with banking, insurance, and non-organizational accounting personnel in order to facilitate financial activities. Coordinate and direct the financial planning, budgeting, procurement, or investment activities of all or part of an organization. Develop internal control policies, guidelines, and procedures for activities such as budget administration, cash and credit management, and accounting. Analyze the financial details of past, present, and expected operations in order to identify development opportunities and areas where improvement is needed. Advise management on short-term and long-term financial objectives, policies, and actions. Provide direction and assistance to other organizational units regarding accounting and budgeting policies and procedures and efficient control and utilization of financial resources. Evaluate needs for procurement of funds and investment of surpluses and make appropriate recommendations.

GOE—Interest Area/Cluster: 06. Finance and Insurance. **Work Group:** 06.01. Managerial Work in Finance and Insurance. **Other Jobs in This Work Group:** Financial Managers; Financial Managers, Branch or Department.

Skills: Management of Financial Resources; Management of Material Resources; Judgment and Decision Making; Management of Personnel Resources; Mathematics; Negotiation; Time Management; Persuasion.

Education and Training Programs: Accounting and Finance; Accounting and Business/Management; Finance, General; International Finance; Public Finance; Credit Management; Finance and Financial Management Services, Other. **Related Knowledge/Courses:** Economics and Accounting; Administration and Management; Personnel and Human Resources; Law and Government; Mathematics; English Language.

Work Environment: Indoors; sitting.

Web Administrators

- ❋ Personality Code: CEI
- ❋ Education/Training Required: Bachelor's degree
- ❋ Annual Earnings: $71,510
- ❋ Beginning Wage: $37,600
- ❋ Earnings Growth Potential: High
- ❋ Growth: 15.1%
- ❋ Annual Job Openings: 14,374
- ❋ Self-Employed: 6.6%
- ❋ Part-Time: 5.6%

The job openings listed here are shared with Computer Systems Engineers/Architects, with Network Designers, with Software Quality Assurance Engineers and Testers, and with Web Developers.

Manage Web environment design, deployment, development, and maintenance activities. Perform testing and quality assurance of Web sites and Web applications. Back up or modify applications and related data to provide for disaster recovery. Determine sources of Web page or server problems, and take action to correct such problems. Review or update Web page content or links in a timely manner, using appropriate tools. Monitor systems for intrusions or denial of service attacks, and report security breaches to appropriate personnel. Implement Web site security measures, such as firewalls or message encryption. Administer Internet/intranet infrastructure, including components such as Web, file transfer protocol (FTP), news, and mail servers. Collaborate with development teams to discuss, analyze, or resolve usability issues. Test backup or recovery plans regularly and resolve any problems. Monitor Web developments through continuing education, reading, or participation in professional conferences, workshops, or groups. Implement updates, upgrades, and patches in a timely manner to limit loss of service. Identify or document backup or recovery plans. Collaborate with Web developers to create and operate internal and external Web sites, or to manage projects, such as e-marketing campaigns. Install or configure Web server software or hardware to ensure that directory structure is well-defined, logical, secure, and that files are named properly. Gather, analyze, or document user feedback to locate or resolve sources of problems. Develop Web site performance metrics. Identify or address interoperability requirements. Document installation or configuration procedures to allow maintenance and repetition. Identify, standardize, and communicate levels of access and security. Track, compile, and analyze Web site usage data. Test issues such as system integration, performance, and system security on a regular schedule or after any major program modifications. Recommend Web site improvements, and develop budgets to support recommendations. Inform Web site users of problems, problem resolutions, or application changes and updates. Document application and Web site changes or change procedures. Develop or implement procedures for ongoing Web site revision.

GOE—Interest Area/Cluster: 11. Information Technology. **Work Group:** 11.02. Information Technology Specialties. **Other Jobs in This Work Group:** Computer and Information Scientists, Research; Computer Operators; Computer Programmers; Computer Security Specialists; Computer Software Engineers, Applications; Computer Software Engineers, Systems Software; Computer Support Specialists; Computer Systems Analysts; Computer Systems Engineers/Architects; Database Administrators; Network Designers; Network Systems and Data Communications Analysts; Software Quality Assurance Engineers and Testers; Web Developers.

Skills: Programming; Systems Evaluation; Systems Analysis; Troubleshooting; Operations Analysis; Technology Design; Installation; Equipment Selection.

Education and Training Programs: Computer and Information Sciences, General; Information Technology; Information Science/Studies; Computer Science; Web Page, Digital/Multimedia and Information Resources Design; Computer Systems Networking and Telecommunications; System, Networking, and LAN/WAN Management/Manager; Web/Multimedia Management and Webmaster; Computer and Information Sciences and Support Services, Other; E-Commerce/Electronic Commerce. **Related Knowledge/Courses:** Computers and Electronics; Telecommunications; Design; Communications and Media; Sales and Marketing; Engineering and Technology.

Work Environment: No data available.

Web Developers

- ❋ Personality Code: CIR
- ❋ Education/Training Required: Bachelor's degree
- ❋ Annual Earnings: $71,510
- ❋ Beginning Wage: $37,600
- ❋ Earnings Growth Potential: High
- ❋ Growth: 15.1%
- ❋ Annual Job Openings: 14,374
- ❋ Self-Employed: 6.6%
- ❋ Part-Time: 5.6%

The job openings listed here are shared with Computer Systems Engineers/Architects, with Network Designers, with Software Quality Assurance Engineers and Testers, and with Web Administrators.

Develop and design Web applications and Web sites. Create and specify architectural and technical parameters. Direct Web site content creation, enhancement, and maintenance. Design, build, or maintain Web sites, using authoring or scripting languages, content creation tools, management tools, and digital media. Perform or direct Web site updates. Write, design, or edit Web page content, or direct others producing content. Confer with management or development teams to prioritize needs, resolve conflicts, develop content criteria, or choose solutions. Back up files from Web sites to local directories for instant recovery in case of problems. Identify problems uncovered by testing or customer feedback, and correct problems or refer problems to appropriate personnel for correction. Evaluate code to ensure that it is valid, is properly structured, meets industry standards and is compatible with browsers, devices, or operating systems. Maintain understanding of current Web technologies or programming practices through continuing education, reading, or participation in professional conferences, workshops, or groups. Analyze user needs to determine technical requirements. Develop or validate test routines and schedules to ensure that test cases mimic external interfaces and address all browser and device types. Develop databases that support Web applications and Web sites. Renew domain name registrations. Collaborate with management or users to develop e-commerce strategies and to integrate these strategies with Web sites. Write supporting code for Web applications or Web sites. Communicate with network personnel or Web site hosting agencies to address hardware or software issues affecting Web sites. Design and implement Web site security measures such as firewalls or message encryption. Perform Web site tests according to planned schedules, or after any Web site or product revisions. Select programming languages, design tools, or applications. Incorporate technical considerations into Web site design plans, such as budgets, equipment, performance requirements, or legal issues including accessibility and privacy. Respond to user e-mail inquiries, or set up automated systems to send responses. Develop or implement procedures for ongoing Web site revision.

GOE—Interest Area/Cluster: 11. Information Technology. **Work Group:** 11.02. Information Technology Specialties. **Other Jobs in This Work Group:** Computer and Information Scientists, Research; Computer Operators; Computer Programmers; Computer Security Specialists; Computer Software Engineers, Applications; Computer Software Engineers, Systems Software; Computer Support Specialists; Computer Systems Analysts; Computer Systems Engineers/Architects; Database Administrators; Network Designers; Network Systems and Data Communications Analysts; Software Quality Assurance Engineers and Testers; Web Administrators.

Skills: Programming; Troubleshooting; Operations Analysis; Technology Design; Systems Evaluation; Quality Control Analysis; Systems Analysis; Complex Problem Solving.

Education and Training Programs: Computer and Information Sciences, General; Information Technology; Information Science/Studies; Computer Science; Web Page, Digital/Multimedia and Information Resources Design; Computer Systems Networking and Telecommunications; System, Networking, and LAN/WAN Management/Manager; Web/Multimedia Management and Webmaster; Computer and Information Sciences and Support Services, Other; E-Commerce/Electronic Commerce. **Related Knowledge/Courses:** Computers and Electronics; Design; Sales and Marketing; Communications and Media; Telecommunications; Clerical Practices.

Work Environment: No data available.

APPENDIX A

Occupations Ordered by Two-Letter Personality Codes

This listing is based on the coding used by the O*NET database of the U.S. Department of Labor. It also includes some SOC titles that are not included in the O*NET database; we determined their RIASEC codes by taking the *average* of the ratings for the equivalent O*NET jobs. Other publishers may not create the exact same set of linkages between personality codes and occupations. For example, some sales jobs that are coded as Social by Psychological Assessment Resources, Inc., the publisher of the *Self-Directed Search,* are coded as Enterprising by O*NET.

Realistic

Personality Code	Job
R	Automotive Body and Related Repairers
R	Sheet Metal Workers
RA	Camera Operators, Television, Video, and Motion Picture
RC	Aircraft Structure, Surfaces, Rigging, and Systems Assemblers
RC	Boilermakers
RC	Bus and Truck Mechanics and Diesel Engine Specialists
RC	Drywall and Ceiling Tile Installers
RC	Freight and Cargo Inspectors
RC	Heating, Air Conditioning, and Refrigeration Mechanics and Installers
RC	Mobile Heavy Equipment Mechanics, Except Engines
RC	Painters, Construction and Maintenance

Personality Code	Job
RC	Pipe Fitters and Steamfitters
RC	Plumbers, Pipefitters, and Steamfitters
RC	Radiologic Technicians
RC	Roofers
RC	Sailors and Marine Oilers
RC	Security and Fire Alarm Systems Installers
RC	Surveying Technicians
RC	Truck Drivers, Heavy and Tractor-Trailer
RC	Water and Liquid Waste Treatment Plant and System Operators
RCA	Architectural and Civil Drafters
RCA	Tile and Marble Setters
RCE	Refrigeration Mechanics and Installers
RCI	Aircraft Mechanics and Service Technicians

Personality Code	Job
RCI	Airline Pilots, Copilots, and Flight Engineers
RCI	Aviation Inspectors
RCI	Brickmasons and Blockmasons
RCI	Carpenters
RCI	Civil Drafters
RCI	Civil Engineering Technicians
RCI	Construction and Building Inspectors
RCI	Construction Carpenters
RCI	Heating and Air Conditioning Mechanics and Installers
RCI	Maintenance and Repair Workers, General
RCI	Mechanical Drafters
RCI	Operating Engineers and Other Construction Equipment Operators
RCI	Pilots, Ship
RCI	Plumbers
RCI	Rough Carpenters
RCI	Surveyors
RCI	Transportation Inspectors
RCI	Transportation Vehicle, Equipment, and Systems Inspectors, Except Aviation
RE	Athletes and Sports Competitors
RE	Cement Masons and Concrete Finishers
RE	Telecommunications Line Installers and Repairers
REC	Captains, Mates, and Pilots of Water Vessels
REC	Correctional Officers and Jailers
RI	Automotive Master Mechanics
RI	Automotive Service Technicians and Mechanics
RI	Electronics Engineering Technicians
RIC	Audio and Video Equipment Technicians
RIC	Automotive Specialty Technicians

Personality Code	Job
RIC	Biological Technicians
RIC	Cartographers and Photogrammetrists
RIC	Civil Engineers
RIC	Computer Support Specialists
RIC	Electrical and Electronic Engineering Technicians
RIC	Electrical Engineering Technicians
RIC	Electrical Power-Line Installers and Repairers
RIC	Electricians
RIC	Industrial Machinery Mechanics
RIC	Medical and Clinical Laboratory Technicians
RIC	Telecommunications Equipment Installers and Repairers, Except Line Installers
RIS	Cardiovascular Technologists and Technicians
RS	Bus Drivers, Transit and Intercity
RS	Fire Fighters
RS	Radiologic Technologists
RS	Radiologic Technologists and Technicians
RSC	Surgical Technologists
RSE	Municipal Fire Fighters

Investigative

Personality Code	Job
IA	Anthropologists
IA	Anthropologists and Archeologists
IAR	Astronomers
IAR	Biochemists and Biophysicists
IAS	Political Scientists
IAS	Sociologists
IC	Network Systems and Data Communications Analysts
ICA	Mathematicians

Personality Code	Job
ICE	Industrial Engineers
ICE	Operations Research Analysts
ICE	Survey Researchers
ICR	Computer Software Engineers, Systems Software
ICR	Computer Systems Analysts
ICR	Software Quality Assurance Engineers and Testers
ICS	Pharmacists
IEA	Industrial-Organizational Psychologists
IEC	Management Analysts
IEC	Market Research Analysts
IR	Aerospace Engineers
IR	Atmospheric and Space Scientists
IR	Biomedical Engineers
IR	Chemical Engineers
IR	Electrical Engineers
IR	Electronics Engineers, Except Computer
IR	Geoscientists, Except Hydrologists and Geographers
IR	Hydrologists
IR	Physicists
IR	Prosthodontists
IR	Veterinarians
IRA	Archeologists
IRA	Medical Scientists, Except Epidemiologists
IRC	Chemists
IRC	Computer and Information Scientists, Research
IRC	Computer Hardware Engineers
IRC	Computer Software Engineers, Applications
IRC	Computer Systems Engineers/ Architects
IRC	Coroners
IRC	Environmental Engineers
IRC	Environmental Science and Protection Technicians, Including Health

Personality Code	Job
IRC	Environmental Scientists and Specialists, Including Health
IRC	Forensic Science Technicians
IRC	Mechanical Engineers
IRC	Medical and Clinical Laboratory Technologists
IRC	Network and Computer Systems Administrators
IRS	Anesthesiologists
IRS	Dentists, General
IRS	Engineering Teachers, Postsecondary
IRS	Nuclear Medicine Technologists
IRS	Orthodontists
IRS	Surgeons
IS	Family and General Practitioners
IS	Pediatricians, General
IS	School Psychologists
ISA	Clinical Psychologists
ISA	Clinical, Counseling, and School Psychologists
ISA	Psychiatrists
ISR	Diagnostic Medical Sonographers
ISR	Internists, General
ISR	Obstetricians and Gynecologists
ISR	Optometrists
ISR	Podiatrists

Artistic

Personality Code	Job
AE	Art Directors
AE	Interior Designers
AE	Music Composers and Arrangers
AE	Music Directors and Composers
AEC	Editors
AEI	Film and Video Editors
AEI	Writers and Authors
AER	Commercial and Industrial Designers

Personality Code	Job
AER	Fashion Designers
AER	Merchandise Displayers and Window Trimmers
AES	Hairdressers, Hairstylists, and Cosmetologists
AES	Music Directors
AI	Architects, Except Landscape and Naval
AI	Multi-Media Artists and Animators
AI	Poets, Lyricists, and Creative Writers
AIC	Technical Writers
AIR	Landscape Architects
AR	Fine Artists, Including Painters, Sculptors, and Illustrators
AR	Makeup Artists, Theatrical and Performance
AR	Photographers
AR	Set and Exhibit Designers
ARE	Graphic Designers
ARI	Architectural Drafters
AS	Interpreters and Translators
ASE	Broadcast News Analysts

Social

Personality Code	Job
S	Recreation and Fitness Studies Teachers, Postsecondary
SA	Architecture Teachers, Postsecondary
SA	Art, Drama, and Music Teachers, Postsecondary
SA	Communications Teachers, Postsecondary
SA	Kindergarten Teachers, Except Special Education
SA	Middle School Teachers, Except Special and Vocational Education
SA	Preschool Teachers, Except Special Education

Personality Code	Job
SA	Special Education Teachers, Middle School
SA	Special Education Teachers, Preschool, Kindergarten, and Elementary School
SAC	Elementary School Teachers, Except Special Education
SAC	Training and Development Specialists
SAE	Adult Literacy, Remedial Education, and GED Teachers and Instructors
SAE	Secondary School Teachers, Except Special and Vocational Education
SAE	Self-Enrichment Education Teachers
SAI	Education Teachers, Postsecondary
SAI	English Language and Literature Teachers, Postsecondary
SAI	Foreign Language and Literature Teachers, Postsecondary
SAI	Marriage and Family Therapists
SAI	Philosophy and Religion Teachers, Postsecondary
SAI	Substance Abuse and Behavioral Disorder Counselors
SC	Graduate Teaching Assistants
SCR	Medical Assistants
SE	Health Educators
SEA	Political Science Teachers, Postsecondary
SEC	Education Administrators, Preschool and Child Care Center/Program
SEC	Equal Opportunity Representatives and Officers
SEI	Business Teachers, Postsecondary
SI	Anthropology and Archeology Teachers, Postsecondary

Personality Code	Job
SI	Atmospheric, Earth, Marine, and Space Sciences Teachers, Postsecondary
SI	Biological Science Teachers, Postsecondary
SI	Economics Teachers, Postsecondary
SI	Health Specialties Teachers, Postsecondary
SI	Medical and Public Health Social Workers
SI	Nursing Instructors and Teachers, Postsecondary
SI	Occupational Therapists
SI	Physics Teachers, Postsecondary
SI	Rehabilitation Counselors
SIA	Counseling Psychologists
SIA	Environmental Science Teachers, Postsecondary
SIA	History Teachers, Postsecondary
SIA	Mathematical Science Teachers, Postsecondary
SIA	Mental Health and Substance Abuse Social Workers
SIA	Mental Health Counselors
SIA	Psychology Teachers, Postsecondary
SIA	Sociology Teachers, Postsecondary
SIC	Computer Science Teachers, Postsecondary
SIC	Registered Nurses
SIE	Instructional Coordinators
SIE	Law Teachers, Postsecondary
SIR	Agricultural Sciences Teachers, Postsecondary
SIR	Chemistry Teachers, Postsecondary
SIR	Physical Therapists
SIR	Physician Assistants
SR	Vocational Education Teachers, Postsecondary

Personality Code	Job
SRC	Dental Hygienists
SRC	Radiation Therapists
SRE	Fitness Trainers and Aerobics Instructors
SRI	Physical Therapist Assistants

Enterprising

Personality Code	Job
EA	Copy Writers
EA	Directors—Stage, Motion Pictures, Television, and Radio
EA	Producers
EA	Public Relations Managers
EA	Talent Directors
EAC	Advertising and Promotions Managers
EAC	Producers and Directors
EAS	Public Relations Specialists
EC	Administrative Services Managers
EC	Air Traffic Controllers
EC	Chief Executives
EC	Financial Managers
EC	Financial Managers, Branch or Department
EC	Gaming Managers
EC	Gaming Supervisors
EC	Logisticians
EC	Marketing Managers
EC	Property, Real Estate, and Community Association Managers
EC	Real Estate Brokers
EC	Real Estate Sales Agents
EC	Sales Agents, Financial Services
EC	Sales Agents, Securities and Commodities
EC	Sales Managers
EC	Securities, Commodities, and Financial Services Sales Agents
ECA	Advertising Sales Agents

Personality Code	Job
ECA	Program Directors
ECI	Computer and Information Systems Managers
ECR	Appraisers, Real Estate
ECR	Demonstrators and Product Promoters
ECR	Detectives and Criminal Investigators
ECR	First-Line Supervisors/Managers of Food Preparation and Serving Workers
ECR	First-Line Supervisors/Managers of Housekeeping and Janitorial Workers
ECR	Food Service Managers
ECS	Compensation and Benefits Managers
ECS	Education Administrators, Postsecondary
ECS	First-Line Supervisors/Managers of Non-Retail Sales Workers
ECS	First-Line Supervisors/Managers of Office and Administrative Support Workers
ECS	First-Line Supervisors/Managers of Personal Service Workers
ECS	General and Operations Managers
ECS	Insurance Sales Agents
ECS	Medical and Health Services Managers
ECS	Meeting and Convention Planners
ECS	Personal Financial Advisors
EI	Criminal Investigators and Special Agents
EI	Lawyers
EI	Natural Sciences Managers
EI	Police Detectives
ER	Ship and Boat Captains
ERC	Construction Managers
ERC	First-Line Supervisors/Managers of Construction Trades and Extraction Workers
ERC	First-Line Supervisors/Managers of Landscaping, Lawn Service, and Groundskeeping Workers
ERC	Mates—Ship, Boat, and Barge
ERC	Technical Directors/Managers
ERI	Engineering Managers
ERI	Sales Engineers
ERS	Police and Sheriff's Patrol Officers
ERS	Sheriffs and Deputy Sheriffs
ES	Social and Community Service Managers
ES	Training and Development Managers
ESC	Customer Service Representatives
ESC	Directors, Religious Activities and Education
ESC	Education Administrators, Elementary and Secondary School
ESC	Employment Interviewers
ESC	Employment, Recruitment, and Placement Specialists
ESC	First-Line Supervisors/Managers of Police and Detectives
ESC	Flight Attendants
ESC	Personnel Recruiters

Conventional

Personality Code	Job
CE	Accountants
CE	Appraisers and Assessors of Real Estate
CE	Bill and Account Collectors
CE	Billing and Posting Clerks and Machine Operators
CE	Billing, Cost, and Rate Clerks
CE	Bookkeeping, Accounting, and Auditing Clerks
CE	Brokerage Clerks

Personality Code	Job
CE	Claims Adjusters, Examiners, and Investigators
CE	Claims Examiners, Property and Casualty Insurance
CE	Compensation, Benefits, and Job Analysis Specialists
CE	Cost Estimators
CE	Court Reporters
CE	Court, Municipal, and License Clerks
CE	Executive Secretaries and Administrative Assistants
CE	Insurance Adjusters, Examiners, and Investigators
CE	Insurance Claims and Policy Processing Clerks
CE	Insurance Claims Clerks
CE	Insurance Policy Processing Clerks
CE	Legal Secretaries
CE	License Clerks
CE	Licensing Examiners and Inspectors
CE	Loan Interviewers and Clerks
CE	Medical Records and Health Information Technicians
CE	Municipal Clerks
CE	Production, Planning, and Expediting Clerks
CE	Purchasing Agents, Except Wholesale, Retail, and Farm Products
CE	Sales Representatives, Wholesale and Manufacturing, Except Technical and Scientific Products
CE	Secretaries, Except Legal, Medical, and Executive
CE	Tellers
CE	Treasurers and Controllers
CEI	Accountants and Auditors
CEI	Assessors
CEI	Auditors

Personality Code	Job
CEI	Budget Analysts
CEI	Compliance Officers, Except Agriculture, Construction, Health and Safety, and Transportation
CEI	Insurance Underwriters
CEI	Web Administrators
CER	Cargo and Freight Agents
CER	Court Clerks
CER	Government Property Inspectors and Investigators
CER	Immigration and Customs Inspectors
CER	Office Clerks, General
CES	Human Resources Assistants, Except Payroll and Timekeeping
CES	Interviewers, Except Eligibility and Loan
CES	Loan Officers
CES	Receptionists and Information Clerks
CES	Statement Clerks
CI	Archivists
CI	Database Administrators
CI	Statisticians
CIE	Actuaries
CIE	Financial Analysts
CIE	Paralegals and Legal Assistants
CIR	Computer Security Specialists
CIR	Computer Specialists, All Other
CIR	Environmental Compliance Inspectors
CIR	Network Designers
CIR	Web Developers
CR	Mapping Technicians
CR	Medical Transcriptionists
CR	Occupational Health and Safety Technicians
CR	Pharmacy Technicians
CR	Postal Service Mail Carriers
CR	Surveying and Mapping Technicians

Personality Code	Job
CRE	Billing, Posting, and Calculating Machine Operators
CRE	Dispatchers, Except Police, Fire, and Ambulance
CRE	Insurance Appraisers, Auto Damage
CRE	Police, Fire, and Ambulance Dispatchers
CRE	Shipping, Receiving, and Traffic Clerks
CRI	Police Identification and Records Officers
CRS	Dental Assistants
CS	Medical Secretaries
CSE	Librarians
CSE	Social and Human Service Assistants

APPENDIX B

The Guide for Occupational Exploration (GOE) Interest Areas and Work Groups

The RIASEC classification that this book uses to organizes occupations was originally developed as a way of interpreting the results of an interest inventory. However, it is not the only interest-based way of classifying jobs. The Guide for Occupational Exploration (GOE) was developed by the U.S. Department of Labor as an intuitive way to assist in career exploration. In the *New Guide for Occupational Exploration*, Fourth Edition, JIST revised the GOE scheme to match the 16 career clusters that the U.S. Department of Education's Office of Vocational and Adult Education developed around 1999 and that many states now use to organize their career-oriented programs and career information.

The GOE structure organizes the world of work into large interest areas (or clusters) and more specific work groups containing jobs that have a lot in common. This appendix defines the 16 GOE interest areas and lists the work groups included in each interest area. We thought you would want to see the complete GOE taxonomy so you would understand how any job that interests you fits into this structure.

Interest areas have two-digit code numbers; work groups have four-digit code numbers beginning with the code number for the interest area in which they are classified. These are the 16 GOE interest areas and their work groups:

01 Agriculture and Natural Resources: *An interest in working with plants, animals, forests, or mineral resources for agriculture, horticulture, conservation, extraction, and other purposes.* You can satisfy this interest by working in farming, landscaping, forestry, fishing, mining, and related fields. You may like doing physical work outdoors, such as on a farm or ranch, in a forest, or on a drilling rig. If you have a scientific curiosity, you could study plants and animals or analyze biological or rock samples in a lab. If you have management

ability, you could own, operate, or manage a fish hatchery, a landscaping business, or a greenhouse.

01.01 Managerial Work in Agriculture and Natural Resources

01.02 Resource Science/Engineering for Plants, Animals, and the Environment

01.03 Resource Technologies for Plants, Animals, and the Environment

01.04 General Farming

01.05 Nursery, Groundskeeping, and Pest Control

01.06 Forestry and Logging

01.07 Hunting and Fishing

01.08 Mining and Drilling

02 Architecture and Construction: *An interest in designing, assembling, and maintaining components of buildings and other structures.* You may want to be part of the team of architects, drafters, and others who design buildings and render the plans. If construction interests you, you might find fulfillment in the many building projects being undertaken at all times. If you like to organize and plan, you can find careers in managing these projects. Or you can play a more direct role in putting up and finishing buildings by doing jobs such as plumbing, carpentry, masonry, painting, or roofing, either as a skilled craftsworker or as a helper. You can prepare the building site by operating heavy equipment or installing, maintaining, and repairing vital building equipment and systems such as electricity and heating.

02.01 Managerial Work in Architecture and Construction

02.02 Architectural Design

02.03 Architecture/Construction Engineering Technologies

02.04 Construction Crafts

02.05 Systems and Equipment Installation, Maintenance, and Repair

02.06 Construction Support/Labor

03 Arts and Communication: *An interest in creatively expressing feelings or ideas, in communicating news or information, or in performing.* You can satisfy this interest in creative, verbal, or performing activities. For example, if you enjoy literature, perhaps writing or editing would appeal to you. Journalism and public relations are other fields for people who like to use their writing or speaking skills. Do you prefer to work in the performing arts? If so, you could direct or perform in drama, music, or dance. If you especially enjoy the visual arts, you could create paintings, sculpture, or ceramics or design products or visual displays. A flair for technology might lead you to specialize in photography, broadcast production, or dispatching.

03.01 Managerial Work in Arts and Communication

03.02 Writing and Editing

03.03 News, Broadcasting, and Public Relations

03.04 Studio Art

03.05 Design

03.06 Drama

03.07 Music

03.08 Dance

03.09 Media Technology

03.10 Communications Technology

03.11 Musical Instrument Repair

04 Business and Administration: *An interest in making a business organization or function run smoothly.* You can satisfy this interest by working in a position of leadership or by specializing in a function that contributes to the overall effort in a business, a nonprofit organization, or a government agency. If you especially enjoy working with people, you may find fulfillment from working in human resources. An interest in numbers may lead you to consider accounting, finance, budgeting, billing, or financial record-keeping. A job as an administrative assistant may interest you if you like a variety of tasks in a busy environment. If you are good with details and word processing, you may enjoy a job as a secretary or data-entry clerk. Or perhaps you would do well as the manager of a business.

04.01 Managerial Work in General Business

04.02 Managerial Work in Business Detail

04.03 Human Resources Support

04.04 Secretarial Support

04.05 Accounting, Auditing, and Analytical Support

04.06 Mathematical Clerical Support

04.07 Records and Materials Processing

04.08 Clerical Machine Operation

05 Education and Training: *An interest in helping people learn.* You can satisfy this interest by teaching students, who may be preschoolers, retirees, or any age in between. You may specialize in a particular academic field or work with learners of a particular age, with a particular interest, or with a particular learning problem. Working in a library or museum may give you an opportunity to expand people's understanding of the world.

05.01 Managerial Work in Education

05.02 Preschool, Elementary, and Secondary Teaching and Instructing

05.03 Postsecondary and Adult Teaching and Instructing

05.04 Library Services

05.05 Archival and Museum Services

05.06 Counseling, Health, and Fitness Education

06 Finance and Insurance: *An interest in helping businesses and people be assured of a financially secure future.* You can satisfy this interest by working in a financial or insurance business in a leadership

or support role. If you like gathering and analyzing information, you may find fulfillment as an insurance adjuster or financial analyst. Or you may deal with information at the clerical level as a banking or insurance clerk or in person-to-person situations providing customer service. Another way to interact with people is to sell financial or insurance services that will meet their needs.

06.01 Managerial Work in Finance and Insurance

06.02 Finance/Insurance Investigation and Analysis

06.03 Finance/Insurance Records Processing

06.04 Finance/Insurance Customer Service

06.05 Finance/Insurance Sales and Support

07 Government and Public Administration: *An interest in helping a government agency serve the needs of the public.* You can satisfy this interest by working in a position of leadership or by specializing in a function that contributes to the role of government. You may help protect the public by working as an inspector or examiner to enforce standards. If you enjoy using clerical skills, you could work as a clerk in a law court or government office. Or perhaps you prefer the top-down perspective of a government executive or urban planner.

07.01 Managerial Work in Government and Public Administration

07.02 Public Planning

07.03 Regulations Enforcement

07.04 Public Administration Clerical Support

08 Health Science: *An interest in helping people and animals be healthy.* You can satisfy this interest by working on a health-care team as a doctor, therapist, or nurse. You might specialize in one of the many different parts of the body (such as the teeth or eyes) or in one of the many different types of care. Or you may want to be a generalist who deals with the whole patient. If you like technology, you might find satisfaction working with X rays or new diagnostic methods. You might work with healthy people, helping them eat right. If you enjoy working with animals, you might care for them and keep them healthy.

08.01 Managerial Work in Medical and Health Services

08.02 Medicine and Surgery

08.03 Dentistry

08.04 Health Specialties

08.05 Animal Care

08.06 Medical Technology

08.07 Medical Therapy

08.08 Patient Care and Assistance

08.09 Health Protection and Promotion

09 Hospitality, Tourism, and Recreation: *An interest in catering to the personal wishes and needs of others so that they can enjoy a clean environment, good food and drink, comfortable lodging away from home, and recreation.* You can satisfy this interest by providing services for the convenience, care, and pampering of others in hotels, restaurants, airplanes, beauty parlors, and so on. You may want to use your love of cooking as a chef. If you like working with people, you may want to provide personal services by being a travel guide, a flight attendant, a concierge, a hairdresser, or a waiter. You may want to work in cleaning and building services if you like a clean environment. If you enjoy sports or games, you could work for an athletic team or casino.

09.01 Managerial Work in Hospitality and Tourism

09.02 Recreational Services

09.03 Hospitality and Travel Services

09.04 Food and Beverage Preparation

09.05 Food and Beverage Service

09.06 Sports

09.07 Barber and Beauty Services

10 Human Service: *An interest in improving people's social, mental, emotional, or spiritual well-being.* You can satisfy this interest as a counselor, social worker, or religious worker who helps people sort out their complicated lives or solve personal problems. You may work as a caretaker for very young people or the elderly. Or you may interview people to help identify the social services they need.

10.01 Counseling and Social Work

10.02 Religious Work

10.03 Child/Personal Care and Services

10.04 Client Interviewing

11 Information Technology: *An interest in designing, developing, managing, and supporting information systems.* You can satisfy this interest by working with hardware, software, multimedia, or integrated systems. If you like to use your organizational skills, you might work as a systems or database administrator. Or you can solve complex problems as a software engineer or systems analyst. If you enjoy getting your hands on hardware, you might find work servicing computers, peripherals, and information-intense machines such as cash registers and ATMs.

11.01 Managerial Work in Information Technology

11.02 Information Technology Specialties

11.03 Digital Equipment Repair

12 Law and Public Safety: *An interest in upholding people's rights or in protecting people and property by using authority, inspecting, or investigating.* You can satisfy this interest by working in law, law enforcement, fire fighting, the military, and related fields. For example, if you enjoy mental challenge and intrigue, you could investigate crimes or fires for a living. If you

enjoy working with verbal skills and research skills, you may want to defend citizens in court or research deeds, wills, and other legal documents. If you want to help people in critical situations, you may want to fight fires, work as a police officer, or become a paramedic. Or, if you want more routine work in public safety, perhaps a job in guarding, patrolling, or inspecting would appeal to you. If you have management ability, you could seek a leadership position in law enforcement and the protective services. Work in the military gives you a chance to use technical and leadership skills while serving your country.

12.01 Managerial Work in Law and Public Safety

12.02 Legal Practice and Justice Administration

12.03 Legal Support

12.04 Law Enforcement and Public Safety

12.05 Safety and Security

12.06 Emergency Responding

12.07 Military

13 Manufacturing: *An interest in processing materials into intermediate or final products or maintaining and repairing products by using machines or hand tools.* You can satisfy this interest by working in one of many industries that mass-produce goods or by working for a utility that distributes electric power or other resources. You might enjoy manual work, using your hands or hand tools in highly skilled jobs such as assembling engines or electronic equipment. If you enjoy making machines run efficiently or fixing them when they break down, you could seek a job installing or repairing such devices as copiers, aircraft engines, cars, or watches. Perhaps you prefer to set up or operate machines used to manufacture products made of food, glass, or paper. You could enjoy cutting and grinding metal and plastic parts to desired shapes and measurements. Or you may want to operate equipment in systems that provide water and process wastewater. You may like inspecting, sorting, counting, or weighing products. Another option is to work with your hands and machinery to move boxes and freight in a warehouse. If leadership appeals to you, you could manage people engaged in production and repair.

13.01 Managerial Work in Manufacturing

13.02 Machine Setup and Operation

13.03 Production Work, Assorted Materials Processing

13.04 Welding, Brazing, and Soldering

13.05 Production Machining Technology

13.06 Production Precision Work

13.07 Production Quality Control

13.08 Graphic Arts Production

13.09 Hands-On Work, Assorted Materials

13.10 Woodworking Technology

13.11 Apparel, Shoes, Leather, and Fabric Care

13.12 Electrical and Electronic Repair

13.13 Machinery Repair

13.14 Vehicle and Facility Mechanical Work

13.15 Medical and Technical Equipment Repair

13.16 Utility Operation and Energy Distribution

13.17 Loading, Moving, Hoisting, and Conveying

14 Retail and Wholesale Sales and Service: *An interest in bringing others to a particular point of view by personal persuasion and by sales and promotional techniques.* You can satisfy this interest in various jobs that involve persuasion and selling. If you like using knowledge of science, you may enjoy selling pharmaceutical, medical, or electronic products or services. Real estate offers several kinds of sales jobs as well. If you like speaking on the phone, you could work as a telemarketer. Or you may enjoy selling apparel and other merchandise in a retail setting. If you prefer to help people, you may want a job in customer service.

14.01 Managerial Work in Retail/Wholesale Sales and Service

14.02 Technical Sales

14.03 General Sales

14.04 Personal Soliciting

14.05 Purchasing

14.06 Customer Service

15 Scientific Research, Engineering, and Mathematics: *An interest in discovering, collecting, and analyzing information about the natural world; in applying scientific research findings to problems in medicine, the life sciences, human behavior, and the natural sciences; in imagining and manipulating quantitative data; and in applying technology to manufacturing, transportation, and other economic activities.* You can satisfy this interest by working with the knowledge and processes of the sciences. You may enjoy researching and developing new knowledge in mathematics, or perhaps solving problems in the physical, life, or social sciences would appeal to you. You may want to study engineering and help create new machines, processes, and structures. If you want to work with scientific equipment and procedures, you could seek a job in a research or testing laboratory.

15.01 Managerial Work in Scientific Research, Engineering, and Mathematics

15.02 Physical Sciences

15.03 Life Sciences

15.04 Social Sciences

15.05 Physical Science Laboratory Technology

15.06 Mathematics and Data Analysis

15.07 Research and Design Engineering

15.08 Industrial and Safety Engineering

15.09 Engineering Technology

16 Transportation, Distribution, and Logistics: *An interest in operations that move people or materials.* You can satisfy this interest by managing a transportation service, by helping vehicles keep on their assigned schedules and routes, or by driving or piloting a vehicle. If you enjoy taking responsibility, perhaps managing a rail line would appeal to you. If you work well with details and can take pressure on the job, you might consider being an air traffic controller. Or would you rather get out on the highway, on the water, or up in the air? If so, you could drive a truck from state to state, be employed on a ship, or fly a crop duster over a cornfield. If you prefer to stay closer to home, you could drive a delivery van, taxi, or school bus. You can use your physical strength to load freight and arrange it so that it gets to its destination in one piece.

16.01 Managerial Work in Transportation

16.02 Air Vehicle Operation

16.03 Truck Driving

16.04 Rail Vehicle Operation

16.05 Water Vehicle Operation

16.06 Other Services Requiring Driving

16.07 Transportation Support Work

APPENDIX C

Definitions of Skills and Knowledge/Courses

I n the Part IV job descriptions, you can see the top skills and types of knowledge required by each job.

Definitions of Skills

Because some of the skill names may not be completely familiar to you, we present here the definitions of all the skills referred to in this book.

Skill Name	Definition
Active Learning	Understanding the implications of new information for both current and future problem-solving and decision-making.
Active Listening	Giving full attention to what other people are saying, taking time to understand the points being made, asking questions as appropriate, and not interrupting at inappropriate times.
Complex Problem Solving	Identifying complex problems and reviewing related information to develop and evaluate options and implement solutions.
Coordination	Adjusting actions in relation to others' actions.
Critical Thinking	Using logic and reasoning to identify the strengths and weaknesses of alternative solutions, conclusions, or approaches to problems.
Installation	Installing equipment, machines, wiring, or programs to meet specifications.
Instructing	Teaching others how to do something.
Judgment and Decision Making	Considering the relative costs and benefits of potential actions to choose the most appropriate one.
Learning Strategies	Selecting and using training/instructional methods and procedures appropriate for the situation when learning or teaching new things.

467

Skill Name	Definition
Management of Financial Resources	Determining how money will be spent to get the work done and accounting for these expenditures.
Management of Material Resources	Obtaining and seeing to the appropriate use of equipment, facilities, and materials needed to do certain work.
Management of Personnel Resources	Motivating, developing, and directing people as they work; identifying the best people for the job.
Mathematics	Using mathematics to solve problems.
Monitoring	Monitoring/assessing your performance and that of other individuals or organizations to make improvements or take corrective action.
Negotiation	Bringing others together and trying to reconcile differences.
Operations Analysis	Analyzing needs and product requirements to create a design.
Persuasion	Persuading others to change their minds or behavior.
Programming	Writing computer programs for various purposes.
Quality Control Analysis	Conducting tests and inspections of products, services, or processes to evaluate quality or performance.
Reading Comprehension	Understanding written sentences and paragraphs in work-related documents.
Science	Using scientific rules and methods to solve problems.
Service Orientation	Actively looking for ways to help people.
Social Perceptiveness	Being aware of others' reactions and understanding why they react as they do.
Speaking	Talking to others to convey information effectively.
Systems Analysis	Determining how a system should work and how changes in conditions, operations, and the environment will affect outcomes.
Systems Evaluation	Identifying measures or indicators of system performance and the actions needed to improve or correct performance relative to the goals of the system.
Technology Design	Generating or adapting equipment and technology to serve user needs.
Time Management	Managing one's own time and the time of others.
Troubleshooting	Determining causes of operating errors and deciding what to do about them.
Writing	Communicating effectively in writing as appropriate for the needs of the audience.

Definitions of Knowledge/Courses

Each job description lists certain kinds of knowledge that are used on the job. These may also be thought of as the content of the courses that you take as part of your education or training for the job. Here is how the terms are defined.

Knowledge/Course Name	Definition
Administration and Management	Knowledge of principles and processes involved in business and organizational planning, coordination, and execution. This includes strategic planning, resource allocation, manpower modeling, leadership techniques, and production methods.
Biology	Knowledge of plant and animal living tissue, cells, organisms, and entities, including their functions, interdependencies, and interactions with each other and the environment.
Building and Construction	Knowledge of the materials, methods, and appropriate tools to construct objects, structures, and buildings.
Chemistry	Knowledge of the composition, structure, and properties of substances and of the chemical processes and transformations that they undergo. This includes uses of chemicals and their interactions, danger signs, production techniques, and disposal methods.
Clerical Studies	Knowledge of administrative and clerical procedures and systems such as word-processing systems, filing and records management systems, stenography and transcription, forms, design principles, and other office procedures and terminology.
Communications and Media	Knowledge of media production, communication, and dissemination techniques and methods, including alternative ways to inform and entertain via written, oral, and visual media.
Computers and Electronics	Knowledge of electric circuit boards, processors, chips, and computer hardware and software, including applications and programming.
Customer and Personal Service	Knowledge of principles and processes for providing customer and personal services, including needs assessment techniques, quality service standards, alternative delivery systems, and customer satisfaction evaluation techniques.
Design	Knowledge of design techniques, principles, tools, and instruments involved in the production and use of precision technical plans, blueprints, drawings, and models.
Economics and Accounting	Knowledge of economic and accounting principles and practices, the financial markets, banking, and the analysis and reporting of financial data.

Skill Name	Definition
Education and Training	Knowledge of instructional methods and training techniques, including curriculum design principles, learning theory, group and individual teaching techniques, design of individual development plans, and test design principles.
Engineering and Technology	Knowledge of equipment, tools, and mechanical devices and their uses to produce motion, light, power, technology, and other applications.
English Language	Knowledge of the structure and content of the English language, including the meaning and spelling of words, rules of composition, and grammar.
Fine Arts	Knowledge of theory and techniques required to produce, compose, and perform works of music, dance, visual arts, drama, and sculpture.
Food Production	Knowledge of techniques and equipment for planting, growing, and harvesting of food for consumption, including crop rotation methods, animal husbandry, and food storage/handling techhniques.
Foreign Language	Knowledge of the structure and content of a foreign (non-English) language, including the meaning and spelling of words, rules of composition and grammar, and pronunciation.
Geography	Knowledge of various methods for describing the location and distribution of land, sea, and air masses, including their physical locations, relationships, and characteristics.
History and Archeology	Knowledge of past historical events and their causes, indicators, and impact on particular civilizations and cultures.
Law and Government	Knowledge of laws, legal codes, court procedures, precedents, government regulations, executive orders, agency rules, and the democratic political process.
Mathematics	Knowledge of numbers and their operations and interrelationships, including arithmetic, algebra, geometry, calculus, and statistics and their applications.
Mechanical Devices	Knowledge of machines and tools, including their designs, uses, benefits, repair, and maintenance.
Medicine and Dentistry	Knowledge of the information and techniques needed to diagnose and treat injuries, diseases, and deformities. This includes symptoms, treatment alternatives, drug properties and interactions, and preventive health-care measures.

Skill Name	Definition
Personnel and Human Resources	Knowledge of policies and practices involved in personnel/human resource functions. This includes recruitment, selection, training, and promotion regulations and procedures; compensation and benefits packages; labor relations and negotiation strategies; and personnel information systems.
Philosophy and Theology	Knowledge of different philosophical systems and religions, including their basic principles, values, ethics, ways of thinking, customs, and practices and their impact on human culture.
Physics	Knowledge and prediction of physical principles, laws, and applications, including air, water, material dynamics, light, atomic principles, heat, electric theory, earth formations, and meteorological and related natural phenomena.
Production and Processing	Knowledge of inputs, outputs, raw materials, waste, quality control, costs, and techniques for maximizing the manufacture and distribution of goods.
Psychology	Knowledge of human behavior and performance, mental processes, psychological research methods, and the assessment and treatment of behavioral and affective disorders.
Public Safety and Security	Knowledge of weaponry; public safety; security operations, rules, regulations, precautions, and prevention; and the protection of people, data, and property.
Sales and Marketing	Knowledge of principles and methods involved in showing, promoting, and selling products or services. This includes marketing strategies and tactics, product demonstration and sales techniques, and sales control systems.
Sociology and Anthropology	Knowledge of group behavior and dynamics; societal trends and influences; and cultures and their history, migrations, ethnicity, and origins.
Telecommunications	Knowledge of transmission, broadcasting, switching, control, and operation of telecommunications systems.
Therapy and Counseling	Knowledge of information and techniques needed to rehabilitate physical and mental ailments and to provide career guidance, including alternative treatments, rehabilitation equipment and its proper use, and methods to evaluate treatment effects.
Transportation	Knowledge of principles and methods for moving people or goods by air, rail, sea, or road, including their relative costs, advantages, and limitations.

APPENDIX D

Resources for Further Exploration

The facts and pointers in this book provide a good beginning to the subject of jobs for your personality type. If you want additional details, we suggest you consult some of the resources listed here.

Facts About Careers

The *Occupational Outlook Handbook* (or the *OOH*) (JIST): Updated every two years by the U.S. Department of Labor, this book provides descriptions for 270 major jobs covering more than 85 percent of the workforce.

The *Enhanced Occupational Outlook Handbook* (JIST): This book includes all descriptions in the *OOH* plus descriptions of more than 6,000 more-specialized jobs related to them.

The *O*NET Dictionary of Occupational Titles* (JIST): The only printed source of the 950 jobs described in the U.S. Department of Labor's Occupational Information Network database. It covers all the jobs in the book you're now reading, but it offers more topics than we were able to fit here.

The *New Guide for Occupational Exploration* (JIST): An important career reference that allows you to explore all major O*NET jobs based on your interests. (An outline of the interest areas and work groups included appears in Appendix B.)

Career Decision Making and Planning

Overnight Career Choice, by Michael Farr (JIST): This book can help you choose a career goal based on a variety of criteria, including skills, interests, and values. It is part of the Help in a Hurry series, so it is designed to produce quick results.

10 Best College Majors for Your Personality, by Laurence Shatkin, Ph.D., and The Editors at JIST (JIST): Built around the six Holland personality types, this book includes an assessment to help you identify your dominant and secondary personality types, plus lists and descriptions of college majors linked to jobs with high pay, high growth, and many openings.

Job Hunting

Same-Day Resume, by Michael Farr (JIST): Learn in an hour how to write an effective resume. This book includes dozens of sample resumes from professional writers and even offers advice on cover letters, online resumes, and more.

Job Banks by Occupation. This is a set of links offered by America's Career InfoNet. At www.acinet.org, find the Career Tools box, click Career Resource Library, then Job & Resume Banks. The Job Banks by Occupation link leads you to groups of jobs such as "Construction and Extraction Occupations" and "Arts, Design, Entertainment, Sports and Media Occupations," which in turn lead you to more specific job titles and occupation-specific job-listing sites maintained by various organizations.

Index

skills, list of definitions, 467–469

Social and Community Service Managers,
42, 52, 74, 75, 124, 389, 456

Social and Human Service Assistants,
44, 53, 58, 64, 77, 78, 107, 108, 125,
442–443, 458

Social Perceptiveness skill, 468

Social personality type

application to people/jobs, 19

best jobs for, 40–41

best-paying jobs for, 47–48

educational levels for best jobs,
119–122

fastest-growing jobs for, 52

job descriptions for, 271–335

most openings, jobs with, 56–57

number of occupations/workers with,
21

older workers, best jobs for, 72–73

part-time workers, best jobs for, 84–86

personality codes, jobs ordered by,
454–455

self-employed workers, best jobs for,
93–94

women, best jobs for, 104

young workers, best jobs for, 62–63

Sociologists, 39, 47, 61, 62, 70, 71, 82, 83,
119, 244, 269, 452

Sociology and Anthropology knowledge
area, 471

Sociology Teachers, Postsecondary, 41,
84, 86, 122, 329–330, 455

Software Quality Assurance Engineers
and Testers, 244–245, 453. *See also*
Computer Specialists, All Other

Speaking skill, 468

Special Education Teachers, Middle
School, 39, 70, 71, 102, 103, 118, 269,
330–331, 454

Special Education Teachers, Preschool,
Kindergarten, and Elementary School,
38, 51, 56, 70, 71, 102, 103, 118, 269,
331–332, 454

Statement Clerks, 443–444, 457. *See also*
Billing and Posting Clerks and Machine
Operators

Statisticians, 44, 49, 77, 78, 109, 127,
444–445, 457

Substance Abuse and Behavioral Disorder
Counselors, 38, 40, 51, 52, 56, 70, 71,
72, 73, 82, 85, 118, 120, 270, 332–333,
454

Surgeons, 36, 46, 55, 68, 69, 91, 116,
245–246, 453

Surgical Technologists, 35, 50, 59, 60, 80,
97, 98, 113, 184–185, 452

Survey Researchers, 38, 115, 246–247,
453

Surveying and Mapping Technicians, 44,
53, 64, 77, 78, 109, 125, 445, 457

Surveying Technicians, 185–186, 451.
See also Surveying and Mapping
Technicians

Surveyors, 35, 45, 50, 66, 99, 114,
186–187, 452

Systems Analysis skill, 468

Systems Evaluation skill, 468

T

Talent Directors, 389–390, 455. *See also*
Producers and Directors

Technical Directors/Managers, 390–391,
456. *See also* Producers and Directors

Technical Writers, 38, 47, 51, 70, 71, 117,
270, 454

Technology Design skill, 468

Telecommunications Equipment Installers
and Repairers, Except Line Installers,
36, 45, 66, 67, 99, 100, 113, 187–188,
452

Telecommunications knowledge area, 471

Telecommunications Line Installers
and Repairers, 36, 46, 98, 100, 112,
188–189, 452

Tellers, 44, 58, 64, 65, 77, 78, 87, 88, 107,
108, 125, 445–446, 457

10 Best College Majors for Your Personality
(Shatkin), 474

Therapy and Counseling knowledge area,
471

Tile and Marble Setters, 35, 50, 59, 60,
89, 90, 98, 100, 112, 189–190, 451

Time Management skill, 468

Training and Development Managers, 42,
48, 53, 74, 75, 124, 391–392, 456

Training and Development Specialists,
38, 41, 51, 56, 70, 71, 72, 73, 102, 103,
104, 118, 120, 270, 333–334, 454

Transportation, Distribution, and
Logistics interest area, 466

Transportation Inspectors, 36, 45, 50, 66,
67, 99, 113, 190, 452

Transportation knowledge area, 471

Transportation Vehicle, Equipment, and
Systems Inspectors, Except Aviation,
190–191, 452. *See also* Transportation
Inspectors

Treasurers and Controllers, 446–447, 457.
See also Financial Managers

Troubleshooting skill, 468

Truck Drivers, Heavy and Tractor-Trailer,
35, 54, 66, 67, 89, 90, 98, 99, 112,
191–192, 451

U–V

U.S. Census Bureau, 1

U.S. Department of Education, 1

U.S. Department of Labor, 1, 23

Veterinarians, 37, 50, 67, 69, 90, 91, 116,
247–248, 453

Vocational Education Teachers,
Postsecondary, 40, 57, 84, 85, 119,
334–335, 455

W–Z

Water and Liquid Waste Treatment Plant
and System Operators, 35, 66, 67, 98,
100, 113, 192, 451

Web Administrators, 447–448, 457. *See
also* Computer Specialists, All Other

Web Developers, 448–449, 457. *See also*
Computer Specialists, All Other

work experience in a related occupation

Artistic jobs, 117

Conventional jobs, 126

defined, 110

Enterprising jobs, 123

Realistic jobs, 113

Social jobs, 119

work experience plus degree

Artistic jobs, 118

Conventional jobs, 127

defined, 111

Enterprising jobs, 124

Investigative jobs, 115

Social jobs, 120

work groups (GOE), list of, 459–466

Writers and Authors, 38, 56, 70, 71, 82,
83, 92, 118, 270, 453

Writing skill, 468